JFK

Who, How, and Why

Solving the World's Greatest Murder Mystery

Also by Mike Palecek

Fiction:

SWEAT: Global Warming in a small town,
and other tales from the great American Westerly Midwest
Joe Coffee's Revolution
The Truth
The American Dream
Johnny Moon
KGB
Terror Nation
Speak English!
The Last Liberal Outlaw
The Progressive Avenger
Camp America
Twins
Iowa Terror
Guests of the Nation
Looking For Bigfoot
A Perfect Duluth Day
American History 101:
Conspiracy Nation Revolution
One Day In The Life of Herbert Wisniewski
Operation Northwoods: . . . the patsy
Red White & Blue
Welcome To Sugar Creek
CRUSHER vs. The Empire

Non-Fiction:

Cost of Freedom (with Whitney Trettien and Michael Annis)
Prophets Without Honor (with William Strabala)
The Dynamic Duo: White Rose Blooms in Wisconsin,
Kevin Barrett, Jim Fetzer & the American Resistance
And I Suppose We Didn't Go To The Moon, Either? (with Jim Fetzer)
Nobody Died At Sandy Hook (with Jim Fetzer)
And Nobody Died in Boston, either (with Jim Fetzer)
America Nuked on 9/11 (with Jim Fetzer)
From Orlando To Dallas and Beyond
White Rose Blooms in Wisconsin

JFK

Who, How, and Why

Solving the World's Greatest Murder Mystery

Jim Fetzer and Mike Palecek
Editors

MOON ROCK BOOKS

Save the World /Resist the Empire Series

And I suppose we didn't go to the Moon, either?
Nobody Died at Sandy Hook
And Nobody died in Boston, either
America Nuked on 9/11
From Orlando to Dallas and Beyond
White Rose Blooms in Wisconsin
Chronicles of False Flag Terror

Mike Palecek, Jim Fetzer
Series Editors

JFK: Who, How, and Why
Solving the World's Greatest Murder Mystery

James H. Fetzer, Ph.D. & Mike Palecek

ISBN: 978-0-9982625-7-4

Ordering more copies: Order more copies of *JFK: Who, How, and Why* from MOON ROCK BOOKS, 6256 Bullet Drive, Crestview, FL 32536 or *MoonRockBooks.com.*

Special thanks to David R. Gahary and Tom Kimball, Ph.D. for the excellence of their work in copy editing this book.

MOON ROCK BOOKS
6256 Bullet Drive, Crestview, FL 32536
www.MoonRockBooks.com

Cover design by Ole Dammegård

CONTENTS

Part V: The Man in the Doorway

Part VI: Special Cases Inside JFK Research

Preface

On JFK and the Unspeakable

by Mike Palecek

I waited my whole life to read James W. Douglass' new book, *JFK and the Unspeakable.*

The wait was not worth it.

I should not have had to wait, at all.

This is supposed to be America, but it is not.

That is why I was made to wait.

Americans should not have to wait.

We like to have it right now.

We want what we want when we want it.

Now.

Please.

Sister Ellen walked into our third grade classroom, hands tucked neatly into the opposite brown sleeve.

She was the principal at Sacred Heart Elementary, and she only came to the classrooms to announce that the poorest kid in our class and his large family had run off a bridge this morning on the way to school, or lead us down to the gym for the Christmas movie and extra chocolate milk.

So on November 22, 1963, when lean, tall, straight Ellen floated in just after lunch recess—pre-Vatican II sisters had no feet, legs, arms, no hair—we saw the Franciscan specter of death.

Later, Mom ironed while she watched the caisson and "Black Jack," the riderless horse, on the black and white television in the front room.

This was Norfolk, Nebraska.

The *Norfolk Daily News* and WJAG told us it was Oswald. We just assumed, along with the *Omaha World-Herald,* that the Warren Commission had been commissioned by God.

Hometown hero Johnny Carson grilled an actual hero, attorney Jim Garrison, because Garrison had the gall to think for himself.

Then followed days and decades of lies.

My mother and I watched out the back door at the turn of the `70s, toward the railroad track, to see if Dad might go past, while grandma Josie sat in her room in the dark, afraid to speak at all.

My dad died to open the `80s, the day before Ruth and I were married.

Football on TV, and lies.

Pot roast on Sunday, with lies.

Turkey and dressing for Thanksgiving. White lies? Dark lies?

Most recently Peter Jennings and ABC News felt the need to cement the lies some 40 years after the Kennedy coup.

The program includes a computer-generated reconstruction of the shooting that confirms that Oswald was the lone gunman. And it finds no persuasive evidence of a conspiracy to kill the president.

Through it all, through the fog of American cultural propaganda, some persisted, some wanted the truth, some like Oliver Stone in *JFK* in 1991, hit hard enough to make the ground quiver for a moment, crack in some places.

But the cracks were quickly filled by volunteers with footballs, turkey, dressing, cranberries, credulity.

Now comes James W. Douglass, long-time peace activist, professor, Catholic Worker.

Why is his book the one I've been waiting for?

Maybe it's because of the flood of new information, at least new to me.

Maybe it's the way Douglass lays it out, on the line, straight and true, brick by brick, looking us in the eye and telling us it was the CIA who killed John F. Kennedy.

And that it was because of money.

Of course.

Is there something else?

I'm not an assassination expert.

I am an expert in living in America.

I am a Ph.D. in suffering through America, its propaganda, its holiday dinners, football afternoons, coffee conversations, newspaper articles, television news shows, entertainment shows.

If there were one thing worth listening to or hearing out of all those, there would be no need to excuse oneself to go stand in the garage smoking hidden cigarettes, holding the knife at your neck, then putting the cigarettes back into the hiding spot and the knife as well, and going back, to try once more to think and live and act as an American.

I happen to hold several advanced degrees in American Culture—years and decades spent sitting in comfortable chairs wearing new Christmas pajamas, balancing a Jethro Bowl of cherry black walnut ice cream in my lap, seeking enlightenment by watching Johnny Carson, Don Rickles, Dean Martin, Ed McMahon.

And then going to bed convinced beyond any reasonable doubt there is nothing more.

This is what there is.

This is life.

All there is to see and know is what I can see in my peripheral vision while watching *Big Red Football, Gunsmoke, Mayberry RFD, Happy Days, Survivor.*

That is all our Norfolk High School "U.S. History" books, all my parents, Isabel and Milosh, the parish priests, mailman have to tell us.

They were my Socrates and I was their Plato, and in our daily discourse I learned not to ask certain questions.

Over the years and decades I had it drilled into me the beauty and wonderment and majesty that the rain was good for the farmers and that it would get cold again this winter.

In the Athens that I imagined Norfolk to be, with its Central Park band pavilion and its "world's largest stockyard," which was also a lie, I learned not to learn.

But now . . . an unknown stone falls from the sky.

Well . . . someone pick it up.

What's this?

There is more?

A lot more.

The land of the free and the home of the brave murders its own presidents when they threaten the men with the money, like the ones who contributed to the schools we grew up in and the newspapers and the . . .

Oh, my.

The amber waves of grain will roll right over you, your children, your house if you stand in their path in any meaningful way.

Murder, Inc.

The business of America is business.

To protect and to serve.

We will kill you and you and your sons and daughters, grandmothers to get what we want.

What we want is to eat and watch television in the dark.

While we grow wrinkles trying to figure out two plus two, those who have made that their profession, manipulate . . . everything.

We vote and we work and we study and we worry about our children having Ho Ho's in their lunchbox and friends on the bus.

And we pay money earned on our knees to hire men and women to kill leaders and overthrow governments to make more money for those who built our schools and run our newspapers, and . . .

And if those people also decide that our president should die, then we can do that, too.

And we pay to have that done. Like having the carpet cleaned, the lawn mowed, the oil changed.

And no newspaper or radio station or TV station will ever talk about it.

Unless telling us that it never happened.

And we will believe them.

Because not believing them means figuring out something else to believe.

And we have things to do. We have lives . . . to live.

And those lives mean nothing, less than nothing, because they are built, constructed . . . days laid down unevenly, brick by brick . . . on lies and murder.

Lies. Murder.

Lies. Killing.

Lies. Death.

And it goes on and on as if it will never stop.

And then one unexpected day, along comes a brave man, like those brave men murdered, who is not like the weak men with the lies.

And everything changes.

A revolution without guns.

A cultural revolution, an undelicate purging of turkey and cranberries, a detoxification.

A new enlightenment, like the one that spawned the men who made this country—that the recent men have destroyed.

And the time does not seem quite so long.

Then and now are connected. Brought together.

Come together.

And now maybe.

Maybe our children will not live within lies, houses of lies, schools of lies, lives of lies.

Just maybe.

POSTSCRIPT

I once wrote a review of James W. Douglass' book, *JFK and the Unspeakable.*

This is a reprinting of that review. It says all I have to say about the JFK murder and the feelings I believe those my age have for that time.

There is nothing more important than getting to the bottom of that day, that time.

Or rather, getting the truth to the American people and forcing them to swallow it like castor oil, because it's good for you, that's why.

I am honored to be part of this new book on the JFK murder, and I offer this essay from 2008, in homage to JFK and to the writers of this new book.

Things do not change, not yet, some 50 years after. But this is not old news.

As a person gets older himself he realizes that he does not get further away from the events of his life, but somehow closer, like somehow traversing around the world and the further you get away, the closer you come.

That is how it is.

And it is my hope that this new book will finally, finally, bring us face to face with the truth about the events in Dallas on November 22, 1963 about 12:30 p.m. Central Time.

Let me say that again. It's not that we don't know the official story is a lie, it's not that. It's more that "what's puzzling you is the nature of my game."

It is still today, still that day, still important. On a grade school textbook timeline of world history at the bottom of the page it is still the same day.

If the truth would come out into the wide open about the death of John F. Kennedy, if the killers be named, we might still live, might still be the people we think we are.

Contributors

Judyth Vary Baker, an American artist, writer, poet and social scientist, is the author of *Me & Lee* (2010), which recounts her affair with Lee Oswald the summer before Dallas, *David Ferrie: Mafia Pilot* (2014), and the futuristic *Letters to the Cyborgs* (2016). Her relationship with Lee has been reported in Part 7, "The Love Affair" (2003), of the Nigel Turner TV documentary, *The Men Who Killed Kennedy* and in *Dr. Mary's Monkey* (2007) by Edward Haslam. *60 Minutes* conducted the most extensive investigation in its history for a feature about Judyth and Lee, but the project was censored and never broadcast for political reasons. In 2010, Judyth did a series of interviews with Jim Fetzer, which can be found by searching for "Jim Fetzer interviews Judyth Vary Baker". Judyth is currently working on three new books, the first about Lee Harvey Oswald's writings (tentatively, *The Mind of Lee Harvey Oswald*) the second about her close friend, Lt. Col. Dan Marvin (a Green Beret who worked as an assassin for the CIA) and a third book about social systems and linguistics. She is also coauthor with Edward Schwartz of *Kennedy & Oswald: The Big Picture* (2016–2017). Judyth currently sponsors a series of conferences on the assassination of JFK—which are held in Dallas—on an annual basis.

Ralph Cinque is a retired chiropractor who graduated from UCLA and Western States Chiropractic College. He has been a student of the JFK assassination since 2000. In 2012, he co-founded the Oswald Innocence Campaign (OIC) with Jim Fetzer and Larry Rivera. Centered around Oswald in the doorway, the OIC has grown to become the largest JFK research and advocacy organization in the world. In addition to his contributions to establishing that Lee Oswald in the doorway of the Texas School Book Depository (TSBD) as the motorcade passed by, Ralph has been at the forefront of the discoveries that the footage of Billy Lovelady standing outside the TSBD after the shooting and of Lovelady sitting at a desk in the Squad Room at the Dallas Police Department (DPD) are fabrications and that alterations were made to Wiegman, Towner, Hughes, and Bell films to conceal Oswald's presence in the doorway. His most recent research has been on the identity of the man who shot Lee in the basement of the DPD.

John P. Costella was born in East Melbourne, Australia, in 1966. He graduated with Electrical Engineering Honors at the University of Melbourne in 1989, but turned to physics and earned a Ph.D. in 1994 specializing in electromagnetism. After teaching for eight years at Mentone Grammar and The Peninsula School, he took a position as Reliability Engineer with the Australian Department of Defense in 2006, analyzing statistical data for defense equipment. He moved into the financial sector in 2007, working as Data Manager and Senior Research Scientist for a leading investment firm. In 2010 he moved to the Peter MacCallum Cancer Centre in East Melbourne, analyzing prostate cancer data to Intelematics Australia, as Senior Data Scientist for vehicle traffic data in 2010. In 2012 he accepted an offer to join Facebook in Menlo Park, California, as a Software Engineer. Since 2013, he and his wife Sally have been residents of San Francisco. He is Threat Infrastructure Data Scientist, bolstering Facebook's cyber defenses. John is the leading expert in the world on technical aspects of the Zapruder film.

Ole Dammegård, receiver of the Prague Peace Prize, nominated for the Light Tower Award, as well as an expert on false flag operations and international assassinations, has spent more than 30 years on solving major murder mysteries like the assassination of the Swedish Prime Minister Olof Palme, which has turned out to be a very dangerous task and has cost the lives of two dear friends. His two-volume work, *Coup d'état in Slow Motion,* provides an intense study of one of the biggest murder investigations in modern history (with some 900 pages with lots of photos, documents, detailed maps and images). What is still claimed to be the deed of a madman has turned out to have its roots within the international military complex and world finance at the very highest level. The book has been called 'a true Bomb of Truth'. Ole's extensive research has revealed incredible links to other big political 'events', such as the deaths of JFK, John Lennon, Robert Kennedy, Che Guevara, Salvador Allende, and Pablo Neruda as well as the sinking of m/s Estonia, killing almost 1,000 people. He is also the author of *Shadow of Tears, Re-Mind Me, The Elusive Enigma, A Global Tour of Terror Parts I-II*, and the children's book *Yolanda Yogapanda,* translated to multiple languages.

Jim Fetzer, a former Marine Corps officer, has published widely on the theoretical foundations of scientific knowledge, computer science, artificial intelligence, cognitive science, and evolution and mentality. McKnight Professor Emeritus at the University of Minnesota Duluth, he edited what Vincent Bugliosi has described as "the only exclusively scientific books" on the death of JFK: *Assassination Science* (1998);

Murder in Dealey Plaza (2000); and *The Great Zapruder Film Hoax* (2003). Jim has chaired or co-chaired five national conferences on JFK (Minneapolis 1999, Dallas 2000, Dallas 2001, Duluth 2003, Santa Barbara 2013. The founder of Scholars for 9/11 Truth, his latest books include *The 9/11 Conspiracy* (2007), *The Place of Probability in Science (*2010), *Nobody Died at Sandy Hook* (2015), *And I suppose we didn't go to the Moon, either?* (2015), *And Nobody Died in Boston, either* (2016), *America Nuked on 9/11* (2016) and *From Orlando to Dallas and Beyond* (2016)

Don Fox began researching the JFK assassination after seeing the movie *JFK* in 1992. He studied books such as Prouty's *JFK: The CIA, Vietnam and the Plot to Assassinate John F. Kennedy*, Garrison's *On the Trail of the Assassins*, Lifton's *Best Evidence* and Jim Marr's *Crossfire*. After listening to an interview of Michael Collins Piper by Jim Fetzer in 2012, Don read his masterpiece, *Final Judgment*. He went public with his writing and research in 2013 with an article in *Veterans Today,* "The JFK War: The Disturbing Case of Jim DiEugenio, LBJ and Israel". He has been a regular on "The New JFK Show" with Gary King, Larry Rivera and Jim Fetzer since 2014. Currently, he is researching the power structure that was behind the JFK assassination, which also appears to be responsible for the French Revolution, the Bolshevik Revolution, the Federal Reserve, WWI, WWII, the Lavon Affair, the USS *Liberty* event and numerous other black ops.

Richard M. Hooke, a student of anthropology at UC Santa Barbara and former computer systems analyst for Bank of America, is also a writer and researcher regarding the death of President John F. Kennedy. He has done brilliant work in identifying the man in the doorway and George H.W. Bush at the Dal-Tex Building in Dallas. Among his publications are (with Rod MacKenzie) *Letter to MacKenzie* (2014), (with Larry Rivera) *The Man with the Mona Lisa Smile* (2014), *Letter to Beverly Oliver* (2015), (with Rod MacKenzie) *The Men that Don't Fit In* (2015) and *Twelve Shots that Shook the World* (2016). Richard has been celebrated for his posters of Lee Oswald and his studies that demonstrate the points of similarity between Lee Oswald and Doorman, who was caught in a famous photograph taken in Dealey Plaza during the shooting by AP photographer James "Ike" Altgens.

Douglas P. Horne, among the most widely respected of all students of the assassination of JFK, graduated *cum laude* from The Ohio State University in 1974, with a B.A. in History. He served for 10 years as a Surface Warfare Officer in the U.S. Navy and then worked for the Navy for 10 more years as a federal civilian. In 1995, he joined the staff of the President John F. Kennedy "Assassination Records Review Board," and rose to the position of Chief Analyst for Military Records. In that capacity, he focused on the medical evidence surrounding the JFK autopsy; the Zapruder film; and ensured the release of military records on Cuba and Vietnam. In 2009 he published the extensive five-volume work, *Inside the Assassination Review Board (Inside the ARRB),* which documents the U.S. government's cover-up of the medical evidence surrounding JFK's assassination and the alteration of the Zapruder film of President Kennedy's assassination.

Peter Janney grew up in Washington, D.C. in the 1950s and 1960s. His father Wistar Janney was a high-level CIA officer who was recruited by Allen Dulles in 1949. The Janney family socialized with other CIA families including Mary and Cord Meyer, the Angletons, Desmond FitzGerald, Richard Helms, and many other Washington dignitaries, including Ben and Tony Bradlee. Peter and Michael Meyer, Cord and Mary's second child, became best friends in childhood and went to the same school together. After Michael's accidental death in 1956, Peter grew closer to Mary Meyer. When he learned of her death in 1964 and then became aware of her affair with President Kennedy in 1976, he began to suspect that Mary's murder was not "a random act of violence," but something much more sinister. Increasingly haunted, fueled by the emerging evidence of conspiracy in JFK's assassination, he embarked on a mission that would take over 30 years to complete. Finally reckoning with his own father's complicity in the CIA's cover-up of the JFK assassination, as well as the murder of Mary Meyer, *Mary's Mosaic* is the story of a truly remarkable woman who helped JFK turn away from the Cold War toward world peace initiatives, before both would be assassinated by elements of the National Security apparatus and the CIA. A graduate of Princeton, Peter earned a doctorate in psychology at Boston University, followed by an MBA from Duke University. He has been a practicing clinical psychologist, health consultant, and lecturer for over 35 years. He lives by the sea in Beverly, Massachusetts.

Clare Kuehn is a Toronto native with a U.S. citizenship as well as Canadian, because of her patriotic American mother, who always kept her citizenship. She grew up with critical thinking lessons, because her mother was a college teacher of philosophy of science and logic. She is more inclined to the arts, but with solid training in interdisciplinary history and studies in thought, through university and beyond. She has applied herself to studying modern cases of intelligence services and mass media lies, after focusing on older cases for so long. She discovered novel lines of reasoning about physical and testimonial evidence in the case of JFK's death and 9/11 applied this rigor to studying modern cases of intelligence services and mass media lies, after focusing on older cases for decades. During The Vancouver 9/11 Hearings in 2012, she presented Dr. Judy Wood's case for the demolition of the Twin Towers in contrast to the mini nuke hypothesis. She assists others who have specific case interests to determine the best (if any) evidence and reasoning about various claims (theories/explanations) and government lies and cover-ups (conspiracy). Her Vancouver slides are archived at *https://donaldfox.wordpress.com/2012/07/01/clare-kuehns-vancouver-powerpoint.* Clare maintains a personal blog at *Youcanknowsometimes.blogspot.com*.

Jim Marrs, an award-winning journalist and author, has earned acclaim for his research on JFK and a wide-range of other controversial subjects. After graduating from the University of North Texas with a degree in journalism, he worked for and owned several Texas newspapers before becoming an independent journalist/author. Jim is the author of *The New York Times* bestseller, *Crossfire: The Plot That Killed Kennedy*, which, together with Jim Garrison's *On the Trail of the Assassins*, became the basis for Oliver Stone's magisterial film, *JFK.* He is also the author of *Rule by Secrecy*, *The Rise of the Fourth Reich* and *The Terror Conspiracy,* among others. His in-depth overview of the UFO phenomenon, *Alien Agenda*, is the best-selling non-fiction book on UFOs in the world, having been translated into several foreign languages. He is a frequent guest on several nationwide radio talk-shows and television programs.

Mike Palecek lives in Saginaw, Minnesota, west of Duluth. A writer, he is a former federal prisoner for peace and the Iowa Democratic Party candidate for the U.S. House of Representatives, 5th District in the 2000 election, gaining 65,000 votes on an anti-war platform in a conservative district. A former award winning reporter, editor, publisher in Nebraska, Iowa, Minnesota, the small newspaper that Mike & Ruth Palecek owned and operated in Byron, Minnesota, won the MNA Newspaper of the Year Award in 1993. He co-hosts "The New American Dream" radio show and has published over a dozen books that offer fictional but insightful studies of the American character and the plight in which we lend ourselves in the world today. Mike is the founder of Moon Rock Books and the co-editor of this volume.

Mike Pincher is a practicing civil law attorney in Palmdale, California who was admitted to the bar in December, 1977. He was educated at the State University of New York at Plattsburgh and the State University of New York at Albany. His interest in the JFK assassination was first piqued by reviewing the Zapruder film at the suggestion of a friend and recognizing early that the film did not match the Warren Report's basic description of the close-up. It was patently obvious that not only was there at least one frontal shot, instantly eliminating Oswald as a sole shooter, but that the actions of both Secret Service agents in the Presidential limo's front seat and of those even in the trailing Queen Mary did not meet expectations of competence that would be given their commitment to protecting the President. It perplexed him why the Zapruder family appeared to have a stranglehold on the Zapruder film's usage that frustrated scholarly analysis of the assassination. He researched legal precedents to determine the film's entitlement to copyright protection and found it lacking for the reasons enunciated in his chapter, which elaborates the basic copyright principles disqualifying the Zapruder film from protection where, given the trend displayed by the cases covered there, the author would expect that subsequent case law would only further buttress the conclusions reached therein.

Larry Rivera is the chairman of the Oswald Innocence Campaign. He was born in Alaska, the son of a career military man who served as a Criminal Investigation Division officer in the Army. He was in Germany on 22 November 1963, age six, and will never forget his father's reaction upon hearing of JFK's murder ("Johnson!") He has made a lifelong study of the JFK assassination, making his first trip to Dealey Plaza in 1991, and attended the Assassination Symposium on Kennedy in 1993 for the 30th anniversary. He has given interviews about the assassination to Spanish media and has published many articles on the assassination, especially on the issue of the Altgens doorway of the TSBD and also the Wiegman doorway. Larry has given presentations at Santa Barbara for the 50th observance of the assassination on Buell Wesley Frazier, and at Judyth Baker's Conference at Arlington on the DPD motorcycle escort officers. Currently, he helps host the Internet radio show "The New JFK Show" with Gary King and Jim Fetzer, conducting interviews and discussing new information on the JFK assassination.

Sherwood Ross is a native of Chicago, Ill. He holds a degree in race relations from the University of Miami, where he was a member of the varsity debate team. After graduation, he worked at the City News Bureau of Chicago, and the news departments of the City of Chicago under Mayor Richard J. Daley and in the National Urban League in New York, under Whitney M. Young, Jr. After leaving the Urban League, he became public affairs director for the Sonderling Broadcast Group, operating out of rhythm-and-blues Radio Station WOL in Washington, D.C. In June 1966 he covered James Meredith's "March Against Fear" in Mississippi for WOL and Sonderling Group, also serving as Meredith's "press coordinator" to draw national media coverage to the event. After Meredith was shot on the second day of the march south of Hernando, Miss., Ross's eyewitness account to WOL was redistributed by *The Washington Post-Los Angeles Times* wire nationally. Ross has also worked on political campaigns for Democratic candidates in Chicago, Washington, and Nassau County, N.Y., and contributed speeches to the presidential campaigns of Senator George McGovern and Governor Michael Dukakis. For 15 years starting in 1969, from his offices in the National Press Building, Ross publicized the editorial content of approximately 100 national magazines, including *American Demographics, The New Yorker, The Atlantic, BusinessWeek, Harper's, Psychology Today, The Nation,* and *Harvard Business Review*. He has worked as a reporter for the City News Bureau of Chicago, *The Miami News,* the *Miami Herald,* the *Chicago Daily News* and for 10 years through 2002 wrote the weekly "Workplace" column for Reuters. His bylines have appeared in virtually all major U.S. dailies.

Prologue

On Solving the World's Greatest Murder Mystery

by Jim Fetzer

Jim: "Gordon, sometimes I think half of the JFK research community is working the other side". Gordon: "No, Jim. It's 90%".—Exchange between Jim Fetzer and Gordon Duff (CIA)

Since my retirement following a 35-year career offering courses in logic, critical thinking and scientific reasoning, I have been devoting myself to taking "conspiracy theories" from "theories" in the weak sense of rumors, conjectures and speculations to "theories" in the strong sense of empirically testable explanatory hypotheses, which can then be assessed by applying inference to the best explanation of the available relevant evidence.

That entails separating the authentic evidence from fabricated or fake, which has proven to be especially relevant in the case of the assassination of John F. Kennedy (JFK), where most of the evidence used to implicate Lee Harvey Oswald as "the lone assassin" was manufactured for that purpose.

The backyard photos are a perfect example, where Marina was induced to say that she had taken them, when they show the same face pasted onto someone else's body, which was Lee's response when Will

Fritz, the homicide detective who interrogated him, showed him one of several. Lee said he knew something about photography and would, with time, be able to prove it. He wasn't given that time, but students of the case, such as Jack White, who testified before the House Select Committee on Assassinations (HSCA) during its hearings in 1977–78, offered multiple lines of proof that they were fake. And, as you will discover here, Jim Marrs and I long since concluded that, while the face belonged to Lee, the body appears to have been that of Roscoe White.

Once you separate the authentic from the fabricated evidence—which includes the home movies taken in Dealey Plaza that day, where the Zapruder was used as a guide to alter the others (but with less than complete success)—the case becomes much easier to solve. In my earlier work on JFK, I published studies by David W. Mantik, M.D., Ph.D., who discovered that the "official" X-rays had been altered, in one instance, to conceal a massive blowout at the back of the head and, in another, to add a 6.5mm metallic slice to implicate an obscure WWII Italian carbine, which was known as "the humanitarian rifle" for never harming anyone on purpose, and it begins to unfold. Indeed, in the course of 10 visits to the National Archives, he has been able to establish that none of the X-rays is an original.

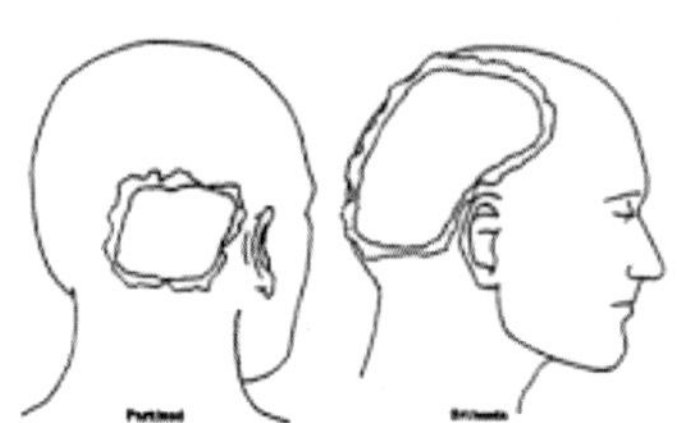

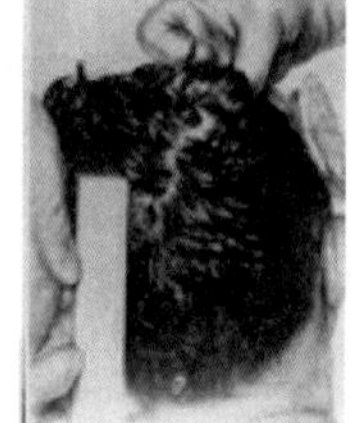

Three Views of the Head Wound

Bob Livingston, M.D., a world authority on the human brain and an expert on wound ballistics, observed that the brain shown in diagrams and photographs at the National Archives could not possibly be that of JFK, who had had half his brains blown out in Dealey Plaza, because the physicians at Parkland had reported extruding cerebellar as well as cerebral tissue, while the brain in the diagrams and photographs had an intact cerebellum.

Not the least of the major indications of a massive cover-up with respect to the medical evidence is that witnesses in Dealey Plaza and at Parkland observed a fist-sized blowout at the back of the head, while the official Bethesda autopsy report shows about half of his skull missing, which the HSCA reconstituted to a small entry wound at the crown of the head. These are completely inconsistent depictions of the same decedent.

Although the Secret Service and the Federal Bureau of Investigation (FBI) concluded the day of the shooting that there had been three shots and three hits—where the first hit JFK in the back (about 5.5" below the collar just to the right of the spinal column), another hit Texas Governor John Connally in the back and the third hit JFK in the back of the head, killing him—the belated discovery that one of the three shots attributed to "the lone gunman" had missed and injured the bystander, James Tague, the President's Commission on the Assassination of President Kennedy (the Warren Commission), was confronted with a dilemma: *admit there had been more than three shots* (thereby conceding there had been at least two shooters and therefore a conspiracy) or *revise the wounds to accommodate them as having been caused by only two shots*, which led to the "magic bullet" theory, where the wound to the back was elevated to the back of the neck and alleged to have passed through and hit John Connally.

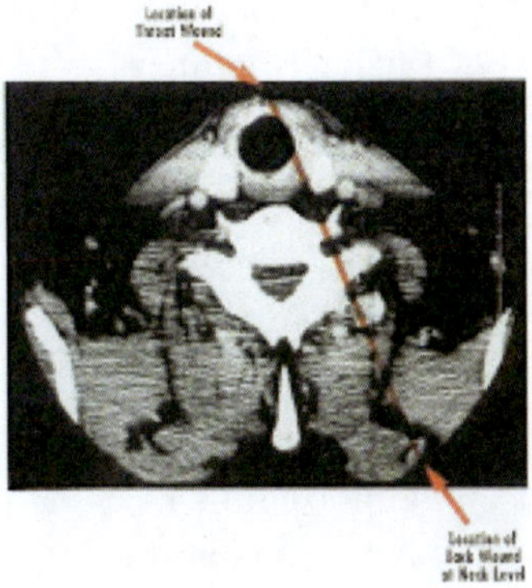

The Non-Existent "Magic Bullet"

It was a preposterous claim, which has been ridiculed by every serious student of the assassination. While there have been many attempted reconstructions of the assassination using dummies or animations as stand-ins for JFK, those replacements suffered from the stunning defect that they lacked *a spinal column*, where David W. Mantik, M.D., Ph.D., took a patient with chest and neck dimensions similar to those of JFK and plotted the official trajectory, which turns out not to be even anatomically possible because cervical vertebrae intervene.

Which means that the option of accounting for the wounds on the basis of only two shots cannot be sustained—unless, of course, JFK had no backbone, which is absurd. Like every other normal human being, he had *a backbone*, where it was because he also had *backbone*, which most others do not have, that he was taken out.

Extensive and meticulous research has confirmed that JFK was hit at least four times: once in the back (from behind); once in the throat (from in front); and at least twice in the head (once from behind and once from the right/front). In his most recent publication, *John F. Kennedy's Head Wounds: A Final Synthesis* (2015), David advances reasons for his tentative conclusion that he was hit a third time in the head (a second from the right/front). As Douglas Horne, the author of the five-volume *Inside the Assassination Records Review Board: The*

U.S. Government's Final Attempt to Reconcile the Conflicting Medical Evidence in the Assassination of JFK (2009) has written—where the Assassination Records Review Board (ARRB), a five-person civilian panel created by Congress to declassify documents and records held by the Central Intelligence Agency (CIA), FBI and other agencies in the wake of the resurgence of interest the case brought about by Oliver Stone's film, *JFK*—in his review of David's book on *amazon.com*, Mantik's work proves that there was "a massive U.S. government cover-up" regarding JFK.

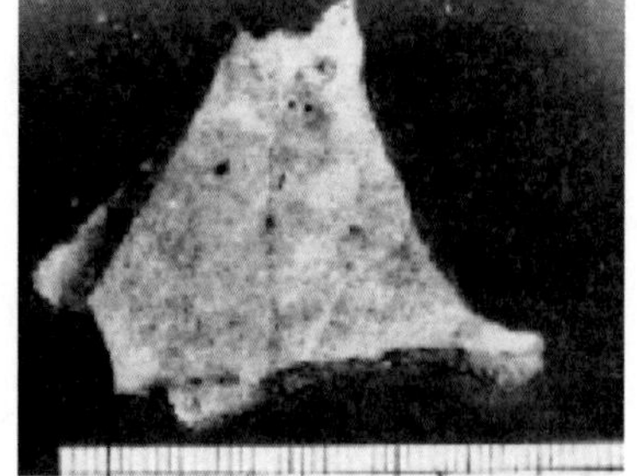

The Harper Fragment

This study also provides the final placement for (what is known as) "the Harper fragment", a triangular chunk of skull found the day after the shooting by a medical student by the name of Billy Harper (hence, the name).

David Mantik not only establishes that the Harper fragment has to be occipital in origin—meaning, *from a specific region of the back of the skull*—but also confirms an entry wound (from behind) at its extreme right edge, thereby verifying that JFK was hit in the back of the head by a shot that appears to have been fired from the Dal-Tex Building (where no shots appear to have been fired from the alleged 6th floor's "assassin's lair", but rather from at least six other locations in Dealey Plaza).

Notice, in particular, that the Harper fragment by itself disproves *The Final Report of the HSCA* (1979), because its depiction of the entry wound (at the top of the skull) shows no missing skull from the back of the head, which not only refutes its medical studies but demonstrates that it was not a serious investigation but another whitewash.

In addition to as many as five hits to JFK, there were several misses, where the shot sequence appears to have been (more or less) as follows: the first shot was fired from the top of the County Records Building and hit JFK in the back; the second was fired from inside the Triple Underpass and went through the windshield hitting him in the throat; then the hits to the head occurred after the driver,

William Greer, had pulled the limo to the left and to a halt, where three shots were fired from the Dal-Tex Building—one missing and injuring the bystander, James Tague; another missing and hitting the chrome strip over the windshield; the third hitting him in the back of the

head—and where at least one shot was fired from the intersection of the Triple Underpass and the picket fence, which hit JFK in the right temple and blew his brains out the back of his head. Another from the grassy knoll was pulled to avoid hitting Jackie and was found in the grass, while one, two or three shots were fired at Connally from the TSBD.

Controlling the Body

We have more than 15 indications of the Secret Service setting up JFK for the hit: two agents were left behind at Love Field; the vehicles were in the wrong order; the motorcade route was changed just four days earlier; the manhole covers were not welded and windows were opened and uncovered throughout the route; the motorcycle escort was cut down to four and ordered not to ride ahead of the rear wheels; the 112th Military Intelligence Unit was ordered to stand down; the crowd was allowed to spill into the street, 8, 10 or even 12 deep; the flatbed press truck that should have preceded the Presidential Limousine was canceled; the President's personal physician and his military aide were moved to the last vehicle; the vehicles were of different makes and colors; the driver took more than a 90° turn onto Elm Street; he pulled the car to the left and to a halt after bullets began to be fired; an agent took a bucket of water and sponge and began washing the blood and brains out of the back seat at Parkland; the autopsy X-rays and photos were gathered at Bethesda and when they later appear, they have been altered; and more.

The key to the cover up was the forcible removal of the body from Parkland, even though the only offense that had been committed was murder, which was a local and state crime, not a federal offense.

By removing the body and transporting it to Air Force One, over the objections of the local justice of the peace, and then moving it from the bronze ceremonial casket into a body bag, which was stored in a secret compartment of the plane and off-loaded on the opposite side (while the attention of the world was focused on Bobby and Jackie with the bronze ceremonial casket) and flown to Walter Reed (where the best forensic pathologists in the military removed bullet fragments), then transporting the body in a black hearse to the rear entry of the morgue (while television was following the enormous entourage following the gray Navy ambulance to Bethesda and only arriving when the body was already undergoing autopsy), the public was deceived about the true causes of his death, which were further concealed by altering the body, the X-rays and photos, and issuing a false official autopsy report.

The Zapruder Film

There are those who, to this day, insist that the Zapruder film and other home movies taken in Dealey Plaza during the shooting are authentic. But the proof that that is not the case is simply overwhelming. Josiah Thompson has advanced the denial with the claim that the chain of possession shows that it could not have been out of the hands of the Secret Service as its custodians in order to be revised. But the Secret Service was in on it.

We know, on the basis of brilliant research by Douglas Horne, who was the Senior Analyst for Military Records of the ARRB, that a copy of the original—an 8mm, already split film developed in Dallas—was taken to the National Photographic Information Center in Washington, D.C., on Saturday (where they had to ask a shop owner to open his store to obtain an 8mm projector in order to view it) and was replaced the following day with a 16mm, unsplit film, developed in Rochester, N.Y., where the CIA has a secret photo lab called "Hawkeye Works".

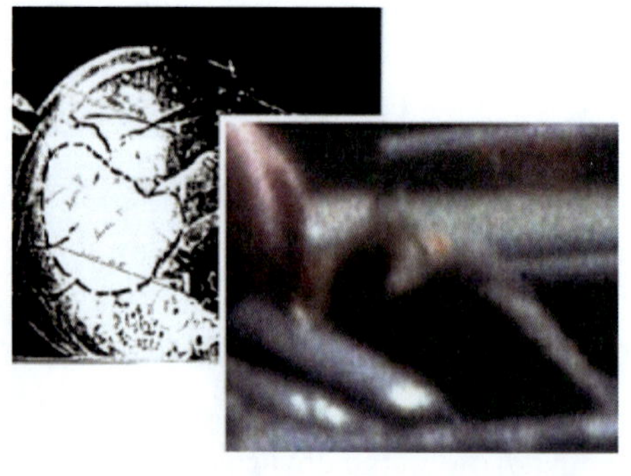

The blowout at the back of the head had been covered in black and the shots to the head—one from behind and at least one from the right/front—were merged to inadvertently create the violent left-and-to-the rear motion no one observed in Dealey Plaza, because it had not happened at the time of the shooting itself. The most striking disproof of authenticity—although there are many—may have been my discovery that, in frame 374, you can actually see the blowout, which those altering the film had overlooked. There is a pinkish skull-flap from the use of a frangible (or "explosive") bullet, where the bluish-gray matter shows what can be seen and is in striking agreement with the area at the back of the lateral cranial X-ray that David Mantik defined as "Area P" (for "patch") in his optical-density studies of the X-rays.

But this means that, in spite of its technical excellence in most respects, the film is not even internally consistent! And when you take into account that, in the Nix film (taken from the side opposite the grassy knoll), shows Jackie moving further back on the trunk than in the Zapruder, you do not even have to take into account the inconsistencies between the film, the witnesses on Elm Street, and the medical evidence to prove—conclusively!—that the Zapruder and other films were subjected to extensive alteration.

Who Was Responsible?

In order to understand who was responsible and why, the story begins in Los Angeles in 1960 during the Democrat Convention, where Jack had invited Sen. Stewart Symington (D-MO) to be his running mate. When Bobby went by the Johnson Suite to make a *pro forma* gesture to Lyndon Johnson, he was stunned when LBJ jumped on it. Jack and Bobby tried to figure a way out of it, but Lyndon—using information provided to him by FBI Director, J. Edgar Hoover—threatened to expose that he had had dalliances with beautiful women, some of whom were spies for other countries (East Germany, specifically) and that he suffered from Addison's Disease and was not expected to live a long, healthy life. Moreover, he told Bobby that, if he were not on the ticket, then any legislative proposals sent to Congress by the White House would be DOA, because he, as the powerful Majority Leader of the Senate, would kill them. They tried to find a solution, but couldn't devise one. JFK was forced to accept LBJ as his running mate.

When a wealthy Lyndon backer burst into the Johnson Suite cursing and swearing because he was going to help JFK to win the presidency, Bobby Baker took him into a bedroom and explained what they had in mind.

He came out all smiles, saying he thought that was "an excellent plan!" Bobby Baker would later state that JFK would not live out his term and would die a violent death. As it played out, LBJ would be in deep trouble politically, where a vote in the Senate on 22 November 1963 over the Bobby Baker scandal (where Bobby was LBJ's bag man in the Senate) was widely expected to tarnish Lyndon so badly that JFK could not run with him again.

But Jack had already informed his personal executive secretary, Evelyn Lincoln, that he was not going to run with LBJ again and was thinking of asking Terry Sanford, governor of North Carolina, to be his running mate. Richard Nixon was even quoted in *The Dallas Morning News* as affirming that he did not believe JFK would be able to run again with Lyndon Johnson.

Disentangling the Assassination

Many conjectures have been advanced as to who was responsible, including the CIA, KGB, Fidel Castro, the anti-Castro Cubans, the Joint Chiefs, the Mafia, the Texas oil men, the Eastern Establishment surrounding the Federal Reserve and Israel.

Securing clarity from confusion requires differentiating between the SPONSORS (individuals and institutions who wanted JFK out, preferring the policies of Lyndon Johnson for diverse reasons), the FACILITATORS (who were the key players in bringing it about and in covering it up), and the MECHANICS (the shooters themselves with their supervisors and coordinators).

Noel Twyman, *Bloody Treason* (1997), got it right. The perfect conspiracy to take out JFK would involve combining the CIA with the Mafia (which conducted domestic hits while "the Agency" conducted international) with the Secret Service and FBI (led by Lyndon's close friend, its director), which was exactly how it was done. The CIA was concerned because JFK was talking about shattering it into a thousand pieces. The Joint Chiefs were upset because he had not invaded Cuba, contrary to their unanimous recommendation, had signed the Above Ground Test Ban Treaty, against their unanimous opposition, and believed that a stand had to be taken opposing the expansion of "international, godless communism" in Vietnam, where he was pulling out our forces.

The anti-Castro Cubans wanted revenge for (what they believed to have been) his betrayal at the Bay of Pigs. The Mafia wanted him out because Bobby was cracking down on organized crime with unprecedented severity and success. The Texas oil men were concerned that he would cut the oil depletion allowance. And the Federal Reserve was threatened with extinction by JFK's decision to have the Department of the Treasury print United States Notes on the basis that it was absurd for the government to pay a consortium of private banks to publish its currency. And JFK was butting heads with David Ben-Gurion over Israel's plans to develop nuclear weapons, which JFK opposed.

Debunking JFK Disinformation

None of the proffered suspects, such as the KGB or Fidel Castro, had anything to do with it—other than that Lee Oswald, who had been recruited by the Office of Naval Intelligence (ONI) as a Marine Corps recruit in San Diego, was portrayed as a pro-Castro communist sympathizer in New Orleans the summer before the shooting by handing out flyers for the Fair Play for Cuba Committee, which is known in the trade as "sheep dipping".

Neither the KGB nor Fidel could have directed the Secret Service to set JFK up for the hit. Neither the KGB nor Fidel could have obtained the autopsy photographs and X-rays in order to alter them. Neither the KGB nor Fidel could have arranged for the revision of the Zapruder film. Once the cover-up's complexity is understood, the very idea that either was involved becomes completely absurd. The world leaders most profoundly affected were Nikita Khruschev and Fidel Castro, who were utterly despondent. Castro and Kennedy representatives were even meeting in Paris to normalize relations at the time.

A recent book, *The Devil's Chessboard: Allen Dulles, the CIA, and the Rise of America's Secret Government* (2016), by David Talbot suggests that the assassination was the work of Allen Dulles, the Director of the CIA, whom JFK retired with fanfare in the wake of the Bay of Pigs fiasco.

Jim Fetzer at the Eternal Flame

The book deserves to be taken seriously by everyone who wants to understand the rise of the national security state. While Talbot has successfully described the means by which a president could be taken out, the motive and the opportunity required to complete his case only arose *after* JFK became president and moved in directions that were contrary to those desired by the national security state. Talbot's conjecture cannot accommodate the mutually reinforcing considerations (a) that Lyndon forced himself onto the ticket with JFK using threats that were based upon information provided by J. Edgar and (b) that only his successor could guarantee that no one would ever pay for participating in the assassination of JFK. Lyndon had the plan in mind when he played Bobby and Jack during the Democrat Convention in 1960. Dulles was not the pivotal player.

We know better from the brilliant work of Phil Nelson and others, including those who knew Lyndon up close and personal: Madeleine Duncan Brown, Billy Sol Estes, Barr McClellan, E. Howard Hunt, Jack Ruby and others still. JFK did not wind up in Dallas because of random political commitments. He was manipulated to go there by LBJ.

So the crucial elements in setting him up for the kill were managed by Lyndon, where his close personal friend, J. Edgar Hoover, used his own FBI to cover it up. They were the FACILITATORS. LBJ took a personal, hands-on role both in relation to the hit—where he sent his chief executive assistant, Cliff Carter, down to Dallas to make sure all the arrangements for the assassination were in place.

You will find extensive documentation and evidence galore in the pages that follow. Plots against kings were commonplace in England. This was a classic palace coup of Shakespearian dimensions—just one that was "Made in the USA".

Part I

JFK: Illusions vs. Reality

1

Dealey Plaza Revisited: What Happened to JFK?

by Jim Fetzer

The application of principles of scientific reasoning to the assassination of JFK can contribute to resolving any lingering questions over whether or not he was murdered as the result of a conspiracy. The likelihood L of an hypothesis h, if evidence e were true, is equal to the probability of e, if h were true. And, because the evidence has "settled down", it warrants acceptance as true.

The hypotheses are viewed as possible causes of the evidence as effects. This assumes that evidence e includes all of the available relevant data, which may include findings that specific items of evidence have been planted, altered, or fabricated, discoveries that lend weight of their own. This chapter cannot exhaust the evidence in this case, but presents a sample sufficient to demonstrate that the conspiracy hypothesis has

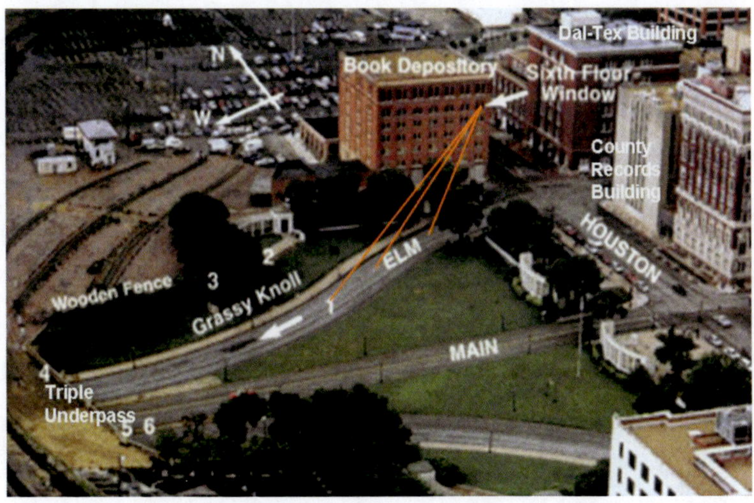

Stewart Galanor, Cover-Up (1968), Expanded

high likelihood and the lone assassin low. It should not have been necessary to frame a guilty man.

According to the Warren Commission (1964), a lone gunman fired three shots from the sixth floor of the Texas School Book Depository (TSBD), scoring two hits and one miss, which injured a distant bystander, James Tague, who was observing from location #6.

Prior to this discovery of a shot that had missed, even the Commission supposed all three had hit—the first hit JFK in the back, the second hit Governor John Connally in the back, and the third hit JFK in the head, killing him.

The backyard photograph, which was published in *Life*, was a fake. His fingertips were cut off; the shadows from his nose and eyebrows were inconsistent with the shadow cast by his figure; the chin was not Oswald's pointed chin with a cleft but a block chin with an insert line.

Jack White used the newspapers as an internal yardstick and discovered that either the person shown was only 5'6" tall—too short to be Oswald, who was 5'10"—or the image of the newspapers was too large.

Two shots were widely reported on radio and television that day, one to the throat, the other to the right temple, which blew his brains out the back of his head.

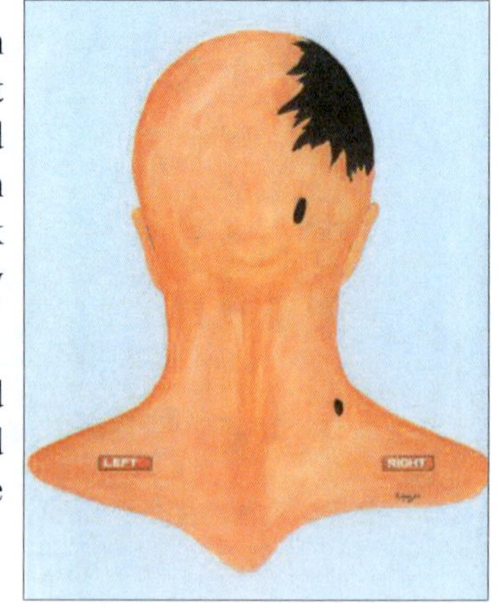

Nevertheless, when the Warren Commission would release its report nine months later, those trajectories had been reversed and JFK had only been hit at the base of the neck and the back of his head, thereby reducing as many as four or more hits to just these two.

The arrest report for Lee Oswald stated, "This man shot and killed President John F. Kennedy and Police Officer J. D. Tippit.

He also shot and wounded Governor John Connally." The time was 1:40 PM. That was very fast work. The assassination had taken place at 12:30 PM and virtually no investigation had yet taken place.

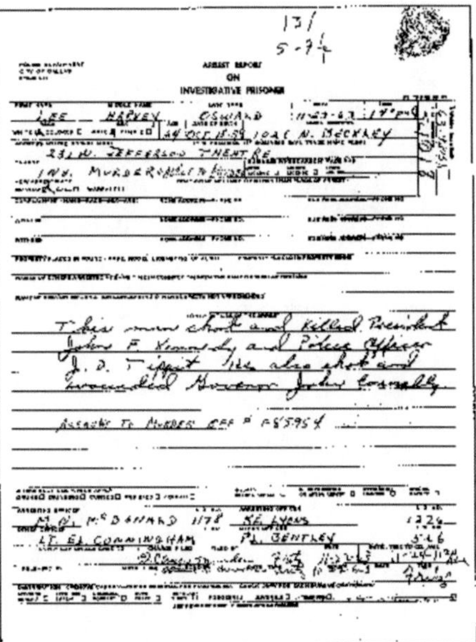
ARREST REPORT
ON
INVESTIGATIVE PRISONER

LEE HARVEY OSWALD 11-22-63
24 OCT 18-39 1026 N. BECKLEY
231 W. JEFFERSON THEATRE
INV. MURDER

This man shot and killed President John F. Kennedy and Police Officer J. D. Tippit. He also shot and wounded Governor John Connally.

ASSAULT TO MURDER OFF # F85954

M. N. McDONALD 1178 K. E. LYONS
LT. E. L. CUNNINGHAM P. L. BENTLEY

Jesse Curry, JFK Assassination File (1969)

The alleged assassination weapon—a Mannlicher-Carcano carbine—was photographed in Dallas by the Dallas Police and in Washington, D.C., by the FBI.

Remarkably, they are not the same. With a muzzle velocity of only 2,000 feet per second (fps), the Mannlicher-Carcano is not a high velocity weapon. According to the official account, the President was killed by high velocity bullets, which means Oswald could not have fired the bullets that killed JFK.

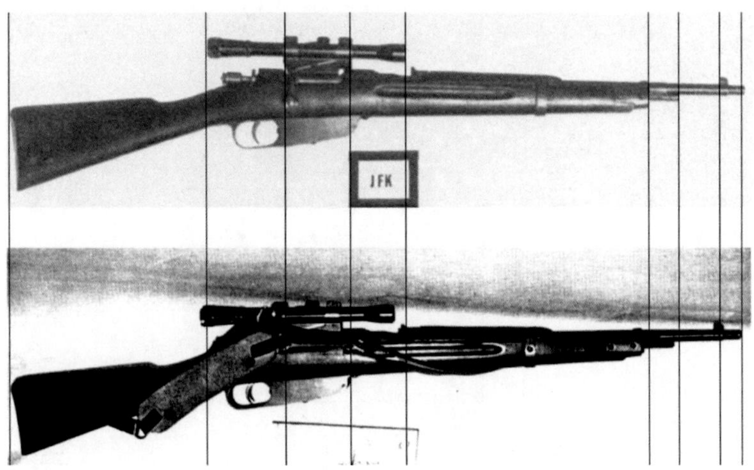

A nitrate test revealed traces on his hands but not on his cheek. While he might have fired a revolver, he had not fired a carbine. Washing his face would have washed his hands, too. He worked in a depository with books printed in ink, which contain nitrates.

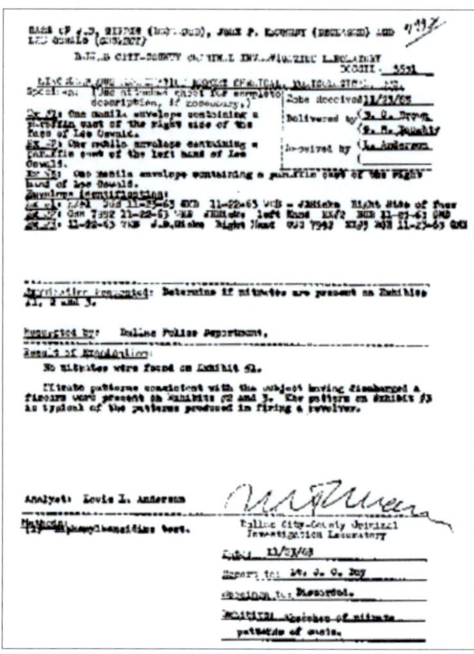

Date received 11/23/63

Ex #1: One manila envelope containing a paraffin cast of the right side of the face of Lee Oswald.
Ex #2: One manila envelope containing a paraffin cast of the left hand of Lee Oswald.
Ex #3: One manila envelope containing a paraffin cast of the right hand of Lee Oswald.

Examination requested: Determine if nitrates are present on Exhibits #1, 2 and 3.

Requested by: Dallas Police Department.

Result of Examination:

No nitrates were found on Exhibit #1.

Nitrate patterns consistent with the subject having discharged a firearm were present on Exhibits #2 and 3. The pattern on Exhibit #3 is typical of the patterns produced in firing a revolver.

Analyst: Louis L. Anderson

Jesse Curry, *JFK Assassination File* (1969)

So this test exonerated him of the commission of the crime in two ways.

11:50 AM: William Shelley saw him near the lunchroom when he (Shelley) came down to eat lunch.

Noon: Eddie Piper saw him on the first floor when he (Oswald) told him he was going up to eat.

12:15 PM: Carolyn Arnold observed him sitting in the lunchroom.

12:25 PM: She saw him again, but on the first floor near the front door.

Oswald appears to have been in a lunchroom on the second floor when the assassination took place. He was confronted there within 90 seconds of the shooting by Motorcycle Patrolman Marrion Baker, who held him in his sights until Roy Truly, Lee's supervisor,

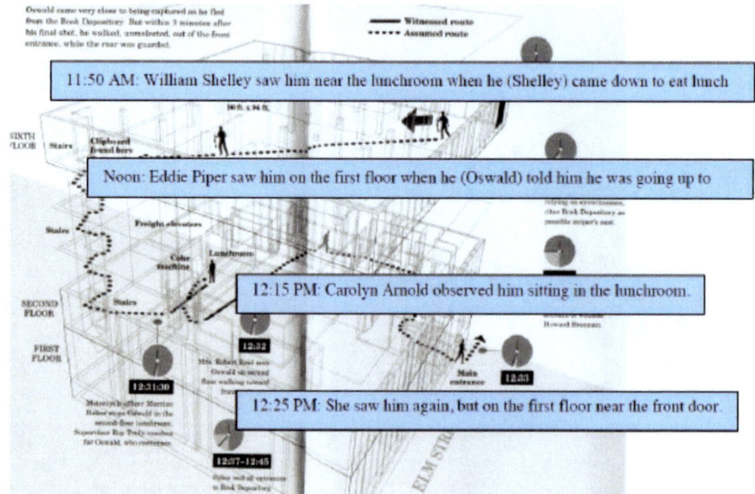

Gerald Posner, *Case Closed: Lee Harvey Oswald and the Assassination of JFK* (1993), Expanded

assured Baker he was an employee who belonged in the building. Both described him as acting perfectly normal, neither agitated nor out of breath, but—Truly added—somewhat startled to find an officer pointing his revolver at him.

Two Secret Service agents, who would have accompanied the limousine, were left behind at Love Field by Emory Roberts, Agent-in-Charge of the presidential protective detail. Here one of them, Henry Rybka, expresses dismay at being called off.

The motorcycle escort was reduced to four, who were instructed not to ride forward of the rear wheels of the Presidential limousine.

One of them observed that it was "the damnedest formation" he'd ever seen. JFK's military aide, who normally sat between the driver and the agent-in-charge, was moved to the last vehicle along with the President's personal physician.

There are more than 15 indications of Secret Service complicity in setting JFK up for the hit.

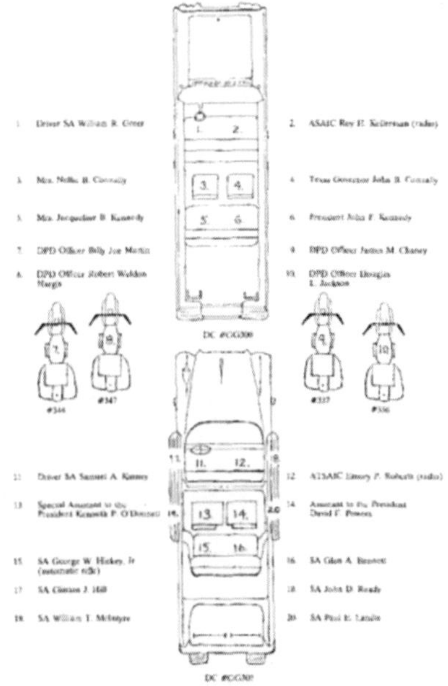

Richard Trask, Pictures of the Pain (1994)

In addition to the agents being left behind at Love Field, the manhole covers were not welded, open windows were not covered, and the crowd was allowed to spill into the street.

Governor Connally was instrumental in making a change to the motorcade route on November 18. Normally, a motorcade route, once fixed, is never changed, so the Secret Service can check every building and screen its occupants. This change brought the President past the Texas School Book Depository building.

Most tellingly, the vehicles were in an improper sequence. The Presidential limousine was placed first.

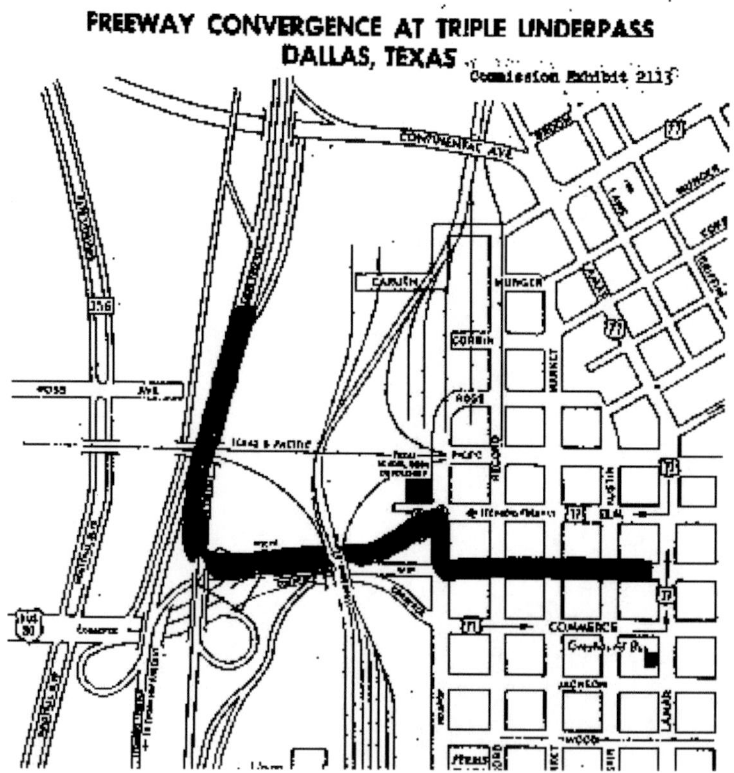

Lower ranking dignitaries, such as the mayor of Dallas and the vice president, should have preceded him.

Reporters were moved to the rear and the President's personal physician to the last car, which put him in the worst location should his patient require emergency medical treatment.

At Parkland Hospital, where the moribund President was taken, a Secret Service agent took a bucket and sponge and began cleaning up the blood and brains from the limousine. When onlookers noticed a through-and-through hole in the windshield, the vehicle was moved.

By Monday, 25 November 1963, the day of the formal state funeral, the vehicle had been sent back to Ford to be completely stripped down to bare metal and rebuilt, including replacing the windshield, which had a bullet hole (the black spot at the center of the small, white spiral nebula) close to the right-center (facing the vehicle from the front). The Secret Service would produce yet a third, different windshield (with cracks) in its place to misrepresent the original damage.

During a press conference at 3:15 PM, Malcolm Perry, M.D., who had performed a tracheotomy through a small

Richard Trask, Pictures of the Pain (1994)

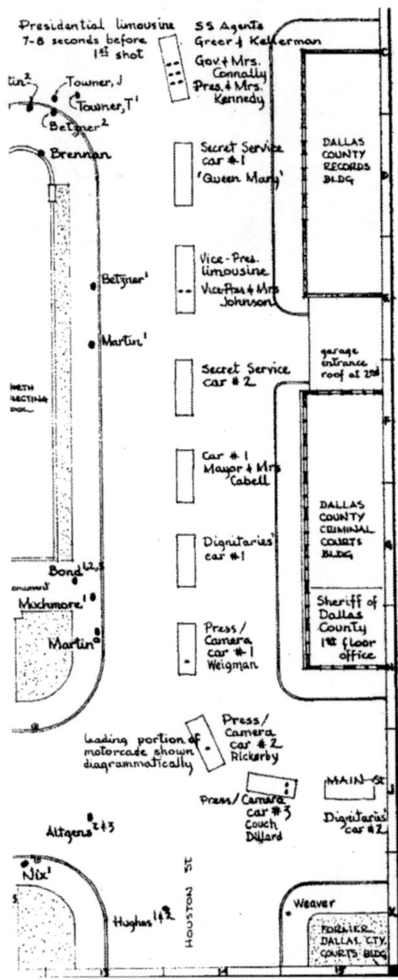

Richard Sprague, Computers and Automation (May 1970)

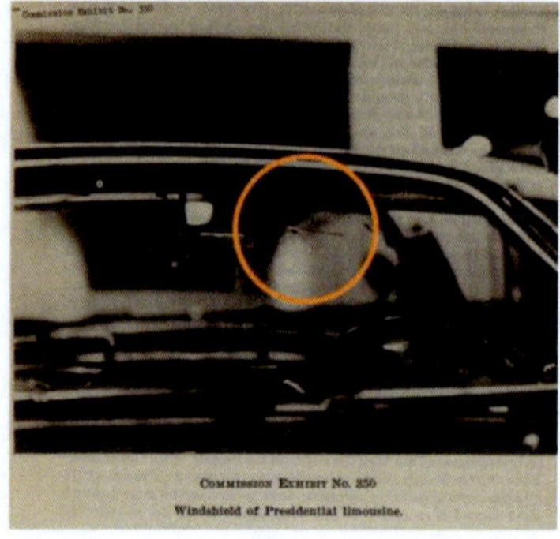

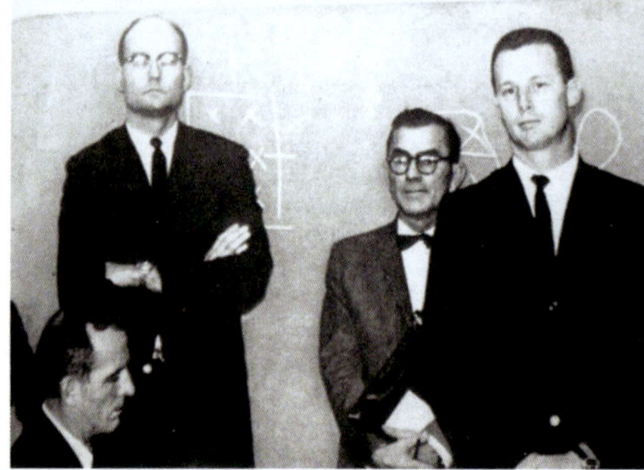

wound in the President's throat, explained three times that the wound was a wound of entry. A transcript of this event would not be provided to the Warren Commission, but would be published in *Assassination Science* (1998).

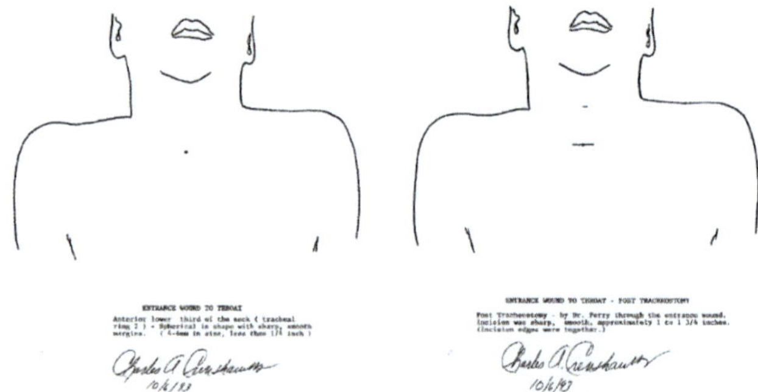

Charles Crenshaw, M.D., who was present during the efforts to revive JFK at Parkland, drew these diagrams of the appearance of the throat wound before and after the tracheotomy incision, which are consistent with Dr. Perry's description of it as a wound of entry.

Officially, one shot hit the President in the back of his neck, passed through his neck without hitting any bony structures, and entered the back of Governor John Connally, inflicting multiple wounds. It shattered a rib, exited his chest, damaged his right wrist, and entered his left thigh. Since this trajectory is so implausible and the alleged missile virtually

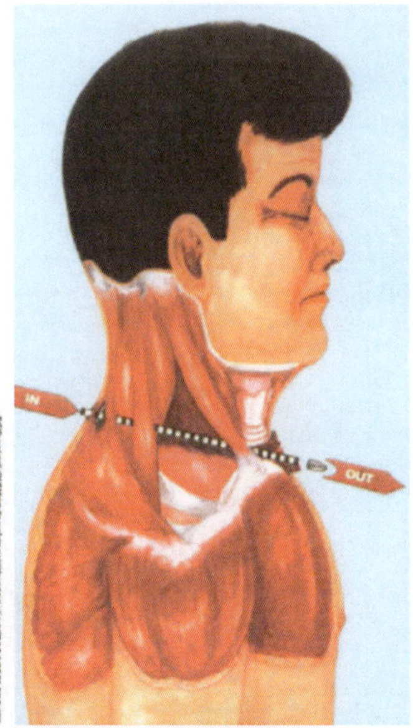

pristine, it has come to be known as "the magic bullet".

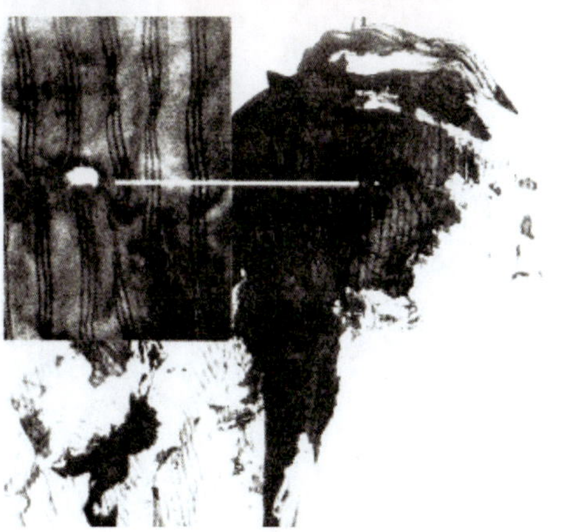

The jacket JFK was wearing shows a hole about 5.5" below the collar, which contradicts the official location of the wound. If the bullet entered here, especially at a downward angle, it is difficult to imagine how it could have passed through his neck and exited at his throat.

A bullet hole in the shirt turns out be about 5.5" below the collar, too low to correspond to the official location at the base of the back of the neck.

Neither the shirt nor the jacket were sent forward to Bethesda for the autopsy, a violation of autopsy protocol. The Bethesda autopsy was conducted by James Humes, who was assisted by J. Thornton Boswell. Neither of them had ever performed an autopsy on a gunshot victim before. Boswell's diagram of the wounds shows a wound to the back about 5.5" below the collar. It was verified by Admiral George Burkley, the President's personal physician.

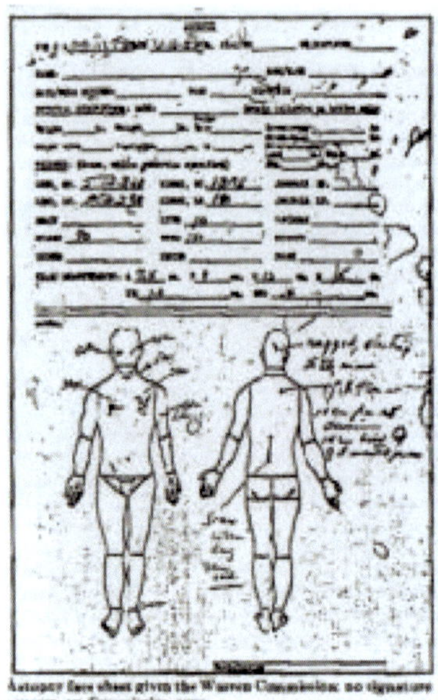

Autopsy face sheet given the Warren Commission: no signature appears on Commission copy.

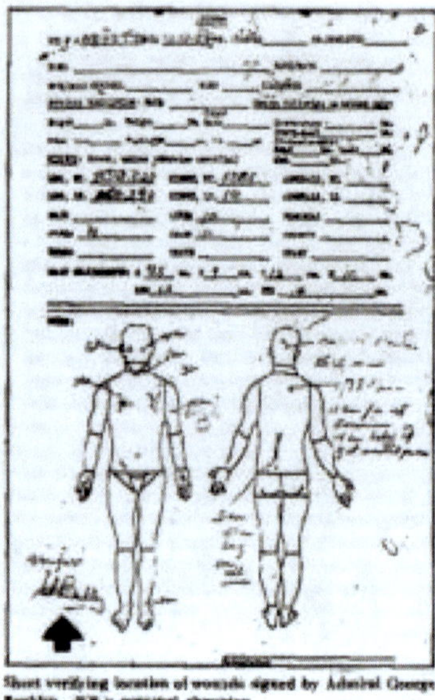

Sheet verifying location of wounds signed by Admiral George Burkley, JFK's personal physician.

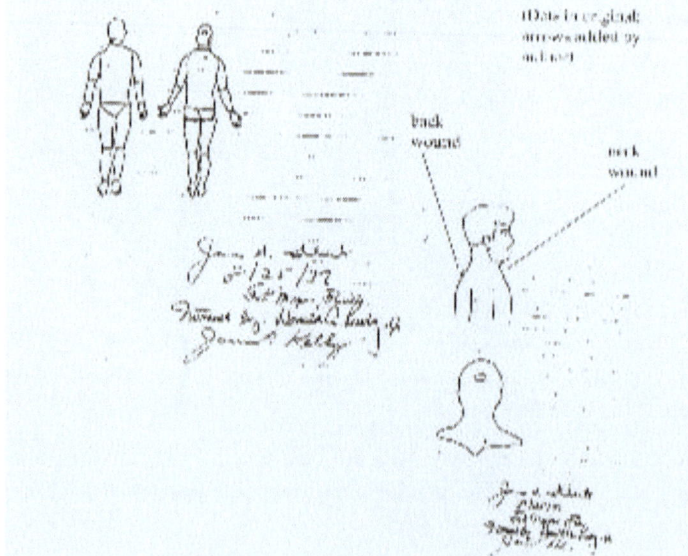

Noel Twyman, Bloody Treason (1997)

One of two FBI agents who witnessed the autopsy, James Sibert, drew a diagram showing the relative location of the wounds, where the back wound is lower than the throat wound, making it most unlikely that they were connected by a shot that had been fired from above and behind.

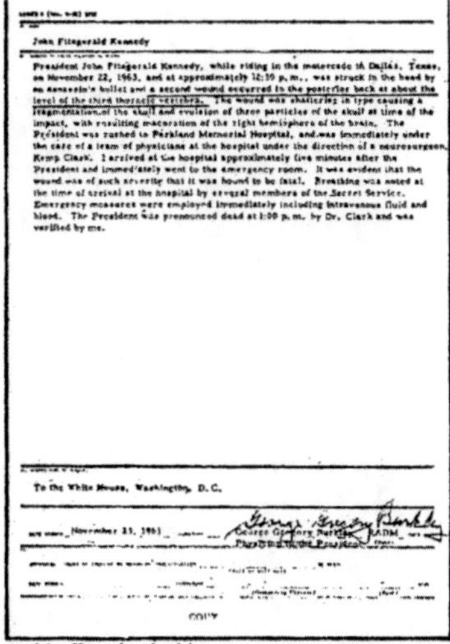

John Fitzgerald Kennedy

President John Fitzgerald Kennedy, while riding in the motorcade in Dallas, Texas, on November 22, 1963, and at approximately 12:30 p.m., was struck in the head by an assassin's bullet and a second wound occurred in the posterior back at about the level of the third thoracic vertebra. The wound was shattering in type causing a fragmentation of the skull and evulsion of three particles of the skull at time of the impact, with resulting maceration of the right hemisphere of the brain. The President was rushed to Parkland Memorial Hospital, and was immediately under the care of a team of physicians at the hospital under the direction of a neurosurgeon, Kemp Clark. I arrived at the hospital approximately five minutes after the President and immediately went to the emergency room. It was evident that the wound was of such severity that it was bound to be fatal. Breathing was noted at the time of arrival at the hospital by several members of the Secret Service. Emergency measures were employed immediately including intravenous fluid and blood. The President was pronounced dead at 1:00 p.m. by Dr. Clark and was verified by me.

To the White House, Washington, D.C.

November 23, 1963 — George Gregory Burkley

COPY

Admiral Burkley composed a death certificate on JFK, which said he had been "struck in the head" by one shot and that "a second wound occurred at the posterior back at about the level of the third thoracic vertebra." He added that the head wound involved "evisceration of the right hemisphere of the brain."

The third thoracic vertebra turns out to be approximately 5.5" below the collar to the right of the spinal column. Some apologists for the official account suggest that his jacket was "bunched up", which made the hole lower than the wound.

But that would not explain the diagrams of the wound showing it at the same location on the body itself. Nor would it account for Admiral

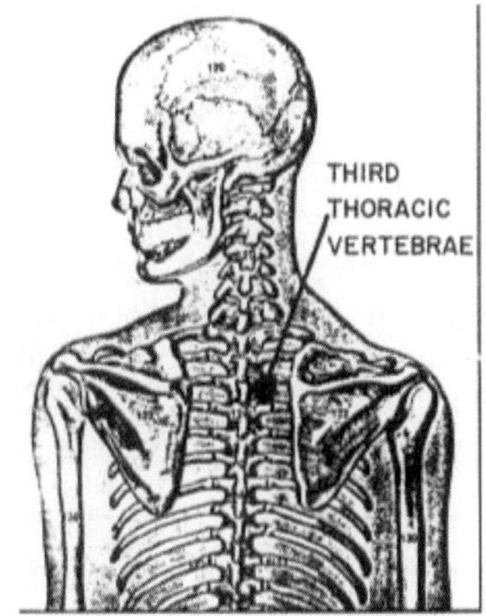

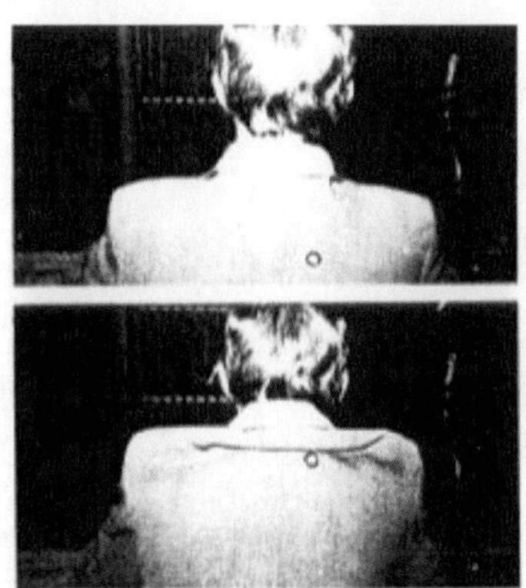

Defenders of the "Report" are resigned to creating outlandishly absurd explanations—like these—to explain why bullet holes in JFK's shirt and coat are nearly six inches below the spot designated by the Commission as the point of entry for the missile.

Gary Shaw, Cover-Up (1976)

Burkley's death certificate description or the FBI sketch of their relative locations.

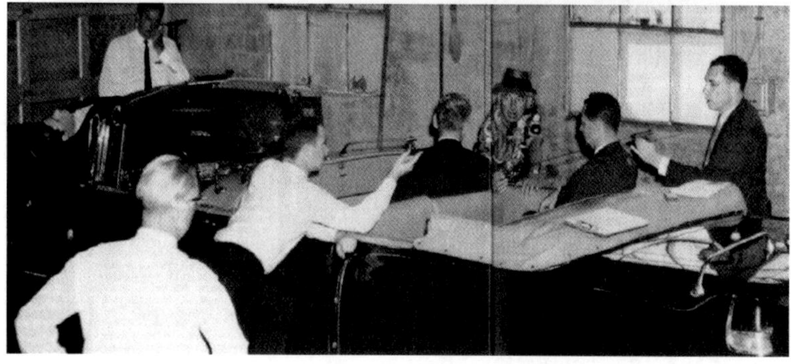

Newsweek (November 22, 1993)

Even the Warren Commission staff concluded that the back shot had been at that location, as the reenactment photograph on the next page displays. The larger circular patch on the back of the stand-in's jacket represents the back wound, the smaller above it the official entry wound to the head.

Arlen Specter, then a junior counselor to the Warren Commission, uses a pointer here to exhibit the path the "magic bullet" would have had to have taken, in order to account for all the wounds with only two shots. Since the larger circular patch visible below his left hand indicates the back shot, a photo intended to illustrate the theory actually refutes it.

An early document released by the Assassination Records Review Board (ARRB) showed that Gerald Ford (R-MI), then a commission member, had had the back wound re-described from "his uppermost

Ford Made Key Change In Kennedy Death Report

WASHINGTON, July 2 (AP) — Thirty-three years ago, Gerald R. Ford changed — ever so slightly — the Warren Commission's main sentence on the place where a bullet entered President John F. Kennedy's body when he was killed in Dallas.

Mr. Ford's change strengthened the commission's conclusion that a single bullet passed through Kennedy and wounded Gov. John B. Connally, — a crucial element in the commission's finding that Lee Harvey Oswald was the sole gunman.

Mr. Ford, who was a member of the commission, wanted a change to show that the bullet entered Kennedy "at the back of his neck" rather than in his uppermost back, as the commission originally wrote.

Mr. Ford said today that the change was intended to clarify meaning, not alter history.

"My changes had nothing to do with a conspiracy theory," he said in a telephone interview.

But his editing was seized upon by conspiracy theorists who reject the commission's conclusion that Mr. Oswald had acted alone.

"This is the most significant lie in the whole Warren Commission report," said Robert D. Morningstar, a computer systems specialist in New York City who said he has studied the assassination and written an Internet book about it.

If the bullet had hit Kennedy in the back, it could not have struck the Governor in the way the commission said it had, Mr. Morningstar said.

The New York Times (July 3, 1997)

back," already an exaggeration, to "the base of the back of his neck" in an effort to make "the magic bullet" hypothesis appear more plausible. David W. Mantik, M.D., Ph.D., who is board certified in radiation oncology, took a CAT scan of a patient with chest and neck dimensions similar to those of JFK. When he plotted the official trajectory, it turned out to be anatomically impossible. Cervical vertebrae intervene. Dr. Crenshaw also drew the massive blowout to the back of the head, which he described as the size of a baseball or of your fist when you double it up. During an interview broadcast on television, he also described an entry wound at the right temple, consistent with the mortician's description.

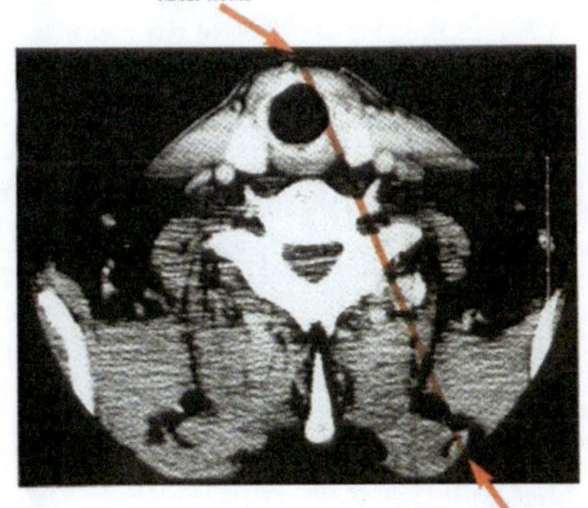

Stewart Galanor, Cover-Up (1998)

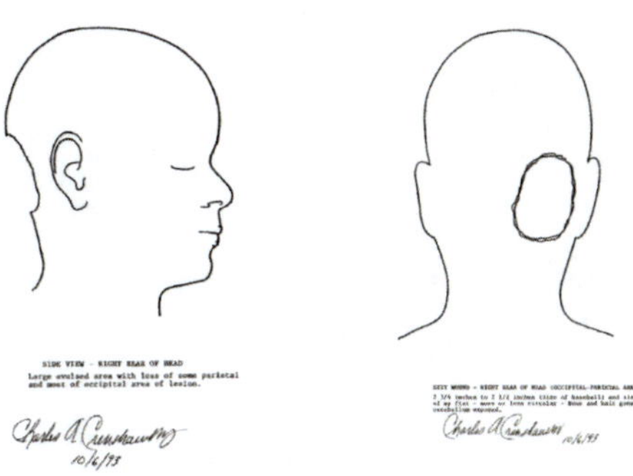

Charles Crenshaw, Assassination Science (1998)

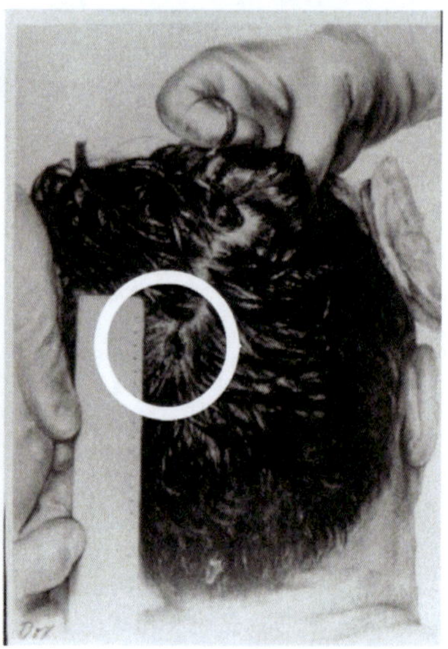

When the House Select Committee on Assassinations (HSCA) re-investigated the case in 1977-78, its medical panel concluded that the entry wound was actually four inches above the entry location previously specified. It was depicted in diagrams (top right) but not visible in photographs (top left).

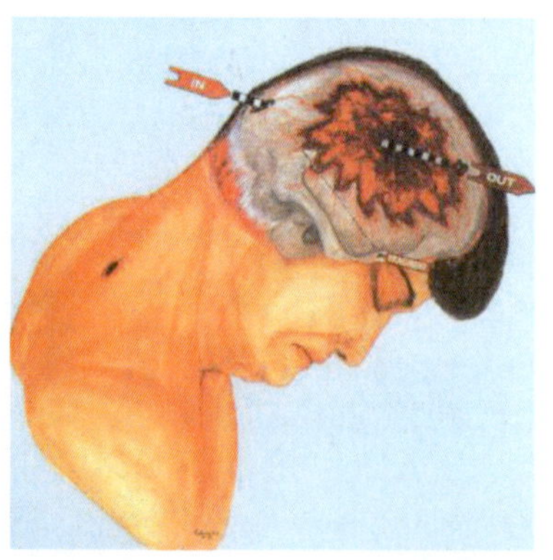

According to the autopsy report, the fatal head shot entered at the back of his head and blew out the top of his skull. The Navy artist who was instructed to prepare these sketches was not allowed to observe the body and drew what he was told to draw.

Beverly Oliver:
"The whole back of his head went flying out the back of the car."

Phillip Willis:
"It took the back of his head off."

Marilyn Willis:
"A red 'halo.' Matter [was] coming out the back of his head."

Dr. Kenneth Salyer:
"This wound extended into the parietal area."

Dr. Charles Carrico:
"There was a large — quite a large — defect about here [pointing] on his skull."

Dr. Richard Dulaney:
"It was up in this area."

Theran Ward
"[It was] right back here."

Aubrey Rike
"You could feel the sharp edges of the bone at the edge of the hole in the back of his head."

Frank O'Neill
". . . a massive wound in the right rear."

Ed Hoffman:
"The rear of his head was gone, blasted outward."

Dr. Robert McClelland:
"It was in the right back part of the head — very large . . . a portion of the cerebellum fell out on the table."

Dr. Paul Peters:
". . . right there, occipital parietal."

Dr. Charles Crenshaw:
"The wound was the size of a baseball."

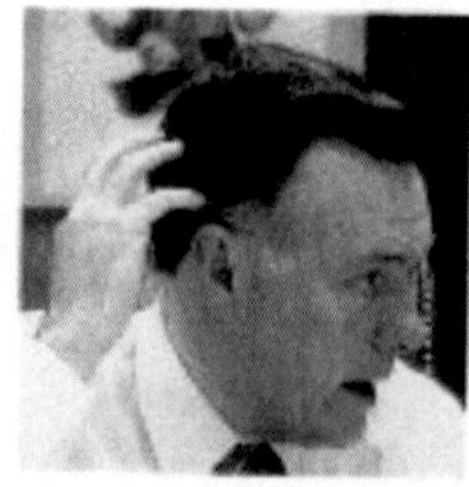

Dr. Ronald Jones:
"My impression was there was a wound in this area of the head."

Nurse Audrey Bell:
"There was a massive wound at the back of his head."

Jerrol Custer
"From the top of the head, almost to the base of the skull, you could see where that part was gone."

Paul O'Connor
"[There was] an open area all the way across into the rear of the brain."

Floyd Riebe
". . . a big gaping hole in the back of the head."

Robert Groden, The Killing of a President: The Complete Photographic Record of the JFK Assassination *(1993), Expanded*

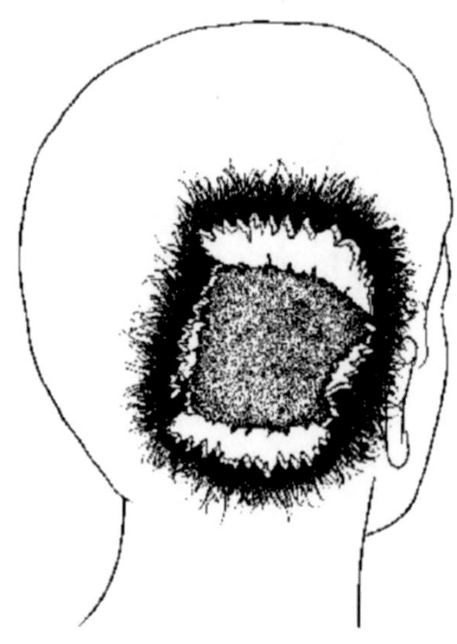

Some 40 witnesses from Dealey Plaza, Parkland and from Bethesda—including bystanders, physicians, medical technicians, and agents of the FBI—reported that JFK had a massive blowout to the back of the head, the location of which they demonstrated with their hands.

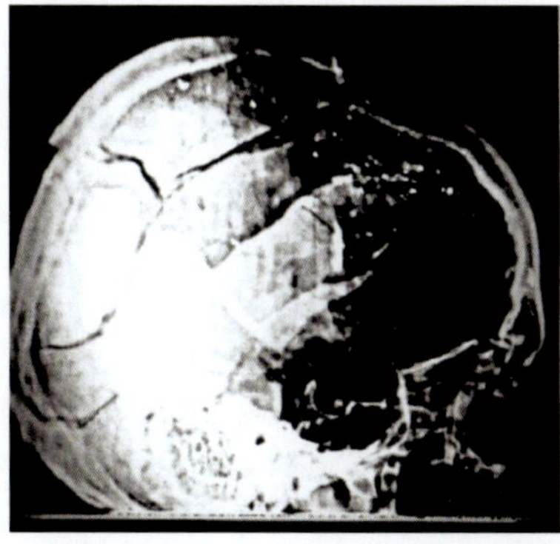

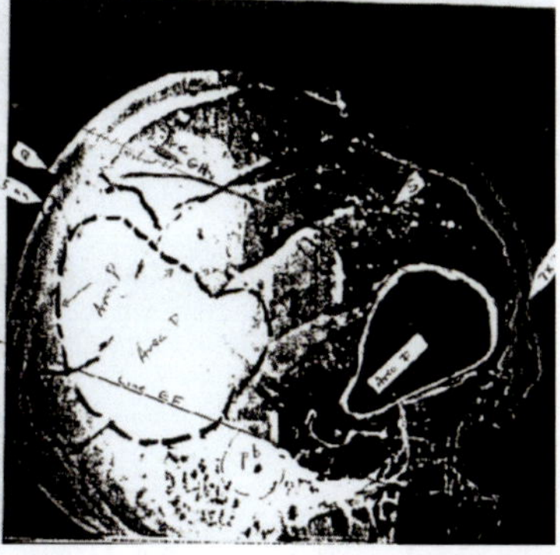

Another diagram of the head wound by Robert McClelland, M.D., who was also present at Parkland, depicts a massive blowout that fits Dr. Crenshaw's description. It was a terrible wound.

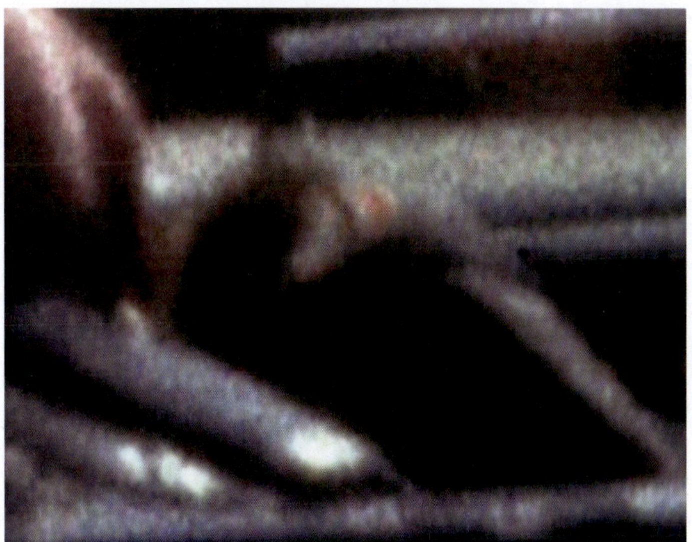

David W. Mantik, Assassination Science (1998)

These reports were discounted on the grounds that the autopsy X-rays don't show it. Mantik, a Ph.D. in physics, used the simple technique of optical densitometry to prove that an area—identified here as "Area P"—had been "patched" using material far too dense to be human bone.

It was my suspicion that those who were involved in reconstructing home movies of the assassination, including the Zapruder film, might have overlooked frames past 313-316 that display the wound to the back of the head. I found this image of the blowout in frame 374.

Damage to the cerebellum

A. According to the autopsy photographs there is no damage to the cerebellum.

B. *According to Dr. Crenshaw*

Dr. Crenshaw says the cerebellum was hanging out of the rear head wound, with strands of brain tissue extending into the brain itself.

C. According to the other Parkland doctors

- Dr. Marion Jenkins
  - CE 392--"herniation and laceration of great areas of of the brain, even to the extent that the cerebellum had protruded from the wound." (WR, p. 530)
  - WC testimony--"Part of the brain was herniated; I really think part of the cerebellum...was hanging out from the wound." (6 H 48)
  - HSCA deposition--"He [Jenkins] noted that a portion of the cerebellum was hanging out from a hole in the right-rear of the head." (HSCA, 7 H 287)
- Dr. Charles Carrico
  - WC testimony--"...skull was fragmented and bleeding cerebral and cerebellar tissue." (6 H 3)
  - HSCA deposition--"One could see blood and brains, both cerebrum and cerebellum fragments in that wound." (HSCA 7 H 268)
- Dr. Malcolm Perry
  - HSCA deposition--"There was visible brain tissue in the macard and some cerebellum was seen." (HSCA 7 H 302)
- Dr. Robert McClelland
  - WC testimony-- "...brain tissue, posterior cerebral tissue and some of the cerebellar tissue had been blasted out." (6 H 33)
- Dr. Charles Baxter
  - WC testimony-- "...the cerbellum was present--a large quantity of the brain was present on the cart." (6 H 41)
- Dr. Kemp Clark
  - WC testimony-- "...cerebral and cerebellar tissue being damaged and exposed." (6 H 20) "...the loss of cerebellar tissue..." (6 H 26)

D. IT IS CLEAR THAT DR. CRENSHAW AND SEVERAL OTHER DALLAS DOCTORS SAW THE CEREBELLUM DAMAGED AND PROTRUDING FROM THE OCCIPITAL HEAD WOUND.

E. AGAIN, DR. CRENSHAW'S OBSERVATIONS ARE CONSISTENT WITH THOSE OF THE OTHERS IN THE EMERGENCY ROOM.

[illegible] PHOTOGRAPHS OF THE BRAIN SHOW THE CEREBELLUM TO BE COMPLETELY INTACT. THIS IS IN FUNDAMENTAL DISAGREEMENT WITH THE DALLAS DOCTORS, INCLUDING CRENSHAW.

Multiple competent physicians with extensive experience in gunshot wounds observed both cerebral and cerebellar tissue extruding from the massive blowout to the back of the head. These observations were inconsistent with a blowout to the top of the head that blew his brains to the right-front, which therefore also impeach the Zapruder film.

The cerebellum is situated at the base of the skull. The cerebrum is a larger mass that comprises the upper portions of the brain. Blown-out tissue of these kinds would look very different in their appearance. Even first year medical students would not confuse them.

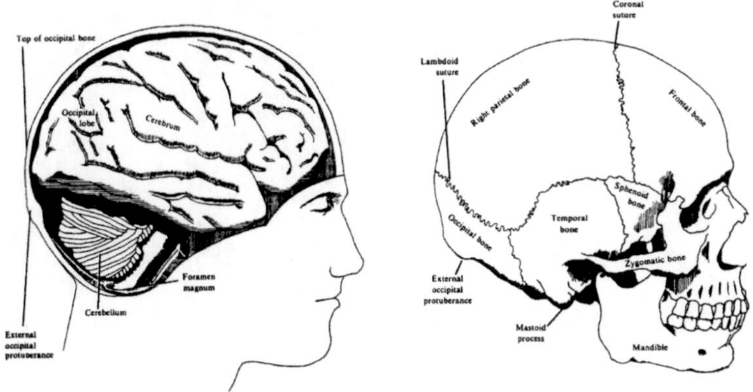

David Lifton, Best Evidence (1980)

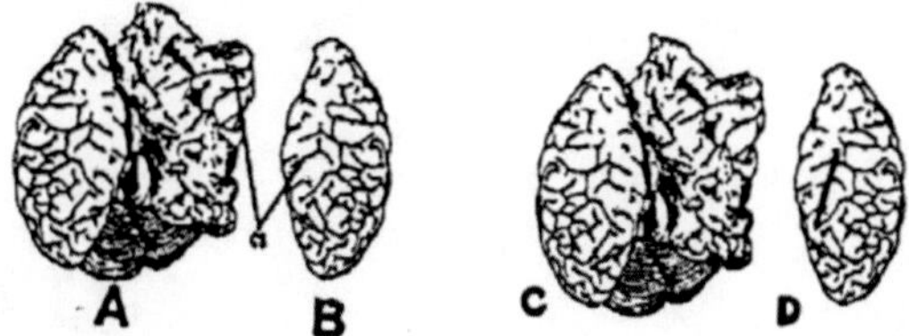

A. HSCA exhibit F-302. Drawing made from photograph of brain illustrating subcortical damage.
B. Mirror image drawing of left hemisphere in Figure A. Distortion due to damage and/or post-fixation artifact is minimal.
C. HSCA exhibit F-302 (again). Drawing made from photograph of brain to show subcortical damage.
D. Mirror image drawing of left hemisphere in Figure A. Black line illustrates schematically the direct cortical damage predicted based upon skull X-rays, which Dr. Mantik has now demonstrated to be composites.

These figures are from Joseph N. Riley, Ph.D., "The Head Wounds of John Kennedy: 1. One Bullet cannot Account for the Injuries," in: *The Third Decade* (March, 1993), pp. 1-15. These particular drawings appear on page 5.

It simply cannot be true that the cerebellum could have been seen extruding from the occipito-parietal wound--by several experienced and thoroughly competent physicians--*and for the same brain* to be seen in superior and lateral photographs, and depicted in a drawing (superior view) showing the cerebellum as being apparently intact. A conclusion is obligatorily forced that the photographs and drawings of the brain in the National Archives are those of some brain other than that of John Fitzgerald Kennedy.

Robert B. Livingston, Assassination Science (1998)

Robert B. Livingston, M.D., a world authority on the human brain and an expert on wound ballistics, studied reports of cerebral and cerebellar damage from Parkland. He concluded that the brain in diagrams and photographs at the National Archives cannot be that of JFK, as he explains above.

Mantik also discovered that a 6.5mm metallic slice had been added to other cranial X-rays in an evident attempt to implicate the obscure Mannlicher-Carcano carbine Oswald is alleged to have used.

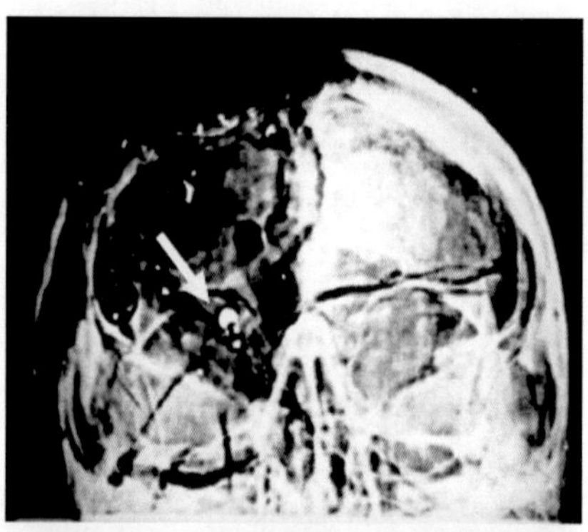

But the weapon is not high-velocity and cannot have fired the bullets that killed JFK, which means that mistakes were made by using the wrong weapon to frame him.

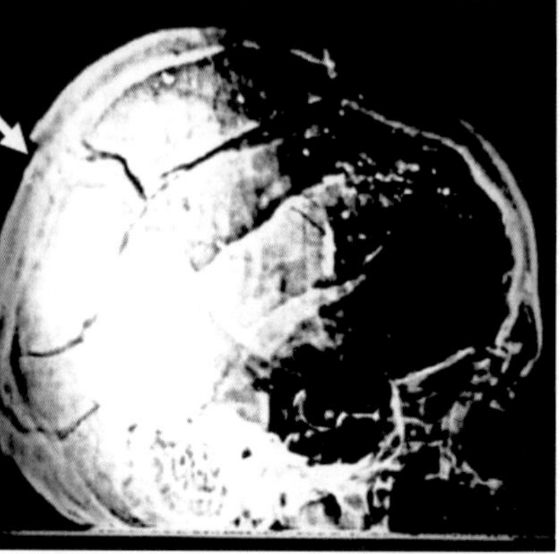

David W. Mantik, Assassination Science (1998)

At 1 PM, 22 November 1963, Malcolm Kilduff, acting press secretary, announced that the President was dead, explaining it was a simple matter of a bullet through the head while pointing to his right temple, attributing that finding to his personal physician, Admiral George Burkley.

The mortician who prepared the body for burial told an investigator that, in addition to a large gaping hole in the back of the head, there was a small wound in the right temple, and a wound on the back, 5”–6” below the shoulder to the right of the spinal column.

When the actual entry location is combined with the rest of the “magic” trajectory, the theory lends itself to ridicule as in Oliver’s Stone’s *JFK*.

The bullet alleged to have performed these feats was nevertheless virtually pristine with only slight longitudinal distortion.

Thomas Evan Robinson

ADDRESS AND PHONE INFORMATION DELETED
FOR MR. ROBINSON'S PRIVACY

lay 26, 1992 (phone)

Wounds:

- large gaping hole in back of head. patched by ~~pa~~stretching peice of rubber .... over it. Thinks skull full of Plaster of Paris
- smaller wound in right temple. cresent shape, flapped down (3")
- (approx. 2) small shrafnel wounds in face. packed with wax.
- wound in back (5 to six inches) below shoulder. to the right of back bone.
- Adrenlin gland and brain removed.
- other organs removed and then put back.
- No swelling or discoloration to face. (died instantly)

Dr. Berkley (family Physician) came in an ask.... "How much longer ??? He was told (Funeral Director) "Take your time"

Is in favor of Exuming Body ... to settle once and ... for all. "Good Pathologists would know exactly"

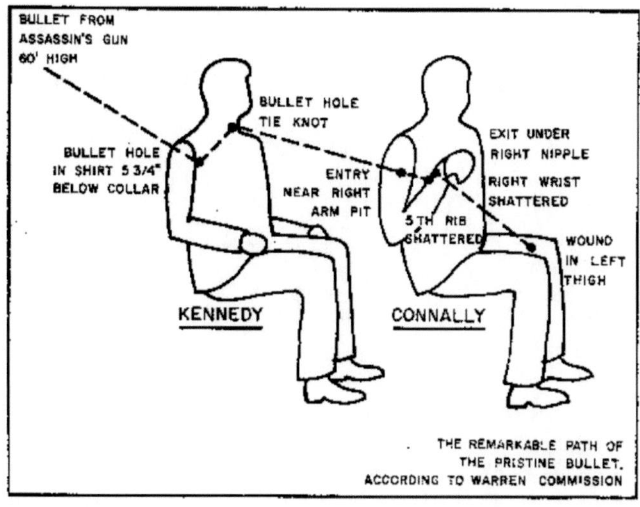

Gary Shaw, Cover-Up (1976)

James H. Fetzer, ed., Murder in Dealey Plaza *(2000)*

Taken by James Altgens, this famous photograph shows (1) the through-and-through hole in the windshield, (2) an Oswald look-alike—probably a coworker named Billy Lovelady—in the doorway of the building; (3) the open window of a closet belonging to a uranium mining company that was a CIA asset, from which three shots appear to have been fired; and (4) the Secret Service assigned to Vice President Johnson responding, even while the Presidential detail still seems to be unaware what's going on.

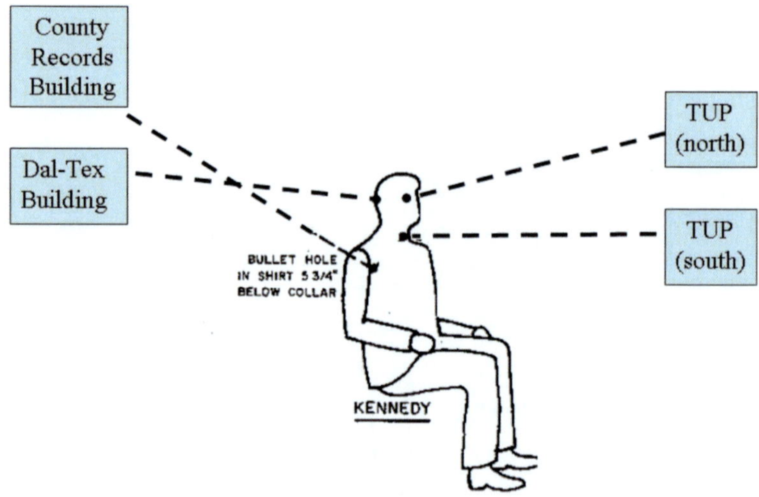

JFK appears to have been hit four times: once in the throat (from in front); once in the back (from behind); and at least twice in the head (once from behind and at least once from the right/front). The shot to his throat appears to have been fired from inside the Triple Underpass and to his right temple from an above-ground-level sewer opening on the north side of the Triple Underpass

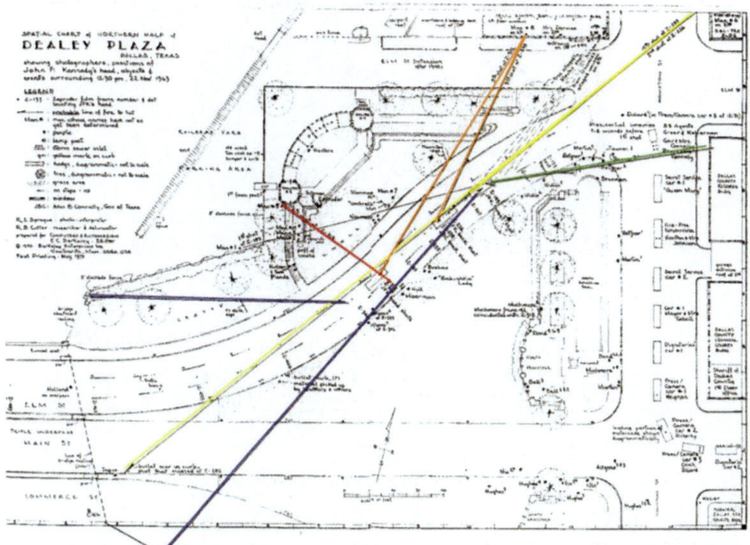

Richard Sprague, Computers and Automation (May 1970), Expanded

The most probable sequence: A shot fired from the top of County Records Building struck the President's back shortly before the shot to the throat from inside the Triple Underpass.

Then a shot from the Dal-Tex Building missed and injured Tague. A shot from the TSBD hit John Connally. The driver pulled the limo to the left and stopped.

A second shot from the Dal-Tex Building hit JFK in the back of the head. He fell forward and Jackie eased him up. She was looking him in the face when a shot from the north side of the Triple Underpass hit his right temple with an exploding bullet.

A third shot fired from the Dal-Tex Building missed and hit the chrome strip. Other shots probably hit John Connally or missed and were found in the grass. No shots were fired from the "assassin's lair".

The first frames from the Zapruder film to which the public had access were published in *Life* (2 October 1964).

Most were unremarkable, but this one—frame 313—posed special problems. The plate was broken twice to revise description (6), which appears to be unique in the history of publishing. There are many indications this and other films have been edited, including the all-but-motionless spectators, the driver's head turns (twice as fast as humanly

Color sequence shows how the President was killed

1. A moment before the first bullet was fired, the President and Mrs. Kennedy, *Governor and Mrs. Connally*, smiling and waving, were passing in front of the brick building *where the assassin was taking aim.*

2. President Kennedy clutched his hands *to his throat. The commission* determined that a bullet had entered the back of his neck and ripped through the lower front portion of his throat. They believe the wound would not necessarily have been lethal.

3. As Mrs. Kennedy reached to help her husband, Connally twisted around. He told the commission he heard a shot and turned to see if Kennedy was all right. It is still not *absolutely clear which bullet hit* the governor. Though he believes it was another bullet—the second fired by Oswald—the commission concluded that it probably was this same one that had passed through the President's throat.

4. Both Kennedy and Connally began to slump. A Secret Service agent sitting beside the driver turned to look back while onlookers, unaware that anything was amiss, applauded.

5. The President's head fell forward into Mrs. Kennedy's arms just before the assassin fired again.

6. *The direction from which shots* came was established by this picture taken at instant bullet struck the *rear of the* President's head and, passing through, caused the front part of his skull to explode forward.

7. As the President lay dying beside her, Mrs. Kennedy pulled herself out of the seat.

8. Crawling across the rear deck of the limousine, Mrs. Kennedy reached out to Secret Service man Clinton Hill.

possible), and the "blob" and blood spray, which appear to have been painted in. Blood and brains across the trunk and the driver's pulling to the left and bringing the vehicle to a halt had to be removed, because it

Zapruder Frame 313

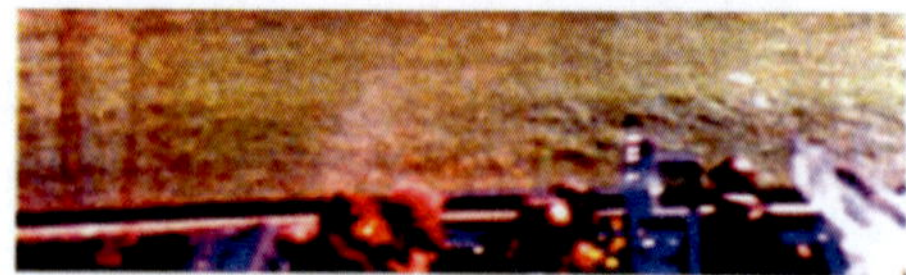

Zapruder Frame 314

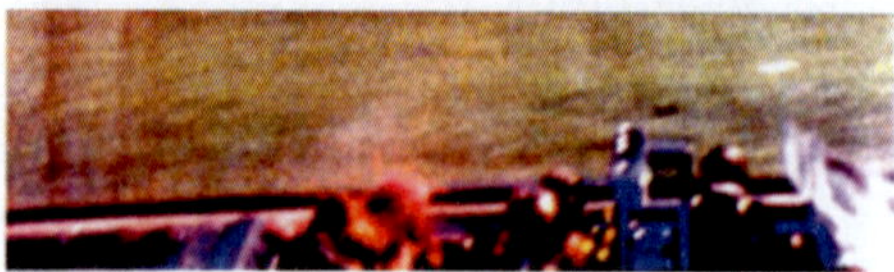

Zapruder Frame 31[illegible]

was such an obvious indication of Secret Service complicity in setting up JFK for the hit.

When the frames were published in the 26 volumes of supporting evidence, they were in the wrong sequence, greatly mitigating the back-and-to-the-left motion of JFK's head in the extant—still existing—film.

David S. Lifton had a friend write to J. Edgar Hoover, Director of the FBI, and Hoover acknowledged they were in the wrong order. Michael Baden, M.D., head of the medical panel for the HSCA, has observed that, if the "magic bullet" theory is false, there had to have been at least six shots from three directions. That turns out to be correct.

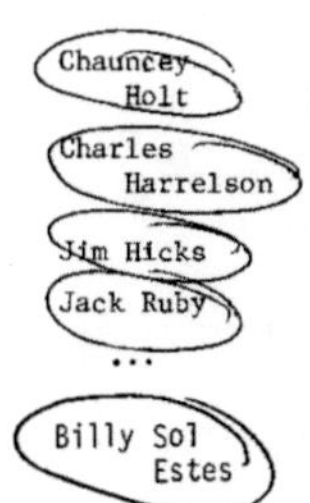

SAM GIANCANA

A question that has been asked many times is: "If the killing of Kennedy was a conspiracy involving many people, how could it possibly have been kept secret all this time? Why hasn't somebody talked?" The answer to that question is simple. A lot of people *have* talked. The talking started before the assassination and has continued to this day. There are many examples: Carlos Marcello bragged in front of Ed Becker that Kennedy would be killed and described how it would be done; Santo Trafficante, Jr., bragged that Kennedy would be killed; Joseph Milteer, right-wing nut, bragged that Kennedy would be killed and how it would be done; Johnny Rosselli, Sam Giancana's right-hand man, told Jack Anderson (years later) that Ruby was "their man and was ordered to silence Oswald." David Atlee Phillips, suspected of being the mysterious Maurice Bishop and perpetrator of the multiple Oswalds, said before he died that fringe elements of U.S. intelligence may have been involved in the conspiracy. As earlier noted, Lyndon Johnson's mistress, Madeleine Brown, has said that Lyndon Johnson implied before Kennedy was killed that it was going to happen. Marita Lorenz, CIA contract agent, stated in depositions for a courtroom trial that Frank Sturgis told her that he and a group of anti-Castro Cubans had been involved in the Kennedy assassination. And, finally, Sam Giancana's brother, Chuck Giancana, revealed in a recent book *Double Cross* that his brother Sam Giancana confessed to the entire crime in 1966 (in an hour-long discussion at Chuck Giancana's suburban home in Chicago), just before Sam Giancana was to move to Mexico City.

Noel Twyman, Bloody Treason (1997)

The claim has often been made that the strongest proof against any conspiracy is that no one has talked. This is false. As Noel Twyman, *Bloody Treason* (1997), has observed (above), at least eight prominent figures talked about it before or after the event.

Others include Chauncey Holt, Charles Harrelson, Jim Hicks, and Jack Ruby. Reinforcing the conclusions of Lyndon's mistress, Madeleine Duncan Brown, *Texas in the Morning* (1997), and of Barr McClelland, *Blood, Money & Power* (2003), Billy Sole Estes, *A Texas Legend* (2005), implicates LBJ in the assassination, as has E. Howard Hunt in his *Rolling Stone* "Confession" (2007).

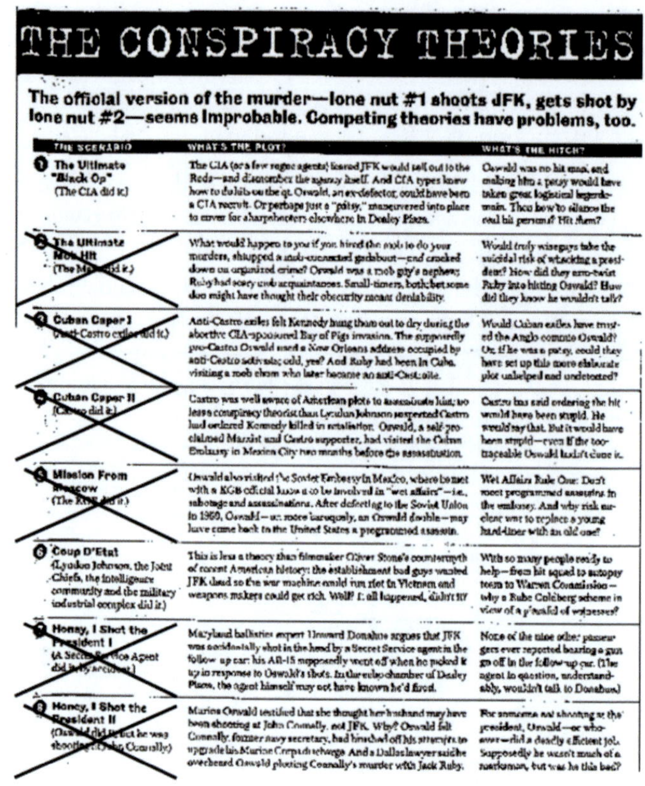

THE CONSPIRACY THEORIES

The official version of the murder—lone nut #1 shoots JFK, gets shot by lone nut #2—seems improbable. Competing theories have problems, too.

THE SCENARIO	WHAT'S THE PLOT?	WHAT'S THE HITCH?
1 The Ultimate "Black Op" (The CIA did it.)	The CIA (or a few rogue agents) feared JFK would sell out to the Reds—and dismember the agency itself. And CIA types knew how to do hits on the q.t. Oswald, an ex-defector, could have been a CIA recruit. Or perhaps just a "patsy," maneuvered into place to cover for sharpshooters elsewhere in Dealey Plaza.	Oswald was no hit man, and making him a patsy would have taken great logistical legerdemain. Then how to silence the real hit persons? Hit them?
2 The Ultimate Mob Hit (The Mafia did it.)	What would happen to you if you hired the mob to do your murders, shtupped a mob-connected gadabout—and cracked down on organized crime? Oswald was a mob guy's nephew; Ruby had scary mob acquaintances. Small-timers, both; but some don might have thought their obscurity meant deniability.	Would truly wiseguys take the suicidal risk of whacking a president? How did they arm-twist Ruby into hitting Oswald? How did they know he wouldn't talk?
3 Cuban Caper I (Anti-Castro exiles did it.)	Anti-Castro exiles felt Kennedy hung them out to dry during the abortive CIA-sponsored Bay of Pigs invasion. The supposedly pro-Castro Oswald used a New Orleans address occupied by anti-Castro activists; odd, yes? And Ruby had been in Cuba, visiting a mob chum who later became an anti-Castroite.	Would Cuban exiles have trusted the Anglo commie Oswald? Or, if he was a patsy, could they have set up this more elaborate plot unhelped and undetected?
4 Cuban Caper II (Castro did it.)	Castro was well aware of American plots to assassinate him; no lesser conspiracy theorist than Lyndon Johnson suspected Castro had ordered Kennedy killed in retaliation. Oswald, a self-proclaimed Marxist and Castro supporter, had visited the Cuban Embassy in Mexico City two months before the assassination.	Castro has said ordering the hit would have been stupid. He would say that. But it would have been stupid—even if the too-traceable Oswald hadn't done it.
5 Mission From Moscow (The KGB did it.)	Oswald also visited the Soviet Embassy in Mexico, where he met with a KGB official known to be involved in "wet affairs"—i.e., sabotage and assassinations. After defecting to the Soviet Union in 1959, Oswald—or, more baroquely, an Oswald double—may have come back to the United States a programmed assassin.	Wet Affairs Rule One: Don't meet programmed assassins in the embassy. And why risk nuclear war to replace a young hard-liner with an old one?
6 Coup D'Etat (Lyndon Johnson, the Joint Chiefs, the intelligence community and the military industrial complex did it.)	This is less a theory than filmmaker Oliver Stone's countermyth of recent American history: the establishment bad guys wanted JFK dead so the war machine could run riot in Vietnam and weapons makers could get rich. Well? It all happened, didn't it?	With so many people ready to help—from hit squad to autopsy team to Warren Commission—why a Rube Goldberg scheme in view of a plenitude of witnesses?
7 Honey, I Shot the President I (A Secret Service Agent did it by accident.)	Maryland ballistics expert Howard Donahue argues that JFK was accidentally shot in the head by a Secret Service agent in the follow-up car: his AR-15 supposedly went off when he picked it up in response to Oswald's shots. In the echo chamber of Dealey Plaza, the agent himself may not have known he'd fired.	None of the nine other passengers ever reported hearing a gun go off in the follow-up car. (The agent in question, understandably, wouldn't talk to Donahue.)
8 Honey, I Shot the President II (Oswald did it, but he was shooting at John Connally.)	Marina Oswald testified that she thought her husband may have been shooting at John Connally, not JFK. Why? Oswald felt Connally, former navy secretary, had blocked his attempts to upgrade his Marine Corps discharge. And a Dallas lawyer said he overheard Oswald plotting Connally's murder with Jack Ruby.	For someone not shooting at the president, Oswald—or whoever—did a deadly efficient job. Supposedly he wasn't much of a marksman, but was he this bad?

Newsweek (November 22, 1993)

The Mafia could not have extended its reach into Bethesda to alter X-rays under the control of medical officers of the U.S. Navy, agents of the Secret Service, and the President's personal physician. Neither pro- nor anti-Castro Cubans could have substituted another brain for the original. Even if the KGB had the same abilities as the CIA to recreate films, it could not have gained access to the Zapruder film. Nor could any of these things have been done by Oswald, who was incarcerated or already dead.

Among the photographs of onlookers in Dealey Plaza discovered by James Richards and Allan Eaglesham, some include persons who appear to be high CIA officials, such as this one. Lucien Conein was among the most notorious of CIA assassins. His presence in Dealey Plaza thus lends further weight to the inference that the CIA played a leading role in the assassination.

Officials of the CIA apparently gathered at Houston and Main to pay their "last respects" to JFK. The findings presented here would be

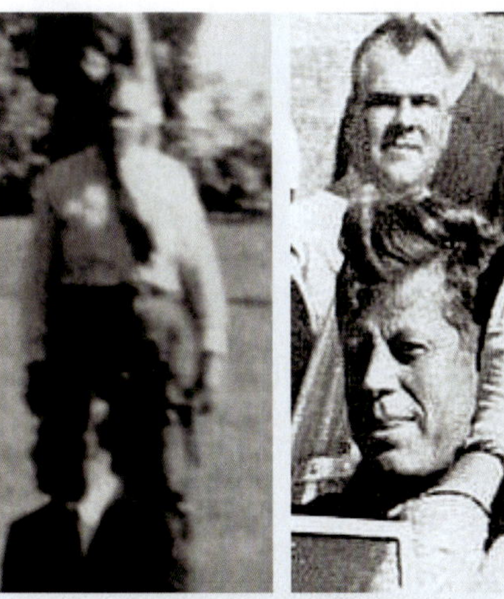

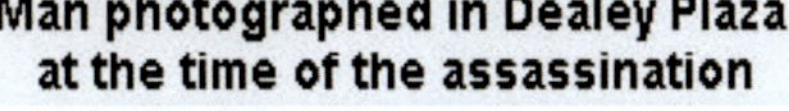

Man photographed in Dealey Plaza at the time of the assassination | **Lucien Conein**

Allan Eaglesham, "Familiar Faces in Dealey Plaza"

highly probable on a conspiracy hypothesis and have a very low—even zero—probability on its lone-assassin alternative. The strength of the evidence of conspiracy is overwhelmingly greater than that of a lone-assassin. Since the evidence has "settled down" (when you separate the authentic from the fake evidence) and points in the same direction, the conspiracy hypothesis is acceptable as true (where the fabricated evidence demonstrates the cover up).

For more on the principles of scientific reasoning, see James H. Fetzer, *Scientific Knowledge* (1981), *Philosophy of Science* (1993), and "Propensities and Frequencies: Inference to the Best Explanation", *Synthese* 132/1-2 (July-August 2002).

On the specifics of the assassination, see James H. Fetzer, ed., *Assassination Science* (1998), *Murder in Dealey Plaza: What We Know Now That We Didn't Know Then About the Death of JFK* (2000), and *The Great Zapruder Film Hoax: Deceit and Deception in the Death of JFK* (2003). Visit *assassinationresearch.com*, which I edit with John P. Costella.

Source note: This chapter first appeared as *"Dealey Plaza Revisited: What Happened to JFK?", http://www.und.edu/org/jfkconference/UNDchapter30.pdf.*

2

Framing the Patsy: The Case of Lee Harvey Oswald

by Jim Fetzer and Jim Marrs

Matte found in desk of Dallas Police Department Detective

The deliberate dissemination of false information about JFK continues to this day. Professor Hany Farid, a member of the computer science faculty at Dartmouth College, affords a stunning illustration. He has injected himself into a long-running dispute concerning the authenticity of photographs related to the assassination of JFK. These photos reportedly of the accused assassin Lee Harvey Oswald are collectively known as "the backyard photographs." What Farid has done, however, simply perpetuates the fraud.

Claiming to have studied one feature of one of these photographs and declaring his support for their authenticity, Farid's analysis immediately raised the ire of many assassination researchers, who for years have known the photos are clever fakes. In an article published in *The Huffington Post* on 5 November 2009 however, Farid asserts his conclusion that it is "extremely unlikely" that backyard photographs of Oswald are fake, based upon his digital analysis of the shadows.

Claiming to have studied one feature of one of these photographs and declaring his support for their authenticity, Farid's analysis immediately raised the ire of many assassination researchers, who for years have known the photos are clever fakes.

In an article published in *The Huffington Post* on November 5, 2009, however, Fraid asserts his conclusion that it is "extremely unlikely" that backyard photographs of Oswald are fake, based upon his digital analysis of the shadows.

Apparently referring to the more famous of the backyard photos—the one published on the cover of *Life* on 21 February 1964 nearly eight months before the Warren Commission handpicked by Kennedy's successor, Lyndon B. Johnson, concluded that Oswald was the lone assassin—Farid says, "You can never really prove an image is real, but the evidence that people have pointed to that the photo is fake is incorrect. As an academic and a scientist, I don't like to say it's absolutely authentic . . . but it's extremely unlikely to have been a fake."

Farid, who has previously conducted research on how poorly the human visual system can be at correctly judging how shadows are cast, admitted, "[W]e are really bad at judging shadows. I'm bad at it and this is what I do for a living."

Despite this caveat, Farid jumped feet first into the controversy of the backyard photos, causing further tumult in the issue. While his announcement of no fakery, propelled by an unquestioning mass media, caused a sensation with some segments of the public, serious students of the photos expressed dismay and concern that Farid had further muddied the issue without seriously delving into the abundant literature on the issue, which remains quite important as the *Life* cover-photo was successfully used to convince the public of Oswald's guilt.

Most researchers into the backyard photos, which includes an official with the Canadian Defense Department and a retired British detective expert, consider the evidence of fakery to be simply overwhelming. But Farid appears to be unaware that other experts have studied them before him.

To appreciate the magnitude of the issue, consider the words of Robert Blakey, now a professor of law at Notre Dame but who served as Chief Counsel to the House Select Committee on Assassinations (HSCA) during its reinvestigation of the deaths of JFK and of Martin Luther King, Jr., in 1977–78. Speaking to the committee about these very photographs, Blakey stated,

> *"If [the backyard photographs] are invalid, how they were produced poses far-reaching questions in the area of conspiracy, for they evince a degree of technical sophistication that would almost necessarily raise the possibility that [someone] conspired not only to kill the President, but to make Oswald a patsy."*

It might be recalled that Oswald himself used that same word—"patsy"—meaning a person set up to take the blame for a crime. In light of the major importance of the backyard photograph issue, Farid immediately drew critics, who claimed his research was superficial and not as definitive as he implied.

No Literature Search

If Farid had only conducted a literature search, he would have known that the shadows were but one of multiple indications of fakery and that, even if he were right about the shadows, he would be wrong about the photos.

Unfortunately, neither the news reporters nor the professor seems to have known enough to appreciate that his conclusion is contradicted by multiple lines of proof, including digital analyses, which are easily accessible—even by Google!

Such proofs include that the chin in the photos is not Oswald's chin; that there is an insert line between the chin and the lower lip; that the fingertips of one hand are missing; and that the figure in the image is too short to be Oswald. Farid's involvement therefore raises serious questions about the integrity of his research and the abuse of his standing as a Dartmouth professor to make public pronouncements impressionable to a wide general audience.

According to the Manchester, *New Hampshire Union Leader* (6–7 November 2009), Farid created a 3-dimensional model of Oswald's head using a computer program called "Facegen" to determine if he could replicate the shadow beneath his nose by manipulating a source of light that simulated the sun. He said he had a difficult time until he realized that he had modeled the neck "too thin".

Farid told the *Leader* that, given the technology available 46 years ago, "there is no way someone would have been able to get the internal and external elements of the photo just right in order to fabricate not only the one photo, but two others in the series." But his own conclusions make it difficult to believe that he was even aware of, much less that he had studied, even two of them.

The professor could have learned much more had he only conducted a search of the literature. Even YouTube includes this documentary, *FAKE: The Forged Photograph that Framed Lee Harvey Oswald*. One of the most interesting has been posted by Judyth Vary Baker, whom we believe to be who she claims—a cancer researcher who became acquainted with Oswald in New Orleans.

In her study, she notes that digitizing a backyard photo creates a problem of trustworthiness, where the strongest conclusion he is justified in drawing is that the pixels in the copy of a copy of a copy he analyzed were not tampered with. He simply reconstructed portions of a backyard photo—we do not know which one he chose—but only seems to have reconstructed the head and neck, not a full figure corresponding to the image.

Nor does he appear to have used the sun as his light source, which means that his "conclusion" is based upon a flawed methodology. Since digital photography did not exist in 1963, it is also relatively effortless to state—with a high degree of confidence—that no digital tampering of the original photos took place.

Misleading JFK Studies

The manipulation of the scene and pre-positioning of the elements to achieve a desired effect is reminiscent of a recent Discovery Channel program, *Inside the Target Car*, in which a rifle anchored to scaffolding was fired into a carefully-designed wooden box representing Kennedy's limousine striking dummies with gelatin heads. The resultant splatter of matter was then studied in an attempt to prove the Warren Commission's theory of one bullet causing seven wounds to both Kennedy and Texas Governor John Connally.

The program assured its audience that all the elements were exactly the same as in Dealey Plaza in 1963—*except that a modern telescopic sight was used for greater accuracy*. Of course, Oswald did not have the advantage of a modern telescopic sight and no mention was made of the fact that, even according to the official version of the assassination,

Oswald was firing at a target moving laterally and downhill away from him with tree branches obscuring the line of sight.

And this is far from the only time that "documentaries" and other studies that claim to have vindicated the Warren Commission have appeared, many of which attempt to support the "magic bullet" theory, even though it has not only been proven to be false but is not even anatomically possible. If you have any doubt, Google "Reasoning about Assassinations". And there are many more.

There appear to have been at least four photos—plus a negative and a missing color transparency—in the entire set. We suspect Farid thought there was only one. Oswald's face is tilted in different directions in different photos, yet the v-shaped shadow under the nose never varies, which is an obvious indication of fakery. Since he studied the nose shadow, he should have discovered this.

The most charitable interpretation of his work is that he naively assumed that the shadow beneath the figure's nose in the image that was published in *Life* was the basis for rejecting the photographs as fakes—and nothing else.

Had Farid simply entered the words, "backyard photographs, Oswald", on Google, he would have found a study entitled, "EXAMPLES OF DIGITAL EVIDENCE ANALYSIS AND PRESENTATION // BACKYARD PHOTOS EVIDENCE OR FAKERY // PRESENTED BY RALPH THOMAS". It should have captured his attention, since Farid was planning to do a digital analysis himself.

Thomas illustrates and explains not only that there is an apparent inconsistency in the shadow of the nose in relation to the shadow of the body but also that the body shadows in different photos indicates they were taken at different times. And, under the heading, "Close Ups Of The Two Faces", he makes key points about two of the backyard photographs:

For many years researchers have said these faces were faked. (1) A fine line runs through the chin. (2) The shadows appear to be the same under the nose. (3) The second head has merely been tilted to fit into the rest of the photo. (4) Although taken just seconds or minutes apart, the tilt of the head on the second photo also tilts the nose shadow. Under the heading, "Overlay Of The Two Faces", he also explains that, when the second face is turned into a transparency and titled to the same angle of the first one and the photos are overlaid on top of each other, (5) they match up perfectly, as indeed he shows in an additional third photo. But this would be impossible if the photos were authentic.

These studies contradict Farid—even about the shadows that he claims to have studied. They raise serious questions about the integrity of Farid's research and suggest he considered only a single aspect of a single photograph. And this is far from the only contrary evidence that a Google search would have produced.

Ignoring Expert Testimony

The day following the assassination, two photographs and the negative to one of these were found by Dallas police in the garage of the Irving home where Oswald's wife was staying. These two were designated as Warren Commission Exhibits (CE) 133-A and B.

In 1976 the Senate Intelligence Committee discovered yet another backyard photo in the hands of the widow of a Dallas policeman. Mrs. Roscoe White said her husband once told her the picture would be very valuable someday. In this heretofore unknown version of the backyard photo, Oswald is depicted holding the rifle in his left hand and newspapers in his right.

This is the same pose used by Dallas police in reenacting the photo for the Warren Commission—clear evidence that authorities were aware of the suppressed picture long before it became known to the public. This photo has been identified as CE 133-C by researchers.

In the same study, Thomas himself provides a summary of far more detailed testimony from Jack White, a long time analyst of JFK photos and films, who presented his findings of fakery to the HSCA but which the HSCA chose to disregard. Here are his observations:

1) STANDING OFF CENTER: White concluded that Oswald is standing off center and outside the weight bearing alignment of his feet. A person could not stand in such a position.

2) PROPORTIONS: When the body proportions are brought into alignment from the knees to the head by adjusting the size of the photographs, one head is much larger than the other.

3) OVERALL BODY SHADOWS: Although the photos were supposed to have been taken just seconds apart, the overall body shadows in the photographs are all different. In 133-A the photograph has a 10 o'clock shadow, 133-B a 12 o'clock shadow and 133-C a 10 o'clock shadow again.

4) ARM AND ELBOWS: White said that the elbow is too high in one photograph and the elbow doesn't show up on the one photograph of the arm were Oswald is holding the rifle. Attempts to duplicate this pose have been unsuccessful.

5) HANDS AND FINGERS: In the photographs, the left hand and finger look normal. Yet the right hand is missing fingernails and the hand appears too stubby to be normal.

6) WATCH: The photographs reveal that Oswald is wearing a watch but all witnesses have stated that Oswald did not wear and didn't own a watch. No watch was found among the possessions of Oswald and he was not wearing one when he was arrested.

7) RIFLE: When the photographs are blown up to the actual height of Oswald that was 5'9", the rifle in the photograph is too long. When the rifle is adjusted in the photograph to its proper length, Oswald's height is six inches too short.

8) SCOPE: White noted that in the photograph the rear end of the rifle scope is missing and pants wrinkles appear where the end of the scope is supposed to be, raising the prospect that the photo was retouched before being found by the Dallas police.

Different chins and an insert line between lower lip and chin

9) FACE: The face shows Oswald with a broad flat chin but Oswald's Dallas Police mug shots depicted him with a pointed and cleft chin. There is a line that breaks up the grain of the photograph that runs across the chin that many say is where a cut took place to paste Oswald's face

onto the photograph. This strongly supports Oswald's complaint to police that someone had pasted his face onto another's body.

10) PHOTOGRAPHIC OVERLAY: When Mr. White took 133-A and 133-B, adjusted and overlaid them, nothing in the background or figure matched up as expected in two separate photos made moments apart with a handheld camera, as stated in the official testimony. However, the face of Oswald was a complete match on both photographs. This could only be explained if someone made a composite photo by pasting the same Oswald face on both pictures.

11) FACE SHADOWS: Both photos show the same V-shaped shadow below the nose. However, on one of the photos Oswald's head is tilted but the shadow does not adjust for this tilt.

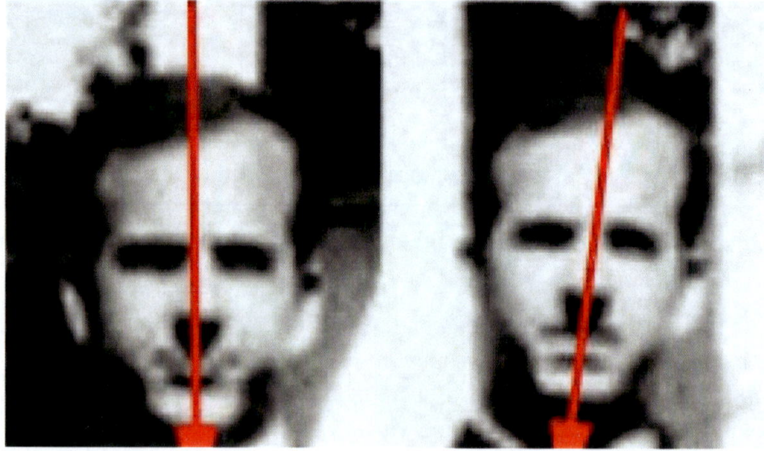

12) NECK SHADOWS: On one of the photos there is light on the right side of the neck but the same photo shows the rifle casting a shadow in the opposite angle.

13) COLLAR SIZE: The figure's collar size can be determined from the photograph using a mathematical formula, which came out to size 16". Oswald wore a size 14.5" collar and all his clothes found among his personal belongings were in the 14.5"–15" range.

14) BACKGROUNDS: White determined that one photograph had the top cropped off and the other photograph had the bottom cropped off making it appear as if they were two separate pictures. However, except for small differences, the backgrounds matched on both photographs, meaning the camera never changed position which contradicts the official story of Oswald's wife reluctantly walking into the backyard to take the photo.

15) SMALL DIFFERENCES: For many months White was puzzled by the small differences he noted in the backgrounds as they were not off by much. After looking at the photographs some more he determined that on the background of one, the camera appeared to be slightly tilted. He then took another copy of the photo by tilting it on a board and everything came perfectly into alignment.

An elementary "literature search" would not only have revealed to Farid that much more than the shadows he claims to have studied themselves afford multiple indications of fakery, as White notes in points (3), (11) and (12)! If he had been determined to conduct a serious and objective study, it's difficult to imagine how he could have missed them.

Questions of Authenticity

These photos are authentic only if they are authentic in every respect. Even if he had been successful in his study of the nose shadows, disproving one out of more than a dozen proofs of photo fakery cannot show that these photos are "unlikely to have been faked", much less that they are authentic. There turn out to have been five versions of these photographs—plus a negative of one and a separate color transparency—as we explain below.

The more we have thought about this, the more obvious it becomes that Farid was unaware of any problem besides the nose shadow or of any photos than the one he studied. Either Farid does not understand the requirements to prove their authenticity—which is absurd, since this is one of his areas of specialization—or he did not conduct a literature search and did not know the history of research on these photos.

The only alternative would appear to be that he has deliberately perpetrated a fraud.

Incredible as it may seem, the photo shown here—a "ghost" image, in the words of researcher Robert Groden—was discovered in the files of the Dallas Police files more than 20 years after the fact. In his classic study, *The Search for Lee Harvey Oswald* (1995), Groden provides an excellent introduction to the problems with the backyard photos on pages 90–95. Indeed, 404 evidence photos that have now been released from an official archive not only include 10 photographs of the backyard without figure—which would have been indispensable to fake them, which using multiple lines of proof we know was done in this case—and two "ghost" images, which suggest that they were either produced or planted by members of the Dallas Police Department.

Farid has in fact published numerous articles regarding the use of digital analysis of photographs, which suggests that he possesses the academic ability to have analyzed them properly. Even on our charitable interpretation—that he was simply unaware of other problems and had not done a search of the literature to dispel his ignorance—then at the very least we would expect that his analysis of the nose shadows would be competent.

His conclusion supports our inference. If Farid studied more than one of these photographs, as he claims, then he should have noticed that the nose shadow remains constant across different photos, an obvious indication of fakery. In fact, the figure's entire face remains constant in these different photographs. Either he did not know there was more than one or he is deliberately deceiving us.

Clearly, Farid has violated a basic canon of scientific research, which is that all the available evidence that makes a difference to a conclusion must be taken into account. It is impossible to demonstrate that a photo is not fake by selecting one issue, excluding consideration of the rest of the evidence, and showing that it would have been possible under special conditions.

Farid focused on the nose shadow, but ignored inconsistencies between the nose shadow and the shadows the figure casts, the similarity in the nose shadow from one photograph to another, and problems with the shadows on the neck. Farid was competent to investigate the shadows, but he did not perform that task in a competent fashion. The question becomes, why was he doing this at all?

Jim Marrs' Response

The author of *Crossfire: The Plot that Killed Kennedy* (1989), Jim Marrs has long been persuaded that the backyard photos are indeed composites, just as Oswald asserted. When separate photographs made at different times with a hand-held camera are turned into transparencies and placed on top of each other, nothing should match. The problem is Oswald's face (above the chin) is a near-perfect match when they are superimposed, as shown here.

The only difference that Marrs has detected is slight distortion of the mouth in one of the photos, which could have been done with retouching. In "The Many Faces of Lee Harvey Oswald" (YouTube), Jack White has compared the thick neck and block chin of the figure with the narrow neck and pointed chin of Oswald. He also noticed a bump on the backyard figure's wrist (CE-133A) not on Oswald. A rookie with the Dallas Police Department, Roscoe White, had a thick neck and a block chin, like the image in the photographs, and a similar bump on his wrist.

The first, depicting a man holding a rifle up over his head with both hands, was shown by Marina to Oswald's mother. Marguerite, the night of the assassination and then again at the Executive Inn, where Marguerite burned it and flushed it down a toilet (WC Vol. I, pp. 146-152). So that photo is no longer available.

The second is the version of CE 133-A with "Hunter of Fascists" handwritten on the back in Russian, which was found long after the assassination in the belongings left behind by George de Mohrenschildt, who appears to have been Oswald's CIA handler and had filed several reports with "the Agency."

Jeanne de Mohrenschildt, George's widow, told Marrs during an interview that she had never seen the photo before and believed it was planted in their belongings while they were traveling in Haiti.

Another copy and a third version (CE-133-A and B) were both found in the garage of Ruth and Michael Paine on the Saturday following the assassination, but Marrs has observed there is a major discrepancy in the record. Detectives Guy Rose and R. S. Stovall of the Dallas Police Department told the Warren Commission that they arrived at the Paine home after noon ("about 1 p.m." quoting Stovall in Vol. VII of the Warren Commission Supporting Volumes, p. 193) on Saturday, 23 November 1963, but only brought the backyard photos discovered in the Paine's garage back to DPD headquarters around two hours later (Rose, WC Vol. VII, p. 231).

Yet, in his statement to the Warren Commission, Capt. Will Fritz, who was in charge of the JFK homicide, related how Oswald was brought back to his office for further interrogation at 12:30 p.m. that same day, "… in an effort to find where he was living when the picture was made of him holding a rifle which looked to be the same rifle we recovered. This picture showed [by its own internal features] to be taken near a stairway with many identifying things in the backyard…. He was placed back in jail at 1:10 p.m." (WC Report, Appendix XI, p. 607.)

> *This raises the question, how could Fritz have seen a backyard photo before Stovall and Rose found two of them in the garage and had brought them back to police headquarters?*

This account lends great support to the stories of Pat and Robert Hester, a husband and wife team called from home on 22 November 1963, the day of the assassination, to help process assassination-related photos for the FBI and the Dallas police at National Photo in Dallas.

Both of the Hesters told Marrs that they had seen an FBI agent with a color transparency of one of the backyard photos and that one of those Robert processed had no figure in the picture. Hester's claim was corroborated by his wife, Patricia, who also helped process film on the day of the assassination.

Marrs believes that the FBI had the photos as early as Friday evening and either passed them to the Dallas police (who lied about finding them) or planted the photos in the Paine garage (where a thorough search of the Paine home Friday had not produced them) in order to be found by the detectives prior to the police search during which they claimed to have found the photographs.

He suspects that the fabrication of the photos can be traced back to J. Edgar Hoover, the Director of the FBI, who was intent on having proof that Oswald would have been convicted of the assassination had he lived to stand trial. And, indeed, there are multiple indications that Hoover took the steps necessary to block a real investigation, which made him at least guilty as an accessory after the fact.

Crossfire (1989)

Most of what Marrs wrote in *Crossfire: The Plot that Killed Kennedy* (1989), one of the main sources for Oliver Stone's *JFK*, remains valid today. The book is a classic in this field and one that anyone with a serious interest in the case should have read. If Farid had only read it, he would have known that multiple experts had studied the photos long before and concluded that they were fakes as well as a great deal more.

The Warren Commission heard from Oswald's accommodating wife, Marina, that she had taken these snapshots with a hand-held Imperial Reflex camera at the insistence of her husband.

Dallas Policeman Roscoe White is on the left, and the alleged Lee Harvey Oswald is on the right.

The Commission, based on Marina's testimony and the order form for Oswald's rifle, pinpointed the date as 31 March 1963, a date which later investigation with the U.S. Weather Bureau showed had been overcast and cloudy, making it impossible to have made them that day, since they evince bright sunlight and dark shadows.

She said she took one shot then handed the camera back to Oswald, who advanced the film and had her take another picture.

When shown one of the backyard photographs by Dallas police, Capt. Will Fritz has said, Oswald made the following remarks:

> *"He said the picture was not his, that the face was his face, but that this picture had been made by someone superimposing his face, the other part of the picture was not him at all and that he had never seen the picture before. . . . He told me that he understood photography real well, and that in time, he would be able to show that it was not his picture, and that it had been made by someone else."*

Photo experts told the HSCA that the most famous backyard picture—CE 133-A, which was used on the cover of *Life*—was obviously made from the original negative while in the hands of Dallas authorities. And yet the negative itself was never accounted for by the Dallas police. As the Committee astutely observed, "There is no official record explaining why the Dallas Police Department failed to give the Warren Commission the other original negative."

Marrs also discusses questions regarding the Imperial Reflex camera that was said to have been used to make these photographs. Oswald's brother Robert claimed to have obtained the camera from the Paine home on 8 December 1963. He said he did not mention it to authorities because he didn't realize anyone would be interested.

Robert was only told the camera belonged to his brother by Ruth Paine; and the FBI did not receive the camera until 24 February 1964. About that time, Marina was shown two cameras but failed to identify either as belonging to her husband.

When the government received the camera, it was inoperable. FBI photographic expert Lyndal L. Shaneyfelt told the Warren Commission, "In order to be able to make a photograph with the camera, I had to make slight repairs to the shutter lever, which had been bent. I straightened it and cleaned the lens in order to remove the dirt which had accumulated."

Then, in June 1964, Marina identified the camera as the one she used to take the photographs. Marina, who originally claimed to have only taken one picture, had revised this statement in her testimony to the Commission in February 1964. She said, "I had even forgotten that I had taken two photographs. I thought there was only one. I thought there were two identical pictures, but they turned out to be two different poses."

She never mentioned any other photos. But this incident was not the only time Marina's testimony reflected inconsistencies and rehearsal.

Experts told the House Select Committee on Assassinations (HSCA) that the most famous backyard picture—the one used on the cover of Life *magazine—was obviously made from the original negative [and the fifth of the total set of five] while in the hands of Dallas authorities.*

Yet the negative itself was never accounted for by the Dallas police. The Committee noted: "There is no official record explaining why the Dallas Police Department failed to give the Warren Commission the other original negative.

Internal Problems

As Marrs notes, objective viewing of the three available backyard photographs reveals internal problems aplenty. Although all three pictures were reportedly taken with a hand-held camera, the background of all three is identical when brought to the same size.

That is, while they are cropped differently, in the three photos, the elements of the background—shadows, leaves, branches, stairs, etc.—are exactly identical. This sameness of background could be produced with a stationary camera on a heavy tripod, but it is almost impossible with a hand-held camera.

In addition to the v-shaped shadow under Oswald's nose, the photos all show a discernible line marking a break in the print's emulsion across Oswald's face just above a flat, broad chin. In Dallas police photos, it is clear that Oswald had a sharply pointed, cleft chin.

It was pointed out in Marrs' 1989 book that when all three photos are brought to the same size and placed on top of each other as transparencies, nothing matches except the face of Lee Harvey Oswald—strong evidence that he was telling the truth when he said his face had been superimposed on another body.

Oswald's assessment that the photos are superimposed fakes has been confirmed by two foreign authorities. In 1977, Major John Pickard, commander of the photographic department at the Canadian Defense Department, made these statements after studying the backyard pictures:

"The pictures have the earmarks of being faked. The shadows fall in conflicting directions. The shadow of Oswald's nose falls in one direction and that of his body in another. The photos were shot from a slightly different angle, a different distance, with the gun in a different hand. So, if one photo is laid on top of another, nothing could match exactly. Yet, impossibly, while one body is bigger, in the other the heads match perfectly, bearing out Oswald's charge that his head was pasted on an incriminating photograph."

Author and British Broadcasting Corporation investigative reporter Anthony Summers had the photos studied by retired Detective Superintendent Malcolm Thompson, a past president of the Institute of Incorporated Photographers in England. Thompson said he detected retouching in the photos around the area of Oswald's head and on the butt of the rifle. He also noted inconsistencies in the location of shadows and the different chin on Oswald.

Thompson stated: "One can only conclude that Oswald's head has been stuck on to a chin which is not Oswald's chin. . . . My opinion is that those photographs are faked. . . . I consider the pictures to be the result of a montage." However, like Farid, neither Pickard nor Thompson had access to the original photos.

Astonishingly, the Photographic Evidence Panel of the House Select Committee on Assassinations, which did study the originals, concluded in 1978 that it could find "no evidence of fakery" in the backyard photos.

This conclusion rested primarily on studies that showed markings on the edges of the negative of one of the original photographs were identical to markings on other photographs made by the Imperial Reflex camera. This ballistics-type evidence convinced the panel that the photos must be genuine.

However, Texas graphics expert White pointed out that if a knowledgeable person wanted to fake the backyard pictures, it would have been a simple matter to produce a high-quality montage photograph using one backyard scene, a figure with rifle and papers and a head shot of Oswald, which then could be photocopied using the Imperial Reflex camera. This procedure would produce a backyard photo that could be proven to have come from the camera traced to Oswald. Another method to achieve the same results, according to White, would be to make an exposure through the Imperial Reflex camera that would include the markings on the edge but nothing else. Then, when the composite photo is combined with this, the markings become part of the negative.

Asked to study the sameness of the different photos' backgrounds, the House Committee's experts said they measured the distances between certain objects in the pictures—such as wooden fence posts—and determined differences in distance, indicating that the photos were indeed separate shots. White, on the other hand, claimed that the differences were simply the result of "keystoning" or tilting the easel on which the photograph was exposed in an enlarger. He said he, too, had been concerned with what appeared to be differences in the photos but discovered that, by simply tilting the photographic print in an enlarger's easel, the backgrounds of the supposedly separate pictures overlapped and matched perfectly.

Furthermore, in recent years White discovered other problems with the backyard photos. In one picture, the tips of Oswald's fingers appear to be missing as does one end of the rifle's telescopic scope. White believes this resulted from sloppy airbrushing.

In another, the figure can be seen to be wearing a large ring on his right hand, yet the ring is missing in the other photos. That point alone ought to have been enough to prove that these photos are fakes.

JFK Evidence Fakery

A search of the literature on a subject is usually the first stage in defining the scope of a research project, since it would be pointless to undertake studies that have been previously conducted, unless there happen to be good reasons to suppose they had not been conducted properly. That has occurred in relation to the autopsy X-rays, which David W. Mantik, M.D., Ph.D., demonstrated to have been altered in studies published in *Assassination Science.*

A Ph.D. in physics who is board-certified in radiation oncology, the treatment of cancer by using X-ray therapy, Mantik used a simple technique from physics called "optical densitometry" to evaluate the X-rays in the National Archives and found evidence that none of them are originals, that there are indications of a second shot to the head in the lateral-cranial X-ray, and that a 6.5 mm diameter, metallic sliver had been added to the anterior-posterior X-ray.

Mantik's discovery of X-ray alteration has been substantiated by Jerrol F. Custer, the Bethesda Naval Hospital radiation technician who actually took the JFK X-rays. In May 1992, Custer told the news media that the negatives in the National Archives presented by the government as assassination evidence were "fake X-rays," which has been reinforced by other research by serious students of the crime.

Blakey's words concerning conspiracy surely apply with even greater force to the alternation of X-rays that were under the control of the Secret Service, medical officers of the U.S. Navy, and the president's personal physician. Adding a 6.5 mm metallic slice was an obvious attempt to implicate an obscure WWII Italian Mannlicher-Carcano as "the assassination weapon".

But the conspirators committed a blunder by this choice of weapon. As other authors—Harold Weisberg, *Whitewash* (1965), Peter Model and Robert Groden, *JFK: The Case for Conspiracy* (1976) and Robert Groden and Harrison Livingstone, *High Treason* (1989), among others—have observed, the Mannlicher-Carcano is not a high velocity weapon. Since the Warren Commission (1964), the final report of the U.S. House Select Committee on Assassinations (1979), and articles published in *the Journal of the American Medical Association* (1992) all affirm that JFK was killed by the impact of high-velocity bullets, Oswald cannot have fired them.

It seems preposterous that, with instance after instance of conclusive proof that Lee Harvey Oswald could not have assassinated JFK, the debate continues. As Martin Schotz, *History Will Not Absolve Us* (1996), has observed, the objective of disinformation is not to convince us of the official account but to create enough uncertainty that everything is believable and nothing is knowable.

As Marrs has noted relative to the backyard photos in spite of the sameness of backgrounds and especially of Oswald's face, conflicting shadows and distances, and the loss of portions of the photos, this vital piece of evidence remains "controversial" even though their inconsistencies can be viewed by any layman and their lack of authenticity has been the studied opinion of multiple experts.

"Of course, this is the cover-up in the Kennedy assassination," said Marrs.

"There has been no real cover-up from the standpoint of lack of evidence. Instead, it has been a cover-up of obfuscation, with one expert countering another expert in order to create controversy and confusing the issue—until the public grows tired and turns away."

And now Hany Farid continues a "controversy" long thought resolved, not by government officials or a formal investigation, but by private experts who have contributed their time and effort in the only sincere search for truth about the death of JFK.

The Dartmouth Dilemma

Anyone who wants to know the latest research on the administration of JFK and the assassination that brought it to an abrupt end should read James Douglass, *JFK and the Unspeakable* (2008), and Phillip Nelson, *LBJ: Mastermind of JFK's Assassination* (2010). Or they can access *John F. Kennedy: History, Memory, Legacy* (2009), including "Revisiting Dealey Plaza: What Happened to JFK?", which features a backyard photograph.

James H. Fetzer, who presented this material during the conference held at the University of North Dakota on 22–23 November 2008, was introduced by John R. Tunheim, now a federal judge in Minneapolis, who served as the Chair of the Assassination Records Review Board (ARRB), a five-member civilian panel with the authority to declassify documents and records held by CIA, FBI, U.S. Secret Service, and other agencies.

Created by legislation that was motivated by the resurgence of public interest in the case after the release of *JFK*, the ARRB succeeded in declassifying some 60,000 documents and records, which was a remarkable achievement and where their work is discussed in his edited book, *Murder in Dealey Plaza* (2000), which begins with 16 "smoking guns," each refuting the official account.

Dartmouth, alas, confronts a dilemma. Hany Farid is not a teaching assistant but a full professor of computer science. He has immersed himself in a controversy that he could have avoided had he conducted due diligence in his research. A literature search would have revealed the full dimensions of the problem and have afforded ample indication that the photos are fakes.

Farid appears to have proceeded on the false assumption that the nose shadows were the source of concern about their authenticity. Yet, even in relation to the nose shadows, his work has been incompetent, as we have demonstrated here—unless controversy was his goal. Even if he were right about the shadows, he would still be wrong about the photos. If Dartmouth wants to perform a service on behalf of the nation, then it should conduct an objective and comprehensive review of Hany Farid's research and publish the results. Unless this bastion of Ivy League academia desires to bear the stain of incompetence in a matter of this magnitude, this appears to be the least that it can do.

Source note: This chapter previously appeared as "*Framing the Patsy: The Case of Lee Harvey Oswald", http://jamesfetzer.blogspot.com/2015/10/framing-patsy-case-of-lee-harvey-oswald.html.*

Did George H.W. Bush Coordinate a JFK Hit Team?

by Richard Hooke

George H. W. Bush (GHWB) was working for the CIA at least as early as 1961; more than likely he was recruited in his college days, at Yale, when he was in the Skull and Bones society.

He and his wife Barbara moved to Houston where he ran an offshore oil drilling business, Zapata Offshore Co., which was a CIA front company with rigs located all over the world, making it very convenient for him to vanish for weeks at a time on CIA business where one would suspect what he was doing.

George H.W. Bush, at the Texas School Book Depository, 22 November 1963

Bush was a major organizer and recruiter for the Bay of Pigs invasion, which was codenamed Operation Zapata. Colonel Fletcher Prouty, former Pentagon high ranking official, who was the basis for the "Mr. X" character in Oliver Stone's *JFK*, obtained two Navy ships for the operation that were repainted to non-Navy colors and then renamed *Houston* and *Barbara*.

George H.W. "Poppy" Bush is one of the few who could never

recall where he was or what he was doing when JFK was assassinated; as a matter of fact, for over 20 years, he could not recall any details at all. He was 39 years old at the time and chairman of the Harris County (Houston) Republican Party and an outspoken critic of JFK.

But on 21 November 1963, GHWB was staying at the Sheraton Hotel in downtown Dallas and spoke that very evening to the American Association of Oil Drilling Contractors. Sometime later, he was reportedly at "the ratification meeting" at the home of Clint Murchison, Sr., receiving last minute instructions and toasting JFK's murder the night before it happened.

[NOTE: Madeleine Duncan Brown has written about this event in her book, *Texas in the Morning* (1997). It was corroborated by Nigel Turner in Part 9, *The Guilty Men, of The Men who Killed Kennedy*.]

Deputy Sheriff Roger Craig reported to Jim Garrison he knew of 12 arrests made in Dealey Plaza that day. One, in particular, was made by R.E. Vaughn of the Dallas Police Department, was of a man coming out of the Dal-Tex Building, who said he was "*an independent oil operator from Houston, Texas*."

The prisoner was taken from Vaughn by Dallas Police detectives, and that was the last he saw of him: no mug shot, no interview, no fingerprints, or name is in existence of this mystery man. "Independent oil operator from Houston" was always George Bush's (CIA) cover.

Exactly why was he arrested? Garrison reported the man came running out of the Dal-Tex Building and authorities could hardly avoid arresting him because of the clamor of onlookers. He was taken to the Sheriff's Office for questioning, although there is no record of it.

Afterward, two officers escorted him out of the building to the jeers of the waiting crowd. They put him in a police car and he was driven away; presumably right back to Dealey Plaza, because that is where he would be photographed with USAF General Edward Lansdale.

Ed Landsdale was identified walking past "the three tramps" (center) by no less authorities than L. Fletcher Prouty, the liaison between the Pentagon and the CIA for covert activities—who was the basis for the figure, "Mr. X", in Oliver Stone's *JFK*, and Victor Krulak, former Commandant of the Marine Corps, both of whom knew him well.

CIA IN DEALEY PLAZA 11/22/1963

As for the identity of GHWB, we have these observations from Ralph Cinque, a professional chiropractor, who is an expert in dealing with person's bodies and clothing, *"The case for George HW being there is cinched. What's the serious alternative? That a simply amazing coincidence occurred in which a man who looked strikingly like him just happened to be there? How many times does V (for Vendetta in the film, "V for Vendetta") have to tell us that he, like God, does not play dice and does not believe in coincidences? Neither do I nor any other serious student of murder, especially not when it involves the JFK assassination."*

We have a photo of him standing in front of the Texas School Book Depository; we have photos of Ed Lansdale in Dealey Plaza at the time; and we have yet another in which Lansdale, who was famous for arranging assassinations around the world, is waiting to speak to him. In this case, it may justifiably be said that "these pictures really are worth more than a thousand words".

The Phony Alibi

The next that we hear of George H.W. Bush on 22 November 1963 comes from an FBI Memorandum according to which GHWB, having been cut loose from his anonymous interrogation at the Dallas sheriff's office, called into Special Agent in Charge Graham W. Kitchel of the FBI Office in Houston alleging that he was establishing a phony alibi in saying he recalled hearing, in recent weeks, a man named James Parrott talking of killing the President when he came to Houston.

Shortly after Bush made this call, FBI agents were dispatched to the Parrot house. In another FBI memo, Parrot's mother said James, who was not home when the FBI arrived, had been home all day helping her care for her son Gary.

Mrs. Parrot advised that shortly after 1 PM a Mr. Reynolds came by and talked to her son about painting some signs at Republican Headquarters on Waugh Drive. The net effect was Kerney Reynolds, George Bush's assistant, gave Parrot an alibi and Parrot was Bush's alibi; everyone's ass was covered. A bogus phone call reporting a would-be assassin who was one of Bush's Republican Party sign-painters; who himself is also freed by an alibi from one of Bush's buddies, really doesn't cut it; this is CIA Alibi 101. This type of stuff cannot be allowed to stand in history; if Bush was so concerned about his sign painter, why didn't he call in to alert the FBI before President Kennedy came to Dallas?

Bush has handed us his head on a silver platter with this memo; that's why he always said he didn't remember what his was doing on 22 November 1963; he was hoping this incredibly stupid memo never surfaced. Bush was worried he had been seen and subsequently panicked and stupidly called the FBI, thinking he was being clever by providing evidence that it wasn't him that was arrested in front of the Dal-Tex Building that day.

It seemed like a good idea, at the time, but he was actually creating a permanent record of his involvement. The memo identifies Bush as an oil man from Houston placing a long distance call from Tyler, Texas. Bush was trying to establish he was not in Dallas during, or shortly after, the assassination. He must have been worried that someone would identify him as the oil man detained running out of the Dal-Tex Building and being ushered in and out of the Dallas sheriff's office.

This FBI memo, dated 22 November 1963, states that Bush called from Tyler, Texas but there is no proof he was actually there. For over 20 years after the assassination, Bush said he did not remember where he was when the assassination took place at 12:30 PM in Dallas. The only other person of whom I have heard such a story was Richard Nixon, who flew out of Love Field just two hours before JFK flew in.

Conspicuously, this FBI memo fails to provide an answer to where George Bush actually was. The memo, however, does tell us that the first moment Bush was free to create a phony alibi was at 1:45 PM. Bush was staying in downtown Dallas at the Sheraton Hotel, just a few blocks from Dealey Plaza, yet he's trying to tell us he was in Tyler, Texas at 1:45 PM.

George Bush's CIA assignment was obviously in Dallas, that's why he was staying there, so what would he have been doing in Tyler? JFK had just been shot at 12:30 PM. Would Bush not have been in Dallas at 12:30 PM as well, like everyone else, which was presumably the reason

UNITED STATES GOVERNMENT

Memorandum

TO : SAC, HOUSTON

DATE: 11-22-63

FROM : SA GRAHAM W. KITCHEL

SUBJECT: UNKNOWN SUBJECT;
ASSASSINATION OF PRESIDENT
JOHN F. KENNEDY

At 1:45 p.m. Mr. GEORGE H. W. BUSH, President of the Zapata Off-shore Drilling Company, Houston, Texas, residence 5525 Briar, Houston, telephonically furnished the following information to writer by long distance telephone call from Tyler, Texas.

BUSH stated that he wanted to be kept confidential but wanted to furnish hearsay that he recalled hearing in recent weeks, the day and source unknown. He stated that one JAMES PARROTT has been talking of killing the President when he comes to Houston.

BUSH stated that PARROTT is possibly a student at the University of Houston and is active in political matters in this area. He stated that he felt Mrs. FAWLEY, telephone number SU 2-5239, or ARLINE SMITH, telephone number JA 9-9194 of the Harris County Republican Party Headquarters would be able to furnish additional information regarding the identity of PARROTT.

BUSH stated that he was proceeding to Dallas, Texas, would remain in the Sheraton-Dallas Hotel and return to his residence on 11-23-63. His office telephone number is CA 2-0395.

ALL INFORMATION CONTAINED
HEREIN IS UNCLASSIFIED
DATE 10-15-93 BY 9803 [illegible]
(JFK)

GWK:djw
(2)

Schmidt –
of
Jackson

62-2115-6
SEARCHED ... INDEXED ...
SERIALIZED ... FILED ...
NOV [illegible] 1963
FBI - HOUSTON

for him having been in town at the Dallas Sheraton Hotel? Would Bush not have driven down the road to Parkland Hospital to check on the President's condition, like everyone else? Except Bush was being interrogated at the Sheriff's office.

The FBI Memorandum

Bush appears to be a candidate for prosecution for treason: his alibis for 22 November 1963 are fabricated and we have evidence that shows he was there. An FBI memo of a call from Tyler, Texas does not prove his location, except that he had concocted a textbook CIA alibi, that he was lying and probably was an accessory to JFK's murder.

As a matter of fact, he had no explanation even in his autobiography; and then, all of a sudden, he concocted a story that he was speaking in Tyler, Texas to a Rotary club. Aubrey Irby said Bush was speaking when the bellhop came over and informed Aubrey that JFK was dead. Mr. Aubrey passed the info on to Mr. Wendell Cherry Irby, who passed it onto Bush, who stopped his speech. According to Irby, Bush explained he thought a political speech was inappropriate under the circumstances, concluded speaking and simply sat down.

It is inconceivable that George Bush could not have recollected this event for more than 20 years. Walter Cronkite's announcement to the world that JFK was dead came on TV at 1:38 PM ET. *Does anyone think that Bush was making a speech at that time, in Tyler, Texas, to the Rotary Club, after the president and Governor Connally were known to have been shot at 12:30 PM?*

President Kennedy had been scheduled to give a speech for lunch at the Dallas Trade Mart, after he passed through Dealey Plaza. Everyone who was anyone around Dallas was going to attend that speech; and after JFK was shot, most rushed to Parkland Hospital to find out the latest news concerning the gravely wounded president and governor.

A speech being given in Tyler, Texas, inside a building owned by right wingers, to a group of Republican JFK haters, hardly qualifies as evidence Bush was not in Dallas, where the available evidence suggests that he was on assignment for the CIA and was supervising the Dal-Tex hit team, from which three shots appear to have been fired with a Mannlicher-Carcano, which appears to have been the only non-silenced weapon that was used.

Next, George Bush can be seen in photos of Dealey Plaza, next to the TSBD doorway and Ed Lansdale, shortly following the assassination (see below). These photos, unmistakably George Bush, tell us where he went after he left the Dallas Sheriff's office: back to the crime scene to get an update on all that he had missed.

He must have made his call to the FBI reporting James Parrot from the Dallas Sheriff's office, at 1:45 PM, because Bush is seen in Dealey Plaza with Lansdale, who would leave the plaza at about 2 PM and walk past "the three tramps" toward the parking lot. Bush obviously had to go straight back to Dealey Plaza for him to be photographed with Lansdale, who remained around Dealey Plaza until Oswald was arrested at the Texas Theater at 1:50 PM.

Bullet hole/Doorway Man/Dal-Tex window/Danny Acre and Johnny Rosselli (?)

If Lee had not been arrested, then Lansdale, as "Plan B", might have framed the three tramps—Charles Rogers, Charles Harrelson and Chauncey Marvin Holt (often misidentified as E. Howard Hunt)—who had been directed to go to a boxcar and the assassination have been blamed on them. Holt (CIA), the tramp with the hat, reported that they were found in the boxcar and taken through the plaza right after Oswald was arrested, which he knew because he was listening in on a CIA provided radio concealed inside the paper bag that he is carrying in the familiar photos.

An Incriminating Memorandum

An FBI Memo from Director J. Edgar Hoover, discovered by John McBride in 1988 but written just seven days after the assassination, provides verification George H.W. Bush was an officer of the CIA in 1963 and was provided updates on the anti-Castro Cubans. George Bush has said this memo was referring to another "George Bush" because he wasn't in the CIA at the time.

But while there was another man by that name, he was a file clerk and would not have been receiving a memorandum about the Bay of Pigs operation. And other information has surfaced showing the George Bush in the document was indeed George H.W. Bush and had the same address. In 1976, President Ford appointed Bush as the Director of the CIA, replacing William Colby. Bush served in this role for 357 days, from 30 January 1976 to 20 January 1977. Bush falsely testified before

Congress that he had never worked for the CIA, and it was widely reported that this was the first time that a civilian would be appointed to run "the Agency." But that was more poppycock from Poppy. George Bush appears to have been a CIA lifer, probably recruited right out of Yale.

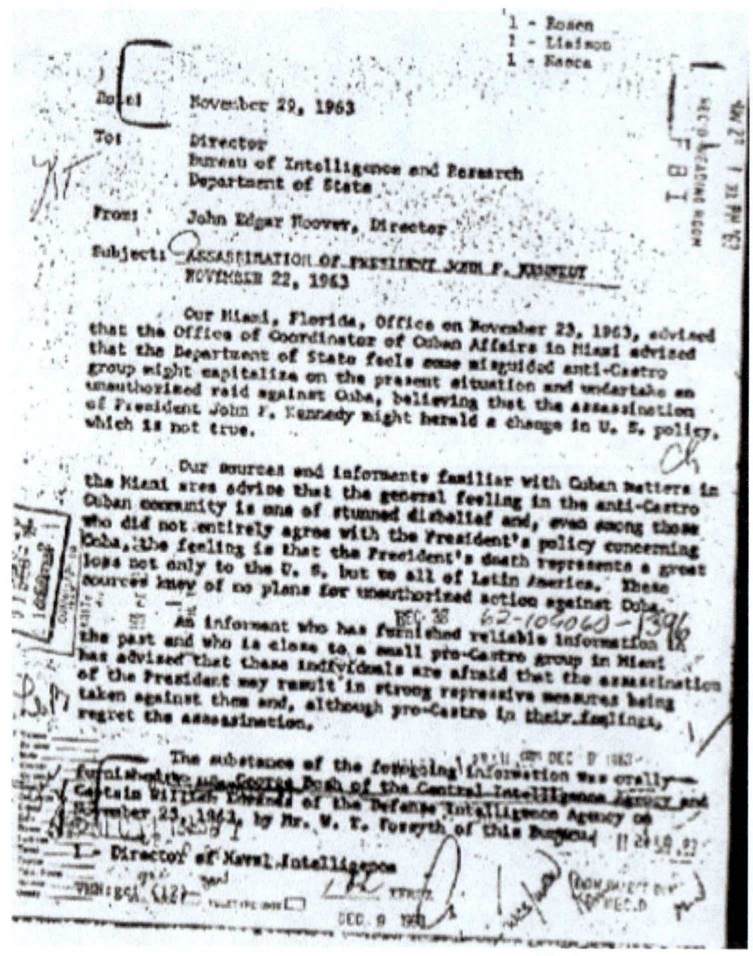

1 - Rosen
1 - Liaison
1 - [illegible]

Date: November 29, 1963

To: Director
Bureau of Intelligence and Research
Department of State

From: John Edgar Hoover, Director

Subject: ASSASSINATION OF PRESIDENT JOHN F. KENNEDY
NOVEMBER 22, 1963

Our Miami, Florida, Office on November 23, 1963, advised that the Office of Coordinator of Cuban Affairs in Miami advised that the Department of State feels some misguided anti-Castro group might capitalize on the present situation and undertake an unauthorized raid against Cuba, believing that the assassination of President John F. Kennedy might herald a change in U. S. policy, which is not true.

Our sources and informants familiar with Cuban matters in the Miami area advise that the general feeling in the anti-Castro Cuban community is one of stunned disbelief and, even among those who did not entirely agree with the President's policy concerning Cuba, the feeling is that the President's death represents a great loss not only to the U. S. but to all of Latin America. These sources know of no plans for unauthorized action against Cuba.

An informant who has furnished reliable information in the past and who is close to a small pro-Castro group in Miami has advised that these individuals are afraid that the assassination of the President may result in strong repressive measures being taken against them and, although pro-Castro in their feelings, regret the assassination.

The substance of the foregoing information was orally furnished to Mr. George Bush of the Central Intelligence Agency and Captain William Edwards of the Defense Intelligence Agency on November 23, 1963, by Mr. W. T. Forsyth of this Bureau.

1 - Director of Naval Intelligence

DEC 18
62-109060-1396

DEC. 9 1963

George H.W. Bush (CIA) was also a close friend of George de Mohrenschildt (CIA), including they were both members of the Dallas Petroleum Club.

After de Mohrenschildt was found shot dead the day before he was to be questioned by Gaeton Fonzi for the HSCA reinvestigation of the deaths of JFK and MLK in the late 1970s, Bush's name and address were found in de Mohrenschildt's address book: "Bush, George H.W. (Poppy) 1412 W. Ohio also Zapata Petroleum Midland."

CIA documents reveal that during the planning of the Bay of Pigs Operation (Operation Zapata), de Mohrenschildt made frequent trips to Mexico and Panama and gave reports to the CIA. His son-in-law also told the Warren Commission that he believed de Mohrenschildt was spying for the planned Cuban invasion. George de Mohrenschildt, notably, was Lee Harvey Oswald's best friend and appears to have been his handler after Oswald was brought to Dallas in the fall of 1963 and would find work at the TSBD.

Was Bush in the Window?

In *The Killing of a President: The Complete Photographic Record of the JFK Assassination* (1994), *Robert* Groden observes that a dark-complected man was seen in the window whom James Richards has identified to Jim Fetzer as having been Nestor "Tony" Izquierdo, for whom there is a statue in Freedom Park of "Little Havana", Miami, Florida. He was an anti-Castro Cuban, whom GHWB may have known from the Bay of Pigs. I have built upon the prior research of Duncan MacRae,"Dal-Tex Shooter 2nd floor" , which provides the most suggestive interpretation of the location from which three rifle shots appear to have been fired.

Given that Bush was in the building at the time, I infer that he was there in the background, inside the window of a broom closet of a

uranium mining company on the second floor of the Dal-Tex Building (which was a CIA asset). My interpretation is that someone with GHWB's preppy haircut, large left ear, tall height, body language (head tilt), hairline part and forehead profile, was supervising the Dal-Tex hit team (see collage below).

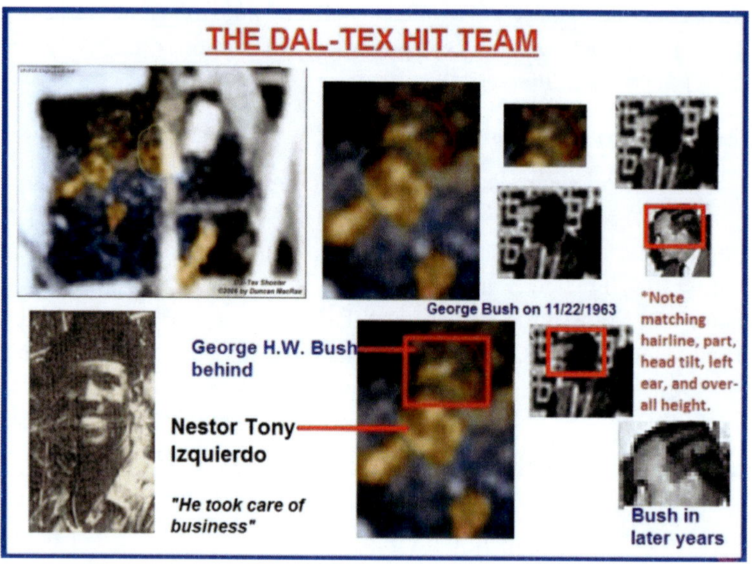

He was in Dallas for a reason, which was not to watch the presidential motorcade, and appears to have been a supervisor rather than a shooter, where it is very likely he was communicating using a radio device with a spotter.

That spotter may have been Danny Arce (CIA), who can be seen speaking into a walkie-talkie, out on Houston Street (in the Altgens6 photo above), standing next to Johnny Roselli (CIA/Mafia). Arce was talking with someone as multiple shots were fired. Ruth Ann (CIA) was reported (by complicit witness Loy Factor) to have been counting down a cadence and to have been receiving information by walkie-talkie from the 6th floor of the TSBD.

Umbrella Man's companion, possibly Orlando Bosch (CIA) [NOTE: or Filipe Vidal Santiago], was not talking on his radio as the limousine passed the Stemmons Freeway sign and the Umbrella Man pumped his umbrella up and down, which appears to have been a signal to "keep firing" because the target was still alive.

[NOTE: It was at a location that was visible from all of the shooting locations that I have identified above.] Chauncey Holt (CIA), the oldest of the tramps, said he had a CIA-supplied radio, concealed in his brown paper bag that kept him updated on events even from inside the Rock Island Railroad boxcar. Holt had delivered 15 sets of fake Secret Service IDs and left them in a red pick-up truck parked in the lot behind the grassy knoll, which was used by the Dallas Police Department, earlier that morning, facilitating the escape of the grassy knoll shooters. And Lee Bowers, the railway tower switchman, also testified to the Warren Commission that he observed strange people driving behind the picket fence and noticed one using a walkie-talkie.

CIA GEORGE BUSH DEALEY PLAZA COORDINATOR

Proof Sketch GWHB Was There

(1) The FBI report (memo) Bush called in at 22 November 1963 1:45 PM identified him as an oil businessman from Houston, Texas and the FBI office he called was the Houston office.

(2) The man arrested running out of the Dal-Tex Building at approximately 12:35 PM on 22 November was said (per Deputy Sheriff Roger Craig) to have identified himself as "an oil man from Houston". Bush was arrested by R.E. Vaughn of the Dallas Police Department.

(3) Bush called his FBI warning about James Parrot by long distance to his friend, FBI Special Agent Graham W. Kitchel, at the FBI office in Houston.

(4) James Parrot had no history as a subversive but was a sign painter for George Bush's Republican Senate campaign.

(5) James Parrot was quickly provided an alibi by another friend, who was also an assistant of Bush, Kerney Reynolds.

(6) George Bush was staying in Dallas at the downtown Sheraton Hotel and had spent the previous night (of the 21st) there.

(7) There are at least two photos of George Bush (CIA) in Dealey Plaza speaking with police shortly after JFK was shot at 12:30 PM.

(8) One of those photos has Bush (CIA) standing next to Ed Lansdale (CIA).

(9) One of the photos shows Bush near the TSBD doorway in a zone police had cordoned off, which would have taken special ID (CIA).

(10) The photo next to Lansdale most likely was taken between 1:45 PM, when Bush called in his bogus FBI memo, and 2 PM, when Lansdale is pictured exiting the plaza passing the three tramps. The tramps were taken from the boxcar at approximately 1:50 PM, when Oswald was arrested at the Texas Theater.

(11) For over 20 years, George H.W. Bush said he did not remember what he was doing during the assassination, then he suddenly remembered he was giving a speech to the Rotary Club in Tyler at 1:38 PM, while his FBI call reporting James Parrot was placed at 1:45 PM.

(12) His attendance with Malcolm "Mac" Wallace at Yale, when "Mac" was LBJ's personal hit man, and his attendance at the ratification meeting at the home of Clint Murchison, Sr., are powerful circumstantial evidence of his complicity in the assassination of JFK.

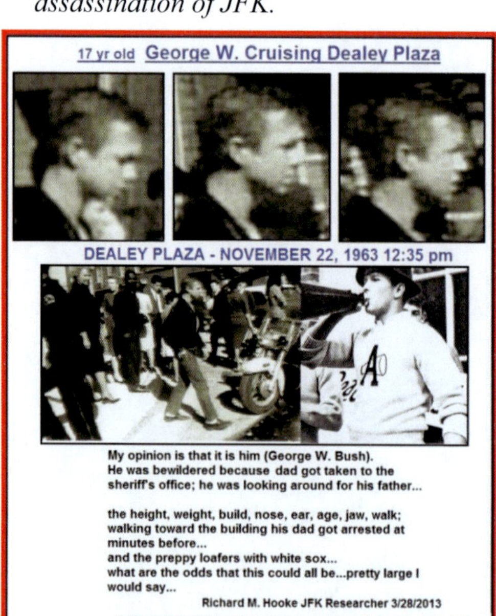

(Collage provided by JFK Researcher Larry Rivera; obtained from the Cook-Cooper Collection)

POSTSCRIPT

Remarkably, there is a figure in the Dallas Cinema Associates film walking off the corner of Houston and Elm and toward the Dal-Tex Building, where "the oil man from Houston" (George H.W. Bush) had been arrested minutes earlier, who looks a great deal like his son, 17-year-old George W. Bush. This figure's ear, nose (where a crude effort to change the nose has been made in the second of these three images), bridge indent and jawline are a very close match to George W. Bush, where the preppy loafers and white socks he's wearing are cheerleader appropriate. It looks like W. was there, too.

Source note: This chapter previously appeared as *"Did George H.W. Bush Coordinate a JFK Hit Team?", http://jamesfetzer.blogspot.com/2015/09/did-george-hw-bush-coordinate-jfk-hit.html.*

4

Six JFK Shooters Named, Three with Ties to CIA

by Sherwood Ross with Jim Fetzer

Six shooters who participated in the assassination of President John F. Kennedy, including three with ties to the Central Intelligence Agency (CIA), were named by a prominent critic of the Warren Commission. Remarkably, Lee Harvey Oswald, the Warren Commission's lone-assassin-designate, was not among them.

During an interview published this past November 20th in the *Santa Barbara Independent,* Warren Commission critic/researcher Dr. James

According to researcher Penn Jones Jr., Weatherford was a "crackshot" and was on top of the Dallas County Jail building at the time of the assassination. A researcher had once asked him if he had shot JFK. Weatherford replied, "You little son of a bitch, I shoot lots of people." Jones also wrote that a custom-made silencer for a rifle had been delivered to Weatherford "a few weeks" before the assassination.

Fetzer of Madison, WI, and first chairman of the Oswald Innocence Campaign, revealed the names of five of those who appear to have been shooters, where he has identified the sixth separately:

(1) The first shot that hit, which struck Kennedy in the back, appears to have been fired from the top of the County Records Building by Dallas Deputy Sheriff Harry Weatherford.

He used a .30-06 to fire a Mannlicher-Carcano bullet fitted with a plastic collar known as a sabot, which hit JFK 5.5" below the shoulder just to the right of the spinal column. This was a shallow wound with no point of exit.

(2) Jack Lawrence, a U.S. Air Force expert, who had gone to work for the automobile dealership that provided vehicles for the presidential motorcade just a few days before the assassination, fired the shot that passed through the windshield and struck JFK in the throat from the south end of the Triple Underpass.

Jack Lawrence

Jack Lawrence worked for the Downtown Lincoln-Mercury car dealership in Dallas. Lawrence claimed that Lee Harvey Oswald asked to test-drive a car in early November. Afterwards Lawrence reported the incident to the Federal Bureau of Investigation.

On 21st November, 1963, Lawrence borrowed one of the firm's cars. The following day he failed to turn up for work. According to Jim Marrs (Crossfire): "about thirty minutes after the assassination, he came hustling through the company's show room, pale and sweating with mud on his clothes. He rushed into the men's room and threw up. He told co-workers he had been ill that morning, and that he had tried to drive the car back to the dealership but had to park it due to the heavy traffic. Later, employees found the car parked behind the wooden picket fence on top of the Grassy Knoll overlooking Dealey Plaza."

Lawrence's strange behaviour was reported to the Dallas police. He was interviewed by officers investigating the assassination of John F. Kennedy. They discovered that Lawrence was a marksman in the United States Air Force.

According to Beverly Oliver, Lawrence was a regular at the Carousel Club (owned by Jack Ruby) and a close friend of George Senator.

(3) Nestor "Tony" Izquierdo, an anti-Castro Cuban recruited by the CIA, fired the shot that hit JFK in the back of the head after the limousine was brought to a halt. He fired three shots with two misses using a MannlicherCarcano, which were the only unsilenced shots fired, from the Dal-Tex Building, which housed a uranium mining corporation, Dallas Uranium and Oil, that was a CIA front.

(4) Roscoe White, a Dallas police officer with ties to the CIA, fired from the grassy knoll adjoining the motorcade route, but seems to have "pulled his shot," Fetzer said, "because it would have hit Jackie, so his shot went into the grass." His son subsequently discovered his diary, but gave it to the FBI and it has not been seen since.

THE MIAMI HERALD, FRIDAY, MAY 29, 1992 A

PETER PORTILLA / Miami Herald Staff

STATUE FOR A WARRIOR

Friends and relatives unveil a bronze statue in Little Havana honoring Nestor A. 'Tony' Izquierdo. Izquierdo, born in Matanzas province, Cuba, fought the Castro regime at the Bay of Pigs and later the Sandinistas in Nicaragua. He died there in 1979 in a plane crash. Among those at the ceremony Thursday were Gilberto Casanova, upper left, who raised $18,000 for the monument; Rene Martinez, upper right; and Edith Izquierdo, Izquierdo's widow. The statue was created by sculptor Tony Lopez.

Roscoe White

v Primary Sources v

Roscoe White joined the United States Marines and left for Japan in August, 1957. He was stationed at Atsugi and worked on the U-2 project.

Whitejoined the Dallas Police Force in September, 1963. Soon afterwards, his wife Geneva White, claimed that she overheard her husband and Jack Ruby plotting the assassination of John F. Kennedy.

White left the police force and was employed by a company called M & M Equipment. On 23rd September, 1971, White and a fellow worker, Richard Adair were both badly burnt in an industrial fire. Adair recovered but White died the following day.

On 4h September, 1990, Roscoe's son, Ricky White, revealed to a meeting at the University of Texas that his father had been involved in killing the president: "The diary said after my father shot the President he handed his 7.65 Mauser to the man standing beside him, hurled over the fence, took the film from the military man, whirled around the fence and went through the parking lot."

White added that Lee Harvey Oswald had also taken part but had not fired any of the shots. White then went on to kill J. D. Tippit. Ricky White claimed he had got this information from his father's diary. This

(5) Malcolm "Mac" Wallace, who shot from the TSBD, may have murdered a dozen people for Lyndon B. Johnson. "Mac" appears to have fired from the west side of the TSBD at Texas Governor John Connally in the mistaken belief he was Senator Ralph Yarborough, whom LBJ despised. Wallace's fingerprint was found on one of the boxes in the "assassin's lair" in the book depository from which Oswald allegedly fired.

(6) Frank Sturgis, later complicit in the Watergate break-in, who also appears to have been connected to the CIA, is said by Fetzer to have

Malcolm (Mac) Wallace v Primary Sources v

Malcolm (Mac) Wallace, the son of a farmer, was born in Mount Pleasant, Texas, in October, 1921. Four years later the family moved to Dallas.

In 1939 Wallace joined the U.S. Marines. After completing basic training Wallace was sent to Hawaii where he served on the aircraft carrier USS Lexington. The following year Wallace fell from a ladder and badly injured his back. On 25th September, 1940, he was medically discharged and he returned to Dallas.

In 1941 Wallace became a student at the University of Texas in Austin. He began to take an interest in politics and was elected president of the Student Union. In October, 1944, Homer P. Rainey, president of the University of Texas and an outspoken supporter of the American Socialist Party, was fired. Wallace led a protest march of 8,000 students but the campaign to have Rainey reinstated ended in failure. Wallace graduated in June, 1947. The following month he married Mary DuBose Barton, the daughter of a Methodist preacher.

While he was working on his doctorate at Columbia University he taught at Long Island University, the University of Texas and the University of North Carolina. It was at this time that Edward Clark introduced Wallace to Lyndon B. Johnson and in October, 1950, he began working with the United States Department of Agriculture in Texas.

fired the shot that entered Kennedy's right temple, from the north side of the Triple Underpass. Sturgis is known to have ties to Meyer Lansky, a notorious crime syndicate kingpin, and confessed his role to a New York City Gold Shield Detective when he was arrested attempting to kill Marita Lorenz.

In his interview with the *Santa Barbara Independent,* Fetzer said "there were shooters at six different locations," with a total of up to 10 shots fired, three of which missed. He asserted JFK was hit four different times: in the back from behind, in the throat from in front, and twice in the head after the driver had brought the car to a halt to make sure he would be killed. Another shot missed and injured bystander James Tague, while "one or more shots hit Connally."

Sturgis became involved with Marita Lorenz, who was having an affair with Fidel Castro. In January 1960, Sturgis and Lorenz took part in a failed attempt to poison Castro. It is also believed that Sturgis was involved in helping the CIA organize the Bay of Pigs invasion. Sturgis was also a member of Operation 40.

A memo sent by Patrick Gray, Director of the FBI, to H.R. Haldeman in 1972: "Sources in Miami say he (Sturgis) is now associated with organized crime activities". In his book, Assassination of JFK (1977), Bernard Fensterwald claims that Sturgis was heavily involved with the Mafia, particularly with Santos Trafficante and Meyer Lansky in Florida.

In January 2004, E. Howard Hunt gave a taped interview with his son, Saint John Hunt, claiming that Lyndon Baines Johnson was the instigator of the assassination of John F. Kennedy, and that it was organized by Sturgis, Cord Meyer, David Atlee Phillips and David Sanchez Morales.

By contrast, the Warren Commission concluded that a single bullet struck Kennedy in the back, exited through his throat and then wounded

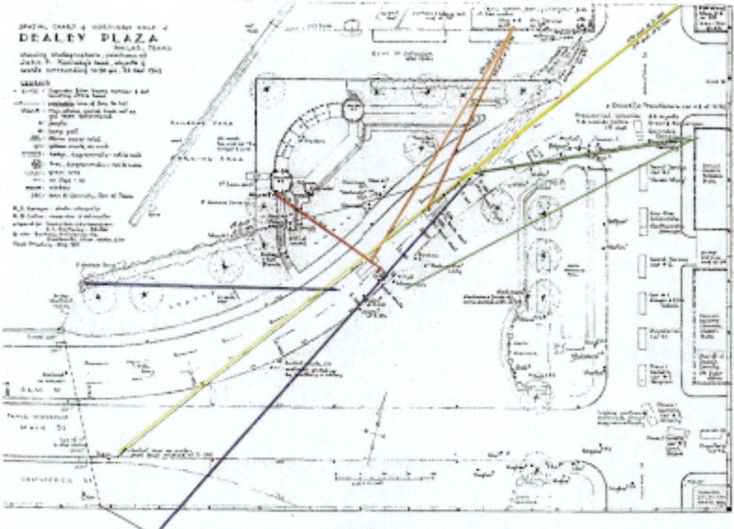

Richard Sprague, Computers and Automation (May 1970), Expanded

Connelly. Fetzer explained that the "magic bullet" theory propounded by the Warren Commission is not only false but provably false and not even anatomically possible, because cervical vertebrae intervene.

Ruth Paine, who appears to have been working for the CIA, arranged for Oswald to go to work for at the TSBD "just weeks before the assassination, which was part of the whole project to set him up as a patsy," Fetzer said. Right up to the time of the assassination, Oswald was a paid FBI informant, collecting $200 a month, which explains why his W-2 forms have never been released by the government.

As for the motivation to kill JFK, Fetzer noted that he was threatening to shatter the CIA into a thousand pieces, that the Joint Chiefs believed

he was soft on communism, that the Mafia was unhappy because Attorney General Robert Kennedy was cracking down on organized crime, that he was going to abolish the Federal Reserve and cut the oil depletion allowance.

Fetzer said Vice President Johnson, who had forced his way onto the ticket with JFK in Los Angeles in order to succeed him when he would be taken out, "was a pivotal player" facilitating the assassination. LBJ sent his chief administrative assistant, Cliff Carter, down to Dallas to make sure all the arrangements for the assassination were in place. And his close friend, J. Edgar Hoover, used the FBI to cover it up.

Fetzer said further there where "more than 15 indications of Secret Service complicity in setting Kennedy up for the hit": two agents assigned to the President's limousine were left behind at Love Field; that JFK's limousine, which should have been in the middle of the motorcade, was put first; that the motorcycle escort was reduced to four and instructed not to ride ahead of the limousine's rear wheels; and after the first shots were fired, the driver pulled the limo to the left and stopped.

What's more, Fetzer produced an AP photograph that appears to show Oswald standing in doorway of the TSBD at the time JFK was shot. They may be compared with Oswald's photograph taken later that afternoon in Dallas police headquarters. When questioned, Oswald told Dallas homicide detective Will Fritz that during the shooting he had been standing with Bill Shelley, one of his supervisors, in front of the building.

Note the missing left shoulder and the figure who is in front of and behind the man in the doorway at the same time, which are obvious indications the photo has been altered. Facial features have been distorted, but the clothing is the key. "If you look at the height, weight,

build, and the clothing he's wearing—especially the highly unusual shirt and the T-shirt he has on—they correspond very closely to what Oswald was wearing when he was arrested," Fetzer said.

For more proof that the man in the doorway (Doorman) was Lee Oswald, visit the Oswald Innocence Campaign online. While they altered features of Doorman's face, the only other candidates for having been there were not wearing comparable clothing or did not fit the height, weight and build of the man in the doorway. When you consider the totality of the evidence, no alternative explanation is reasonable.

In his *Santa Barbara Independent* interview, Fetzer said public opinion polls "have shown over the years that as much as 85% of the public has expressed disagreement with the Warren Commission and the lone assassin theory." Fetzer elaborated on the points he made in great detail during his keynote address, "The Assassination of America", for the Santa Barbara JFK conference that he organized and moderated, which is now available at jfk50santabarbara.com.

Source note: This chapter previously appeared as "*Six JFK Shooters Named, Three with Ties to CIA—Oswald Not Among Them*", http://jamesfetzer.blogspot.com/2013/12/six-jfk-shooters-including-three-tied.html.

Part II

The Zapruder Film: Frame by Frame

5

The Zapruder Film: The Costella Combined Cut

by John P. Costella

Among the first results of the 2003 Zapruder Film Conference was the discovery that the copies of the film available to the public, including David Lifton's "Z Film" (undated), the Macmillan CD (1993), Robert Groden's "The Assassination Films" (1965), and MPI Media Group's (MPI) "Image of an Assassination" (1998), all differ significantly in the amount of pixel information they provide. Even MPI's "Image of an Assassination" (1998) does not include frames 155 and 156; does not include frames 208, 209, 210, and 211; has reversed frames 331 and 332; and does not include (what ought to be) frames 341, 350, and (even) 486!

John P. Costella, Ph.D., has produced a fresh version of the film, which overcomes these deficiencies and introduces improvements never before seen in any Zapruder film, namely: corrections for pincushion and aspect ratio distortion; inclusion of the so-called "ghost panels"; and masking of open sprocket holes to make information more accessible. In the interest of advancing the frontiers of knowledge, education, research, science, and inquiry, this new, improved version is being made available to the public free of charge. For the complete set of frames and the fresh version of the film, go to assassinationscience.com. (To save space and show more of the images, we have cut away the lower black part of all frames).

Z001 *Z002* *Z003*

Z004 Z005 Z006

Z007 Z008 Z009

Z010 Z011 Z012

Z013 Z014 Z015

Z016 Z017 Z018

Z019 Z020 Z021

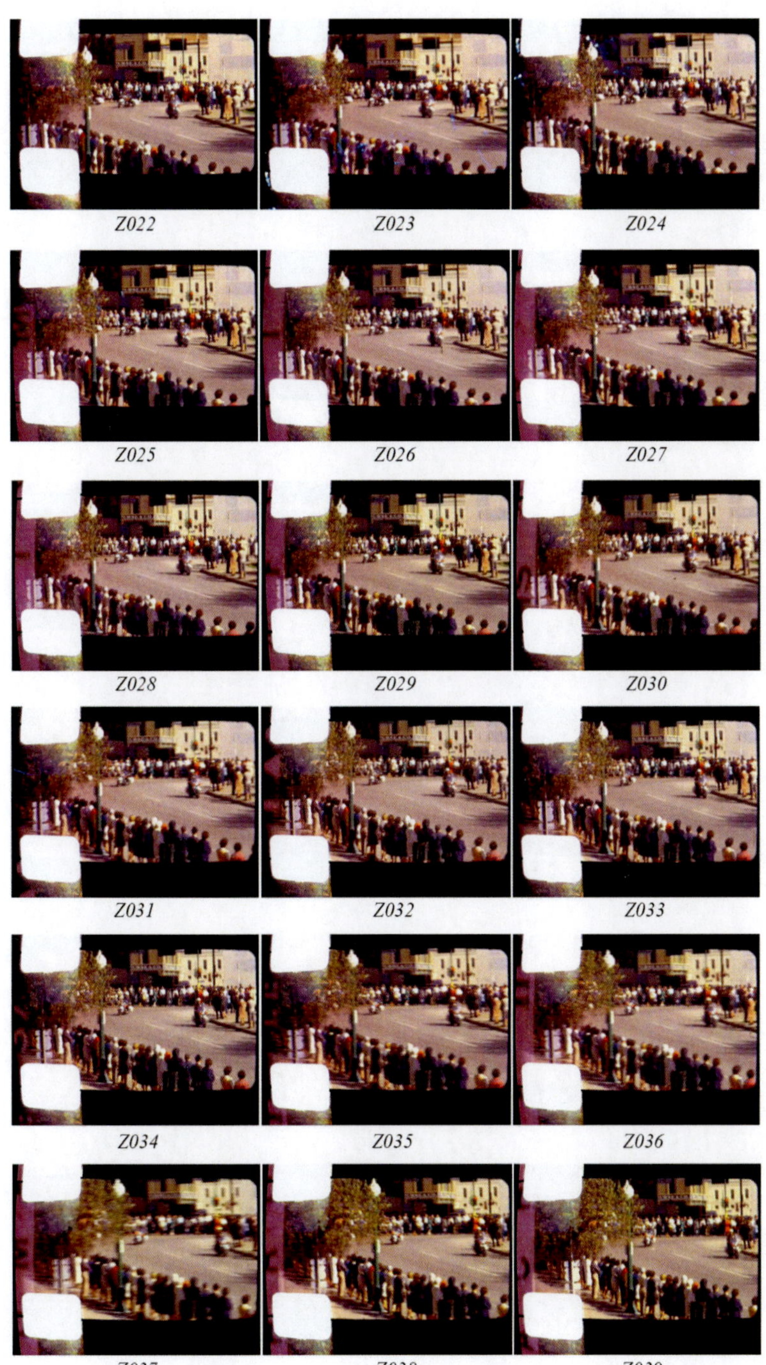

Z022 Z023 Z024

Z025 Z026 Z027

Z028 Z029 Z030

Z031 Z032 Z033

Z034 Z035 Z036

Z037 Z038 Z039

Z040
Z041
Z042
Z043
Z044
Z045
Z046
Z047
Z048
Z049
Z050
Z051
Z052
Z053
Z054
Z055
Z056
Z057

Z058 *Z059* *Z060*

Z061 *Z062* *Z063*

Z064 *Z065* *Z066*

Z067 *Z068* *Z069*

Z070 *Z071* *Z072*

Z073 *Z074* *Z075*

Z076 Z077 Z078

Z079 Z080 Z081

Z082 Z083 Z084

Z085 Z086 Z087

Z088 Z089 Z090

Z091 Z092 Z093

Z094 Z095 Z096

Z097 Z098 Z099

Z100 Z101 Z102

Z103 Z104 Z105

Z106 Z107 Z108

Z109 Z110 Z111

Z112 *Z113* *Z114*

Z115 *Z116* *Z117*

Z118 *Z119* *Z120*

Z121 *Z122* *Z123*

Z124 *Z125* *Z126*

Z127 *Z128* *Z129*

Z130 *Z131* *Z132*

Z133 *Z134* *Z135*

Z136 *Z137* *Z138*

Z139 *Z140* *Z141*

Z142 *Z143* *Z144*

Z145 *Z146* *Z147*

Z148 Z149 Z150

Z151 Z152 Z153

Z154 Z155 Z156

Z157 Z158 Z159

Z160 Z161 Z162

Z163 Z164 Z165

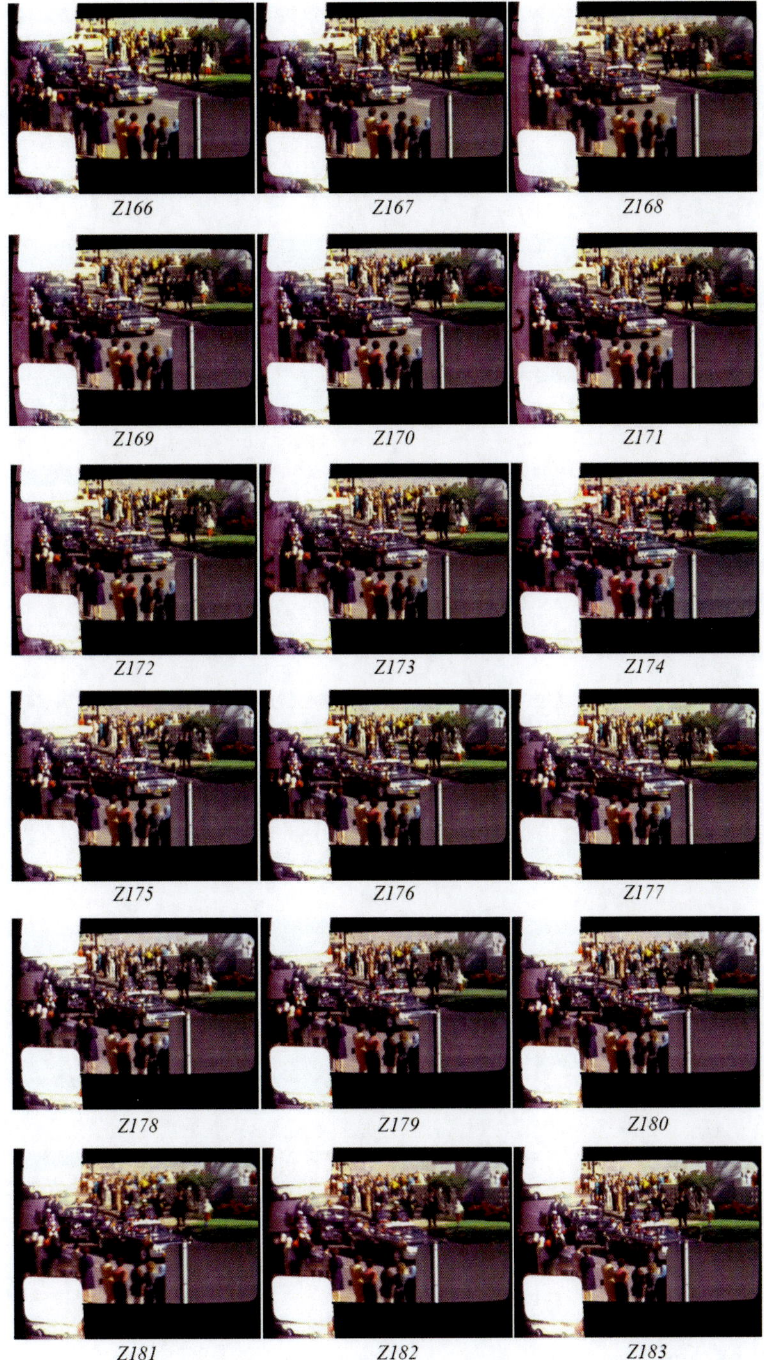

Z166 *Z167* *Z168*

Z169 *Z170* *Z171*

Z172 *Z173* *Z174*

Z175 *Z176* *Z177*

Z178 *Z179* *Z180*

Z181 *Z182* *Z183*

Z184 Z185 Z186

Z187 Z188 Z189

Z190 Z191 Z192

Z193 Z194 Z195

Z196 Z197 Z198

Z199 Z200 Z201

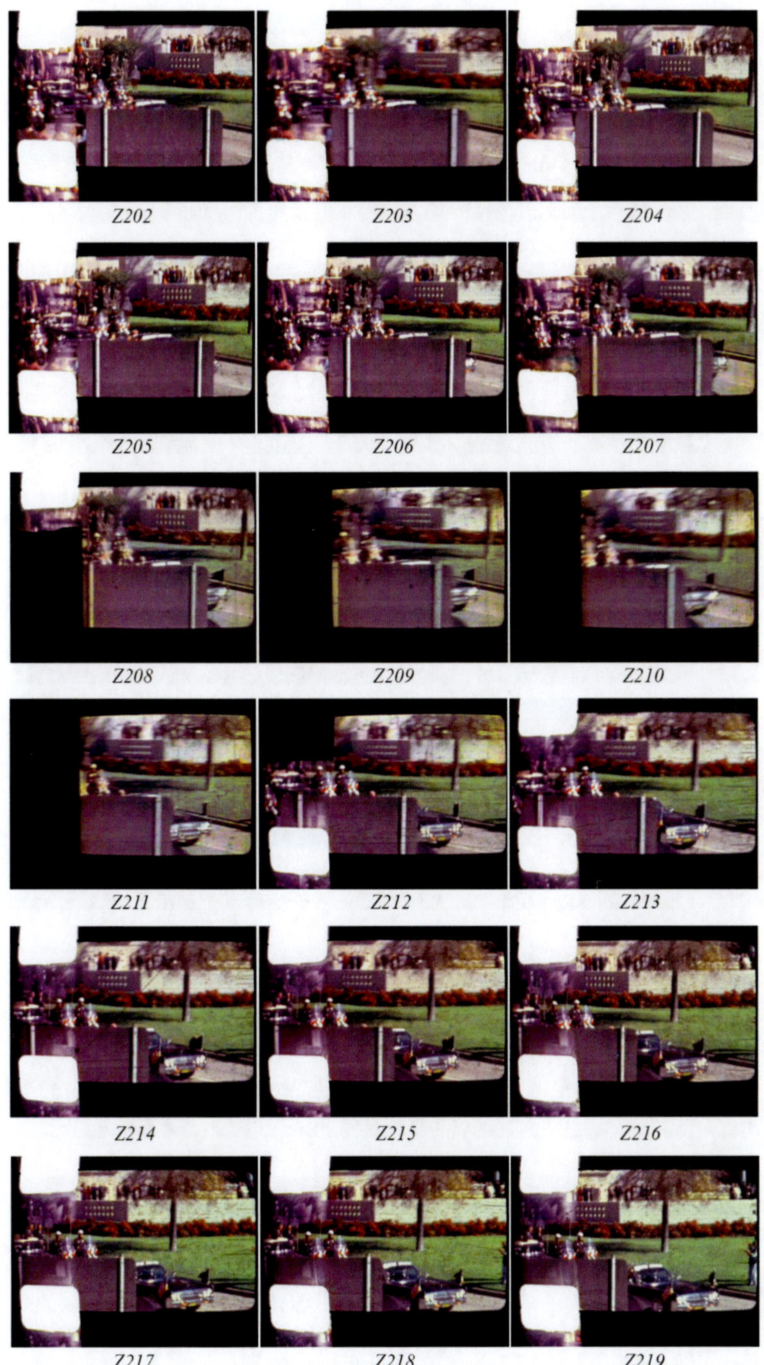

Z202 *Z203* *Z204*

Z205 *Z206* *Z207*

Z208 *Z209* *Z210*

Z211 *Z212* *Z213*

Z214 *Z215* *Z216*

Z217 *Z218* *Z219*

Z220 Z221 Z222

Z223 Z224 Z225

Z226 Z227 Z228

Z229 Z230 Z231

Z232 Z233 Z234

Z235 Z236 Z237

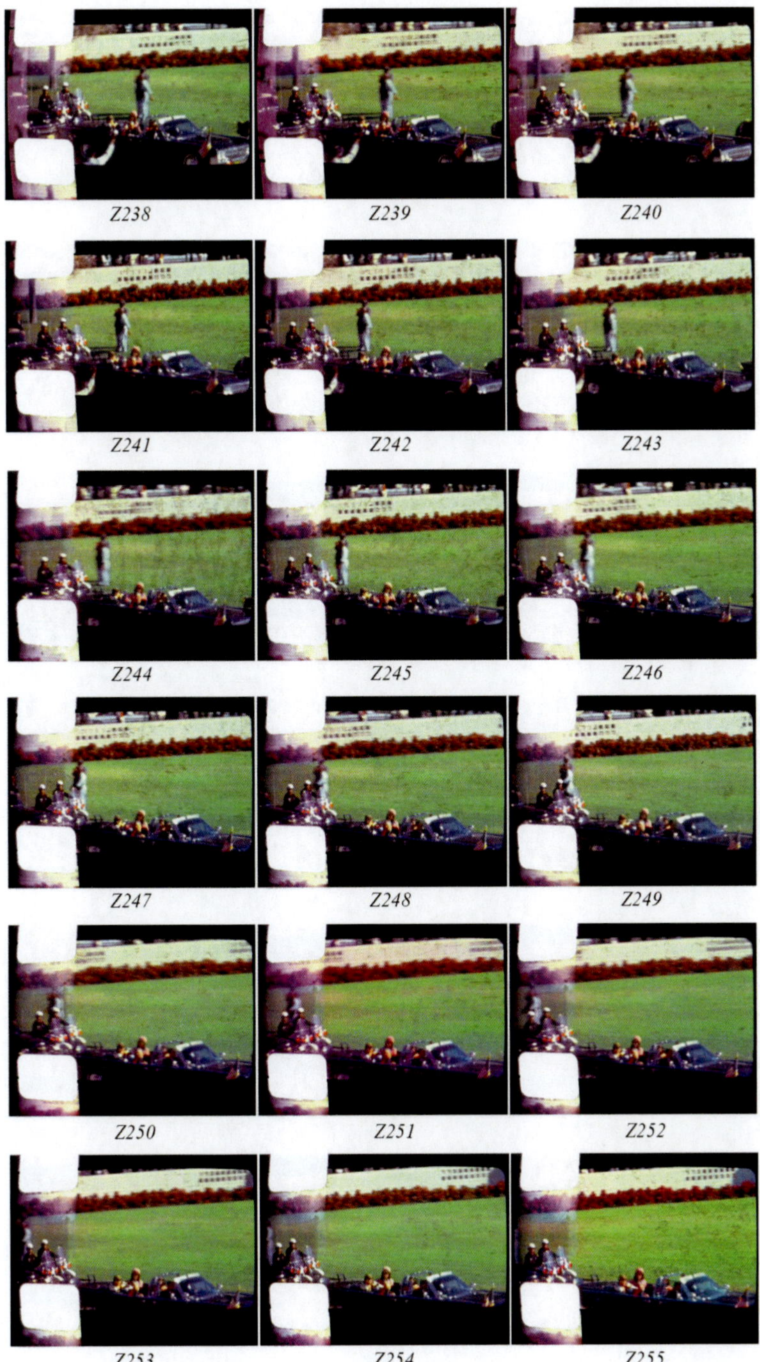

Z238 Z239 Z240

Z241 Z242 Z243

Z244 Z245 Z246

Z247 Z248 Z249

Z250 Z251 Z252

Z253 Z254 Z255

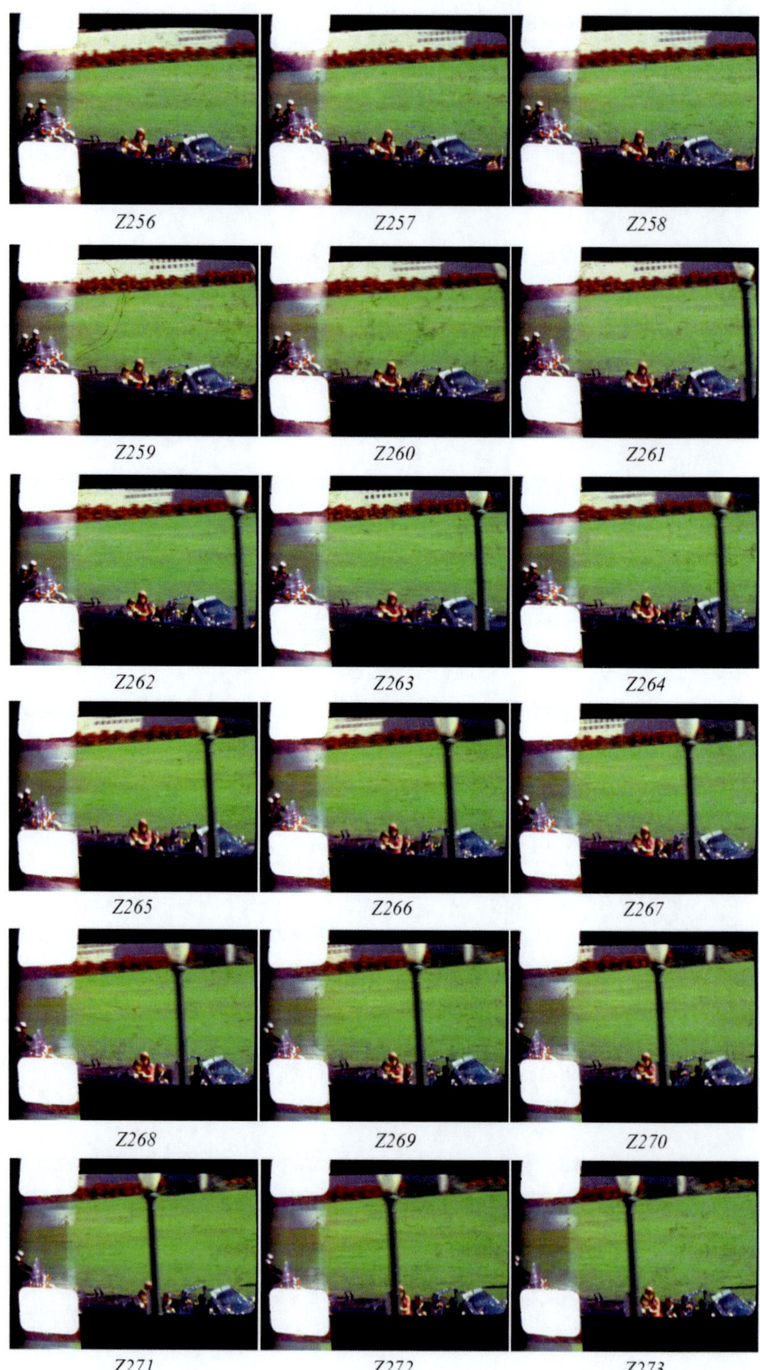

Z256 Z257 Z258

Z259 Z260 Z261

Z262 Z263 Z264

Z265 Z266 Z267

Z268 Z269 Z270

Z271 Z272 Z273

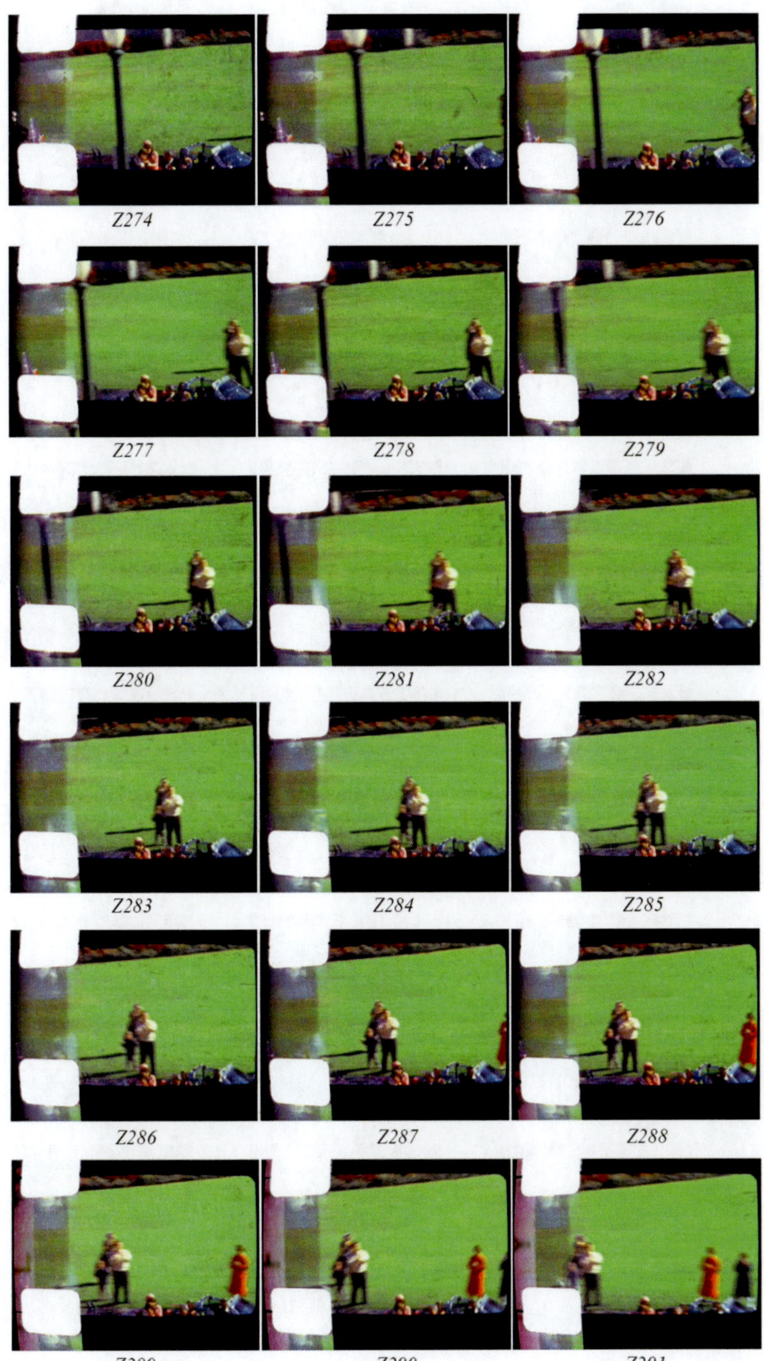

Z274 Z275 Z276

Z277 Z278 Z279

Z280 Z281 Z282

Z283 Z284 Z285

Z286 Z287 Z288

Z289 Z290 Z291

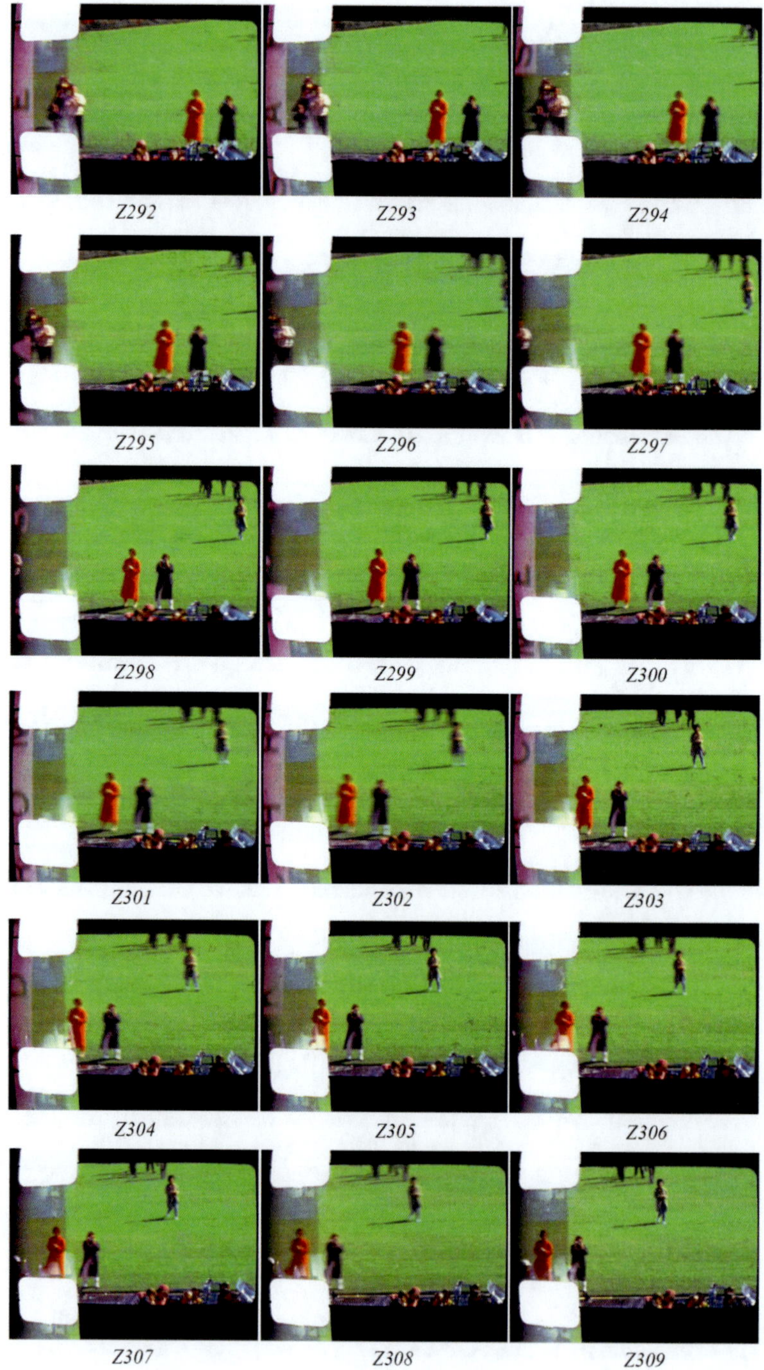

Z292 Z293 Z294

Z295 Z296 Z297

Z298 Z299 Z300

Z301 Z302 Z303

Z304 Z305 Z306

Z307 Z308 Z309

Z310 Z311 Z312

Z313 Z314 Z315

Z316 Z317 Z318

Z319 Z320 Z321

Z322 Z323 Z324

Z325 Z326 Z327

Z328 Z329 Z330

Z331 Z332 Z333

Z334 Z335 Z336

Z337 Z338 Z339

Z340 Z341 Z342

Z343 Z344 Z345

Z346 Z347 Z348

Z349 Z350 Z351

Z352 Z353 Z354

Z355 Z356 Z357

Z358 Z359 Z360

Z361 Z362 Z363

Z364 *Z365* *Z366*

Z367 *Z368* *Z369*

Z370 *Z371* *Z372*

Z373 *Z374* *Z375*

Z376 *Z377* *Z378*

Z379 *Z380* *Z381*

Z382 Z383 Z384

Z385 Z386 Z387

Z388 Z389 Z390

Z391 Z392 Z393

Z394 Z395 Z396

Z397 Z398 Z399

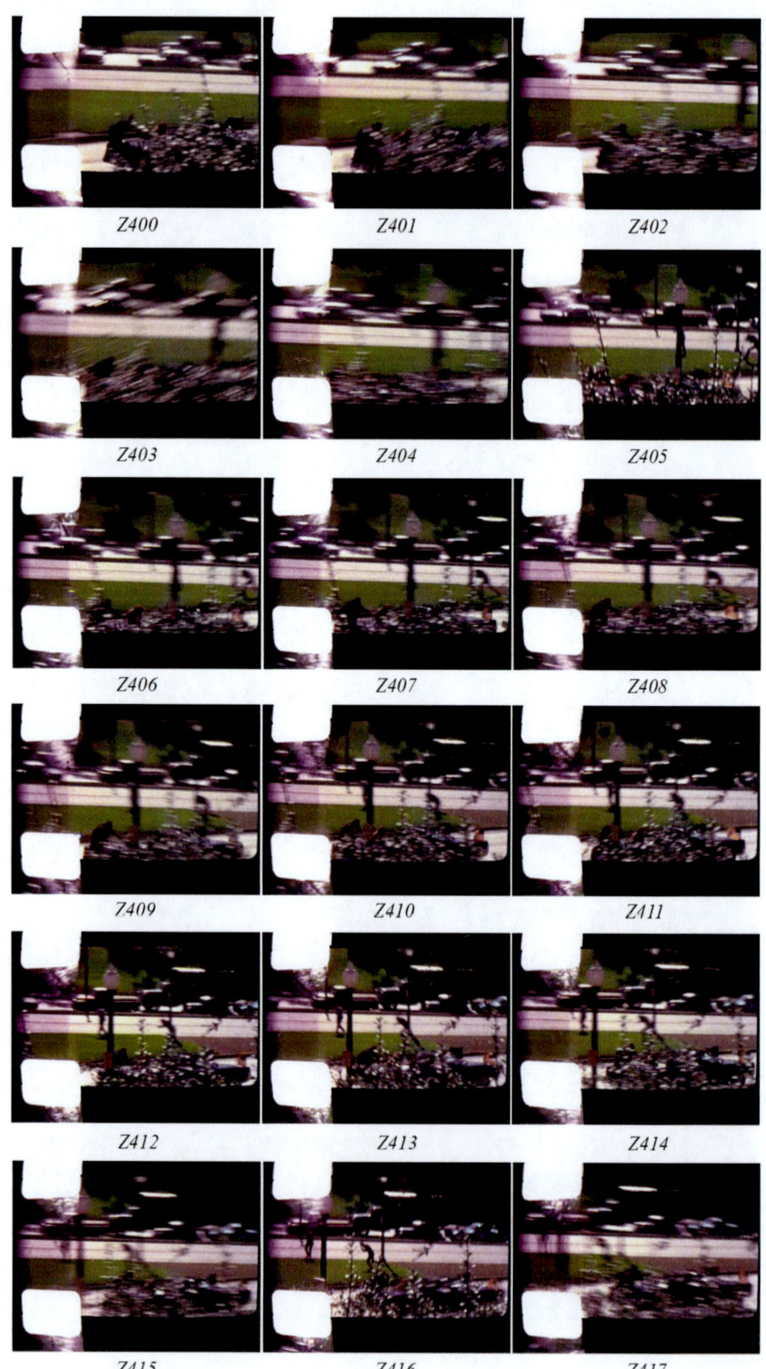

Z400 *Z401* *Z402*

Z403 *Z404* *Z405*

Z406 *Z407* *Z408*

Z409 *Z410* *Z411*

Z412 *Z413* *Z414*

Z415 *Z416* *Z417*

Z418 Z419 Z420

Z421 Z422 Z423

Z424 Z425 Z426

Z427 Z428 Z429

Z430 Z431 Z432

Z433 Z434 Z435

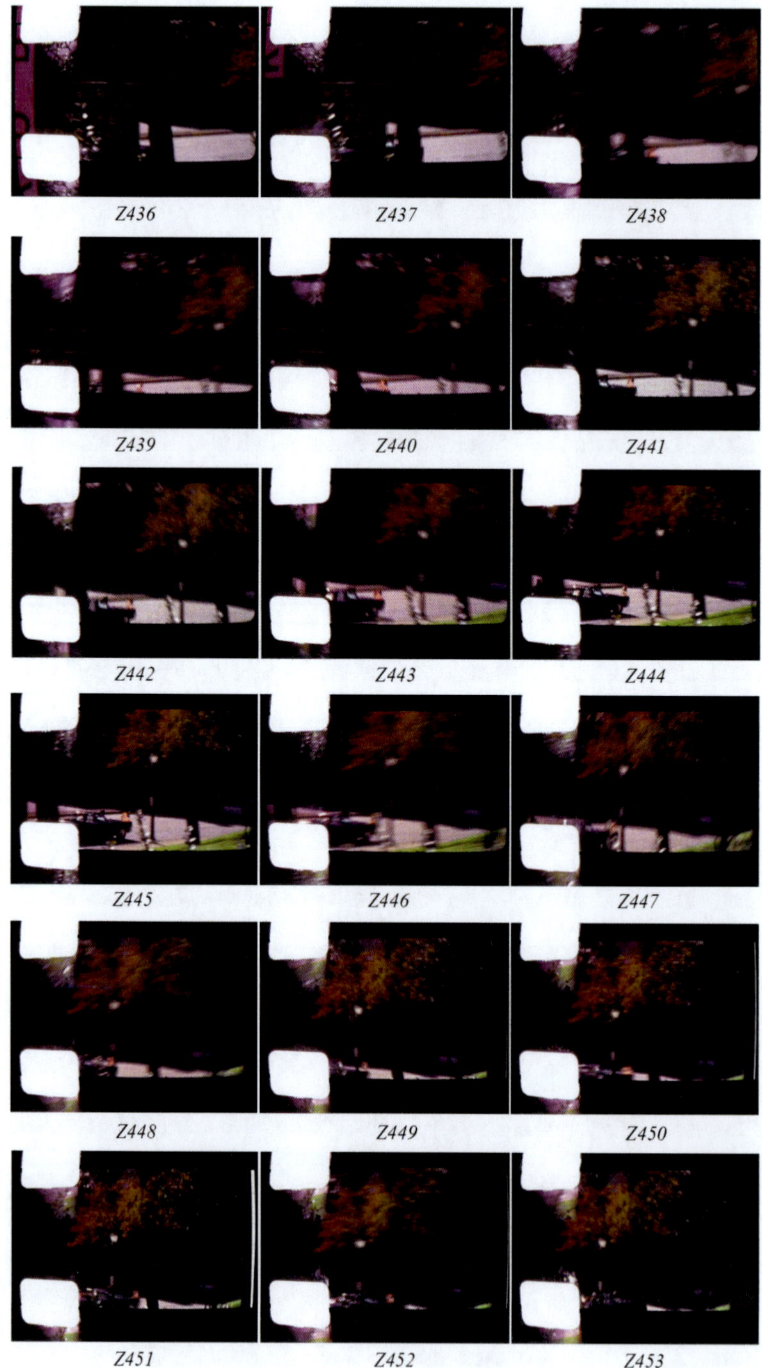

Z436 Z437 Z438

Z439 Z440 Z441

Z442 Z443 Z444

Z445 Z446 Z447

Z448 Z449 Z450

Z451 Z452 Z453

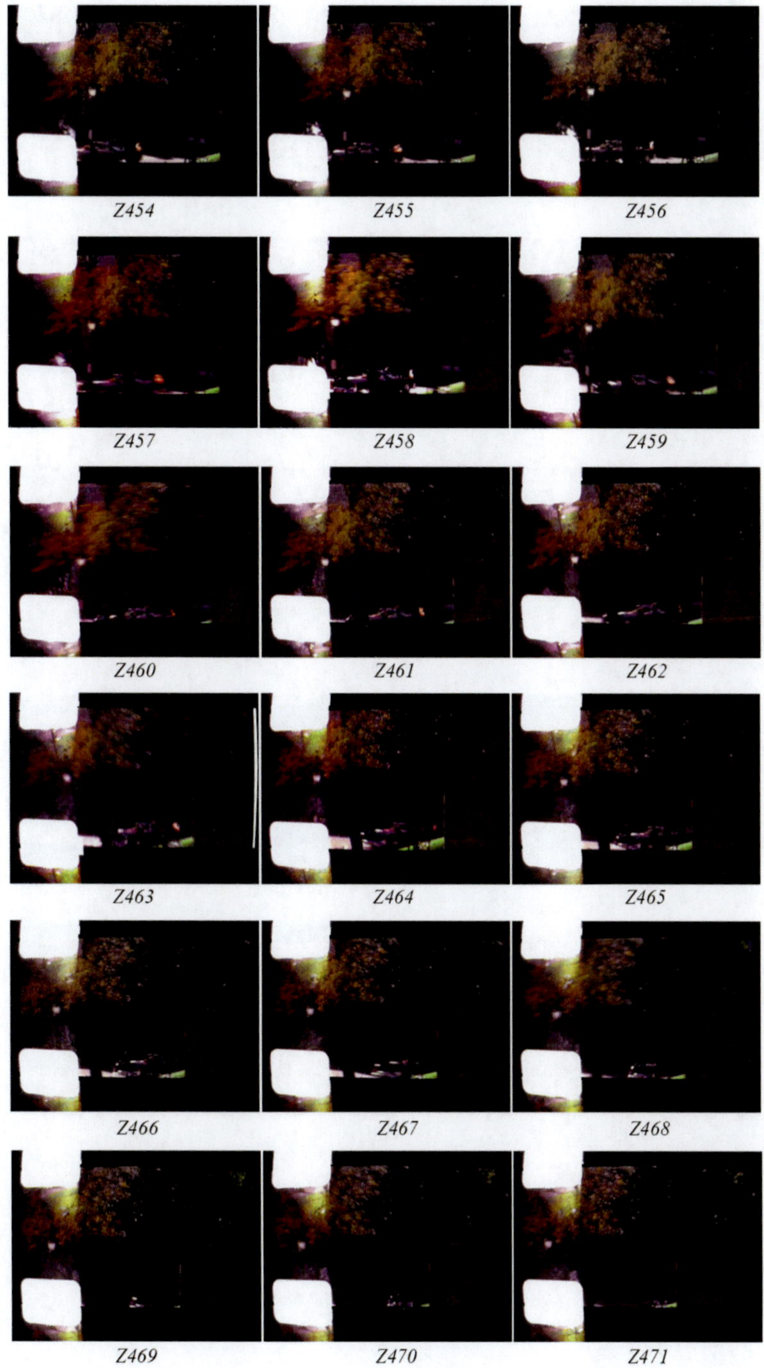

Z454 Z455 Z456

Z457 Z458 Z459

Z460 Z461 Z462

Z463 Z464 Z465

Z466 Z467 Z468

Z469 Z470 Z471

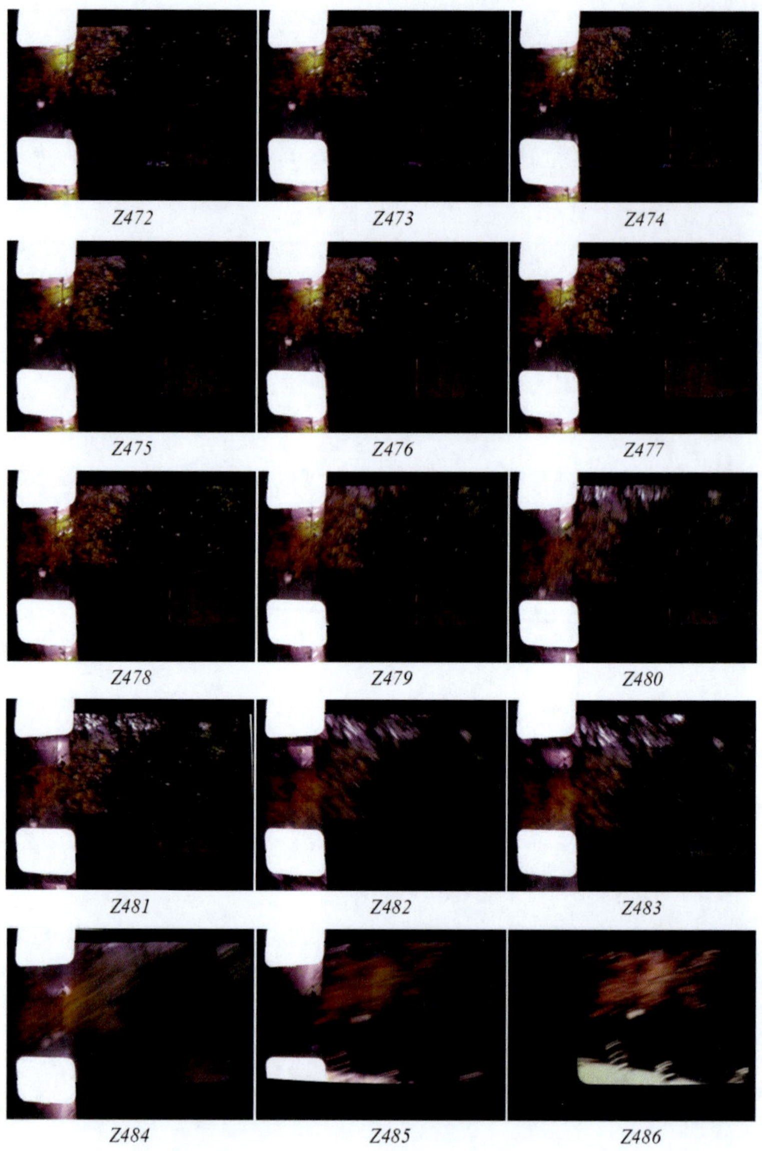

Z472 Z473 Z474

Z475 Z476 Z477

Z478 Z479 Z480

Z481 Z482 Z483

Z484 Z485 Z486

Source note: This chapter previously appeared as *"The New Zapruder Film Frames", http://www.assassinationresearch.com/zfilm*

Part III

The Zapruder Film: Real or Illusion?

6

Who's Telling the Truth: Clint Hill or the Zapruder Film?

by Jim Fetzer and John P. Costella

- Agent's reports contradict JFK film, autopsy X-rays and other crucial photographs

"In the midst of the mayhem the agents were calm, but ready to react in a millisecond"–Jerry Blaine, The Kennedy Detail: JFK's Secret Service Agents Break Their Silence

According to Jerry Blaine, the author of *The Kennedy Detail: JFK's Secret Service Agents Break Their Silence* (2010), his purpose in writing this book was "to set history straight, to leave a book for [his] grandchildren that they could read and know the truth beyond any measure of doubt." What Blaine has actually done, however, moves us further toward the truth by revealing that the words of Clint Hill, the only agent to respond during the assassination, contradict his actions as shown in the Zapruder film, in which his efforts to protect Jackie Kennedy are among its most indelible features. They also impeach autopsy X-rays and other photographs.

We therefore have in Clint Hill's own words stunning new proof that the extant film has been faked. The book—and presentations to promote it—thus contributes to "setting history straight", but not in the sense its author intended.

JACK READY

Clint Hill was not the only agent to attempt to respond after shots rang out. Secret Service agent John Ready, who was on the right running board whereas Clint was on the left, began to respond but was called back by Emory Roberts, Agent in Charge of the Presidential Protection Detail. This is stunning in itself, but is only one of more than 15 indications that the Secret Service set up JFK for the hit, which include that two agents were left behind at Love Field, that the vehicles were in the wrong order, that the 112th Military Intelligence Unit was ordered to "stand down" rather than provide protection throughout the city, and that the motorcycle escort was reduced to four, who were instructed not to ride forward of the rear wheels. Open windows were not covered, manhole covers were not welded shut and the crowd was allowed to spill out into the street.

When I discovered that Jerry and Clint had made presentations at book signings, I sent out a notice to several of my closest collaborators, all of whom contributed to the three JFK books I edited, *Assassination Science : Experts Speak Out on the Death of JFK* (1998), *Murder in Dealey Plaza: What We Know Now That We Didn't Know Then About the Death of JFK* (2000), and *The Great Zapruder Film Hoax* (2003). I had reported there that we had found multiple indications the film had been reconstructed, where rather important events, such as the driver, William Greer, bringing the limo to a halt, had been removed and the film redone. An expert on special effects, Roderick Ryan, had told Noel Twyman, *Bloody Treason: On Solving History's Greatest Murder Mystery : The Assassination of John F. Kennedy* (1997), that the "blob" of brains exploding to the right/front had been painted in, while, as Doug Horne, *Inside the Assassination Records Review Board: The U.S. Government's Final Attempt to Reconcile the Conflicting Medical Evidence in the Assassination of JFK Volume IV* (2009), has explained, a new group of Hollywood experts has found that a massive defect to the back of JFK's head had been concealed by being (crudely) painted over in black.

The Costella Response

John Costella, Ph.D., the leading expert on the film in the world today, who earned his doctorate in physics with a specialization in electromagnetism—the properties of light and images of moving objects—responded almost immediately. "Forget about the book", he wrote. "That YouTube video [of Blaine and Hill at a book signing, which can be found here: https://www.youtube.com/watch?v=lYpY8zI_wwA#t=239], is worth its weight in gold!"

A few years ago, after he did a compilation of eyewitness reports from Dealey Plaza, (*http://assassinationresearch.com/v5n1/v5n1costella.pdf*) and created a stabilized version of the Zapruder film (*https://www.youtube.com/watch?v=0aBqRBDsFQ*,) in which the limousine does not move vertically within frames. John recognized that what Clint has described from the days after the assassination, to his testimony to the Warren Commission and right up to his last public interviews in the 1970s or 1980s, was consistent, but contradicts the film. At the book signing,

> *24:30: "As I approached the vehicle there was a third shot. It hit the President in the head, upper right rear of the right ear, caused a gaping hole in his head, which caused brain matter, blood, and bone fragments to spew forth out* ***over the car, over myself****. At that point Mrs. Kennedy came up out of the back seat onto the trunk of the car. She was trying to* ***retrieve something that had gone off to the right rear****. She did not know I was there.* ***At that point I grabbed Mrs. Kennedy, put her in the back seat.*** *The President fell over into her lap, to his left.*
>
> *His right side of his head was exposed.* ***I could see his eyes were fixed. There was a hole in the upper right rear portion of his head about the size of my palm. Most of the gray matter in that area had been removed, and was scattered throughout the entire car, including on Mrs. Kennedy. I turned and gave the follow-up car crew the thumbs-down,*** *indicating that we were in a very dire situation. The driver accelerated; he got up to the lead car which was driven by Chief Curry, the Dallas Chief of Police . . . ".*

This is completely consistent with every account Clint has ever given. He insists that he reached Mrs. Kennedy, pushed her down into the back seat, and was lying over the President, close enough to view the exact wounds, before the driver accelerated away—and certainly before they got to the lead car.

The problem is that the extant Zapruder film—together with the less familiar Nix and Muchmore films—has Clint never actually touching Mrs. Kennedy; indeed, the extant Zapruder film shows that **he never got further than the rear foothold until the time that the limo passed the lead car and went under the Triple Underpass.** Instead, it shows him stuck there on the rear foothold.

According to Clint Hill (shown here on the rear foothold of the limousine as the vehicle is about to enter the Triple Underpass), he had already reached Mrs. Kennedy and pushed her down in the back seat. JFK had fallen to the left into her lap, where the right side of his head was exposed to Clint, who was lying over them. This photo is supposed to have been taken by Ike Altgens and corresponds with late Zapruder frames. Clint's testimony not only falsifies the Zapruder film, but also shows that this photograph was faked to agree with it.

Lest there be any doubt on this crucial point, in Clint Hill's written statement dated 30 November 1963, which was published as Commission Exhibit CE 1024, he wrote:

"As I lay over the top of the back seat I noticed a portion of the President's head on the right rear side was missing and he was bleeding profusely. Part of his brain was gone. I saw a part of his skull with hair on it lying on the seat." [18H742]. And in his testimony to the commission on 9 March 1964, "The right rear portion of his head was missing. It was lying in the middle of the car. His brain was exposed." [2H141]. Since he has told us he made these observations before the limousine had reached the pilot car driven by Chief Curry (shown above), this photo has to

have been faked. Clint could not have made these observations from the rear foothold as it represents.

(His descriptions of the wound to the right rear of JFK's head are discussed later.)

The Limo Stop

Not the least fascinating aspect of Clint Hill's latest remarks is his observation that he was covered with brains and gore as he ran forward from the left running board of the Secret Service Cadillac—called "The Queen Mary"—which, according to Emory Roberts (*The Kennedy Detail: JFK's Secret Service Agents Break Their Silence,* page 215), was 15 feet back.

This is consistent with the report of Officer Bobby Hargis riding to the left/rear of the limousine, who was hit so hard by the brains and debris that he thought he himself might have been shot. Agents who saw JFK's brains splattered across the trunk in Washington, D.C. would be nauseated by the sight, as I explained in *The Great Zapruder Film Hoax,* page 27. But it is not in the film. So John wrote to Clint—and he got it, because John has the signed Registered Mail receipt card—urging him to be certain to record his version of events for posterity.

Now he is on the road, participating in book signings and talking publicly again, for the first time in decades.

His story is still exactly the same and, most important, still does not agree with his actions as seen in the film. Here is a clip featuring what is represented as Clint Hill's actions in the film: https://www.youtube.com/ watch?v=0aBqRB-DsFQ.

The film itself thus demonstrates that the Zapruder version of Clint Hill's actions up to the Triple Underpass contradict Clint Hill's words describing what he actually did.

John's collation of eyewitness reports about the assassination includes dozens and dozens about the limo stop. Some reported seeing it slow dramatically and others that it came to a complete stop, which makes sense since, from different positions, different witnesses would have seen it slow dramatically as it came to a complete stop. Among them is Toni Foster, who was interviewed by Debra Conway in 2000.

As Daniel Gallup has observed, Foster seems to have no idea that her recollections contradict the official record. Toni told Debra, "For some reason, the car stopped. It did stop for seconds. I don't even know why it stopped and all of a sudden it sped up and they went under the underpass. I could never figure out why the car stopped." "The way she delivers these lines," Gallup observed, "I doubt Toni had ever seen the extant Zapruder film, and had no idea her recollections contradicted that film."

He said he was reminded of David Lifton's early (1971) interviews with the Newmans, who also said the limo had stopped. "They had no way of knowing at the time that the Zapruder film showed no such stop. All of this is to say, the earliest recollections of individuals are likely to be the most significant," he added, "especially if there is evidence of a lack of exposure to contrary viewpoints that might influence memory."

For a few more:

> ***Billy Lovelady*** *(on the steps of the Texas School Book Depository), 19 March 1964: "I recall that following the shooting I ran toward the spot where President Kennedy's car had stopped." [FBI statement: 22H662]*
>
> ***Roy Truly*** *(on the north side of Elm Street in front of the building), 24 March 1964: "The car—I saw the President's car swerve to the left and stop somewhere down in this area" [Later:] (Mr. Belin: "When you saw the President's car seem to stop, how long did it appear to stop?) Mr. Truly: It would be hard to say, over a second or two, something like that. I didn't see—I just saw it stop. I don't know. I didn't see it start up." [Warren Commission testimony: 3H221]*
>
> ***Mrs. Earle Cabell*** *(four cars behind the Presidential limousine, at the top of Elm Street at the time of the shots), 13 July 1964: "I was aware that the motorcade stopped dead still. There was no question about that." [Later:] "As I told you, the motorcade was stopped." [Later:] (Mr. Hubert: "That was when your car at least had come to a standstill?") Mrs. Cabell: "Every car in the motorcade had come to a standstill." [Later:] "... we were dead still for a matter of some seconds—" [Warren Commission Testimony" 7H486–7]*

These reports are significant from multiple points of view. Roy Truly was Oswald's supervisor in the TSBD and would reassure Officer

Marrion Baker, when he confronted Oswald in the 2nd floor lunchroom 90 seconds after the assassination, that he was an employee and belonged there. Billy Lovelady was another employee who looked enough like Oswald to be mistaken for him. And Earle Cabell, the Mayor of Dallas at the time, was the brother of Lt. Gen. Charles Cabell, USAF (ret.), whom JFK removed as a Deputy Director of the CIA after the disastrous Bay of Pigs fiasco.

The limo stop—during which JFK was hit twice in the head, once from behind and once from in front—was such an obvious indication of Secret Service complicity that it had to be taken out, which is undoubtedly the principal reason for fixing the film. But it had other ramifications. What Clint Hill has consistently described is not in the Zapruder film: he describes several actions in those seconds around the limo stop that were deleted from the extant film. In editing the timeline of the extant film, it was necessary to delete his pushing of Mrs. Kennedy back into the seat—there just wasn't enough time left in the film once the limo stop had been deleted.

There is no possible way in which Clint could possibly have seen what he claims to have seen **before** the car accelerated away and passed the lead car when he was stuck on the back of the speeding limo as he is shown doing in the extant film. And from his initial reports right up to his latest "book signing" interview, he has insisted that that was when he saw those things, that he did reach Mrs. Kennedy and that he did push her down into the car, unlike what the film shows. Which means that the film is a fake.

The Head Wound

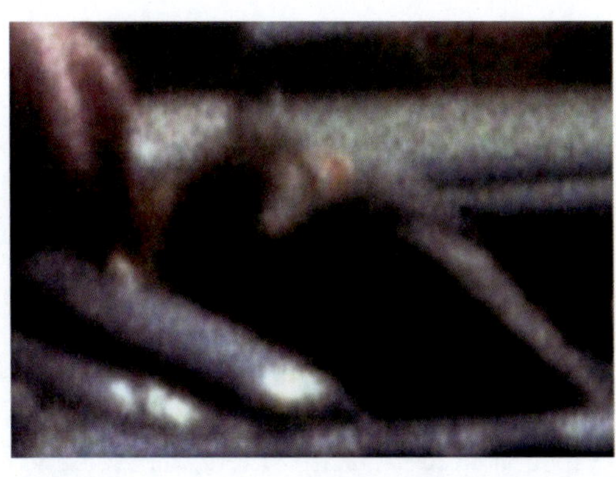

Other proofs of the alteration of the film derive from his description of the wound itself and of the debris that was blown over the car. *"As I approached the vehicle there was a third shot. It hit the President in the head, upper right rear of the right ear, caused a gaping hole in his head, which caused brain matter, blood, and bone fragments to spew forth out over the car, over myself. . . . His right side of his head was exposed.* ***I could see his eyes were fixed. There was a hole in the upper right rear***

portion of his head about the size of my palm. Most of the gray matter in that area had been removed, and was scattered throughout the entire car, including on Mrs. Kennedy." Clint's description corresponds with the image of the blowout that can be seen in later frames of the film, such as 374:

In the belief that those who were altering the film around the head shot in frame 313 might have overlooked later frames, I began to study later frames and found that the blowout could be seen in frame 374. The bluish-gray image is brain matter, while the pinkish extension is the back of a skull flap that was blown open by the frangible (or exploding) bullet when it hit. But the blowout is not seen in frames like 313-316, another proof of fakery.

Even if Clint actually touched Jackie, the films do not show him pushing her into the seat, which is what he has always maintained. In his formal report dated on 30 November 1963 about the events of 22 November 1963, a copy of which is archived at www.assassinationscience.com/ce-1024-clinthill.pdf he reports, "As I lay over the top of the back seat I noticed a portion of the President's head on the right rear side was missing and he was bleeding profusel[y]. Part of his brain was gone. I saw a part of his skull with hair on it", which is consistent with frame 374 but not with frames 313–316.

Indeed, since this record was Warren Commission Exhibit CE-1024, at least some of its members and staff had to have been aware of observations of the first person to observe the head wound, apart from Jackie herself.

But even *The Kennedy Detail* (2010) includes this sentence, "And slumped across the seat, President Kennedy lay unmoving, a bloody, gaping, fist-sized hole clearly visible in the back of his head," (*The Kennedy Detail*, p. 217), an observation of enormous significance in relation to the autopsy photographs and X-rays as well as to the authenticity of the Zapruder film.

As I have observed, Doug Horne, *Inside the Assassination Records Review Board, Volume IV*, (2009), has reported that a new group of Hollywood experts studying the film has found that, in frames 313-316, the blowout to the back of the head was (crudely) painted over in black. Their finding complements the earlier report by Roderick Ryan, an expert in special effects, that the "blob" of brains and blood that bulges out to the right/front had also been painted in, as Noel Twyman, *Bloody Treason: On Solving History's Greatest Murder Mystery: The Assassination of John F. Kennedy* (1997), explained. (Roderick Ryan would receive

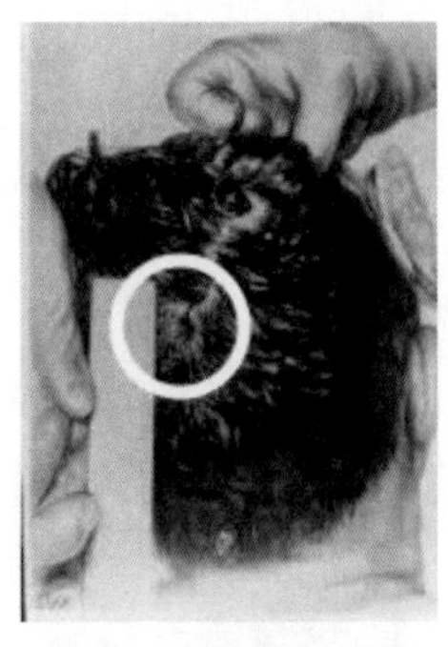

the Academy Award for his contributions to cinematography in 2000.)

Since the blowout is visible in frame 374 but not visible in frames 313–316, we have yet another proof of the film has been altered. But these observations also extend to the autopsy photographs and X-rays. Here, for example, are drawings and photographs of the back of the head, which were assumed to be authentic by the House Select Committee on Assassinations (HSCA) when it reinvestigated the case in 1977–78:

There are several important features of these images. One of the most stunning is that when the two pathologists who had conducted the autopsy at Bethesda Naval Hospital testified to the HSCA about the location of the alleged entry wound to the back of his head, they raised its location by 4" from above and to the right of the external occipital protuberance (EOP) to the crown of the head (or "cowlick"), an astounding variation from their autopsy report.

Notice, too, that while the alleged entry wound is visible in the diagram on the right, it is not visible in the photograph on the left. Most important, however, is that, as in the case of Zapruder frames 313–316, the blowout to the back of the head at the right rear, which Clint so vividly described, is missing. The skull flap is present, but the defect is not. Based upon his observations—he has been consistent about all this for more than 40 years—this diagram and photograph, even apart from the EOP entry wound, have been faked.

The Witnesses and the X-rays

Clint Hill, moreover, was hardly the only witness to have reported that the President had an enormous blowout to the right rear of his head. More than 40 witnesses from Dealey Plaza, Parkland Hospital, and even Bethesda reported a blowout to the back of his head, including Beverly Oliver, Phillip Willis, Marilyn Willis, Ed Hoffman, Dr. Robert McClellan, Dr. Paul Peters, Dr. Kenneth Salyer, Dr. Charles Carrico, Dr. Richard Dulaney, Dr. Charles Crenshaw, Dr. Ronald Jones, Nurse Audrey Bell, Justice of the Peace Theran Ward, ambulance driver Aubrey Rike, FBI Agent Frank O'Neill, as well as Bethesda Naval medical technicians Jerrol Custer, Paul O'Connor and Floyd Reebe, as Robert Groden, *The Killing of a President: The Complete Photographic Record of the JFK Assassination* (1994), pp. 86–88, has recorded, and as Gary Aguilar, M.D., has confirmed *(Murder in Dealey Plaza: What We Know Now That We Didn't Know Then About the Death of JFK*, 2000, pp. 175–217).

Beverly Oliver: "The whole back of his head were flying out the back of the car."

Phillip Willis: "It took the back of his head off."

Marilyn Willis: "A red 'halo.' Matter [was] coming out the back of his head."

Ed Hoffman: "The rear of his head was gone, blasted outward."

Dr. Robert McClelland: "It was in the right back part of the head — very large . . . a portion of the cerebellum fell out on the table as we were doing the

Dr. Paul Peters: ". . . right there, occipital parietal."

Dr. Kenneth Salyer: "This wound extended into the parietal area."

Dr. Charles Carrico: "There was a large — quite a large — defect about here [pointing] on his skull."

Dr. Richard Dulaney: "It was up in this area."

Dr. Charles Crenshaw: "The wound was the size of a baseball."

Dr. Ronald Jones: "My impression was there was a wound in this area of the head." When shown

Nurse Audrey Bell: "There was a massive wound at the back of his head."

Theran Ward "[It was] right back here."

Aubrey Rike "You could feel the sharp edges of the bone at the edge of the hole in the back of his head."

Frank O'Neill ". . . a massive wound in the right rear."

Jerrol Custer "From the top of the head, almost to the base of the skull, you could see where that part was gone."

Paul O'Connor "[There was] an open area all the way across into the rear of the brain."

Floyd Riebe ". . . a big gaping hole in the back of the head."

The highly consistent and mutually reinforcing testimony of all these eyewitnesses—including the physicians who were present in Trauma Room #1 when JFK's moribund body was brought to Parkland Hospital and even Special Agents of the FBI who were present to observe the conduct or the autopsy at Bethesda Naval Hospital—were all discounted on the basis of the claim that the autopsy X-rays did not show any such blowout.

This inconsistency would not be resolved until late 1992, when David W. Mantik, M.D. Ph.D., would enter the National Archives to study the X-rays and in the process transform our understanding of the assassination and the cover-up.

A medical doctor with board certification in radiation oncology, which is the treatment of cancer using radiation therapy because of which he is an expert in the interpretation of X-rays, he drew on his background as a Ph.D. in physics and applied a simple technique known as "optical densitometry", which enabled him—by measuring the amount of light

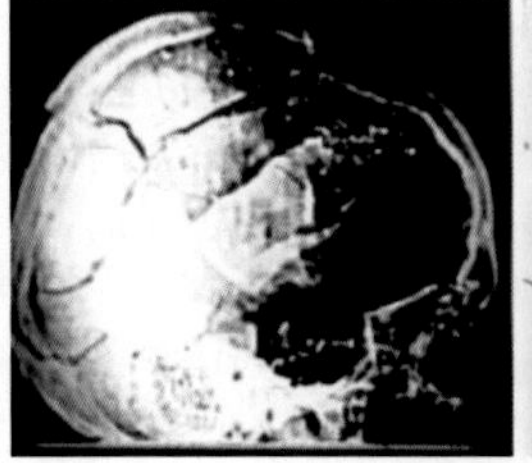
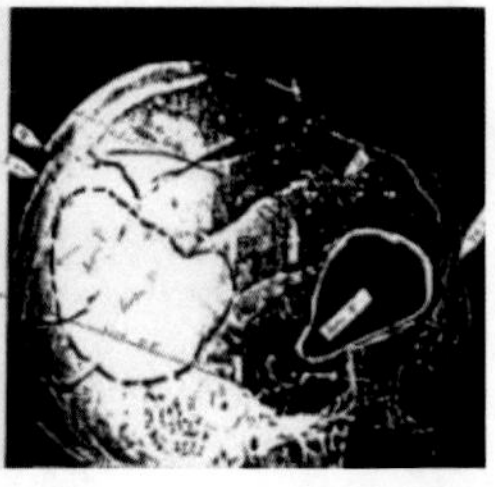

that passes through an X-ray to determine the relative density of objects whose exposure to radiation had created the image—to discover that the lateral cranial X-ray (of the skull taken from the side) had been altered by imposing a kind of patch over the blowout.

Here we can see the "official" X-ray on the left and the patch ("Area P") on the right, which bears a striking correspondence in size and shape to the image in Frame 374:

David's discoveries and those of Robert B. Livingston, M.D., a world authority on the human brain and an expert on wound ballistics, were the centerpiece of my first of three books on the death of JFK, *Assassination Science: Experts Speak Out on the Death of JFK* (1998), where I brought together experts on different aspects of the case. Livingston compared the multiple, consistent reports of qualified and experienced physicians at Parkland Hospital with the diagrams and photographs of the brain in the National Archives.

The physicians reported both cerebral and cerebellar tissue extruding from the blowout, while the diagrams and photographs—the brain itself is missing—show a virtually undamaged brain with a complete cerebellum.

You or I might have drawn the same conclusions, but it carries more weight when it's the finding of a world authority on the brain. For those who may not have access to the book, a summary of our findings as well as of the shooting sequence is archived at "*Dealey Plaza Revisited: What Happened to JFK?*"

"Ike" Altgens and Clint Hill

In his comprehensive study of the Zapruder film in *The Great Zapruder Film Hoax* (2003), Costella discusses the ambiguity that Altgens has displayed regarding the photos he allegedly took in Dealey Plaza on 22 November 1963. The identity of the person who took them was important in part because an Oswald look-alike (allegedly Billy Lovelady) can be seen in the photo with which this article begins—published in *The Saturday Evening Post* following the assassination. So the name of the photographer was widely sought but difficult to come by.

Even J. Edgar Hoover skirted the issue. It would not be until 24 May 1964 he was identified by name and then questions arose of why neither the FBI nor the Warren Commission had interviewed him. While his office at the Associated Press was a short walk away from the FBI in Dallas, the FBI only interviewed him on 2 June 1964 and produced a rather garbled report of his actions that day. As Richard Trask, *Pictures of the Pain: Photography and the Assassination of President Kennedy* (1994), reports, Altgens himself would subsequently deny that he had taken all of the photos that had been attributed to him. And that, no doubt, is for a very good reason. *No one can have taken a photo that was faked.*

Costella is certainly right about the importance of Clint Hill's book signing statement in comparison with the book itself, which is rather sketchy and vague relative to the sequence of events of greatest interest here. The video captures more detail and his demeanor in relating his extraordinary experiences. But even *The Kennedy Detail* (2010) includes this sentence, stunning in simplicity but pregnant in ramifications:

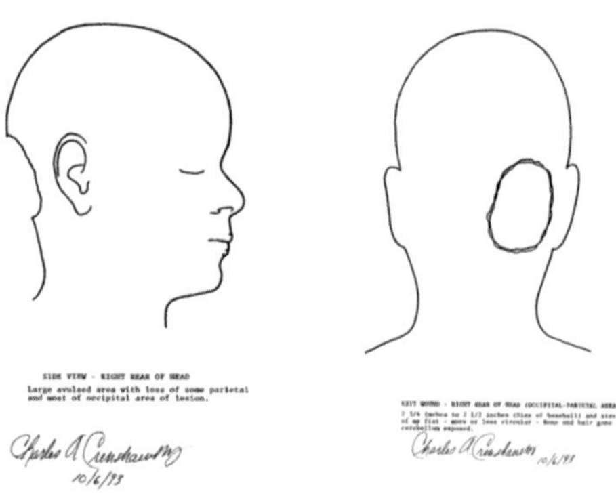

And slumped across the seat, President Kennedy lay unmoving, a bloody, gaping, fist-sized hole clearly visible in the back of his head. (*The Kennedy Detail*, p. 217)

After all, if JFK had a fist-sized hole clearly visible in the back of his head, it follows that (1) the eyewitnesses were right about its location, (2) the HSCA photograph and diagram are fake, (3) the autopsy X-rays were altered, and (4) the Zapruder frames that don't show it when they should were changed, precisely as we have found above. In fact, Clint Hill was far from the only expert who described that wound as "fist-sized". When I edited *Assassination Science* (1998), I invited Charles Crenshaw, M.D., to contribute a chapter and asked him to diagram the wounds as he had witnessed them at Parkland Hospital, where he was the last physician to observe them before he closed JFK's eyelids as he was being wrapped in sheets and placed in the casket.

Charles told me that this defect was the size of a baseball or else the size of your fist when you double it up. The best witnesses and the best studies thus converge on the conclusion that strenuous efforts were made to conceal the true causes of the death of JFK from the American people. For over 50 years, Clint has maintained that he pushed Jackie down into her seat and observed the blowout to the head in his report of 22 November 1963,

www.assassinationscience.com/ce-1024-clint-hill.pdf,

in this 1975 interview,

www.assassinationscience.com/clint-hill-1975.mp4

and in this 1995 interview, where he describes it all in detail, and not just once but twice:

www.assassinationscience.com/clint-hill-1995.mp4.

He and Jerry Blaine have thereby contributed to the resolution of one of the most contentious questions in the history of assassination research with corroborating proof the Zapruder film was altered.

Disturbing Reflections

Charles gave more than one interview in which he explained that the bullet that had blown out the back of JFK's head had *entered at the right temple*. He suggested that it had taken a tangential trajectory and blown out the back of his skull, whereas Bob Livingston believed that shock waves created by the explosion of the frangible bullet had caused his brains to be blown out the back of his skull, which had already been weakened by the shot that entered the back of his head near the EOP. If Crenshaw was mistaken in detail about the trajectory, he was right that the autopsy photos he was being shown did not resemble the wounds that he had observed, which meant that there had been alteration of the evidence—either by faking photos and films or by the physical alteration of the wounds—both of which appear to have taken place.

Toward the end of this book, which is unintentionally revealing, Blaine relates the story of an exchange between Clint Hill and Mike Wallace for a planned *60 Minutes* segment. Mike asked Clint if he had any doubt that Oswald was the lone gunman, to which Clint replied, "There were only three shots," Clint shrugged. "And it was one gun. Three shots." (*The Kennedy Detail*, p. 387)

What troubles me is that, given his consistent description of the blowout to the back of the head, it ought to have been obvious that that shot had been fired from the right front. While there was an entry wound in the vicinity of the EOP, as Mantik explains in his masterful synthesis of the medical evidence in *Murder in Dealey Plaza* (2000), the massive, gaping wound that Clint observed was clearly fired from another location by someone else.

And that is not the only anomaly in Clint's testimony as it is reported in the pages of this book. In the most puzzling passage of them all, Blaine reports' "The Zapruder film was being used for Secret Service training and sometimes Clint was called on to comment" (*The Kennedy Detail*, p. 375). Given Clint's consistent depiction of the actions he took which are inconsistent with the extant film, I am taken aback by the ghoulish prospect that the Secret Service may be using the authentic film, while the public has only the fake. Surely Clint would have been unable to miss the difference between his actions as he lived them and those depicted in the fabricated film. But perhaps even this extraordinary possibility cannot be ruled out. It might also help to explain Clint's consistency in his depiction of the actions he took over 50 years ago, if his memory has been periodically refreshed by seeing the original over again.

So Clint's descriptions and observations both have significant ramifications for the autopsy X-rays, photos and the Zapruder film. Notice, for example, that the Mafia could not have altered X-rays under the control of medical officers of the U.S. Navy, agents of the Secret Service, or the President's personal physician.

Neither pro- nor anti-Castro Cubans could have substituted another brain for that of JFK. And even if the Soviets had the capacity to fabricate movies comparable to that of the CIA and Hollywood, it would have been unable to get its hands on the Zapruder film. JFK had antagonized many of the most powerful individuals and groups in the USA, as Douglass', *JFK and the Unspeakable* (2008), and Phillip Nelson's, *LBJ: The Mastermind of JFK's Assassination* (2010), have explained. We now have another piece of a puzzle that implicates officials at the highest levels of the American government as complicit in an elaborate cover-up that has to have been planned in detail and in advance of the commission of the crime. It is long past time the truth be known to the public.

Source note: This chapter previously appeared as *"Who's Telling the Truth: Clint Hill or the Zapruder Film?", http://jamesfetzer.blogspot.com/2015/09/ whos-telling-truth-clint-hill-or.html.*

7

Two NPIC Zapruder Film Events Pointing to its Alteration

by Douglas Horne

Douglas P. Horne, who served as the Chief Analyst for Military Records for the ARRB (formally, the Assassination Records Review Board), a five member civilian panel that was entrusted with the mission of locating and declassifying documents and records held by the CIA, the FBI, the Secret Service, ONI, and other federal agencies under the President John F. Kennedy Assassination Records Collection Act of 1992 (the JFK Records Act, which was passed by Congress in the wake of the resurgence of interest in the death of JFK, which was brought about by Oliver Stone's monumental film, *JFK*), has become a personal hero of mine (Jim Fetzer).

Those in that category are few and far between, but include JFK, RFK, Mohammed Ali, Bill Russell, and other figures from JFK assassination research, including David W. Mantik, M.D., Ph.D., John P. Costella, Ph.D., and Jack White, who have been among my closest associates and collaborators for more than 20 years. When I published, *Murder in Dealey Plaza* (2000), I included two chapters by Doug Horne, which concerned certain discoveries that had been made during the proceedings of the ARRB, the first of which concerned the occurrence of two supplemental brain examinations following the Bethesda autopsy on JFK's body, the first of the original brain, and the second of a substitute brain.

That the brain shown in diagrams and photographs in the National Archives could not be the brain of JFK had been previously established by Robert B. Livingston, M.D., a world authority on the human brain and expert on wound ballistics, in his contributions to *Assassination Science* (1998).

He had noticed that, while physician after physician from Parkland Hospital, who had examined the body, had reported cerebral and cerebellar tissue extruding from a fist-sized hole in the back of the head, the HSCA artist's rendering of the autopsy photographs of "JFK's brain" displayed a completely intact cerebellum and a virtually intact (although dislodged) cerebrum, even though roughly half of President Kennedy's brains had been blown out in Dealey Plaza during the shooting, where he was hit at least four times: once in the back from behind; once in the throat from in front; and twice in the head, once from behind and once from the right/front, as I have explained in "*What Happened To JFK And Why It Matters Today*."

In order to conceal that blowout at the back of his head, the two authentic lateral cranial X-rays had been altered to conceal the blowout, which initially appeared to have been done by "patching" using material that was much too dense to be human bone, as David W. Mantik, M.D., Ph.D., discovered through the use of optical densitometry during nine visits to the National Archives. While he would subsequently conclude that the defect had been concealed by means of "light blasting" into that area (thereby removing evidence of a fatal shot from the right/front), JFK's real brain (which also offered evidence of a shot from the right/front) could no longer be used as evidence, so they effected a substitution.

By photographing another brain during *a second post-autopsy supplemental brain examination* and introducing those photographs into the medical record, they were able to produce autopsy X-rays and photographs that were, at least in general, more consistent with the "official account" of three shots having been fired from above and behind, where two of those shots had hit, one of which would become the "magic" bullet that was supposed to have passed through his neck, the other the shot that purportedly hit the back of his head and killed him.

The other chapter by Horne concerned a crucial briefing board from the National Photographic Interpretation Center (NPIC), which had been prepared for presentations about the assassination for one or more high-ranking government official(s), probably either J. Edgar Hoover or Lyndon B. Johnson. In 1997, the ARRB staff was aware of only one briefing-board event at the NPIC, but we now know that two films had been brought there on successive evenings: the first was an 8mm, split film that had been developed in Dallas and appears to have been the Zapruder original, which arrived on Saturday; the second was a 16mm, unsplit film that had been developed in Rochester, N.Y. and appears to have been an extensively revised version.

These events involved "Zapruder films" in different formats and two groups of NPIC personnel, who were unaware of one another; and led to the preparation of two different briefing boards. There is no room for doubt that the NPIC was dealing here with two different films, which Doug has discussed in his five-volume study, *Inside the Assassination Records Review Board* (2009), where I summarized some of his most important discussions related to the film in "*U.S. Government Official: JFK Cover-Up, Film Fabrication*". In the remarkable study that follows, Doug expands upon the events at the NPIC that weekend. Those who want to learn more about the film and its fabrication may want to review *The Great Zapruder Film Hoax* (2003). In the meanwhile, what we have here is a great place to start.

The Two NPIC Zapruder Film Events: Signposts Pointing to the Film's Alteration

by Douglas Horne

Most Americans don't know anything about the two significant events involving the famous Zapruder film of President Kennedy's assassination that took place back-to-back, on successive nights, at the CIA's National Photographic Interpretation Center (NPIC)—in Washington, D.C.—on the weekend immediately following JFK's assassination.

But anyone evenly remotely interested in what is perhaps the key piece of film evidence in the Kennedy assassination—what for decades was viewed as the "bedrock evidence" in the case, the "closest thing to ground truth"—needs to become acquainted with what happened to Abraham Zapruder's home movie of JFK's assassination during the three days immediately following President Kennedy's death. Why should that be the case?

Because the hottest debate raging within the JFK research community for the past several years is about whether the Zapruder film in the National Archives is an authentic film from which sound, scientific conclusions regarding JFK's assassination can be divined, or whether it is an altered film indicative of a government cover-up, which yields tainted and suspect information, and leads us to false conclusions, about what happened in Dealey Plaza. The resolution of this debate hinges on the answers to two essential questions: First, is the film's chain of custody immediately after the assassination what it has been purported to be for many years, or is it, in reality, quite different? Second, are there visual indications within the film's imagery which prove it has been tampered with, i.e., altered?

If the film's chain of custody has been misrepresented for decades, and if the opportunity and means existed that weekend to alter the film, then suspect imagery within the film takes on a crucial new level of importance, and is not simply of academic interest.

This paper will first, and primarily, address questions about the chain of custody of the Zapruder film immediately following President Kennedy's assassination, for new scholarship teaches us that the actual chain of custody of Abraham Zapruder's home movie, from 23--25 November 1963, is not anything close to what it was represented to be for years, and in fact indicates an extremely high level of interest in Abraham Zapruder's home movie by the U.S. government during the three days immediately following President Kennedy's assassination in Dallas on Friday, 22 November 1963.

The relatively new chain of custody evidence presented here will not only prove that the camera-original Zapruder film was in the custody of the CIA and Secret Service—not *Life* magazine—from late Saturday evening through Monday morning that weekend, but is of such a provocative nature that it strongly suggests—indeed, virtually proves—the original film was altered that weekend, prior to the publication of any of the film's frames in *Life* magazine, and prior to its use by the Warren Commission. After the startling new facts about the Zapruder film's actual chain of custody are thoroughly explored, I will summarize briefly some of the key evidence indicating that the film's imagery has been altered.

Backstory

I served on the staff of the Assassination Records Review Board (ARRB) during the last three years of its four-year lifespan, from August 1995-September 1998. I was hired as a Senior Analyst on the Military Records Team, and was promoted midway through my tour to the position of Chief Analyst for Military Records. In addition to working with military records on Cuba and Vietnam, I was privileged to work extensively with the JFK medical evidence, and on all issues related to the Zapruder film. Before launching into the story of the two NPIC events with the Zapruder film the weekend of the assassination, and my personal involvement in interviewing all three of the key NPIC witnesses, it's essential that the reader gain some familiarity with the historical background of the Zapruder film.

Even though Time, Inc. (more commonly referred to in this instance as *Life* magazine) had purchased the Zapruder film on 25 November 1963 (the Monday following JFK's assassination) for $ 150,000, it was never shown publicly by Time, Inc. or *Life* as a motion picture. (Only selected still frames were published by *Life*, from time to time, on special occasions, when the magazine deemed it appropriate.) The Warren Commission staff studied a grainy, second-generation FBI copy of the film for seven days during late January and early February of 1964; again in April of 1964; and viewed the purported original on one day only—25 February 1964—when it was brought over by *Life* magazine, at the Commission's request.

On 6 March 1975 a bootleg copy of the Zapruder film was shown on television, for the very first time, by ABC and the host of its program *Good Night America,* Geraldo Rivera; in the ensuing uproar about the film's 12-year suppression as a motion picture, Time, Inc. decided to rid itself of the albatross, and sold the film, and all rights, back to Abraham Zapruder's heirs for $1 on 9 April 1975.

Zapruder's heirs (the LMH Co.) subsequently placed the film in courtesy storage at the National Archives on 29 June 1978 so that it would be protected in a low temperature (25° Fahrenheit), low humidity environment specifically designed for archival film storage. The legal status of the film became uncertain with the passage of the President John F. Kennedy Assassination Records Collection Act on 26 October 1992, since the goal of the "JFK Records Act" was to seek out assassination records and place them in the National Archives, in a permanent new collection.

Zapruder's heirs failed in their attempt to remove the film from courtesy storage on 15 March 1993, when the Archives decided that the terms of the courtesy storage agreement signed with the LMH Co. on 10 July 1978 were in possible conflict with the requirements of the JFK Records Act—namely, securing assassination records for the American people in a special collection at the National Archives. The impasse was finally resolved on 24 April 1997, when the Review Board formally voted to designate the Zapruder film as an "assassination record," and to implement a legal "taking" of the film in order to preserve it in perpetuity, for the American people, as part of the JFK Records Collection. The "taking" was to be implemented on 1 August 1998. (The film never left the custody of the National Archives; 1 August 1998 was simply the date the film would be formally transferred from courtesy storage, and officially become part of the JFK Records Collection.)

Well after the sunset of the ARRB's operations at the end of September 1998, a Justice Department binding arbitration panel decided on 16 June 1999 (by a split vote of 2–1) that Abraham Zapruder's heirs should be given $16 million in "just compensation" for the taking of the film by the U.S. government, and the U.S. Congress obediently ponied up the money. [1] Strangely—and inappropriately, in view of its windfall profit—the LMH Co. (Zapruder's heirs) was allowed by the Justice Department to keep the copyright, and all of the legal control over use of the film's images that comes with the copyright. On 30 December 1999 the LMH Co. contractually transferred the copyright for the Zapruder film, and all of its film holdings (including large format transparencies and various copies of the motion picture film), to the Sixth Floor Museum in Dallas, Texas. [2]

Prior to the implementation of the taking on 1 August 1998, the Review Board—at my recommendation—commissioned a limited authenticity study of the Zapruder film (based primarily on examination of its edge print, the markings and script imposed on the film at the factory where it was produced, and at the developing plant after it was exposed). The ARRB staff first approached the Eastman Kodak Co. for film assistance and advice in 1996, and asked in 1997 if Kodak would perform the Zapruder film study pro bono; Kodak agreed, and hired a noted retired Kodak film chemist, Mr. Roland Zavada, as a paid consultant to perform the one-man study.

Mr. Zavada studied the film's edge print; perceived anomalies in the bleed-over imagery in the intersprocket area of the film; its forensic chain of custody on the day of JFK's assassination; and educated himself on the basic characteristics of Zapruder's Bell & Howell movie camera by purchasing several models and experimenting with them—but at our request, he did not study the film's image content. Zavada's report was signed out on 25 September 1998, and arrived in Washington, D.C. on 28 September, two days before the ARRB shut down its operations on 30 September.

The Key Witnesses

During the summer of 1997, following the announcement that the film would be "taken" by the government, and while the authenticity study by Kodak was effectively already underway, the ARRB staff became aware that there were two former CIA/NPIC employees who had, in 1963, worked with the Zapruder film at "the Agency's" National

Photographic Interpretation Center (NPIC) immediately after JFK's assassination: their names were Homer A. McMahon (the former Head of the NPIC Color Lab), and Morgan Bennett ("Ben") Hunter (his assistant at the time). The ARRB staff interviewed each man three times that summer, and I was present at all of those interviews. [3] I was the lead interviewer at the one interview that was recorded on audiotape—this was my questioning of Homer A. McMahon at Archives II, in College Park, Maryland on 14 July 1997.

The tape of that interview has been available to the American people through the JFK Records Collection at Archives II since November of 1998; I finally produced a long-overdue verbatim transcript of the interview in May of 2012, which I make available on request to anyone who is interested. ARRB staff interview reports—written summaries—were produced after each interview of these two NPIC employees, and those interview reports are also available to the public in the JFK Records Collection at Archives II.

The activity McMahon and Hunter were involved in on the weekend following President Kennedy's assassination was the making of photographic enlargements from individual frames of the Zapruder film; the purpose of this activity was to support the creation of "briefing boards" that would be assembled by others at NPIC, using the color prints they made, for purposes and audiences unknown. The customer requesting the activity was the U.S. Secret Service. Homer McMahon, following the instructions of a person who identified himself as Secret Service agent "Bill Smith," presided over this "briefing board event" at NPIC. Unknown to the ARRB staff at the time, this round of interviews with Homer McMahon and Ben Hunter was only the first half of the story of what happened at NPIC the weekend of the assassination. I would not become aware of the second half of the story until 2009, about 11½ years later.

NPIC Panel 1

Then, in February of 2009, I was contacted by JFK researcher Peter Janney of Massachusetts (author of *Mary's Mosaic,* 2012), who had just commenced a long series of interviews with a third former NPIC employee who had also participated in an NPIC "briefing board event" the weekend following JFK's assassination. This witness, who had spoken only briefly and cursorily to a few other JFK assassination researchers, was the prestigious Dino A. Brugioni, who had served as the Chief Information Officer (the "briefing board czar") at NPIC for about two-and-a-half decades; Mr. Brugioni was, and remains today, the world's foremost living expert on the U-2 and SR-71 aerial reconnaissance imagery, and on the Corona and early Keyhole satellite reconnaissance imagery; and when first contacted by Peter Janney, was already the author of several books, including *Eyeball to Eyeball* (an account of aerial reconnaissance during the Cuban Missile Crisis), and *Photo Fakery.*

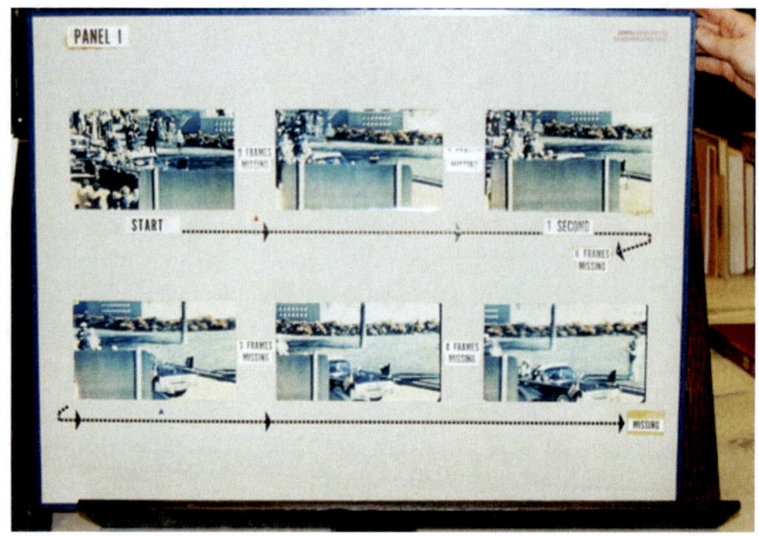

At Peter's request, I helped him develop an evolving list of questions for Mr. Brugioni, and also helped him evaluate the answers as they came in following each interview. Peter Janney conducted an exhaustive series of MP3-recorded telephonic interviews of Dino Brugioni throughout the late winter and spring of 2009 (seven interviews altogether, beginning on 30 January and ending on 27 June), [4] and the upshot was that without any doubt whatsoever, Mr. Brugioni presided over a distinctly different "briefing board event" at NPIC the weekend following the assassination, using a distinctly different Zapruder film.

Mr. Brugioni, like Mr. McMahon, also presided over the making of enlargements—blowup prints—from individual frames of the Zapruder film, which were then mounted on briefing boards. But his work crew was entirely different than McMahon's; the numbers of enlargements made differed significantly; the number of briefing boards made was different; and the format of the briefing boards made at Brugioni's event was distinctly different.

Most significantly, the format of the Zapruder film delivered at Brugioni's NPIC event was distinctly different from the format of the Zapruder film delivered at McMahon's NPIC event. Yet each man believed, without any doubt, that he was working with the original film. And the two events occurred only one day apart. Mr. Brugioni was contacted again in 2011, and the information that he had previously provided in 2009 was reconfirmed by Peter Janney in an MP3-recorded interview at Mr. Brugioni's home on 28 April 2011; as well as in a four-hour-long HD video interview conducted by me on 9 July 2011. Mr. Brugioni's memory remained sharp, and his credibility high—very high. Indeed, his good memory and credibility is recorded for posterity on the HD video recording.

What the two NPIC events point to, the weekend immediately following President Kennedy's assassination, is a compartmentalized operation, in which the first NPIC work crew (Brugioni's) made briefing boards, using enlargements of individual frames from the true camera-original Zapruder film; and in which the second NPIC work crew (McMahon's) also made briefing boards, the very next night, using enlargements of frames from an altered Zapruder film, masquerading as the camera-original. I characterize the operation as compartmentalized because neither group was aware of the other group's activity that weekend, nor were they intended to be. At the time, back in 1963, both McMahon and Brugioni were each led to believe they were working with the "original film," but clearly, only one of them could have been. Fantastic, you say? Certainly. But all true. The evidence will be clearly laid out before you, below, along with an analysis of what the evidence likely means, and why.

Before I present to you a detailed summary of what happened at each of the two NPIC "briefing board events," let us examine what we thought we knew, before the two NPIC events were made known to us, about the Zapruder film's chain of custody during the critical four days following JFK's assassination. This short digression is vital to understanding the significance of the differences between the two versions of the Zapruder film delivered to NPIC the weekend following the assassination.

The Traditionally Understood Zapruder Film Chain of Custody, from Friday, 22 November 1963 through Tuesday, 26 November 1963

Here is the commonly-agreed-to chain of custody for the cameraoriginal Zapruder film, as it was known prior to our new understanding of the implications of the two NPIC events:

Friday, 22 November:

Zapruder's home movie of the assassination was developed at the Kodak plant in Dallas. When developed, it was a 16 mm wide, 25-foot-long "double 8" film, with sprocket holes running along both outside edges, and was unslit. What does this mean? Simply put, as shot in the camera, and then as developed, all "double 8" home movie films consisted of two 8mm wide image strips going in opposite directions, and upside down when compared to each other.

The normal practice immediately following developing was for the developing lab to "split," or slit, the 16 mm wide film in half, vertically, and then join the two sides of the movie (known as the A side and the B side) together with a splice, so that it could be projected in an 8 mm home projector. A "double 8" movie that has been slit only has sprocket holes on one side (the left side), and is 50 feet long (instead of 25).

In the case of the Zapruder film, the A side (family scenes) and the B side (the Kennedy assassination) were not initially split, or slit apart, so that Mr. Zapruder could get three copies (contact prints) exposed at another lab (the Jamieson film lab in Dallas), in Mr. Jamieson's 16 mm contact printer. That is, the 16 mm out-of-camera format (with opposing image strips going in opposite directions) was temporarily preserved on Friday afternoon, so that Zapruder's film could be copied.

Before departing for the Jamieson lab to have three contact prints exposed, the 16 mm wide, out-of-camera-original was viewed once by the production supervisor (Mr. Chamberlain) and Mr. Zapruder, on a Kodak 16 mm processing inspection projector, at twice the normal projection speed—to simply ensure that Zapruder had indeed captured the assassination on film. [5]

Following his return from the Jamieson lab with the three exposed contact prints, all three contact prints were developed at the Kodak plant in Dallas. After the three dupes were found satisfactory, the original film was slit down the middle to 8 mm in width, and the two halves of the movie spliced together, end-to-end (per normal procedure).

The original film, now 8mm in width, was viewed at least twice on an 8 mm projector by several laboratory personnel (including Production Supervisor Phil Chamberlain, and Customer Service Manager Dick Blair), Mr. Zapruder, and his attorney. [6] At least one of the three dupes was also viewed, and was noted to have a "softer" focus than the original film (as would be expected).

The original film, now 8mm in width, was viewed at least twice on an 8 mm projector by several laboratory personnel (including Production Supervisor Phil Chamberlain, and Customer Service Manager Dick Blair), Mr. Zapruder, and his attorney. [6] At least one of the three dupes was also viewed, and was noted to have a "softer" focus than the original film (as would be expected).

Zapruder departed Kodak's Dallas plant at about 9 PM, and turned over two of the three "first day copies" to the Secret Service. One was sent to Washington, D.C.—to Secret Service headquarters—by Dallas Secret Service agent Max Phillips, who placed it on a commercial flight late Friday night. It arrived in Washington after midnight, and sometime before dawn, on Saturday, 23 November 1963.

The second "same day copy" relinquished to the Secret Service by Zapruder on Friday night was loaned by the Secret Service to the FBI in Dallas the next day, on Saturday; and then flown by the Dallas office of the FBI to FBI headquarters, in Washington, on Saturday evening. [7]

Zapruder went home Friday night with the camera-original film, and one of the "first day copies" in his possession. He was contacted on the phone late Friday night by Richard Stolley, L*ife* magazine's Pacific Coast editor out of Los Angeles, and Zapruder agreed to meet with Mr. Stolley and discuss the film's potential sale the next morning in his office.

We have now accounted for the whereabouts of all three "first day copies" that weekend. However, the primary focus in this paper should remain on the original film. ARRB consultant Roland Zavada's formal conclusion in his report was this: "After the dupes were found satisfactory, the original film was slit to 8 mm." [8] There was absolutely no doubt in his mind about this, for he had interviewed the surviving employees from the Kodak plant in Dallas, and both high level supervisors present that day concurred in this.

Saturday, 23 November:

Abraham Zapruder met with Secret Service officials and Mr. Stolley of *Life* in his office on Saturday morning, 23 November 1963, and projected the original film for them on his 8 mm projector. [9]

He then struck a deal with Richard Stolley, selling to *Life,* for $50,000, worldwide print media rights to the assassination movie (but not motion picture rights). Zapruder agreed in this initial contract that he would not exploit the film as a motion picture, himself, until Friday, 29 November. Zapruder immediately relinquished the camera-original film to *Life* for a six-day period, and kept in his possession the one remaining "same day copy." By the terms of this initial contract with LIFE, Zapruder was to have the original film returned to him by *Life* on or about 29 November, and in exchange he was then to give *Life* the remaining first-day copy. [10]

Richard Stolley immediately put the film on a commercial flight bound for Chicago, where *Life's* principal printing plant was located.

[11] The presses for the 29 November edition had been stopped on Friday, the day of the assassination, and the plan was to make major use of the imagery from Zapruder's film as the issue was reconfigured.

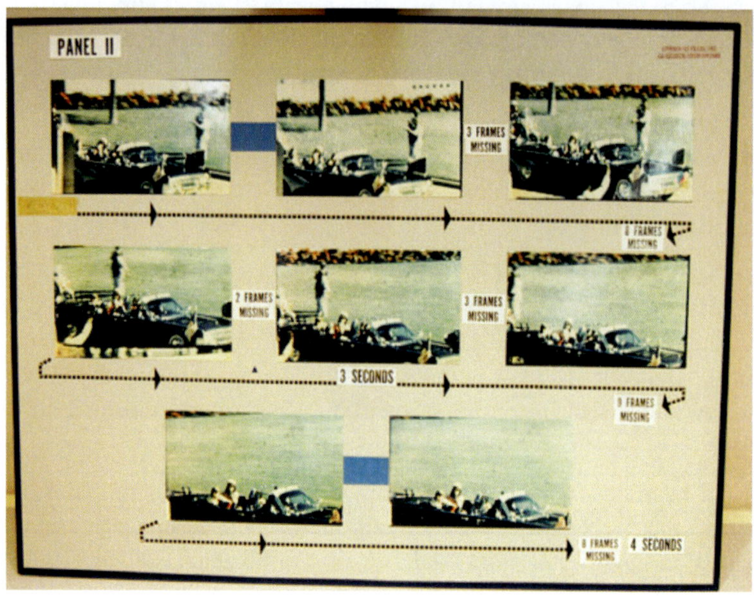

NPIC Panel II

Now, here is the doubtful part of the chain of custody story that will require modification after we study the two NPIC events the weekend of the assassination: the traditional belief, for decades, was that the original Zapruder film remained with *Life* in Chicago from early Saturday evening, until Tuesday, 26 November, when the first issues of the reconfigured 29 November issue began to appear on local newsstands.

The principal reference supporting this traditional view of the Zapruder film's chain of custody, from Saturday through Tuesday, has been pages 311–318 of Loudon Wainwright's 1986 memoir, titled *The Great American Magazine: An Inside History of Life.* In his book, Wainwright recounts hearsay passed along to him from others at *Life* about how the film was processed in Chicago—who was on the team that prepared the use of blowups from the film, how they worked on the layout, etc. [12]

The magazine was actually printed at Chicago's R.R. Donnelley & Sons Company printing plant; prior to the actual layout and graphics work at the printing plant, numerous 8 x 10 inch prints were run off at a separate Chicago photo lab. [13] We shall further discuss the activities in Chicago, and what was actually published in the 29 November issue, toward the end of this article. The only part of the Chicago story that is subject to doubt is the exact timing of when the *Life* editorial and technical team actually performed its layout of the Zapruder frames for the 29 November issue: was it actually Saturday night, or was it really Sunday night, or perhaps even early Monday morning before dawn?

Sunday, 24 November:

On Sunday evening, Richard Stolley, on behalf of *Life,* approached Abraham Zapruder on the phone and requested that they meet to negotiate *Life's* acquisition of additional rights to the film. "Something" had happened that caused the magazine to seek all rights to the film, including motion picture rights, and outright ownership of both the original film, and all copies. These additional rights would prove extremely expensive to Time, Inc., *Life* magazine's parent company.

Monday, 25 November:

After the conclusion of President Kennedy's funeral on Monday—the funeral ended at about 2 PM Dallas time (CST), with Air Force One flying over the gravesite at 2:54 PM EST, and with the former First Lady, Jacqueline Bouvier Kennedy, lighting the eternal flame at 3:13 PM EST—Stolley, Zapruder, and his attorney for this purpose, Sam Passman, met to renegotiate the sale contract for the film. Earlier that day *Life's* publisher, C.D. Jackson, had relayed to Stolley the formal approval of the board of Time, Inc. for him to renegotiate the contract. [14]

For a renegotiated total price of $150,000 ($100,000 more than the original contract signed on Saturday), Time, Inc. now gained all rights to the Zapruder film's imagery (domestic and foreign; and newsreel, television, and motion picture); and permanent ownership of the original and all three copies of the "8 mm color films," thus erasing any doubt that the original and the copies had been slit to 8 mm on Friday. In addition, the new contract stipulated that Time, Inc. would pay to Zapruder an amount equal to one half of all gross receipts for use of the film, above and beyond the new $150,000 sale price. (The contract stipulated that Time, Inc. would also own the two "first-day copies" that Zapruder had loaned to the Secret Service, once they were returned; they never were returned.) [15]

Tuesday, 26 November:

The first newsstand copies of the 29 November issue of *Life* began to trickle out; the issue displayed a total of 31 fuzzy, poor resolution, black-and-white images of blowups from individual frames of the film. [16] Twenty-eight of them were quite small; two were medium sized;

and one was a large format reproduction. What is hard to understand, in retrospect, is why *Life* magazine published such muddy, indistinct images of a film that its parent company, Time Inc., had spent an additional $100,000 to repurchase. We will revisit this question following our examination of the two NPIC "briefing board events," below.

NPIC EVENT # 1 (Presided over by Dino Brugioni)

The summary below recapitulates information gleaned from the seven recorded (MP3) Peter Janney-Dino Brugioni interviews in 2009; an eighth recorded (MP3) Peter Janney-Dino Brugioni interview on 28 April 2011; and my own HD video interview of Mr. Brugioni on 9 July 2011.

Time and date:

This event commenced about 10 PM, EST, on Saturday evening, 23 November 1963, when two Secret Service officials (estimated to be in their late 30s or early 40s) brought an 8 mm home movie of the JFK assassination to the CIA's National Photographic Interpretation Center, located in Building 213 in the Washington Navy Yard. (At no time could Mr. Brugioni recall either of their names.) They had not yet seen the film themselves, and Mr. Brugioni is of the distinct impression that they had just gotten off of an airplane and had come directly to NPIC from the airport. They did not volunteer where they had come from, or where the film had come from. The event at NPIC went on all night long, until about dawn on Sunday, 24 November. [Note: The home movie of the assassination brought to NPIC by the two Secret Service officials was not copied as a motion picture that night; nor did NPIC even have the capability to do so.]

How notified:

Dino Brugioni was the Duty Officer at NPIC that weekend, and was personally notified about the impending visit by NPIC's Director, the legendary Arthur C. Lundahl. Lundahl, in turn, had been notified by CIA Director John McCone that the Secret Service would be bringing in a film, and would require NPIC's assistance.

Work crew called in (and not called in):

Mr. Brugioni personally notified and called in, as his primary assistants, Mr. Bill Banfield (the Head of the Photography and the Graphics Departments), and Ralph Pearse, the Lead Photogrammatrist at NPIC. Bill Banfield had in turn ordered in three or four photo technicians, and two or three people from the graphics department, to assist in the work that evening.

During the course of several interviews, Mr. Brugioni was asked whether any of the following people were present, and he emphatically stated that they were not: neither Captain Pierre Sands, U.S. Navy; Homer A. McMahon; nor Morgan Bennett ("Ben") Hunter was present that night, according to Mr. Brugioni. He was quite certain, and unequivocal, about this. When asked if he had sighted, and knew, the photography and graphics technicians assisting the management team that night, he affirmed that he had indeed seen them that night, and that none of them were either Homer McMahon, or Ben Hunter. (Brugioni knew both men, and knew Ben Hunter particularly well.)

Format of film delivered:

Mr. Brugioni clearly recalls that the film delivered was an 8 mm film. He is positive about this because one member of his team had to go out that night and, through special arrangement, purchase a brand-new 8 mm projector, so that the film could be viewed as a motion picture. [NPIC had a state-of-the-art 16 mm projector installed in its briefing room, but had no 8 mm movie projectors.] He clearly recalls that the film strip only had sprocket holes down one side, which is consistent with a slit, 8mm wide "double 8" film.

He is also positive in his own mind that it was the original film, and not a copy. Mr. Brugioni personally owned an 8 mm "double 8" camera in 1963, and was familiar with the differences in quality between an original film and a copy film. He recalls that the images on the film were extremely sharp. Furthermore, the extreme nervousness and anxiety demonstrated by the two Secret Service officials convinced him that he had the original film, since they were terrified he would damage it when projecting it. All factors he observed, Brugioni insists, pointed to the film being the camera-original.

The Secret Service Couriers—the Customer:

The two Secret Service officials, after examining the film at least four or five times as a motion picture, wanted it timed with a stopwatch, to gain an appreciation of time between perceived shots. They were warned by NPIC personnel that this would not yield precise or reliable results, since the Bell & Howell movie camera used was a spring-wound camera, and hence its frame rate, or running speed, would have varied throughout the filming of the assassination.

The customer persisted in this desire, however, and therefore the NPIC crew complied. After viewing the film as a motion picture several times, the Secret Service officials requested that specific frames be enlarged and blown-up as photographic prints, and that the prints be mounted on briefing boards. The two segments of the film they focused on were the limousine on Elm Street as it went behind, and emerged from behind, the Stemmons Freeway sign; and the head shot. Mr. Brugioni could not remember any specific conclusions reached that night as to the number of shots fired, but he says the agents came with no pre-conceptions about this, for they had not yet seen the film.

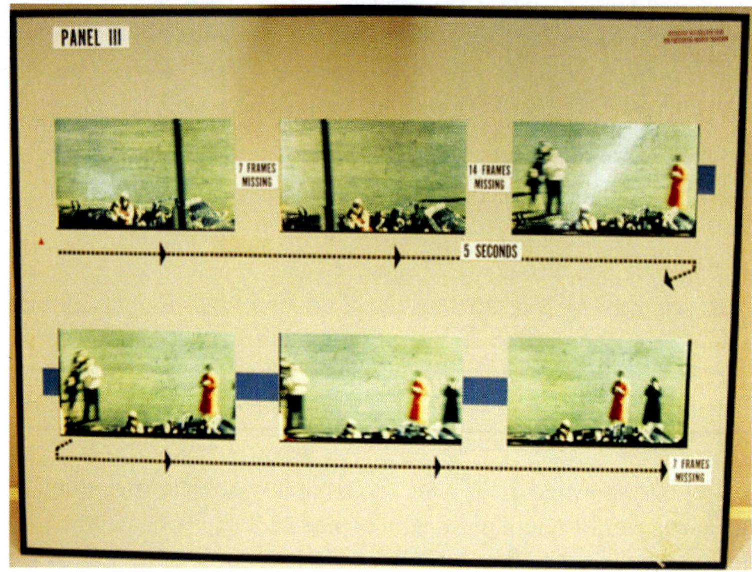

NPIC Panel III

Briefing Boards created: After the customer selected individual frames to be enlarged and printed, the NPIC work crew made internegatives of each of those frames using a precision, high-quality enlarger, and then made two photographic prints from each internegative. Between 12 and 15 frames on the home movie, total, were selected for enlargement, and two small prints, about 4 x 5 inches in size, were printed from each internegative. Using these prints, two sets of briefing boards were made at NPIC, one for the customer (the Secret Service), and one for CIA Director John McCone. (It was standard procedure for the CIA Director to receive duplicates of briefing boards made for other customers within the federal government.)

The two briefing board panels that constituted each set were 22 x 20 inches in size, and joined by a plastic hinge in the middle, that allowed each briefing board set to be folded in half for easier transportation; thus, the overall size of each briefing board set was 44 inches wide from left to right, and 20 inches tall. (Mr. Brugioni had originally estimated in 2009 that the conjoined, two panel briefing boards were each about six-feet-wide-by-three-feet-tall; but prior to the 2011 HD video interview, he had refreshed his recollection by examining old photos of NPIC staff members holding standard briefing boards used at NPIC; and in July of 2011, he more accurately recalled that the standard size of each pre-cut briefing board was 22 x 20 inches—and modified his answers accordingly.)

The only textual information that Mr. Brugioni recalls being posted on each briefing board set was: (1) the magnification factor, listed at the top of each panel; and (2) the frame number of each print, displayed above each print. [In 2009, Brugioni recalled the frame numbers being posted below each print.]

Accompanying Textual Material: Mr. Brugioni personally prepared and typed a one-page set of notes for Mr. Arthur Lundahl, NPIC's Director, to use when delivering the two sets of briefing boards to CIA Director McCone, and briefing him, on Sunday morning. The set of notes contained the names of all the NPIC people involved; the NPIC's admonition against using a stopwatch to time shots depicted on a film shot with a spring-wound camera; and other technical information about how the briefing boards were prepared. Two sets of notes were prepared, one to go with each briefing board.

The departure of the Secret Service officials: The two Secret Service officials departed at about 3 AM on Sunday morning, or 4 AM at the latest, as soon as they had seen what one of the blowup enlargement prints looked like, and were satisfied with its quality and resolution. They departed without the briefing boards, for the boards were not even close to being completed when they departed.

The only textual material the two officials took with them was a list they had requested of Brugioni, listing the names of all of the NPIC employees involved in the briefing board event. The two Secret Service officials took the film with them, and departed without saying where they were going.

Mr. Lundahl's role on Sunday: Brugioni notified Mr. Lundahl by phone about 7 AM on Sunday morning that the work was finished, and Mr. Lundahl arrived at NPIC at about 8 AM to pick up the two sets of briefing boards; the two sets of briefing notes; and deliver them to Director McCone. Lundahl briefed McCone on Sunday morning, 24 November 1963. It would be up to McCone, as per standard procedure, to deliver one set of briefing boards and one set of briefing notes to the customer. Mr. Brugioni assumes that John McCone personally delivered one briefing board set and one set of notes to the Secret Service.

End of the event: Mr. Brugioni went home shortly after Mr. Lundahl departed to deliver the two briefing board sets to Mr. McCone, and was never notified again that weekend about any other activity at NPIC, of any kind. He said that if there had been additional activity, as duty officer that entire weekend (including Monday, the day of President Kennedy's funeral), he should have been the person notified.

Briefing boards placed in the National Archives by the CIA in 1993 are not the briefing boards prepared by Dino Brugioni's team: In 1993, the CIA's Historical Review Group, as required by the JFK Records Act, deposited with the National Archives one set of briefing boards identified in 1975 at NPIC—a four panel set (four loose panels, not joined to each other in any way)—mounting frame enlargements of the Zapruder film.

In both 2009 and 2011, Mr. Brugioni was shown good photographs of each of these four briefing board panels (which together constitute one set) and he consistently and emphatically denied that the four panels in the JFK Records Collection (in Flat 90A) are the ones he made in 1963.

His reasons were as follows: first, the frame numbers his group placed above each print, and the magnification factor his group placed at the top of each board, are not present; second, this briefing board set consists of four loose panels, not two conjoined panels; third, the four panels together contain 28 prints, not the 12 to 15 prints he recalls making for his briefing boards; fourth, each panel in the Archives is labeled "Panel I, Panel II, Panel III, and Panel IV," which is not what was done on his briefing boards, where there were no identifying numbers placed on each panel; and fifth, the four briefing board panels at the Archives contain different information, and a different layout, than placed on his briefing boards.

Working notes associated with the four briefing board panels at the Archives were not produced by Mr. Brugioni's team at his event: There are five (5) pages of NPIC working notes (also identified in 1975) stored with the four briefing board panels at the National Archives, in Flat 90A; one is a half-sheet of yellow legal pad paper with writing on both sides; one page is a typewritten summary of the prints (by frame number) on each of the four briefing board panels; and the three other pages consist of a shot and timing analysis of shots that may have hit President Kennedy and Governor Connally (three possible scenarios), keyed to frame numbers and taking into account the amount of time between postulated shots in each scenario. [The first of the three scenarios is the one written about in the 6 December 1963 issue of *Life* magazine.]

Mr. Brugioni, in both 2009, and again in 2011, denied having anything to do with these notes, and said he had not ever seen them until 2009, when Peter Janney first showed them to him. He furthermore volunteered that his group would not have had the time to conduct such a shot and timing analysis at the event he presided over, commencing late on 23 November 1963, so busy were they simply counting frames, making internegatives, printing photographic enlargements, and creating the two briefing boards from the photographic prints.

A startling revelation in 2011—the "head explosion" seen in the extant Zapruder film, in the National Archives today, is not at all consistent with the head explosion seen by Mr. Brugioni in the Zapruder film he viewed on the evening of 23 November 1963: During the follow-up interview at Dino Brugioni's home on 28 April 2011, Peter Janney showed Mr. Brugioni a good image of frame 313 from the extant Zapruder film—the so-called "head explosion"—scanned from a 35 mm dupe negative of the film obtained from the National Archives. [The provenance of the frame used therefore unquestionably represents what is in the National Archives today.]

Mr. Brugioni was quite startled to find out that this was the only frame graphically depicting the "head explosion" in the extant film, which the National Archives has characterized as "the original film." He insisted that the head explosion he viewed multiple times on 23 November 1963 was of such a great size, and duration (in terms of time), that there should be many more frames depicting that explosion than "just the one frame" (frame 313), as shown in the Zapruder film today. Furthermore, he said the "head explosion" depicted in the Zapruder film today is too small in size, and too low in the frame, to be the same graphic depiction he recalls witnessing in the Zapruder film on Saturday, 23 November 1963 at NPIC.

Mr. Brugioni viewed the Zapruder film as a motion picture several times during the HD video interview I conducted with him on 9 July 2011—using the 1998 MPI DVD product, *Image of an Assassination,* made by the LMH Co. in 1997 from the film in the National Archives—and reiterated those comments that he made on 28 April to Peter Janney, insisting that "something was missing" from the film in the National Archives today.

While viewing the video on 9 July 2011, Mr. Brugioni also stated that the head explosion he viewed was a large "white cloud" that surrounded President Kennedy's head, and was not pink or red, as shown in the extant Zapruder film. The words below are excerpted from Dino Brugioni's 28 April 2011 interview with Peter Janney, as he recounted what he recalled seeing when he watched the head explosion in the Zapruder film on 23 November 1963:

"…I remember all of us being shocked…it was straight up [gesturing high above his own head]…in the sky…There should have been more than one frame…I thought the spray was, say, three or four feet from his head… what I saw was more than that [than frame 313 in today's film]…it wasn't low [as in frame 313], it was high…there was more than that in the original… It was way high off of his head…and I can't imagine that there would only be one frame. What I saw was more than you have there [in frame 313]." [17] [emphasis as spoken]

In repeatedly viewing the Zapruder film as a motion picture during his July 2011 video interview, Dino Brugioni definitively confirmed that it was indeed the Zapruder film he was working with at NPIC on 23 November 1963, even though the Secret Service couriers did not refer to it by that name; they simply referred to it as a "home movie."

But Brugioni confirmed to me unequivocally that it was the Zapruder film he was working with, and not some other film. Aside from the head shot, he recalled one other thing about the extant film that was inconsistent with what he saw on 23 November 1963: prior to viewing the film on 9 July 2011, he had independently recalled Secret Service agent Clint Hill either physically striking, or violently pushing Jackie Kennedy to force her from atop the trunk lid, back into the rear seat of the limousine. Brugioni spent a considerable portion of the interview attempting to find evidence of Clint Hill "striking Jackie" in the extant film, to no avail. He was quite mystified.

NPIC EVENT # 2 (Presided over by Homer McMahon)

As stated earlier, as a member of the ARRB staff, I interviewed Homer McMahon and Ben Hunter three times each between June and August of 1997. [18] A written call report was produced following each interview; additionally, the second of three Homer McMahon interviews—on 14 July 1997—was tape-recorded, and that recording may be obtained from the National Archives, along with all of the written interview reports. In May of 2012, I completed a verbatim transcript of the audiotaped interview with Mr. McMahon on 14 July 1997. The summary below recapitulates the totality of the information provided by McMahon and Hunter over the course of all of their interviews in the summer of 1997.

Time and date:

The strong and final consensus of opinion between the two men was that the NPIC event they participated in took place "about two days after" JFK's assassination, and "before the funeral." [The funeral was

Monday afternoon, 25 November.] They both agreed that their NPIC activity took place before the funeral of the 35th President. McMahon initially recalled the event as taking place one or two days after the assassination, and Hunter initially recalled it as taking place two or three days after the assassination; but both men consistently agreed that their NPIC activity definitely occurred prior to President Kennedy's funeral. The work commenced after dark, and lasted all night long. [Note: The home movie of the assassination brought to NPIC for McMahon and Hunter to work with was not copied as a motion picture; nor did NPIC even have the capability to do so.]

How notified:

Homer McMahon did not recall specifically how he was notified to go into work, but during his tape-recorded ARRB interview, he stated, "I was not contacted." [By this he meant, in my opinion—based upon the context of the questioning—that he was not called in by the duty officer at NPIC—that is, he was "not contacted" by the normal procedure.] Ben Hunter recalled a Navy Captain named "Sands" being present, but did not initially recall a Secret Service agent being present, only someone in civilian clothes; Homer McMahon did not independently recall Captain Sands, but when informed of Hunter's recollection, McMahon did subsequently remember the presence of a Navy Captain, who had met the customer and granted him access to NPIC.

Homer McMahon vividly remembered that the "customer" at NPIC that night was a single Secret Service agent named "Bill Smith." This was a very strong recollection of McMahon's, and, although Ben Hunter never remembered this name, McMahon was most persuasive and credible in this regard. (See the repeated references to Bill Smith in the May 2012 transcript of the ARRB-McMahon interview.) In subsequent interviews, Ben Hunter did recall the presence of a Secret Service official, after I asked him that question.

NPIC Panel IV

Work crew called in (and not called in): The only NPIC employees present for the making of internegatives and prints from the Zapruder film delivered to NPIC by "Bill Smith" were McMahon (the Head of the Color Lab) and Hunter (a new-hire trainee fresh out of the Air Force, who assisted McMahon that evening). McMahon and Hunter did not make any briefing boards themselves, but they were aware that others in their building were going to create briefing boards mounting the enlargements, i.e., the photographic prints that they were running off from internegatives they had made from individual frames from the assassination film.

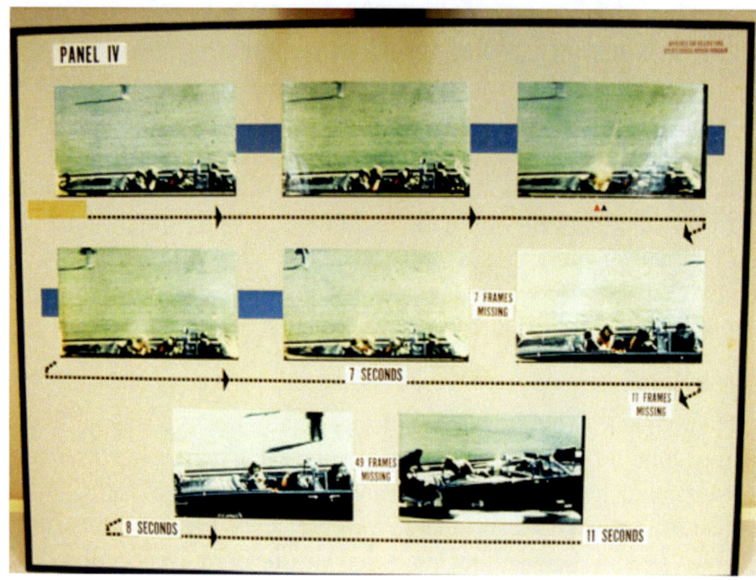

Captain Sands was present that night to allow the Secret Service courier/ customer to gain entry, but Sands did not participate in the making of internegatives or prints. [It was Dino Brugioni who revealed in both 2009, and 2011, that Captain Pierre Sands, U.S. Navy, was the NPIC Executive Director—the No. 2 man in the chain of command—in November of 1963. This has been confirmed by referencing an Internet biography of "Pierre Sands, U.S. Navy."]

No mention was made during the 1997 interviews, by either McMahon or Hunter, of Dino Brugioni; Bill Banfield; Ralph Pearse, or any other NPIC personnel.

In his second interview, McMahon remembered one young man who was assigned to assist in the making of the actual briefing boards after he and Hunter ran off the photographic enlargements, but could not remember his name; in his third interview, McMahon told me that he now remembered who made the briefing boards, but that he wasn't going to reveal his name to me. [McMahon was afraid that that employee might still be "current," and was therefore being very protective of his name.]

Format of film delivered:

Homer McMahon vividly and independently recalled during his first interview that an unslit,"double 8" home movie film, 16 mm wide, was delivered to him at NPIC by "Bill Smith" of the Secret Service. This was confirmed by him during his second, tape-recorded interview. He remembers being told by Bill Smith that the unslit double 8 movie was the camera-original film, and he believed this, because of its unslit format, as well as because of the sharpness of the image.

He remembered seeing opposing image strips going in opposite directions on the 16 mm film, with one of the image strips upside down when the other was right side up. McMahon definitely remembered himself, Ben Hunter, and Bill Smith projecting a version of the home movie using an installed 16 mm projector in a briefing room, but was unsure whether the movie projected was the unslit double 8 film, or a dupe of that film. He definitely remembered seeing an unslit, "double 8" film in his 10x20x40 precision enlarger that night as he was making internegatives from individual frames on the home movie. He also remembered that Bill Smith told him that dupes had been run off, and repeatedly said that it may have been a dupe that was projected using the 16 mm projector in the NPIC briefing room.

The Secret Service Customer—Bill Smith—and what he reported about the film's provenance

Homer McMahon said he was told by Bill Smith that a patriotic citizen in Dallas had donated the camera-original film to the Secret Service out of a sense of duty, and that the individual did not want to make any money off of the film, and so had given it to the Secret Service for free. Bill Smith told McMahon he had personally couriered the undeveloped film himself to a Top Secret Kodak film lab called "Hawkeyeworks," which McMahon knew to be in Rochester, N.Y. at Kodak headquarters; that it had been developed there; and that the personnel at the Top Secret lab had subsequently referred Bill Smith back to his home base of Washington, D.C., to NPIC, for the making of individual frame enlargements and briefing boards, since those specific tasks could not be performed at the lab in Rochester.

McMahon was extremely sensitive about the code-name "Hawkeyeworks" during the interview, and regretted mentioning it. [NOTE: In 1997, the CIA's Historical Review Group asked the ARRB staff to expunge the use of the code-word from our written interview reports, and from the audiotape of the interview to be released to the public.

Thus, in 1998, a sanitized (i.e., redacted) tape was provided by the ARRB staff for public release by the JFK Records Collection at the National Archives and Records Administration (NARA), and the Archives placed the unredacted, original tape-recording under lock-and-key, for automatic release not later than 2017, in accordance with the JFK Records Act. The point is now moot, for the code-name

"Hawkeyeworks" has since been effectively declassified, per the mention of this facility ("Eastman Kodak's Hawkeye Film Processing Facility in Rochester, N.Y.") in Dino Brugioni's 2010 book, *Eyes in the Sky: Eisenhower, the CIA and Cold War Aerial Espionage*, which was thoroughly vetted and approved for publication by the CIA. [19]

Furthermore, Dino Brugioni himself repeatedly mentioned the "Hawkeye Plant," and the capabilities of that state-of-the-art, high-tech laboratory, during his interviews with Peter Janney and me in 2009 and 2011.] McMahon explained that the government had classified contracts with Kodak in 1963, and that both the CIA and Kodak had their best people working together on classified projects. He was absolutely certain that the film had been developed at Rochester, and had come from Rochester, for Bill Smith had indicated this by using the unique code-word ("Hawkeyeworks") that unmistakably referred to the "other Top Secret lab" in Rochester, to the exclusion of all other locations. (The "Hawkeyeworks" lab and its capabilities, as defined by Dino Brugioni, will be further discussed later in this chapter.)

Opinions About the Assassination of JFK Expressed by Bill Smith of the Secret Service:

According to Homer McMahon, Bill Smith came to NPIC in Washington, D.C., having already examined the home movie, expressing the opinion that only three (3) shots had been fired at the occupants of President Kennedy's limousine on Elm Street, and that they had all been fired from the TSBD by Lee Harvey Oswald. Homer McMahon, who had been a trick-shot artist as a child, and a champion in National Rifle Association shooting competitions as a teenager, felt otherwise, and told Jeremy Gunn and me during our interview of him, on 14 July 1997, that he believed six to eight shots had hit President Kennedy, and that they had been fired from at least three directions.

But he could not change Bill Smith's mind; for as McMahon said to me, "Oh yes, I expressed my opinion—but you know, it, it, it was pre-conceived. That's the way I felt about it—it was pre-conceived, so you don't fight City Hall. I wasn't there to fight 'em, I was there to do the work." In truth, Bill Smith did not want Homer McMahon or Ben Hunter to do any analysis whatsoever; he only wanted them to make internegatives and blowup prints, or enlargements, for the frames he selected during his visit to NPIC.

Photographic Products created at NPIC:

With the full understanding that they were going to be used in briefing boards created by their colleagues "upstairs" at NPIC, McMahon and

Hunter created internegatives of frames selected by "Bill Smith," using a full immersion "liquid gate" procedure in the optical precision 10x20x40 enlarger. Each internegative created was of a "40x" magnification, and three (3) each contact prints of about 5 x 7 inches in size were then made from each 40x internegative. Ben Hunter initially recalled a very limited number of frames selected—perhaps as few as only eight (8). Homer McMahon recalled that somewhere between 20 and 40 internegatives were made from the home movie of the assassination.

Bill Smith selected all of the frames for which internegatives were made, and enlargements were later printed. Smith told McMahon that the work was to be treated as "above Top Secret;" that it was on a strictly "need-to-know" basis; and that not even Homer McMahon's boss was to know anything about it. McMahon and Hunter were instructed that they could not even answer questions about why they were putting in for overtime, and that any such questions from their immediate supervisors would have to be referred to Captain Sands. McMahon reported that Bill Smith took custody of all discards, and all scraps and trash that night, and that he and Hunter were not allowed to throw anything into the burn bags, or classified trash receptacles.

The Four Briefing Board Panels at NARA are examined:

Both McMahon and Hunter agreed that the prints mounted on the four briefing board panels in the National Archives were indeed the prints they made the night of their "NPIC event." Neither man had seen the completed briefing boards before, but they both agreed that the 28 prints mounted on the four panels were the prints they had made. McMahon stated that the prints had been trimmed down to a slightly smaller size from what had been printed. McMahon also noted, with dispassionate professional interest, that the prints had deteriorated badly over time, due to the instability of the dyes.

When McMahon examined the 28 prints mounted on the four panels, he immediately expressed the opinion that some of the prints they had made were missing from the briefing boards, and had not been used—most likely additional views of the limousine before it went behind the Stemmons Freeway sign, and additional views of Clint Hill mounting the vehicle after the head explosion.

Neither McMahon nor Hunter had any direct or indirect knowledge of how the four briefing board panels were used. McMahon could only speculate that they may have been used to brief the Warren Commission, but this was not something told to him by Bill Smith; indeed, there was no Warren Commission yet created when Bill Smith visited NPIC.

[The Warren Commission was not even created by President Lyndon B. Johnson until Friday, 29 November 1963,]

The five pages of NPIC "working notes" are examined: Neither McMahon nor Hunter had seen four of the five pages of notes that are found in Flat 90A at the Archives, along with the four briefing board panels. (Specifically, they said they had never seen the three-page shot and timing analysis, nor the typewritten summary of briefing board panel contents.) The one page that they both agreed contained their handwriting was the half-sheet with writing on both sides. Of particular interest to McMahon was the back side of the half sheet, which contains the following pencil notations: "shoot internegs, one-and-a-half hr; proc and dry internegs, two hr; print test, one hr; make three prints (each), one hr; proc and dry prints, one-and-a-half hr;" and the total is listed as "seven hrs."

McMahon stated with assurance that these notations were in his handwriting; and that they referred to the time required to create the internegatives from the Zapruder film frames, and to make the contact prints. [Note: In my judgment, the prints mounted on the four briefing board panels are clearly from the extant version of the Zapruder film, for they appear to match the Zapruder film frames published throughout the years in numerous books. So clearly, McMahon and Hunter were also working with a version of the Zapruder film, just as Brugioni was during his "briefing board event," even though the assassination film was not identified through the use of Zapruder's name by Bill Smith.]

Source note: This chapter previously appeared as "Two NPIC Zapruder Film Events Pointing to its Alteration", *http://jamesfetzer.blogspot.com/2015/09/ two-npic-zapruder-film-events-pointing.html.*

Notes:

[1] The panel voted its decision on 16 June 1999, but did not announce its decision publicly until 3 August 1999, due to its sensitivity over the death of John F. Kennedy Jr. in a plane crash.
[2] Richard B. Trask, *National Nightmare on Six Feet of Film: Mr. Zapruder's Home Movie And the Murder of President Kennedy* (Yeoman Press, 2005); David R. Wrone, *The Zapruder Film: Reframing JFK's Assassination* (University Press of Kansas, 2003); and Douglas P. Horne, *Inside the Assassination Records Review Board: The U.S. Government's Final Attempt to Reconcile the Conflicting Medical Evidence in the Assassination of JFK* (self-published, 2009).
[3] Horne, 2009, p. 1220–1226
[4] Ibid., p. 1231.
[5] Roland J. Zavada, Analysis of Selected Motion Picture Photographic Evidence (25 September 1998), Attachment A1-8 (Meeting Minutes of Discussion between Roland Zavada, Phil Chamberlain, and Dick Blair), and Attachment A1-11 (Phil Chamberlain's original manuscript regarding events related to the handling and processing of the Zapruder film at the Kodak plant in Dallas).
[6] Zavada, 1998, Attachment A1-8.
[7] Trask, 2005, p. 119–122; and Wrone, 2003, p. 22–28.
[8] Zavada, 1998, Study 1, p. 27.
[9] Trask, 2005, p. 127–131; and Wrone, 2003, p. 32–35.
[10] Horne, 2009, p. 1200.
[11] Trask, 2005, p. 131; and Wrone, 2003, p. 34–35.
[12] Horne, 2009, p. 1346–1350.
[13] Trask, 2005, p. 152–155; and Wrone, 2003, p. 34–35, and 52–53.
[14] Wrone, 2003, p. 34–37.
[15] Horne, 2009, p. 1200–1201.
[16] Trask, 2005, p. 154–155.
[17] Peter Janney, *Mary's Mosaic* (Skyhorse Publishing, 2012), p. 293.
[18] Horne, 2009, p. 1221.
[19] Dino A. Brugioni, *Eyes in the Sky* (Naval Institute Press, 2010), p. 364.

8

Two NPIC Zapruder Film Events: Analysis and Implications

by Douglas Horne

The authenticity of the Zapruder film and of the other home movies purportedly taken of the assassination in Dealey Plaza has been hotly contested since I (Jim Fetzer) first organized and moderated the first Zapruder Film Symposium during the JFK Lancer Conference in 1996.

We have accumulated an enormous quantity of confirming evidence since that time, where those who want to know what actually happened are better off reading the compilation of witness reports from those who were present, which John P. Costella, Ph.D., has compiled, "*What Happened on Elm Street? The Eyewitnesses Speak*", than they are watching the extant version of the film.

Indeed, John, who earned his Ph.D. in electromagnetism and is an expert on the laws of optics and the physics of moving objects, has a brilliant visual introduction to the study of Zapruder film fakery, "*JFK Assassination Film Hoax: A Simple Introduction*".

Some of the most stunning proof of alteration comes from one of the most prominent figures in the extant film, Clint Hill, the Secret Service agent who was assigned to protect Jackie Kennedy. As the volley of shots that blew JFK's brains out to the back rear is virtually complete, Hill rushed forward to protect Jackie.

As he has consistently maintained for over 50 years now, he climbed up on the limo, where Jackie was reaching across the trunk to pick up a chunk of Jack's skull and brains, pushed her back down into the seat, lay cross her and JFK's body, peered into a massive, fist-sized hole in the back of his head, and gave his colleagues a "thumbs down", all before the limousine had reached the Triple Underpass.

Yet, in the Zapruder film and the complementary photograph shown here–which also has to have been fabricated–we only see him climbing on the back of the limo and reaching out toward Jackie before it zooms toward Parkland Hospital and passes beneath the underpass. What Clint Hill has been reporting—in written reports as well as during spoken presentations—contradicts the extant version of the film.

The principal reason for altering it was that William Greer, the driver, pulled the limo to the left and to a halt after bullets had begun to be fired.

This was such an obvious indication of Secret Service complicity in setting up JFK for the hit that it had to be removed. That caused a time contraction, which was inconsistent with retaining Clint Hill's activities, which therefore had to be contracted.

It also did not allow the inclusion of Officer James Chaney's motoring forward to notify Chief of Police Jesse Curry that JFK had been hit, which provides yet another line of proof demonstrating that the film has been fabricated.

The simplest and easiest to understand, however, is that in revising the original, they blacked out the gaping wound at the back of the head,

which Clint Hill has so vividly described, which was observed by a host of witnesses to the assassination or who witnessed the body thereafter.

Try as they might, however, they overlooked a late frame—374—in which the blowout is visible. So while they even altered the X-rays to conceal the wound reported by these witnesses, *the film itself is not even internally consistent!*

We have ample proof that the film was fabricated, but knowing exactly how it was done and when has posed a challenging task, which, I am proud to say, Douglas Horne has nailed down in his remarkable studies of events at the National Photographic Interpretation Center the weekend following the assassination.

An 8mm, split film developed in Dallas–which appears to have been the original–was brought on Saturday, the 23rd, and another film, this time a 16mm unsplit film developed in Rochester–which appears to have been the revised version–was brought on Sunday, the 24th.

Doug's first reports about these events appeared in Murder in Dealey Plaza (2000), where more definitive studies about the fabrication of the film were published in *The Great Zapruder Film Hoax* (2003) and in its latest incarnation in *Inside the Assassination Records Review Board* (2009), which is supplemented by the studies that Doug Horne has authored here. I must conclude that those who persist in sincerely denying that the extant film is a fabrication are either unfamiliar with the evidence or cognitively impaired.

ANALYSIS & IMPLICATIONS OF THE TWO NPIC EVENTS

by Douglas Horne

So what does all this mean? Let us explore the obvious implications, and let us not pull any punches.

Brazen Deception by "Bill Smith" of the Secret Service:

"Bill Smith" of the Secret Service (and yes, Homer McMahon did express some degree of whimsical, bemused doubt about his true identity) [20] "lied his eyes out" to Homer McMahon about the origins of the assassination film he brought to NPIC with him from "Hawkeyeworks" in Rochester, New York.

We know definitively from the examination of the four briefing board panels by both Homer McMahon and Ben Hunter, in the summer of 1997, that Bill Smith did bring with him to NPIC a version of the Zapruder film, and not "some other film."

This is crucially important, for from this basic fact we know that "Bill Smith of the Secret Service" lied to Homer McMahon and Bill Hunter about a number of things:

(1) he lied when he said a private citizen donated the assassination film out of patriotism because he did not want to make any money on it; for Abraham Zapruder was determined to make as much money as he could off of the film, and did;

(2) he lied when he said he carried the undeveloped film to Rochester and had it developed at "Hawkeyeworks;" for it is well-documented that the camera-original Zapruder film was developed at the Kodak plant in Dallas on Friday, 22 November 1963;

(3) clearly, the film brought to NPIC from "Hawkeyeworks" by Bill Smith was created there, but it was not just "developed"—it was a re-creation of the Zapruder film after its alteration at that facility, intended to masquerade as an original out-of-camera, unslit (16 mm wide), "double 8" film.

It had to have been produced in an aerial-imaging optical printer with an animation stand affixed, such as that shown in Figures 9.4 and 9.5 of Professor Raymond Fielding's seminal 1965 textbook, *The Technique of Special Effects Cinematography* (Focal Press, Fourth Edition, 1985).

The technique undoubtedly used—aerial imagery—was widely employed in Hollywood during the 1950s and 1960s, and can be read about on pages 224–232.

Those orchestrating the Zapruder film cover-up the weekend of the assassination were determined to call in a different work crew when the altered film (now "reassembled" optically in an "aerial imaging" optical printer as an unslit, 16 mm wide "double 8" film again) was returned to NPIC the night after Brugioni's "briefing board event."

The goal was obviously to make a "sanitized" set of briefing boards, from the "sanitized" film, which would now necessarily be absent the more egregious evidence of frontal shots, and therefore of crossfire, and conspiracy. This need is the only reasonable explanation for calling in a different work crew and telling them that the work was "need-to-know" and "above Top Secret," and that not even their bosses were allowed to know what activity they had been involved in.

Simply put, it was easy to fool McMahon and Hunter and whoever assembled the four panel briefing boards using their prints; the hard part, and the necessary part, was to keep the Brugioni team ignorant of the activity of the McMahon team.

This succeeded remarkably well because of the culture of secrecy within "the Agency," and Brugioni never found out about the second NPIC event until 2009. McMahon, who cannot be located today in 2012, and who is presumably deceased, never found out about it.

This does not speak well for Arthur Lundahl, or Navy Captain Pierre Sands, however, who both must have understood "the Big Picture", and known what was afoot at the facility they managed.

So the operative question remains, did the "Hawkeyeworks" facility have the capability to perform aerial imaging? Was there an optical printer with an aerial imaging animation stand installed, present at Hawkeyeworks?

"Hawkeyeworks" Explained:

After the Homer McMahon interview was released in 1998, JFK researchers loyal to the concept of an authentic Zapruder film that is "ground truth" in the Kennedy assassination downplayed the importance of the "Hawkeyeworks" story, either doubting its existence because there was no documentary proof, or alternately saying that the "Hawkeyeworks" lab was solely dedicated to U-2 and Corona satellite photography. But these critics were wrong on both counts.

First, Dino Brugioni, during his 2009 and 2011 interviews with Peter Janney and me, not only confirmed the existence of the state-of-the-art Kodak lab in Rochester used by the CIA for various classified purposes, but confirmed that he visited the place more than once, including once prior to the JFK assassination. (He also confirmed its existence in his recent book, *Eyes in the Sky,* on page 364.)

Second, Dino Brugioni made clear to me, when I interviewed him in July of 2011, that the "Hawkeye Plant" (as he called it) was an enormous state-of-the-art private-sector laboratory founded and run by Kodak, which performed far more tasks than "just" Corona satellite and U-2 "special order" film services. He said that the Hawkeye Plant was involved in developing new film products and in manufacturing and testing special film products of all kinds, including new motion picture films, and that it definitely had the capability to process motion pictures.

He did not see such equipment himself, but was told by Ed Green, a highranking Kodak manager at "Hawkeyeworks" with whom he had a relationship of trust, that the "Hawkeye Plant" could, and did, definitely process motion pictures. When repeatedly questioned about this capability by Peter Janney throughout the 2009 interviews, Brugioni said with great reverence, on several occasions, "They could do anything." [21]

The CIA refused to provide me with any information about "Hawkeyeworks" when "the Agency" finally responded to my 12 September 2009 Freedom of Information Act (FOIA) request on 27 January 2010. But that was hardly surprising, since over one year earlier, on 27 January 2010, the CIA wrote to me, cautioning:

"The CIA Information Act, 50 U.S.C. Section 431, as amended, exempts CIA operational files from the search, review, publication, and disclosure requirements of the FOIA."

What this meant, in rather blunt language, was that if the CIA was running an "op," such as the alteration of the Zapruder film immediately after JFK's assassination, then they didn't have to search for those records or tell me about it, in any way. So the failure by the CIA to answer any of my many questions about "Hawkeyeworks" means literally—nothing.

NPIC Panel I

The plain facts are these:

(1) the 8 mm (already slit!) camera-original Zapruder film was delivered to NPIC late on Saturday evening, 23 November 1963, and the two Secret Service officials who brought it to NPIC for the making of briefing boards left with the film at about 3 AM Sunday morning; and

(2) a 16 mm, unslit version of the Zapruder film was returned to NPIC the next night, after dark, on Sunday evening, 24 November 1963; and its courier ("Bill Smith") said it had been processed at "Hawkeyeworks," and that he had brought it directly to NPIC in Washington, D.C. from Rochester (using the unmistakable code word "Hawkeyeworks") himself.

"Double 8" home movies which have already been slit at the processing facility do not miraculously "reassemble" themselves from two 25-foot strips 8 mm in width, and connected with a splice in the middle, into 16 mm wide unslit double 8 films. A new Zapruder film was clearly created at "Hawkeyeworks" in Rochester, in an optical printer. Bill Smith told the truth when he said the film he carried had been developed there at "Hawkeyeworks;" he lied when he said that it was the camera-original film taken by the photographer in Dallas.

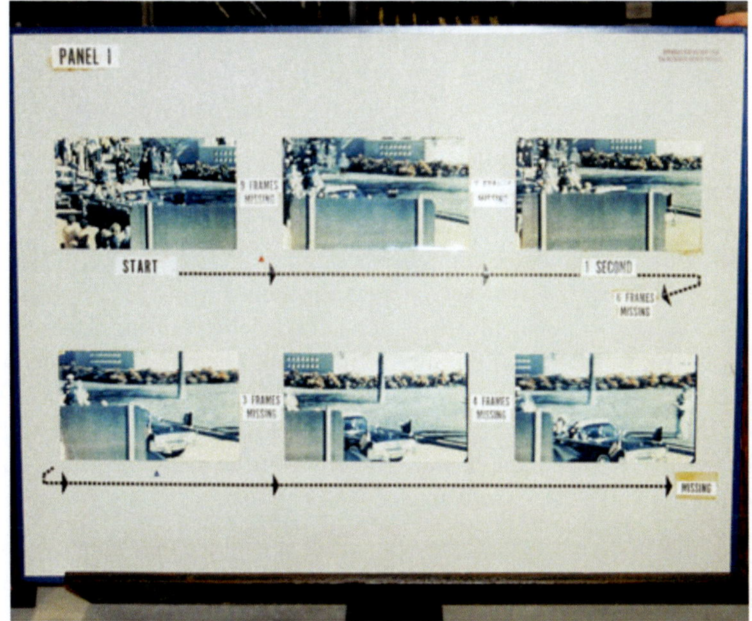

If "Hawkeyeworks" truly had the physical capability "to do anything," as Ed Green informed Dino Brugioni, then all that would have been required that weekend would have been to bring in some experienced personnel—an animator or two, and a visual effects director—experienced in the "black arts" of Hollywood.

Those personnel, if not already on-site, employed at "Hawkeyeworks," could have been brought into Rochester on Saturday, 23 November, the same day the JFK autopsy photographs were being developed in Washington, D.C. at Naval Photographic Center, Anacostia. The JFK autopsy photos developed on Saturday (per Robert Knudsen's 1978 HSCA deposition transcript) would have provided the guide for the image alteration necessary on the Zapruder film the next day, on Sunday.

The JFK autopsy photos document the massive head wound created by clandestine, postmortem surgery on JFK's head wounds at Bethesda Naval Hospital, and would have provided a rough guide for the massive head wound in the top and right side of the skull that had to be painted onto selected Zapruder film frames the next day, on Sunday. No such parietal-temporal-frontal wound was seen at Parkland Hospital in

Dallas by any of the treatment staff the day Kennedy was shot and treated there, but it had to be added to selected Zapruder film frames, to match the illicit postmortem cranial surgery at Bethesda that was being misrepresented in the autopsy photos as "damage from the assassin's bullet." [22] In addition to painting on a false wound, of course, the forgers at "Hawkeyeworks" would have had to obscure—black out—the real exit wound, in the right rear of JFK's head, that was seen in Trauma Room One at Parkland Hospital. (More on this below.)

What is undeniable is that there are undisputed "facts on the ground" which indicate that an optically edited Zapruder film—a re-creation—arrived at NPIC in Washington, D.C. on Sunday night, 24 November 1963, after the film had been in Rochester, at "Hawkeyeworks," all day long. Remember, the two Secret Service officials who had the original 8 mm camera-original film departed NPIC with the film at about 3 AM (4 AM at the latest) on Sunday morning. They may have been at "Hawkeyeworks" with the film as early as 6 AM; and since the Zapruder film did not reappear at NPIC until well after dark on Sunday evening, approximately 12 hours (or more) may have been available to those at "Hawkeyeworks" who were engaged in its alteration.

A final comment here: those who insist upon injecting "Hollywood" expertise into the equation here, must respect "the facts on the ground." The film that arrived at NPIC Sunday night did not come from anywhere else other than Rochester, N.Y.—it was not couriered from Hollywood, or New York City, or anywhere else other than Rochester—it came from "Hawkeyeworks," per the words of the courier who brought it to NPIC Sunday night, Bill Smith. And the code word "Hawkeyeworks" meant one thing only—the state-of-the-art, Top Secret Kodak lab located at Kodak headquarters, in Rochester, New York. Hollywood talent may very well have been involved in altering the Zapruder film, but if so, it was talent employed at the Kodak facilities at "Hawkeyeworks" in Rochester.

Anyone who suggests otherwise is not employing the necessary intellectual rigor, for it is undeniable that the camera-original film was developed on 22 November 1963 in Dallas; undeniable that Zapruder took it home with him Friday night; undeniable that he projected the camera-original film himself on an 8 mm projector in his office Saturday morning, and that he then struck a deal with *Life*; and undeniable that Richard Stolley of *Life* magazine then put the camera-original film on a plane for Chicago on Saturday afternoon. This timeline does not allow for alteration in Hollywood or New York City, based on what we now know about the film's true chain of custody on 23 November 1963, for we know without a doubt that the original film showed up at NPIC at about 10 PM on Saturday night, 23 November 1963.

The Chicago Timeline Reconsidered:

It is obvious to me, in view of what happened at the "Dino Brugioni event" at NPIC, that the camera-original Zapruder film was intercepted, either at the Chicago airport as soon as it arrived from Dallas, or as soon as it arrived at the offices of *Life,* by the Secret Service. In my view this explains the very late arrival (about 10 PM) of the film at NPIC in Washington, and its delivery by two Secret Service officials who had not yet seen it projected. In his July 2011 video interview with me, Dino Brugioni expressed the opinion that the two Secret Service officials had just gotten off of an airplane, and had come directly to NPIC.

This is a very important fact, for it reinforces the extremely high likelihood that the film brought to Brugioni truly was the original film, and not a copy. Let us re-examine where the three copies were that day, on Saturday, 23 November 1963. One "first day copy" remained with Zapruder in Dallas; one had been loaned to the FBI in Dallas by the Secret Service in Dallas, and was flown to FBI headquarters in Washington, D.C. on Saturday night, via the Baltimore airport; [23] and the third "same day copy" had been flown to Secret Service headquarters in Washington, D.C. on Friday night, and had arrived sometime between midnight and dawn.

Let us assume that the Secret Service copy in the nation's capital had arrived by sunrise (a conservative estimate), and that officials at Secret Service headquarters had spent all morning Saturday reviewing it. Even if those conservative timelines were the case, then if it were the film brought to Brugioni for the briefing board work, WHY WAS IT NOT DELIVERED AT NOON, OR ONE O'CLOCK PM ON SATURDAY?

The fact that the film delivered to him arrived at 10 PM, and the fact that it had not been seen by the two men who couriered it to NPIC, mitigates against the film he worked with having been the "first day copy" sent to Washington by the Dallas Secret Service (Max Phillips) on Friday night.

That is most unlikely for another reason, as well. Enlargements of tiny 8 mm frames for briefing boards would not have been made from a copy film if the original film were available. Furthermore, Dino Brugioni himself would have noticed the soft focus if he had been working with a copy film, instead of an original.

So in my view, it is clear that the camera-original Zapruder film was intercepted in Chicago by federal agents identifying themselves as Secret Service late on Saturday afternoon or early Saturday evening, and then flown directly to Washington D.C., and taken immediately to NPIC, in the Navy Yard, from Washington National Airport. What this means is that the timing of the activities in Chicago reported by Loudon Wainwright in his memoir (mentioned above) was simply off by 24 hours. No doubt he got all the names of those involved correct, and their various roles in preparing the layout in the 29 November issue correct, but was just off by one day in recounting when it happened. After all, he was not present at those events, and was reporting hearsay.

We know that the alteration at "Hawkeyeworks" was finished sometime before the middle of the evening on Sunday, 24 November. We know that because the altered film, now in 16 mm wide, "double 8" format again, arrived at NPIC Sunday night, after dark. We even know that "dupes" of the film were made at "Hawkeyeworks," according to Bill Smith. [24]

And there is strong evidence that such dupes—or at least one such dupe—known in the trade as "dirty dupes," were run off as black and white copies at "Hawkeyeworks," and then rushed to Chicago Sunday night so that the magazine could begin its layout for the revised 29 November issue. Three such "dirty dupes"—all unslit, 16 mm wide, "double 8" versions of the Zapruder film—surfaced in January of 2000 when the LMH Co. materials were physically transferred to the Sixth Floor Museum, in Dallas. They are all black and white products (as are the 31 poor quality blow-up prints of the Zapruder film published in the 29 November issue of *Life*).

As noted by author Richard Trask, one of them, a "reversal black-andwhite positive," does contain markings that "...appear to be markings used to determine selected images for inclusion in *Life* magazine." [25]

Unfortunately, both Roland Zavada and Richard Trask (who has endorsed Zavada's view) have gotten carried away by the discovery of these three black-and-white "dirty dupes," and have drawn entirely the wrong conclusion from these materials discovered about 12½ years ago. They have both concluded that the camera-original Zapruder film was not slit after all, at the Kodak plant in Dallas, the day of the assassination.

This absurd conclusion flies in the face of the expert testimony collected by Zavada himself in 1997 and 1998 as he repeatedly interviewed and corresponded with the surviving managers and technicians who worked at the Kodak plant in Dallas on the day of JFK's assassination; flies in the face of the manuscript written by Mr.

Phil Chamberlain (the Production Supervisor of the Kodak plant in Dallas) in the late 1970s; and flies in the face of the many witnesses who saw Mr. Zapruder project his 8 mm camera-original film, using an 8 mm projector, on Saturday, 23 November. [26]

I have an alternative, and more reasonable, explanation for the origin of these "dirty dupes"—one more in line with Occam's Razor, and which respects expert eyewitness testimony (instead of disrespecting it). I believe that at least one of the three unslit "double 8" Zapruder film "dirty dupes" found at the Sixth Floor Museum in January of 2000, among the donated materials from the LMH Co. (that once belonged to *Life* magazine), was run off in a contact printer at "Hawkeyeworks" on Sunday evening after the alteration of the Zapruder film was completed.

It was then, I believe, rushed to Chicago from Rochester so that *Life* magazine, now behind schedule, could get going on its layout for the delayed 29 November issue.

Arrival of just one "dirty dupe" at the Donnelley printing plant on Sunday night would have provided the imagery necessary for the first mail-out issues of the magazine to be ready for mailing Monday afternoon, 25 November, and would also have been consistent with the first newsstand issues hitting the shelves on Tuesday, 26 November, as reported by Trask.

In his 2005 book, *National Nightmare on Six Feet of Film,* Trask writes (on p. 117): "The cardboard container associated with the 16 mm films included a printed address reading 'Allied Film Laboratory, 306 W. Jackson, Chicago 6, Illinois.'"

In my view, this might merely indicate that one "dirty dupe" was received from "Hawkeyeworks," and that the lab in question ran off two more copies of the first "dirty dupe" after it arrived in Chicago Sunday night. Or it might indicate nothing at all related to the provenance of the dupes. Even if the box does indicate a connection between Allied Film Laboratory and the dupes, the presence of the box alone does not indicate that all three of the dupes were run off in Chicago, nor does it tell us that they were copied from the camera-original film.

As Trask himself says, Kodak lab personnel interviewed in "recent years" (presumably he means the 1980s through 2005, when his own book was published) "…seem to recall that in 1963 all four films were slit into 8 mm format." Yes, that's what they have recalled, because that is what happened—all four films (the camera-original, and the three first-day copies) were all slit down to 8 mm on Friday night in Dallas, after the three copies were developed, and before Zapruder departed the Kodak plant. There is no serious or believable reason to doubt their consistent recollections.

In conclusion, a highly significant fact about the 29 November issue of *Life,* and the four briefing board panels at NARA, that even many "alterationists" have not dealt with adequately, is that the frames in that early issue of *Life* that depict JFK's head wound appear to show the same head wound seen in the extant film today. [This makes perfect sense to me; no cabal at "Hawkeyeworks" in charge of altering the film to hide evidence of shots from the front would have dared to allow *Life* to have a print of the movie before the film was altered.]

My main point here, though, is that the prints posted on the four briefing board panels at the Archives (from the McMahon event) are also consistent with the frames published in *Life* on 29 November, and have frame numbers assigned to them in the NPIC working notes that are consistent with the frame numbers used today in association with those same frames in the extant film.

About five or six of the frame numbers denoted in the NPIC notes (which describe the photos mounted on the four briefing board panels) are off by one frame (denoting human fallibility—obvious counting errors attributable to fatigue, or haste that night), but the frame numbers and images associated with the briefing boards are consistent with the extant film today.

That is to say, there are no major deviations, or patterns in the frame numbering indicating that the film McMahon worked with was structured differently than the one we know today. The obvious implication of these facts discussed above is that at least the major alterations to the Zapruder film (such as frame excisions and deletions, and alterations of the head wound images) were completed by Sunday night, 24 November 1963—and that perhaps all of the alterations were completed by Sunday night, when the film left "Hawkeyeworks," on its way to NPIC in Washington, D. C.

Rockefeller Commission Issues:

In 1975, President Gerald Ford appointed the U.S. President's Commission on CIA Activities Within the United States—headed by Vice President Nelson Rockefeller—in response to allegations in the media of widespread illegal CIA domestic activities, including mind-control-drug experiments upon unsuspecting American citizens; illegal mail opening; and illegal surveillance of domestic political groups. On 24 March 1975, an American citizen named Paul Hoch (a Berkeley, California computer programmer) submitted a long list of

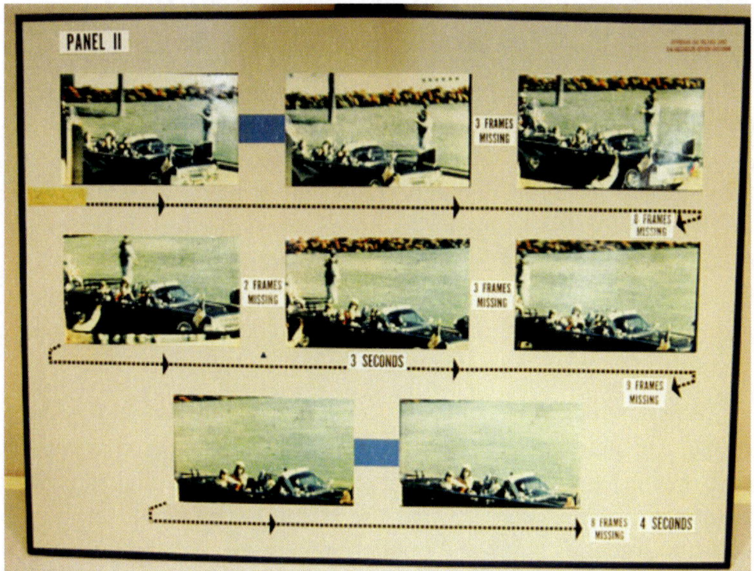

interrogatories to the Rockefeller Commission, one of which was the timely question—in the immediate wake of the airing of the bootleg copy of the Zapruder film by the ABC television network on 6 March 1975—"…what use did the Agency make of the Zapruder film?"

NPIC Panel II

This one simple question from Paul Hoch resulted in a series of exchanges in May of 1975 between Rockefeller Commission Senior Counsel Robert B. Olsen, and the CIA, about the Zapruder film. These exchanges quickly drew Dino Brugioni of NPIC and the new NPIC Director, John Hicks, into the search for Zapruder film records, and forced the CIA to: (1) admit to the Commission, in writing, on 14 May 1975, that it still possessed four surviving briefing board panels mounting Zapruder frame enlargements that had been created sometime in late 1963; and (2) to turn over the previously mentioned six pages of NPIC working notes (along with a handwritten memo from NPIC Director John Hicks) to the Rockefeller Commission, in response to Senior Counsel Robert Olsen's oral request on 8 May 1975 for textual materials about the Zapruder film that may have been provided to the Secret Service by the CIA.

These working notes (referred to above in this article) were finally, belatedly released to the public in 1978 under FOIA, and based on the long, administrative FOIA document number assigned by the CIA, became commonly known to JFK researchers by the shorthand of "CIA Document 450." The notes created a significant stir among JFK researchers, since they indicated a high level of CIA/NPIC interest in the Zapruder film shortly after President Kennedy's assassination.

But of significant interest here is the very first response sent by the CIA to Senior Counsel Robert B. Olsen, on 7 May 1975, for the story surrounding this response—what it said, and what it did not say—involves deep levels of duplicity, both within the CIA, and between the CIA and the Rockefeller Commission's staff. And that duplicity surrounds the first set of briefing boards—briefing boards made from the original, unaltered, camera-original Zapruder film—those made by Dino Brugioni at the Zapruder film "briefing board event" over which he presided, commencing late on 23 November 1963 at NPIC.

It went down like this. After the Rockefeller Commission forwarded the Paul Hoch list of questions to the CIA, it stimulated a massive search within "the Agency" for ways to "come clean" and satisfy the Rockefeller Commission, so that the Commission would eventually leave "the Agency" alone and publicly report its cooperation with the Commission.

Sometime in late April or early May of 1975, in response to the Commission's inquiries about domestic activities (and more specifically, the Paul Hoch memo asking about the Zapruder film), Dino Brugioni reported to the NPIC Director, John Hicks, that he possessed one of the two-panel briefing boards he had made during his Zapruder film event at NPIC; the board had been returned to NPIC when John McCone retired, and the then-Director of NPIC, Arthur Lundahl, had given it to Dino Brugioni and told him to lock it up, saying that no one was to see it except for Lundahl or Brugioni. Since that time, Arthur Lundahl had retired.

Dino Brugioni not only informed John Hicks about the existence of the two-panel briefing board; he showed it to him. Hick's response was both profane, and violent. Hicks said to Brugioni, when shown the two-panel briefing board made from the unaltered Zapruder film: "Goddammit, what the hell are you doing with that?" Hicks followed with immediate instructions: "Get the goddamn thing out of here!" A shaken Dino Brugioni, who is still mystified today about the anger expressed by Hicks, wrapped up the two panel briefing board, sent it over to the office of CIA Director William Colby, and never saw it again. [27]

Mr. Hicks, the key player in this drama, then proceeded to withhold from the Rockefeller Commission the existence of the two-panel briefing board, and to withhold from Dino Brugioni the fact that a four panel briefing board (different from Dino's) had also been found at NPIC, along with working notes indicating substantial NPIC activity with the film. [28] (This was peculiar behavior, since Brugioni was the Chief Information Officer at NPIC, and in this capacity was the "briefing board czar" for Mr. Hicks.) Not only was Hicks maintaining the compartmentalization put in place at NPIC the weekend following the assassination, but he is the one and only persuasive candidate who fits the bill as the "probable author" of what can only be viewed as an intentionally misleading communication sent to the Rockefeller Commission about the NPIC Zapruder film activity.

On 7 May 1975 Mr. E. H. Knoche, an intelligence officer who was a special assistant to CIA Director William Colby, signed out a letter to Senior Counsel Robert B. Olsen, which forwarded an unsigned "addendum" (one typewritten page) which summarized Zapruder film activity—the making of briefing boards—at NPIC "in late 1963." Not only does the addendum provide no specific dates for the activity, but the two separate briefing board events have been conflated into one event, and as described in the addendum, there was only one briefing board event that took place with the Secret Service (which we now know is not true).

Mention is made of the creation at NPIC of two sets of briefing boards (consistent with the Brugioni event), but the addendum also states that those two sets consisted of four panels each (which we now know is consistent only with the McMahon event). The addendum also states that Secret Service representatives (plural, and consistent with the Brugioni event, but not with the McMahon event) left by Mr. Knoche to Olsen on 7 May, and that Hicks' intention in writing the addendum in the way that he did was to hide the fact that there were two compartmentalized operations with the Zapruder film at NPIC the weekend of President Kennedy's assassination.

If, for example, it became known that Dino Brugioni had retained a briefing board set returned by Mr. Cone, Hicks could explain that away to outsiders by showing them the four panel briefing board set made at the second event. His failure to inform Dino Brugioni, who was supposedly his right-hand man, about the discovery of the four panel set (the set in the Archives today), or the NPIC working notes, speaks to his duplicity within his own organization. [29]

Wrapping up this tale, it was the Knoche letter to Olsen of 7 May (and its intentionally confusing addendum about NPIC activity in support of the Secret Service) that stimulated Olsen's oral request on 8 May to receive copies of "any memoranda or other textual information provided to the Secret Service by CIA after NPIC's analysis of the Zapruder film."

Hicks wrote a handwritten internal memo on 13 May, admitting that NPIC had the four briefing board panels and the working notes, but withholding the fact that a two-panel briefing board panel had been found, and shown to him, by Brugioni.

It was this Hicks memo and the six pages of notes that were forwarded to Olsen by Knoche on 14 May 1975. In doing so, the CIA (Hicks and Knoche) withheld from the Rockefeller Commission the existence of a different set of briefing boards, and refused to divulge that two different Zapruder film "briefing board events" occurred at NPIC the weekend of the assassination. [Hicks even briefed Olsen in person, at NPIC on 14 May, so presumably Olsen was shown the four briefing board panels which, of course, contain the same image frames seen in the extant Zapruder film today.] [30]

So I am forced to conclude that NPIC Director John Hicks (the replacement for the eminent Arthur Lundahl), the engineer of all this legerdemain, must have known that there were two compartmentalized operations at NPIC on 23 and 24 November 1963, and that if he were to reveal that, he would be revealing that the Zapruder film had been altered at Hawkeyeworks by the CIA and Kodak and the Secret Service, all working together on the project.

It must have been for this reason that Hicks felt the Rockefeller Commission did not have a "need-to-know" about the two-panel briefing board retained by Brugioni; and it must have been for this reason that Hicks felt Brugioni did not have a "need-to-know" about the four panel briefing with the film and one set of briefing boards. We now know that this is not true, for Brugioni was clear in his interview with me that the Secret Service left with the film, but not with the briefing boards, which had not been completed yet. Secret Service agent "Bill Smith," at the McMahon event, probably did leave with his briefing board products, so concerned was he with secrecy and tight security.

The addendum also states that Mr. McCone retained one set of boards; while this is true, the set of boards he retained was a two-panel set joined with a hinge in the middle (made from an unaltered Zapruder film), not the four panel set that the CIA would soon acknowledge having to the Rockefeller Commission. It is my considered opinion—after my four-hour interview with Dino Brugioni in July of 2011—that Mr. Hicks wrote the addendum forwarded board set which Hicks was showing to Olsen on 14 May. One final thought: since Brugioni sent the two-panel briefing board back to the CIA Director's office by special CIA courier, and since Mr. E. H. Knoche worked as a special assistant to the Director of CIA in 1975, and had been working in that capacity at the time of the JFK assassination under Director John McCone, [31] Mr. Enno Henry "Hank" Knoche may very well have known about the compartmentalized operations at NPIC in 1963 as well, and may have been willfully cooperating with Hicks in deceiving the Rockefeller Commission.

Summary of Visual indications of Alterations

The two NPIC "briefing board events" the weekend following President Kennedy's assassination have together definitively proven: (1) that the film's chain of custody is not what we thought it was for decades; and (2) that the film was located that weekend in a facility where the means almost certainly existed to alter its image content.

First, based on Dino Brugioni's very clear recollections of his NPIC "briefing board event," the camera-original, 8 mm Zapruder film was not in Chicago, at the *Life* printing plant, on the Saturday night following JFK's assassination; but rather, was in Washington, D.C. at NPIC on Saturday, 23 November 1963, from about 10 PM that night, until 3 or 4 AM the next morning, on Sunday, 24 November 1963.

Second, the statements of the Secret Service courier who brought the altered, and reformatted 16 mm wide, unslit, "double 8" Zapruder film back to NPIC on Sunday night, 24 November 1963—"Bill Smith"—revealed to Homer McMahon that the Zapruder film delivered to him for the making of prints had been processed at "Hawkeyeworks," a state-of-the-art, world class photo laboratory at Kodak headquarters, that was regularly used in support of classified CIA contracts.

The two major classified CIA-Kodak contracts at the time were in support of "special orders" for U-2 high-altitude and Corona satellite photography, but the overall physical capabilities of the "Hawkeye Plant" went well beyond these two areas, and included much work in the motion picture field, according to what Mr. Brugioni was told by the Kodak employees who managed the Rochester lab, and who were his points of contact there.

We know from the historical record that the two key statements made by "Bill Smith" about the Zapruder film were outright fabrications—to wit, the original film was not donated to the government for free by Mr. Zapruder; and the camera-original Zapruder film was not developed at "Hawkeyeworks" in Rochester, as Smith had claimed. [Zapruder had negotiated an initial sales contract with *Life* magazine for $50,000 on

Saturday morning; and the camera-original film had been developed in Dallas, not at "Hawkeyeworks" in Rochester.]

Dino Brugioni's knowledge of the "Hawkeyeworks" facility in Rochester, gained from Mr. Ed Green of Kodak and others whom he knew at the facility, was that it could indeed process motion picture film, and that the Kodak technicians at the Top Secret laboratory "could do anything" with film. Because "Bill Smith" of the Secret Service delivered a Zapruder film to NPIC on Sunday, 24 November 1963, whose format had miraculously been transformed, within 24 hours, from a slit, 8 mm wide "double 8" film, to an unslit, 16 mm wide, "double 8" film, it is reasonable to conclude that the Zapruder film's image content was indeed altered on Sunday, 24 November 1963, and that the alteration occurred at "Hawkeyeworks," from whence Bill Smith had come with the film, which he readily admitted had been processed at that facility.

For all of the foregoing reasons, it is therefore appropriate to briefly review three of the major indicators that the Zapruder film's imagery has undergone alteration.

The Head Explosion:

As discussed earlier in this paper, Dino Brugioni opined during his 9 July 2011 interview with the author that the head explosion seen today in the extant Zapruder film is markedly different from what he saw on 23 November 1963, when he worked with what he is certain was the camera-original film.

The head explosion he recalls was much bigger than the one seen today in frame 313 of the extant film (going "three or four feet into the air"); was a "white cloud" that did not exhibit any of the pink or red color seen in frame 313 today; and was of such a duration that he is quite sure that in the film he viewed in 1963, there were many more frames than just one graphically depicting the fatal head shot on the film he viewed in 1963. Mr. Brugioni cannot, and does not, accept frame 313 of the extant Zapruder film as an accurate or complete representation of the fatal head shot he saw in the camera-original Zapruder film on the Saturday evening following President Kennedy's assassination.

He is supported in this view by two other opinions.

Erwin Schwartz, Abraham Zapruder's business partner, told interviewer Noel Twyman on 21 November 1994 that when he viewed the original film on Friday, 22 November 1963, he saw biological debris from the head explosion propelled to the left rear of the President when he viewed the film. This debris pattern is not visible on the film today, but dovetails with the consistent recollections of motorcycle officer

Bobby W. Hargis, who was hit with great force at the time of the head shot by debris traveling to the left rear. [32]

Similarly, professional surveyors Robert West and Chester Breneman performed the first of several site surveys of Dealey Plaza that they participated in on Monday, 25 November 1963—for *Life* magazine. Breneman was quoted in the *Fort Worth Star-Telegram* on 14 April 1978 as saying that in using the color prints of individual Zapruder frames provided by *Life,* he could see in some of the prints "large blobs of blood and brain matter flying from Kennedy's head to the rear of the car." [33]

Whether his remembered date for the *Life*-sponsored survey is precisely accurate or not, the important factor here is that he saw debris traveling to the rear of the President in enlargements made from individual frames of the Zapruder film—imagery that is not seen in the extant film today. If his recollection that those images were provided by *Life* was correct, it suggests covert collusion between some at *Life* magazine and the U.S. government—namely, a joint effort to determine exactly what did happen in Dealey Plaza, apparently using frames from the unaltered Zapruder film.

Given the decades-long ties between *Life's* publisher, C. D. Jackson, and the U.S. intelligence community, such collusion would not be surprising, particularly given *Life* magazine's history of false reporting in its 6 December 1963 issue about the imagery in the Zapruder film, and its suppression of the film as a motion picture for almost 12 years. [34] It seems clear to me that David Wrone got it all wrong in his book when he assessed *Life's* primary motive in its dealings with the Zapruder film as profit-driven. On the contrary, spending an additional $100,000 on Monday, 25 November (beyond the original $50,000 spent on Saturday, 23 November) to secure motion picture rights and total ownership of the film, and then never exploiting the film commercially as a motion picture for 12 years, speaks to suppression as the primary motive, rather than profit.

Altered Head Wound Imagery:

California resident Sydney Wilkinson purchased a 35 mm dupe negative of the Zapruder film from the National Archives in 2008—a third generation rendition, according to the Archives—and with the assistance of her husband, who is a video editor at a major post-production film house in Hollywood, commissioned both "HD" scans (1920 x 1080 pixels per scan) of each frame of the dupe negative, as well as "6K" scans of each frame. Because the Zapruder film's image,

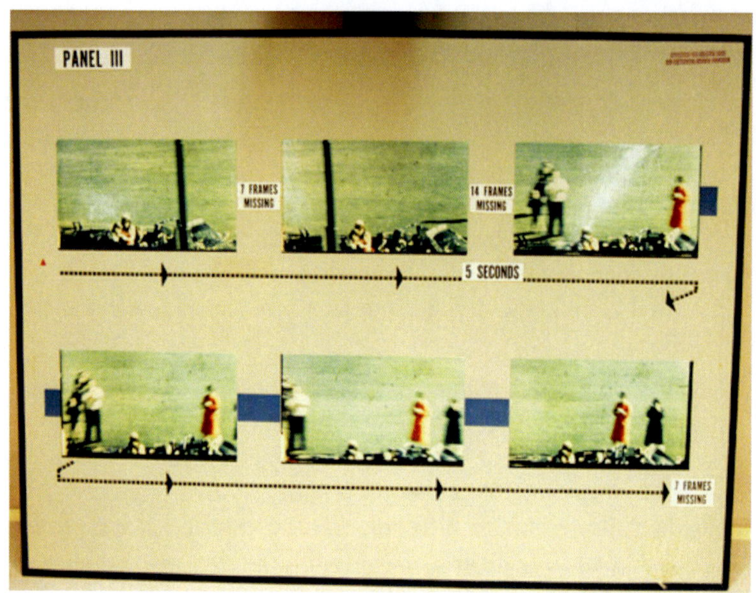

from edge to edge, only partially fills each 35 mm film frame obtained from the Archives, the so-called "6K" scan of each frame is therefore 'only' the equivalent of a "4K" image, i.e., 4096 x 3112 pixels, for each Zapruder frame imaged. Each Zapruder frame scan still constitutes an enormous amount of information: 72.9 MB, or 12.7 million pixels per frame.

These "4K equivalent" scans of the Zapruder film used by this couple to conduct their forensic, scientific study of the assassination images are 10-bit log color DPX scans, otherwise known in common parlance as "flat scans." These logarithmic color scans bring out much more information in the shadows than would the linear color normally viewed on our television screens and computers. Therefore, much more information in each Zapruder film frame is revealed by these logarithmic scans, than would be revealed in a linear color scan of the same frame.

As reported in the author's book, numerous Hollywood film industry editors, colorists, and restoration experts have viewed the "6K" scans of the Zapruder film as part of the couple's ongoing forensic investigation. In the logarithmic color scans there are many frames (notably 317, 321, and 323) which show what appear to be "black patches," or crude animation, obscuring the hair on the back of JFK's head.

The blacked-out areas just happen to coincide precisely with the location of the avulsed, baseball-sized exit wound in the right rear of JFK's head seen by the Parkland Hospital treatment staff, in Dallas, on the day he was assassinated. In the opinion of virtually all of the dozens of motion picture film professionals who have viewed the Zapruder film "6K" scans, the dark patches do not look like natural shadows, and appear quite anomalous. Some of these film industry professionals—in particular, two film restoration experts accustomed to looking at visual effects in hundreds of 1950s and 1960s era films—have declared that the aforementioned frames are proof that the Zapruder film has been altered, and that it was crudely done. [35] If true, this explains *Life's* decision to suppress the film as a motion picture for 12 years, lest its alteration be discovered by any professionals using it in a broadcast.

The extant Zapruder film also depicts a large head wound in the top and right side of President Kennedy's skull—most notably in frames 335 and 337—that was not seen by any of the treatment staff at Parkand Hospital.

The implication here is that if the true exit wound on President Kennedy's head can be obscured in the Zapruder film through use of aerial imaging (i.e., self-matting animation, applied to each frame's image via an animation stand married to an optical printer)—as revealed by the "6K" scans of the 35 mm dupe negative—then the same technique could be used to add a desired exit wound, one consistent with the cover story of a lone shooter firing from behind.

The apparent alteration of the Zapruder film seen in the area of the rear of JFK's head in the "6K" scans is consistent with the capabilities believed to have been in place at "Hawkeyeworks" in 1963.

In a recent critique of the author's Zapruder film alteration hypothesis, retired Kodak film chemist (and former ARRB consultant, from 1997-1998), Roland Zavada, quoted professor Raymond Fielding, author of the famous 1965 textbook mentioned above on visual special effects, as saying that it would be impossible for anyone to have altered an 8 mm film in 1963 without leaving artifacts that could be easily detected. I completely agree with this assessment attributed to professor Fielding, and I firmly believe that the logarithmic color, "6K," 10-bit, DPX scans made of each frame of the 35 mm dupe negative of the Zapruder film have discovered just that: blatant and unmistakable artifacts of the film's alteration.

Critics of this ongoing forensic investigation in California have tried to dismiss the interim findings by displaying other, dissimilar images from the Zapruder film that have been processed in linear color (not logarithmic color), and in some cases are also using inferior images of the Zapruder film of much poorer resolution than the 6K scans, or images from the film in which the linear color contrast has been adjusted and manipulated (i.e., darkened). Saying that "it just isn't so" is not an adequate defense for those who desperately cling to belief in the Zapruder film's authenticity, when the empirical proof (the untainted and raw imagery) exists to back up the fact that it is so. Anyone else who purchases a 35 mm dupe negative of the Zapruder film from the National Archives for $795, and who expends the time and money to run "6K" scans of each frame, will end up with the same imagery Sydney Wilkinson has today, for her scans simply record what is present on the extant film in the National Archives; she and her husband have done nothing to alter the images in any way. Their scans simply record what is present on the extant film.

The Missing Car Stop:

One final imagery-related indication that the Zapruder film has likely been altered is the simple proof that about 16 persons in Dealey Plaza indicated that the President's limousine stopped, very briefly (for approximately .5–1.5 seconds), during the head shot sequence on Elm Street. No such "car stop" is seen on the extant Zapruder film. And yet, many of the witnesses who claim the limousine stopped were those closest to President Kennedy when he was killed, including Jean Hill, Hugh Betzner, Bill Newman, Mary Woodward, Roy Truly, Phil Willis, Alan Smith, DPD patrolmen Earle Brown and J. W. Foster, and DPD motorcyclists Bobby W. Hargis and James Chaney. [36]

(Incidentally, none of them recalled seeing the violent back-and-to-the- left "head snap" seen in the extant Zapruder film today, which reinforces the likelihood that it is an optical artifact in the extant film, created by the removal of several exit debris frames during optical editing at "Hawkeyeworks.")

If Abraham Zapruder was really operating his movie camera at 48 frames per second (the accelerated frame rate required to play back the film in "slow motion" on a home movie projector—three times the normal speed), vice 16 frames per second (the normal frame rate), then anyone engaged in altering the film would have had a much easier time optically excising frames of exit debris, and removing the car stop, through use of an optical printer. All that was required to operate Zapruder's Bell & Howell camera at the accelerated frame rate of 48 frames per second was a slight downward pressure on the trigger with the operator's index finger.

It could have happened this way—consider this: the extant film (that is, the assassination movie, not the Zapruder family scenes present on the two Secret Service copies) in the National Archives (not counting leader) consists of a strip of film 8'10" long (of which only 6'3" contains the imagery of the assassination film, and 2'7" is black, unexposed film with no image showing); then there is a physical splice; then there is a segment of black film containing no imagery that is 19'3" long; then there is another physical splice; then there is another segment of black film containing no imagery which is 5'8" long. Summarizing, after the first splice at the end of the assassination segment, there are a total of just over 24' of black film with no image showing. If the camera-original film had actually been shot at 48 frames per second—three times normal speed—then conceivably it would have required approximately three times the length of film in the present assassination segment (i.e., 3' x 6' = 18').

Currently, there is more than 18' of black film that is not contiguous with the assassination movie—that is, there is actually 24' of black film that has not been shot, but the problem is, it is not physically connected to the assassination film. The rhetorical question becomes, how do we know the actual, camera-original Zapruder film wasn't shot at 48 frames per second, and then edited down to normal speed during the alteration process by removing two thirds of the frames when the new film was created in an optical printer? The answer is, we don't know that—there is room for subterfuge here—because the black, unexposed film on the reel of the extant Zapruder film has been attached with a splice. [37]

Summation

An indefensible position:

In his 2003 book, *The Zapruder Film: Reframing JFK's Assassination,* author David Wrone wrote the following on page 125:

"Regarding the CIA, no scrap of paper, legitimate witness, or indirect source of any merit places the agency or any of its surrogates indirectly or directly in connection with the film on November 22 or the following two days."

In view of the two NPIC events discussed above, this statement is demonstrably wrong in every particular. Homer McMahon (Head of the NPIC Color Lab in 1963) and Dino Brugioni (Chief Information Officer at NPIC) were certainly "legitimate witnesses" and "sources of merit," as was Ben Hunter, a CIA career man who was still working for "the Agency" when the ARRB staff interviewed him in 1997. The CIA's code name "Hawkeyeworks," referring to the Top Secret lab at Kodak headquarters in Rochester, N.Y., with which the CIA had a close association through several classified contracts, was where the second Zapruder film delivered to NPIC, on 24 November 1963, had been processed; thus "Hawkeyeworks" certainly qualifies as one of "the CIA's surrogates."

The "thoroughly documented lack of official interest in the Zapruder film" that David Wrone writes about on page 125 is a figment of his imagination. The two NPIC events detailed by Brugioni (event # 1, commencing 23 November 1963) and McMahon and Hunter (event # 2, commencing 24 November 1963) indicate a great deal of interest, indeed, by the U.S. government, immediately following the assassination of President Kennedy, and precisely within the two-day period that David Wrone so falsely characterized.

Two compartmentalized operations took place on the weekend of 23–25 November 1963, at the CIA's National Photographic Interpretation Center (NPIC) in the nation's capital. Secret Service couriers were shuttling the Zapruder film to Washington, D.C. from Chicago, and then the next day from Rochester, N.Y., back to Washington again. Even as late as 1975, Mr. Hicks, the Director of NPIC, was withholding important information from one vital and trusted employee (Dino Brugioni), and was withholding other important information from the Rockefeller Commission, in an attempt to keep the lid on what had happened with the Zapruder film at NPIC.

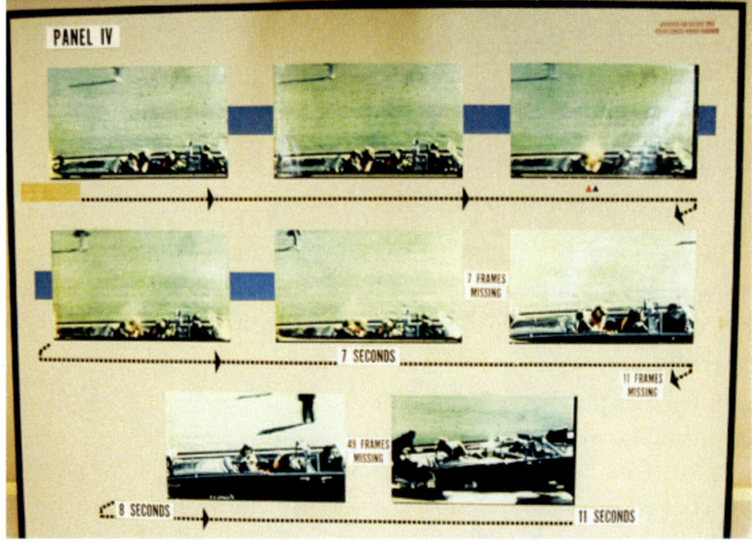

The two NPIC events are indeed "signposts" to the Zapruder film's alteration. The only way in which the two NPIC events can be properly understood or explained is in the context of the film's alteration at "Hawkeyeworks" on the very weekend immediately following President Kennedy's assassination.

Why Do So Many in the JFK Research Community Resist the Mounting Evidence that the Zapruder Film is an Altered Film?

I do not include here, in this question, those who have written books defending the Zapruder film's authenticity; their obstinacy and closedmindedness is related to ego, reputation, and to lifelong defense of their established turf. The old orthodoxy always resents the new paradigm that threatens established ways of thinking. [38]

There is a bigger problem within the JFK research community, and it revolves around the following question commonly posed by perplexed members of the "old guard," first-generation JFK researchers, to whom the concept of an altered Zapruder film seems dangerous heresy. They usually ask, "Why would anyone alter the film, and yet still leave evidence of conspiracy in the film?" (By this they usually mean the "timing problem" in the extant film which makes the single bullet theory impossible; and the "head snap" of JFK's upper torso and head to the left-rear after frame 313—which they equate with a shot, or shots, from the right front, and not from the Texas School Book Depository.)

The answers to this valid question are clear to me: (1) those altering the Zapruder film at "Hawkeyeworks" on Sunday, 24 November 1963 were extremely pressed for time, and could only do "so much" in the 12-to-14 hour period available to them; (2) the technology available with which to alter films in 1963 (both the traveling matte, and aerial imaging) had limitations—there was no digital CGI technology at that time—and therefore, I believe the forgers were limited to basic capabilities like blacking out the exit wound in the right-rear of JFK's head; painting a false exit wound on JFK's head on the top and right side of his skull (both of these seem to have been accomplished through "aerial imaging"—that is, animation cells overlaid "in space" on top of the projected images of the frames being altered, using a customized optical printer with an animation stand, and a process camera to re-photograph each self-matting, altered frame); and removing exit debris frames, and even the car stop, through step-printing.

In my view, the alterations that were performed were aimed at quickly removing the most egregious evidence of shots from the front (namely, the exit debris leaving the skull toward the left rear, and the gaping exit wound which the Parkland Hospital treatment staff tells us was present in the right-rear of JFK's head).

I believe that in their minds, the alterationists of 1963 were racing against the clock—they did not know what kind of investigation, either nationally or in Texas, would transpire, and they were trying to sanitize the film record as quickly as possible before some investigative body demanded to "see the film evidence."

There was not yet a Warren Commission the weekend following the assassination, and those who planned and executed the lethal crossfire in Dealey Plaza were intent upon removing as much of the evidence of it as possible, as quickly as possible.

As I see it, they did not have time for perfection nor the technical ability to ensure perfection, in their "sanitization" of the Zapruder film. They did an imperfect job, the best they could in about 12-14 hours, which was all the time they had on Sunday, 24 November 1963, at "Hawkeyeworks."

Besides, there was no technology available in 1963 that could convincingly remove the "head-snap" from the Zapruder film; you could not animate JFK's entire body without it being readily detectable as a forgery, so the "head-snap" stayed in the film. The "head snap" may even be an inadvertent result—an artifact of apparently rapid motion—caused by the optical removal of several "exit debris" frames from the film.

When projected at normal speed at playback, any scene in a motion picture will appear to speed up if frames have been removed.

Those altering the film may have believed it was imperative to remove the exit debris traveling through the air to the rear of President Kennedy, even if that did induce apparent "motion" in his body which made it appear as though he might have been shot from the front.

The forgers may have had no choice, in this instance, but to live with the lesser of two evils. Large amounts of exit debris traveling toward the rear would have been unmistakable proof within the film of a fatal shot from the front; whereas a "head snap" is something whose causes could be debated endlessly, without any final resolution.

Those who altered the Zapruder film knew that the wound alteration images in frames 317, 321, 323, 335, and 337, for example, were "good enough" to show investigators the film on a flimsy movie screen coated with diamond dust, but they also knew the alterations were not good enough to withstand close scrutiny.

That is why I believe C.D. Jackson—the CIA's asset at *Life* and its best friend in the national print media—instructed Richard Stolley to again approach Abraham Zapruder on Sunday night, and to offer a much higher sale price for Zapruder's movie, in exchange for *Life's* total ownership of the film, and all rights to the film.

By Sunday night, the name of the game at *Life* was suppression, not profit-making. By Sunday night, 24 November, C. D. Jackson was wearing his CIA hat, not his Time, Inc. businessman's hat. After striking the new deal with Time, Inc. on Monday, Zapruder received an immediate $25,000, and the remainder of his payments $25,000 per year, each January, through January of 1968), were effectively structured as "hush money" payments. His incentive to keep his mouth shut about the film's alteration would clearly be his desire to keep getting paid $25,000 each January, for the next five years. The alterationists in 1963 also had a "disposal" problem, for they had three genuine "first day copies" of the Zapruder film floating around which threatened to proliferate quickly, unless they could get them out of circulation immediately, replaced with new "first generation copies" struck from the new "Hawkeyeworks" master delivered to NPIC on Sunday night.

For them, speed was of the essence, not perfection. I believe that once the new "master" was completed at "Hawkeyeworks" early Sunday evening, three new first generation copies were struck from it, as well as at least one "dirty dupe" for the *Life* editorial crew standing by in Chicago.

Only after these products were exposed at Rochester, early Sunday evening, was the "new Zapruder film" (masquerading as an unslit, 16 mm wide camera-original "double 8" film) couriered down to NPIC by "Bill Smith," who took his cock-and-bull story along with him, to his everlasting discredit.

Of course, the cock-and-bull story worked, since Homer McMahon and Ben Hunter knew nothing about the event with the true camera-original film at NPIC the previous night. McMahon and Hunter had no reason, on Sunday night, 24 November 1963, to disbelieve "Bill Smith" when he told them that he had brought "the camera-original film" with him, after it had been "developed" at Rochester.

After all, the product handed to them looked like a camera-original "double 8" film: it was a 16 mm wide unslit film, with sprocket holes on both sides, and exhibited opposing image strips, upside down in relation to each other, and going in reverse directions.

I am quite sure that by Tuesday, 26 November, all of the original "first day copies" had been swapped out with the three replacements made at "Hawkeyeworks" Sunday night from the new "original."

NPIC finished up with the new "original" Zapruder film by some time Monday morning, 25 November, or perhaps by midday Monday at the latest. McMahon went home after the enlargements (the 5 x 7 prints) were run off, but the graphics people at NPIC still had to finish assembling the three sets of four panel briefing boards.

And the rest is history. Now, through the magic of high resolution digital scans—technology undreamed of in 1963, in an analog world—the forgery and fraud of November, 1963 is being exposed, slowly but surely. Alterations that were "good enough" to hold up on a flimsy, portable 8 mm movie screen back in 1963, look quite bad—very crude—today, under the magnifying glass of today's digital technology.

The two back-to-back "briefing board events" the weekend of President Kennedy's assassination at the CIA's National Photographic Interpretation Center (NPIC) in Washington, D.C.—compartmentalized operations bracketing the Zapruder film's alteration at the "Hawkeyeworks" lab in Rochester, N.Y.—are the signposts that illuminate for us, like two spotlights piercing the night sky, the hijacking of our nation's history over 50 years ago.

The Zapruder film was altered by the U.S. government, using clandestine, state-of-the-art Kodak resources in Rochester, to remove the most egregious evidence within the film of shots that came from in front of JFK's limousine. The true exit wound in the rear of his head was blacked out in many frames; frames showing exit debris from the fatal head shot propelled violently to the left rear were removed from the film; and a false "exit wound" was added to many of the image frames, in an attempt to support the lone assassin cover story. The altered film is one of the strongest proofs of a massive government cover-up following President Kennedy's death, and the intelligence community's third party surrogates are doing all they can, today, to deny that the film was ever altered, and discredit this story. I believe the facts speak for themselves.

I will close now with this cautionary quote for those skeptics, unwilling to let go of a discredited paradigm, who still feel compelled to defend the Zapruder film's authenticity:

> *"It is misleading to claim that scientific advances and scholarly experiments can cause all photo fakes to be unmasked. Questions about authenticity remain. Many photos that once were considered genuine have recently been determined to be faked."*
>
> ~ Dino Brugioni, author of *Photofakery: the History and Techniques of Photographic Deception and Manipulation* (1999).

Source note: This chapter previously appeared as *"Two NPIC Zapruder Film Events: Analysis and Implications", http://jamesfetzer.blogspot.com/2015/09/ two-npic-zapruder-film-events-analysis.html.*

Notes:

[20] ARRB interview of Homer A. McMahon conducted on 14 July 1997 by Douglas Horne.
[21] Horne, 2009, p. 1326–1327.
[22] Horne, 2009, p. 987–1013.
[23] Trask, 2005, p. 122.
[24] ARRB interview of Homer A. McMahon conducted on 14 July 1997 by Douglas Horne.
[25] Trask, 2005, p. 118.
[26] Trask, 2005, p. 117–119; and Horne, 2009, p. 1277–1281.
[27] HD Video interview of Dino Brugioni conducted on 9 July 2011 by Douglas Horne.
[28] Ibid.
[29] Ibid.
[30] Handwritten Memo for File written by H. Knoche on 14 May 1975.
[31] Dino A. Brugioni, *Eyeball to Eyeball* (Random House, 1991), p. 66.
[32] Horne, 2009, p. 1295–1296
[33] Ibid., p. 1296.
[34] Ibid., p. 1201–1205.
[35] Ibid., p. 1352–1363.
[36] Ibid., 1299–1302.
[37] Zavada, 1998, Attachment A1-1C, "Film Map of Original Zapruder Film" (prepared by ARRB staff member Douglas Horne following examination of the extant Zapruder film on 4 April 1997, at the National Archives)
[38] Thomas S. Kuhn, *The Structure of Scientific Revolutions* (University of Chicago Press, 1962).

9

Did Zapruder Film "the Zapruder Film"?

by Jim Fetzer

At first consideration, the question sounds very odd on its face. How could Zapruder have not taken "the Zapruder film"? So here is some background.

As many readers may be aware, I organized a JFK research group in 1992 of the most highly-qualified persons to ever study the case, including a world authority on the human brain, who was also an expert on wound ballistics; a Ph.D. in physics who was also an M.D. and board-qualified in radiation oncology; another M.D. who had been present in Trauma Room #1 when JFK was brought in for care and, two days later, was responsible for the treatment of his alleged assassin, Lee Harvey Oswald, in Trauma Room #2; a legendary photo-analyst, who had testified before the House Select Committee on Assassinations (HSCA) and later advised Oliver Stone on the production of *JFK*; and another Ph.D. in physics, this time with a specialization in electromagnetism, which includes the properties of light and of optics and images of moving objects.

We discovered that the autopsy X-rays had been altered to conceal a massive blowout at the back of the head; that another person's brain shown in diagrams and photographs at the National Archives had been substituted for that of JFK; and that the most famous footage in history, the Zapruder film, had been recreated by the removal of some frames and by the introduction of others, using the sophisticated techniques of optical printing and special effects applied to original footage to create a new film. I organized and moderated the first symposium on the authenticity of the film in Dallas in 1996 and would subsequently organize and moderate a conference on this subject in Duluth in 2003. (The conference is now available on YouTube in 66 segments, under the heading,"*Zapruder Fakery*".)

Later that year, I would publish my third collection of studies by experts on different aspects of the case, *The Great Zapruder Film Hoax* (2003), one of the greatest photographic scams of history.

Which film is "the Zapruder film"?

This may sound like a lot to swallow, so I will break it down for accessibility. One of the first results of the Zapruder Film Conference was the discovery that the films currently available to the public, including David Lifton's *Z Film* (undated), the Macmillan CD (1993), Robert Groden's *The Assassination Films* (1995), and MPI's *Image of an Assassination* (1998), differ significantly in the amount of information they provide. It we take the MPI version, which is the most complete, as the base of 100% (with a total of 411,305 pixels), the least complete is only about half of that:

COMPARISON: FRAME/	WIDTH (pixels)	HEIGHT (pixels)	AREA (pixels)	AREA/MPI VERSION
Lifton:	620	360	223,200	54.3%
Macmillan:	645	445	287,025	69.8%
Groden:	674	451	303,974	73.9%
MPI (frames):	671	484	324,764	78.9%
Sprocket area:	273	317	86,541	100.0%

These considerations suggest that the MPI version is the best available for research. Somewhat surprisingly, however, even MPI's *Image of an Assassination* (1998) has frames missing and others out of order. MPI's version does not include frames 155 and 156 or frames 208, 209, 210, and 211; it has reversed frames 331 and 332; and it is also missing (what ought to be) frames 341, 350, and even (the last frame) 486.

As it happens, John P. Costella, Ph.D., has produced a fresh, new version of the film, which overcomes all of these deficiencies and introduces improvements never before seen in any other version of the film, namely: corrections for pincushion and aspect ratio distortion; the inclusion of the so-called "ghost panels"; and masking of open sprocket holes to make information more accessible. In the interest of advancing the frontiers of knowledge, education, research, science and inquiry, this new, improved version is being made available to the public at no charge and is accessible at *The New Zapruder Film Frames.*

Here is an example of frame 317 from Costella's version, which is of special interest. When a frangible—exploding—bullet entered his right temple, it not only set up shock waves that blew his brains out the back of his head but it also blew open a skull-flap on the right side of his head, which some have mistaken for the blowout itself. As we shall see, they are not the same, nor should either of these genuine effects be confounded with the whitish "blob", which, as Roderick Ryan, a Hollywood expert, explained to Noel Twyman, was painted in. (See "*The JFK 'Head Shot' Paradox*".)

The Skull-Flap is Visible but the Blowout is not in Frame 317

Notice, especially, that while a skull flap is extending from the right side of his head, which is also visible in the HSCA diagram and photograph below, like them, no blowout to the back of his head is visible, even though it can be seen in frame 374 below. A stabilized real-time version is also available at *www.assassinationscience.com* toward the bottom of the home page. The frames and the stabilized version can be downloaded for further study, where this is the best available version for serious research.

Was it Copyrightable?

The study of the film has been inhibited by the control that has been exercised over it by a private company and now by The Sixth Floor Museum. A brief I commissioned by Mike Pincher, J.D., an attorney from California, was published as *"The Zapruder Film: "No" to Copyright Protection".* He contends—with complete justification, in my opinion—that the film was never entitled to copyright from the start.

There are two separate questions that have to be addressed. The first is that if the film is genuine as an accurate depiction of an historical event, is it entitled to copyright protection? The second is that if the film has been altered and is no longer an accurate film of an historical event, especially when it is marketed as genuine, does it deserve copyright protection? Interestingly, the answer to both questions seems to be the same, "No!" It appears obvious to me that this abuse of copyright has been deliberate to inhibit the serious study of the extant film, which has become an expensive proposition. In certain respects, the question of whether the film is properly subject to copyright is even more intriguing than whether a reworked film is deserving of such a protection.

Even if the film were judged to be authentic and complete, there are good reasons why it still should not be entitled to copyright protection. The predominant one is the 1990's federal legislation popularly known as the JFK Records Act that was a direct countermand to the veil of secrecy pervading the subject matter (arguably already placing the film in the public domain), but also because of language in judicial case law. In 1998, the government purchased the film for $16 million, but did not also acquire its copyright.

As Pincher argues in his study, while one 1968 federal district court case called it copyrightable, it is highly doubtful, based on subsequent case law, that even the U.S. Court of Appeals for the Second Circuit would agree. More significantly, it is doubtful that the U.S. Supreme Court would support it. Pincher contends—and I agree—that the film was never properly copyrightable to begin with, both because of its great public interest as a news event, and, no doubt more importantly, in that the assassination cannot be properly understood without public access to this source *in toto*. The idea of the event and its precise Zapruder film depiction cannot be properly treated separately. Even if the film were authentic, it would not deserve copyright protection.

And if the Film is Fake?

In considering the issue of copyright, a sharp line must be drawn between not only fiction and non-fiction, but between non-fiction and the recording of an historical event. There is no latitude of expression for the latter. Substantial similarity, as in the case of Oliver Stone's *JFK*, has no bearing. An historical record per se is either accurate or not, has no creative value otherwise and cannot be tampered with.

The Zapruder family and assignees have no entitlement of copyright protection relative to the extant film, when the film that came out of Zapruder's camera and what we see in that film are two different depictions—and, indeed, depictions that are drastically different—and by design. The Kennedy assassination can only be accurately studied based upon the original film as a whole, with its expression appreciated as a whole uncompromised by change or alteration. Even individual frames are incapable of doing the occasion justice. Privilege only attaches to the real film seen as a whole in real time. Thus, no copyright protection can attend to the extant version of the film.

Those who study the individual frames or the stabilized version of the film archived at *www.assassinationscience.com* may notice a feature that they have probably not seen in earlier versions, in particular, the "ghost panels" that surround the sprocket holes. These are double-exposures due to the design of the camera that was originally used by Zapruder to take the original film, which link one frame to another and cannot be duplicated. When those who were recreating the film had made the content changes they desired, then had to re-shoot most of its frames in a laboratory to recreate the ghost panels, in the absence of which the deception involved in its re-editing would have been immediately apparent.

It is for this reason that the film as a whole had to be recreated, which makes the film as a whole a "fabrication". That does not mean that none of it is real, but only that it takes a great deal of investigation and study to separate the authentic from the fake parts, as I am about to explain. But the answer to the intriguing question with which we began should be evident: Zapruder did not film the Zapruder film for the simple reason that no one took a film that was revised!

How we know it's fake

The reason the chapter *Who's Telling the Truth: Clint Hill or the Zapruder Film?* is so very important, therefore, is that we now have new proof of its alteration from an unexpected source. Clint Hill, a Secret Service agent on the Kennedy detail, is, along with Jack and Jackie, *the most conspicuous figure in the Zapruder film,* where he is the only agent who responded in an attempt to protect Jackie. What Clint has to tell us about his actions at the time—which he has maintained for over 50 years!—contradicts what we see in the film. Another agent on the opposite side of the limousine, John Ready, also started to respond when the first shots were fired, but was called back by Emory Roberts, Agent in Charge of the Secret Service Detail in Dallas.

This makes Roberts one of the principal suspects in setting JFK up for the hit, where we have discovered more than 15 indications that that was the case. The other key players were the driver, William Greer, who, unbelievable as it may sound, actually pulled the limo to the left and to a complete halt to make sure that JFK would be killed, and Floyd Boring, the Assistant Agent in Charge of the White House Detail, who was not in Dealey Plaza, as Vincent Palamara has also explained in *Murder in Dealey Plaza* (2000).

That Clint Hill has been saying the same thing for 50 years might make this sound like "old news". But the discovery that Clint had been saying this for so long only became apparent when John Costella viewed the video of what he had to say at La Jolla, California's Warwick's bookstore in December 2010.

John took a closer look and recognized that Clint had been saying the same thing, but that its importance for the authenticity of the Zapruder film had up until now gone unnoticed. Mike Pincher has also pointed out to me that, insofar as the film appears to have been recreated at a highly-classified photographic and film laboratory run by the CIA at Kodak headquarters in Rochester, N.Y., the extant film appears to be a product of the government.

Products of the government, which are financed at taxpayer expense, however, like other government documents, studies, and reports, do not qualify for copyright protection. Ironically, the discovery that the film has been faked also nullifies any arrangements that even the government itself has made regarding its copyright protection. There thus appear to be a variety of grounds for denying copyright to the extant film, which Mike Pincher has explained.

Resistance to Zapruder fakery

Among those in the JFK research community who have been the most outspoken in opposition to Zapruder film fakery are Robert Groden and Josiah Thompson. Robert Groden has a vast collection of JFK memorabilia, including what appears to be an early copy of the film. Josiah Thompson published his book *Six Seconds in Dallas: A Micro-Study of the Kennedy Assassination* (1967), based upon the study of the film to which he had access through a special arrangement with *Life* magazine.

In my opinion, they both have serious conflicts of interest in being objective about the proof we have adduced, since the value of Groden's collection and the significance of Thompson's book would be seriously compromised were the fabrication of the film to become widely accepted by the public.

The arguments that they have given for its authenticity, moreover, have not withstood critical scrutiny. Josiah, for example, has argued that it would have been impossible to fake the film because of an unbroken chain of custody from Dallas to *Life* magazine and after, a claim that was recently dismantled by the Assassination Records Review Board (ARRB), a civilian panel created by the JFK Records Act.

Its former senior analyst for military affairs, Douglas Horne, has now published *Inside the Assassination Records Review Board* (2009), in which he traces the discoveries that occurred during its years of operation in declassifying more than 60,000 documents and records that had been withheld from the public by the CIA, the FBI, the Secret Service and other government agencies.

Among those discoveries was that one version of the Zapruder film was brought to the National Photographic Interpretation Center (NPIC) in Washington, D.C., on Saturday, 23 November 1963, and another on Sunday, 24 November 1963.

The first was an 8mm film that had been developed in Dallas. The second was a 16mm film that had been developed in Rochester, N.Y. There were five physical properties of the strips of celluloid which distinguished them, as I have explained in "US Government Official: JFK Cover-Up, Film Fabrication". So the chain of custody argument, which Thompson, especially, has championed, has no merit.

In addition, we have discovered a great many changes in the content of the extant version of the film from what it should have shown, based upon studies of the medical evidence, the physical evidence, and the reports of a large number of eyewitnesses in Dealey Plaza, none of whom, interestingly, reported observing the dramatic, back-and-to-the-left motion of JFK's body that is so striking in the film.

Clint also describes peering into a hole in the back of JFK's head, a gaping, fist-sized blowout, which by itself contradicts the official X-rays, some of the autopsy photographs and diagrams, and early frames of the Zapruder film, where, as a new group of Hollywood experts has found, it was (crudely) painted over in black.

Some years ago, on the hunch that the conspirators who were redoing the film might have spent so much time concentrating on those early frames, especially 313-317, that they could have overlooked the wound in later frames, I made a search and found that it is clearly visible in frame 374, as I emphasized in *The Great Zapruder Film Hoax*.

So the simplest proof that the film has been altered is that the head wound is visible in some frames but has been concealed in others, which is something that you can confirm for yourself.

Algorithmic Proofs of Fakery

Here is how you can prove for yourself that what I am telling you is true. Go to the chapter, *"Who's Telling the Truth: Clint Hill or the Zapruder Film?"*, then do as follows:

(1) Scroll down to frame 374, where you can see the blowout in his head;

(2) Compare that with the HSCA photo and diagram, the next image in line;

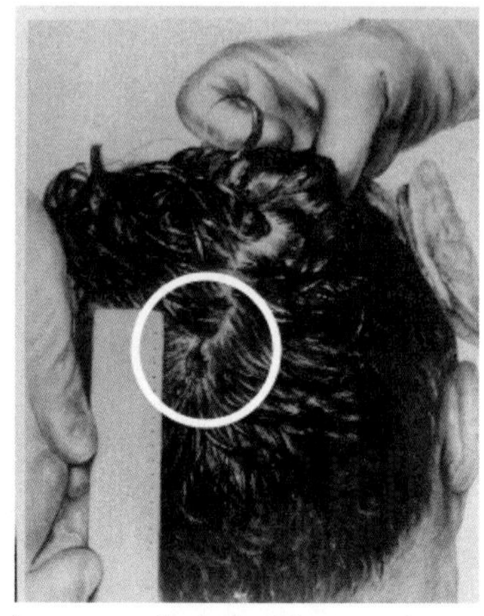

(3) Do you observe that the skull flap is present but the blowout is not?

(4) Scroll down to the witnesses reporting the location of the blowout;

(5) Do you see that it corresponds with the blowout seen in frame 374?

(6) Scroll down to the X-ray on the left and "Area P" defined on the right.

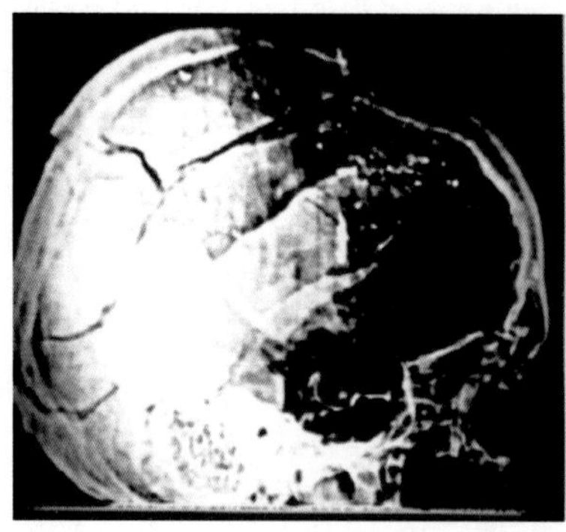

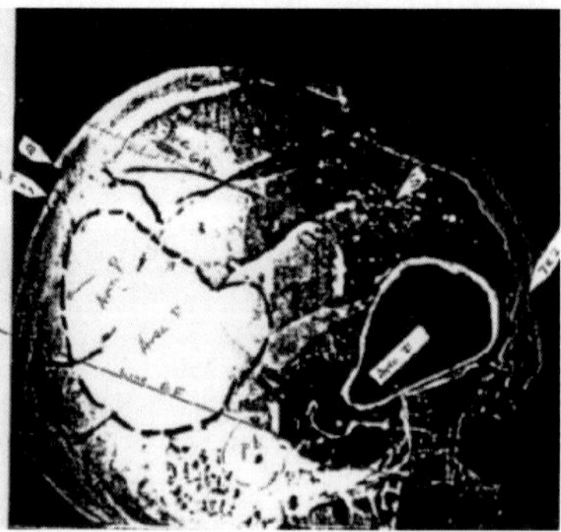

(7) Do you see where "Area P" closely resembles the blowout in frame 374?

(8) Do you see where "Area P" is unusually bright in the X-ray on the left?

(9) Scroll down to the diagrams of the head wound by Charles Crenshaw, M.D.

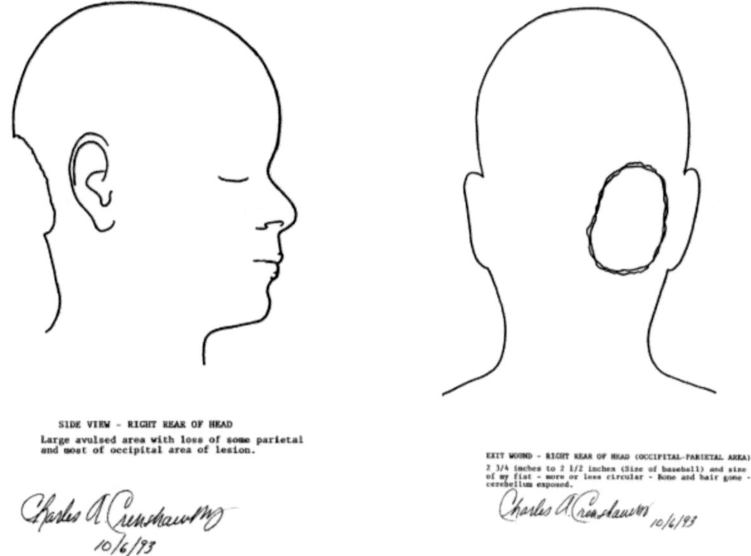

(10) Do you see how his diagram agrees with frame 374 and X-ray "Area P"?

(11) Go to the Zapruder film as individual frames or in its stabilized version.

(12) Compare what you see in frames 313-317 with what you see in frame 374.

Since the blowout is visible in frame 374 but not in earlier frames, such as 313-317, what does that tell you? Hollywood experts have determined it (the blowout) was painted over in black in those early frames, which means that the film has been altered. The limo stop was also taken out, where we have around 60 witnesses who reported seeing it dramatically slow or come to a complete stop. But the car *had to slow dramatically as it came to a complete stop.*

Notice in the section entitled, "The Limo Stop", I quote witnesses—Toni Foster, Billy Lovelady, Roy Truly, and Mrs. Earle Cabell—who report seeing the limo stop with their own eyes. Is there anything you question about what they are reporting? But if the limo came to a stop—and all four of the motorcycle patrolmen said the same thing—since the stop is not in the film, what happened to it? Did it simply disappear? Or did it have to be removed when the film was reworked, because it was an obvious indication of Secret Service complicity in setting JFK up for the hit? Which is the principal reason the Zapruder film had to be faked, the ramifications of which clearly extend far beyond recreation of the film.

The Commission's Dereliction

Indeed, there are more than 15 indications of Secret Service complicity in setting JFK up for the hit, including leaving two Secret Service agents (who would have been with the limo) at Love Field, placing the vehicles in the wrong order (with the President's limo first, when it should have been preceded by those of the Mayor of Dallas and of the Vice President), removing the flat-bed truck that should have accompanied the President's vehicle to provide for press and television coverage), not welding down the manhole covers, not covering the open windows, ordering the 112th Intelligence Unit to "stand down", allowing the crowd to spill out into the street, taking a turn of more than 90°, changing the motorcade route three days before the event, reducing the motorcycle escort to four and directing them not to ride forward the rear wheels, not responding after bullets began to be fired, pulling the limo to the left and a stop to make sure JFK would be killed, getting bucket and sponge to wash the brains and blood off the limo at Parkland Hospital before he had even been pronounced dead; and more that involve the autopsy X-rays and photos, which suggests the direction in which responsibility lies for the assassination of JFK.

Greer's bringing the limo to a halt and Kellerman's silence and inaction over blatant violations of protocol for which he was responsible confirms both of their roles among the crucial conspirators.

Moreover, whether someone personally finds Hill credible or not does not detract from impugning the integrity of the Warren Commission itself. Clint Hill's account so severely contradicts the Zapruder film that the commission had a duty to inquire of him, which it failed to do.

Thus, neither the accuracy of the film nor the integrity of the Secret Service appear to have been of the least concern to the commission, which was operating—with tacit or overt complicity of the FBI and its own staff—to substantiate the predetermined conclusion that Oswald was "the lone gunman" regardless of truth.

His testimony is sufficient, at the least, to either establish that the film wasn't what it was presented to be (which eliminates it as authoritative evidence for assassination research) or that he, as a member of the President's protective detail, was lying and should have been removed as an agent or criminally prosecuted or both. The corruption of the Warren Commission becomes all the more glaring from these reflections on what it did not do as well as what it did.

Source note: This chapter previously appeared as "Did Zapruder Film 'the Zapruder Film'"?", *http://jamesfetzer.blogspot.com/2015/09/did-zapruderfilm-zapruder-film.html*

Part IV

The Limo Stop

10

JFK Escort Officers Speak: The Fred Newcomb Interviews

by Larry Rivera

Among the most disputed issues in JFK research is whether or not the presidential limousine came to a halt after bullets began to be fired.

New information about what happened during this crucial interval has now been made available in "The JFK Horsemen", an article included in a new CD-ROM, "The Man with the Mona Lisa Smile", by Richard Hooke and Larry Rivera (with special contributions by Jim Fetzer).

As Jim has explained in many places, including several presentations on the assassination that are accessible on YouTube, such as *What Happened To JFK And Why It Matters Today* (*https://youtu.be/slPUe2NCt7I* University of Wisconsin-Madison, 22 November 2011), there are more than 60 witnesses who reported seeing the limo either slow dramatically or come to a complete halt, where it slowed dramatically as it came to a complete halt, which has been confirmed by a half-dozen others who have seen a more complete film. For a summary of lines of proof that support this conclusion, see "*The JFK War: The Challenging Case of Robert Groden*". Remarkably enough, interviews of the four JFK motorcycle escort patrolmen conducted in 1971 by Fred Newcomb for his book, *Murder From Within: Lyndon Johnson's Plot against President Kennedy* (2011), reveal significant details about the duration of

the event and the multiple activities that occurred when it stopped on Elm Street.

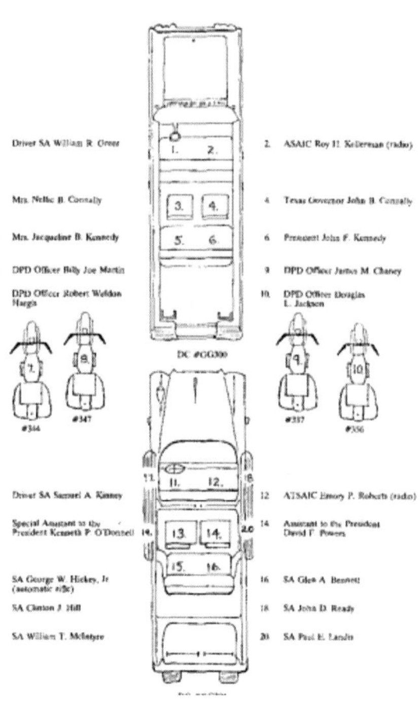

The officers were Billy Joe Martin on the outside/left (#7), Robert Weldon Hargis the inside/left (#6), James M. Chaney on the inside/right (#9) and Douglas L. Jackson the outside/right (#10).

In these excerpts, which are transcribed from the Newcomb interviews, all four of them claimed that it stopped or almost stopped after the "first" shot, which was actually the second or third, since JFK had already been hit in the back by a shot fired from the top of the County Records Building.

The sound of a firecracker

The reason many reported the second or third as "the first shot" is that it made the sound of a firecracker as it passed through the windshield en route to JFK's throat, where, according to Bob Livingston, M.D., a world authority on the human brain and expert on wound ballistics, it hit bone and fragmented, one part going downward into his right lung, the other upward into his brain.

Whitney: Do you remember how long it stopped when it was on Elm Street.
Hargis: Oh - you mean after that first shot?
Whitney: Right.
Hargis: Only about uh, oh 3-4 seconds. Maybe about 5-6. That's all.
Whitney: You say it stopped for about 5 or 6 seconds.
Hargis: Yeah, but you won't find that in the Warren Commission Report.
Whitney: Don't they claim that it stopped?
Hargis: Huh?
Whitney: Don't they claim that it stopped?
Hargis: Ah no I don't think it didn't - you've seen a rolling stop have you? It's going less than one mile an hour?
Whitney: Right, right.
Hargis: Well that's what he was doing he wasn't completely stopped or dead still.

Whitney: 'Cause we see a lot of things in there. In fact we see one thing which is very disturbing, that the car doesn't even stop in that film, doesn't even slow down.
Martin: Doesn't slow down at all?
Whitney: No, somebody's monkeying around with, some things...
Martin: I would've sworn that, that it was, uh, the time that he, uh, tried to get up, that the car stopped....
Whitney: You say who was trying to get up.
Martin: ..the agent - after the shooting? That when he came up to, and jumped up to the back of the car - at that instant is when it stopped, and I believe he lost his balance. Then they started again, and of course was throwing him off and that's when she turned around and - I thought was trying to help him get up on the, help him up on the back of the limousine.

In these transcripts, "Whitney" on behalf of Fred Newcomb is questioning Officers Hargis and Martin. When Hargis refers to "that first shot", therefore, he is speaking of what happened after the sound of a firecracker, not the actual first shot. He has told Whitney that the limo stop lasted for "about five or six seconds". Officer Martin is troubled the Zapruder film does not show a limo stop:

What is also significant about Martin's replies is that he is describing an agent–presumably, Clint Hill–who was trying to get up on the limo during the stop. Jackie is out on the trunk and, Martin believes, was reaching out to help him get up on the back of the vehicle, where she had gone after a chunk of JFK's skull and brains and which she would hold in her hand all the way to Parkland.

Chaney: I don't know whether the lead car stopped or not but I know that uh, I mean uh, Kennedy's car, the one behind them,..apparently did because it was officers that run from the left hand side, in front of me -
Whitney: U huh.
Chaney: I know I stopped.
Whitney: Right
Chaney: Whenever I seen what happened there, then, I know Hargis, the motorcycle escort on the other side run across the front.
Whitney: Yeah, Bobby, I just spoke to him just a few minutes ago. Yeah, you know I think at least between 60 and 75 people that day who claimed the car stopped. But even if it didn't stop...
Chaney: Whether the lead car did or not - I don't believe that it did....it slowed down enough that this agent, whats his name Clint Hill?,
Whitney: Right, right.
Chaney: ...slowed down enough that he did get on that car, now whether or not he was on there or not you know - several different times during the procession there, he would run up and jump on this little step and ride there for a couple of seconds and jump off, and - that all depends on how fast it was going along and where we were at - so whether, I don't believe that it actually stopped, it could have, but I don't know - I know that the second car did 'cause I recall the officers....and Officer Hargis jumped off the motor and run in front of me. .
Whitney: Right, right, that's another thing -
Chaney: I don't recall myself stopping - I must have or come almost to a stop. Hargis did, he got off of his motorcycle over on the left hand side and run between those two cars...and run in front of me, so apparently I did too. I don't recall stopping, but I'm not sure.

This one with James Chaney offers further proof that the limo stopped on Elm Street for quite some time. Chaney describes how Bobby Hargis, after dismounting from his cycle and leaving it on the left lane of Elm Street, ran in front of him–*and in between the two limos*–on his way up the grassy knoll and up to the pedestal, where Zapruder had been standing (WC6H 295):

For Bobby Hargis to have had enough time *to park his motorcycle and then pass in between the two vehicles in front of Chaney means that both limos stopped for a substantial amount of time, perhaps at least as*

Hargis at the lamppost and across the street

long as five or six seconds, as Hargis himself had observed above. The only problem with this is that none of the films that exist today show Bobby Hargis doing any of that.

The Bell Film Tracks Hargis

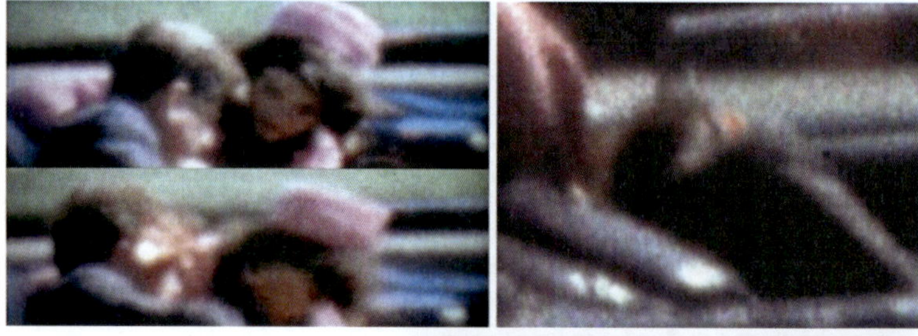

The Bell film initially tracks Hargis as he stands by the lamppost on the north curb, then shows him turning around and crossing Elm Street to get back on his motorcycle, after which he rides underneath the Triple Underpass and then back on the other side to help search the railroad yard, but it does not show him moving between the two vehicles to get to the north side of Elm Street.

The absence of Bobby Hargis' initial movements across Elm Street and in between the limos after he dismounted his motorcycle, therefore, indicates that the Bell film has been edited and revised, like so much of the rest of the JFK photo and film record. Since frame 374 shows the blowout at the back of the head but earlier frames do not, the Zapruder film itself is internally inconsistent. (See: *https://youtu.be/xkl0ECGmU58*)

Since the Nix film shows Jackie moving further back on the trunk and Clint Hill further forward than they do in the Zapruder, the Nix and Zapruder films are mutually inconsistent. These are among the simplest proofs that these films have been altered, where the altered Zapruder appears to have been used as a guide in fixing the others–except that it was done with only mixed success.

Who climbed on the limo?

The extant Zapruder and Nix films show a smooth rolling limousine cruising around 12-15 miles an hour, which slows down slightly when Clint Hill boards the vehicle via the back, by climbing over the trunk, who according to Bobby Hargis, did so in order to prevent Jackie Kennedy from climbing out of the back seat of the car. Was Clint Hill the only Secret Service Agent to climb into the limousine? Hargis was emphatic about a second agent boarding and entering the back seat:

Whitney: Were they the guys who jumped out of their car and pursued it to the car in front of them?
Whitney: Well uh, two of them did. Uh-huh. Two.
Hargis: Uh-huh. Ran up to the back of the uh, Continental.
Whitney: Two ran out to the back of the Continental
Hargis: Huh?
Whitney: Two ran out to the back of the Continental.
Hargis: Uh, there was two Secret Service men you know they've got them steps up there...
Whitney: Right, right.
Hargis: ...that they ride on. This one on the left hand side stopped Jackie Kennedy from coming out.
Whitney: Uhh, one of them got up on the back and stopped Jackie, that was probably Clint Hill, the other one how did - did he get into the car?
Hargis: Yeah a huh.
Whitney: When did he get into the car?
Hargis: Well, I'm not sure exactly there if it was one on the left and one on the right, one of them - put his body over the President where no harm could come to him - I don't know, all you could see was his feet sticking out.

The Miller Photograph

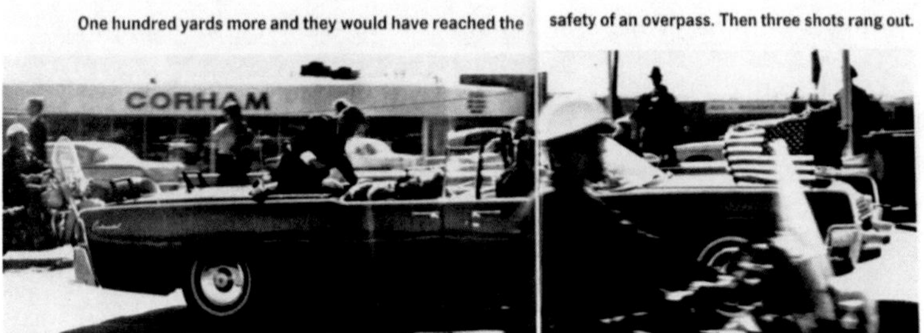

Rivera Scan from Original Copy of
The Saturday Evening Post *14 December 1963*

The Miller photograph, which was widely circulated in *The Saturday Evening Post* (14 December 1963) shows a left foot sticking out which has always been assumed belonged either to Agent Clint Hill—who was bent in an unusual, contorted position—or else to JFK, mortally wounded with half his brain blasted out, but who had somehow lifted his left foot over the side quarter panel of the Continental (CD87, p. 418). So whose left foot does this really belong to?

Sergeant Stavis Ellis, who was in very close contact with all of the patrolmen who were under his supervision, had this to say:

> Whitney: Did you notice who was in the car.
> Ellis: It was the Governor, Governor Connally and his wife, the driver and a Secret Service man and uh, Jackie Kennedy in the back with the dead President. One or two agents by then were on there 'cause we nearly lost one of em hanging on as fast as we were going he had a hard time hanging on there. In fact of the two agents this one old boy that Jackie knew had made the trip overseas with her, **he come running and jumped on there and another one, and - by the time we pulled out of there we had two of them agents hanging on the back.**
> Whitney: You had two in the back. You don't remember-
> Ellis: **I believe - I know we had one and possibly two.**

This information, if accurate, is devastating to the official version, because it confirms not only that the limo did stop on Elm Street, but that it stopped, as Hargis said, perhaps for as long as five to six seconds, giving not just one agent time to get in, but a second agent time to get in and cover the President and First Lady.

This would have been in line with protocol established by the Secret Service, where each one was assigned a personal shield in case of an emergency such as this one.

Photographic Confirmation

Three to four seconds is a long time, but five to six seconds is an eternity when the President of the United States is being murdered in a triangulated crossfire in broad daylight in the streets of Dallas. *But the person seen in the Miller photograph is not wearing any sunglasses!*

The hair pattern seems fair, the hairline is entirely different from Hill's, and he seems to be wearing a bulletproof vest of some kind. Notice also how Hill's undershirt extends well below and into the chest area.

As the motorcade advanced on Stemmons Freeway, note this closeup of a photo credited to the Dallas Times Herald, and published in former Dallas Chief of Police Jesse Curry's book, *Retired Dallas Police Chief, Jesse Curry reveals his personal JFK Assassination File* (1969) on

Rivera Scan from Original Copy of
The Saturday Evening Post *14 December 1963*

page 31, which shows "Agent Hill" still straddling the back seat of the limousine.

All of a sudden, "Agent Hill" is wearing sunglasses again! But a careful comparison of Clint Hill's sunglasses with the person in the image reveals the sunglasses have been painted in, in crude fashion. Notice the real Agent Hill's shades with a discernible and well-defined bridge.

The simple examination of these images indicates something is not right about the back seat limo rider. The inconsistencies are pretty obvious. But wait, the story does not end here.

Sergeant Ellis revealed what was reported to him by the motorcycle officers under his command that the limo stopped for as long as five to six seconds, where evidence is mounting that two agents climbed upon it:

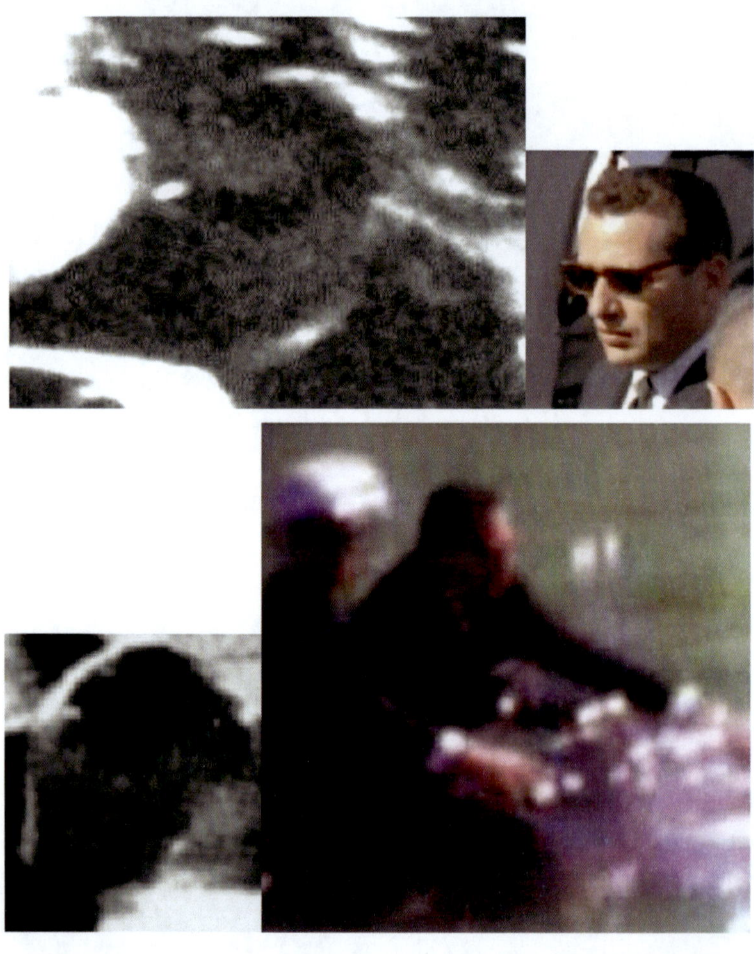

Reconstructing the two head shots that JFK sustained during the limo stop, he slumped forward after having been hit in the back of the head by the first, Jackie eased him back up and was looking right in his face when he was hit in the right temple by the second and then slumped to the left. She would have been left in the street when she climbed out onto the trunk after a chunk of his skull and brains, had the limo been accelerating. Jim Fetzer has suggested that, given the activities of the Secret Service, it might have even been as long as 20–30 seconds.

Reports that Hargis passed between the cars supports a stop of this longer duration.

The Chunk of Skull

Apparently a large chunk of JFK's skull was blown to the left and onto the inner grass beyond the south curb of Elm Street. Since the motorcade was at a standstill, an unidentified boy picked up the piece of skull and a Secret Service Agent snatched it from him and threw it into the back seat of the limo. As far-fetched as it may seem, Sergeant Stavis Ellis was quite sure this happened:

> Whitney: Did you see any of the wounds on him at all?
> Ellis: No I didn't, I didn't get that close, I know that down on the street a piece of his skull blew out of the car and blew over on the grass, and a kid picked it up, a Secret Service man took it away from him and threw it in the back of the car. (pause) We, our people, right there at the motor knew how bad he was hurt, I knew he was hit, I didn't know how bad he was hit until my man Chaney came up there and said he - no chance, he ain't got no chance but let's go - he said his head was just - well I didn't really know for sure until we got to the hospital, there wasn't any chance for him, after talking to how often they come in. (last part unintelligible)
> Whitney: That piece of bone that the Secret Service man took from that young boy you say in the grass - when he came to the hospital he threw it in the car there.
> Ellis: No, he put it in the car back at the - right there as it happened as I remember.
> Whitney: As it happened at the street there on Elm?
> Ellis: Yes sir.
> Whitney: The President's limousine stopped for a while, right at that point?
> Ellis: Well no it didn't stop, it almost stopped. If you've ever ridden a motor, you know if you go so slow, your motor will want to lean to one side, you have to put your foot down and balance it, but we were going so slow, that's what was happening we were having to kick our foot down, a very slow pace, this was, after the first shot was fired, we were - we cut the speed, the Secret Service cut the speed, on the convoy.
> Whitney: You know for how long?
> Ellis: Well, it was just momentarily, it never did stop, it almost stopped, it got so slow, we were just barely moving - and then they hollered Go Go Go! Lets go. Get him to the hospital as quick as you can.

While he is equivocal about whether the limousine came to a complete stop or not, he is entirely unambiguous that "a kid" picked up a large piece of JFK's skull, which one of the agents–either Chaney or Jackson–took from him and "threw it back in there" (into the rear seat of the limo), where Whitney mistakenly presumed that this event had happened later at Parkland Hospital:

> Whitney: So much stuff coming into my head, I can hardly hold it all together. Ah, I'm trying to think, you saw the SS, Secret Service man put the piece of skull in the car was that as you said at the hospital he did that you said?
> Ellis: He put it in there, I think, I believe he put it, threw it back in there, right..... (pause) right there where it happened there I remember, cause the kid that gave it to him it was on the grass on the side of the street there that - where it happened..

Whitney: He picked it up right there on Elm St.
Ellis: The kid picked it up, had it and gave it to the Secret Service man took it away from him.
Whitney: You remember seeing that, you say over on Elm Street.
Ellis: I beg your pardon?
Whitney: You say you remember seeing that over on the by the Depository, when the Secret Service man took the skull...
Ellis: No I didn't see him put it in there at all.
Whitney: You didn't,
Ellis: No I just...
Whitney: What made you feel - how'd it get in there?
Ellis: One of my men saw him do it - motorcycle officer...
Whitney: You don't remember who that was.
Ellis: It was either Chaney or Jackson, one of the two.

Richard Hooke has proposed the possibility that this same piece of skull might have been placed or planted much further down Elm Street, in line with the southeast window of the sixth floor of the TSBD, which was later found by Billy Harper the following Saturday evening, more than 24 hours after the assassination (5:30 PM, Saturday, 23 November 1963, see HSCA Vol 7, p. 122).

The Harper Fragment

The discovery of the Harper Fragment and its location had never made any sense at all, given the fact that Dealey Plaza was cordoned off and thoroughly combed and searched that Friday after the assassination for evidence. It may have been moved to make it look more like the result of a shot from behind. Here's the approximate location of where it was officially found (map inverted):

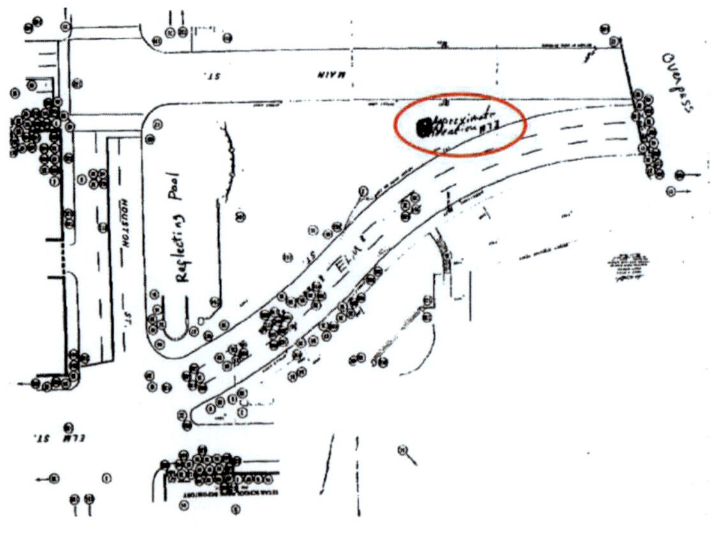

The significance of the interviews conducted by Fred Newcomb of these policemen back in 1971 are only now being understood. After discussing this with Richard Hooke and Ted Coeyman, the possibility has been raised that the boy who seems to have been closest to the point where the piece of skull landed was Charles Brehm's son, Joseph. Coeyman has reported that Brehm was immediately sequestered after the shots, which may have been to intimidate him from talking about it.

The information gleaned from these recordings tends to confirm what researchers have long suspected and why the investigative bodies involved wanted no part of their testimony. The escort officers' supervisor, Sergeant Stavis Ellis, had been ordered not to allow them to disperse and to report to the second floor of City Hall as soon as they were done at Parkland Hospital and Love Field with the new President aboard Air Force One. The reasons are becoming obvious.

Source note: This chapter previously appeared as *"JFK Escort Officers Speak: The Fred Newcomb Interviews", http://jamesfetzer.blog,spot.com/2015/09/jfk-escort-officers-speak-fred-newcomb.html.*

11

The "Grassy Knoll" Rider and JFK Limo Backseat

by Larry Rivera

During the House Select Committee on Assassinations (HSCA) meetings reinvestigating JFK's assassination (197778), it was very odd that Secret Service personnel were required to read from their notes what transpired.

The president was face down on the back seat. Mrs. Kennedy made a cradle of her arms around the president's head and bent over him as if she were whispering to him.

Notice how on 11/23, Merriman Smith changed his story to the president being face down on the back seat, which coincides with what they tried to establish with the altered Miller photograph.

Anonymous writes, "I lived next door to Adrian G. (Mr. Pete) Vial, and he confided to me that after the assassination they (SS) were ordered to turn over all of their records, including their field notes, to the FBI. He was very bitter about this. [It means that] if their testimony to HSCA was from any SS person, it had to be provided back to them by the FBI."

The author has followed up Beverly Brunson's lead, where she wrote, "[T]he (news) papers were full of the event of this cyclist riding up the knoll."

I found these newspaper clipping from, of all places, Robin Unger's site where he posts the front page of 81 newspapers dated 22 and 23 November 1963. Furthermore, I found astounding reference to both JACKIE AND JFK being on the floor of the limousine as it pulled up to Parkland, where Merriman Smith filed a report for UPI on the 22nd indicating they were on the floor, then REVISED it on the 23rd to say they were on the seat instead.

Circulation 313,289 A.M.-P.M. Daily Average, October 1963

OKLAHOMA CITY TIMES

VOL. LXXIV, NO. 240 42 PAGES—500 N BROADWAY, OKLAHOMA CITY FRIDAY, NOVEMBER 22, 1963 FINAL HOME FIVE CENTS

3 Shots—'It Was Horrible'

By Allan Cromley (Washington Bureau)

Wall Hurdled

The first tip-off of tragedy was when several spectators jumped over a stone wall and started running toward what apparently was the scene of the shooting.

A motorcycle patrolman rode pell-mell up a railroad embankment, apparently in pursuit of the assassin.

As the deadly gunfire sounded, motorcycle police raced up the grassy knoll of a park nearby where a man and woman were huddled.

Mrs. Kennedy was on her knees on the floor of the rear seat with her head toward the president.

KENNEDY ASSASSINATED DURING DALLAS PARADE

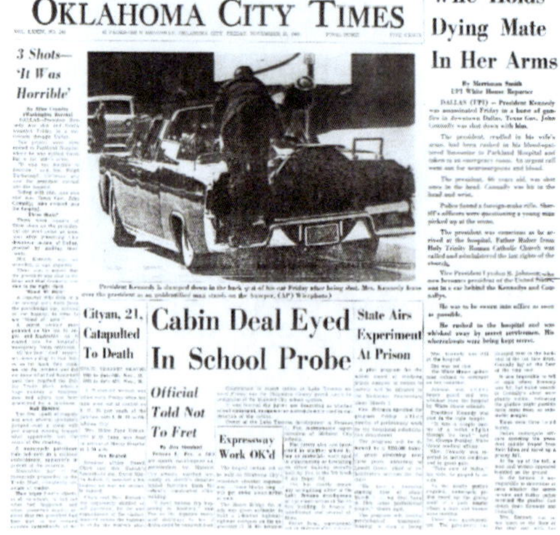

Circulation 313,289 A.M.-P.M. Daily Average, October 1963

OKLAHOMA CITY TIMES

3 Shots—'It Was Horrible'

Wife Holds Dying Mate In Her Arms

Cityan, 21, Catapulted To Death

Cabin Deal Eyed In School Probe

Official Told Not To Fret

State Airs Experiment At Prison

Expressway Work OK'd

The photo featured here, technically known as the "Altgens7", was faked to conceal what happened.

The Atlanta Jou

"COVERS DIXIE LIKE THE DEW"

Vol. LXXXI, No. 231 Tel. JA. 2-5050—P.O. Box 4689 Atlanta (2), Ga., F

As it neared the triple underpass leading toward the Trade Mart where Kennedy was to address a lunch, three bursts of gunfire sounded.

As the deadly gunfire sounded, motorcycle police raced up the grassy knoll of a park nearby where a man and woman were huddled.

There was pandemonium. The President's car cut out of the line of travel and raced behind screaming motorcycle police sirens to Parkland Hospital. Two litters were brought out for the President and the governor.

Mrs. Kennedy and Mrs. Connally appeared in shock.

The President lay face down on the floor of the limousine, which had its bubble top down. Mrs. Kennedy crouched over him.

The first of Larry Rivera's reports based on Fred Newcomb's interviews of the escort officers (https://youtu.be/jlMwxZPNpTM)

"The President lay face down on the floor of the limousine . . . . Mrs. Kennedy crouched over him."

Circulation 313,289 A.M.-P.M. Daily Average, October 1963

OKLAHOMA CITY TIMES

VOL. LXXIV, NO. 240 42 PAGES—500 N BROADWAY, OKLAHOMA CITY, FRIDAY, NOVEMBER 22, 1963 FINAL HOME FIVE CENTS

Wife Holds Dying Mate In Her Arms

By Merriman Smith
UPI White House Reporter

DALLAS (UPI) – President Kennedy was assassinated Friday in a burst of gunfire in downtown Dallas. Texas Gov. John Connally was shot down with him.

Mrs. Kennedy was on her knees on the floor of the rear seat with her head toward the presi-

Here, Jackie was on her knees on the floor of the rear seat, with her head toward the president.

St. Paul Dispatch

20 PAGES ST. PAUL, MINN., SATURDAY, NOVEMBER 23, 1963 Northwest

Editor's note—Merriman Smith, UPI White House reporter since 1941 was on the scene in Dallas Friday when President Kennedy was assassinated. Smith was in the motorcade not far from Kennedy when the shooting took place. He followed the president's car to the hospital. He was there for the swearing-in of President Johnson in an air force jet and came on back to Washington aboard the aircraft bearing the new president and the body of the slain Kennedy. He was the only news agency reporter on the aircraft.

By MERRIMAN SMITH

WASHINGTON — (UPI) — It was a balmy, sunny noon as

The president was face down on the back seat. Mrs. Kennedy made a cradle of her arms around the president's head and bent over him as if she were whispering to him.

Notice how on 11/23, Merriman Smith changed his story to the president being face down on the back seat, which coincides with what they tried to establish with the altered Miller photograph.

HOUSTON CHRONICLE EXTRA

"Miss Classified" CA 4-6868 • Circulation Service CA 4-2061 • Other Depts. CA 7-2211

Vol. 63 No. 40 FRIDAY, NOVEMBER 22, 1963 HOUSTON, TEXAS—THE NATION'S SIXTH CITY ★★ 72 PAGES

There were three loud bursts.

Dallas motorcycle officers escorting the President quickly leaped from their bikes and raced up a grassy hill.

* * *

THE PRESS-COURIER

VOLUME 56 NUMBER 125—PRICE TEN CENTS OXNARD, CALIFORNIA, FRIDAY, NOVEMBER 22, 1963

The President lay face down on the floor of the limousine, which had its bubble top down. His wife crouched over him.

Dallas motorcycle officers escorting the President quickly leaped from their bikes and raced up a grassy hill.

Now they are on the back seat, where Jackie is cradling JFK's head and whispering to him (which no doubt happened at Parkland), where they had to exert effort to pry his lifeless body from her arms.

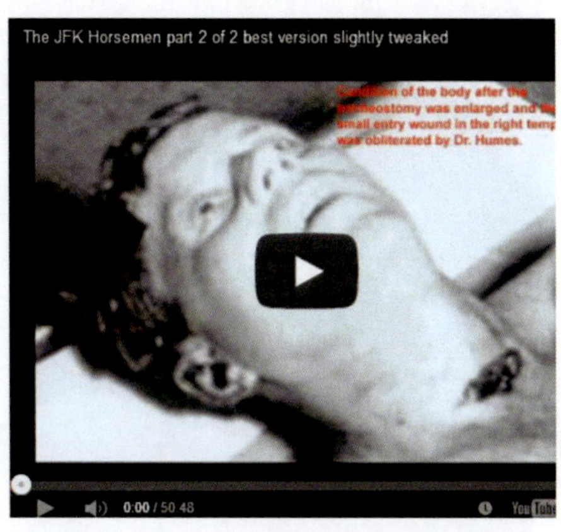

Here is the second of Larry Rivera's YouTubes based upon Fred Newcomb's interviews *(https://www.youtube.com/watch?v=DP7YvelagHA)*.

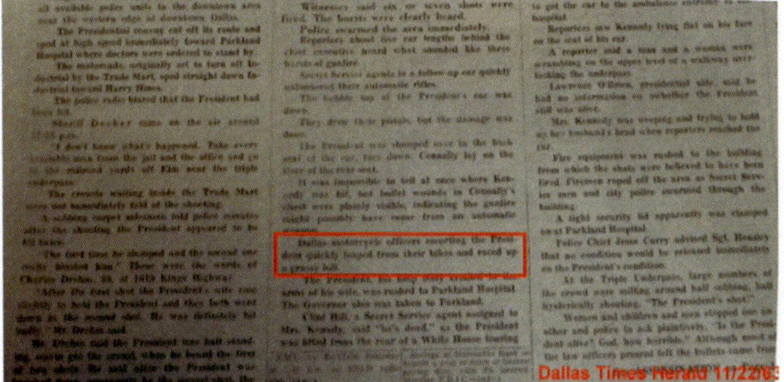

These have come from Unger's site, hiding in plain sight! Notice how Merriman Smith changed his story the very next day! On 22 November, most dispatches reported the escort motorcycle cops dismounted and ran up the knoll, but by 23 November, all these reports had been removed. I don't think that anybody has previously bothered to actually read the 81 front pages at Unger's site.

Source note: This chapter previously appeared as "*The 'Grassy Knoll' Rider and JFK Limo Backseat*", *http://jamesfetzer.blogspot.com/2015/09/the-grassyknoll-rider-and-jfk-limo.html.*

12

Tampering with the JFK Limo in the Altgens6

by Dennis Cimino

A significant amount of speculation has taken place over the years, regarding the photograph known to the world as the Altgens6, taken by AP photographer James "Ike "Altgens in Dealey Plaza, with his camera, on the day that President John F. Kennedy was brutally murdered by the CIA and other elements of the U.S. government, including the Secret Service and even the Joint Chiefs of Staff of our own American Armed Forces.

In the following work, some layers of the onion will be peeled back to expose that Altgens6 is not only the key to establishing that *Lee Harvey Oswald wasn't even a shooter*—because he was clearly photographed in the doorway of the Texas School Book Depository at the moment that a shot from in front of the President's limousine penetrated the vehicle's windshield, struck and spun the vehicle's rear view mirror and caused the passenger seat Secret Service Agent, Roy Kellerman, to gawk in astonishment at the spun mirror, necessitating his face be obscured by later alterations–but that a disinformation program to alter evidence has been ongoing for over 50 years.

For a bullet to have obviously come from forward and to the left of the vehicle, as it came down Elm Street, means that at least one assassin who took part in this "turkey shoot" was located forward of the vehicle, which means that not all the shots came from above and behind. In addition, Oswald wore such a unique shirt that day that it was impossible for the CIA murderers to obtain that same shirt for Billy Lovelady to claim that he had been in that doorway standing on the left, when he was instead standing on the right (as we view the photo). That shirt was so distinctive it forced the CIA to try to alter it out of existence, where alterations to Altens6 were even made to impose facial features of Lovelady on Lee.

The Faxed Photo

Ironically, that very shirt is one and the same with the shirt worn by Lee Oswald when arrested by the Dallas Police Department, where a series of studies published on *Veterans Today* have confirmed that Lee was wearing the same shirt as Doorman and have refuted the alternatives that Doorman could have been either Billy Lovelady or "Checkered Shirt Man", which illustrates the importance of falsification in the study of these questions.

Although the claim has been made that the photograph was faxed shortly after the film was processed, Roy Schaeffer, who was working for a Dayton, OH, newspaper at the time, took it off the photo-fax the next morning. This time window created ample opportunity for the initial alterations and reshooting of the negatives in a photo lab, so that Altgens did not get his original negative back. Here is a partial of the faxed photo, which was the subject of an important article by Douglas Weldon, J.D., "The Kennedy Limousine", which appeared in *Murder in Dealey Plaza* (2000):

Weldon identified the hole in the windshield, which Douglas P. Horne, who served as the Senior Analyst for Military Records for the Assassination Records Review Board (ARRB), has discussed in a 2012 article on Lew Rockwell's website. This specific image was faxed (clearly visible as a fax) showing the location that Horne (in 2009) believed proved that alterations to the photo to hide the bullet hole had not yet occurred. In later versions of this photo, this area has been so modified to obscure Agent Roy Kellerman's facial reaction to the bullet impact and the rear view mirror which was struck by the bullet as it passed through the glass, but the hole itself remains visible.

The Throat Wound

The bullet hit the President in the throat, the second of four hits he would sustain, where Malcolm Perry, M.D., would subsequently perform a simple tracheotomy incision through the wound after JFK was brought to Parkland. Dr. Perry thereafter described it three times as a wound of entry during the Parkland Press Conference, the transcript of which appears in *Assassination Science* (1998), as Appendix C; and Charles Crenshaw, M.D., who was also present in Trauma Room #1, drew diagrams at Jim Fetzer's request based upon his direct personal observations, which also appear there as Appendix A:

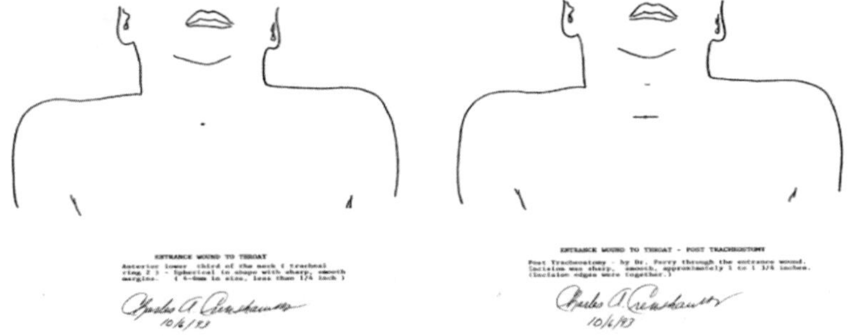

In this much clearer shot (next page, top), which was not faxed and lacks the grainy pattern of pixels that are features of the fax, the approximate location of the hole that Weldon and Horne identified in the windshield is distinguishable as a small, white spiral nebula with a dark hole in the center, where lateral cracks (discussed below) that appear to have been made by the bullet impact are not visible, because they had been masked out of the shot before THIS VERSION was released to the photographer.

As we are about to discover, multiple alterations were made to the image of the limousine in the Altgens6, where simply whiting out the dark hole at the center was the simplest move that tended to conceal the

existence of the bullet hole, but it can still be seen where JFK's left ear would be visible had it not been obscured by that image. Well aware of the problem that it posed, which revealed the existence of at least one shooter who was firing from in front of the limo rather than above and behind, as the "lone assassin" scenario requires, the Secret Service would deftly respond by effecting a substitution.

The Windshield Switch

The limo was sent to Ford its manufacturer, Ford Motor Company in Detroit, MI, on Monday, 25 November 1963, stripped down to bare metal and completely rebuilt, including replacing it with a new windshield, where the presence of the through-and-through hole was confirmed by the Ford official, George Whitaker, Sr., who had supervised its replacement, whom Doug Weldon had tracked down and interviewed.

The Secret Service, however, would later release the image of yet a third windshield and claim that it had actually been on the limousine in Dealey Plaza:

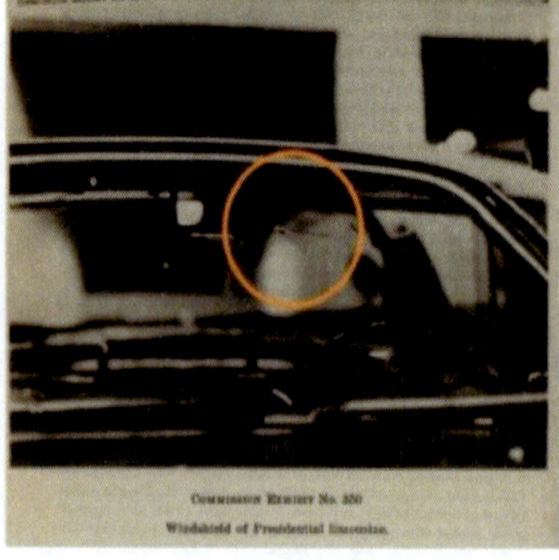

In addition to Doug Weldon's brilliant study, Douglas Horne would pursue this issue and published his confirmations of Doug Weldon's work in his own masterful five-volume work, *Inside the Assassination Records Review Board* (2009), Vol. V, pages 1439–50. There and in several other articles, including "JFK Conspiracy: The bullet hole in the Windshield" (2012), Horne summarized the testimony of a half-dozen witnesses who had observed the through-and-through bullet hole, whose existence is not in doubt, as the following testimony confirms.

The Witnesses Speak

(1) Dallas motorcycle patrolmen Stavis Ellis and H. R. Freeman both observed a penetrating bullet hole in the limousine windshield at Parkland Hospital. Ellis told interviewer Gil Toff in 1971:

"There was a hole in the left front windshield . . . You could put a pencil through it . . . you could take a regular standard writing pencil . . . and stick [it] through there." Freeman corroborated this, saying: "[I was] right beside it. I could of [sic] touched it . . . it was a bullet hole. You could tell what it was." [David Lifton published these quotations in his 1980 book, *Best Evidence: Disguise and Deception in the Assassination of John F. Kennedy*.]

(2) *St. Louis Post-Dispatch* reporter Richard Dudman wrote an article published in *The New Republic* on 21 December 1963 [and reprinted in *Assassination Science* (1998)], in which he stated: "A few of us noted the hole in the windshield when the limousine was standing at the emergency entrance after the President had been carried inside. I could not approach close enough to see which side was the cup-shaped spot which indicates a bullet had pierced the glass from the opposite side."

(3) Second year medical student Evalea Glanges, enrolled at Southwestern Medical University in Dallas, right next door to Parkland Hospital, told attorney Doug Weldon in 1999: "It was a real clean hole." In a videotaped interview aired in the suppressed Episode 7 of Nigel Turner's series, *The Men Who Killed Kennedy*, titled "*The Smoking Guns*", she said: "... it was very clear, it was a through-and-through bullet hole through the windshield of the car, from the front to the back . . . it seemed like a high-velocity bullet that had penetrated from front-to-back in that glass pane."

At the time of the interview, Glanges had risen to the position of Chairperson of the Department of Surgery, at John Peter Smith Hospital, in Fort Worth. She had been a firearms expert all her adult life.

(4) Mr. George Whitaker, Sr., a senior manager at the Ford Motor Company's River Rouge Complex in Dearborn, Michigan, told attorney (and professor of criminal justice) Doug Weldon in August of 1993, in a tape-recorded conversation, that after reporting to work on Monday, 25 November 1963, he discovered the JFK limousine—a unique, one-of-a-kind item that he unequivocally identified—in the Rouge's B Building, with the interior stripped out and in the process of being replaced, and with the windshield removed.

He was then contacted by one of the vice presidents of the division for which he worked, and directed to report to the glass plant lab, immediately. After knocking on the locked door (which he found most unusual), he was let in by two of his subordinates and discovered that they were in possession of the windshield that had been removed from the JFK limousine.

They had been told to use it as a template, and to make a new windshield identical to it in shape—and to then get the new windshield back to the B Building for installation in the Presidential limousine that was quickly being rebuilt. Whitaker told Weldon (quoting from the audiotape of the 1993 interview): "And the windshield had a bullet hole in it, coming from the outside through…it was a good, clean bullet hole, right straight through, from the front. And you can tell, when the bullet hits the windshield, like when you hit a rock or something, what happens? The back chips out and the front may just have a pinhole in it…this had a clean round hole in the front and fragmentation coming out the back."

Whitaker told Weldon that he eventually became superintendent of his division and was placed in charge of five plant divisions. He also told Weldon that the original windshield, with the bullet hole in it, had been broken up and scrapped—as ordered—after the new windshield had been made.

When Doug Weldon interviewed Whitaker in August of 1993, his witness insisted on anonymity. Weldon reported on the story without releasing Whitaker's name in his excellent and comprehensive article titled: "*The Kennedy Limousine: Dallas 1963*," which was published in Jim Fetzer's anthology, *Murder in Dealey Plaza,* in 2000. After Weldon interviewed Whitaker in August of 1993, Mr. Whitaker subsequently—on 22 November 1993 (the 30th anniversary of President Kennedy's assassination)—wrote down all he could remember about the events he witnessed involving the Presidential limousine and its windshield.

After George Whitaker's death in 2001, his family released his written testament to Nigel Turner, who with their permission revealed

Mr. Whitaker's name, as well as the text of his "memo for history," in Episode 7 of *The Men Who Killed Kennedy, "The Smoking Guns."*

In *"The Smoking Guns,"* the text of Whitaker's memo can be read on the screen employing freeze-frame technology with the DVD of the episode. It said, in part: "When [I] arrived at the lab the door was locked. I was let in. There were 2 glass engineers there. They had a car windshield that had a bullet hole in it. The hole was about 4 or 6 inches to the right of the rear view mirror [as viewed from the front]. The impact had come from the front of the windshield. (If you have spent 40 years in the glass [illegible] you know which way the impack [sic] was from."

(5) The sixth credible witness to a bullet hole in the windshield of the limousine was Secret Service Agent Charles Taylor, Jr., who wrote a report on 27 November 1963 in which he detailed his activities providing security for the limousine immediately after the car's return to Washington following the assassination. The JFK limousine and the Secret Service follow-up car known as the "Queen Mary" arrived at Andrews Air Force Base (AFB) aboard a C-130 propeller-driven cargo plane at about 8:00 PM on 22 November 1963.

Agent Taylor rode in the Presidential limousine as it was driven from Andrews AFB to the White House garage at 22nd and M Streets, N.W. In his report about what he witnessed inside the White House garage during the vehicle's inspection, he wrote: "In addition, of particular note was the small hole just left of center in the windshield from which what appeared to be bullet fragments were removed."

Outward Cracking

As Horne emphasizes, six credible witnesses—Stavis Ellis, H.R. Freeman, Richard Dudman, Evalea Glanges, George Whitaker, and Charles Taylor (who was subsequently forced to recant his report)—all testified to observing a through-and-through bullet hole in the windshield *either on the day of the assassination itself (for five of the six) or the following day (for Whitaker, who observed it at Ford when he came in to work on Monday, 25 November 1963).* Two were positive it had been caused by a shot fired from in front, which by itself falsifies the "official account" of the death of our 35th President.

Moreover, Dennis Cimino has discovered that the rear view mirror of the vehicle had bullet scuff marks on the front side facing the windshield, where it was struck by the bullet passing through from front to rear. In the below photo, taken at the Parkland Memorial Hospital after the slain president was removed from the car, both the bullet hole and some lateral outward cracking from both sides of the hole is discernible. He has marked that area with CYAN to highlight the bullet strike area:

Close examination of the vehicle's rear view mirror also seems to show the possibility of a hairline crack running from one side of that to the other side of it. The mirror partially obscures the actual bullet entry hole and some of that stress cracking, which extends for at least six or more inches behind the mirror blocked portion of the windshield, as other photos show. Some of the crack extends from upper windshield down to about mid-level on passenger front.

[NOTE: Evidence of patching done to the flip up driver's visor as well seems visible in this shot, but because it was taken so soon after the assassination, it's difficult to imagine them taping that over so quickly; but it does look very odd and appears to be worth mentioning.]

The Deeper Tint

Below is a shot of the limo, taken on 23 November 1963, the day after the assassination. Carefully compare the visibility of the doctor's coat above in this shot, showing how 'non tinted' the windshield is in the upper region, because in the lower shot, this is clearly NOT THE SAME WINDSHIELD when compared to the deeper tint below the top of the windshield, an extension of the tinting in the REPLACEMENT.

One might ask why a six or more inch strip of window tinting could be acceptable on a vehicle with any dignitary in it, let alone the President.

The Secret Service's job is to see ahead and upwards with clarity, looking for snipers or anyone who could harm the passengers of this particular car.

It doesn't make much sense that the glass would have much more than a modest narrow tint across the very top, as was the case in the Parkland Memorial Hospital photograph clearly showing. The doctor's smock is easily seen just inches from the rear view mirror. From this photograph in the garage at the White House, it's evident that this windshield is not the same one. The tinting extends easily six or more inches downward and is NOT PRESENT in the photo above, taken at Parkland Memorial the day before.

Below is a side shot, where you can again see the tint gradient, much deeper down into the windshield compared to the top photo taken immediately after the assassination occurred in Dealey Plaza that day.

So, one might well ask, given the other damage to the vehicle, including the blood and brain tissue and other parts of the now dead President, why was it imperative to change out the windshield and replace it with a much more heavily TINTED ONE?

That is a very interesting question—especially on a car where exceptionally unobscured forward visibility not only was desired, but mandatory for protection of the President and any dignitaries who may ride with him in this vehicle.

A couple of glitches

Take a good look at this one. They masked the windshield to hide the tinting, but overlapped the mask onto the chrome frame of the windshield and blowing it badly. This reveals their concern about the tint:

Following is another shot taken in the garage, from behind, showing that someone now has dropped down the glare shields on both sides to make sure we don't really get a good look at the heavy tinting of this windshield. Why? I don't think sun was a problem in the parking garage.

The Rear View Mirror

Here's a shot of the rear view mirror, facing the windshield, showing the bullet scuffing that was evident at Parkland that day after

the assassination took place. There is a scuff center of the mirror, and further to the left, another scuff, as well as the possible hint of clear adhesive tape from one side of the mirror to the other, covering the dark outer rim on both sides of the inexplicably damaged mirror.

This mirror appears to have been dented in and scratched by the entering bullet, after spinning it on its post, which comes down from the top of the windshield frame. Normal hand wear on this mirror using the anti-glare rotator tab, for example, would not account for these scuffs.

And, once again, the tinting gradient is positively not there in this mirror shot, certainly not to the extent it is in the "changed out"

windshield put in before the car went back to Washington, D.C. the next day. In this photo, the adhesive tape is much more clearly evident.

It appears to extend from one side of the mirror to the other, covering the dark outer rim on both sides. Did it crack when it was struck by the bullet?

Back at Parkland

Below is another shot of the limousine at Parkland, showing the tint gradient is not there on the car at Parkland Memorial not long after the shooting took place. Notice the bulletproof glass leaning against the leftrear fender, which was NOT USED that day, which may have protected the president had it been installed. But of course the plan was NOT TO PROTECT THE PRESIDENT BUT TO SET HIM UP. If you look closely at the second nurse on the right, her hands and smock are clearly visible with minimal tint.

Now, I have taken the liberty to add in this shot of the very very visible windshield and rear view mirror scuffing, taken at Parkland, where the bullet hole and lateral cracking is clearly evident and clearly visible to the eye.

If you look closely at the rear view mirror, you can easily see the scuffing on it. It's very evident on the lower portion of the mirror.

This is an especially important photograph, because this appears to be the third of the three windshields, which the Secret Service would

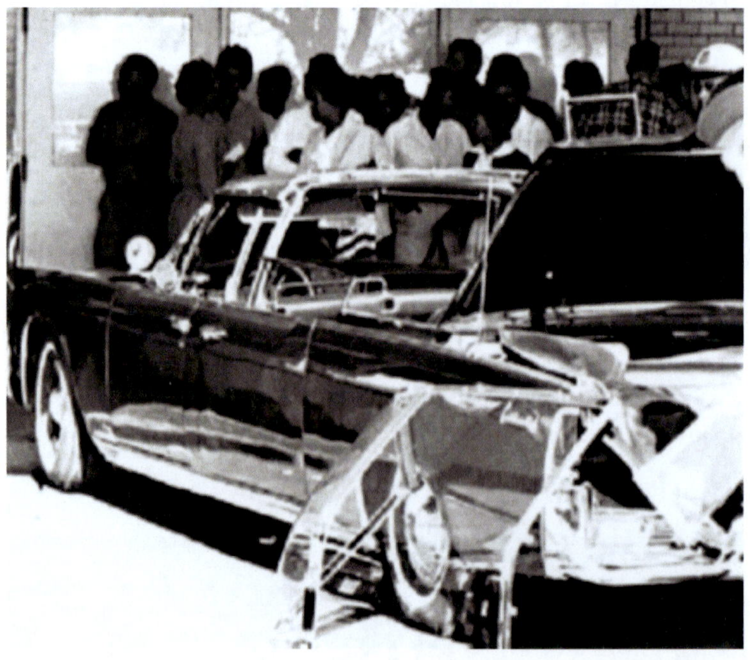

produce and which would become Warren Commission Exhibit 350 (shown above). It shows cracking caused by (what would be claimed to have been) a fragment of a shot fired from in front, where the through-and-through hole visible in some versions of the Altgens6, which six witnesses confirmed having observed, no longer exists. Notice, moreover, the absence of tinting.

And another look at the mirror. Something struck this mirror pretty

hard in the front side of it, facing the windshield, and scuffed it not only on the middle but on the left (to us) side. With such a long scuff pattern on the rear view mirror, something more than the driver's hand has to have done this. (SCUFFS MARKED IN CYAN)

Clearly the mirror is dented in based on the shading there as well. Unfortunately for the CIA, which modified the Altgens6 extensively, they had no idea that many photos of the limousine were out there that would in fact show that the vehicle took a bullet hit in the windshield, which struck the mirror, at precisely the same moment that the President is clutching at his throat just before the limo stop takes place and the fatal head shots occur.

The Beat Goes On

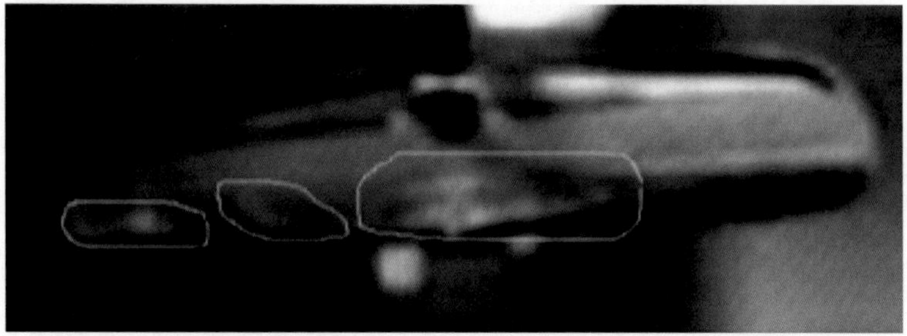

With regard to the Altgens6 shot, we have barely touched upon the other much more significant alterations done to hide the fact that Lee Harvey Oswald was standing in the doorway at the TSBD at precisely the moment this bullet made a hole in the windshield and struck the rear view mirror and JFK that morning. Other alterations to the photo, however, are the result not only of what the CIA did on that day to the original negatives and their processing but later, through the years, DIGITAL ALTERATIONS to this photo have been facilitated by the emergence of new technology.

Here is a much, much later version of Altgens6, which came from the Internet and cannot be tracked or validated as to whose custody it was in before it was published online. In this shot, you can clearly see that the Secret Service agents are very concerned, as they look at Lee Harvey Oswald and others in a very retouched portion of the photograph.

Notice the fact that JFK is clutching his throat and Texas Governor John Connally is turning. The face of Roy Kellerman is obscured here, whereas in FACSIMILE VERSION, you can see facial features much more clearly. NOTE: In this photo, the windshield damage has been altered out so it is not visible to the naked eye, and there is heavy digital alteration as well as manual cut and paste alteration in the top of the windshield. By taking that shot and turning it into a NEGATIVE, Dennis has been able to highlight the areas of alteration with regard to the windshield itself.

Thus, Dennis has marked the most heavily altered portions of the

photo with RED. Once again, comparison to the grainy FAX shot on the top of this article shows much more detail in some of these areas.

Clearly, the upper windshield area has been hazed out or altered, which is much more visible in NEGATIVE, revealing the tinting gradient on the day of the assassination. The windshield tinting was not there, which means that someone made an effort to add it in or obscure the upper windshield. The area where the bullet damage has occurred has been altered here, while the face of Agent Roy Kellerman has been

obscured. What is also evident is that in the area where Jackie Kennedy and Agent William Greer, the vehicle driver, are situated, has also been ALTERED to obfuscate them.

If you look closely at this shot in both NORMAL and in NEGATIVE, you can see what appear to be alterations to the shot. On some of these later Altgens6 photos, indications of DIGITAL alteration are in place over the more crudely done alterations when the film was first remastered by the CIA, proof that "the Agency" has an ongoing program to fake evidence in the death of our 35th President that continues to this day.

Dennis has also zoomed in to accent the obfuscation of Kellerman's face, presumably because his expression would have drawn attention to the occurrence of something that had startled him as the bullet passed through the windshield.

The scuffing on the mirror is discernible, where making a change from the white of the spiral nebula to the dark of his ear and head must have been regarded as too conspicuous to undertake.

The upper portion of the windshield appears to have been masked using a rectangular pasted object in black (on our right), then later it was decided to dab on black to obscure the upper windshield. Notice again, there is no tint on the upper portion of this windshield or it would be over Kellerman's face and uniformly across the upper portion of the windshield. Dennis has identified the portions that appear to have been altered in CYAN.

What this means is that interior portions of the limousine have also been heavily altered to obscure collateral damage from the impact while obscuring the facial expressions of both Agents Kellerman and Greer from the photograph. It also would appear that obscuration of Jackie's face took place here as well. The reason may have been that she was looking at and reacting to the bullet hole in the windshield as she held her husband's arm.

Source note: This chapter previously appeared as *"Tampering with the JFK Limo in the Altgens6", http://jamesfetzer.blogspot.com/2015/09/tamperingwith-jfk-limo-in-altgens6.html.*

13

The James "Ike" Altgens Photo Timeline

by Larry Rivera

The chronology of one of the most famous photographs in history has been deliberately obscured

Much has been written and speculated as to the authenticity and timing of the photographs taken by James "Ike" Altgens, an Associated Press photographer, on 22 November 1963.

This chapter brings forward some unknown facts and dispels some of the myths that prevail in the research community to this day.

The movements of James Altgens

In May 1964, two key articles were published which brought national attention to 42-year-old James "Ike" Altgens and his photograph. The first was Dom Bonafede's "A picture with a life of its own", published in the *New York Herald Tribune* on 24 May, which detailed Jones Harris' quest to find out who the man in the doorway really was.

The second was published the following day by Maggie Daly in the *Chicago American,* where she publicized the fact that Altgens had been within 15' of the President, yet he had not been brought to testify before the Commission. These two articles had the FBI up in arms about how to resolve the Altgens6 and its "man in the doorway" dilemma.

By the time Altgens was brought before the Commission on 22 July, he lamented how he wished it had been sooner, because he admitted that time had dulled his memory somewhat:

> "*Well I wish I would have been able to give you this information the next day when it was fresh on my mind because 6 months or so later, sometimes the facts might be just a little bit off and I hate to see it that way." (WC7H525) (it was actually 8 months)*

Altgens stated in his FBI interview 2 June 1964 that after the final shots in Dealey Plaza, and after following Secret Service men and motorcycle cops up the embankment, then placing a phone call to his office, he headed straight to the AP facilities located at *The Dallas Morning News* building, five blocks away on Houston and Young, to deliver his film for processing.

The FBI then established 12:57 PM Central Time as the time at which the Altgens6 "moved" on the wire. Quite a feat when one considers the time it would have taken for Altgens to make sure no more bullets were flying in Dealey Plaza, the time he took to follow Secret Service men and policemen into the parking lot adjacent to the railroad yard, making sure there were no other victims to photograph, make a phone call, then "dash" back to AP to develop the film. (WC7H519)

Bear in mind that Altgens never provided a precise timeline of his activities after the shots. The severely cropped photograph, however, did not appear in newspaper print until the last evening editions in only a handful of newspapers on the West Coast, and was not shown on national TV until 6:35 PM by Walter Cronkite. The rest of the nation's newspapers did not publish the Altgens6 until the following Saturday, 23 November.

From Yahoo.com: How long does it take to develop black and white film?

Best Answer: To develop negatives, the film has to be in the developer for a period of between 5 and 10 minutes (usually). Subsequent steps are required to make your negatives permanent and then the negatives must dry before printing. Plan on two darkroom sessions, 30 min. minimum for negatives and a couple of hours for printing. You probably want to contact print first. It's fairly straightforward, and you should be able to make a good one in 10-30 minutes the first time.

What really happened?

Over the years, most researchers have accepted the official version, and have never questioned the timing involved. Richard Trask interviewed Altgens back in 1985 and maintained contact with him over the years for his 1994 volume *Pictures of the Pain*. His timeline for Altgens and his photographs, has been accepted without questioning the logistics. For the sake of our discussion, and to put things into proper perspective, here is a possible timeline for James Altgens and his roll of film:

1. 12:30 PM shoots Altgens6 and Altgens7 (one to two minutes)

2. Snaps the Altgens8 photograph from his position on the south curb of Elm Street. Runs up the embankment following Secret Service agents and motorcycle cops. Amid the confusion, he must stay at least a few minutes to take in what is happening because he wants to make sure he captures the moment in which someone is arrested. (WC7H519)

Checking out the scene

3. Makes sure there are no other victims for him to photograph. (Ibid)

4. Comes down from the grassy knoll and calmly stands at the north curb for a few minutes. (Ibid)

Altgens walking down past the Newmans to the sidewalk and curb of Elm Street.

Altgens at the curb. Newmans still on the ground. Dark complected man and Umbrella man have already sat down on the lawn. Estimated time elapsed - 5 minutes.

This four image sequence shows Altgens in the Mal Couch film. While everyone is running around, he calmly stays, "to take a long look around", (WC7H519) and does not look to be in any hurry.

Bill and Gayle Newman

Ike Altgens (back towards the camera) in one of the Cancellare photographs

Bill and Gayle Newman estimated they were on the ground for three minutes. Gayle, however, stated in an affidavit taken on 22 November that they got up and laid down a second time. This could have stretched this closer to five minutes.

The Dallas Morning News — Saturday, November 22, 1986

Caught up in history

Couple, sons stood watching only feet away as JFK was slain

By John Kirkpatrick
Staff Writer of The News

Building." No names of the mother ... Newman says.

They stayed on the grass for maybe three minutes. Tentatively, they stood up. A Channel 8 reporter spotted them. Billy recognized him as the same man, Jerry Haynes, who starred in a kiddie TV show. "That man is Mr. Peppermint!"

After a TV interview, the New-...

Altgens and his "gadget bag"

5. Altgens crosses Elm Street to retrieve his gadget bag before moving on to find a "nearby phone."

Looking for a phone

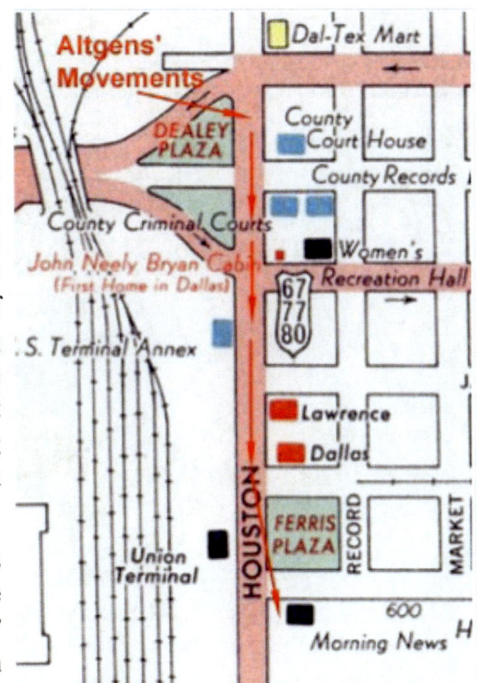

6. Locates a "nearby phone" and makes phone call to his office to inform that he has witnessed the assassination (FBI 2 June 1964 DL100-10461) (anywhere from five–10 minutes). Every member of the media was scrambling to find a phone—witness Robert McNeil who went into the TSBD looking for one! Phones were at a premium in Dealey Plaza.

7. After talking to his office about witnessing the assassination, he "dashes" or "sprints" down Houston Street, (FBI 2 June 1964 DL10010461, and WC7H519) a quarter of a mile, carrying his camera and gadget bag, five blocks to Houston and Young, to the AP office located on the third floor of *The Dallas Morning News* building. Enters building, catches an elevator, runs down the hallways, etc. (Total time six minutes)

8. Hands his camera to "someone" who rewinds unused film and removes his roll of film for processing. (five minutes)

9. Depending on the efficiency of the personnel, the film must be removed from its roll in a dark room and placed in developer solution between five and 10 minutes.

10. Film is placed in fixer solution.

11. Film is placed in washing solution.

12. Negative film is dried at least another 10 minutes.

13. First contact prints made of film roll Altgens 2-8. *Altgens1 is missing.* (10 minutes)

14. Two positive 8 1/2" x 11" prints are printed, one for processing, one for the "morgue" for storage.

15. Photographs are captioned and stamped for transmission.

16. AP supposedly sends A4, A5, A6 and A7 out on the wire (five minutes) A4, A5 and A7 are the first to be published in newspapers. A4 and A6 are shown by Cronkite at 6:35 PM on CBS.

Total minimum time: 60 minutes

Altgens4 at 6:34:29PM

Altgens6 at 6:34:46PM

The Trask Timeline

The 1994 book by Richard Trask, *Pictures of the the Pain,* dedicated an entire chapter titled "The AP Man", to the Altgen6 photograph. Trask had Altgens arriving at his office at AP by 12:39 PM, and then sticking around for a few moments to take phone calls to relay what he had witnessed. He would be sent to Parkland Hospital with AP photographer Henry Burroughs, Jr., known as the "dean of the Washington photographers," to continue covering the tragedy:

> *"Someone grabbed my camera, removed the film and took it to process it, because they wanted me on the telephone reporting what I saw. We did an extraordinary good job, because within 20 minutes of the assassination we had a picture rolling on the wire–and that's good. All over the world, at the same time that people got it in the U. S. of A. It was fantastic. I saw some of the cable photos that came back in that night, and one or more of the pictures I had taken were on page one of many of the world newspapers." (Trask p. 318)*

Trask never mentions the fact that Altgens called his office from "a nearby phone" as documented in his FBI interview (FBI 2 June 1964 DL100-10461). The report states he sprinted back *after talking on this phone.* Trask writes that Altgens informed AP Bureau Chief Bob Johnson about Kennedy being shot, when he arrived at the AP offices, after his mad dash down Houston Street. Trask concluded his timeline by asserting that Altgens6 was sent out at 1:03 PM, which is also in conflict with the time of 12:57 PM established by the FBI in the interview of 2

June 1964. Trask conducted his interviews of Altgens on 21 November 1985, 22 years after the assassination.

Someone grabbed his camera

Another issue that is not explained by Trask, is that if someone grabbed his camera as he entered the AP offices, *it had to have been because they already knew about his pictures,* of which he informed Johnson in his phone call beforehand, while he was still in the field. The "someone" who grabbed his camera was never identified, despite Altgens having been on the job there for 26 years and probably knew everyone who worked there.

It must be noted here that Altgens was primarily a wirephoto operator and photographer who did all of the processing of the photographs that he took, from developing negatives, to printing and captioning, to actually working the transmitting equipment thermofax machines, during all of his career at AP in Dallas. It seems odd that on this particular day he would have been sent to continue covering the assassination at Parkland, especially when they already had Henry Burroughs carrying out that task. (Trask p. 318)

Usually Altgens captioned the photographs that he sent on the wire. According to Trask, the sign-off of the captioned wirephoto read: "AP Wirephoto cel61303 stf- jwa." This indicates that one Carl E. Linde operated the wirefax machine and sent out a photograph taken by James

W. Altgens on a Friday, at 1:03 PM. Trask writes that Altgens witnessed the transmission. (The rest of this study will argue for the improbability of this timeline.)

Problems with the official timeline

This FBI Report by itself derails the Trask timeline:

ALTGENS advised that as the President's car disappeared he observed some Secret Service Agents and police officers with drawn guns on the north side of Elm Street running in the direction of the top of the triple overpass. He said he thought they were chasing someone who had fled from somewhere behind the President. ALTGENS related he also ran in this direction. After proceeding across Elm Street and up toward the triple overpass, ALTGENS stated he met the police officers returning. At this juncture, ALTGENS advised he then ran to a nearby telephone and informed his office that the President had been shot and that he had witnessed it. He then sprinted to his office in the Dallas News Building with the pictures he had taken. ALTGENS stated the pictures showing the President slumping in his seat with Mrs. KENNEDY bending over him moved on the Associated Press Wirephoto Network at 12:57 p.m. which was 17 minutes after the first news bulletin was sent out by Associated Press

on 6/2/64 at Dallas, Texas File # DL 100-10461

by Special Agent A. RAYMOND SWITZER and EUGENE F. PETRAKIS:vm Date dictated 6/3/64

This document contains neither recommendations nor conclusions of the FBI. It is the property of the FBI and is loaned to your agency; it and its contents are not to be distributed outside your agency.

The obvious question that needs to be answered here is why the FBI misrepresented the time the cropped Altgens6 was sent out on the wire on 22 November 1963.

In his Warren Commission testimony, Altgens made it quite clear that Secret Service men and motorcycle policemen went up the embankment toward the picket fence area. Amazingly **[Note: although today we know why],** Wesley Liebeler cut him off at that moment to ask him to elaborate as to the "little incline":

There was utter confusion at the time I crossed the street. The Secret Service men, uniformed policemen with drawn guns that went racing up this little incline and I thought—— WC7H519

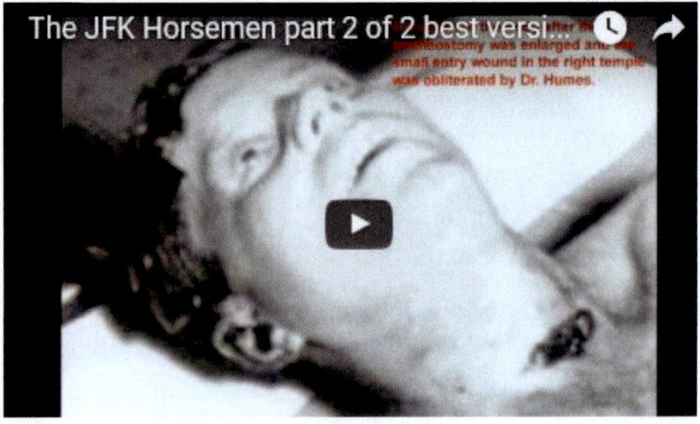

https://youtu.be/DP7YvelagHA

Lingering at Dealey Plaza

He then explained why he stuck around Dealey Plaza for quite some time:

> Mr. ALTGENS. Yes, sir.
>
> I started up the incline with—or, after the officers, because they were moving well ahead of me and I was moving behind them thinking perhaps if they had the assassin cornered I wanted a picture, but before I had gotten over one-quarter of the way up the incline, I met the officers coming back and I presumed that they were just chasing shadows, so to speak, because there was no assassin in the area apparently, but I didn't learn the location of the sniper's nest until I was en route out to Parkland Hospital to continue my assignment and I heard it on the radio, that the assassin's nest was in the sixth floor window of the Book Depository Building.
>
> After that I made a good look through this area to see that no one else had been hit. I noticed the couple that were on the ground over here with their children, I saw them when they went down and they were in the area and laid there some time after the Presidential car had disappeared.
>
> Mr. LIEBELER. They threw themselves on the ground in this grassy area that I have just described previously where you ran across after this last shot?
>
> Mr. ALTGENS. Yes; but they were not hit. I looked at them and they weren't hit by a bullet, so I took another long look around before I started my dash back to the office, and as it turned out, my report was the first that our service had on the assassination and my pictures were the only pictures we had available for a period of about 24 hours. **WC7H519**

Interestingly enough, when one compares his Warren Commission testimony vis-à-vis his FBI interview of 2 June 1964, we note that in his Warren Commission testimony he does not mention placing his phone call to his office, conversely, in his FBI interview he does not mention staying to make sure there were no other victims, and taking another "long look around". Perhaps that is the reason why the Warren Commission decided to drag their feet and were not overly excited about deposing James Altgens.

Needless to say, the timeline claimed by the FBI in their report of 2 June 1964 is physically impossible. Altgens would have taken at least 20–25 minutes, just to get back to his office. It would have taken 30-35 minutes just to process his roll of film. The earliest Altgens' photographs could have been sent out via thermofax would have been 1:30 PM.

Another interesting tidbit about his Warren Commission testimony and the Trask timeline is the fact that he continued his assignment on to Parkland Hospital. This confirms that he was not around when his film was processed, therefore, Altgens did not really know the results of what he shot that day. Roy Schaeffer has been more specific about this, stating, "*They sent him to Parkland to get him out of the way.*"

The Roy Schaeffer Timeline

Recently, Mr. Roy Schaeffer and this author have painstakingly reviewed and revisited the Trask timeline and Altgens' FBI and Warren Commission interviews. Roy grew up in Dayton, Ohio and was reared in the newspaper business. In the 1950s his father was president of the typographical union in Dayton, Ohio, where his responsibilities included negotiating labor contracts between the union and newspapers all over the United States, including most major newspapers such as *The New York Times, Los Angeles Times, San Francisco Chronicle,* to name just a few. Roy can be considered an expert of the highest order, with intricate knowledge of the newspaper business of the late '50s and early '60s and beyond.

As fate would have it, Roy happened to be the person at the *Dayton Daily News* who received the Moorman and Altgens6 photographs and removed them from the thermofax machine at 7:15 AM on Saturday 23 November 1963. Schaeffer is extremely well-informed on alteration techniques and procedures, and the equipment necessary to make these changes. Immediately he noticed opaquing techniques on the images that were received that morning.

The very first thing we wanted to know from Roy was specifically, if the image taken off of a unifax machine was of sufficient quality that it could have been used to make alterations. Mr. Schaeffer answered this would not have been possible. Any alterations had to have been made locally in Dallas using the original negative, or the original negative flown that afternoon to a place with the proper equipment to realize any alterations. Here is what Schaeffer had to say about this:

> "*Only the negative from Altgens film was ready to be altered in about 2 1/2 hours after it being delivered to* [The Dallas Morning News]. *Two positives then had to be made off the original negative. One print went into the AP morgue and the other to the wire operator who wrote the caption prior to it being sent over the wire. So either the negative had to be altered by a film stripper or a print of the original was made and then masking and opaquing of the positive had to occur prior to it being sent over the wire. This would take about two hours.*
>
> *My best guess that the altered original ran five hours later in altered condition over the wire with its caption. Then after a newspaper receives the AP wire it takes another 2 hours to use a*

line camera and make two copies. One with a 55 line screen on it. Then a zinc engraving has to be made for a newspaper to run the AP altered wire."

"I think the main reason Altgens made his statement as such was he knew the negative film was replaced with an altered negative. I pointed this out to Burl Osborn, Pres. of [The Dallas Morning News] *in 1994. He then referred it over to his lawyer who declined to expose this fact."*

"In about 2004 I contacted the president of World Wide who then owned Altgens which was altered. I proved this in 1989 when I was sent 5 and 6 for book publication." (email 19 March 2015)

"Once a fax comes off the wire, crude opaquing could be used. If it did occur, the opaque area would be darker or lighter than the rest of the altered photo. All the alterations of the Moorman and Altgens#6 were done prior to them being sent over the wire." (email 21 March 2015)

Schaeffer tried for many years to get *The Dallas Morning News* to admit to the alterations of the Altgens and Moorman photographs, but to no avail. The fact that the original "morgue" copies of Altgens photographs were never shown, speaks volumes of the secrecy with which the photographs were treated.

He believes the original, unaltered Altgens first generation positive prints still exist somewhere.

Why the alterations were made in Dallas

In completing our discussion of the Altgens timeline it is important to establish when his images showed up in newspapers that day. The first Altgens photos that were published on the East Coast and middle America newspapers were Altgens4 and Altgens7. Here is a sampling:

Altgens7: *OKC Times, The Evening Press* (Binghamton, N.Y.), *The Sun* (Lowell, Mass.), *Daily News* (5 PM Late News edition), *The Bay City Times* (Mich.), *The Sheboygan Press* (Wisc.)[1] *Tulsa Tribune, The Muncie Star, Chattanooga Times Free Press* (night final), *Atlanta Journal* (3rd Extra)

Altgens4: *The Daily News* (Longview, Wash.), *The Seattle Times* (final)

[1] Note: One very strange case was *The Sheboygan Press,* where Ralph Cinque has proven that two different front pages are in circulation, an original one which did not contain the Altgens6 and a second one which contained both the Altgens6 and Altgens7 photographs.

In the hypothetical case that the negative was flown out of Dallas early that afternoon, the time of transportation via flight would have been added onto the time required for alteration, in order to make it on time to publish on the West Coast and shown by Cronkite at 6:35 PM EST.

CBS, ABC and NBC first photos not Altgens'

Despite the claims by Trask—that with unprecedented efficiency, Associated Press had the Altgens images distributed on the wire—there is nothing further from the truth. At 2:08 PM EST, 1:08 PM CST 38 minutes after the assassination, Cronkite showed this UPI photograph and it was not one of Altgens' photographs (lower left):

CBS (left) and NBC (right) showed the same UPI photograph, which was transmitted and received on the wirephoto thermofax machine, around the same time of 2:08PM Eastern.

And ABC showed it almost simultaneously:

ABC News Ron Cochran shows the first UPI wirephoto on national television

Furthermore, this same UPI photograph was the very first one published in afternoon newspaper and extra editions that day. This one is from the *New York World-Telegram:*

And this is the original, non-cropped UPI photograph:

The race to publish was on

It is quite obvious that the media were competing with each other to get the "scoop" in before the competition. AP and UPI were mortal enemies in this battle. (Trask p. 391) the *Dallas Times Herald* and *The Dallas Morning News* had couriers who were scooping up and catching rolls of film from photographers riding in the camera cars, (Trask top of pg, 312 Featherstone, p. 439 top).

One particular instance, which came to the attention of the Warren Commission was when *Dallas Times Herald* photographer Bob Jackson tossed a roll of film to courier Jim Featherstone as camera car #3 was on Main Street and close to making the turn onto Houston Street. He misjudged its flight in the wind and allowed it to fall and roll onto the pavement, much to the amusement of his colleagues in camera car #3. (WC2H158, Trask 439) Featherstone then rushed this roll of film over to the *Times Herald* installations on Pacific Avenue for immediate distribution nationwide via wirephoto.

Cronkite showed this cropped photo (left) at 2:32PM (1:32PM Dallas Time), wired by *The Dallas Times Herald*. ABC followed suit and showed the same photograph (right) at around the same time. NBC did not show this photograph.

The next photo, taken as JFK's limousine made the turn onto Main Street, which was in that specific roll of film, was made available to the media roughly within an hour of the assassination. The photo was severely cropped, see entire photograph below.

John Caldbick was 17-years-old and had just started working the day before as a copyboy at the *Seattle Post Intelligencer.*

This is how he described the scene that day:

"Smaller groups gathered around the UPI Wirephoto and AP Telephoto machines, primitive faxes that took about five minutes to squeeze out a bad picture on wet, tissue-like paper that always made my fingers feel weird. It was like watching a movie in extreme slow motion, the image burned into the chemicals of the paper one thin scanned line at a time, slowly building up to an entire picture and caption.

Then there'd be a brief pause, and another one would start its slow vertical climb out of the machine. One of the staff artists' main and most hated jobs was retouching these things to make them passably usable. The first photo I remember seeing that day was of the Kennedys smiling and waving from the limousine, taken just a few minutes before the shots were fired:" (See image above Dallas Times Herald) (From: http://www. historylink. org/_content/printer_friendly/pf_output.cfm?file_id=10670)

Original, non-cropped version of the Dallas Times Herald photograph

Here is a sample of a retouched wirephoto as noted by Caldbick above:

This scan by Richard Hooke of the *Oakland Tribune* of the late afternoon of 22 November 1963 shows an extremely cropped wirephoto with obvious retouching showing tracing around JFK's head, the rear view mirror, Connally's head, Kellerman's shoulders and head, sun visors, to name just a few. Exactly the procedure described by Caldbick above: *"One of the staff artists' main and most hated jobs was retouching these things to make them passably usable."*

The competition continues

The Associated Press was definitely in this horse race to get photographs out nationwide. The first Associated Press wirephoto shown on 22 November by NBC was this one:

AP wirephoto showing JFK, Governor Connally, and Jackie at Love Field shown by NBC at 2:07PM Eastern

Robert Groden's 1993 book *The Killing of a President* credited AP/ Worldwide with the following photograph. This proves that the Associated Press was actively transmitting photographs early that afternoon, and raises the question as to why the Altgens photographs were delayed when compared to the rest of the photographs that they were distributing that day.

Amazingly enough, the next photograph to make its way on television was the Cancellare photograph shown earlier in this study, which depicts the backside of Ike Altgens. It was broadcast by NBC at 2:40 PM that afternoon!

This simple chronological order of the wirephotos that were transmitted by different media that day suggests that they were taking no prisoners when it came to getting the scoop over the competition. Conspicuous by its absence, however, were Altgens photographs. Simply put, they were not shown on television that afternoon, and only made their way onto newspapers very late that day.

Coupled with our analysis of the time it would have taken James "Ike" Altgens to make his film available to the media, and the obvious delay his photos underwent, this now raises serious questions as to the real trajectory of his roll of film. We must now consider a more nefarious scenario.

The Jaggars-Chiles-Stovall Connection

"I have long suspected that all is not right with that firm" –Beverly Brunson

JFK researchers are very familiar with the firm Jaggars-Chiles-Stovall, Inc. (JCS). It was Lee Oswald's second place of employment after he came back from the Soviet Union, and he worked there for six months between October 1962 to April 1963. As we shall now see, many loose ends and unanswered questions remained in the investigation of this company, some of which we will now attempt to bring into focus.

JAGGARS-CHILES-STOVALL INC
522 Browder-RI 1-5501
Jaggars Prntg Co—See
Jaggars-Chiles-Stovall Inc
[1965 Phone Book listing]

We decided to take another look at the physical layout of downtown Dallas and noted that the address of Jaggars-Chiles-Stovall, at 522 Browder Street, was in close proximity to Dallas City Hall, which in 1963 was on Harwood Street, and to *The Dallas Morning News* Building at Houston and Young (see map). In the 2014 article "The Cartha Deloach Memorandum", we inferred the possibility that JCS, a company which did contract work for the CIA in the area of top secret maps for the U.S. military, appears to have had a role in the alteration of the Altgens6 photograph that afternoon, before it was sent on the wire to newspapers.

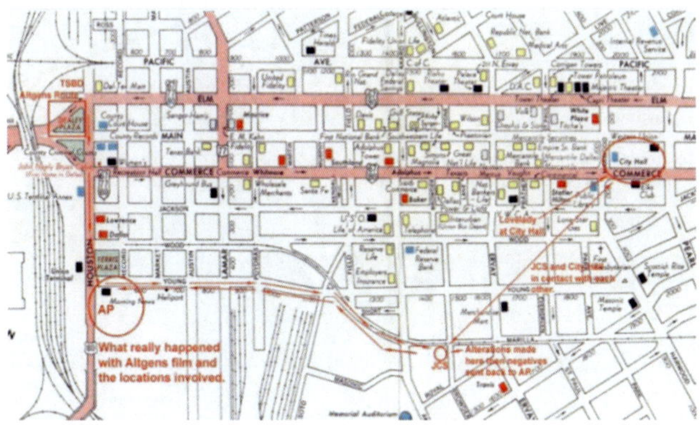

Citing British researcher Paul Rigby's timeline, the article established at least a three-hour window before the Altgens6 was published in newspapers on the West Coast. The East Coast papers did not publish the photograph until the following Saturday, and Walter Cronkite did not show the photograph until 6:35 PM Eastern Time. Brunson's suspicion of JCS was well founded. On 26 October 1991, author Harry Livingstone interviewed the Reverend Jack Shaw in relation to his research on Roscoe White.

In passing, Reverend Shaw stated that JCS, which was located downtown at 522 Browder Street, was used as a base of operations for the assassination. (HT2 466). Brunson in her studies notes that Seth Kantor had written an account of his experiences that day which was published as an exhibit in Volume 20.

The fact that Seth Kantor reported that a JCS employee was responsible for spreading a "rumor" about another wounded victim makes this information extremely significant. It indicates that at least one JCS employee was actively involved in the propagation of information (or disinformation) during the assassination. (Kantor Exhibit 4 Vol 20):

1 p.m.) I went ot an office down the hall and placed a call to Washington. It was difficult getting a line out of the hospital. The nurses in this office-- there were a handful-- seemed to be stunned-- and they looked at each other dreadfully as they listened to my conversation to Washington. A western union man who had been with us since we came down from from Andrews Air Force Base came into the office. A nurse asked him about a report that a Secret Service agent had been killed out on the street. He said then it was true. This was one of the immediate rumors which sprung up . It took several days for this particular rumor not to be believed in Dallas itself (fellow in Jaggars-Chiles-Stovall) who got it from a friend who got it from a postman supposed to have been at the death scene that the shot and bleeding SS man was picked up and whisked away and it was all hushed up. Why? I asked. Because they even have to die in secret, he said. He and others hinted that maybe the SS man was in on the plot to kill the President.)

Kantor Exhibit 4, WC20H410

In a very rare 1978 letter from the great Sylvia Meagher to Harold Weisberg, after reviewing Edward Epstein's book *Legend: The Secret World of Lee Harvey Oswald*, Sylvia had this to say about her suspicions of JCS, and their role in setting up Lee Oswald as the patsy:

The interesting thing about this rumor is that Kantor gives someone from Jaggars Chiles Stovall part of the credit for spreading the rumor. I have long thought, because of the "Walker" letter, which denotes a time when Oswald had to be working for Jaggars-Chiles Stovall. and was yet engaging in some mysterious activity,(which Jaggars must have covered at least when they turned over work reports that indicated Oswald was regularly employed from Oct. 13 to April 6th) -I have long suspected that all is not right with that firm. Ofstein their employee thought so too. If Jaggars-Chiles-Stovall was interested in spreading a rumor that a secret service man was wounded (Kantor also says that the rumor incorporated that the secret service man was in on the plot to kill Kennedy), then it could only have been to explain that spot of blood which so many saw that day, and to scotch the rumor that it was ~~xxx~~ the motorcycle officer who was wounded.

"The second item is Epstein's claim in the body of the book that John Bowen (at JCS) and Gary Taylor both saw the rifle in Oswald's possession (in the footnote, this is changed to Gary Taylor and Alexandra de M. Taylor, with Bowen dropped). But Gary Taylor said no such thing in his Warren Commission testimony–why should one believe him now? As for Bowen, he is an ex-convict, using an alias, and I would like to know if he was paid for giving Epstein an interview."

What *was* Jaggars-Chiles-Stovall doing?

In his book *Spy Saga: Lee Harvey Oswald and U.S. Intelligence*, Phillip Melanson observes that this company had been practically ignored by previous researchers. When he dug a little deeper, he noted that Lee Oswald had annotated two intriguing terms in his address book below the reference to the company: "Typography" and "microdots." This led Melanson to try to contact ex-employees of the company and on 14 May 1981 he spoke to Mr. Steven Baker. Baker confirmed for Melanson what John Graef had already told the Commission in 1964 in this excerpt from *Spy Saga:*

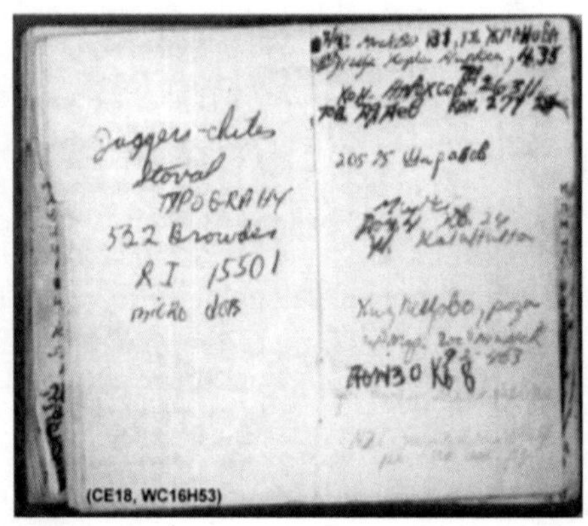

(CE18, WC16H53)

"These references have been only partially deciphered by previous research. 522 Browder Street was the Dallas address of the Jaggars firm; RI1 1150, its telephone number. Typography can refer to almost any aspect of the advertising or printing trade, from typesetting to photographic composition. In May 1981 the author talked with Mr. Steven Baker, who then worked in Jaggars' advertising department."

He indicated that at Jaggars, typography had a more specialized meaning: it described the sophisticated techniques of photographic reduction and modification performed by the firm in its advertising work.

In 1962–63, Baker asserted, Jaggars used "modification cameras" and other complex equipment which were more sophisticated than the photographic equipment available in most photo labs. 67Microdot is a system employed in espionage to store and transmit intelligence data.

Using sophisticated techniques of photographic reduction, the system affords the storage of large volumes of strategic information within a tiny spot the size of a semicolon or an exclamation point. Such a spot is then concealed within the text of a letter or document for storage or transmittal. It might be fruitful to examine all of Oswald's correspondence, notes and documents to see if any contain microdot.

Neither the Warren Commission nor the House Committee did that. If microdot data could be found, it might reveal much about Oswald's spy missions and about the identity of those who controlled him. If the Commission or the Committee had become curious about microdots, however, they most likely would have asked the nation's premier espionage agency to analyze Oswald's papers."

Melanson also acknowledged that Jaggars employees and management claimed ignorance about microdots, but in the final analysis, it is obvious that this type of classified work would have been denied in any investigative setting.

Photo manipulation capabilities

Surely, any outfit equipped to manufacture microdots would have had unlimited capabilities of photographic manipulation. A microdot is in effect *a reduced negative, and as we shall see, the re-generation of the Altgens negatives after alteration of the photographs, is fundamental to the production of positive prints for later dissemination.*

This is how John Graef, who was director of the photographic department at JCS, (Vol 10 p. 175) described their capabilities:

Mr. GRAEF. That's correct. All our cameras are different from the ordinary cameras you find in commercial printing shops or printing establishments.

Mr. JENNER. Are these portable cameras or fixed cameras?

Mr. GRAEF. No, fixed cameras—dark room cameras.

Mr. JENNER. When I used the expression "fixed," I had in my own mind that they would be these large-size cameras, fixed in the sense that they would be adjacent to a wall or a bench or a table.

Mr. GRAEF. Or the floor?

Mr. JENNER. Or the floor.

Mr. GRAEF. Yes.

Mr. JENNER. And be so heavy as not to be portable or so firmly secured as not to be removable?

Mr. GRAEF. Yes; that's right.

Mr. JENNER. Would you indicate their size?

Mr. GRAEF. I would say approximately 8 feet long total length, with 6 or 7 feet of the front of the camera projecting through a wall, which on the outside of that wall have the exposure lights to light whatever you are going to shoot. Then, the back of the camera sticks through the wall in the darkroom and on the back of the camera, of course, you place your light-sensitive film and make your exposure this way.

Mr. JENNER. And do you use light-sensitive film plates?

Mr. GRAEF. No; ordinary commercial Litho film or Ortho film that are generally available from large companies.

Mr. JENNER. Indicate the size of the frames?

Mr. GRAEF. Approximately 20 by 24 inches. The difference in these cameras—they are commonly known as modification cameras. As I said previously, you could take a line of type and twist it or curve it or stretch it out of proportion. As they are different compared with ordinary cameras that are used in most places throughout the country in that they do not have any scales on them. Ordinarily you measure a piece of copy and you set the cameras on a certain number, and for example, the same size—if you wanted to make the same size shot, you would set your copy board on No. 1, and you would set your film carrier on No. 1, put your film in and make your exposure, and you get a same size shot, but our cameras have no scales and you have to find visually and manually your sizes, everything is flexible on the camera. The boards move——

Mr. JENNER. What boards?

Mr. GRAEF. The copy boards can twist. The film carrier can twist.

Mr. JENNER. When you say "twist" do you mean twist the image?

Mr. GRAEF. On its axis—actually twist on its axis.

Mr. JENNER. You mean "twist" as distinguished from "turn"?

Mr. GRAEF. Well, let me say "turn"—then. Can turn on its axis. The lens camera can be shifted up or down or to the right or left. There are various devices that are supplied with the camera, consisting of prisms through which you can make distortions, various other forms which can be used to make various complicated bends and waves in type or illustrations, or what have you.

Mr. JENNER. Now, the bends or waves—when you say bends or waves in type, you mean you do not bend or twist the copy itself—that is, the thing to be photographed, but by use of prisms and other distortion devices, the image implanted on the film is a twist or distortion of the copy or photograph?

Mr. GRAEF. Yes; except we do both.

Clearly, these passages describe very specialized work in the field of photographic optics, enhancement and manipulation using equipment not normally found in commercial facilities. In his effort to please the Commission, perhaps Graef was just a little bit too revealing about the capabilities of JCS.

Mr. JENNER. You do straight photographing as well as distortion photography?

Mr. GRAEF. Well, many times, we will take the actual copy and twist it. Anything goes to get the final results, whatever has to be done, for example if we want to make a curved shot of a label, a flat two-dimensional label, a printed label, and we wanted to curve that label, we might take an empty tin can and paste that on the tin can and tip the tin can so that the lens looking at it would pickup the curve. We would tilt the can to such a degree that the lens in its position would pickup this curve of the label, and, of course, we would make an exposure, so anything goes in camera modification.

You start with the fundamentals of learning film and paper; the characteristics of them—we have many grades of paper, many contrasts of paper; we have several different varieties of film; the time developing these various papers—all of these have to be learned by an applicant before he can go on to beginning the camera, so it is a progression of a trade that takes time.

Mr. JENNER. Does this include color work?

Mr. GRAEF. No; all black and white.

Mr. JENNER. Oh, all black and white?

Mr. GRAEF. All black and white. We shoot color copy occasionally, but we don't do color work.

Mr. JENNER. That is, when I say color work, I intended two things—first, color film and secondly, colored ultimate product.

Mr. GRAEF. Colored film, no; we do not develop colored film and we don't shoot colored film. We might, in black and white, make a two-color a set of two-color negatives or something, for example, we might shoot part of a label and furnish a negative that would print the black on something and we might furnish an additional negative that would register with the first, that would print a color. For example, a colored border around the black copy and we

Which again brings us back to the Altgens6 and Altgens7 photographs. It has been pointed out by researchers how fast key TSBD witnesses Billy Lovelady, Bill Shelley, Danny Arce, Bonnie Ray Williams, Charles Givens, and others were taken to City Hall for affidavits that day, literally before there had been a chance for the smoke to clear in Dealey Plaza.

Other witnesses like Bill and Gayle Newman were taken to the sheriff's office on Main Street, a classic example of divide and conquer tactics. Furthermore, Buell Wesley Frazier, another employee and possible patsy, who was on the steps of the entrance, was missing in action, and was not heard from until 6 PM later that day. The logistics would have dictated the need to divide and control these key witnesses.

In Lovelady's case, we know that Detective James Leavelle took his affidavit at City Hall that afternoon:

After the arrest of Oswald at the Texas Theatre I was told over the police radio that Squad 91 had the witness to the shooting and was enroute to the city hall. I then returned to the city hall and my office. I assisted other officers in taking affidavits an answering the telephone. I took affidavits from Charles Douglas Givins and Billy Nolan Lovelady.

James Leavelle #36 Report

Because of the obvious reactions of Secret Service agents John Ready and Paul Landis, who are seen looking in the direction of the TSBD, Altgens6 offered the conspirators a perfect opportunity to show the world from where the shots should be perceived.

If you were trying to frame the patsy, this image was perfect "evidence" that the shots were fired from behind Kennedy, the building where Lee Oswald worked.

The unwanted evidence

The only problem they confronted was a plethora of unwanted evidence captured in the photograph, specifically the people in the doorway, and the reactions of Roy Kellerman, Bill Greer and Emory Roberts.

Other people standing at the curb had to be air-brushed out as well, apparently people who were not supposed to be in Dealey Plaza that day.

As mentioned earlier, the very first versions of the photograph were severely cropped. The first attempt to show the non-cropped photograph was this one by *The Saturday Evening Post* of 14 December 1963:

Even this version of Altgens6 was not intact, where the top portion had been cropped to remove the upper parts of the fire escape of the Dal-Tex Building in the background. To this day it is unknown how far up the original photograph reached. (Weisberg WWII)

By far, the largest obstacle preventing the immediate dissemination of Altgens6 had to be the presence of *Lee Oswald, Buell Wesley Frazier, Billy Lovelady and Joe Molina in the doorway. All of them were potential patsies.*

That would have been the primary reason to send the negatives on to JCS for alteration. All four of these men were altered in one way or another.

Then, the government tried desperately to convince the critics that the man in the doorway was really Billy Lovelady, by co-opting and intimidating a couple of witnesses into identifying Doorman as Lovelady.

The prize for identifying Oswald—that they themselves would not be accused of pulling the trigger.

As mentioned earlier in the article by Bonafede, Jones Harris actually commissioned a thorough study by an expert by the name of Bernard Hoffman, which enhanced the extant photograph, and only served to raise even more questions which prevail to this day.

To his credit, Harris tried everything in his power to obtain a photograph of Billy Lovelady for comparison, and was met with hostile resistance in Dallas every time.

This photograph immediately induced early researchers Harold Weisberg, Shirley Martin, Beverly Brunson and many others to break out their magnifying glasses and study every last pixel of the image.

The alterations are numerous and need to be broken down in left and right halves as shown in these brightness adjusted images:

But the alterations were not limited to Altgens6. Many researchers have discovered that Altgens7 is also rich in alterations:

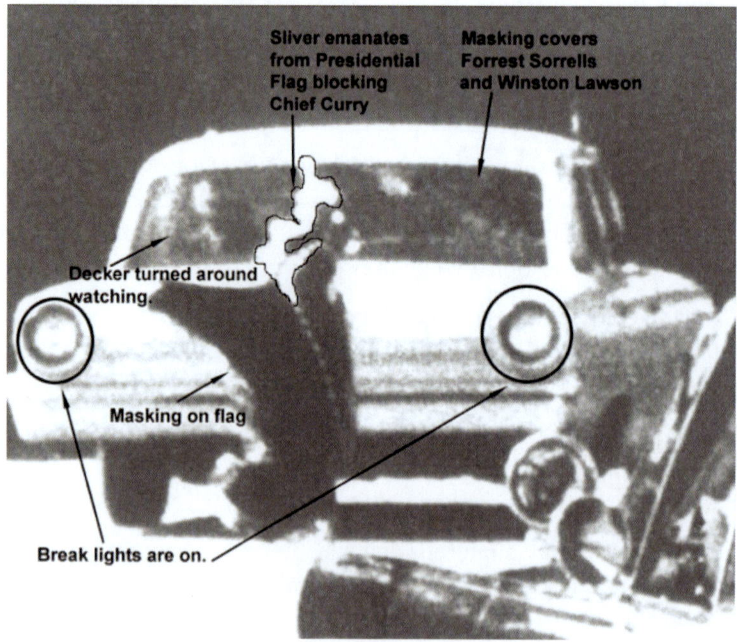

The Presidential Flag

The key to understanding the alterations to Altgens7 can be found in the Presidential Flag. As seen above in Willis slide number two, the border of the flag contained a golden fringe, which was uniform on three sides—top, bottom and outer.

(Fringes on flags are used in formal settings such as parades, inaugurations, dedication ceremonies, etc.) Furthermore, this particular Presidential Flag had no loose tassels or any other loose ornaments.

Altgens7 contains a prominent sliver of sorts which conveniently splits the rear windshield, facilitating masking and opaquing on the right side of the glass, while covering Chief Curry.

Altgens 5

Altgens 6

Altgens 7

Presidential Flag comparison in Altgens photos

Schaeffer describes this alteration: *"They added a slight white opaque to the top of the flag to conceal the slight masking on the rear of Curry's back car windshield to help hide their view in the plaza."*

Altgens7

Altgens7, the next photograph, which was sent on the wire, scanned from the original copy of *The New York Times* of 23 November 1963. Sheriff Bill Decker and the left tail light have been cropped out, as well as the upper portion of the photograph which showed the top portion of the overpass:

WHEN THE BULLETS STRUCK: Mrs. Kennedy moving to the aid of the President after he was hit by a sniper yesterday in Dallas. A guard mounts rear bumper. Gov. John B. Connally Jr. of Texas, also in the car, was wounded.

After showing that alterations were indeed performed on these photographs, the obvious question remains: where could these alterations have taken place?

Roy Schaeffer breaks this down:

> *"In truth, I think three places could have altered Altgens6 photo. Assuming that JCS could have done it,* The Dallas Morning News *had the equipment to do so. The key thing is where the negative was developed and looked at."* (email 20 March 2015)
>
> *"The Altgens photo could have been altered at JCS or* The Dallas Morning News. *For example, the* Dayton Daily News *would use what is called a Job Shop, Craftsman photo craft. The newspaper would use this if they didn't have the necessary equipment to*

change a photo or mask out or opaque certain things in the photo or negative that the newspaper didn't want published.

"I am on the fence about as whether The Dallas Morning News *or JCS altered the Altgens film. One thing for sure, a copy of the original film strip was remade or re-shot after it was altered. This could have been done at the JCS. No newspaper has this equipment. Period."* (email 25 March 2015)

Once more, *the revelations of the Reverend Shaw, who told Harry Livingstone that JCS was used as a base of operations for the assassination, make this outfit the primary suspected culprit for the* activities whereupon the Altgens photographs would have been altered. We have shown here that they certainly had the capability and equipment to do so. *The Dallas Morning News* building, which housed the AP office, was a hub of frenzied activity that afternoon and weekend.

Any activity involving photos of the assassination would have attracted an inordinate amount of attention. The physical proximity of JCS, only eight short blocks east, in a very quiet and unassuming setting, and in relative proximity of City Hall on Harwood Street, would have made JCS the ideal venue for this type of operation.

Once the altered negative was produced, it would quietly make its way back to *The Dallas Morning News* building at Houston and Young for nationwide distribution.

One final argument in favor of JCS, has to be the simple fact that Oswald had worked there for six months from 13 October 1962 to 6 April 1963: his appearance and physical characteristics were very well-known to the company.

A possible scenario

Based on the arguments presented so far, which casts great suspicion JCS, ***here is one possible scenario:***

Altgens arrives at 12:50–12:55 PM at the AP facilities on the third floor of the *Dallas Morning News* building at Houston and Young, and "someone" grabs his camera because they already know he has witnessed the assassination, and has potentially explosive photographs, having discussed this by telephone with his boss Bob Johnson prior to arriving, while he was still in Dealey Plaza. This "someone" has never been identified. In trying to beat out the competition to put photographs on the wire as soon as possible, the negative is developed and examined on a light table. The first 8½" x 11" prints are made, one of which goes to the "morgue".

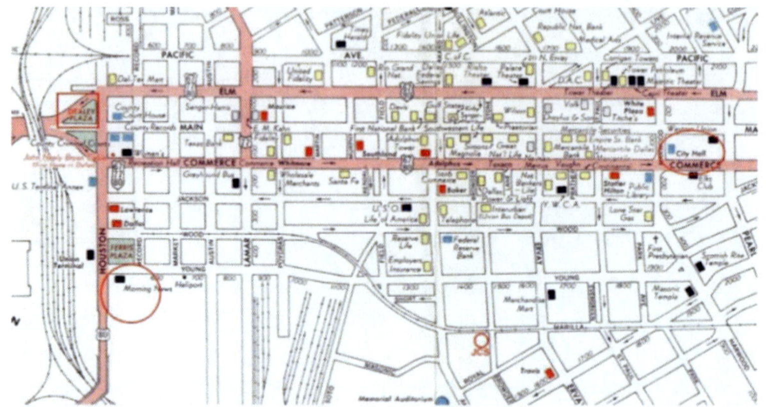

Judging by the swiftness with which competitors the *Dallas Times Herald* and UPI have put some of their photos on the wire that day, with couriers intercepting photographers riding in camera cars, it can be safely assumed that Altgens' negatives are available within an hour of his arrival at AP, 1:50 PM CST. AP, via live television, is aware that CBS News with Walter Cronkite, NBC with Bill Ryan and Frank McGee, and ABC with Ron Cochran, are already showing photos shot by the competition.

They are now frantic and trying to catch up. It is our opinion that a major mistake was made when they send out the photograph which is shown by NBC around 2:07 PM Eastern, depicting the President with John Connally and Jackie at Love Field immediately after deplaning. This shows they are actively in competition to wire photographs to the rest of the country. It also shows the efficiency which they are capable of. Altgens4 and Altgens6, however, do not make it onto television until 6:35 PM.

At least four images are identified, which show the President immediately before and after the shots, Altgens4, 5, 6 and 7. Schaeffer believes that at least one other photograph is possible to have been shot by Altgens between 6 and 7. (This one was scratched entirely—could it have shown what several motorcycle escorts and at least 60 different witnesses said about the complete stoppage of the motorcade that day, and Secret Service Agents dismounting and running past the JFK limo and others going up the embankment, as reported by Altgens himself.)

At this moment, the images must be thoroughly inspected by "someone" who knows what needs to be taken out. In following the timeline of UPI and the *Dallas Times Herald* photographs, which were the first images put on the wire, by 1:50 PM CST, the Altgens' photos should have been sent out via thermofax, yet they were not. As mentioned earlier, *Cronkite shows the Times Herald photograph within an hour of the assassination, but does not show Altgens' photographs 4 and 6 until 6:35 PM EST, 5:35 Dallas time.* This leaves a time void of three hours and 45 minutes, where his photos are unaccounted for. (It is important to realize that in the case of Altgens' photographs, it had to be all or none because the suppression would have been obvious.)

Altgens 6 and 7 are deemed unsuitable for public consumption and the negative strip is sent down the street to JCS. The positive prints are enlarged so they can be worked on. Airbrushing, masking and opaquing are the only techniques available at the time. As noted above, Altgens6 undergoes at least a dozen alterations. Altgens 7 is altered in the area of the rear window of Chief Jesse Curry's lead car to hide the actions of Forrest Sorrells, Winston Lawson and Curry, who are turned around like Sheriff Bill Decker, watching the events behind them unfold while the motorcade is at a standstill.

The upper portion is chopped off to remove the cement railing at right of the Triple Underpass. Once the alterations are in place and new negatives are produced, the images are re-shot, and a new negative produced on Tri X Pan film. The original negatives are destroyed. The resultant negatives are sent back to the AP offices at the *Dallas Morning News* building and these are then processed in the normal manner and distributed nationwide. Here is what happened next (as described by Roy Schaeffer):

> *"Working backwards, the original negative had a print made to go over the wire service from Dallas to the* Dayton Daily News *on the AP wire Saturday morning 11/23/1963 at 7:15 pm. After I watched it print out on the wire machine I noticed on the way to engraving to have a zinc plate made from it, I noticed the editing in the area of the front windshield. Mainly the area on the passenger side of the Presidential limousine. I also noticed that the motorcyclist was much more clear or darker that the front windshield of the limousine. I also notice that the flag was darker than than the persons in the front of the Presidential limousine.*
>
> *While in the engraving department, Sony Delator shot the AP fax using a line camera to crop the photo so it would fit in a three column space. So working backwards the AP fax when received by me was 18 hours later. When Altgens called the AP Dallas, he gave the info the caption writer would write when he received the photo after it was developed. After checking the* Cincinnati Enquirer, Indianapolis Star *later that week all had the same ALTERED (photo), what is now referred to as the AP6,*

or DN5. The process is the negative has to be developed and dried. Someone then examined the emulsion side of the developed Altgens film strip and then altered it for some reason that I didn't know at that time.

If the Cronkite #6 positive photo was shown as it appears in a altered state at 6:30 pm that Friday, 11/22/1963, so now we have a time line of 5 hours. My photograph training tells me that the Altgens #6 was altered by someone who knew what he was doing."

"On 12/14/1963 The Saturday Evening Post *ran an almost full photo of it. I found at least 8 places where the photo has been retouched. I think in this case the AP photo editor had already typed out the caption with a time date but the photo wasn't attached to the photo to be sent out. ONE MUST REMEMBER ONE THING—THE FAX SENT OVER THE WIRE WAS SEVERELY ALTERED. This suggests that one can't trust the time stamp as to when the AP went over the wire in a unaltered state."*

"My work started on the altered Altgens photo from the beginning. My problem in telling workers at the newspaper of the altered Altgens I had no reason for this to occur in December of 1963. The fly in the ointment is the entire negative had to be re-shot using Pan X film on a duplicating film stock. The (proof) of the correct time line is when the AP photo arrived at the newspaper it was sent to over the AP wire. In my opinion the time line was at about 5:30 pm Dallas time. The time to alter the Altgens #6 would be about 4:30 pm. for the altered AP photo to be sent out to various newspapers who bought the AP wire service. Roy Schaeffer

Conclusion

The surviving CBS, ABC, and NBC television videos, which take us back to 22 November 1963, as riveting as they are, show a blow-by-blow account of the tragedy that was unraveling when this nation lost its innocence to a conspiracy that claimed our 35th President. Within these videos, we are unequivocally able to discern the order in which early images and photographs were propagated and disseminated to the world that day.

In the case of the Altgens photographs, unfortunately, it is clear that these were set aside and were not sent out until later that afternoon. Despite concerted attempts to establish their dissemination early that afternoon, the truth of the matter is that the two most important photographs—Altgens6 and Altgens7—were delayed long enough to undergo extensive alteration by forces unknown to this day.

Source note: This chapter previously appeared as "The James 'Ike' Altgens Photo Timeline", *http://jamesfetzer.blogspot.com/2015/09/the-james-ikealtgens-jfk-photo-timeline.html.*

Part V

The Man in the Doorway

14

Oswald was in the Doorway, After All!

by Ralph Cinque and Clare Kuehn

This is a sequel to "JFK Special: Oswald was the Man in the Doorway, after all!" (25 January 2012), which was co-authored by two of us. We are going to look further at the Altgens photo and the reasons why the evidence shows that Doorman has to have been Lee Harvey Oswald and could not have been Billy Lovelady. But, we are also going to look further at the images of Billy Lovelady that were taken after the assassination, and it will show clearly that manipulation, alteration, and fakery were involved. Billy Lovelady even masqueraded as Doorway Man, and it was a concerted effort, for which he had help.

To a great extent, this analysis is based on the new observations of Kelly D. Ruckman, a Canadian researcher, who was interviewed for two hours by Dr. Fetzer on his Internet radio program, "The Real Deal,

20 February 2012, archived at *radiofetzer. blogspot. com.*

We will begin with the work of Ralph Cinque and add discussion of the contributions of K.D. Ruckman as appropriate, especially in the final three sections of this study. Clare Kuehn, who is another Canadian student of JFK, authored several sections beginning with "Multiple Versions of the Altgens". Those who have not read the earlier article may not appreciate the evidence that has already been presented that establishes proof that the man in the doorway was Lee Oswald and not Billy Lovelady, especially based on analysis of the shirts they were wearing.

So, let's begin by going back to the doorway of the TSBD as seen in the Altgens photo. This image, by Robert Groden, may be the clearest one we have. Some say that the face of Doorman is that of Billy Lovelady, but even the House Subcommittee on Assassinations wasn't sure. They said:

"Due to the blurred quality of the enlargements of the spectator's image in the Altgens photograph, it was not possible either to identify or exclude positively Lovelady or Oswald."

They also went on to say that there was a greater probability that he was Lovelady than Oswald, and that was based on very small "anthropometric" measurements such as facial length, lower jaw breadth, nasal breadth, forehead breadth, and such, which were based on feature of the face, which we believe to have been superimposed on Oswald's body. If Lovelady's face was superimposed, those features would be Lovelady's.

It's the shirt, stupid! (with Ralph Cinque)

But, that was ridiculous because they looked at those tiny elements while ignoring the big, looming elements in the picture, such as the V-neck T-shirt which was a match to Oswald not Lovelady, the form and fit of the outer shirt which was a match to Oswald not Lovelady, and the manner of dress (unbuttoned) which was a match to Oswald not Lovelady, and the slender build of the man which was a match to

Oswald not Lovelady. If tiny facial measurements were a match to Lovelady while the big, visible, physical elements of the picture were a match to Oswald, isn't that suspicious? So, how did they deal with it? Simple; they didn't. They just ignored the large, physical elements.

But, notice that the face is surrounded by murky darkness, almost completely, while the junction of Doorway Man and Black Tie Man is also murky. That face has an island quality to it, and it looks like it could have been super-imposed-pasted in there. It was the reverse of the backyard photos, which Jim Fetzer has explored with Jim Marrs, "*Framing the Patsy: The Case of Lee Harvey Oswald*", in which Oswald's face was imposed over that of another man. This time, it was another man's face imposed above Oswald's body.

Doorman's clothing are a perfect match to Oswald's, and that includes the right collars, the V-necked T-shirts, the left lapels, the loose fit, and the major unbuttoning, all of which powerfully confirm that it's Oswald standing there.

The only aspect of the clothing that has ever been linked to Lovelady is the shirt pattern, but that's not true. Doorman's shirt pattern is not identical to Lovelady's–far from it. For instance, Lovelady's shirt only had white lines, whereas Doorman's had white *blotches.* Lovelady's shirt had pattern and contrast all the way up to the collar, whereas Doorman's right collar—and the whole upper right side of his shirt—was completely devoid of pattern. It simply looks GRAINY–like Oswald's shirt. Here, take a look:

Which one is the odd man out? It's obvious that someone tried to impose some pattern and contrast to other parts of Doorman's shirt, but they did a crude, sloppy, inadequate job of it. Again, look: are these the same shirts? This isn't horseshoes or hand grenades. Close doesn't count. The weak, shoddy imitation of Lovelady's shirt pattern should sound an alarm that it is just another fakery in a long list of fakeries.

No Match to Lovelady

So again, there is absolutely nothing about the clothing that is a match to Lovelady–not even the shirt pattern. The entire clothing ensemble is a match to Oswald, and so is the slender build of Doorway Man, and that means that—geographically speaking—at least 80% of Doorway Man matches Oswald, and only 20% or less of him (the face—that extracted face in a sea of murkiness) is a match to Lovelady.

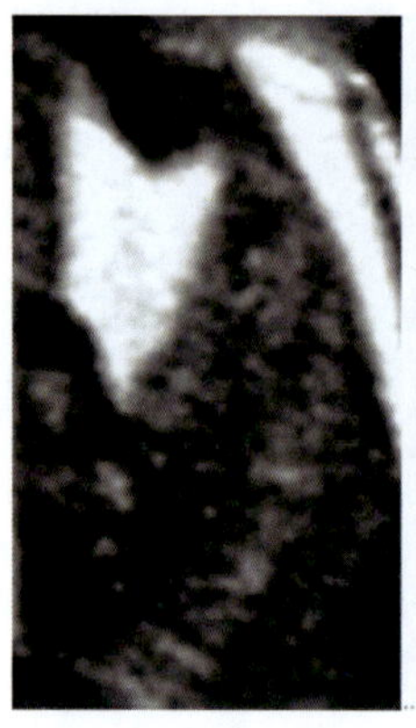

So, considering that imbalance in proportionality, was it ever reasonable to say that Doorman leaned more towards looking like Lovelady? I hardly think so.

Where did the face of Lovelady come from to superimpose on Doorway Man? We suspect it came from “Obfuscated Man”—so named by Dr. Fetzer. Look to Doorman’s left, which is our right. Do you see that big white splotch which looks like a cloud? Surrounding it, you can see the outline of a man’s head. And below it you can see, in black, the outline of his torso as it merges with the afro hairdo of the woman with a radiant smile who is in front of and below him. That whole man was obfuscated, his face in white and his body in black, and that is why Dr. Fetzer refers to him as “Obfuscated Man”. He may have been the real Lovelady.

Obfuscated Man

In this image, K.D. Ruckman has highlighted the features of the Altgens that have been obfuscated. He agrees with me about the other anomalous figures, including “Black Tie Man”, who seems to be fused to Doorman, and although he is standing behind him, he is also overlapping him. The word “overlap” is Kelly’s choice of word, and it’s a good one.

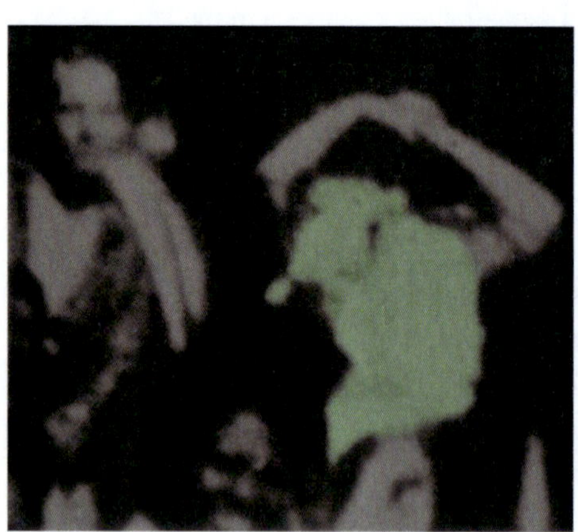

Black Tie Man definitely looks like he was inserted there in a forged placement. There is also the faceless Black Hole Man with his arms up shading his eyes from the sun–except that his face is in complete, utter darkness. So, why is he doing that? And concealing the right arm of Doorway Man is the face of a black man, to whom we may refer as “the Black Profile Guy” as follows.

The Black Profile Guy

So let's discuss someone whom I have not mentioned previously but whom Kelly Ruckman noticed: the African-American man who is right in front of and below Doorman. Is he supposed to be sitting or standing? I presume he is sitting. But, how can he be comfortable with Doorman wrapping his arm under his chin and breathing down his neck like that?

That's what you call encroaching on someone's "personal space." It's odd for Doorman to be doing it, and it's odd for the black guy to be OK with it. It goes against everything we know about normal human boundaries. And where is the black guy looking? Not at Kennedy, that's for sure. He is looking off in the opposite direction. But why?

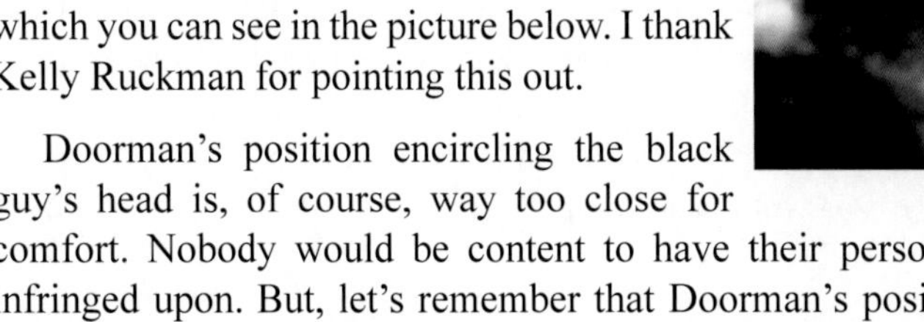

So, is the black guy another super-imposed figure in the photograph? We suspect he is. And we believe the purpose of putting him there was to hide the tattered condition of Oswald's shirt, particularly on his left side, which you can see in the picture below. I thank Kelly Ruckman for pointing this out.

Doorman's position encircling the black guy's head is, of course, way too close for comfort. Nobody would be content to have their personal space so infringed upon. But, let's remember that Doorman's position with his arm swung over like it is to the inside of his body is very unnatural, abnormal, and uncomfortable- for him, even without the black guy being there. If you try to duplicate his position yourself, you'll see how uncomfortable it is to hold your arm swung-over like that to the inside. All your instincts will tell you to let it go, to just drop your arm and let it dangle.

Is Doorman leaning on something, such as a railing? There was no railing there in 1963. Could he have been leaning on the molding of the pillar? That's theoretically possible, but it's a strange thing to do. Who does such a thing? I have never done it or seen anybody do it. Why would anyone do it? What is practical about it? What is comfortable about it? Nothing.

Fedora Hat Man

Before we leave this picture of the doorway, I want to mention my uneasiness with the Fedora Hat Man, the fact that he is turned and looking directly at Doorman instead of at Kennedy. Why is he more interested in Doorman? And what about that woman and child who are in front of him? How is she supporting the weight of that child? The boy seems perfectly vertical, and he's not that small, and she's not that big. So, how is she able to hold him up so seemingly effortlessly? And how exactly is she holding him? How is she keeping him from falling? We can't see her arm around him nor his arm around her.

> *And how is he perched so perfectly straight? To me, it looks like he is standing on something, and she is standing next to him. But, there is nothing there that he could be standing on. And why is the boy wearing a winter wool cap pulled down over his ears when other people nearby are in short-sleeves or T-shirts? It was reportedly an unseasonably warm day for November.*

I want to elaborate about this because I think it is important. Recall when you have seen a mother holding a child; not a baby, but a child. Recall that often the mother does things to lessen the load. Sometimes, she will have the child straddle her hip bone, sitting on her, which transfers the load from her relatively weak arms to her relatively strong legs. Or, she may lean back so that the child is lying on her chest, and by leaning back it causes passive structures, such as the ligaments and spinal facet joints, to bear some of the load, taking the strain off her arms. And, there are other shifts she could make to ease the burden. But, this woman isn't reacting to the weight at all, even though he is a rather big kid for such a tiny woman to support. Yet, she looks totally unfazed. Take a look:

So, the question is: was the image of the boy and his mother put there to cover up Jack Ruby's face? We know from reading Jim Douglass, *JFK and the Unspeakable* (2008), that Jack Ruby was in Dealey Plaza that day. So, was that Jack Ruby in the Fedora hat? If so, it's understandable that he'd be looking at Oswald. After all, the patsy was not supposed to be standing outside in plain view. I'm sure that was not part of the plan. Note that even if he were facing the right direction, towards Kennedy, he would hardly be able to see anything. His orientation is very peculiar. It makes no sense for him to be standing behind that woman and child.

Another TSBD employee, Vicki Adams, was on the fourth floor when the shots rang out. She ran down the stairs—the same stairs that Oswald was supposedly bolting down at the same time, but of course, she didn't see him—and when she reached the ground floor, she saw Bill Shelley and Billy Lovelady standing together by the elevator, and when she went outside, she saw Jack Ruby. She said he was asking questions and ordering people around "like a cop." So, that places Ruby outside the TSBD, and it makes it even more likely that Fedora Hat Man was Jack Ruby. Barry Ernest has published a book about Vicki Adams, *The Girl on the Stairs: The Search for a Missing Witness to the JFK Assassination* (2010).

Billy and the FBI

Now, let us move on to Billy Lovelady, and we are going to compare his FBI image from March 1964 (which definitely was him) to his alleged image from the day of the assassination at the Dallas Police Department (DPD). But first, let me remind you that there is controversy about which shirt he wore on 22 November 1963. He first claimed to have worn a red and white striped short-sleeve shirt. He told to the FBI he wore that shirt, and he told the same to at least one reporter: Jones Harris. But, the DPD said Lovelady was wearing a plaid checkered shirt, and that is the one that became part of the official story.

But first take a look at this official letter from the FBI to the Warren Commission stating that Lovelady claimed to have worn the red and white striped shirt. The exact wording is: "He stated he was wearing a vertical red and white striped shirt and blue jeans," which has been underlined at the end of the second paragraph:

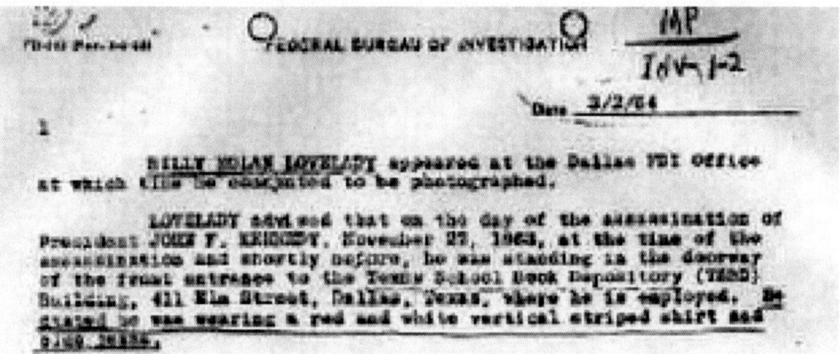
FEDERAL BUREAU OF INVESTIGATION

Date 3/2/64

1

BILLY NOLAN LOVELADY appeared at the Dallas FBI Office at which [illegible] to be photographed.

LOVELADY advised that on the day of the assassination of President JOHN F. KENNEDY, November 22, 1963, at the time of the assassination and shortly before, he was standing in the doorway of the front entrance to the Texas School Book Depository (TSBD) Building, 411 Elm Street, Dallas, Texas, where he is employed. He stated he was wearing a red and white vertical striped shirt and blue jeans.

LOVELADY stated his picture has appeared in several publications which picture depicts him on the far left side of the front doorway to the TSBD. LOVELADY was exhibited a picture appearing on pages 4-5 of the magazine entitled "Four Dark Days in History," Copyright 1963 by Special Publications, Inc., 6087 Hollywood Blvd., Los Angeles 28, California. He immediately identified the picture of the individual on the far left side of the doorway of the TSBD as being his photograph. He stated this same photograph or one identical to it has appeared in the Dallas Times Herald newspaper of November 22, 1963, and in the Cincinnati Inquirer of December 3, 1963. He stated it also appeared in an edition of the Saturday Evening Post the date of which he does not know.

Mr. LOVELADY stated his close resemblance to LEE HARVEY OSWALD has become somewhat embarrassing. He stated his step-children, [illegible], age 6, and stepdaughter, ANGELA [illegible], age 4, were watching television shortly after the assassination at a time when LEE HARVEY OSWALD was shown while in custody of the Dallas Police Department and both of these children remarked that they thought their daddy was on television referring to his close resemblance to LEE HARVEY OSWALD.

The following physical description and background information was obtained from interrogation and observation of LOVELADY:

Name	BILLY NOLAN LOVELADY
Race	White
Sex	Male
Born	2/10/37, Myrtle Springs, Texas
Height	5'8"

on [illegible]/64 at Dallas, Texas File # DL 100-10461

by Special Agent ROBERT P. GEMBERLING [illegible]:vm Date dictated [illegible]/64

735

And notice that in the pictures taken in March 1964 (below), they had him pose with his shirt unbuttoned, like Doorman. But, why would they do that if he was wearing a different shirt? What would be the point of it? Obviously, they thought at the time that he was wearing the shirt from 22 November. And notice how differently his unbuttoned shirt sprawls open compared to Doorman's. It's a totally different look,

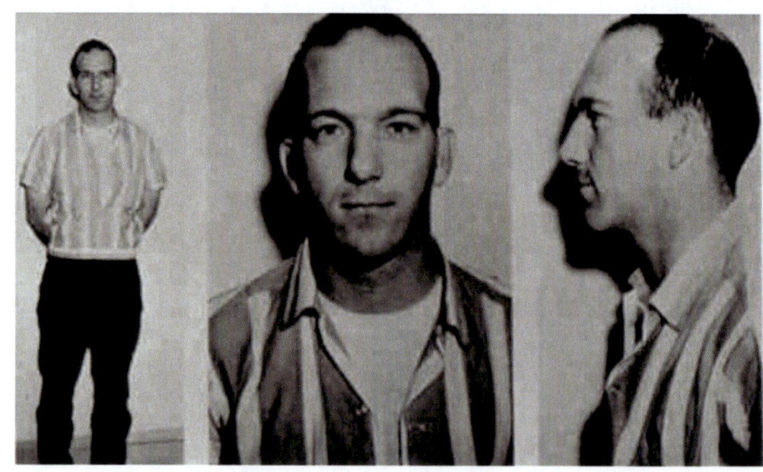

and that's because every shirt is different and behaves differently. It is obviously not the same presentation that we saw on Doorman. Notice also that the shirt is short-sleeved, whereas Doorman's shirt was long-sleeved. So they had to do something pronto to get him out of that shirt.

Comparing the "Loveladys"

But before we go on, let's observe how well the layout of the unbuttoned shirts matches between Doorman and Oswald. And you can compare them to what you see on Lovelady above, especially in the above left. I consider what you see below to be very comparable spreads. Would anyone care to differ?

Kelly makes the interesting observation that both shirts bulge a little where the lapel folds over, except that it's higher on Oswald than on Doorman. On Oswald, you see the bulge right at the middle of the lapel whereas on Doorman, the bulge is at the bottom above where the shirt is finally buttoned. Remember that it was a rough fold and not really following a crease, so at times, it bulged. But, that's still the same behavior of the same material, and it doesn't matter that it bulged in different places at different times. So, you are looking at the same guy wearing the same shirt.

But now, let's compare the images of FBI Lovelady from March 1964 to that of DPD Lovelady from 22 November 1963, which they crucially needed in order to place Lovelady in a long-sleeved shirt, supposedly like Doorman. Here they are side by side.

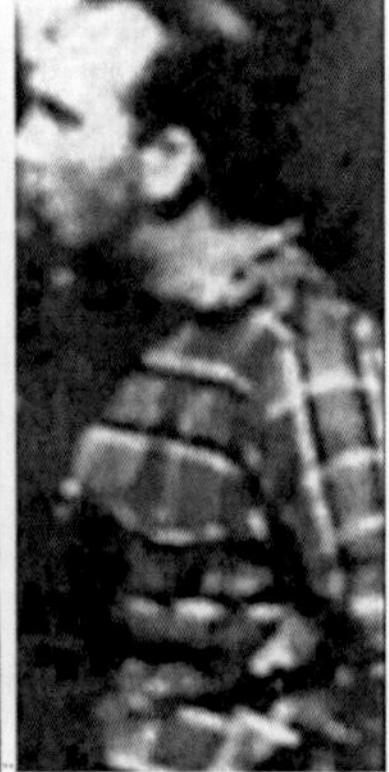

Kelly Ruckman noticed the following comparative differences:

First, DPD Lovelady's head (right) is wider from front to back than is FBI Lovelady's (left). *Second,* the slope of FBI Lovelady's head is more vertical, and the angle of his forehead with the top of his head is more rectangular. On DPD Lovelady, there is no angle at all, rather there is just a long, gentle, slope, like a ski slope, and it reminds me of the images we have seen of Cro-Magnon Man or Neanderthal.

Third, FBI Lovelady seems to have a longer nose, and DPD Lovelady seems to have a shorter, stubbier nose. *Fourth,* the hairlines are different. FBI Lovelady's hairline at the temple seems to go straight up whereas DPD Lovelady's hairline angles back more. *Fifth,* the ears look different, with the real Lovelady's on the left being longer and narrower. Remember that ears are very distinctive, like fingerprints.

Thank you, Kelly Ruckman, for pointing out the above. But there is a difference between the two of them which jumps out even more at me: *their necks*. DPD Lovelady (on the right) has a condition known as Forward Neck Syndrome. Any orthopedist or chiropractor can see it—at a glance. Instead of going up, his neck is going forward.

FBI Lovelady has a much more vertical neck. The basic, fundamental direction that it is going is UP. But on DPD Lovelady (on the right), his neck isn't going up so much. His neck is going more FORWARD, and that has the effect of shortening his neck. And that is something we can measure. Take a ruler and measure the length of the visible neck on each of them, going from the bottom of the ear to wherever the vertical line reaches the shirt. As I measure it, I get a full inch of neck length on FBI Lovelady, but only 2/3 inch on DPD Lovelady. So, from the perspective of DPD Lovelady, FBI Lovelady has 50 percent more length in his neck.

Next, I want you to drop a plumb line on each of them. And the way you can do it is to take a ruler and place it right behind the ear, and holding it vertical, track it down and see where it goes. With good posture, the ear should not be too much in front of the sagittal plane of the shoulder, and FBI Lovelady is doing quite well in that respect. His isn't bad alignment. I like what I'm seeing.

But DPD Lovelady's ear is much farther forward than that; his plumb line is well forward of his shoulder. He is really quite contorted, and he's the kind of guy who is destined to have osteoarthritis of the neck.

In holding his neck forward like that, he has to do something to maintain his eyes level, that is, parallel with the ground, and what he's doing is cocking his head back sharply at the very top of his neck. You may not be able to see it as well as I can, but if you were to see it on an x-ray, it would jump out at you. So, his neck is going forward, and at the very top of his neck, his head is rocking back on his neck. And that is like putting a heavy weight on a spring and compressing it. That puts pressure on all the cervical joints, and over time, they wear out from it.

The compressed cervical discs thin out until they are practically non-existent. Cervical disc herniations are also possible with this kind of posture.

Another Proof of their Differences

Here's another way you can tell the difference: look at the axis of FBI Lovelady's ear. It's pretty much vertical: straight up and down. Not perfectly so, but close. But, on DPD Lovelady, the ear is rocked back more. It's got more pitch to it.

The line of greatest length through the ear is more diagonal, with the upper part back and the lower part forward. Again, it's rocked back, and the reason it's rocked back is because the whole head is rocked back. This is a very rigid, locked, dysfunctional posture that compromises mobility, flexibility, and coordination.

As a chiropractor, it's a pleasure for me to look at FBI Lovelady because he has such nice lengthening in his neck and that translates into freedom of motion, lightness of being, and a generally expansive state of the body, which is what you want. But, it's very distressful for me to look at DPD Lovelady because he looks solid, rigid, steeped in stiffness, and destined for pain.

Is there any chance that Lovelady was just standing and comporting himself differently on the two days? No. There is absolutely no chance of that. Postural habits are deeply ingrained. They are the MOST deeply ingrained of all the habits you've got. It's extremely hard to break them—even if you try, and there is no reason to think Lovelady was trying.

And the reason that it's so hard to change them is because your habitual way of carrying yourself is the only thing you know; it's the only thing that feels right to you; anything else would feel way out of balance and terribly wrong, like you were going to fall. It's like your own little world that you're living in, your way of responding to gravity and other forces, and it's the only one you can even conceive of.

Having been a chiropractor for 40 years, I can tell you that this one factor of the Forward Neck Syndrome on DPD Lovelady and its absence on FBI Lovelady completely eliminates any possibility that the two of them were the same man. It clinches it like different dental X-rays. It is not just a different position that DPD Lovelady is holding his neck; he is anatomically fixed that way. He could not make his neck look like FBI Lovelady's no matter what he did. It would be anatomically impossible.

Now, let us compare DPD Lovelady with later known pictures of Lovelady from 1971 and 1978. '71 Lovelady, in the middle, looks thinner, and he definitely does not have Forward Neck Syndrome, and there is no chance that it went away in the man on the left. '78 Lovelady, on the right, looks a lot older, but he doesn't have Forward Neck Syndrome either. Apparently,

Lovelady shed a lot of weight after the assassination. But notice that the shirt still fits him. Shouldn't that shirt be hanging on him after having lost all that weight? And notice that the pocket with the big flap that you see on DPD Lovelady (on the left) was not present when he was photographed in 1971 and 1978.

So, what is with that? How can a shirt continue to fit snugly after a man drops a lot of weight? Did he have the shirt altered, taken in? But, that's a major job to reconstruct the shoulders and the core dimensions of a shirt. It is rarely ever done. Shortening the sleeves is one thing, but taking in the shoulders and the core width of the shirt is too much work. Who does such a thing? Nobody.

But, if he did have the shirt altered, maybe it was necessary to remove the pocket because it no longer took up the right place. And rather than relocate the pocket, they just got rid of it completely. Of course, the other option is that it's a totally different shirt—one that did not come with a pocket.

The Dallas PD Lovelady

Now let's look at DPD Lovelady as a still taken from some newsreel footage. As Kelly puts it:

"Since the impostor got caught on camera, they got stuck with the plaid shirt. Lovelady tells the truth at the start, but later recants and begins his role of playing Doorman in plaid shirts similar to the one the impostor wore, until his mysterious death in 1979."

But, I would add that they really had no choice but to go with the plaid shirt because Lovelady's real shirt—the one he actually wore—was shortsleeved, whereas Doorman's was long-sleeved, being Oswald's

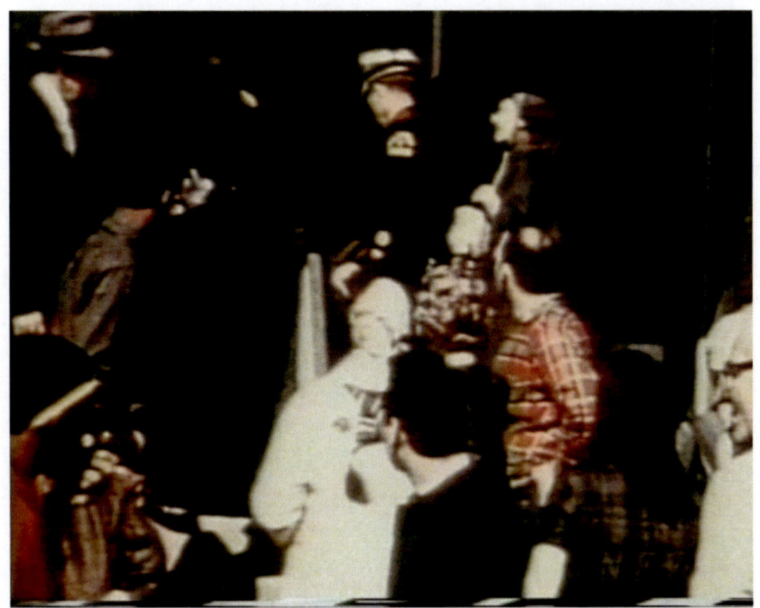

shirt. So, they needed to come up with a long-sleeved shirt, and that's why they were forced to go with this guy in plaid.

But, it's Kelly Ruckman who deserves credit for first recognizing that DPD Lovelady was a fake. And think about what it means: It means that just as there was an Oswald double floating around Dallas on 22 November, there was also a Lovelady double. To learn about the Oswald double, you only have to read *JFK and the Unspeakable* (2008) by James Douglass.

Douglass covers the Oswald double in detail, including his being smuggled out of the state on an Air Force cargo plane hours after the assassination, as reported by Air Force Sergeant Robert Vinson, who rode with him on the plane.

Vinson's experience would be revealed in detail in the book by James P. Johnston and Jon Roe in *Flight from Dallas: New Evidence of CIA Involvement in the Murder of President John F. Kennedy* (2003).

Kelly makes another interesting point about the Altgens photo: that the area around Doorman comprises about 2.5% of the total photo, yet all of the anomalies and strange, beguiling figures happen right there and nowhere else in the picture. The rest of the vast picture is completely straightforward, photographically speaking, with no weird, inscrutable stuff. Why should everything that is puzzling and questionable be happening to and around Doorman? It is a rhetorical question directed at those who proffer "photographic compression", "emulsion bleeding" or other such pseudotechnical excuses for the strange occurrences that are concentrated in that one small area.

But, the bottom line about Billy Lovelady is that he was engaged in an enormous and elaborate fraud. Not only did he pose in a different shirt from the one he wore on 22 November 1963—but he knew very well that he was not the Doorway Man. No doubt, he was in the Altgens photo, but he was not the man standing next to the pillar in the loose-fitting, unbuttoned, longsleeved shirt over a V-neck T-shirt.

Why did he do it? Money may have been a factor. Billy Lovelady was a warehouse worker who suddenly had the financial means to start his own trucking company in Denver, Colorado shortly after the assassination. And fear may have been a factor, fear for his life. He did, after all, die suddenly of a first and fatal "heart attack" in 1979 at the tender age of 41. Billy never even testified before the House Select Committee on Assassinations (HSCA).

Multiple Versions of the Altgens (with Clare Kuehn)

Dr. Ralph Cinque has done much, with Dr. Fetzer, to elaborate on the simpler observations of Penn Jones, Jr. from the 1980s, about how Oswald's shirt matches Doorway Man's. Cinque has also remarked that the male figure wearing a hat and standing behind the woman and a child in front of the TSBD and to the right side of the doorway (to our left, viewing the photograph), might have a Fedora and could be Jack Ruby. His face and most of his body, after all, are covered by a child whose comfortable spinal posture would be erect, yet the child is otherwise positioned as if it belonged with the woman, implicitly being held by her. It is not straining to get straight up and is not tipping in any way from being held in an arm. It could more reasonably be standing on a platform, based upon its posture, but there was no platform of that height. Could he have been Jack Ruby?

As Ralph Cinque has observed, two men in Fedoras can be observed in the Altgens, one of whom is dark-complected, the other of whom has

his face sufficiently obscured to be indeterminate, but where you can see some part of his forehead, which also seems to be dark in complexion. It is very odd to seem to have two men in Fedoras, both of whom are black:

Ralph observes that the person in question is the man in the Fedora to the far left. But Kelly and Clare have another candidate in mind: Black Tie Man, who is standing just behind Doorway Man and to his immediate left. Vicki Adams' testimony makes it likely that Jack Ruby was there, but he could still have been either of these candidates.

Mr. Kelly Ruckman has noticed that there is a significant early close-up of the region of the Altgens showing Doorway man in a documentary based upon Mark Lane's famous early work on the assassination, *Rush to Judgement* (1966). In this version, the high contrast area of Black Tie Man's suit is clearly evident. With little definition in the blacks and in the whites, whatever was light and survived the contrasting could not have been medium toned originally. On Black Tie Man's left breast is a significant white line, fairly thick, enough for a kerchief in a breast pocket. In this version, and this version only, of the Altgens there is this feature which could not be taken away by mere changes in contrast of one print or another. It would not simply disappear unless taken out. This means that more than one version of the Altgens appeared in print somewhere, for Lane to have included it.

Not only this, but Ruby was known to be a natty dresser, who often wore a kerchief in his pocket. At the Friday night press conference, he is dressed just as Black Tie Man was, in Mark Lane's 1967 documentary, where the Altgens (shown here) is complete with white handkerchief. Was Black Tie Man Ruby? Even if not, the Altgens we have from the extant newspapers was provably touched up in one area: the area of the breast pocket of a figure in the doorway: Black Tie Man. Perhaps some newspapers got an early version of the image, and Lane included it. It would have been good for Mark to have come forward with that version before his demise. If anyone has an early Altgens image, please contact us.

The impossible posture of head, hips and shoulder

Mr. Kelly Ruckman noticed some other odd things in later photographs of Lovelady. Before covering them directly, we will have to describe an optical illusion which occurs when we look at Doorway man in different blow-up levels. Once we see how the optical illusion happens, we can be careful to notice the elements in its occurrence, even at lower magnification. Then we can move on to Ruckman's discovery and why what he discovered was done. The following is also the first discussion on record of exactly how the wrong posture of Doorway man comes to set itself in our mind, as if accurate and inaccurate at the same time, and is thus important in its own right.

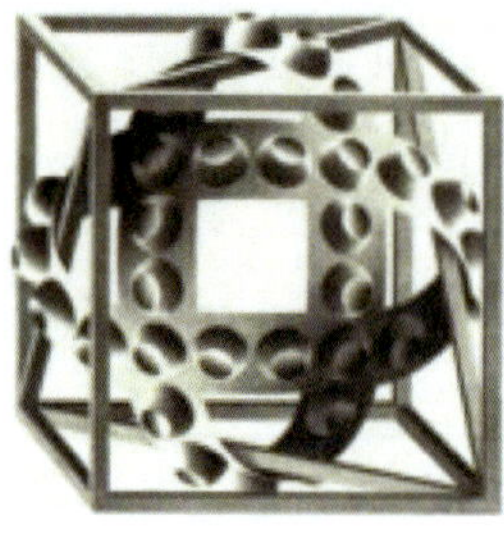

An optical illusion can occur in different ways. Sometimes, as in many playful perspective images by the artist M.C. Escher, we cannot have the image resolve properly into one perspective rationally. Our minds can see the box or column set, or stairway as, in or out, up or down, alternately, but the whole image cannot resolve both interpretations. A simpler problem, using a cube only, is presented here, and it's called the "Impossible Cube", with good reason:

We understand this rationally but cannot see the total at one time in our mind. We can redraw it or re-image it in our mind linearly, but it will always remain one or the other impression as a total object picture. This is what we have with Doorway man's left arm width, left hip and side, versus the width of his shoulder and upper arm and his shoulder line.

In the most general sense, many have noticed that in the Altgens photo, Doorway man has an awkward posture. This is, in fact, due to an optical illusion which, we will see, is in turn due to a botched paint job.

We may choose the line of the arm which extends not far beyond the lighter gray portion. This matches the width of the shoulder area. The arm is too long and forces us to the conclusion, as well, that the man is lunging. His hip area then recedes to the darker gray shadowy area around the Black Profile Guy's face.

The rest of the gray area becomes basically one tone in our mind, then, and even can seem to be the suit jacket and pants of Black Tie

Man. Black Tie Man's true black suit jacket then looks like a shadow from a lapel. It is not his true suit line, which does extend a bit beyond, but for the moment, our mental impression ignores that.

This interpretation is reinforced by the line of the back of the head of the African American person below and in front of Black Tie Man. If, alternately, we try to incorporate this generalized gray area as Doorway man's left side, the lunge of the shoulders and the matching beginning, anyway, of the light gray arm area, we are left with a very awkward posture overall, where the arm is crossed almost violently (and too long) and the rest of the body is erect. We could call it "a Goiter Hip": he lunges from the lighter arm area and shoulder, but his hip still looks straight.

But the conclusion that this is not a natural body is further deepened with a different impression, one from the fuller facts of the arm. The actual, true lower arm extends in a wide arc, below the lighter gray elbow area. In fact, though it is harder to see in lower resolution, it is possible to see that there is more definition below the light gray arm . . . far below it. This true arm line is due to blotchy striped-check blobs in dark-middle and middle gray.

Once we take this line for the arm, and it is the true arm line, we see that the lower arm is a Flat Fat shape, and thus way too thick for the body. As well, the arm would have to be broken to sit like that. The lunge is missing then, the arm even longer by implication, and the true middle gray area begins lower. Now it really is not Black Tie Man's suit, but a kind of straighter posture for this now completely wrong arm. Goiter Hip is back.

We cannot reconcile the new information, the fuller arm line, with our wishful thinking from the lighter arm line. This is like Escher's games with perspective. We must ignore—in the sense of allide, conjoin and eliminate or not notice—certain features of some of his "objects" in order to see an object in each and when we include new information we would have to drop or conjoin aspects of the image we saw before and know also to be there, in order to hold the new object image information in mind.

Reconciling the Shoulders and the Hips

Many have attempted to reconcile the posture by using the shoulders and hips, saying the man is somehow twisted to look lunging yet straight up. They have not realized that the reason for the "awkward" arm is that an impression of lunge comes only from the light gray arm and shoulder—matching in width with each other, where the rest of the body below might be Black Tie Man's body, or be only glossed over in our mind (the way the irreconcilable aspects of one view of Escher's images forces us to ignore or partly generalize what's going on in the rest), while we—but the impression of straight posture comes only from a too-fat lower arm (Flat Fat arm) and distinct gray area for hip (Goiter Hip).

The full image information cannot be reconciled in the visual mind, because it derives from seeing one aspect of the arm (the light gray) and then finding out the full arm width extends to the man's lower belly, and remains that thick. It hangs there, way beyond the normal thickness of the arm from the shoulder.

In fact, it even extends out in a blob beyond the "left side" (our right) of Doorway man's goiter hip, as if it were an elbow or fold, but is actually bad paint. This blob clearly goes beyond the arm, to match with the line of Black Tie Man's black suit line. An elbow would be up higher, more where the light gray arm implies. It was likely from a paintbrush painting too far. It thus looks like a broken lower extremity from the general width of that lower arm and looks flattened for the same reason, but also has an incongruous botched paint job beyond the arm.

This paint job fools you: it goes as far as Black Tie Man's waist. The lighter, slenderer arm of Doorman in the light gray area plus some of the dark gray, puts the elbow much higher. The gray outcropping, putatively a lighter striped-check part of the sleeve again, no longer matches the shoulder and upper arm direction to where the inner elbow and width are reasonable.

Notice how Black Tie Man relates to Doorway Man's left shoulder. Many have thought Black Time Man's image overlaps his left shoulder, which would be blatant proof of fakery by itself, but the situation appears to be just a bit more subtle than that. Doorway Man's wider lower arm implies a wider shoulder; we then see the shoulder as too narrow, when it is the lower arm which drags too wide and too low.

The shoulder matches the thinner lighter arm, and the rest is a widening below it, a paint job of extra-stripey checks. If you put your finger over the mid-gray stripes of the lower side and bottom of the arm, you will see that the lighter arm area width matches the real shoulder roundness.

The illusion is optical and due to a botched paint job. Compared to the shoulder width and its matching light gray arm impression, the lower arm's far greater thickness, and very low, almost broken angle for the shoulder, making a gentle sweep too low, could it be due to a huge, hanging shirtsleeve?

No. Of course, a person might wear or fashion such a shirtsleeve. Remember, our comparison size here is the light gray arm and shoulder area, perhaps adding a bit for shadowed curvature, not the Goiter Hip dimensions of an erect posture which does not fit the shoulder size and lighter arm.

How do we know it wasn't just a very very wide sleeve? We have the later images of Lovelady in a putatively identical shirt, and it does not fit his shoulders and then swell off his lower arm, nearly double the size. Do we have situations where a shirt could look similar to this without being a lower balloon? Well, if one places any used shirt flat on a surface, it can look roughly rounded and wide in its outer curve, around the elbow area and on down.

But these impressions come from different real-world physical processes than a) a man wearing a relatively tight regular shirt, as was claimed for this check-striped shirt, and b) a shirt with no person in it, where the material flattens out and looks wider in two dimensions than when curved, even a bit loosely, around an arm.

And the light gray or medium gray arm itself is always too long (along with the addition of Black Profile Guy). This was clearly partly to cover the bottom of Oswald's nearly open shirt, which was in tatters at the bottom. The medium extent of the true gray lower arm is also kind of broken looking, once one notices its relation to the shoulder and narrower light gray arm. Hence my allusion to the impossible cube. We now return to Ruckman's own work.

Three wrongs don't make a right left arm!

After looking at the "generally awkward" left arm in the Altgens—an arm whose true medium-gray outline is too low and "broken"-looking, but which looks awkward even as a light gray arm, when compared to hips and shoulder and head position—Ruckman noticed that when the House Select Committee on Assassinations (HSCA) received images of Lovelady in the 1970s, his left arm was altered in the recent images! The arm of the Altgens is too long and broken, whereas the new alterations were mostly shatter-broken (cut in multiple places)

or outrightly shortened; this would seem to contrast with the Altgens literally, but it achieves a similar impression, that is, that something is wrong with the arm.

"Keep on moving! Nothing to see here!" might be the motto of these doctorers, but by fearing the Altgens botch job so much that they did more weird edits to new images and actually left MORE evidence of their handiwork for those willing to notice. We see him in the check-striped shirt he supposedly wore (but claimed to the FBI he did not), posing for a CBS interview and in photos by Robert Groden. In some of these, his left arm check-stripes are actually compressed without a rounded fold. They have been cut and shortened in the Jackson '71 and Groden '76 copies. (What does this imply about Groden? Did he realize this was done to his images?) See opposite page for the full set of Groden photos, as submitted to the HSCA.

Here is the Jackson '71 photo, available only in a collage by what Ruckman calls the "notorious disinfo-agent John MacAdams". This is a different doctoring than the others, which were simple cuts in multiple places. This image relies on the impression that a shoulder muscle on the uppermost arm leaves a strong shadow on a naked, buff man, when appropriately lit and high contrast is wanted in the image. Instead, we have really a cut-paste job in the uppermost arm of this image, for the lighting source is front-top and no bend occurs in a human arm at that point, fabric drapes with gravity and flattens out vertically—a spurious fold can only occur under such conditions in that part of an arm and leave other evidence of itself. The putative wrap-around fold disappears into the front upper arm impossibly, cut off by the dark gash. There is no fold at the point of the dark gash. And the arm's general position is more of a flat-on view, as if it was from a side image, or as if the arm were twisted around to the front face. In the case of such a twist, however, the shoulder would be even flatter, for the side of the arm would become the front. But in this image the arm is also shorter, and in that respect it fits with the Groden fakes.

The thing to remember here is not that these images shorten the arm, but rather that they make the arm wrong. In the latter, not in the former sense, they are like the Altgens. Now we noticed that the light gray arm on Doorway man is too long, and the full real arm image is way too long and wide, so why shorten the arm of Lovelady? The impression of SOMETHING wrong with the arm and the broken look of the full lower arm image including the non-light portions, must have led the cover-up to continue. But it's such an obvious break in the image that one might conclude it isn't a break, but a fold, or something else. Would they risk our seeing how broken the arm image is in these later stills?

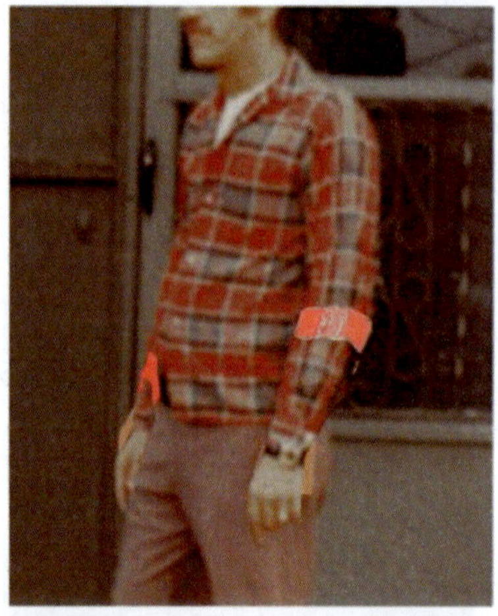

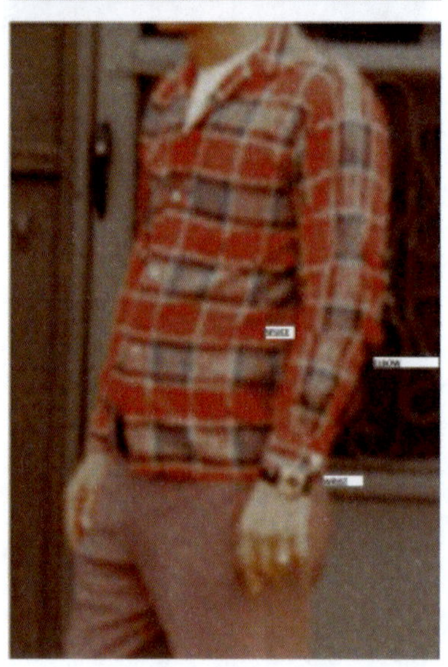

Indeed. For if the left arm always looks a bit "funny", as the English say, it seems as if there's less wrong with the Altgens arm. This is subconscious: hide a man in a mask among others with masks.

Mr. Ruckman noticed the cropped-and-pasted arms for the first time. He had not analyzed exactly what was wrong with the Altgens arm illusion, but he noticed the simpler job done on the later images and they are obvious once one notices them. Folds will not do there. So why?

The Altgens is not cut in such a way, but the true arm width extends past the elbow, lowers widely and Fat Flat. In low resolution and interpretation from the light gray arm's general impression, however, we don't see that lower arm shape properly. When we do, the arm is even more broken for the body. No, it is not a simple cut-paste there, but it is awkward, and moreso even would have to be broken and flattened on a real body.

The general impression of "something"'s being wrong with the arm was maintained in a cover-up into the 1970s.

One of the mistakes that happened that day is their man, the Man in Plaid was caught on film, not once but twice. Since he was doubling Lovelady, they were stuck with the plaid shirt. In the same sense that Oswald's face had to be covered up with the superimposed face of Lovelady, Oswald's shirt had to be painted over with white splotchy lines to mimic the plaid shirts checkered pattern. For more of K.D. Ruckman's work, visit his blog about Billy and Lee.

Lovelady stuck to the truth at the start, shying away from the media and refusing to have his picture taken. Later he must have been "gotten to".

By 1967 he recants and begins his role as Doorway Man in Plaid shirts similar to the one the Man in Plaid wore, again in 1971 and lastly for Groden in 1976. He suffered a fatal heart attack in 1979–or else in 1984 by some accounts.

Just another mysterious death at the bottom of a long list of dead JFK assassination witnesses.

What about Bill Shelly? ***(with Ralph Cinque)***

Let's close by looking at Bill Shelley. Oswald told Detective Fritz that he was "out in front with Bill Shelley."

Yet, Bill Shelley denied it. In fact, he made an emphatic statement that: "At no time during the shooting did I see Lee Harvey Oswald." It seems odd that he would use three names to refer to someone he knew and worked with.

But, it turns out that Shelley knew Oswald well and long before Lee came to work at the TSBD, insofar as they were both involved in the Texas/Louisiana Civil Air Patrol. That was an organization that was founded by the owner of the TSBD building, David Byrd. So, why didn't Shelley mention to the Warren Commission that he knew Oswald from the Civil Air Patrol? Didn't he think it was relevant? The truth is that Bill Shelley was a career CIA man. He worked for Army Intelligence during WWII, and when the CIA was launched in 1947, he immediately got immersed in it. On the morning of the assassination, Bill Shelley spent hours on the sixth floor directing a crew of men who were laying flooring. So, how did he miss seeing the arrangement of the boxes of books that were organized into the "sniper's nest"? Alarm bells should be going off about Bill Shelley.

It is very clear now that, from the beginning, the Altgens photo was the weakest link in the official JFK story. And one can even imagine that the conspirators breathed a sigh of relief when all people wanted to talk about was the "magic bullet", the timeline, the Zapruder film, and other things– because all of that paled in comparison to the photograph of Oswald standing in front of the building while the shooting was going on. It may be that it was always their worst nightmare that the focus would someday return to the Altgens photo.

Well, that someday has arrived, because the focus has returned to the Altgens photo. The Doorman is back! And now we can point to visible evidence that the Doorman was definitely wearing Oswald's clothes. And that means that he WAS definitely Oswald. There is no longer any doubt about it. Oswald was outside watching while President Kennedy was being gunned down. It can't be reasonably denied, where this simple fact makes a complete mockery of all the official lies concerning the murder of JFK and its cover-up. These lies can no longer endure.

Source note: This chapter previously appeared as *"Oswald was in the Doorway, After All!", http://jamesfetzer.blogspot.com/2015/09/jfk-specialoswald-was-in-doorway-after.html.*

More Proof: Oswald was in the Doorway

by Richard Hooke and Jim Fetzer

Those who have been following the "JFK Special: Oswald was in the Doorway, After All !" series are familiar with much of the evidence that has established that Lee Harvey Oswald, the alleged assassin of JFK, actually had a cast iron alibi, because he was captured in a famous photograph taken by AP photographer James "Ike" Altgens, which appeared in most papers the following day, but in some cases, such as *The Sheboygan Press,* which is now a morning paper but was then published in the afternoon–assuming that this is the actual issue that was published and not a substitute—appeared on Friday, 22 November 1963, the day of the assassination itself.

The Sheboygan Press

THE PAST IS GONE — WE FACE TO-DAY

KENNEDY DEAD

Stock Market Closes Down For The Day

Sniper's Bullets Cut Down President, Texas Governor

President John F. Kennedy

Disbelief Numbs News Staff

Altgens6 and Altgens7

Because Altgens shot a sequence of photographs that day, they are commonly referred to by their number in the sequence. Thus, the photograph we have been discussing and analyzing, which is seen on the left, is also known as "Altgens6", while another photograph, which is also attributed to him, known as "Altgens7", was published along side of it in *The Sheboygan*

Press. Although it is not widely known, Altgens7, which shows Clint Hill on the running board at the back of the limousine, appears to be a fabricated photograph.

By Clint Hill's own testimony, written and spoken, for over 50 years now, he had stepped onto the back step, pushed Jackie down, and laid across both of their bodies, while peering into a fist-sized blowout at the back of JFK's head, which in turn caused him to turn to his colleagues and give them a "thumbs down", all before the limousine had reached the Triple Underpass, whose shadow can been seen in Altgens7. That he was lying across their bodies was confirmed by Roy Kellerman in his testimony to the Warren Commission:

Mr. SPECTER. All right. Now, when the flurry occurred then, were you still facing forward talking into the microphone to Lawson?
Mr. KELLERMAN. That is right.
Mr. SPECTER. All right. Then precisely what was your next movement after completing the delivery of that message to Lawson?
Mr. KELLERMAN. When I completed the delivery of those instructions to Lawson, I just hung up the receiver and looked back.
Mr. SPECTER. To your right this time--to your left; pardon me.
Mr. KELLERMAN. To my left; that is right. This is when I first viewed Mr. Hill, who was on the back of the--
Mr. SPECTER. Precisely where was he in that instant?
Mr. KELLERMAN. Lying right across the trunk of the car with Mrs. Kennedy on the left rear, Mr. Hill's head was right up in back of her.
Mr. SPECTER. When you describe the left rear you mean as the car was facing?
Mr. KELLERMAN. As the car is traveling, sir; yes, sir. He was lying across the trunk of this car, feet on this side.
Mr. SPECTER. Was he flat across the trunk of the car?
Mr. KELLERMAN. Flat; that is right.
Mr. SPECTER. What was the position of Mrs. Kennedy's body at that time?
Mr. KELLERMAN. She was sitting up in the corner of this back seat, like this.
Mr. SPECTER. So that she was on the buttocks area of her body at that time?
Mr. KELLERMAN. Yes, sir.
Mr. SPECTER. And what movement, if any, did you observe Mrs. Kennedy make at that time?
Mr. KELLERMAN. I never did see Mrs. Kennedy leave that back seat, sir.
Mr. SPECTER. When you say the back seat, are you referring--
Mr. KELLERMAN. The seat she was sitting on.
Mr. SPECTER. Are you referring to the seat itself of the automobile?
Mr. KELLERMAN. Right.
Mr. SPECTER. Where did you look next; what did you observe following that?
Mr. KELLERMAN. Then I observed how the President was lying, which was-- he was--flat in the seat in this direction.
Mr. SPECTER. On his left-hand side?
Mr. KELLERMAN. Yes, sir. Governor Connally was lying straight on his back with Mrs. Connally over him about halfway.
Mr. SPECTER. Did Governor Connally say anything up to this point?
Mr. KELLERMAN. No.
Mr. SPECTER. Did Mrs. Connally say anything up to that point?
Mr. KELLERMAN. No.
Mr. SPECTER. When was it that Mrs. Kennedy made the statement which you have described, "My God, what are they doing?"
Mr. KELLERMAN. This occurred after the flurry of shots.
Mr. SPECTER. At that time you looked back and saw Special Agent Hill across the trunk of the car, had your automobile accelerated by that time?
Mr. KELLERMAN. Tremendously so; yes.
Mr. SPECTER. Now, to the best of your ability to recollect, exactly when did your automobile first accelerate?
Mr. KELLERMAN. Our car accelerated immediately on the time-at the time--this flurry of shots came into it.
Mr. SPECTER. Would you say the acceleration--
Mr. KELLERMAN. Between the second and third shot.

Now Winston Lawson was in the pilot car driven by Chief of Police Jesse Curry and was already ahead of the limousine around the Triple Underpass at the time. So when Roy Kellerman describes seeing Clint Hill "lying right across the trunk of car with Mrs. Kennedy on the left rear", given what we know from Clint Hill himself, he was lying across their bodies, with JFK beneath him and Jackie to the left of the rear seat. But that means he was *not* still on the back steps of the limousine and that Altgens7 is a fabricated photograph.

That Clint Hill is never shown prone, moreover, is further proof that the home movies of the assassination were revised to remove the limo stop, where William Greer, the driver, had pulled the limo to the left and to a halt to make sure that JFK would be killed, during a brief three to four or more seconds interval, he was hit in the back of the head and fell forward, but Jackie eased him back, where she was looking him in the face when he was hit in the right temple with a frangible bullet that blew his brains out the back of his head to the left/rear.

That some rather obscure newspapers, like *The Sheboygan Press,* should have run Altgens6 when major newspapers did not until the next day or even later has raised the suspicion in my mind that some of those issues may have been redone and replaced for an occasion like this one.

Since there was enough time for Altgens7 to have been fabricated, however, there should be no serious doubt that there was enough time to also tweak Altgens6, where the proof that we have adduced that Altgens6 was indeed altered has become simply overwhelming.

The Altgens6

The reason for explaining how we know that Altgens7 appears to be a fabricated photo—which had to be faked because, once they removed the limo stop, which was such an obvious indication of Secret Service complicity in setting up JFK for the hit—there was no time for Clint Hill's activities. But many witnesses had seen him climb up on the limousine, so they kept that part in and removed other events, including Officer James Chaney, who was riding on the right/rear, motoring forward to notify Chief Curry that the President had been shot.

This, of course, is far from the only indication that we have that the film has been faked, since the "flurry of shots" that Roy Kellerman described to the Warren Commission had to be removed as well. Although there are some who want to insist that the timeline precluded the alteration of the Zapruder film, thanks to the brilliant work of Douglas Horne, we know much better today, where I (Jim Fetzer)

recently published his studies of the two events at the NPIC, where a film was brought there on Saturday, but its replacement was brought on Sunday. One of the oddities of Altgens6, moreover, is that several of the Secret Service agents riding on the right-side of the Queen Mary, as the agents' Cadillac limousine was affectionately called, were looking toward the doorway of the Texas School Book Depository.

Since we have more than 15 indications of Secret Service complicity in setting JFK up for the hit, they may well have known that the designated "patsy" was Lee Harvey Oswald, which might easily have drawn their attention, when they observed him peering out of the doorway of the building.

That is not to take for granted that it was Lee, but the evidence we have marshaled in our earlier studies, "JFK Special", "JFK Special 2", and "JFK Special 3", makes that inference a highly plausible one. The would-be alleged assassin would have had a cast iron alibi had he been featured in this photograph, which was taken at the time of the shooting. Insofar as the photograph shows signs of alteration, when the only reason to have altered it would have been if someone had been there who should not have been, the circumstantial case is highly plausible.

Moreover, notes from Lee's interrogation by Homicide Detective Will Fritz showed that, when questioned about what he was doing during the motorcade, Lee told him he had been "out with Bill Shelley in front", which makes a great deal of sense.

He had been observed in the lunch room by Carolyn Arnold as late as 12:25, he had already had his lunch, and it would have been most peculiar for him to have remained there while a motorcade carrying the President of the United States and his glamorous wife drove by, when he could walk a few steps and watch.

Doorway Man

A conflict has now long endured over whether the man to the left/center in this photograph was Lee Harvey Oswald or a coworker by the name of Billy Lovelady. Notice several odd features right off the bat: (1) to the right/front of the man in the doorway, to whom we shall refer as "Doorway Man" or, for short, "Doorman", a figure has had his face obscured as well as his shirt. Moreover, (2) a man to the left in this photo, who is wearing a Fedora hat, has his own face completely obscured by the presence of a child, who is wearing a wool cap and his mother.

That is not the least of the oddities here, since (3) half-way down Doorman's torso, the half-face of a black man (by his right profile) extends out as though from the wall to cover that part of his shirt and body, while (4) his shoulder appears to be completely missing and his right arm appears to be abnormally long and extended in a most peculiar manner. His right shoulder, moreover, (5) seems to be overlaid by the image of a man in a black tie, who simultaneously appears to be both in front of him and behind him, reminiscent of an Escher cube.

The first question to address, therefore, is whether Doorman more closely resembles Lee Oswald or Billy Lovelady. Here are images of the both, with Lovelady on the left and Lee on the right, where Doorman is in between them.

Initially, most of us would probably suppose that, although it's a close call, his face more closely resembles that of Billy Lovelady than it does the face of Lee Oswald. That was even the conclusion of Oliver Stone, the director of *JFK,* when he gave the matter his professional consideration. He thought it was Billy, too.

And that was even my (Jim Fetzer) conclusion when I first discovered the Fritz notes and that the man to Doorman's right/front had had his face and shirt obscured. I drew the inference Oswald's face and shirt had probably been taken out of the photo in *JFK: What we know now that we didn't know then.*

But Ralph Cinque, a chiropractor experienced in dealing with bodies and clothing, convinced me the shirts and bodies outweighed the faces, where, unless Lovelady was wearing Lee's shirt, Lee had to

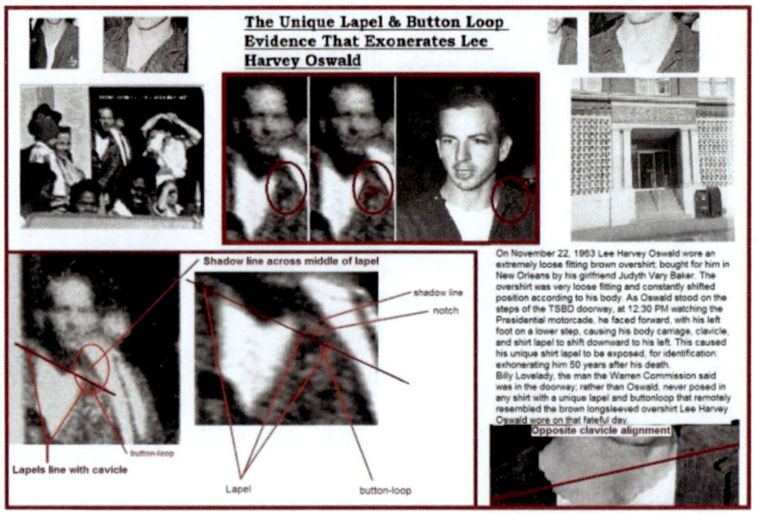

be Doorman. Richard Hooke has summarized some of the key findings that support this opinion:

Billy's Red-and-White Striped Shirt

Although Billy reportedly confirmed that he was Doorman very early on, he would subsequently visit the FBI to show them the red-and-white vertically striped shirt he told them he had been wearing that day, which contradicted what had previously been reported.

The FBI, intriguingly, photographed him in his red-and-white vertically striped shirt and, in their formal report back to FBI Headquarters, duly reported both that he had been wearing this shirt but also that they had identified him as Doorman, which was inconsistent with their own evidence.

Richard has taken Billy's report, which we believe to be true, and has compared it with Altgens6, where anyone can see that Doorman is not wearing a red-and-white vertically striped shirt.

We infer, therefore, that, having been given explicit instructions to show that Lovelady was Doorman, they went as far as they could go by photographing him and then attributing to Billy Lovelady as having identified himself as Doorman, which no doubt circumvented the problem of having proven the opposite and not wanting to incur the wrath of J. Edgar Hoover, who ran the FBI with an iron hand.

So here you have a photograph of Billy Lovelady, wearing the shirt he said he had worn on 22 November 1963, which is obviously *not* the shirt being worn by Doorman; yet being cited here as having "immediately identified the picture of the individual on the far left side of the doorway of the TSBD as being his photograph".

FEDERAL BUREAU OF INVESTIGATION

Idv 1-2

Date 3/2/64

1

BILLY NOLAN LOVELADY appeared at the Dallas FBI Office at which time he consented to be photographed.

LOVELADY advised that on the day of the assassination of President JOHN F. KENNEDY, November 22, 1963, at the time of the assassination and shortly before, he was standing in the doorway of the front entrance to the Texas School Book Depository (TSBD) Building, 411 Elm Street, Dallas, Texas, where he is employed. He stated he was wearing a red and white vertical striped shirt and blue jeans.

LOVELADY stated his picture has appeared in several publications which picture depicts him on the far left side of the front doorway to the TSBD. LOVELADY was exhibited a picture appearing on pages 4-5 of the magazine entitled "Four Dark Days in History," Copyright 1963 by Special Publications, Inc., 6637 Hollywood Blvd., Los Angeles 28, California. He immediately identified the picture of the individual on the far left side of the doorway of the TSBD as being his photograph. He stated this same photograph or one identical to it has appeared in the Dallas Times Herald newspaper of November 23, 1963, and in the Cincinnati Inquirer of December 3, 1963. He stated it also appeared in an edition of the Saturday Evening Post the date of which he does not know.

Mr. LOVELADY stated his close resemblance to LEE HARVEY OSWALD has become somewhat embarrassing. He stated his step-children, TIMMY EKSTEDT, age 6, and stepdaughter, ANGELA EKSTEDT, age 4, were watching television shortly after the assassination at a time when LEE HARVEY OSWALD was shown while in custody of the Dallas Police Department and both of these children remarked that they thought their daddy was on television referring to his close resemblance to LEE HARVEY OSWALD.

The following physical description and background information was obtained from interrogation and observation of LOVELADY:

Name	BILLY NOLAN LOVELADY
Race	White
Sex	Male
Born	2/19/37, Myrtle Springs, Texas
Height	5'8"

on 2/29/64 at Dallas, Texas File # DL 100-10461

by Special Agent ROBERT P. GEMBERLING / EMORY E. HORTON:vm Date dictated 2/29/64

This document contains neither recommendations nor conclusions of the FBI. It is the property of the FBI and is loaned to your agency; it and its contents are not to be distributed outside your agency.

735

That was an ingenious solution to an insuperable problem since now, if Edgar was not pleased with their work, they could attribute responsibility to Billy Lovelady himself rather than to themselves, even though they had to realize there was a problem here:

So Richard took the image where I had assumed Oswald's face and shirt had been obscured and tweaked it by restoring Doorman's missing left shoulder but also by introducing the image of a man in a red-and-white vertically striped shirt, which yielded an visual impression that was far less anomalous than the original but where multiple features remained unaccounted for.

Richard proved so adept at analyzing this photograph and offering suggestions for how it may have been rearranged I (Jim Fetzer) wanted to showcase his work—which I regard as brilliant—to show how it was probably done:

The Missing Shoulder

Another huge problem with Altgens6–and the strongest proof that it was altered–is the anomalous shoulder, which is at once missing and overlapped by the man with the black tie, who is ostensibly standing behind him. One member of The Education Forum, where a battle has raged over these findings, which were bitterly contested, took his own photograph to show that it was possible to replicate Doorman's pose, but as Larry Rivera shows here (on the left), that was only done by

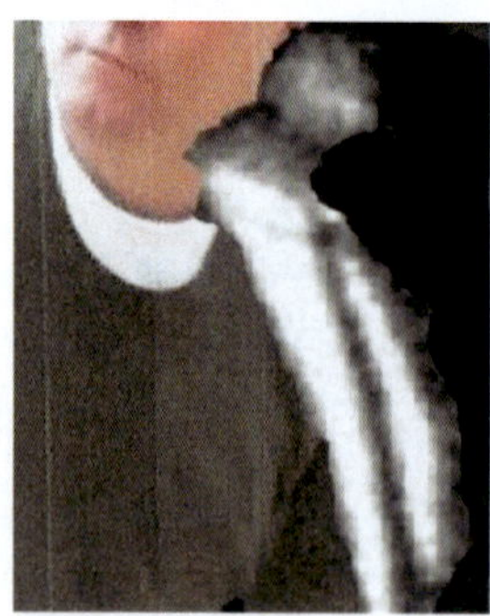

ignoring the extreme slope of what remained of the shoulder and would be impossible for anyone who has one:

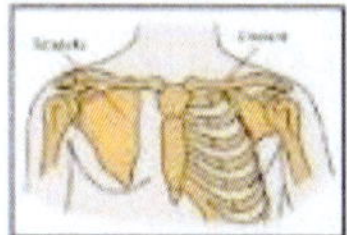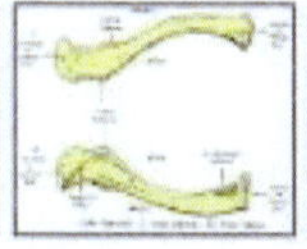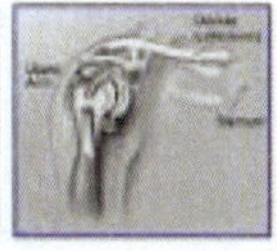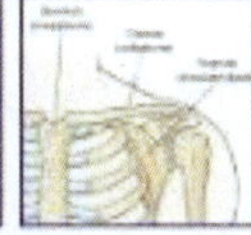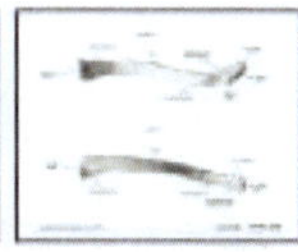

But there can be no serious doubt that, for anyone with a clavicle, this position is anatomically impossible, where, in my opinion, none of those who were disputing our discoveries ever actually succeeded in showing we had anything wrong:

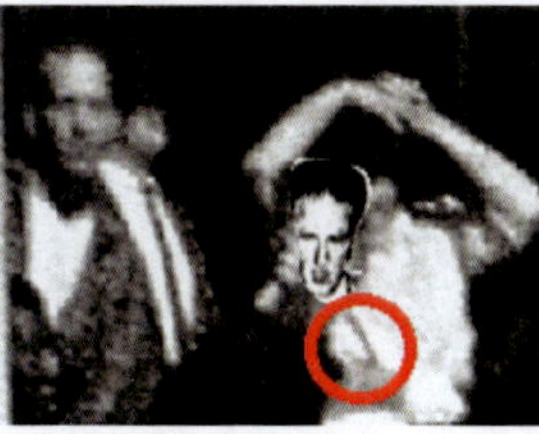

What could be a more stunning proof of the alteration of Altgens6 than that the most important figure is standing in a position that would be anatomically impossible unless he were missing one of his skeleton's most important bones? But Richard was not done yet, and began speculating on how that image itself could have been created using the figure we will call Black-Tie-Man.

Indeed, one more indication that Lee had been set up was that Bill Shelley did not vouch for him, after he told Will Fritz that he had been "out with Bill Shelley in front". Richard has also noticed that he may have been right where Lee said he had been—and why would Lee have said such a thing were it not true?

Shelley turns out to have been a member of the Civilian Air Patrol, which was founded by D. H. Byrd, the oil tycoon who owned the TSBD, and Shelley had known Lee and David Ferrie in an earlier life. He was almost certainly one of those keeping tabs on Lee.

How it was done

What Richard realized—in a series of steps—was, first, that Black-Tie-Man had been deployed to conceal more of the shirt that Lee had been wearing, just as the half-face of the black man at mid-torso had been used to do the same, where, in that case, it was the open lower part of the distinctive shirt he had been wearing, which was completely different from the checkered shirt that those responsible were using as a replacement.

BLACK-TIE MAN EXPOSED!

Most Americans are probably not familiar with Black Tie Man; he is very illusive. Black Tie Man makes an appearance in the famous photo, by Ike Altgens, of President Kennedy being shot, while Lee Harvey Oswald looks on from the doorway of the Texas School Book Depository, on November 22, 1963.

At first, the natural inclination of the human mind is to assume Black Tie Man is a pile of rags, or a gym towel, draped over Lee Harvey Oswald's left shoulder. BUT, make no mistake about it: the Warren Commission position is that Black Tie Man is a man; atop Lee Harvey Oswald's, anatomically impossible; photo shop amputated, left shoulder.

Question: How can Black Tie Man be in front, and behind, of Lee Harvey Oswald at the same time?
Answer: I do not know, but, he must be because Gerry Ford endorsed it.

Explanation: the Black Tie Man illusion is similar to that employed by graphic artist M.C. Escher; as demonstrated in his famous work Waterfall (below) where the human mind is deceived; has trouble determining which way the water is going.

Black Tie Man's Cover is Blown: the truth is Black Tie Man was a ruse to cover up the left collar, lapel, and distinctive button loop on Lee Harvey Oswald's brown, long-sleeved, shirt. None of the, many, shirts the conspirators have claimed Bill Lovelady wore that day were even remotely similar to Lee Harvey Oswald's left collar, lapel, and distictive button loop.

Final Answer: Black Tie Man was neither in front, or behind Lee Harvey Oswald; Black Tie Man was merely a poorly super-imposed photo clip coverup of Lee Harvey Oswald's left collar, lapel, and distictive button loop by the conspirators behind the assassination of President Kennedy.

It was not the red-and-white vertically stripped shirt that Billy had said he was wearing—which was even short-sleeved, but it was available from a member of the crowd:

What Richard also realized—as he considered this further—was that, in order to make the alteration subtle enough to by and large escape casual detection, they needed to use elements that were present in the original photograph, especially if they could thereby solve more than one problem at a time. He conjectured—and the fit is too perfect for Richard to be wrong—that they had take the shirt and tie off of the man wearing the Fedora–who looks a great deal like Jack Ruby–and shift it to conceal the shoulder they wanted to obscure, while moving the image of a woman and child in front of him:

While we have not figured out where the woman holding the child was found, since it is no longer in the extant image, we cannot resolve that question. But no doubt it was there originally, since the texture, focus, and other qualities of the image would have given the fabrication away, had they not used original material from the same approximate location.

Here is another way in which the shift may have been made, where both appear to accommodate the crucial desideratum of covering up Doorman's shirt and, we believe, removing Jack Ruby from close and visible proximity to a dark place:

The Lovelady Impostor

Jack Ruby at Oswald's Midnight Press Conference on Friday night, November 22,

For those who do not know the natty dresser who went by the name "Jack Ruby", here is a photograph of him at the Friday evening press conference, where he does not appear to have changed his clothes. Jack and Lee knew each other, not only in Dallas but also in New Orleans. Beverly Oliver has told me how she had come to Jack's Carousel Club after her own performance as a singer at another near-by nightclub, when Jack called her over and introduced her to "Lee Oswald of the CIA". That they would be in close proximity at the TSBD is not really that surprising, since Jack was no doubt also keeping tabs on Lee.

When you reinsert Billy in his short-sleeved, red-and-white vertically stripped shirt, then the series of moves that those who were altering

Altgens6 appear to have made are represented here, where the original obfuscation of the face and the shirt that I (Jim Fetzer) surmised must have been Lee Oswald were more probably required to obliterate the distinctive shirt that Billy was wearing, which, had it surfaced early on, would have given the game away. I therefore believe that Richard has done a brilliant job of reconstruction of how the original was converted into the anomalous image we have available today:

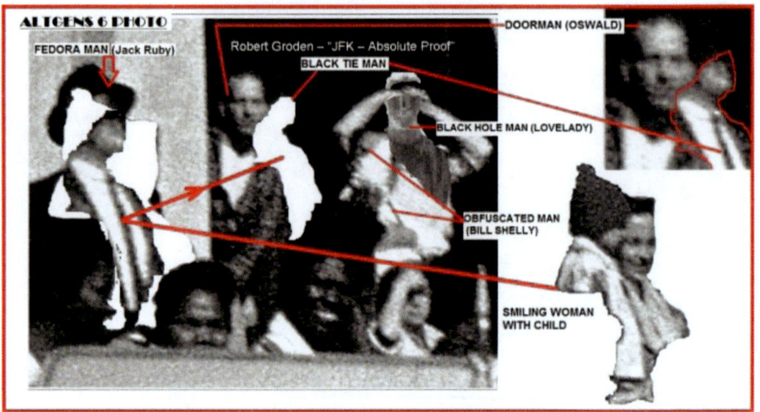

A residual issue, which Ralph Cinque has been relentlessly pursuing, is how the Lovelady impostor was introduced into footage that was purportedly made in the Dallas Police Department (DPD), which appears to have been done to reinforce the impression that Billy Lovelady was wearing a checkered shirt that day rather than his red-and-white vertically striped shirt, where you can see the impostor in the crowd outside the TSBD shortly after the shooting and in the footage

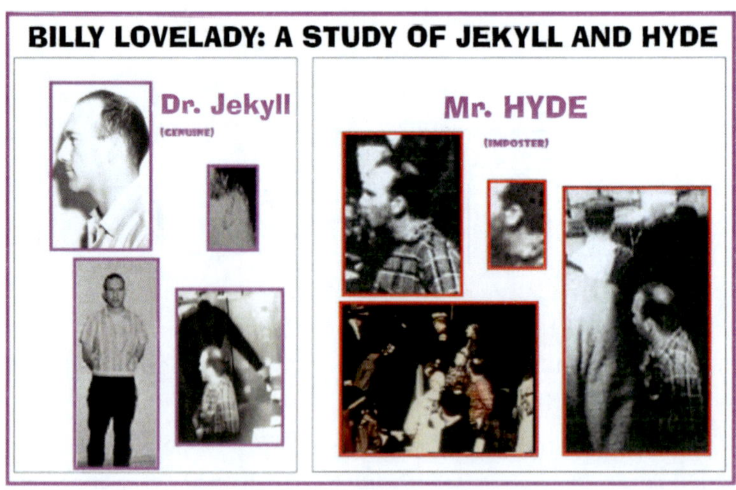

from the DPD on the right hand side, but where the differences between him and Billy Lovelady even extend to their ears:

Ears are as distinctive as fingerprints, which has left all of us astonished that the members of The Education Forum who were opposing us so furiously would not even acknowledge were distinct.

The gross differences in their appearance even caused me (Jim Fetzer) to describe the impostor as "looking like a gorilla," while Billy himself had a relatively normal and even passive appearance. But that Lee Oswald was on the steps of the depository must not be allowed to make its way into the public domain as the simplest possible proof that our government has been lying to us for over 50 years about the death of JFK.

Source note: This chapter previously appeared as "More Proof: Oswald was in the Doorway", *http://jamesfetzer.blogspot.com/2015/09/oswald-was-indoorway-after-all-with.html.*

16

The Oswald, Lovelady and Doorman Shirts: A Study in Pixels

by Judyth Vary Baker

First of all, I approach the matter of "Oswald in the doorway" as an academic study, since there is ample evidence that Lee H. Oswald could not have been on the sixth floor of the Texas School Book Depository (TSBD) at the moment of the assassination, thanks to witnesses such as Victoria Adams, Sandra Stiles and others. I knew Lee Oswald personally (see my book *Me and Lee, How I came to know, love and lose Lee Harvey Oswald*) which has impelled me to speak out in his defense since 1999.

Having been trained as a scientist, I have critically examined two contending "doorway" figures that could be Lee Oswald, generally dubbed "Doorway Man" and "Prayer Man" and the means used to identify those figures and others present. Researcher Larry Rivera and I have spent considerable time and effort doing so, assisted by photo expert Chana Gail Willis, photo enhancement programs, and the work of researchers such as Staffan H. Westerberg and Peter Engwall.(1)

My present focus is on the figure dubbed "Doorway Man," as I am personally familiar with the shirt that Oswald was photographed wearing on 22 November 1963, the day of the Kennedy assassination and his almost immediate arrest. The shirt was photographed numerous times and is distinctive in pattern and design. So far, it has proven impossible to locate a duplicate. The uniqueness of the shirt makes it important concerning Doorway Man.

The famed Altgens6 photo shows a tiny figure in the doorway of the TSBD in the early moments when gunfire first occurred in the Kennedy assassination (where JFK is clutching his throat and the Secret Service agents appear lost). The face of this figure looks troublingly like Lee Harvey Oswald, although a portion of the hairline resembles the hairline of fellow TSBD employee Billy Lovelady.

We note that fellow TSBD employee Roy Lewis, who knew and worked with Oswald, reported to Larry Rivera in 2015 and to the attendees of the JFK Assassination Conference held in Dallas November 2016, that Billy Nolan Lovelady was "too heavy" to be the figure in the doorway.(2)

It is important to note, as well, that in Harold Weisberg's *Whitewash II* ("The Lovelady Caper" pp 185–94) we can see FBI photos of Lovelady taken 29 February 1964, which show Lovelady wearing a "red and white vertical striped shirt."

He had reported to the FBI wearing this shirt: in May, 1964, he described the shirt he wore on 22 November 1963 to Jones Harris of

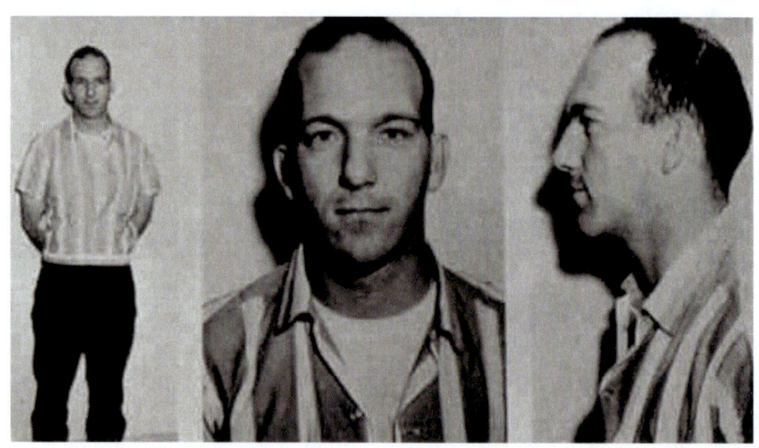

the *New York Herald Tribune* as "a red-and-white striped sport shirt buttoned near the neck" (*Whitewash II,* p. 190).

Lovelady would later claim he wore a plaid shirt that did not

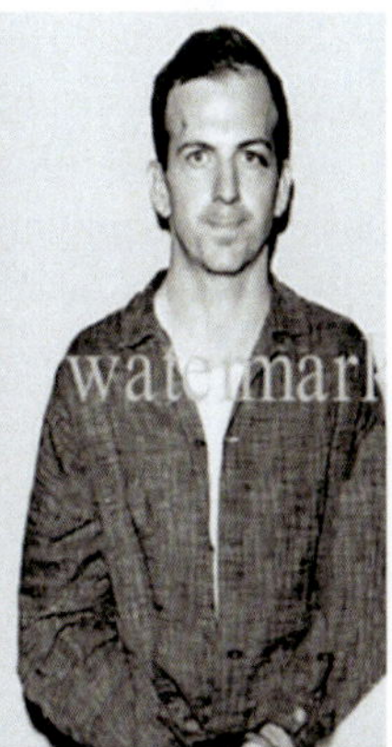

resemble the striped one, but which better resembled the pattern seen in the shirt worn by Doorway Man.

Lovelady showed the short-sleeved shirt to the FBI in 1964 with three buttons open but switched to this shirt for later photographs.

Leaving speculations to others, Lovelady has been sufficiently described as having been seated on the TSBD's front steps eating his lunch (no doubt standing up to get a view when the motorcade appeared), while notes made by Captain Will Fritz during his interrogation of Lee Oswald include Lee's apparent claim that he had been "out with Bill Shelley in front"— presumably indicating that he had been outside and present near the doorway at the time of the shooting.(3)

The Warren Commission presented Billy Lovelady as the man in the doorway. During his testimony to the Commission, Lovelady would be represented as claiming that he had been Doorway Man.

Without the statement from Lovelady, there would have been fierce arguments favoring Oswald as the Doorway Man, largely because the figure appears too slender to be Lovelady (later photos show Lovelady slimmer: they should not be confused with earlier photos).

Hence, for decades, anyone suggesting Doorway Man was not Lovelady was subjected to ridicule in the JFK research community. However, with photo enhancement programs now available, it became possible to conduct a pixel analysis of "Doorway Man's" shirt compared with Oswald's and Lovelady's.

The Doorway figure is so small in the Altgens6 photo that it can scarcely be seen. When this part of Altgens6 is magnified, various smears and lines suggest retouching or rough handling.

In addition, any Brownian motion in the film's emulsion might have helped produce some anomalies.(4) Even so, a significant section of shirt material was available for analysis.

Below, we have a good version of the area of the doorway:

Section of Altgens6 Photo by Robert Groden

Preliminary Considerations

Chana Gail Willis and Larry Rivera have determined, using photo enhancement, that a portion of Doorway Man's face was obscured by some incursion of light (or someone else's face) behind the Doorway Man's face.

I believe the following pixel degeneration study will assist us in asserting that Doorway Man's shirt was neither of the shirts in which Billy Lovelady was photographed. A simple approximation of this study can be repeated over and over, at any time, by anyone who uses what Rivera calls "the blurred method." However, it is important to make sure any comparisons between Oswald's and Lovelady's shirts use photos with the same resolution.

Comparing an Oswald shirt with 50,000 pixels to a Lovelady shirt with 10,000 pixels, for example, can skew results. I used photos of the same resolution, which were then converted to the same psi (pixels per square inch), and then magnified to degrade the pixels. Color photos should be compared to color, black and white to black and white, newspaper photos to newspaper photos, and so on.

Shirt the government claims Oswald was wearing when he was arrested. The author has no problem accepting this shirt as such, due to information presented by researchers Westerberg and Engall regarding the incidents after Lee Oswald left the TSBD and the activities of an imposter.(5)

Discussion

The original Doorway Man image is a tiny part of a much larger photograph, originally developed as a film composed not of pixels, as photos today are usually created, but of photosensitive chemicals in a colloid gel that was then processed in a transfixing fluid.

What appears to some as a hasty and sloppy attempt to retouch the area just under Doorway Man's left cheek with white-out, including a smear that crosses the mouth area and extends into the white-shirted figure to the right, for example, might have been caused by hasty film processing, where the result contributing to obscuring essential facial features.

Nevertheless, many observers agree that there are more features in Doorway Man's face that correspond to Oswald's face than those that correspond to Lovelady's.

In November, 2016, researcher Larry Rivera, his research supplemented by Chana Gail Willis' contributions, presented some stunning work, accomplished using photogrammetric analysis techniques, that revealed a higher correlation of Lee Oswald's face with Doorway Man's face than for Billy Lovelady's.

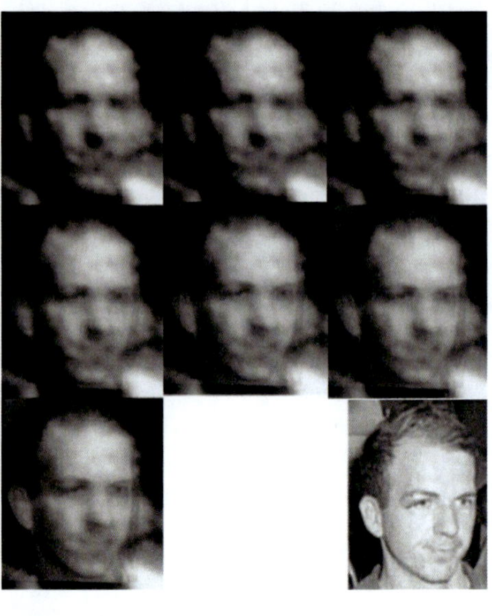

Discrepancies ruling out Lovelady included pupillary distance, size of head, shape of jaw, width of head, and location of eyes in the skull. Only by resizing Lovelady's head as the same size as Oswald's (which it was not) could it be made to fit Doorway Man's, but even then, Lovelady's jawline extended too far. In contrast, Oswald's head size, shape and features were a comfortably good fit. Only a few of hundreds of examples of Rivera's work is shown here:

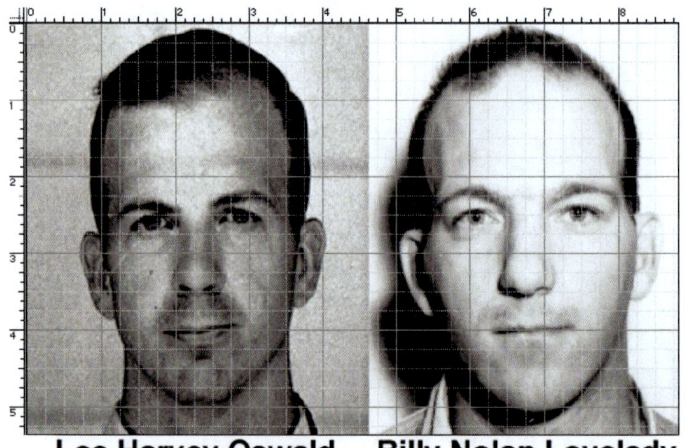

Lovelady's eyes were farther apart than Oswald's. In addition, Lovelady's chin was longer than Oswald's or Doorway Man's.

With these considerations in mind, it seemed logical to look closer at the shirt. A large portion of the shirtsleeve can be seen in the Altgens6 photo. Arguments that this was Roy Lewis' arm and hand—and waving—could be dismissed because that would have been the only part of Lewis that had the exact pattern of Doorway Man's shirt. It thus seemed reasonable to compare sections of Lovelady's and Oswald's shirtsleeves with the shirtsleeve in Altgens6.

To make a proper comparison, the photos of such sections would have to be degenerated to the same degree as the Altgens6 shirtsleeve. On the Internet, the Altgens6 photo is pixelated, as indeed are other photos of Lovelady's and of Oswald's shirts.

Magnifying the sleeve at first seems to support the idea that the pattern was a plaid. But further magnification would reveal something different.

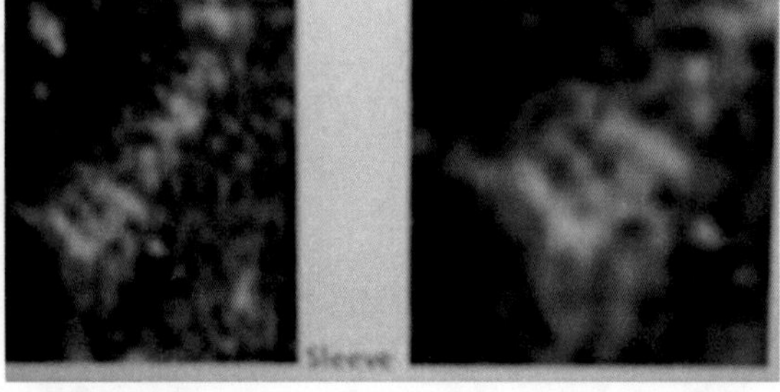

A Definition for "Pixelation": in computer graphics and digital photography, to cause an image to break up into pixels, as by over-enlarging the image.

Over-enlarging sections of pixelated photos of Lovelady's and Oswald's shirtsleeve would cause them to break up, a reproduction of such a magnified photo would create new pixels.

The resulting degeneration of the image creates a pattern that is comparable to those seen in the Altgens6 photo of the Doorway figures, especially Doorway Man's shirt sleeve.

Similar sections of the degenerated images of Lovelady's and of Oswald's shirtsleeves could then be compared with the (similarly degenerated appearance of the) Altgens6 shirtsleeve.

Lovelady's Shirt vs. Doorway Man's Shirt

It could be argued that Lovelady's shirt might be a candidate, due to what appear to be stripes or wriggling lines. In contrast, no stripes appear in the shirt Lee wore when he was arrested.

But what happens when both photos get degenerated, in a manner similar to how the Altgens6 photo showed a degenerated pattern in Doorway Man's shirt?

I chose a photograph that had been taken by Robert Groden of Billy wearing what is supposed to be the shirt that he had worn on 22 November 1963, as Groden reported:

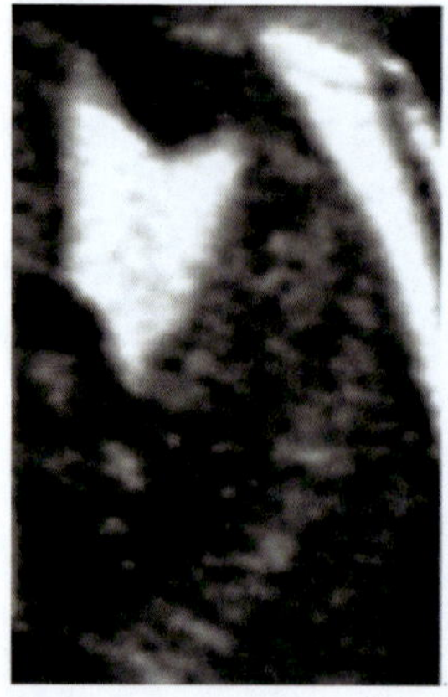

In order to create images that are appropriate for comparison, here are sections of Billy's later shirt and Lee's arrest shirt—both in black and white:

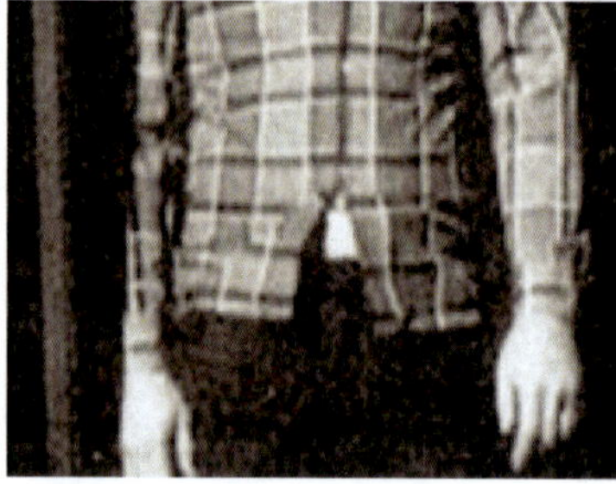

Comparing the left sleeves

We'll take sections from each left sleeve for the study and tilt them to the same angle as it appears in Altgens6. First, Lovelady's sleeve appears on the left (original and L-tilted). Second, Oswald's sleeve appears on the right (original and O-tilted) to attain a proper basis for their comparison:

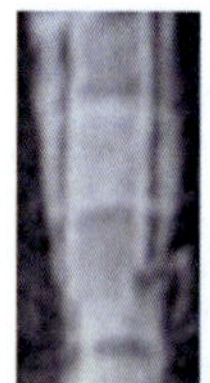

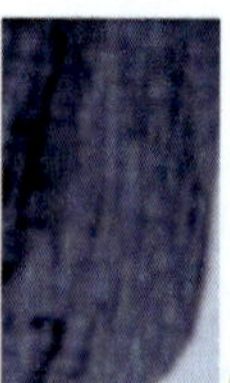

Note that the "plaid" effect in "L" (Lovelady's shirt) remains intact, even when it has been magnified, in spite of pixel degeneration, while a surprising pattern of boxes and stripes develops in "O" (the Oswald shirt) as pixels degenerate:

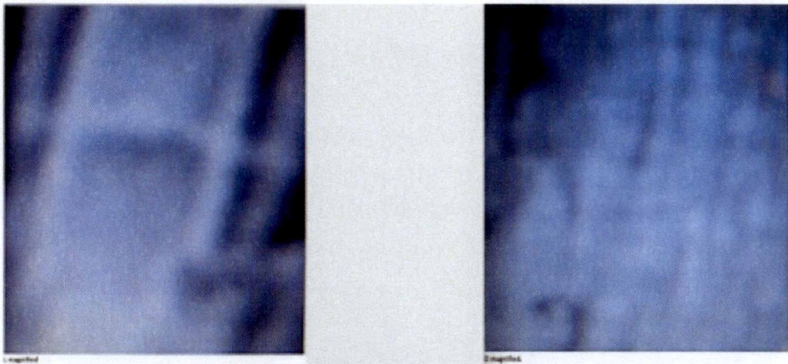

Comparing Similar Section from Doorway Man's Sleeve

The crucial comparison can now be made between these images and the image of Doorway Man's sleeve in the Altgens6 photograph to ascertain similarities and differences: Oswald's sleeve sample is to the left; Lovelady's sleeve sample is to the right in these side-by-side diptychs.

A distinctive pattern always emerges when Lovelady's shirt is subjected to this process. Below is another section of Lovelady's shirt, from a different black and white photo: The difference in patterns

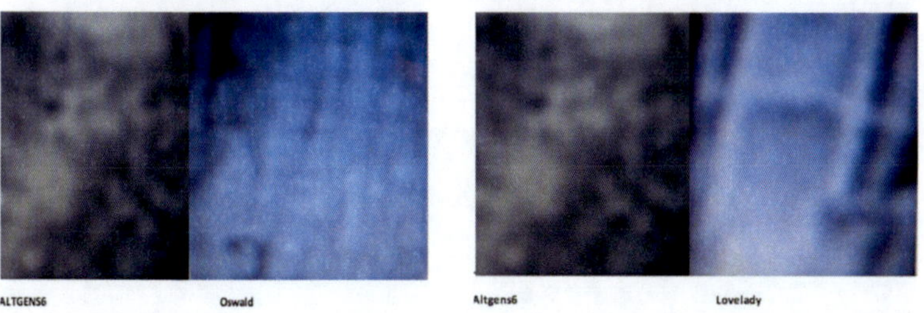

between Altgens6 and Lovelady samples is in contrast to the similarity that emerges when comparing the Altgens6 samples with samples from Oswald's shirt. Here is a different section of the Altgens6 sleeve (left), compared with a corresponding section of the Oswald sleeve (right, sample tilted to the same angle as the Doorway Man sample), through a blue filter:

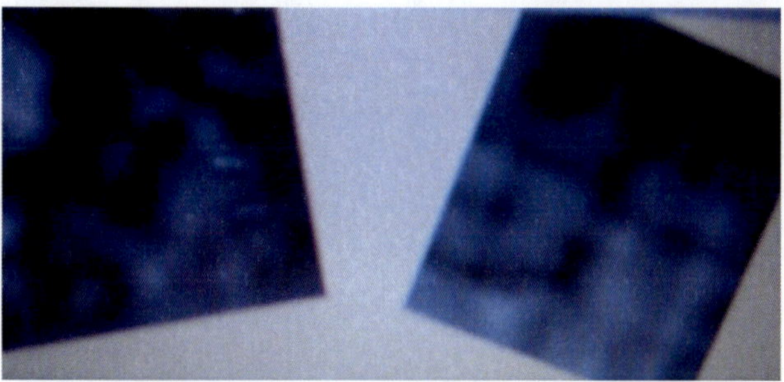

Who would have thought that Oswald's shirt, under these constraints, would develop such a pattern, and that it would resemble Doorway Man's sleeve?

It was important to see if other shirt samples would give results consistent with the above. For this purpose, other shirts with patterns resembling the patterns of Lovelady's and Oswald's shirts were tested, including these samples:

"Similar to Lovelady" shirt pattern

"Similar to Oswald" shirt pattern

Below, we first show the "similar to Lovelady shirt pattern" example.

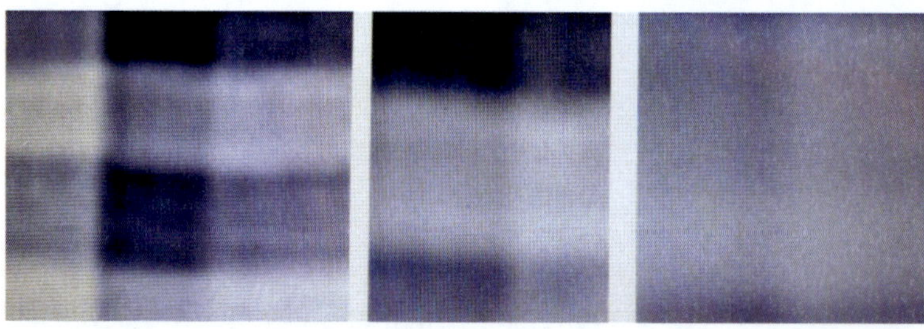

Next, we show the "similar to Oswald shirt pattern" example:

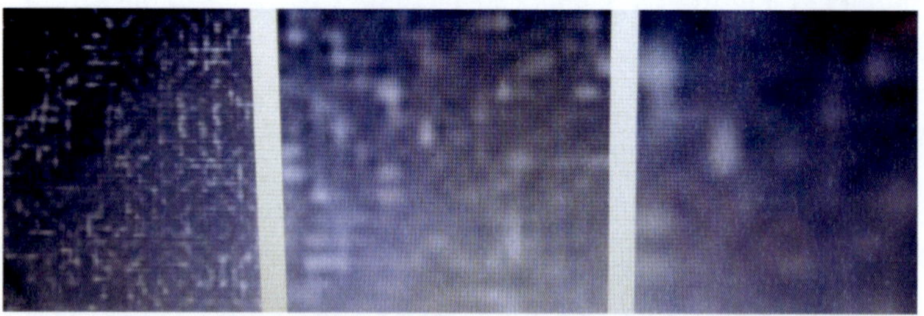

On the next page is another well-known photo of Lee Oswald's shirt, with a section that has some "crisscross" pattern magnified:

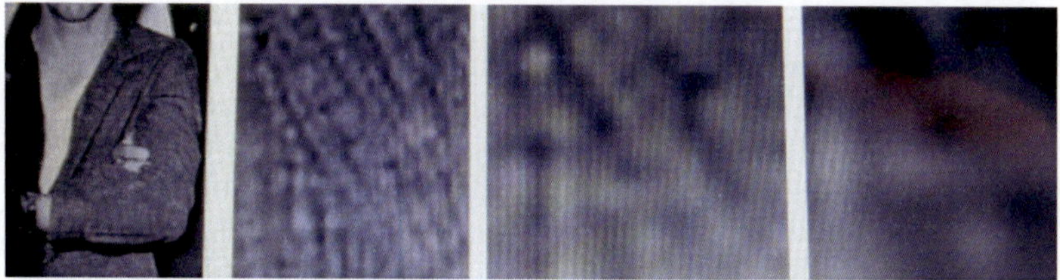

Compare to a section of Doorway Man's shirtsleeve where there is a white "plaid" effect:

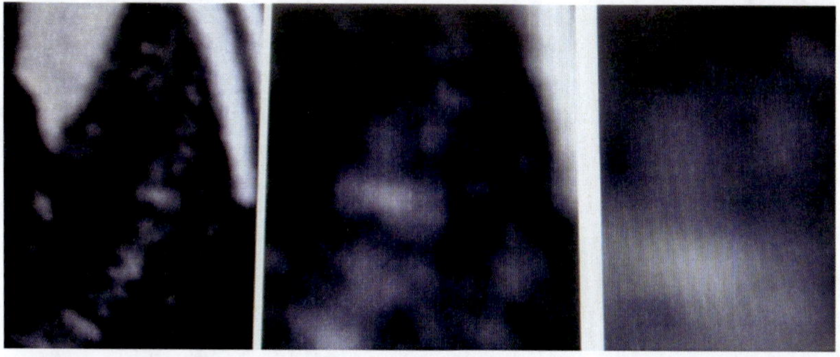

Here is another, less-known photo of Billy Lovelady's shirt, with a "criss-cross" section magnified:

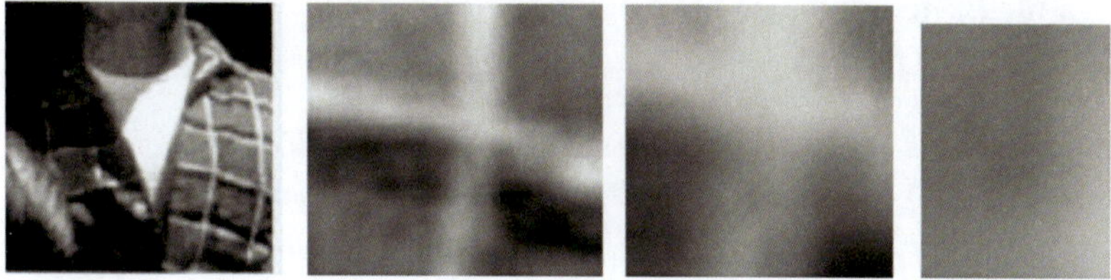

Compare to a section of Doorway Man's shirtsleeve, where there is a white "plaid" effect:

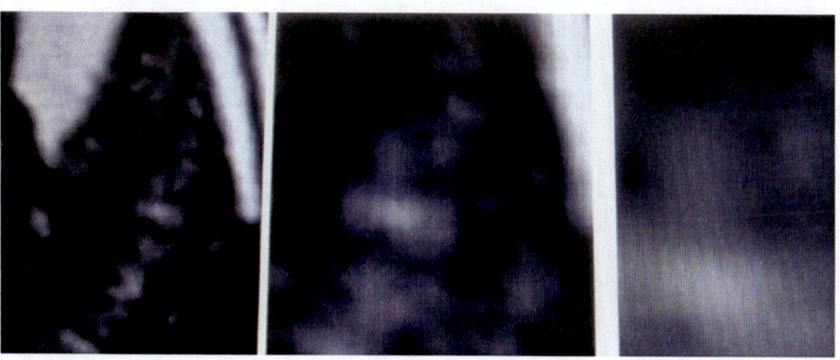

Conclusion

Judyth Vary Baker

The Lovelady shirt retains a distinctive lighton-dark pattern even under severe degeneration, whereas Oswald's shirt forms surprising marks and blobs similar to that seen in the Altgens6 shirtsleeve when the pattern is magnified, which degenerates the pixels. Therefore, **the shirt seen on the Doorway cannot be the shirt alleged to have been worn by Billy Lovelady.** Further, the pattern of Lee Oswald's shirt when he was arrested resembles the pattern of the shirt worn by Doorway Man, when both shirts are subjected to a similar degree of pixel degeneration.

Concerning the question as to whether Oswald is "Doorway Man" or "Prayer Man," the reader should be aware that researcher Larry Rivera has discovered several reasons to dispute the identification of key persons supposedly eliminated as contenders for "Prayer Man." Those who have been convinced by the Warren Commission, the FBI or the HSCA that Lovelady is standing in the doorway in the Altgens6 photo are encouraged to repeat the experiments conducted here to assist them in a final determination.

Source note: This chapter expands and revises *"Judyth Vary Baker Cements Oswald in the Doorway", http://jamesfetzer.blogspot.com/2015/09/judythvary-baker-cements-oswald-in.html.*

Notes

1. Rivera, Baker and Willis presented information supporting this work at the morning session of 18 November 2016, at the 4th Annual JFK Assassination Conference in Dallas, Texas. There exists sufficient evidence to support the contention that Dallas Police Officer Marion Baker first encountered Oswald in or near the vestibule on the first floor of the TSBD, according to the earliest statements (including Baker's and Roy Truly's), which then evolved to move the encounter to the second floor. This matter is addressed by Westerberg and Engall in their papers and publications in Europe. We anticipate publication of their material in the U.S. in the near future.
2. Witness Roy Lewis was filmed at the conference on 18 November 2016, which was attended by over 300 people.
3. For the sake of brevity, this paper will not be citing well-known facts in the case, discussions of which extend decades into the past.
4. Slight deformities in film emulsions, which are colloids, might help produce some blurring of such a tiny bit of film. See *http://pubs.acs.org/doi/ abs/10.1021/la00031a021?journalCode=langd5*: "Coalescence Dynamics of Deformable Brownian Emulsion Droplets" by Danov, Denkov, Petsev, et al, Langmuir, 1993, 9 (7), pp 1731–17401; also, "The coefficient of diffusion of the suspended particles . . . depends only on the coefficient of viscosity of the liquid and on the size of the suspended particles.." Diffusion and motility depends on the viscosity of the liquid (wet emulsion, a colloid) on the surface of the film at the moment chemical processing of the film begins working to stabilize the final photo product. The mobility of the suspended particles on the surface of the film, though admittedly small, could exert some influence on the visible results at the moment processing begins: since the temperature involved is known, and the composition of the colloid, the diffusion coefficient can be calculated. See *http://cds.cern.ch/record/382609/files/9903033.pdf*: "Notes on Brownian motion and related phenomena" by Deb Shankar Ray, Department of Physical Chemistry, Jadavpur, Calcutta 700032, India. (23 March 1999).
5. Westerberg and Engall's research is as yet unpublished, but has been widely distributed among researchers in the JFK Historical Group assembled by researcher David Denton. The presence of an imposter has been a credible theory for some time, based on witness reports such as those from Acquila Clemons and Butch Burroughs. It can now be posited, based on Westerberg's and Engall's research, that not only was evidence planted and testimonies distorted or falsified concerning Lee Oswald's route between the TSBD and the Texas Theater, but that an imposter also entered the Beckley boarding house where Lee Oswald

had rented a small room. The author is currently working with a team of researchers dedicated to determine who was involved in the murder of Dallas Police Officer J. D. Tippit. Witnesses who identified Oswald as Tippit's killer were exposed to rigged lineups, as described by researcher Michael T. Griffith and were, in addition, variously coerced, influenced, or otherwise compromised, and would be dismissed in court proceedings.

17

Doorman's Identity Confirmed: Oswald was Watching the Motorcade

by Larry Rivera

Abstract/Hypothesis

The man in the doorway in the Altgens6 photograph can now be positively identified using modern computer graphics techniques. The techniques used here can be completely and reliably reproduced using the materials and methods described herein.

Introduction

At 12:30 PM, on 22 November 1963, John F. Kennedy was assassinated in broad daylight, on the streets of Dallas in the presence of a multitude of people who were hoping to get a glimpse of the President of the United States as he drove through that city in a motorcade.

As soon as AP photographer Ike Altgens fifth photograph, now known as the Altgens6, was published nationwide and around the world, many people noticed a figure in the background standing in the entrance of the Texas School Book Depository (TSBD), who resembled the accused assassin, Lee Oswald. The obvious implication being that the image offered the perfect alibi for Oswald.

On the weekend of the assassination, the FBI immediately went out of its way to proclaim the man in the doorway as another employee of the TSBD company by the name of Billy Nolan Lovelady. The issue was further

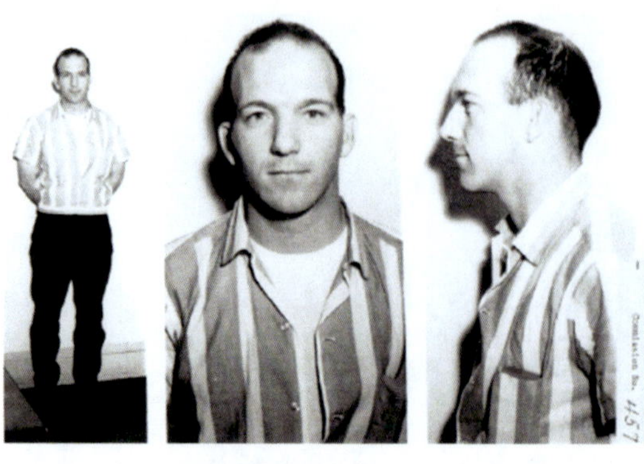

Commission Exhibit 4576, Commission Document 457

compounded when the FBI photographed Lovelady on 29 February 1964 in the shirt he claimed to have worn, which was a short sleeved vertical stripped red and white shirt, a shirt which in no way resembled the one worn by the man in the doorway.

Within months, Jones Harris would become the first person to commission special enhancement studies of the photograph, by having Bernard Hoffman scan the image and construct a mosaic which detailed every last pixel, which at the time technologically offered the most sophisticated enlargement for study. (1) According to Dom Bonafede, this exercise proved inconclusive because Harris could not obtain contemporary photographs of Lovelady for comparison basis.(2)

Lovelady and his employer fiercely resisted every attempt by photographers to obtain images of the famous “man in the doorway”. (3) Lovelady claimed that he did not want some “crazy S.O.B. take a shot” at him.(4) Despite all of this, Mark Lane was successful in taking this photograph of Lovelady, some time after the assassination.

Even though the area in question is extremely small, one of the arguments among early critics was the fact that the shirt worn by Doorman very closely resembled and seemed to match the shirt worn by the accused assassin Lee Oswald. Harold Weisberg was the first author to publish a nine-point study which documented these similarities.(5)

The FBI, the Warren Commission, and the House Select Committee on Assassinations (HSCA) never conducted reenactments of the figures in the doorway using the same equipment and film Altgens had used that day. Weisberg complained repeatedly that they should have brought Lovelady with the shirt he claimed to have worn and simply stood him in the doorway and taken pictures to settle the matter once and for all. (6)

It was not until November 2012, 49 years later, that a Texas researcher by the name of Ralph Cinque decided to commission a thorough reenactment of the figures in the doorway of Altgens photograph by utilizing the exact same equipment, position, camera, film and focal length settings that Altgens had used. (7)

Cinque conducted his experiment at the exact same time of day (12:30 PM) that the photograph had been taken in order to ascertain the effect of the shadows cast by the figures seen in the doorway. Moreover, despite the passage of time, Cinque was able to prove the exact position of Doorman in the center of the stairway, standing on the landing that led to the glass door of the front entrance.

Because of the strange parallax effect seen in the photograph, many had assumed that Doorman was standing against the West wall of the entrance. The first clear enlargement of the photograph was later conducted by Robert Groden, where he also proclaimed the figure as Lovelady.

This paper will explain the procedures of image processing and overlay in facial recognition as it is applied to biometrics, and offer new empirical data that should enable us to draw comparisons and make an informed decision as to the true identity of the man in the doorway.

Image overlaying in facial recognition

Facial recognition using image overlaying software is widely used and accepted in the field of Forensic Science. (See "Face Recognition in Forensic Science (Part 1)" pp. 4–5: *http://what-when-how.com/face-recognition/face-recognition-in-forensic-science-facerecognition-applications-part-1/*) The following is quoted verbatim from this source:

"The procedure of the comparison can be qualitative or quantitative, using relative or absolute dimensions. In a morphological comparison, the location and size of facial features is measured relatively, not absolutely. If the perspectives of the questioned and known images are similar and the position of the head is similar, the image depicting the known individual can be scaled to that of the questioned individual by

using the interpupillary distance or other consistent features within the image.

An overlay of the scaled known image and the questioned image can then be made in order to determine if the relative alignment of other facial features is consistent. This overlay of images is also referred to as the superimposition method and can be performed with video editing or image processing equipment [19].

A variation of the overlay approach is a photogrammetric one: a side-byside of the images is prepared and two sets of 3 or more parallel lines are drawn through facial features, such as the jawline, pupils, nasal bridge, on both images and compared by position [4].

For both a photogrammetric and overlay approach, the images must be of the same perspective, but the key difference is that an overlay allows one to view the length and width simultaneously although viewing the lines in the photogrammetric approach leaves more to human perception as one looks across both images.

Superimposition can appear to be doctoring the evidence if not properly explained because scaling implies changing the images to effect alignment, but the method is sound. (Emphasis ours) Consider that if you scale an image of Abraham Lincoln to the same eye corner-to-corner distance as that of George Washington, that scaling will not force the length of the face or shape of the jaw to match up, and rightly so because they are different individuals.

Just as scaling two images of Abraham Lincoln to the same interpupillary distance will demonstrate the similar locations of facial marks and the consistent sizes of facial features because the images do depict the same individual. Therefore a superimposition can provide extremely beneficial information to determine if features appear to be the same and if the relative locations and dimensions relate.

With an overlay, the examiner can "blink" back and forth between questioned and known imagery to assist in the comparison by identifying similarities and dissimilarities. In this type of comparison, facial landmarks, standard reference marks generally defined by the underlying structure of the skull [6, 10], are used in the main as guides and are not typically measured."

Biometric parameters and identifiers

The digital era of computers has opened up a vast field in the science of biometrics which goes hand-in-hand with forensic science photogrammetrics.

> "Biometric recognition, or simply biometrics, is a rapidly evolving field with applications ranging from accessing one's computer, to gaining entry into a country. Biometric systems rely on the use of physical or behavioral traits, such as fingerprints, face, voice and hand geometry, to establish the identity of an individual. The deployment of largescale biometric systems in both commercial (e.g., grocery stores, amusement parks, airports) and government (e.g., US-VISIT) applications, increases the public's awareness of this technology.
>
> This rapid growth also highlights the challenges associated with designing and deploying biometric systems. Indeed, the problem of biometric recognition is a grand challenge in its own right.
>
> The past five years have seen a significant growth in biometric research resulting in the development of innovative sensors, robust and efficient algorithms for feature extraction and matching, enhanced test methodologies and novel applications. These advances have resulted in robust, accurate, secure and cost effective biometric systems." (See *http://www.springer.com/us/book/9780387710402#otherversi on=9781441943750*)

Biometric parameters are now being used from individual applications in medicine to assess fetal development, to the deployment of security systems of mass recognition as cited above. Identification systems ranging from finger, hand and palm recognition to retinal scans, all fall under the umbrella of biometrics. Photogrammetric, side-by-side comparison can be used as a key component of biometrics, which can subsequently be used to verify and quantify the results of facial image overlaying.

Examples of facial overlaying and calibration of the system

A simple example of overlay techniques used in facial recognition can be seen when we compare these two images, who are obviously not the same person:

The very first task is to match interpupillary distance between the two individuals, followed by scaling, in this manner:

When we try to line up the rest of the features such as nose, lips, chin, ears, etc, the rest of the features fail to line up, obviously because they are not the same person.

Our next example compares two females who at first glance look very much alike:

When we apply the same overlay techniques, it is quite evident that eyebrows, nose, and mouth do not line up, and overall facial structures differ in shape and general contour.

Marilyn Monroe-Jane Mansfield comparison

Now we try two different photos of the same person—in this case Marilyn Monroe:

Both components of this overlay fall into perfect alignment and are a match in all biometric and photogrammetric parameters.

Yet another example

In 1971 Ramón Flores was accused of murder in Ohio and fled that state to hide out in Puerto Rico, in the southern town of Juana Diaz. After 40 years on the lam and in hiding, authorities caught up with Flores, and the following photographs were released (see: *http://elvocero.com/arrestan-en-juana-diaz-fugitivo-buscado-hace-40-anos/*)

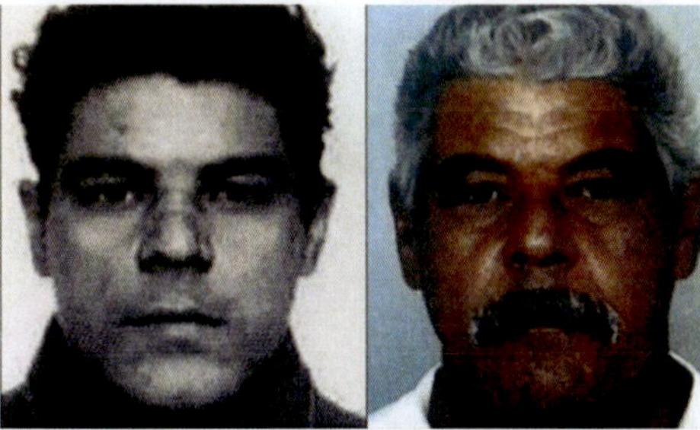

The difference between the two photographs is approximately 40 years.

When we applied the same overlay techniques to these two photographs, the results were as seen alongside.

Despite there being 40 years difference between the photographs, once the interpupillary distance was set and images scaled appropriately, the rest of the features lined up perfectly.

A small difference in ear size can be attributed to normal cartilage enlargement as the human body ages.

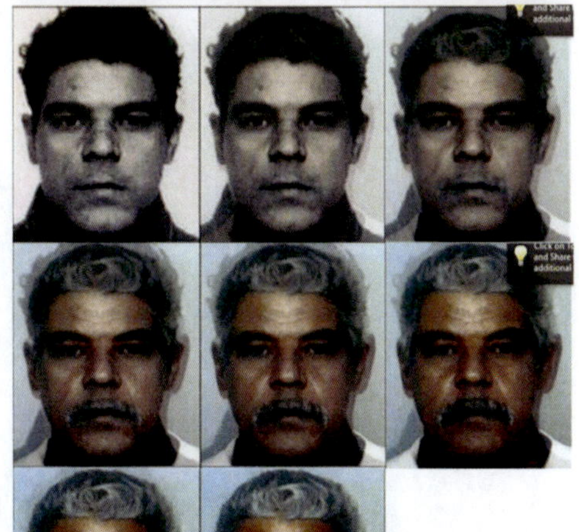

Ramón Flores
1971 and 2015

The preceding exercises have allowed us to calibrate and establish the reliability and accuracy of the system which will now be used to identify the man in the doorway.

Lee Oswald images and overlays

The same procedures and techniques can be applied to known photographs of Lee Oswald and Billy Lovelady. The following is a four-image collage showing Lee Oswald at different times in his life. We have overlaid a grid and ruler to facilitate comparison.

The top two images are from the late '50s, first a photograph when he was in the Marines, and the second his passport photograph. The bottom two are the mug shots in New Orleans and Dallas, respectively left and right:

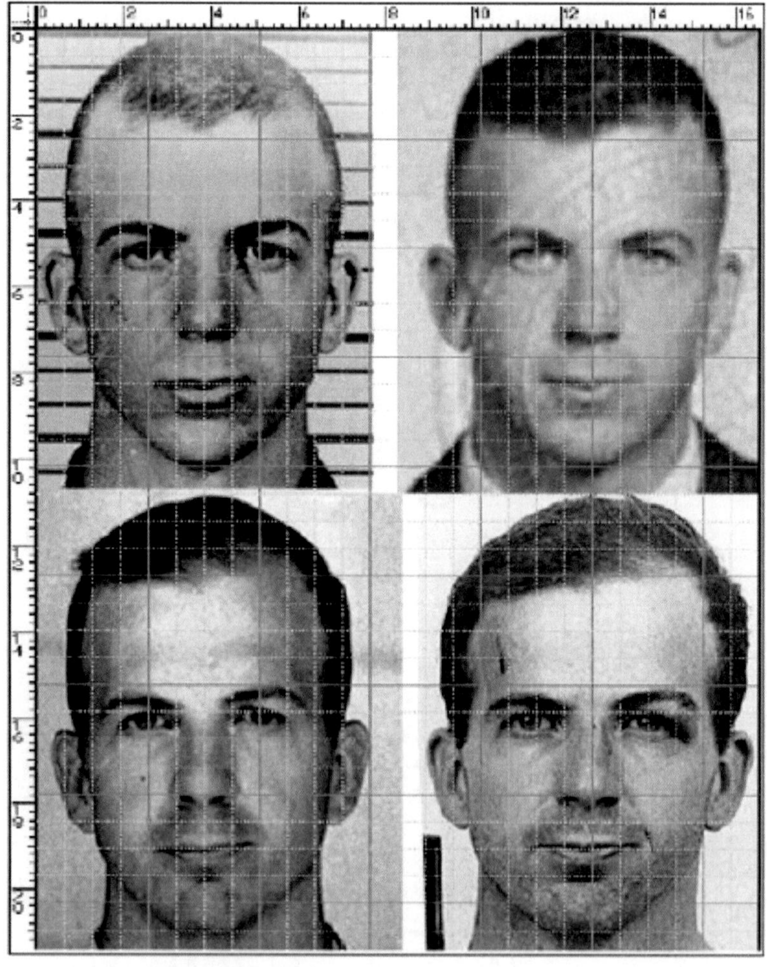

When we color code each individual photograph, we come up with this:

This exercise shows a relatively consistent pattern in features and cranial size. Here is the color-coded overlay onto the first image at top left, with the next three images at 50% opacity:

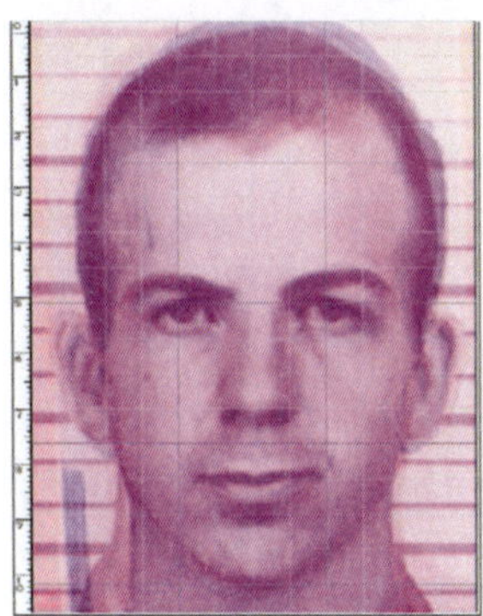

This overlay contains all four photographs of Lee Oswald shown in the two collages above.

Next, we compare the Dallas and New Orleans mug shots. These offer a unique opportunity to appreciate the shape and dimensions of Lee Oswald's face and head:

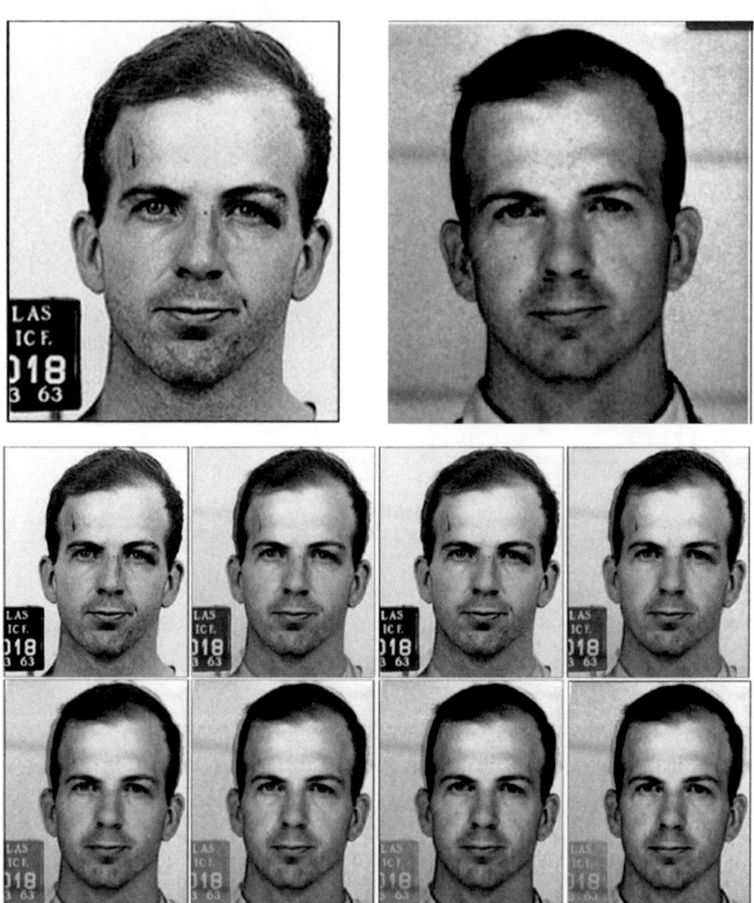

This overlay sequence shows a remarkable degree of similarity between the Lee Oswald arrested in the summer of 1963 and the Lee Oswald arrested in Dallas on 22 November 1963.

As shown in our earlier Marilyn Monroe example, the difference between these two images is almost negligible.

The inescapable conclusion here must be that they are one and the same person.

(Note: there are two small dark spots on the right side of his face—left as seen in photo—of the New Orleans Police Department (NOPD) photo, which are anomalies placed there after it was taken).

Billy Lovelady images and overlays

There are very few images of Billy Lovelady; however, the two that we have picked confirm the identity as the same person who was photographed by the FBI on 29 February 1964:

A

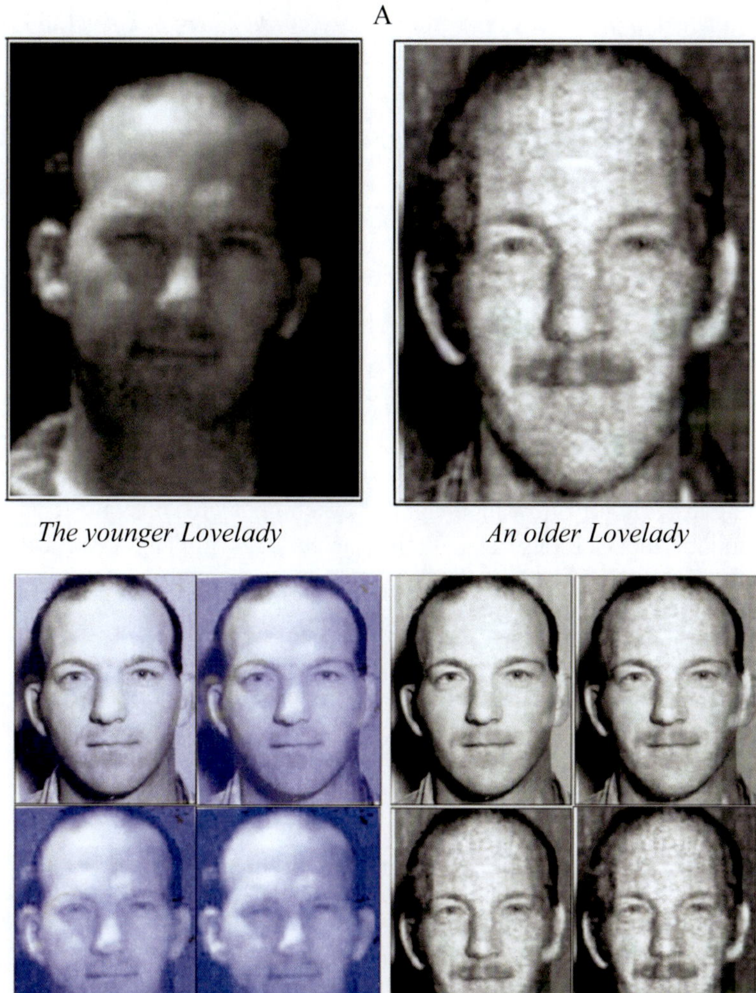

The younger Lovelady *An older Lovelady*

The task at hand

First generation researcher Ray Marcus was the first person to attempt to do overlays of Altgens6 with a clear sheet of plastic in the mid-1960s. Marcus, however, in a reversal of the methodology that will be presented here, attempted to overlay an enlarged image of the man in the doorway over facial enlargements of Oswald and Lovelady. Another limitation of his methodology was the use of frontal shots of the subjects as opposed to Doorman who is at a slight angle, showing 75% of his face.(8) According to interviews of Marcus conducted by John Kelin for his book, *Praise from a Future Generation: The Assassination of John F. Kennedy and the First Generation Critics of the Warren Report* (2007), Marcus reported that: "They (Oswald) seemed to roughly match", and he admitted the limitations of his methods.(9)

Obviously, the technology of the time did not allow for detailed analysis. Besides Marcus, as far as we know, no other researcher has ever undertaken the task of performing overlay experiments using the image of Doorman as a control image, and superimposing confirmed photographs of the two possible candidates cited by those on either side of the issue, Lee Oswald and Billy Lovelady.

The symmetry of the faces of the gallery (test) images

In order to validate the procedures in this study, and even though human faces are not perfectly symmetrical, it is important to first establish the symmetrical properties of the faces of the individuals being tested. The following images show a high degree of symmetry for both individuals. Indications of this near-perfect symmetry are revealed in this photogrammetric comparison, when we overlay a grid and ruler which allows for easy measurable parameters.

By applying the proper biometrics it is possible to demonstrate this degree of symmetry. This exercise will be extremely important when we move on to the methodology portion of this paper. At first glance, this side-by-side, photogrammetric comparison suggests that Lovelady's head was larger, longer, and wider than Lee Oswald's head.

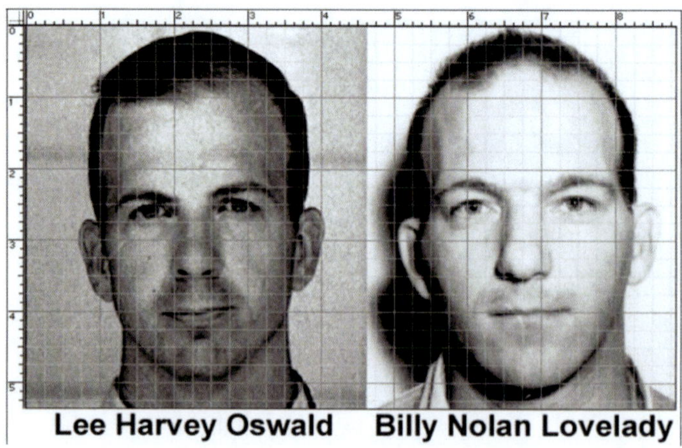

Lee Harvey Oswald Billy Nolan Lovelady

The next two images are enlargements of the Billy Lovelady 29 February 1964 FBI photograph and the Lee Oswald NOPD mug shot. Both have been slightly tilted to adjust the horizontal plane of the eyes.

Again, a grid and ruler have been superimposed, where this time the grid contains intersecting points or cross hairs that line up with the pupils of the eyes. This procedure shows measurable interpupillary distance between the two subjects.

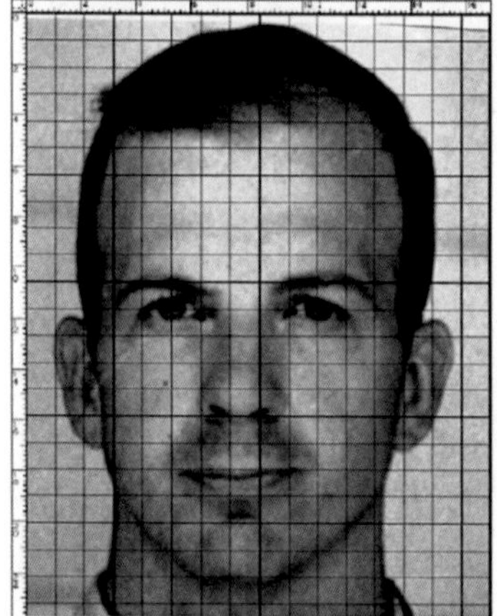

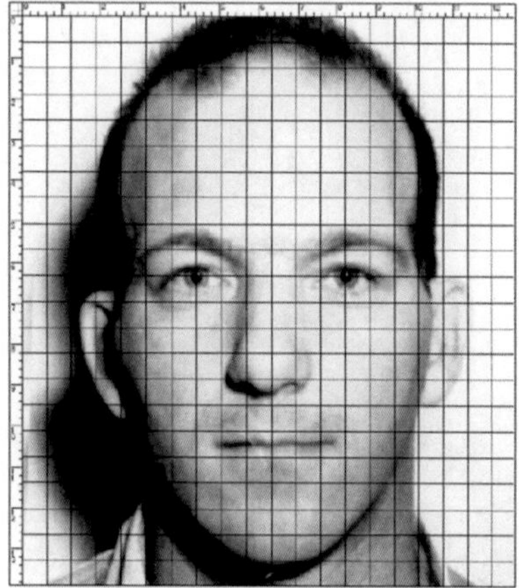

And finally, here we have combined and overlaid both of these photographs after calibrating the interpupillary distances to show the many differences between the two subjects. Lovelady's face is much wider, the chin is rounder, and the nose larger and more bulbous.

When we take a look at both subject's profiles, we note the following important difference in the location of the ears:

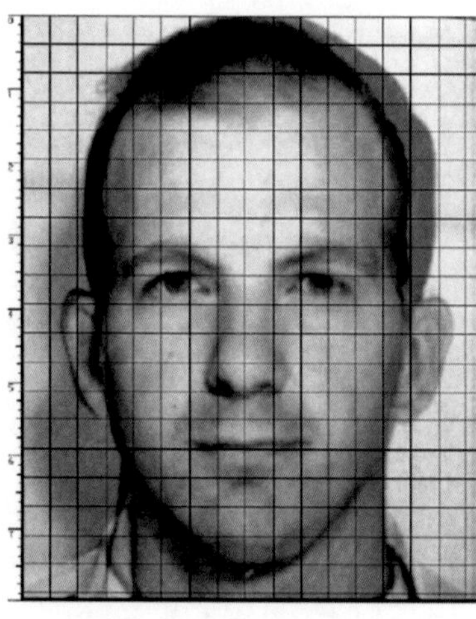

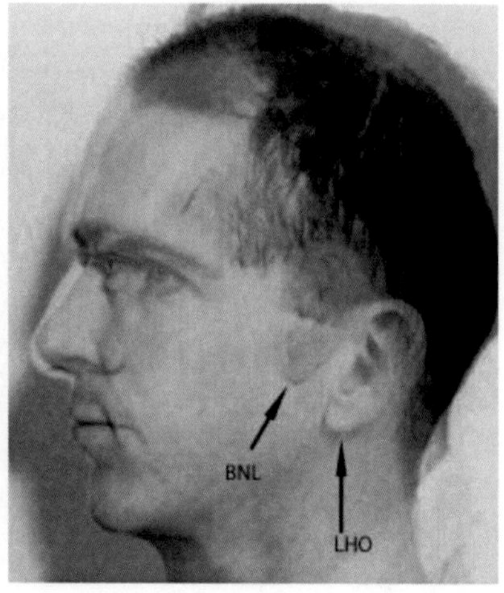

About the Control image or "probe"

The image or photograph to be tested is known as the "probe". The provenance of our probe or control image is an enlargement (or scaling up) of the Groden scan shown earlier above.

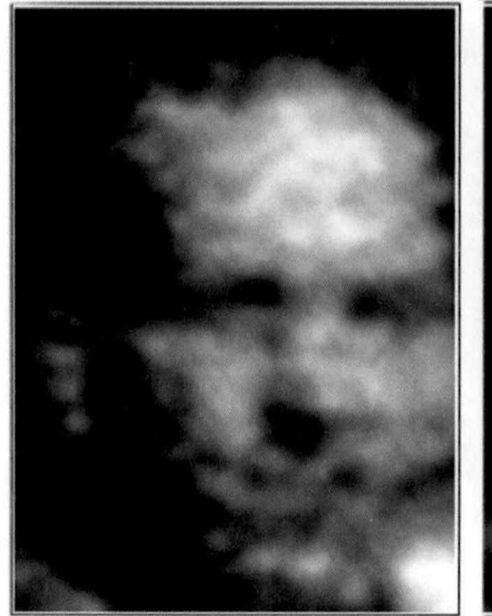
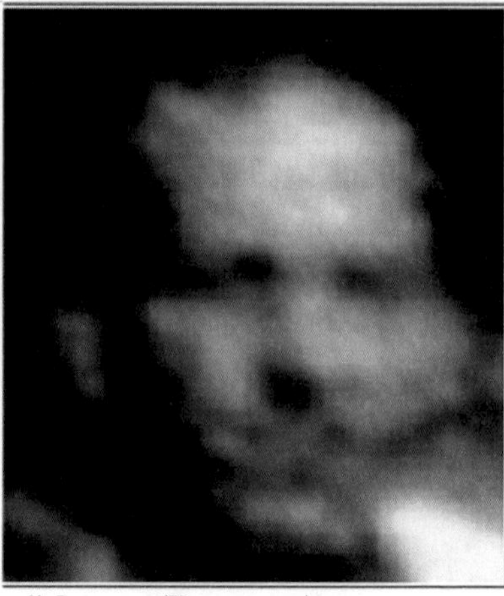

Control or "Probe" Image (Doorman)

The image first appeared in the book by Robert Groden, *The Search for Lee Harvey Oswald: A Comprehensive Photographic Record* (1995). Many in the JFK research community have used the image to either confirm or refute the identity of Lovelady as Doorman. It is not known how Groden enhanced the photograph to obtain the enlargement. Above right, Dennis Cimino has removed the haze and "mottled" condition of Groden's image to facilitate its study.

No other adjustment has been made. Bear in mind that Groden has already used this scan to identify Billy Lovelady as the man in the doorway and has continued to proclaim Lovelady as Doorman as recently as the weekend of 17–18 October 2015, where he addressed a gathering of researchers in New Orleans observing the 76th birthday of Lee Oswald.

To our knowledge, Groden has never submitted the image to any bona fide, peer-reviewed scientific analysis, and published the results in the manner we are doing here. The majority of the JFK research community has merely accepted his proclamation of Lovelady as Doorman.

Groden's argument resides in his contention that Lovelady's shirt was actually a black and red checkered patterned plaid shirt, and cites the "presence" of Lovelady outside the TSBD entrance in the John Martin film.(10) Groden has overlooked the fact that the shirt worn by the man in the Martin film contains a breast pocket on the left side which has a distinctive flap, whereas the shirt that Groden photographed Lovelady wearing in 1976 does not exhibit this feature.

In 1998, researcher Dr. John Johnson published two exquisite articles in *The Fourth Decade: A Journal of Research on the John F. Kennedy Assassination,* which, first, dealt with the man in the doorway issue, and second, pointed out the difference in the plaid shirts. Johnson concluded his study:

"The pattern of Lovelady's shirt is close to that of the shirt in the Martin film—very, very close. But how does the old expression go? Close, but no cigar. If Lovelady's shirt does not exactly match the one in the Martin (or Bell) film, it would be evidence of an elaborate hoax. It is simply inconceivable that a simple man like Billy Lovelady would concoct such a hoax all by himself." (pp. 36–-37)

Johnson's analysis centered on the pocket flap which was noted by Australian researcher Jim Baker. The following enhanced collage shows a breast pocket with a flap and button of some type:

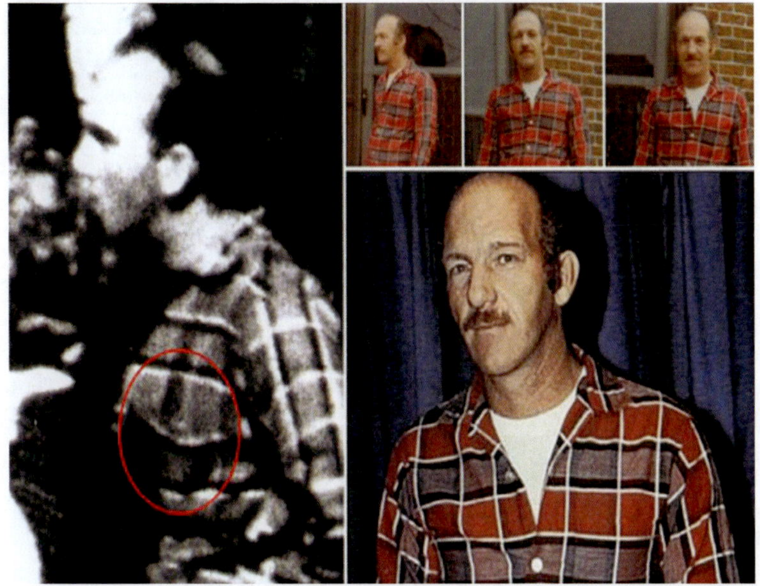

Furthermore, in 2014, Judyth Vary Baker conducted a computerized study of the pixel pattern exhibited by Doorman's shirt and concluded that it most closely resembled the brownish-red, richly textured shirt worn by Oswald the day and night of 22 November 1963.(11)

These issues can certainly be clarified, and all doubts put to rest, if the probe image can be successfully submitted to the same forensic facial recognition overlay tests which have been described here.

Materials and Methods

1. There are three images in the public domain that offer the unique opportunity to perform overlay experiments on Doorman, because of the angle in which he is presented in the Altgens6 photograph, where he is showing the right side of this face and ear, which is an approximate 3/4 profile. There are two photos of our subjects that offer the opposite orientation, which would be the left side of the face and ear. We have shown in our introduction the uncanny symmetrical properties of the faces of these two individuals, so when these images are flipped, we are able to produce these two workable facsimiles, which in forensic face recognition jargon are known as the "gallery":

The third image to be tested is a non-flipped photograph (right) of Lovelady published on 18 January 1979 by the *Dallas Times Herald* at the time of Lovelady's death. The photograph was taken by Bob Jackson.

2. The computer program which allows us to conduct these experiments is one which is extremely popular, powerful and sophisticated—Adobe Photoshop. Another very good and open source program by the name of GIMP can also be used, however we have chosen Photoshop for this study because of our familiarity with the program.

3. A screen capture program which shows precise coordinates on a computer monitor is necessary to copy each individual rendition as the overlay is increased in opacity. In the case that an animation constructed from each progressive image is required, it is of utmost importance to avoid shifting of the resultant images to provide a much smoother transition.

For our purpose we have chosen the program Gadwin PrintScreen 4.7. (www.gadwin.com)

4. Optional. In case animation is required, as mentioned in No. 3 above, a very good open source program to use is Photoscape. (www.photoscape.org)

Procedure

1. The control or probe (background) image is opened in Photoshop, followed by the two gallery or overlay images that will be used for testing. The gallery photos have been tinted magenta for Lovelady and blue for Oswald. This will allow differentiation of the exemplars.

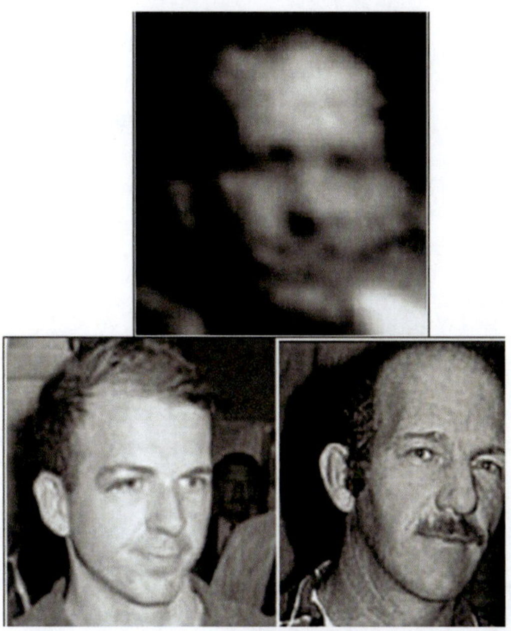

2. In separate procedures, the image which will be superimposed is selected with the select tool:

Alternatively (see right), the user can right-click on the image and select the entire image.

The next step is to copy it into the clipboard, via Edit->Copy.

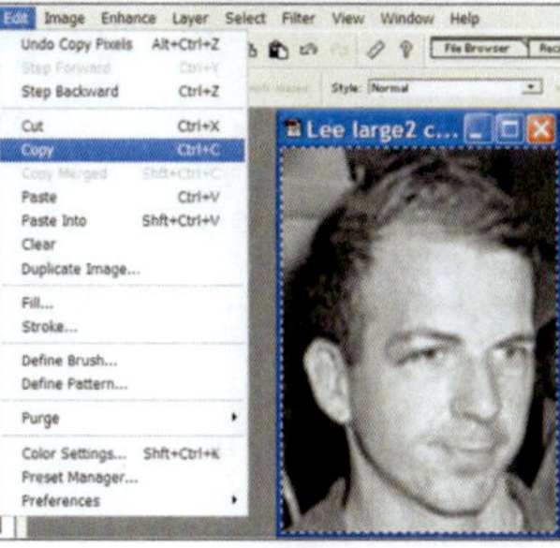

In order to color code the test images we must first modify them by using the color Variations tool, which is under the Enhance tab (right).

This will take us to the Variations page, where the image can be tinted to any color necessary:

Next, cut out and isolate the heads of the individuals using the polygonal lasso tool.

This tool will neatly separate the heads from the gallery photos:

And finally, before trying to do any overlays, we must render the white areas transparent—this is also known as the "alpha channel"—so that only the heads are overlaid onto our probe image, excluding all other elements of the gallery photograph. This is done in different manners, depending on the version of Photoshop.(12) (See notes section for details.)

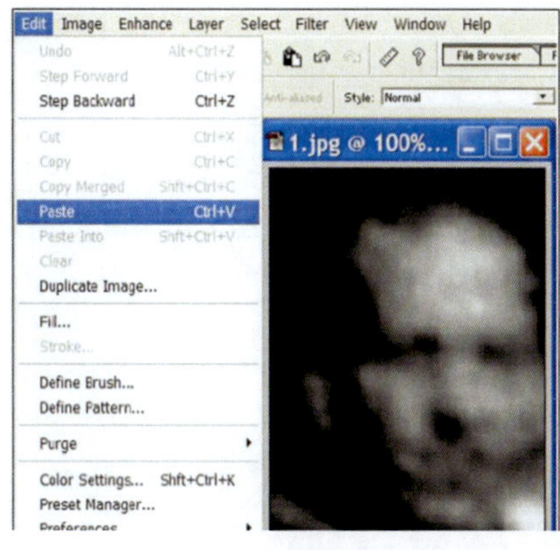

Once the heads have been isolated, right-click on the control image to activate, and paste the contents of the clipboard over the control image:

3. We have thus defined our first layer. We now move over to "Layers" at the top of the screen.

The definition and assignment of layers allows manipulation of opacity values of the test image which can be overlaid onto the control image.

There are two ways to control this function: 1. By directly entering the percentage value in the dialog box, or 2. By sliding the control triangle right or left:

By slightly changing the opacity it is now possible to line up features. In this experiment, we lined up the eyes and ears, and sized the separation and angle to match the control image of Doorman. At this juncture, the move tool is indispensable to tilt, size and move the overlay image to match it as much as possible with the control image:

4. Once satisfied with the position of the overlay, we are ready to start capturing the results.

Unfortunately, this is not a function of Photoshop. In order to capture different degrees of opacity, it is necessary to use the screen capture program mentioned earlier, Gadwin PrintScreen. The process has to be repeated after every adjustment of the opacity levels mentioned above. In this experiment we went from zero, to 5%, 10%, 15%, 20%, 25% and 30% opacity. After each capture, the opacity value is raised to the next level. Gadwin will place the captured image into the clipboard. Returning to Photoshop, we go to File -> New ->OK to create the new image with the correct dimensions:

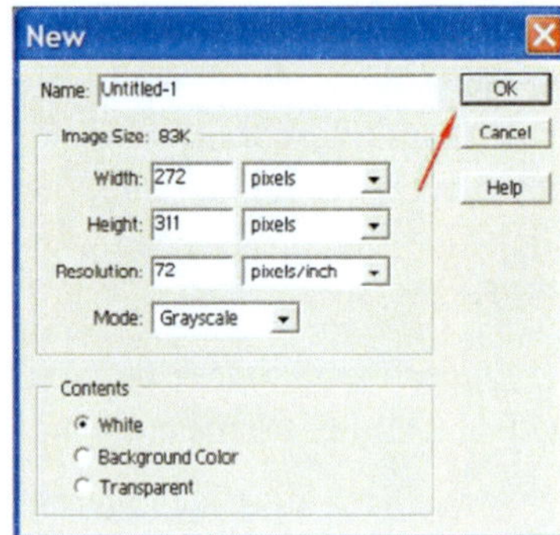

Paste the contents of the clipboard into Photoshop with Edit-> Paste. Each resultant file is saved in JPEG format with a distinctive name which allows and defines an ascending order: (i.e.: LHO5%.jpg, LHO10%.jpg, etc)

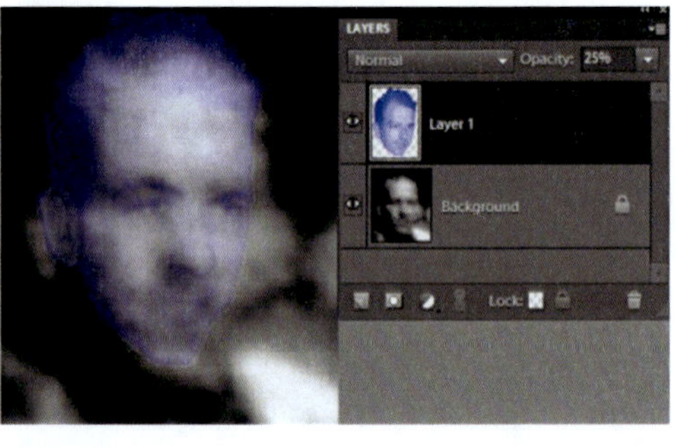

By experimenting with the opacity levels, it is possible to obtain as many different versions of the overlay onto the control image as necessary, with varying intensities and opacity. The next illustration shows one of the gallery images in the process of being scaled, positioned and overlaid onto the probe image with a 25% degree of opacity.

Results and measurements

After superimposing and overlaying all three exemplars onto our control image of Doorman, it is clear that there is quite a bit of difference between them. The following collages and images show the empirical results of our tests and procedures.

Billy Nolan Lovelady

This first collage of results shows our flipped image of Billy Lovelady.

Billy Lovelady-Doorman Overlay Collage

Observations

Once interpupillary distance had been set, we attempted to scale the head of Lovelady as much as possible, to match that of Doorman. Here are some of the anomalies:

1. Nose is rounder, larger and more bulbous. The bridge is different. *Nose shifts to the right, displacing it from the shadow cast by the nose of Doorman.*

2. There is slightly more space between the lower lip and the tip of the chin which brings the mouth slightly higher.

3. Eyebrows are more arched and there is more space between eyes and brow ridge.

4. Shape of the chin is different and the face is wider.

5. The forehead is swept back at a different, lower angle.

Our second set of results show how the *Dallas Times Herald* photograph of Billy Lovelady of the article dated 18 January 1979 lines up in our overlay procedures:

Billy Lovelady-Doorman Overlay Collage using non-flipped Dallas Times Herald photograph

Observations:

Once interpupillary distance had been set, once again, we attempted to scale the head of Lovelady as much as possible, to match that of Doorman. Here are some of the anomalies:

1. Nose is rounder, larger and more bulbous. The bridge is different. *Nose shifts to the right, displacing it from the shadow cast by the nose of Doorman.*

2. There is slightly more space between the lower lip and the tip of the chin which brings the mouth slightly higher.

3. Eyebrows are more arched and there is more space between eyes and brow ridge.

4. Shape of the chin is different and the face is wider.

5. The forehead is swept back at a different, lower angle.

A key aspect of this overlay reveals and confirms that because Lovelady's face was wider than Doorman's, the horizontal adjustment required to match interpupillary distance drew the face inward, making it narrower, to the point of throwing the ear completely out of alignment.

Here the right ear (left on photograph) fails to line up with Doorman's and does not even reach the required position.

And the reason for this is probably because the ear location on both subjects is different, as shown earlier in this study.

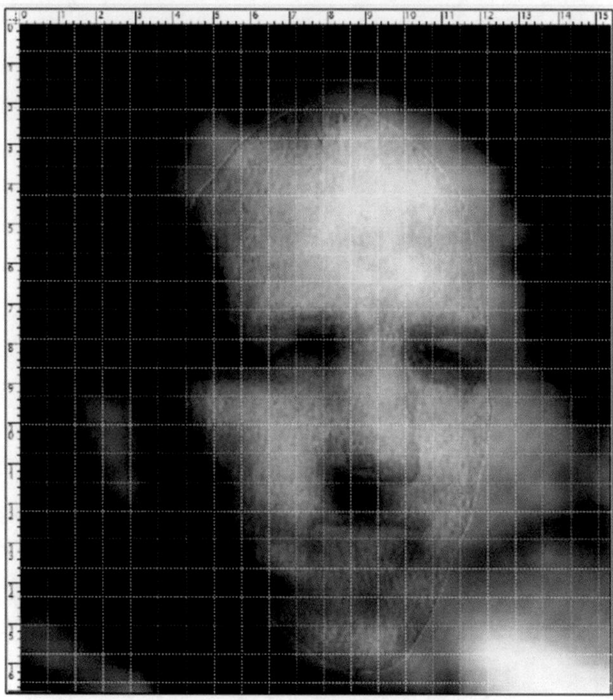

Lee Oswald

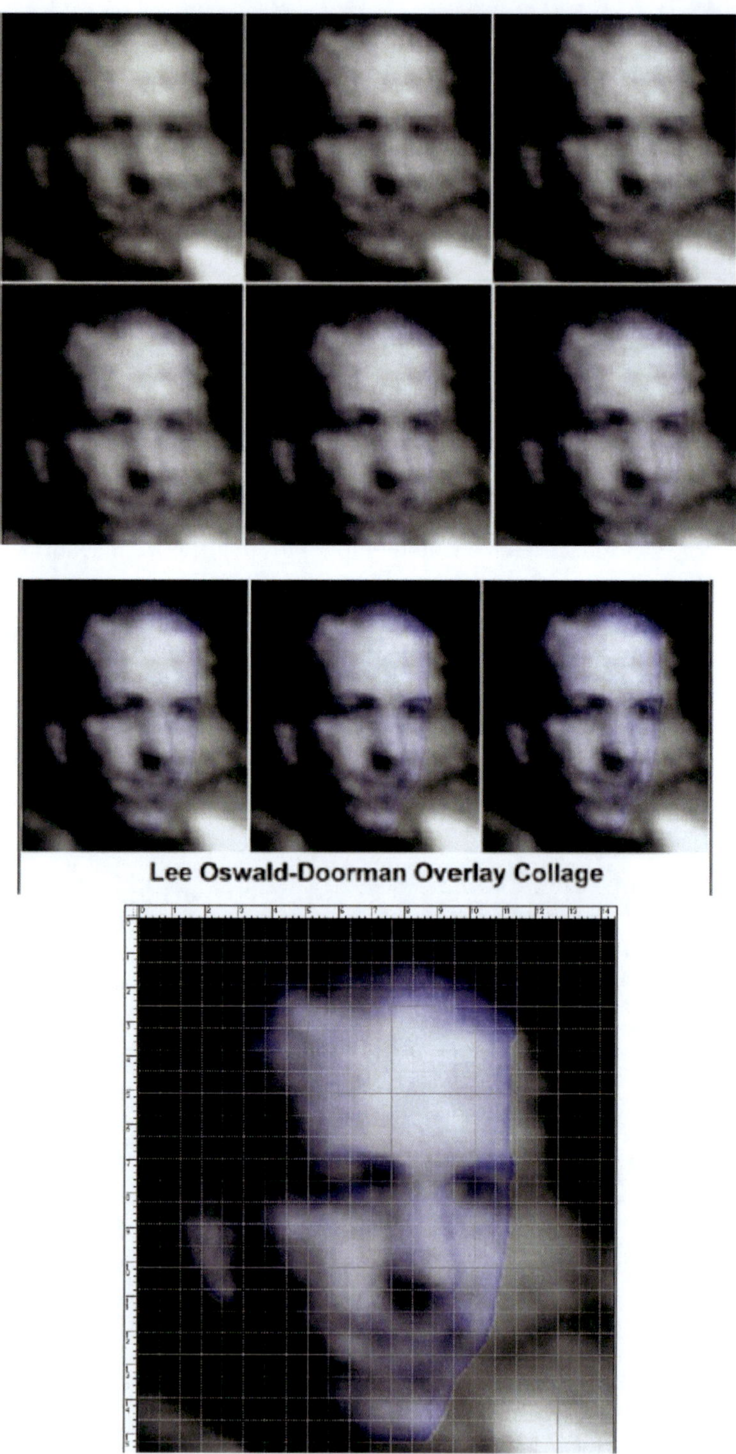

Lee Oswald-Doorman Overlay Collage

Observations—key identifiers

1. Interpupillary distance between Oswald and Doorman is the same. This makes the eyes line up perfectly.

2. Nose matches, including bridge and general conformation. *More importantly, the nose is in perfect position to cast the shadow seen below Doorman's nose, (which was caused by the noon sun).*

3. Lips, which are pursed in a particular and specific manner, are a match.

4. Eyebrows and brow ridge are more horizontal and are a match. High forehead is a match.

5. Chin matches in size and shape. The face matches in both width and height.

6. The ear is a perfect match in location and size. (note: Oswald had suffered a bruise over his left eye, which had caused swelling—when the image is flipped this area stands out somewhat.)

Photogrammetric comparisons

Working backwards, we can now apply photogrammetric techniques using the results obtained above. First by using the flipped image of Billy Lovelady:

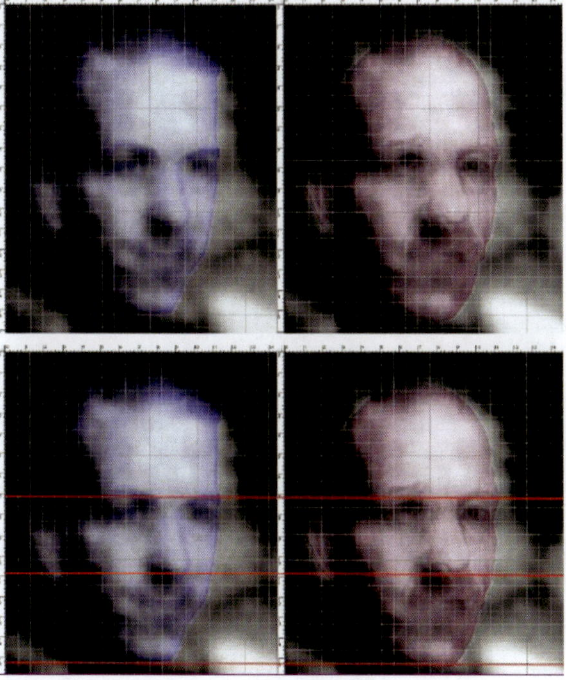

And finally, the photogrammetric comparisons using the *Dallas Times Herald* non-flipped photograph of Billy Lovelady:

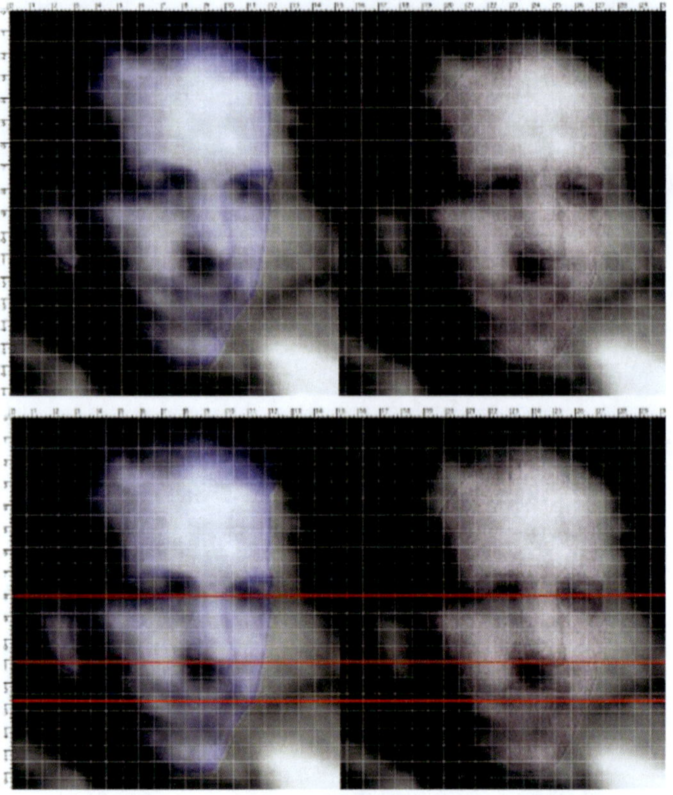

The narrowing of the Lovelady *Dallas Times Herald* photograph when adjusting interpupillary distance is vividly illustrated with the following collage:

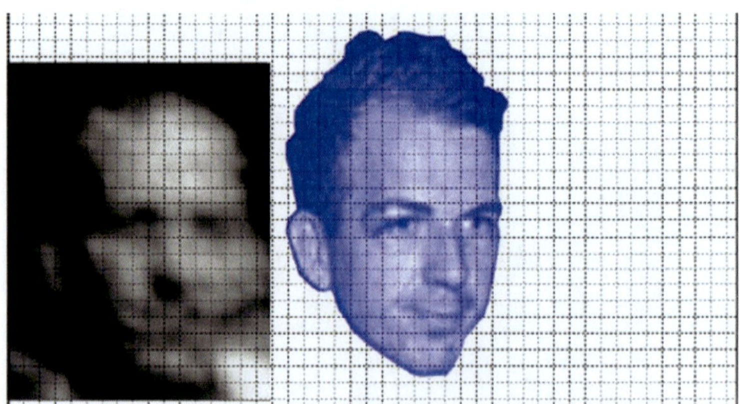

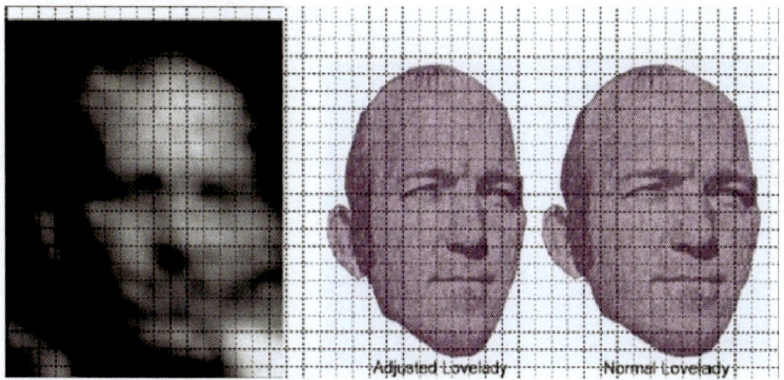

Billy Lovelady does not fit Doorman

The empirical data obtained in this final exercise suggests that even if we were to exclude Lee Oswald as one of the subjects being tested using accepted facial forensic recognition and comparison protocol, both images of Billy Lovelady, flipped and non-flipped, fail to line up with the features of Doorman.

The evidence also clearly suggests that Bob Jackson's covert intention was to pose Lovelady to make his features look like Doorman by pursing his lips and squinting his eyes. In doing so, the results presented here render him an absurd caricature, not unlike the famous "cone heads" *of Saturday Night Live* fame.

Conclusion

This paper has confirmed the reliability of photographic overlays in the assessment and measurement of biometric and photogrammetric parameters, which when properly applied, can aid in the identification and/or refutation of the individuals in question.

The methodology used in this study, and the empirical data obtained, unequivocally prove that the key identifiers stated above, match up perfectly with Lee Oswald, who truly was, "the man in the doorway". Conversely, these same identifiers exclude Billy Lovelady, to a high degree of certainty, as "the man in the doorway". The significance and implications of these findings are beyond the scope of this paper.

Source note: This chapter appears here for the first time.

Notes:

1. Dom Bonafede, *New York Herald Tribune* 5/24/64 "A picture with a life of its own", page 2
2. Ibid page 4
3. Ibid. Francis Beckman, who had been sent by Harris to take a picture, was almost thrown in Jail for "harassing" Lovelady
4. Ibid page 5
5. Harold Weisberg, *Whitewash II: The FBI-Secret Service Cover-Up* 1966
6. Ibid
7. Cinque used the same 35mm Nikkorex camera with 105mm telephoto lens loaded with Eastman Kodak Tri-X film set at 30 feet focal length
8. John Kelin provided copies of the actual sheets of the Ray Marcus overlays.
9. John Kelin, Praise from a future generation, 2007 pg. 227
10. Robert Groden, *The Killing of a President* (1993) p. 187
11. http://jamesfetzer.blogspot.ca/2015/07/jfk-judyth-vary-baker-cements-oswald-in. html
12. Mode-> Indexed color -> Mode-> Color Table -> Select Eyedropper tool -> "touch" white area with eyedropper to render transparency:

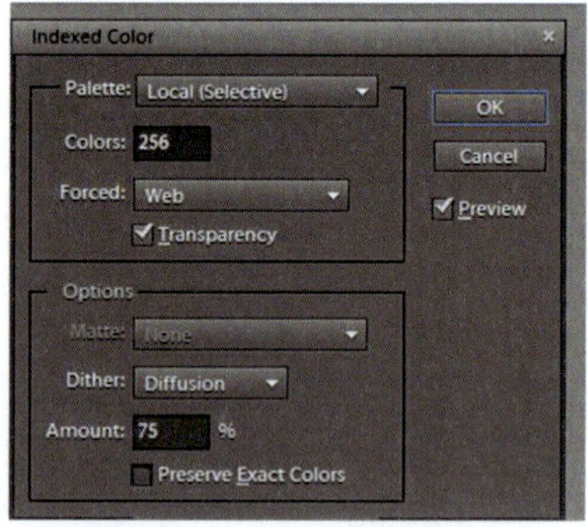

Note: In order to overlay the colorized gallery image, it is necessary to convert the probe to "RGB color" via Mode -> RGB Color.

If this is not done, the gallery image will revert to black and white.

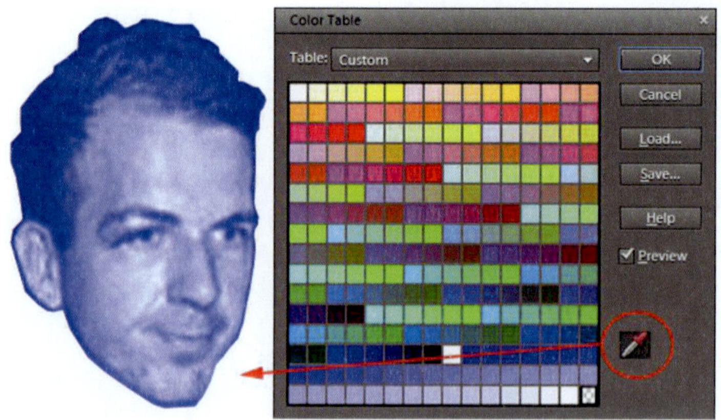

Part VI

Special Cases Inside JFK Research

18

JFK, the CIA and *The New York Times*

by Jim Fetzer

"The Central Intelligence Agency owns everyone of any significance in the major media."—William Colby, former CIA Director

In 1977, Carl Bernstein, who would subsequently co-author *All the President's Men* (1994) with Bob Woodward, one of the most celebrated books in American political history, published "The CIA and the Media", *Rolling Ston*e (20 October 1977), reporting that, with respect to its infiltration of the American media." By far the most valuable of these associations, according to CIA officials, have been with *The New York Times,* CBS and Time Inc." Those who lent their cooperation to the Agency included William Paley of CBS, Henry Luce of Time Inc., Arthur Hays Sulzberger of *The New York Times*, Barry Bingham Sr. of the *The Courier-Journal (Louisville, Ky.),* and James Copley of the Copley Press. Other organizations which cooperated with the CIA included ABC, NBC, AP, UPI, Reuters, Hearst Communications Inc., Scripps-Howard Newspapers, *Newsweek*, the Mutual Broadcasting System, the *Miami Herald* and *The Saturday Evening Post* and the New *York Herald Tribune.*

It was therefore fascinating to discover that *The New York Times,*which has a history of suppressing research on the assassination of JFK, was publishing "*The Umbrella Man: A video interview with the author of* Six Seconds in Dallas (1967)", widely regarded as a classic of conspiracy research on the assassination of JFK.

Its author, Josiah Thompson (whose nickname is "Tink"), was at one time a professor of philosophy at Haverford College and, when I returned from 13 months in the Far East with the 1st Battalion, 12th Marines, 3rd Marine Division, where we had been anchored out in Port of Kaohsiung in Formosa, where I had been awakened at 3:30 AM by the officer of the deck who told me that JFK had been shot and, then again, an hour later that they had caught the guy who had done it, who was a communist, which I thought at the time was "pretty fast work",

I obtained a copy of his book while stationed at Marine Corps Recruit Depot San Diego—as a series commander, supervising 15 DIs and 300 recruits going through the training cycle—which I read with great interest, especially because I had earned my A.B. at Princeton in philosophy and, like myself, Tink had served in the Navy (in the UDT rather than the Marine Corps) and was doing research on JFK, which was attracting my interest as well.

Six Seconds in Dallas

At the time, I thought it was an admirable study, which payed special attention to the Zapruder film, to which the author had had access in conducting research with *Life* magazine, ostensibly for an article about the film. Apparently, Tink took a copy of the film without authorization and there was a falling out. *Life* rescinded permission it had granted for him to use frames from the film, which were replaced by very high-quality charcoal sketches—not as good as the actual frames, but still valuable.

Among the most important features of his book was an analysis of the "double-hit", according to which, in frame 312, JFK's head moves forward under the impact of a shot fired from behind, while in frames 313-316, his head moves violently back and to the left, which is indicative of a shot fired from in front—to the right/front, actually, which many have assumed to have meant from the grassy knoll or even the picket fence.

The book created quite a sensation at the time and lead to Thompson's story being feature on the front page of *The Saturday Evening Post* (2 December 1967).

According to the analysis published there, three assassins had fired four shots, all of which hit. The first, fired from the Texas School Book Depository (TSBD), hit JFK in the back. The second, fired from the roof of the County Records Building, hit Governor John Connally in the back. The third, again from the TSBD, hit JFK in the back of the head, moving it forward, while the fourth was fired from the picket fence and struck him in the right forehead, killing him. For its time, this was excellent work, which offered a stunning contrast to the "official account" of the assassination, which featured three shots with one miss, where one hit JFK at the base of the back of his neck, passed through without hitting any bony structures, and entered Connally's back, while the other hit him in the back of the head, killing him.

We know today that the "magic bullet" scenario is not only provably false but not even anatomically possible, where no bullet could have taken the alleged trajectory, because cervical vertebrae intervene. I even presented a lecture about it at Cambridge during an international conference, which would be published in an international, peer-reviewed journal under the title, *"Reasoning about Assassinations"*.

While Tink's book was very good for its time, his analysis of the shot sequence was superseded by the far more extensive study by Richard Sprague, *Computers And Automation* (May 1970), which demonstrated that there had been more shooters and more shots, which I have refined based upon our studies of the medical evidence and the ballistics published in three books, *Assassination Science* (1998), *Murder in Dealey Plaza* (2000), and *The Great Zapruder Film Hoax* (2003).

The issue over which we have repeatedly clashed, however, concerns the authenticity of the film that was the foundation for his book. I suppose it would be only natural that he would resist evidence that the film has been faked (edited, altered, revised, fabricated), when it pulls the rug out from under his classic study.

The proof is abundant and compelling, as anyone who has followed my columns about JFK can verify for themselves by reading *"JFK: Who's Telling the Truth: Clint Hill or the Zapruder Film?"* . If you read the comments on *Six Seconds in Dallas: A Micro-Study of the Kennedy Assassination* (1967), moreover, you will find those who are adamant that Tink got it right and the rest of us got it wrong. The first "reader's review", for example, makes these claims:

5.0 out of 5 stars *Best book ever about the Kennedy assassination—bar none*, January 22, 2005. By Michael K. Beusch (San Mateo, California United States)—See all my reviews

As an American who believes in his heart that President Kennedy was assassinated as the result of a conspiracy, it pains me to see so many half-baked and flat-out irresponsible studies of the assassination. These run the gamut from the ridiculous defenses of the Warren Report (Gerald Posner, in particular) to the most outlandish conspiracy books hawking absolutely ridiculous theories (James Fetzer's books claiming that the Zapruder film is a fake is the latest). Both the Warren Commission's defenders and the way-out conspiracy theorists do the search for the truth a great disservice. Both groups pick and choose whatever evidence suits their needs . . .

Indeed, Josiah has been attacking me for doing research on Zapruder film authenticity since 1996, when I organized the first symposium devoted to this issue at the JFK Lancer Conference.

I conducted a 10.5 hour preliminary discussion the day before with a dozen or more students of the film, which led to the 4.5 hour presentation the following day with the best half-dozen, including Jack White, Noel Twyman, David Lifton, David Mantik and Chuck Marler, which can be obtained as a 2-disc DVD from Lancer to this day. Our encounters have been relentless since then, numbering in the hundreds.

By now, there may have been as many as a thousand, where he has referred to my first book as *"Assassinated Science"*, even though it published the studies of the autopsy X-rays by David W. Mantik, M.D., Ph.D., which revealed that the X-rays had been altered to conceal the true causes of death of JFK, and by Robert Livingston, M.D., a world authority on the human brain and an expert on wound ballistics, who concluded that, given the consistent and multiple reports from experienced and highly qualified Parkland physicians, who described cerebellar as well as cerebral tissue extruding from fist-sized wound at the back of his head, that the brain shown in the diagrams and photographs at the National Archives could not possibly be of the brain of John Fitzgerald Kennedy.

Since it also included multiple studies of Zapruder film alteration, perhaps that was Tink's overriding concern.

The Umbrella Man

His credibility was not enhanced when he attacked *Murder in Dealey Plaza* (2000), which many regard as the best published on the death of JFK, claiming that a study by Gary Aguilar, M.D., showing the consistency of descriptions of that fist-sized blowout to the back of the head had been highly consistent across witnesses in Dealey Plaza, others at Parkland Hospital, and even those who observed the body at Bethesda Naval Hospital, where the autopsy would be performed.

While we now know that James Humes, who was performing the autopsy, actually took a cranial saw to the head and enlarged the head wound to make it look more like the effect of a shot fired from behind (but inexplicably allowed two witnesses to watch him do this, as Doug Horne, *Inside the Assassination Records Review Board: The U.S. Government's Final Attempt to Reconcile the Conflicting Medical Evidence in the Assassination of JFK* (2009), has documented in detail, which means that Aguilar's study is not quite as accurate as I initially supposed), the case for that massive defect—*or one that was even larger*—is amply established by this study.

When Tink said that Gary's chapter was the only good one in the book, therefore, I knew he had committed a blunder, since if Gary was right, then the film–*which does not show this defect*–had to have been faked.

Indeed, since I had found a late frame, 374, in which the blowout is visible, while it has been blacked out in frames 313-317, for example, the film is not even self-consistent, which means that it cannot, in its totality, possibly be authentic

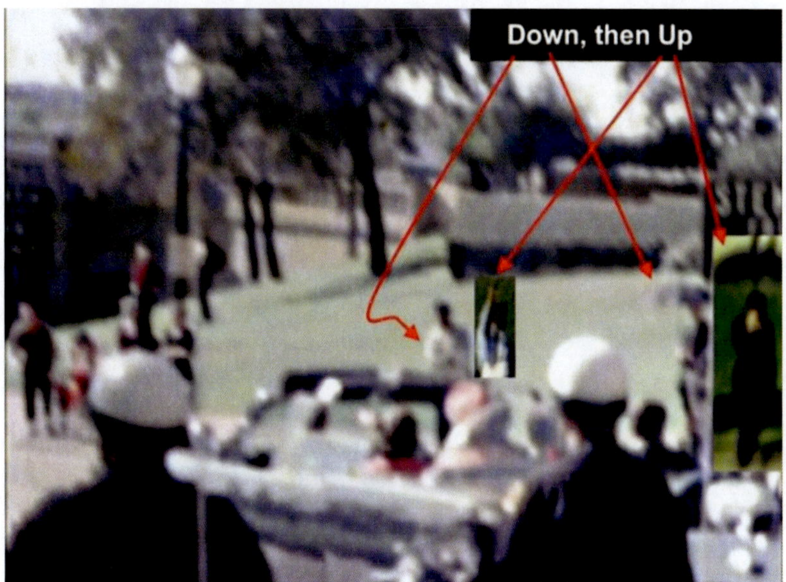

The Umbrella Man pumping his umbrella.

The Umbrella Man Pumping his Umbrella

When I discovered that the estimable Errol Morris, described as "an Academy Award-winning filmmaker—*The Fog of War: Eleven Lessons from the Life of Robert S. McNamara*—and a *New York Times* best-selling author—*Believing Is Seeing: Observations on the Mysteries of Photography*—whose first film, *Gates of Heaven,* is even on Roger Ebert's list of the 10 best movies ever made, and his latest, *Tabloid*, has just been released on DVD", was conducting a series of interviews with Tink, I was fairly incredulous. It was striking to me that he had used "Believing as Seeing" as the title of his study about photography, since we had shown that "Seeing is not Believing" in relation to the Zapruder film.

In agreement with most students of JFK, I had formed the opinion that the Umbrella Man was complicit in the assassination, not only because of his association with the Cuban, but because he had been pumping his umbrella up and down in what we took to be a signal to the assassins that their target was still alive and to continue shooting. The video interview in *The New York Times*, however, portrayed the Umbrella Man as having been completely innocent and present with an umbrella to protest policies, not of JFK, but of his father in relation to an earlier era:

OP-DOCS

'The Umbrella Man': A video interview with the author of *Six Seconds in Dallas: A Micro-Study of the Kennedy Assassination* (1967)

The Umbrella Man: On the 48th anniversary of the assassination of President John F. Kennedy, Errol Morris explores the story behind the one man seen standing under an open black umbrella at the site.

By ERROL MORRIS
Published: November 21, 2011

For years, I've wanted to make a movie about the John F. Kennedy assassination. Not because I thought I could prove that it was a conspiracy, or that I could prove it was a lone gunman, but because I believe that by looking at the assassination, we can learn a lot about the nature of investigation and evidence.

Why, after 48 years, are people still quarreling and quibbling about this case? What is it about this case that has led not to a solution, but to the endless proliferation of possible solutions?

Years ago, Josiah Thompson, known as Tink, a young, Yale-educated Kierkegaard scholar wrote the definitive book on the Zapruder film—"Six Seconds in Dallas." Thompson eventually quit his day job as a professor of philosophy at Haverford College to become a private detective and came to work with many of the same private investigators I had also worked with in the 1980s. We had so much in common—philosophy, P.I. work and an obsessive interest in the complexities of reality. But we had never met.

Last year, I finally got to meet and interview Tink Thompson. I hope his interview can become the first part of an extended series on the Kennedy assassination. This film is but a small segment of my six-hour interview with Tink.

Where this reader's comment (of now 301) spoke volumes to me about Tink's interview and the impression it was conveying to the public:

23. HIGHLIGHT (What's this?)
Mark M, New York, NY, November 22nd, 2011, 6:16 am
This was wonderful. The best—and most convincing—debunking of any and all conspiracy theories I have ever seen, and in just 6 minutes too.

I submitted a comment of my own after listening to what Tink had to say, which was a fascinating effort to undermine not just conspiracy research related to the Umbrella Man but, it turned out, with respect to JFK conspiracy research generally. With the *Times* running performance art like this from Josiah, I regarded it as most unlikely that they would publish my comment, even though I was exposing a false assumption at the foundation of his presentation:

James H. Fetzer, Oregon, WI:

How can Josiah Thompson have written "the definitive book" on the Zapruder film when its fabrication has been proven beyond reasonable doubt? The limo stop was removed, the wounds were changed, and, having reduced the time frame, Clint Hill's activities–about which he has been consistent for more than 47 years–contradict what we see in the extant film. See, for example, "JFK: Who's Telling the Truth: Clint Hill or the Zapruder Film?" For more on how it was done, see "U.S. Government Official: JFK Cover-Up, Film Fabrication". For a tutorial on some of the ways we know the film we have is not the original, see John Costella, "The JFK Assassination Film Hoax", http://

assassination...ella/jfk/intro/ I dismembered Josiah's feeble defense of the authenticity of the film in THE GREAT ZAPRUDER FILM HOAX (2003). Check it out. The American people are entitled to the truth about the assassination of our 35th president. It isn't a close call.

The Umbrella Man Debate

At this point, I was rather incensed that Tink was playing fast and loose with one of the most interesting figures whose image was recorded in the Zapruder film and by others with cameras in Dealey Plaza at the time. I therefore initiated a thread on The Education Forum to discuss it, entitled *"Tink's performance in The New York Times: Josiah Thompson shows his true colors"*.

Among my earliest posts was one laying out arguments that Tink had shaded the evidence in a number of important respects, where I would later add photographs to support my points.

When David S. Lifton, the author of *Best Evidence: Disguise and Deception in the Assassination of John F. Kennedy* (1980), asked for "credible evidence" that former Dallas insurance salesman Louis Steven Witt was not the person he claimed to be to the HSCA, I posted three images that supported my objections to their identification:

(1) As I have previously observed, the Umbrella Man and the Cuban were obviously together, where any explanation of the presence of the Umbrella Man must account for their association:

(2) While everyone else in Dealey Plaza was dumbfounded, the Umbrella Man and the Cuban did not act surprised by the assassination–and their faces have been obscured in certain photos, which is highly suspicious by itself:

(3) Moreover, they hang around together, sitting on the curb, as though nothing especially un-

usual had taken place, where I had supposed virtually everyone would agree that their behavior is abnormal under these circumstances.

When Jim DiEugenio, the author of *Destiny Betrayed: JFK, Cuba, and the Garrison Case* (1992), posted this summary of Witt's testimony, I thought the case against Witt was cinched:

Posted 25 November 2011—07:36 PM

Has anyone read Witt's testimony of late? I don't think so. These are some of the things he said.

1.) He never planned on doing what he did until that morning.

2.) He did not know the exact parade route.

3.) He just happened to wander around for a walk and guessed where it would be.

4.) Contrary to what Cliff says, he did what he did with no relation to JFK's policies, only Joe Sr.

5.) What did the Cuban looking guy say? Words to the effect, They shot those people. (Oh really Louie?)

6.) Admits he sat there for up to three minutes and that he never even looked behind him at the picket fence! (Truly surprising.)

7.) He never did anything like this before or since, and he was not a member of any conservative group or organization.

8.) He placed the umbrella on the sidewalk and then picked it up. He wavers on whether this is definitely the umbrella he had that day.

9.) He often uses the conditional, like I think that is me, or that may be the guy I sat next to.

Felipe Vidal Santiago

Roy Hargraves

At this point in time, I felt very confident that Jim and I were right in debunking Tink's suggestion that the Umbrella Man was Witt, including that Tink was taking that identification for granted, when it is instead a conclusion that requires its own substantiation. In logic, this is called "begging the question" by assuming what requires independent proof.

He was ignoring that more reasonable identifications would be of the Cuban as Felipe Vidal Santiago, a committed anti-Castro Cuban, and of Roy Hargraves, who fit the photos and the scenario, I thought, to a "t".

The very idea that Witt would offer this fantastic story about Joe Kennedy, which is preposterous on its face, and Tink would claim it was "so extraordinary and unbelievable it must be true", struck me as simply absurd.

It seemed far more likely that, by pumping his umbrella, Witt was signaling to the assassins that JFK was still alive, which makes sense, rather than an obscure historical allusion that no one, including Jack, would have grasped.

By remarking that there are always alternative explanations that might be true, when you isolate one element of a complex picture, Tink was employing the technique known as "divide and conquer". If all you knew were what Tink had presented in this little clip, then you could rather easily be taken in; but once you consider the other evidence we have available, his scenario is not remotely plausible. Still, I thought it would be appropriate to review what others have thought, so I turned to Jim Marrs' classic study, *Crossfire: The Plot That Killed Kennedy* (1989), pp. 29-32, for such light as it might shed on the subject.

Jim Marrs in *Crossfire*

About the time that Kennedy was first hit by a bullet, two men standing near each other on the north sidewalk of Elm Street acted most strangely—one began pumping a black umbrella while the other waved his right arm high in the air.

These and subsequent actions by this pair aroused the suspicions of researchers over the years, yet the initial federal investigation ignored both men. Their activities are known only through analysis of assassination photographs.

As Kennedy's limousine began the gentle descent into Dealey Plaza, a man can be seen standing near the street-side edge of the Stemmons Freeway sign holding an open umbrella. He holds the umbrella in a normal fashion and the top of the umbrella almost reaches the bottom of the sign.

In photos taken minutes before Kennedy's arrival, the umbrella is closed and, immediately after the shooting, pictures show the umbrella was closed again. The man's umbrella was only open during the shooting sequence. Furthermore, as seen in the Zapruder film, once Kennedy is exactly opposite the man with the umbrella, it was pumped almost two feet into the air and then lowered.

At the same time, the second man—in photos he appears to be of a dark complexion, perhaps a black man or Hispanic—raised his right hand into the air possibly making a fist. This man was located on the outer edge of the Elm Street sidewalk opposite the umbrella man, who was on the inner edge.

The man with the open umbrella was the only person in Dealey Plaza with an open umbrella. Under the warm Texas sun, there was no reason to carry an open umbrella at that time.

Two main theories have emerged concerning the "umbrella man" and his activities that day. Assassination researcher Robert Cutler has long maintained that the umbrella may have been a sophisticated weapon that fired a dart or "flechette" filled with a paralyzing agent. Cutler's theory has been the object of dirision over the years but it is supported by the 1975 testimony of a CIA weapons developer who told the Senate Intelligence Committee that just such an umbrella weapon was in the hands of the spy agency in 1963.

Charles Senseney, who developed weaponry for the CIA at Fort Detrick, Maryland, described a dart-firing weapon he developed as looking like an umbrella. He said the dart gun was silent in operation and fired through the webbing when the umbrella was open. Senseney said the CIA had ordered about 50 such dart weapons and that they were operational in 1963.

Cutler theorized that the umbrella was used to fire a paralyzing dart into Kennedy immobilizing him for marksmen with rifles. He claims this theory accounts for the small puncture wound in Kennedy's throat described by Dallas doctors, but which was altered by the time of the Bethesda autopsy. According to Cutler, this dart explains Kennedy's lack of motion during the shooting sequence. Since such a weapon existed and since both the actions of Kennedy and the "umbrella man" were consistent with the operation of such a weapon, Cutler's theory cannot be completely dismissed.

They were there together and remained together

However, most assassination researchers prefer the alternative theory that both of these suspicious men may have been providing visual signals to hidden gunmen. This theory suggests that Kennedy was killed by a crossfire coordinated by radiomen. The two men, who were among the closest bystanders to the President when he was first struck, gave signals indicating that he was not fatally hit and therefore more shots were needed.

A fascinating twist on this latter theory came from researcher Gary Shaw, who said the two men may have been providing Kennedy with a last-second sign of who was responsible for his death. Shaw recalled that throughout the planning of the Bay of Pigs invasion, CIA officers had promised an "umbrella" of air protection of the Cuban invaders. This "umbrella" failed to materialize because Kennedy refused to authorize

U.S. military support for the invasion. According to Shaw's theory, the man with the open umbrella symbolized the promise of an air-support "umbrella" while the dark-complected man may have been one of the anti-Castro Cuban leaders known to Kennedy. Thus, in the last seconds of his life, Kennedy may have seen the open umbrella and the face of a Cuban he knew was involved in the Bay of Pigs and realized who was participating in his death.

But this is all speculation. The existence of the "umbrella man" and the dark-complexion man is fact. Their activities after the assassination especially bear study. While virtually everyone in Dealey Plaza was moved to action by the assassination—either falling to the ground for cover or moving toward the Grassy Knoll—these two men sat down beside each other on the north sidewalk of Elm Street.

Here the dark-complexion man appears to put a walkie-talkie to his mouth.

Hand held radio in use?

In a photograph taken by Jim Towner, what seems to be an antenna can be seen jutting out from behind the man's head while his right hand holds some object to his face.

Several photos taken in the seconds following the assassination show both of these men sitting together on the Elm Street sidewalk. Moments later, the man with the umbrella gets up, takes one last look toward the motorcade still passing under the Triple Underpass, and begins walking east in the direction of the Depository. The dark-complexion man saunters toward the Triple Underpass passing people rushing up the Grassy Knoll. He can be seen stuffing some object—the walkie-talkie?—into the back of his pants.

Despite the suspicious actions of these two men, there is no evidence that the FBI or the Warren Commission made any effort to identify or locate them. Officially they did not exist. Yet over the years, this pair became the focal point of criticism by private researchers. Researchers claimed the lack of investigation of these men was indicative of the shallowness of the government's handling of the assassination.

Once the House Select Committee on Assassinations was formed in 1976, researchers urged an investigation of both men. The Committee finally released a photograph of the "umbrella man" to the news media and urged anyone with knowledge of the man to come forward.

Coincidentally—if it was a coincidence—the "umbrella man" suddenly was identified in Dallas a few weeks after this national appeal. In August 1978, a telephone caller told researcher Penn Jones, Jr., that the man with the umbrella was a former Dallas insurance salesman named Louie Steven Witt.

Jones contacted some local newsmen (Jim Marrs being one of them) and together they confronted Witt, who then was working as a warehouse manager. Witt refused to talk with newsmen but acknowledged that he was in Dealey Plaza on the day Kennedy was killed.

Jones later wrote: "I felt the man had been coached. He would answer no questions and pointedly invited us to leave. His only positive statement, which seemed to come very quickly, was that he was willing to appear before the House Select Committee on Assassinations in Washington."

Witt indeed appeared before the Committee during its public testimony. His story was comic relief compared to the intense scrutiny of witnesses like Marina Oswald and Warren Commission critics.

His story was facile and improbable and when the umbrella that Witt claimed was the same one he had had in Dealey Plaza in 1963 was displayed, it suddenly turned wrong-side out, prompting one Committee member to quip: "I hope that's not a weapon."

Witt told the Committee that on the spur of the moment, he grabbed a large black umbrella and went to Dealey Plaza to heckle Kennedy. He claimed that someone had told him that an open umbrella would rile Kennedy. While Witt offered no further explanation of how his umbrella could heckle the president, Committee members—not Witt—theorized that the umbrella in some way referred to the pro-German sympathies of Kennedy's father while serving as U.S. ambassador to Britain just prior to World War II. They said the umbrella may have symbolized the appeasement policies of Britain's Prime Minister Neville Chamberlain, who always carried an umbrella.

According to Witt:

> I think I went sort of maybe halfway up the grassy area [on the north side of Elm Street], somewhere in that vicinity. I am pretty sure I sat down. . . . [when the motorcade approached] I think I got up and started fiddling with that umbrella trying to get it open, and at the same time I was walking forward, walking toward the street. . . . Whereas other people I understand saw the President shot and his movements; I did not see this because of this thing [the umbrella] in front of me . . . My view of the car during that length of time was blocked by the umbrella's being open.

Based on the available photographs made that day, none of Witt's statements were an accurate account of the actions of the "umbrella man" who stood waiting for the motorcade with his umbrella in the normal over-the-head position and then pumped it in the air as Kennedy passed.

Witt's bizarre story—unsubstantiated and totally at variance with the actions of the man in the photographs—resulted in few, if any, researchers accepting Louis Steven Witt as the "umbrella man."

And there continues to be no official accounting for the dark-complexion man who appears to have been talking on a radio moments after the assassination. The House Committee failed to identify or locate this man and Witt claimed he had no recollection of such a person, despite photographs that seem to show the "umbrella man" talking with the dark man. Witt claimed only to recall that a "Negro man" sat down near him and kept repeating: "They done shot them folks."

Interestingly, one of the Committee attorneys asked Witt specifically if he recalled seeing the man with a walkie-talkie, although officially no one has ever admitted the possibility of radios in use in Dealey Plaza.

New Evidence Appears

No one could have been more surprised than I when another student of the assassination, Bernice Moore, sent me a comment that had been posted in response to *The New York Times*, which included an extract of Witt's actual testimony to the HSCA:

> Christopher Marlow, San Diego, CA
> November 22nd, 2011, 6:08 pm
>
> After watching this video, I looked up the interview of the "Umbrella Man" for the House Committee on Assassinations. It

> was very enlightening. The man's name was Louis Steven Witt, a former Dallas insurance salesman. He was questioned by counsel for the committee, Mr. Genzman….
>
> Mr. WITT. Yes. As I moved toward the street, still walking on the grass, I heard the shots that I eventually learned were shots. At the time somehow it didn't register as shots because they were so close together, and it was like hearing a string of firecrackers, or something like that. It didn't at that moment register on me as being shots.
>
> Mr. GENZMAN. What do you next recall happening?
>
> Mr. WITT. Let me go back a minute. As I was moving forward I apparently had this umbrella in front of me for some few steps. Whereas other people I understand saw the President shot and his movements; I did not see this because of this thing in front of me, The next thing I saw after I saw the car coming down the street, down the hill to my left, the car was just about at a position like this [indicating] at this angle here. At this time there was the car stopping, the screeching of tires, the jamming on of brakes, [!!!] motorcycle patrolman right there beside one of the cars. One car ran upon the President's car and a man jumped off and jumped on the back. These were the scenes that unfolded as I reached the point to where I was seeing things.
>
> If you look at the Zapruder film, you will see that the car does not stop. But the Umbrella Man and literally dozens of witnesses testified that the presidential limo came to a stop during the assassination. The Zapruder film has been altered to conceal this and other facts. Any careful examination of the Z film will lead you to this conclusion.

This new evidence, moreover, makes an enormous difference to the evaluation of Witt's testimony. Based upon other evidence we have accumulated about the Zapruder film, which is contradicted by witness reports about the limo having been brought to a halt—which we believe was in response to the Cuban's raised fist—for which there are many witnesses, whose reports have been collated by John Costella in *"What Happened on Elm Street? The Eyewitnesses Speak"* ,*"New Proof of Zapruder Film Fakery"* and *"JFK: Who's Telling the Truth: Clint Hill or the Zapruder Film?"*, what Witt is saying closely corresponds to those other witnesses and to the reports of others who have seen "the other film", which appears to be the original Zapruder before it was subjected to reconstuction, as Doug Horne has explained in his five-volume study, which I summarized in *"U.S. Government Official: JFK Cover-Up, Film Fabrication"*. As I then explained in post #160 on The Education Forum:

> *Well, I'm only beginning to sort this out, but his description of what happened is very close to what happened as we have reconstructed it.* The limo stop, of course, is at the heart of the matter. It was such a blatant example of Secret Service complicity that it had to be taken out.
>
> When you study Clint Hill's report of the sequence of acts he took—running forward, boarding the vehicle, pushing Jackie down, lying over their bodies and peering into a fist-sized hole in the back of JFK's head while giving a "thumbs down" BEFORE THE LIMO REACHED the TUP—which he has been saying and reporting consistently for (then) 47 years–this is hardly the first time we've had a witness who supported the limo stop. I have given several references to studies that document their reports.
>
> *The point is that THIS DESCRIPTION, which was NOT in DiEugenio's summary, POWERFULLY SUGGESTS HE ACTUALLY WAS THERE.* Some of it is rather fascinating, including about the brakes and all that, because it has not come up before. But when you have a motorcade that is proceeding quite uneventually AND THE LEAD CAR SLAMS ON ITS BRAKES, it would not be surprising if the car following should run up against it or if other drivers had to react by slamming on their breaks. So you are making too quick an inference from the sound of breaks to assuming the sound came from the limo! What he is saying needs to be sorted out but, given this stunning and dramatic report (which he cannot have acquired from viewing the Zapruder film), he probably WAS there.
>
> *It's like finding a fingerprint or the DNA of someone who was not previously a suspect at a crime scene.* This guy could not possibly have known some of what he is reporting UNLESS HE HAD BEEN THERE. Even the limo stop is not widely known, even though there are dozens and dozens of witnesses who reported it.
>
> Too many play on the "slowed dramatically" versus "came to a halt" difference, which is splitting hairs, since (1) it had to slow dramatically to come to a halt and (2) the Zapruder film shows NEITHER dramatic slowing NOR coming to a halt. So this is really quite remarkable, because, as in the case of Gary Aguilar's chapter in MURDER, Tink has endorsed Witt, but he turns out to

have witnessed the limo stop, which is further proof that the film is a fake.

What Then About the Umbrella Man?

I have now done what I should have done originally, namely, check his testimony for myself. Here is what I have found:

> Mr. FAUNTROY. All right. Now, the car is moving beyond you now. Are you aware that the President has been hit at this point—after you hear these firecracker-like shots?
>
> Mr. WITT. No, sir. I—my view of the car during that length of time was blocked by the umbrella being open. And my—the next time I saw the car after I saw it coming down on my left traveling west, the next time I saw the car was when this activity of the car stopping, one car rushing up on another, the motorcycle patrolman stopping, there was this screeching of tires, this sort of thing.
>
> One thing I recall there was a movement in the President's car. By this time—I don't recall seeing the President. He must have—I am sure he was down.
>
> The only thing I recall was the—there was a sort of a pink movement, and it was—that was Jackie Kennedy, I think, wearing a pink dress or something. This pink thing stood out in my mind, and all of this happened in very rapid order. The—as soon as the one car ran up behind this one, a man jumped off and I think the first car was pulling out about the time he had jumped on the back.
>
> Mr. FAUNTROY. Your testimony is that you then sat down where you are pictured there?

While there is massive evidence of the limo stop (links to some of which I have cited above), I do not find Witt credible simply because he observed the limo stop but because he is reporting information that only someone who was actually there could possibly have known. The Zapruder film was shown for the first time on the Geraldo Rivera TV program in 1975, but it does not show any of these very specific details that Witt is reporting. Even most students of the assassination would be hard-pressed to say what they think actually happened at that place and time.

The screeching of tires, with one car running up onto the other (the Secret Service Cadillac evidently butting up against the Lincoln limousine) and one man jumping off and climbing onto the back of the other (Clint Hill rushing from the Cadillac to the back steps of the Lincoln) not only fits the scenario to a "t" but adds details that offer more data to consider, including especially the acoustical aspects of this event, which have been under-explored previous to this belated discovery.

This also means that Robert Morrow, another contributor to the forum, may have been closer to the truth than I was in relation to the

Umbrella Man. *A fundamental principle of scientific reasoning is that the search for truth must be based upon all the available relevant evidence.* Witt's remarks about the shots and their sound are also telling. We know many said that the first shot (or "the first shots") sounded like firecrackers. Jim Lewis, who has been experimenting with junked cars, has found that, when high velocity bullets are fired through windshields, they make the sound of a firecracker.

But the fact is we have new evidence to consider in assessing this. When his testimony was vague and ambiguous, my other arguments carried greater weight. But this very detailed and specific testimony outweighs the vagueness of the rest. At the very least, we have found a remarkable additional witness to the limo stop from an expected source—and thanks to Tink! And that underlines a mistake in Jim Marrs' discounting of Witt's story:

> ***According to Witt:***
>
> *I think I went sort of maybe halfway up the grassy area [on the north side of Elm Street], somewhere in that vicinity. I am pretty sure I sat down. . . . [when the motorcade approached] I think I got up and started fiddling with that umbrella trying to get it open, and at the same time I was walking forward, walking toward the street. . . . Whereas other people I understand saw the President shot and his movements; I did not see this because of this thing [the umbrella] in front of me . . . My view of the car during that length of time was blocked by the umbrella's being open.*
>
> *Based on the available photographs made that day, none of Witt's statements were an accurate account of the actions of the "umbrella man" who stood waiting for the motorcade with his umbrella in the normal over-the-head position and then pumped it in the air as Kennedy passed.*

But that is to overlook that the film has been massively revised to conceal the true causes of the death of JFK. One of the first and most obvious oddities of the extant film is that so many figures in Dealey Plaza, including the bystanders on the north side of Elm Street, are virtually motionless and unresponsive, even when the President is immediately before them. This has long since appeared to be a result of taking earlier footage as the foreground and making adjustments to later footage, including the introduction of special effects, such as adding the "blob" and blood spray to make it look as though the head shot in frame 313 was fired from behind and blackening out the actual wound at the back of his head.

In order to achieve consistency between the various films, they had to change them to conform to the revised Zapruder, where removing activities like those that Witt reported would have made that task immeasurably simpler. If he is moving around, the effects of deleting frames would have been conspicuous because of "jumps" in his actions. It was simpler to keep him frozen, more or less as was done with Mary Moorman and Jean Hill on the opposite side of the street.

There are multiple indications that Tink's purpose here and throughout the entire series—which, given there are 10 six-minute segments in an hour and Errol Morris has reported he has six hours of interviews, which may mean as many as 59 more six-minute reports—is to attempt to debunk belief in conspiracy in the assassination of JFK. His remarks about a "wing-nut" who suggested that the umbrella may have concealed a device to fire a flacehette is particularly revealing, since such a device is actually discussed in the HSCA transcript of the testimony of Louie Steven Witt. Richard Sprague and Robert Cutler were among those who took the idea seriously, where it turned out that the CIA actually had devices of this kind in 1963.

So Tink was either faking it (because he was not familiar with the Umbrella Man's testimony) or deliberately distorting an odd aspect of the investigation of the assassination (which was conducted by investigators that no one else familiar with their work would describe as "wing-nuts").

It was not irresponsible for Sprague and Cutler to endorse the flechette hypothesis when, to the best of my knowledge, (i) they did not have access to the Parkland Press Conference transcript (which was not even provided to the Warren Commission), (ii) they did not know there was a through-and-through hole in the windshield, (iii) they were apparently unaware of the tiny shrapnel wounds in JFK's face, and (iv) they did not know that, unless the tentorium had been previously ruptured, even the near simultaneous impact of the shot to the back of his head and the frangible hit around his right temple would not have been sufficient to cause cerebellum to extrude from the wound.

So this appears to be a classic case of acquiring new information and new hypotheses that make a difference to understanding what took place, where, in this case, hypotheses that were previously accepted should be rejected and hypotheses that were previously rejected should be accepted. Another serious student of the assassination, Alan J. Salerian, M.D., moreover, has taken this hypothesis seriously in studies he has presented as recently as 2008.

Anyone with any lingering doubt about Tink's betrayal of JFK research should pay close attention to what he says, where, in particular, he is suggesting there are arbitrarily many innocuous explanations for any evidence that has ever been viewed as "sinister" in the assassination of JFK. As Cliff Varnell has remarked, "Check out the sarcasm dripping from Tink's [use of the phrases] "really sinister" and "sinister underpinning" (*https://youtu.be/QVsPcMFoEnk*).

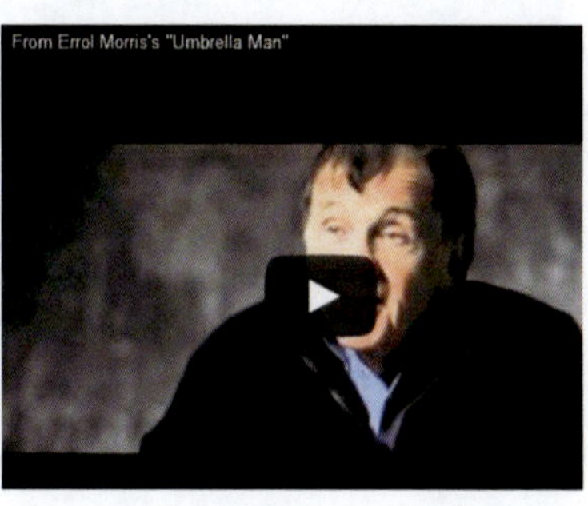

Here's a transcript: (laughing) *What it means it that, if you have any fact which you think is really sinister—it's really obviously a fact which can only point to some sinister underpinning—hey, FORGET IT, MAN, because you can never, on your own, think up all the non-sinister perfectly valid explanations for that fact. A cautionary tale.*

And that, of course, is why Mark M., commented, *"This was wonderful. The best—and most convincing—debunking of any and all conspiracy theories I have ever seen, and in just 6 minutes too."*

I hate to say "I told you so", but I nailed Tink as working the opposite side of the street a long time ago and was attacked for doing so. I also observed earlier that, in disavowing the "double-hit" theory, he was setting himself up to proclaim that there was no conspiracy in the assassination, after all, just in time for the 50th observance. That we have good reasons to believe that Witt was there, however, does not excuse his suspicious activities and association with the Cuban.

That the Secret Service would allow them to act that way in close proximity to the President is one more indication–along with more than 15 others—of Secret Service complicity in setting JFK up for the hit.

While Robert Morrow and I may not completely agree on the activities of Umbrella Man, we converge in our conclusions about the role of Josiah Thompson in this shabby affair; and for that reason, I want to give him the last word for this round of what may well turn out to be the most elaborate CIA *cum New York Times* disinformation campaign in history:

> *I have "fallen into traps" before on the JFK assassination. Then when I see the error of my ways I try to get out of that hole as quick as possible. That means I change my mind when the weight of evidence changes direction.*

As for this NY Times—Josiah Thompson—Umbrella Man thing . . . it looks like it is yet more generalized lone-nutter propaganda given an NY Times platform. Really, instead of debunking one probable fallacy—that Umbrella Man was part of the assassination—they could have used that valuable air space/ print space to document a THOUSAND things that point to a coup d'etat.

So we have yet another pathetic performance by the NY Times. Perhaps not an error of commission, but a thousand errors of omission. How about an article on Fletcher Prouty and Victor Krulak's identification of Maj. Gen. Edward Lansdale at the TSBD and what that probably means? Spend a little time on that photo and the backgrounds of Lansdale and what Prouty has to offer.

That is but one mere example.

*As for Josiah Thompson—count me extremely unimpressed with his smug attitude and *performance*—and that is exactly what he was doing , *performing*—as the JFK expert for the NY Times, playing along with their lone-nutter agenda, much in the way [that] "conspiracy theorist" Gary Mack [who is the official archivist for The Sixth Floor Museum] constantly does.*

Source note: This chapter previously appeared as "JFK, the CIA and *The New York Times*", *http://jamesfetzer.blogspot.com/2015/09/the-jfk-war-whats-going-on-with-len_30.html.*

19

The Challenging Case of Robert Groden

by Jim Fetzer

"The most productive mindset you can have is simply this: always, always, always have a belief system that doesn't resist change. Go wherever the information leads you, without fear, because surely the truth is never something to dread."—Darryl Sloan, *Reality Check*

On the eve of the 50th observance of the death of JFK, it would appear to be timely to make an assessment, not only of what we know now that we didn't know then, but of the contributions of some of the most admired figures in the history of assassination research.

One of those, Josiah Thompson, has been the subject of an earlier study, *JFK, the CIA and* The New York Times, which suggests that he has been preparing to disavow the existence of a conspiracy in the assassination of our 35th President.

Another, Robert Groden, however, presents a more challenging case, because so much of his work has been impressive and has made important contributions, including a JFK video series.

An evaluation of Groden's contributions, especially the positions he has adopted that appear to be mistaken, requires an appreciation of the logical and evidentiary connections and relationships between the witness reports, the available photos and films, and especially the medical evidence.

Groden's Contributions

I personally have greatly valued his books and other contributions, where we agree on many aspects of the events in Dealey Plaza, including a shooting sequence that entailed eight, nine or ten shots, including as many as four misses, as he lays it out in *The Killing of a President: The Complete Photographic Record of the JFK Assassination* (1993), pp. 18-40, which is comparable to my analysis of eight, nine or 10 shots with at least three misses.

Groden's Contributions

Robert J. Groden first became interested in the assassination of John F. Kennedy in 1964. A harsh critic of the Warren Commission, he was the Staff Photographic Consultant to the House Select Committee on Assassinations and a consultant on Oliver Stone's film *JFK*.

Groden is the author of several books on the assassination of *High Treason: The Assassination of President John F. Kennedy: What Really Happened* (1989), *High Treason: The Great Cover-Up: The Assassination of President John F. Kennedy* (1992), *The Killing of a President: The Complete Photographic Record of the JFK Assassination, the Conspiracy, and the Cover-up* (1993) and *The Search for Lee Harvey Oswald: A Comprehensive Photographic Record* (1995).

While we differ on the sequence in which the shots were fired and order of the wounds they inflicted, he and I are very close on the mechanics of the assassination.

Where we differ concerns the authenticity of the evidence, including the Zapruder film and Altgens6, which appears to be consistent with his endorsement of Altgens7, where the evidence I shall review suggests that he is wrong:

(1) Groden denies the existence of a bullet hole in the windshield;

(2) he defends a set of autopsy photos that seem to be fabrications;

(3) he claims the Zapruder film is authentic, which may explain (1);

(4) he maintains that the Altgens6 photograph is also authentic;

(5) he denies Oswald was in the doorway during the shooting; but

(6) he offers an alternative explanation of his location at the time;

(7) which also implies that Lee cannot have been on the sixth floor.

While it may have been reasonable for Groden to maintain these positions in the past, research conducted since the publication of *The Killing of a President* (1993) published in *Assassination Science* (1989), *Murder in Dealey Plaza* (2000), *The Great Zapruder Film Hoax* (2003) and articles that have appeared in *Veterans Today* render (1) through (6) indefensible, even though (7) is true. Since rationality of belief requires us to change our minds on the basis of new evidence or alternative hypotheses, which I am going to summarize here—which displays the complex inter-relations between photographic, medical, and witness evidence—Groden ought to respond with appropriate adjustments to his

(1) to (6), which are no longer defensible, given the available relevant evidence. (*https://youtu.be/thCHTIg_ofc*)

The windshield bullet hole

According to Robert Groden, *The Killing of a President* (1993), p. 36, the photo taken by AP photographer James "Ike" Altgens (technically known as "Altgens6") displays no signs of a bullet hole in the windshield, whereas a larger image that exhibits spiderweb cracks that he, in agreement with the Secret Service, claims to have been caused by a fragment of a bullet that was fired from behind, not by a shot that was fired from in front.

There are many problems with this position, however, including that the bullet hole IS visible in Altgens6, that multiple witnesses reporting observing it at Parkland, and that, as he explained in his chapter on the limo in *Murder in Dealey Plaza* (2000).

taken by the Altgens just after the first four shots, the photo (right) shows the windshield of the President's car with no sign of damage from gunfire. Next came the fatal head shot, followed a half second later by a sixth bullet that hit Connally from the rear. It appears that a fragment cracked the windshield. The photo below was taken by the Secret Service soon after the assassination.

Doug Weldon, J.D., recently deceased, tracked down the official at Ford who had been responsible for replacing the windshield, who confirmed that the original had a through-and-through hole:

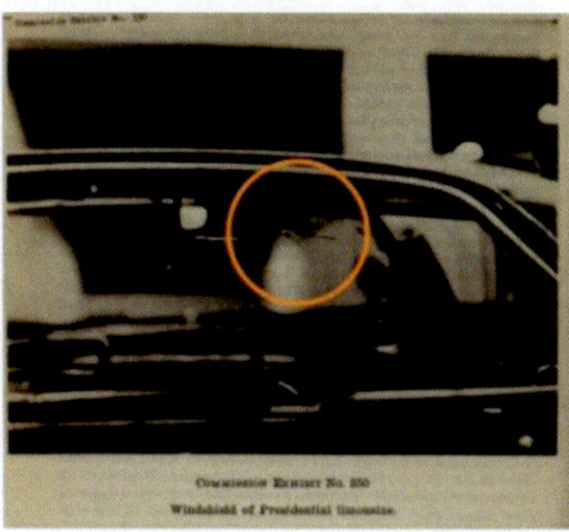

This research, which has been available since 2000, has been confirmed by more recent studies by Doug Horne, "*Photographic Evidence of Bullet Hole in JFK Windshield*" (4 June 2012) and "*JFK*

Conspiracy: The Bullet Hole in the Windshield" (28 June 2012) and, even more recently, by Dennis Cimino, "*Tampering with the Limo in the Altgens6*" (20 March 2013). Indeed, as other students have observed, it can also be seen in Zapruder frame 225:

Moreover, as I explain in *The Great Zapruder Film Hoax* (2003), p. 436, Jim Lewis has been traveling through the South and firing high-velocity rounds through the windshields of junked car to determine whether or not he could hit a dummy in the back seat. Not only have they created small, white spiral nebulae with a dark hole at the center, but passing through, they have made the sound of a firecracker, which many witnesses reported hearing.

The mortician's confirmation

Perhaps most interesting of all, the mortician, Thomas Evan Robinson, discovered that JFK's body had several tiny shrapnel wounds in the face from which embalming fluid leaked, where David W. Mantik, M.D., Ph.D., inferred they had resulted from small shards of glass that broke off when the bullet passed through the windshield, which means that the medical evidence, including the wound to the throat that JFK sustained, supports the conclusion.

Indeed, Charles Crenshaw, M.D., drew diagrams of the wound to the throat both before and after a tracheostomy incision was made by Malcolm Perry, M.D., who described it three times during the Parkland Press Conference that afternoon as a wound of entry.

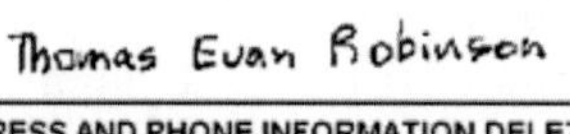
Thomas Evan Robinson

ADDRESS AND PHONE INFORMATION DELETED
FOR MR. ROBINSON'S PRIVACY

May 26, 1992 (phone)

Wounds:

- large gaping hole in back of head. patched by ~~pa~~stretching piece of rubber ... over it. Thinks skull full of Plaster of Paris
- smaller wound in right temple. cresent shape, flapped down (3")
- (approx. 2) small shrapnel wounds in face. packed with wax.
- wound in back (5 to six inches) below shoulder. to the right of back bone.
- Adrenlin gland and brain removed.
- other organs removed and then put back.
- No swelling or discoloration to face. (died instantly)

Dr. Berkley (Family Physician) came in an ask.... "How much longer ???
He was told (Funeral Director)" Take your time"

Is in favor of Exuming Body ... to settle once and ... for all. "Good Pathologists would know exactly"

It was a small, clean puncture wound, where the transcript of the meeting, which was not provided to the Warren Commission, is an appendix of *Assassination Science* (1998).

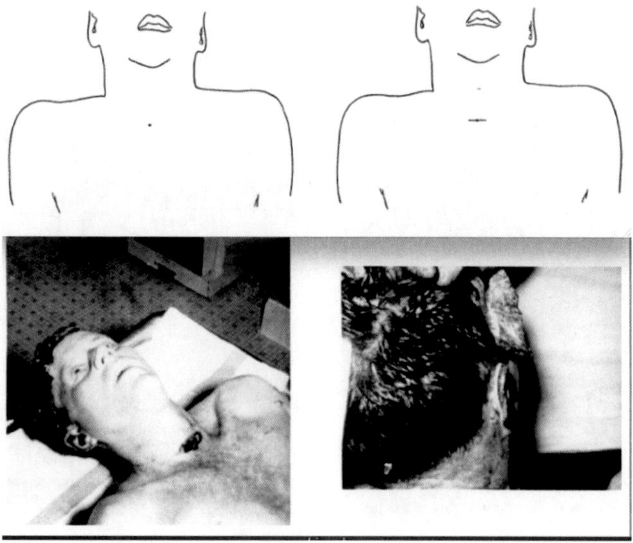

Comparison between the Crenshaw diagrams from Parkland (above) and the autopsy photo from Bethesda (bottom/ left) and the HSCA version of the head wound (bottom/right)—where the small wound in the right temple should not be confounded with the skull flap, which is conspicuous on the bottom/right)—makes it difficult to deny the thesis of David Lifton, *Best Evidence* (1980), that either the body was subject to alteration or autopsy photos were faked.

The dubious autopsy photographs

It is difficult to imagine why anyone, much less Robert Groden, would persist in denying the bullet hole in the windshield when the only evidence to the contrary are photographs from which it has been removed. Perhaps as extraordinary has been Groden's insistence that photographs showing a mass of brains and gunk on the top of the head are authentic, when they are grossly inconsistent with the observations of the Parkland physicians as well as diagrams and photos of the *Final Report of the Select Committee on Assassinations U.S. House of Representatives* (1979), which, if anything, are even more bizarre and indefensible. Compare the Groden photographs with the HSCA versions below.

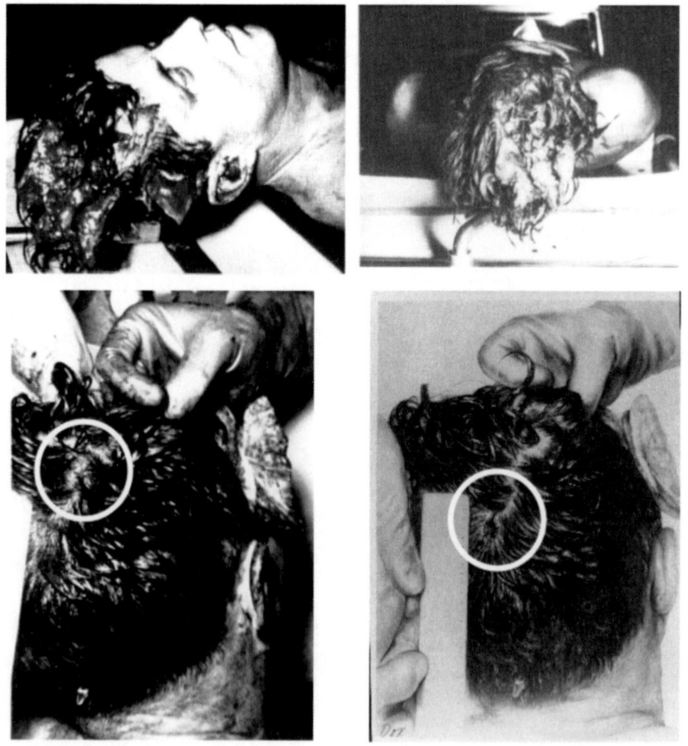

The extraordinary contrast led the Assassinations Record Review Board (ARRB) to ask James Humes, the U.S. Navy medical officer in charge of the autopsy, whether the body had been given a shampoo and a haircut during the procedure, to which he had replied, "No, no, no, no, no, ..." Obviously, both sets of photographs cannot be authentic, although they could both be fabrications—which, as I shall explain, appear to be the case. I have been troubled by the realization that the performance of the HSCA medical panel is completely indefensible, not least of all because it completely ignores the Harper fragment found in the grass the day after the shooting.

Notice the skull flap extending from the right side of the head in both the HSCA photograph and drawing. This is the defect that the mortician, during his conversation with Joe West—a private investigator from Houston—was describing when he told him that in addition to the "large, gaping hole" in the back of JFK's head—an exit wound—there was a smaller wound in the right temple—which Charles Crenshaw, M.D., would confirm as an entry wound in a TV interview—and a "crescent shape[d], flapped-down (3") skull flap that had been blown open by the shock waves generated by the explosion of the frangible bullet entering there—which is clearly not the Harper fragment, for which the HSCA cannot account.

The back-of-the-head wound

The HSCA photograph and diagram not only ignore the Harper fragment but contradict the Bethesda autopsy report and are inconsistent with the Parkland physicians observations, which was of a fist-sized blowout at the back of the head and slightly to the right. These diagrams were drawn by Robert McClellan, M.D. (on the left) and by Charles Crenshaw, M.D. (on the right), who were present in Trauma Room #1 during JFK's treatment:

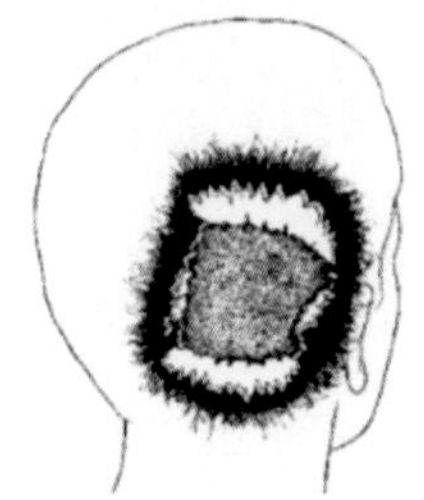

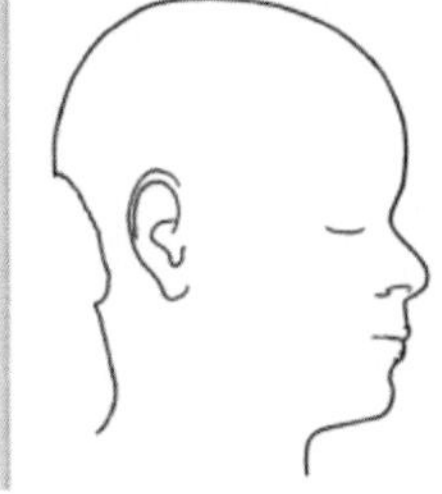

Just two days later, Dr. Crenshaw would be responsible for the treatment of his alleged assassin, Lee Oswald, in Trauma Room #2. They were discounted on the ground that the autopsy X-rays did not confirm them. However, as the extraordinary research by David W. Mantik, M.D., Ph.D., *Assassination Science* (1998), on the basis of meticulous optical densitometry studies have established, those X-rays were "patched" to conceal the blowout, which has now been confirmed by my discovery of the visible blowout in late frame 374, which I emphasized in *The Great Zapruder Film Hoax* (2003). Notice how closely "Area P" (for "patch") defined by the series of broken lines corresponds to the blowout as seen in that frame.

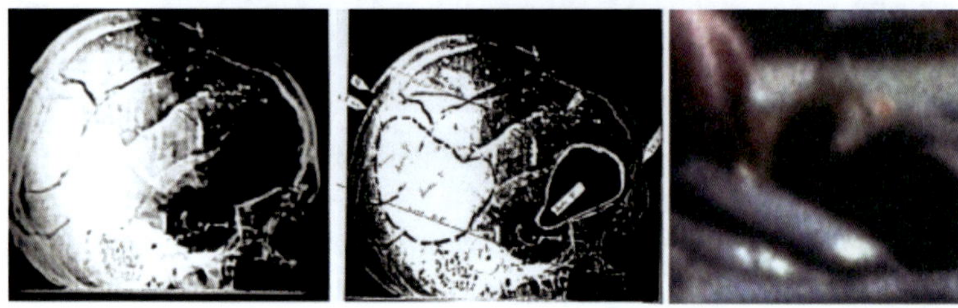

For those who prefer evidence-based history, there is no longer any room for doubt who got it right—the Parkland physicians, the Bethesda pathologists, or the HSCA!

The evidence intersects

What this means—believe it or not!—is that the medical evidence in the assassination of John Fitzgerald Kennedy has undergone an astounding evolution from the appearance of the wounds to thoroughly competent and highly experienced physicians at Parkland Hospital—who were used to dealing with gunshot victims—to the Bethesda autopsy report—by physicians who had never dealt with one—and then was unjustifiably contracted by the HSCA:

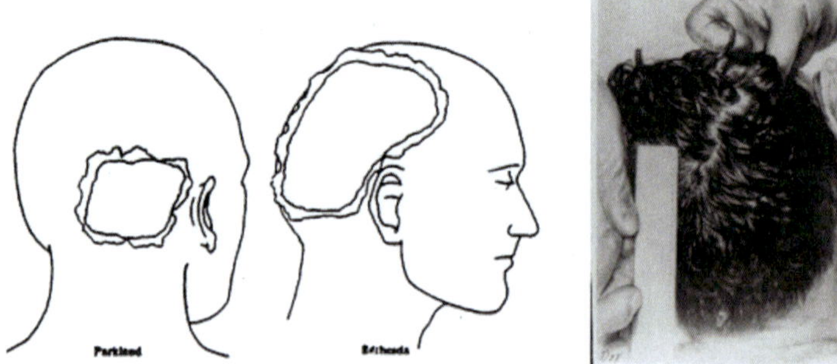

Indeed, we now know from depositions conducted by the ARRB, that Humes took a cranial saw to the skull of JFK and enlarged the wound to make it more consistent with the appearance of (what could have been) a shot fired from behind, since the Parkland observations were obviously of an exit wound from a shot fired from in front. Humes performed that grisly task in front of two witnesses, one of whom was Thomas Evan Robinson, the mortician.

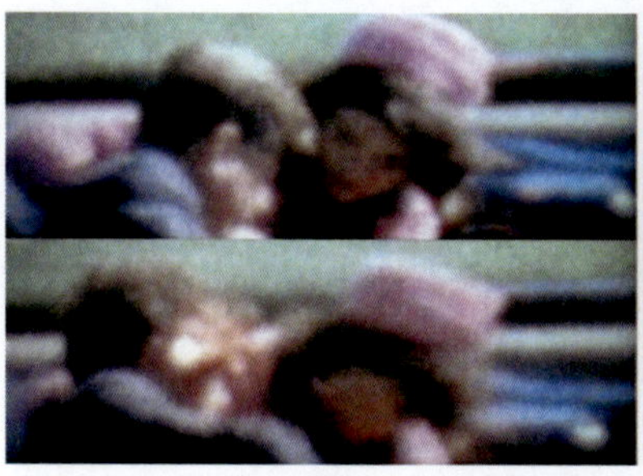

This comparison of earlier frames with frame 374 demonstrates that the blowout observed at Parkland was taken out by the simple expedient of painting over the wound in black—as the Hollywood restoration experts have confirmed.

This means that the film is not even internally consistent, which makes it all the more incredible that experts on film and photos, such as Robert Groden, would persist in contending the film is authentic, when it is provably false.

Zapruder film authenticity

So much proof that the film is a fabrication has been published—where some of those proofs are as simple and straightforward as the one I have just presented—that I shall simply summarize some of the most important proofs that have appeared since the publication of *The Great Zapruder Film Hoax* (2003), where it is beyond belief that any serious student of the assassination of JFK, much less experts on film and photos, would continue to deny them:

(1) We have more than 60 witnesses who reported seeing the limo slow dramatically or come to a complete stop, where it slowed dramatically AS it came to a complete stop, where those witnesses include all four of the motorcycle escort officers: See "What happened on Elm Street? The Eyewitnesses Speak" compiled by John P. Costella, Ph.D.

(2) We also know that Officer James Chaney motored forward to inform Chief Curry the president had been shot, which was confirmed by Chief of Police Jesse Curry, Secret Service Agents Winston Lawson and Forrest Sorrels, as well as Motorcycle

Officers Bobby Hargis, James Chaney, and Marrion Baker: See *New Proof of JFK Film Fakery*. (See **Endnote)**.

(3) We know that, for over 50 years, Clint Hill has described climbing on the trunk, pushing Jackie down, lying across their bodies, peering into the wound, observing a fist-sized blowout and giving a "thumbs down", all before the limo had reached the Triple Underpass: See *JFK: Who's telling the truth: Clint Hill or the Zapruder film?*

(4) We know that the original 8mm, already split film developed in Dallas, was taken to the NPIC on Saturday, the 23rd, and that a substitute 16mm, unsplit film, developed in Rochester, N.Y., was taken there on Sunday, the 24th, where two different teams worked on the different versions: See *U.S. Government Official: JFK Cover-Up, Film Fabrication*.

(5) We also know that a half-dozen or more have viewed another film, apparently the original, including William Reymond, Rich DellaRosa, Gregory Burnham and several others, where Rich DellaRosa's description of its content appears as an Appendix to *The Great Zapruder Film Hoax* (2003): See *Did Zapruder film "the Zapruder film"?*

(6) We have John Costella's precise visual tutorial about evidence internal to the film that explains how we can know that the film is a fabrication, where all of its frames had to be reshot to create the right sequence of "ghost panels": See The JFK Assassination Film Hoax: An Introduction. Here's an informal discussion of his research on the film: *https://youtu.be/UnnxwijxG7Q*

(7) We know that they not only removed the limo stop but painted over the blowout in early frames and that the "blob" and the blood spray were painted in, but that they overlooked that in later frames, especially in frame 374, the blowout can be seen, as I explain in many places, including *What Happened To JFK And Why It Matters Today*.

(8) More recently, in *The Two NPIC Zapruder Film Events: Signposts Pointing to the Film's Alteration* (2012) and *The Two NPIC Zapruder Film Events: Analysis and Implications* (2012), Doug Horne has substantiated that the original was taken to the NPIC on Saturday, the 23rd, and the substitute was brought there on Sunday, the 24th.

The timeline argument—that there was no opportunity for the film to have been faked, which Josiah Thompson has endlessly promoted—

has no basis in fact and was merely a gambit. We know the film was altered, which can be proven by multiple lines of argument. We also know when and where it was altered and when and where the fake film was substituted for the original.

Since rationality requires that we revise our beliefs with the acquisition of new evidence and alternative hypotheses, the time has come to abandon the fantasy that the Zapruder film is authentic.

What about Altgens6?

The proof that Altgens6 was altered may be even more obvious and compelling than the proof that the Zapruder film was fabricated, where each frame had to be reshot in the laboratory to create a new sequence of "ghost panels", in the absence of which the fakery would have been conspicuous. We have another timeline argument about this photo, which also has no merit.

When there is proof that a photo or film has been faked, there must have been time to fake it. You don't have to be a philosopher to appreciate that whatever is actual must be something that is possible.

In this case, however, the CIA took extraordinary measures to conceal that Oswald had been in the doorway at the time of the shooting, which has to be the most direct and obvious proof that the Warren Commission was a sham.

My research on Altgens6 began when I belatedly discovered that the ARRB had released notes that Will Fritz, the homicide detective

who had interrogated them, had taken, during which Lee Oswald had told him he was "out with Bill Shelley in front", which led me to take a closer look to see if he had been caught in this famous photo (above). I discovered a collage on a John McAdams website, in which it was apparent that a face had been obfuscated. It was my initial inference that this had to have been Lee's face, since there was no obvious reason to have removed anyone else's.

But I was soon contacted by Ralph Cinque, who explained I had the right conclusion for the wrong reasons, an area in which he possessed considerable relevant expertise, given his background as a professional chiropractor.

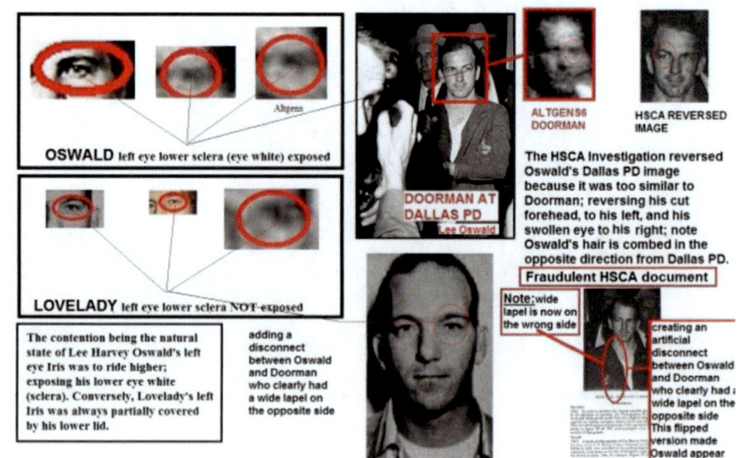

Ralph convinced me that the key to unraveling the ambiguity is their clothing, not their faces, where the shirt that Doorman is wearing is strikingly similar to the shirt that Lee was wearing when he was arrested.

We would publish a series of sequels: we explained that Lovelady visited the FBI and showed them the shirt that he had been wearing, which was a red-and-white, vertically striped short-sleeved shirt; that a man near the doorway in a checkered shirt, who has been claimed to have been Lovelady, has very different cranial and facial features and does not resemble him; that Doorman is missing his left shoulder and that "Black Tie Man" is both in front of him and behind him at the same time and that several videos were doctored to place "Checkered Shirt Man" in the Dallas Police Department (DPD).

Just as we know the actual must be possible, we also know that the impossible cannot be actual.

Since anyone can see that Doorman is missing his left shoulder and that Black Tie Man is both in front of him and behind him at the same time, I have become incredulous that any serious student of the assassination could deny Altgens6 has been altered.

Indeed, Richard Hooke has done a series of studies that place the identity of Doorman as Oswald beyond a reasonable doubt, since no alternative explanation is reasonable.

This study of the right eyes of Billy and Lee lends further support to that conclusion, but also exposes the duplicity of the HSCA in reversing Oswald's image to make it less obvious that he had been the man in the doorway. Many other measures would be taken to obfuscate that fact.

How it was done

Even Billy Lovelady explained to a reporter that it was a mistake to confuse him with Lee Oswald, because he was 3″ shorter and 15-20 lbs. heavier. And, indeed, that appears to be true of the figure we call "Black Hole Man" because his face has been turned into a black hole.

He not only appears to be about 3" shorter and 15-20 lbs. heavier than the man in the doorway, but he also appears to be wearing a short-sleeved shirt! Richard has also suggested that the man whose face was obfuscated—whom I originally mistook for Oswald—was Bill Shelley, no doubt because, had Shelley actually been there, it might have raised too many questions about whether what Lee had told Fritz was true.

The series of moves that were involved here thus appear to have involved several moves using figures in the photo on the next page:

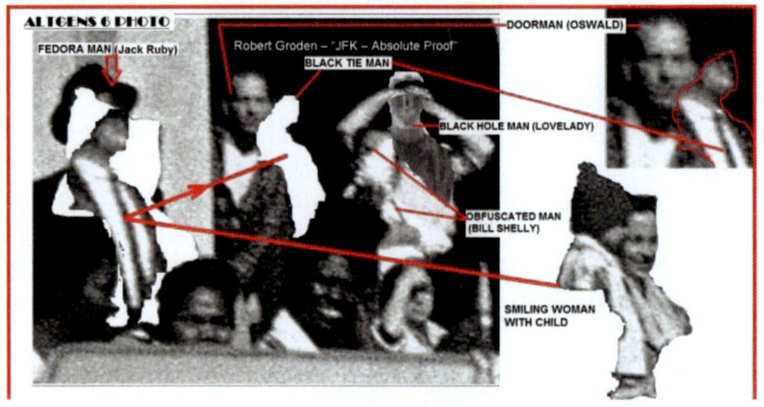

A recent study by Larry Rivera has revealed why Buell Wesley Frazier's image was removed from a location right in the midst of the crowd in front of the doorway, because once they turned Billy into Doorman, they needed someone to replace Billy—even if only in a vaguely defined fashion. And Ralph Cinque has done a reenactment of Altgens6, which has proven to be revealing in several respects, including that the visual image of a man in a checkered shirt would have been very different than what we find in Altgens6. One of the most remarkable ramifications of the study of these questions has been that Robert Groden, *The Killing of a President* (1993), pp. 186-187, has taken several photos of Billy and has promoted the impression that he was Doorman and was wearing a checkered shirt.

The News-Palladium

PRESIDENT KENNEDY IS KILLED BY SNIPER!

Rushed To Dallas Hospital Blood Pouring From Head

EXTRA

Man, Woman Believed To Be Assassins

Courts Urged To Boost Fees

The News-Palladium

PRESIDENT IS SLAIN!

EXTRA

Sniper's Gun Kills JFK In Dallas, Texas

One of Larry Rivera's most remarkable discoveries was that the entry way to the Texas School Book Depository was remodeled, apparently to create space for Buell Wesley Frazier to have stood and leave it vague as to whether or not the "official account" requires him to have been Black Hole Man, where there wasn't originally space for any other inference to be drawn. Most stunning of all, after some of those opposed to the alteration thesis found newspapers that seemed to show Altgens6 had been published on 22 November 1963.

Ralph discovered two "EXTRA" issues of the Beacon Hill, MI *News-Paladium* (22 November 1963), which is a small community of around 10,000 in Michigan. So not only has the Agency altered photographs and films, but it has spared no expense in concealing the truth from the American people, even to the extent of fabricating fake issues of obscure newspapers at taxpayer expense!

Groden's Slight-of-Hand

On pages 186-187 of *The Killing of a President* (1993), Robert Groden not only endorses Billy Lovelady as Doorman, but he asserts (beside photos of Billy in a checkered shirt), "I interviewed Billy in 1976. Lovelady took out the shirt he had worn in Dealey Plaza (he had packed it away for safekeeping) and put it on for the first time in years".

Moreover, he asserts (below the photographs of Billy in the short-sleeved shirt he had worn for his visit to the FBI, "When the FBI called Lovelady to come down and be photographed, they told him not to bother to wear the same shirt. When they released the photographs, they stated that it was the same shirt, creating the controversy over whether it was Oswald or Lovelady in the Depository doorway". But what Robert Groden is claiming in both cases is false.

These photographs are extremely important, not only because Groden is concealing that the statement that Billy had been wearing this shirt on 22 November 1963 was in the formal FBI report to its Director,

J. Edgar Hoover, but, that Billy himself had told them that this was the shirt he had worn at the assassination, which is clear from the report itself.

He also ignores that *Billy had been interviewed by Jones Harris in Dallas and that Lovelady had confirmed to Jones that the short-sleeved, red-and-white vertically striped short sleeved shirt was the one that he had been wearing.*

FD-302 (Rev. 1-25-60)

FEDERAL BUREAU OF INVESTIGATION

MP
Idv 1-2

Date 3/2/64

1

BILLY NOLAN LOVELADY appeared at the Dallas FBI Office at which time he consented to be photographed.

LOVELADY advised that on the day of the assassination of President JOHN F. KENNEDY, November 22, 1963, at the time of the assassination and shortly before, he was standing in the doorway of the front entrance to the Texas School Book Depository (TSBD) Building, 411 Elm Street, Dallas, Texas, where he is employed. He stated he was wearing a red and white vertical striped shirt and blue jeans.

LOVELADY stated his picture has appeared in several publications which picture depicts him on the far left side of the front doorway to the TSBD. LOVELADY was exhibited a picture appearing on pages 4-5 of the magazine entitled "Four Dark Days in History," Copyright 1963 by Special Publications, Inc., 6527 Hollywood Blvd., Los Angeles 28, California. He immediately identified the picture of the individual on the far left side of the doorway of the TSBD as being his photograph. He stated this same photograph or one identical to it has appeared in the Dallas Times Herald newspaper of November 23, 1963, and in the Cincinnati Inquirer of December 3, 1963. He stated it also appeared in an edition of the Saturday Evening Post the date of which he does not know.

Mr. LOVELADY stated his close resemblance to LEE HARVEY OSWALD has become somewhat embarrassing. He stated his step-children, TIMMY EKSTEDT, age 6, and stepdaughter, ANGELA EKSTEDT, age 4, were watching television shortly after the assassination at a time when LEE HARVEY OSWALD was shown while in custody of the Dallas Police Department and both of these children remarked that they thought their daddy was on television referring to his close resemblance to LEE HARVEY OSWALD.

The following physical description and background information was obtained from interrogation and observation of LOVELADY:

Name	BILLY NOLAN LOVELADY
Race	White
Sex	Male
Born	2/19/37, Myrtle Springs, Texas
Height	5'8"

on 2/29/64 at Dallas, Texas File # DL 100-10461

by Special Agent ROBERT P. GEMBERLING EMORY E. HORTON:vm Date dictated 2/29/64

This document contains neither recommendations nor conclusions of the FBI. It is the property of the FBI and is loaned to your agency; it and its contents are not to be distributed outside your agency.

735

Notice that Billy's height is given as 5'8", while Lee was around 5'10" or even 5'11", which corresponds with Billy's statement that he was 3" shorter and 10-15 lbs. heavier than Lee Oswald, who was slight of build, while Billy was quite a bit stockier. Although Groden publishes profile photos of Checkered Shirt Man just above the FBI photos, he does not observe that they look nothing alike: Billy has an ordinary facial profile and normal cranium, while those of Checkered Shirt Man make him look like a gorilla! They are not remotely the same, which we have emphasized in many of our studies. Ralph consulted with nine experts, who unanimously agreed they were not the same man. On the next page you can see one of Richard Hooke's collages, which makes the point so clearly that it is unreasonable to deny.

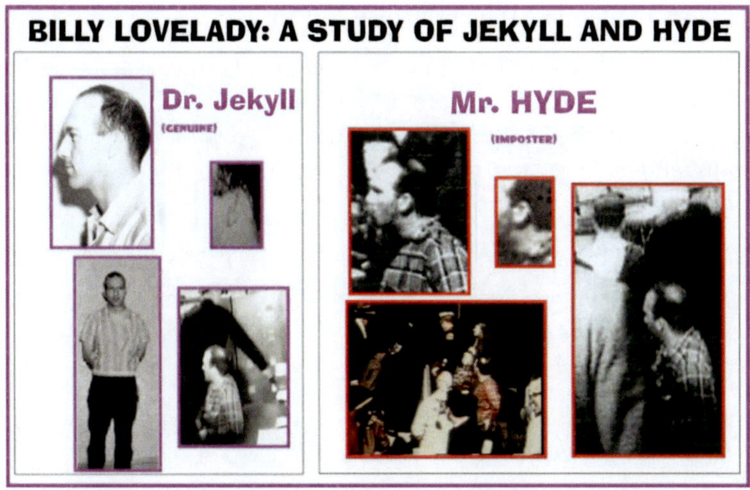

That a point is unreasonable to deny does not mean that otherwise reasonable people might not still deny it, especially if they have an agenda! The crucial distinction must be drawn between rationality of belief and rationality of action, where those who have specific aims, goals or objectives—such as persuading a target audience that something true is actually false, as with swindlers, con men and disinfo ops—may deny that something is true even when the evidence is abundant, objective and compelling. You do not have to be an expert in photography or film to discern that these are photographs of two different persons.

And in *The Search for Lee Harvey Oswald: A Comprehensive Photographic Record* (1995), p. 159, Groden takes another step in the wrong direction by offering a frame from a film into which Checkered Shirt Man has been introduced.

What about Geneva Hine?

It was therefore fascinating for me—and, independently, Richard Hooke, during a separate interview—to discover that Jones Harris had been called down to the Time Life building in Rockefeller Center by

Josiah Thompson, who was working for the company at the time, where he showed Jones some of the footage with Checkered Shirt Man at the DPD.

This suggests to me that Josiah was "on the job" even earlier than some have surmised, although Vincent Salandria was quite explicit in calling him out when his book, *Six Seconds in Dallas* (1967), first appeared, because in the final paragraph of the text, he disclaims that his book proved the existence of a conspiracy in the assassination of JFK, even though the proof it presents is abundant and compelling. So Groden is reinforcing Thompson on this point.

In this context, therefore, I have been intrigued to discover that Robert Groden claims to have "new proof" that Lee was innocent of the crime, which derives from a source—now deceased—who is unavailable for confirmation.

Her name is Geneva Hine. Groden made the following remarks during a 17 September 2009 interview on Black Op Radio:

> *I actually found a woman some years ago. She was terrified. She did not want to come forward. And she finally agreed to give an interview, and I did interview her.*
>
> *When the shots actually went off, she was talking to Lee Oswald on the second floor.*
>
> *We always assumed that Lee had the change, that he had had the change for the machine. He didn't. He went into the office across from the snack room with a dollar bill and asked for change. He said, "No pennies, please."*
>
> *And, as the change was being counted out into his hand, the shots went off. And they looked at each other, this woman and Lee, and [asked], "What was that?" Backfires, firecrack[ers], who knew?*
>
> *He got the rest of the change, walked back across the hall, bought the Coke and then just a little over a minute later there was a gun in his ribs held by Officer Baker. Lee had an airtight alibi. He could not possibly have done this. She told this story to the Warren Commission. They told her to keep her mouth shut. And she did. She told very few people. Very few people. I was one of the few that she did.*
>
> *So I got to speak to her because I had a friend who knew a friend of hers. I had to promise her I would never reveal any of this until after she was gone. And now she is. The whole story, including her name, will be in the next book.*

So it may be worthwhile to consider whether or not Robert Groden has found a "smoking gun" in the form of the testimony of Geneva Hine. It would resolve questions about the timeline for Oswald to have rushed from the sixth floor to the second floor lunchroom and would explain why he was drinking a coke when he was confronted by Officer Marrion Baker.

The timeline is problematic, because several of Oswald's coworkers had observed him in and around the lunchroom shortly before the shooting and, according to the official account—which in this respect appears to be accurate—he was confronted by Officer Baker within 90 seconds of the shooting, which his supervisor, Roy Truly, confirmed.

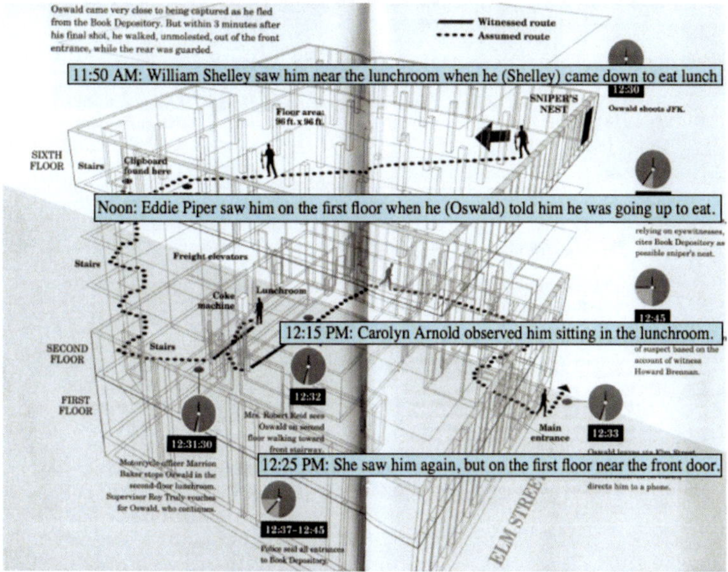

Has Groden "cracked the case"?

Observe that, if Lee was inside the building obtaining change from Geneva Hine, he cannot have also been in the doorway watching the motorcade as it passed by.

Like those who suggest Doorman was someone other than Lee Oswald, their remarkable convergence in their height, build, shirt and other features would defy the odds.

The probability of the evidence we have adduced, on the hypothesis that Doorman was Oswald, is extremely high, while the likelihood that it was someone else is extremely low. There is no good reason to suppose that we are wrong, given the available evidence. His claim about Hine is new evidence and a new hypothesis.

If Groden is right, then we are wrong. But it seems implausible on its face. Geneva Hine was interviewed by the FBI on 18 March 1964, and her Warren Commission testimony on 7 April 1964 also contradicts Groden's position. She acknowledges that she knew Oswald but denied that she had seen him at the time of the shooting. Here are her most interesting comments:

EJR:vm
DL 100-10461

"Dallas, Texas
March 18, 1964

"I, Mrs. Geneva L. Hine, hereby freely and voluntarily make the following statement to E. J. Robertson who has identified himself as a Special Agent of the FBI.

"My name is Geneva L. Hine and I reside at 2305 Oakdale Road, Dallas, Texas. I am 52 years of age, born October 4, 1911, at Martinsville, Ind. I am a white female, and am employed at the Credit Desk, Texas School Book Depository.

"At the time President Kennedy was shot I was on the second floor of the Texas School Book Depository Building, in my office. I was alone at the time. I did not see Lee Harvey Oswald at the time President Kennedy was shot.

"I do not remember seeing any person in the Texas School Book Depository Building on the morning of November 22, 1963 who was a stranger to me.

"I left the Texas School Book Depository Building at about 2:30 PM on November 22, 1963. All employees on the second floor working for the Texas School Book Depository left at the same time.

"I have read the above statement consisting of one and one-fifth pages and it is true and correct to the best of my knowledge.

"/s/ GENEVA L. HINE

"Witnesses: E. J. ROBERTSON, Special Agent, F.B.I., Dallas, Texas 3/18/64
THOMAS T. TRETTIS, Jr., Special Agent, F.B.I., Dallas, Texas, 3/18/64."

41

COMMISSION EXHIBIT No. 1381—Continued

Mr. BALL. Were you alone then at this time?

Miss HINE. Yes.

Mr. BALL. Did you stay at your desk?

Miss HINE. Yes, sir: I was alone until the lights all went out and the phones became dead because the motorcade was coming near us and no one was calling so I got up and thought I could see it from the east window in our office.

Mr. BALL. The east window?

Miss HINE. Yes, sir; going north on Houston Street. I saw it turn left and I saw the President's car coming and I saw the President and saw him waving his hand in greeting up in the air and I saw his wife and I saw him turn the corner and after he turned the corner I looked and I saw the next car coming. Just at the instant I saw the next car coming up was when I heard the shots.

Mr. BALL. How many did you hear?

Miss HINE. Three.

Mr. BALL Could you tell where the shots were coming from?

Miss HINE. Yes, sir; they came from inside the building.

Mr. BALL. How do you know that?

Miss HINE. Because the building vibrated from the result of the explosion coming in.

Mr. BALL. Did you know they were shots at the time?

Miss HINE. Yes, sir; they sounded almost like cannon shots they were so terrific. . . .

The part about hearing three shots and that they sounded as though they had come from inside the building are not very persuasive, but suppose we give her the benefit of the doubt. There appears to be nothing here that would inspire confidence in Groden's story about what she had confided in him. And given the evidence we have amassed that Lee was in the doorway at that time—which also explains how he could have reached the lunchroom for a coke in such a short time—we have to weigh Groden's credibility against his track record, which is what we have been doing here. So how credible is Robert Groden based upon the evidence we have presented in our discussion of his work above?

The Groden Score Card

I find it painful to draw the conclusions that follow from this evaluation, because they are highly unfavorable to his claims to be dedicated to exposing falsehoods and revealing truths about the assassination of JFK.

Robert Groden has done a great deal of good for JFK research, including being the first person to arrange for the extant Zapruder film to be broadcast on television. He has testified before Congress and he advised Oliver Stone on *JFK*, where, alas, he conveyed the false positions that the film is authentic and that Doorman was Billy Lovelady. This chapter provides him with an opportunity to reconsider our findings:

(1) Groden denies the existence of a bullet hole in the windshield; but the evidence for the through-and-through hole is readily accessible and he has to know better. This suggests he is covering it up.

(2) He defends a set of autopsy photos that seem to be fabrications; indeed, they are as fake as those presented by the HSCA, which indicates that the performance of the HSCA deserves more scrutiny.

(3) He claims the Zapruder film is authentic, which may explain (2); but there are multiple lines of argument, each of which supports the other in the conclusion that the extant film is a fabrication.

(4) He maintains that the Altgens6 photograph is also authentic; but it includes impossible features that make its alteration beyond dispute: no authentic photograph can include impossible features.

(5) He denies Oswald was in the doorway during the shooting; but comparisons of the height, build, and shirt with the incompatible properties of the alternatives make it beyond a reasonable doubt.

(6) He offers an alternative explanation of Oswald's location at the time; but the available evidence in relation to Geneva Hine's prior testimony makes that very difficult to accept, especially given (1)-(5).

(7) While this new account also implies that Lee cannot have been on the sixth floor and could not have been a shooter, it pales in comparison with the proof we have adduced that he was in the doorway.

If Robert Groden is rational with respect to his beliefs, then he will take these arguments into account and revise his present beliefs. But, if he has an agenda to ignore reason and promote beliefs that are no longer justifiable, that will be a telling sign that he, like Josiah Thompson, does not deserve continuation of the admiration that he has enjoyed in the past.

So this chapter is an invitation for him to take stock of his past positions and consider revising them. As a token of my own appreciation for much of what he has done, I conclude with a video about Robert Groden's efforts to make the case for conspiracy in Dealey Plaza *(https://youtu.be/zV2d49u8y5g)*. No matter how much we disagree on the facts of the case, here he has clearly excelled.

Endnote: Recent research by Larry Rivera, including on the Jack Daniel's film (which was only released in 1979), shows Cheney well behind the limousine, where this appears to have been a cover story that cannot be sustained

Source note: This chapter previously appeared as "The Challenging Case of Robert Groden," *http://jamesfetzer.blogspot.com/2015/09/the-jfk-war-challenging-case-of-robert.html.*

20

The Disturbing Case of Jim DiEugenio, LBJ and Israel

by Don Fox

For some time and across a broad range of different issues, I (Jim Fetzer) have had concerns about Jim DiEugenio, author of *Destiny Betrayed*, 2nd ed., which explores New Orleans District Attorney Jim Garrison's attempt to prosecute Clay Shaw, and of *Reclaiming Parkland: Tom Hanks, Vincent Bugliosi, and the JFK Assassination in the New Hollywood*, which *amazon.com* describes as investigating Tom Hanks's failed attempt to adapt Vincent Bugliosi's massive book *Reclaiming History: The Assassination of President John F. Kennedy* into a mini-series and as exposing the origins of that book in a mock trial pitting Bugliosi against attorney Gerry Spence.

It is said to include a withering critique of Bugliosi's inflated book, where DiEugenio examines an early draft of the film *Parkland*, the CIA's influence in Hollywood today, Hanks' closeness to Washington, and the actor's spurious claim of being "an historian". It also includes the author's unsuccessful attempt to stop Leonardo DiCaprio from making a film out of *Legacy of Secrecy: The Long Shadow of the JFK Assassination*.

As one who has also criticized Bugliosi's tome and entreated Tom Hanks and Leonardo DiCaprio to abandon those blunders (in *Forrest Gump on the Grassy Knoll*), I applaud these efforts. But he has done other things about which I am decidedly less enthusiastic.

(1) During that long thread about Judyth Vary Baker on "The Education Forum," he discounted her observation that, when

Lee had visited the home of a state senator, his daughter had observed a woman who stayed in the car. Jim argued that she had eventually given up her claim, which does not mean that it was not true: that she made it in the first place suggests it was true; that she later abandoned it was undoubtedly due to pressure applied to her. He has to know that earlier testimony is almost invariably more trustworthy than later testimony, yet he went on a binge to attempt to discredit Judyth on methodologically improper grounds. I fault him for that.

(2) When David Talbot and Jefferson Morley visited David Sanchez Morales home town, they made it entirely obvious that they were there looking for evidence that he had been involved in the assassinations of JFK and of RFK. No one was going to come forth and corroborate that proposition under those circumstances, which I take as proof that they were not there in a serious attempt to investigate the issue but rather to deliberately confuse it and make it all but supportable on that basis. Jim came to their defense, which I found incredible, as I have explained in *RFK: Outing the CIA at the Ambassador*. That is when I began to have serious doubts about him.

(3) Jefferson Morley has subsequently sought to portray himself as a leading student of JFK. He has a website that is very sophisticated and represents a considerable investment in time and money. One of its features is to list the "best" and the "worst" JFK websites. His list includes my *assassinationscience.com* as among the worst and John McAdams' website among the best! If I hadn't seen it for myself, I would not have believed it. When someone challenged him about these points, he justified himself on the ground that I deny the Zapruder film is authentic, which is absurd. We have proven that the film is a re-creation on dozens of grounds. See, for example, *The Challenging Case of Robert Groden*, for a nice compact summary of the proof.

(4) On The Deep Politics Forum, I offered dozens and dozens of posts supporting Phillip Nelson and others in their claim that LBJ played a pivotal role in the assassination, which is evident from the books and testimony of Madeleine Duncan Brown, *Texas in the Morning: The Love Story of Madeleine Brown and President Lyndon Baines Johnson,* Billy Sol Estes, *Billy Sol Estes, a Texas Legend, "The Man Who Knows Who Shot JFK"*, Barr McClellan, *Blood, Money, & Power: How LBJ Killed JFK*, E. Howard Hunt (*Last Confessions* in *Rolling Stone*), Phil Nelson, *LBJ:*

The Mastermind of the JFK Assassination, and Jack Ruby (who observed that this would never have happened had someone else been vice president).

It is also substantiated by Nigel Turner in Part 9 of *The Men Who Killed Kennedy* and there are probably a half-dozen new books that are about to appear that offer further evidence, yet he unleashed Seamus Coogan to attack me and Phil on that forum. It was nasty and disgraceful.

(5) Peter Janney's book, *Mary's Mosaic: The CIA Conspiracy to Murder John F. Kennedy, Mary Pinchot Meyer, and Their Vision for World Peace*, is one of the most courageous and brilliant I have ever read about the death of JFK and its ramifications. Peter knew Mary Meyer as a boy, sat on her lap, and was devastated when he learned she had been killed. During the course of his research on her death, he discovered that his own father, Wistar, who was a CIA official, had been involved in both her death and that of JFK. That he could pursue this with such determination and dedication is one of the most admirable accomplishments I have ever witnessed. The book is especially important because, in his painstaking reconstruction of her death, he reveals a textbook perfect illustration of how this is done by the Agency. I regard attitudes toward this book as a test of research integrity, as I explain in *Mary's Mosaic: A Litmus Test of JFK Research Integrity*. Jim flunks.

Indeed, on all of these issues, DiEugenio is on the wrong side. I have accordingly gradually become convinced that he is not promoting JFK research so much as he is undermining it and that, in his role as co-host with Len Osanic, he has been tarnishing the reputation of Black Op Radio for objective and dispassionate discussion of the issues. DiEugenio is not about that at all. He appears to steer research away from the truth, alas, not to reveal it. I was therefore struck when Don Fox sent me a note about the late Michael Collins Piper, who made the case for Israeli involvement in the death of JFK:

I just downloaded Michael Collins Piper's *Final Judgment: The Missing Link in the JFK Assassination Conspiracy*. Piper mentions Mr. DiEugenio a few times. Here is one passage:

Although James DiEugenio's Destiny Betrayed*, is a fine, fact-filled examination of Jim Garrison's investigation of Clay Shaw, DiEugenio (who has publicly scoffed at* Final Judgment*) has been careful not to explore the multiple Mossad links of the Permindex* *corporation on whose board Shaw served. DiEugenio's book was published by the Sheridan Square Press whose founders received financing from the* ***Stern family of New Orleans who were also contributors to the Mossad intelligence arm, the Anti-Defamation League (ADL).***

Close friends of Clay Shaw, the Sterns were owners of the WDSU media empire which played a central role in Shaw's "sheep-dipping" of Lee Oswald as a "pro-Castro agitator" prior to the JFK assassination. Although we now know Garrison recognized Mossad involvement in the JFK affair, he (perhaps wisely) voiced his suspicions only in an unpublished novel—a fact many choose to ignore.

DiEugenio's publisher received financing from the Stern family who also contributed to the ADL and they were close friends of Clay Shaw!! That explains a lot doesn't it? It seems like if you really dig into 9/11 or JFK you're going to run into the ADL.

I am hardly the first to take exception to DiEugenio, who has been raked over the coals by Gus Russo, the author of *Live by the Sword: The Secret War Against Castro and the Death of JFK* (1998), which suggests the Lee Oswald visited the Cuban Embassy in Mexico City to offer his services to Castro by taking out JFK.

But since *the man the CIA photographed there looks nothing like Oswald, and J. Edgar Hoover even put out a memorandum to his Agents-in-Charge that someone was impersonating Lee in Mexico City—which, in my opinion, is sufficient by itself to establish the existence of a conspiracy in the assassination*—it's not much of a stretch to argue that, if his views on DiEugenio are as well-founded as his work on JFK, then they should not be taken seriously.

In DiEugenio's defense, he has advanced good reasons to believe that the CIA was deeply involved in the assassination of JFK, which is undoubtedly correct. That he fingers Allen Dulles as having played the pivotal role that I and others, such as Phil Nelson—and now Roger Stone, *The Man who Killed Kennedy: The Case against LBJ* (2013), which I recommend—attribute to LBJ can be taken as falling within the ballpark of differences in opinion and evaluation of the evidence, which is defensible. He may be right or he may be wrong, but that difference—at least on first consideration—does not count against him.

But Don believes that DiEugenio has offered up Allen Dulles, who was undoubtedly involved, as a cover for LBJ and for Israel.

DiEugenio appeared recently on "Coast to Coast with George Noory" about the new edition of *Destiny Betrayed*, which he describes as not simply "updated" but having been 90% rewritten, which "for all intents and purposes" is another book. (*www.youtube.com/watch?-feature=player_embedded&v=W0CRaObxlSg)*

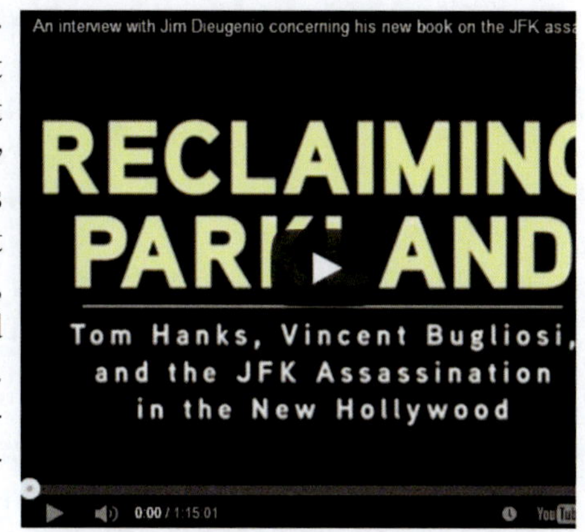

While I don't care for his style, everyone should have the opportunity to judge for themselves. I note that Don's critique of DiEugenio's role in not discussing the role of Israel in relation to the death of JFK might also be applied to me.

Although I have interviewed Michael Collins Piper more than once (see, for example, my interview of 10 August 2012) I have certainly not focused on that aspect in the belief that this was an "all American" affair. But I am willing to consider new evidence and alternative hypotheses, such as those Don Fox presents here, where if I have been remiss in not exploring this dimension of the assassination adequately, I would like to make amends. I therefore offer this article as a prolegomenon to further investigation.

DiEugenio and CTKA: Obfuscating LBJ and Israel's roles in the Assassination of JFK

by Don Fox

Jim DiEugenio has spent decades researching the JFK assassination. He has written two books on the subject, *Destiny Betrayed: JFK, Cuba, and the Garrison Case* and *Reclaiming Parkland: Tom Hanks, Vincent Bugliosi, and the JFK Assassination in the New Hollywood.*

He previously published *Probe* magazine and now runs the CTKA.net (Citizens for Truth about the Kennedy Assassination) website and appears regularly on Len Osanic's Black Op Radio.

DiEugenio never mentions Israel or the Mossad as having a motive to kill Kennedy. Israeli Prime David Ben-Gurion clashed with JFK over Israel's nuclear program. Kennedy was determined to prevent Israel from becoming a Nuclear Weapon State and Ben-Gurion was determined that Israel would. Ben-Gurion viewed atomic weapons as vital to the survival of Israel.

DiEugenio and CTKA downplay the role of Lyndon Johnson and instead promote Allen Dulles as being the pivotal player in the assassination. The motive often cited is the Vietnam War. Indeed, U.S. policy changed abruptly after Kennedy's death and the Vietnam War went into high gear behind the scenes even before Kennedy's body was buried.

CTKA often cite a quote from Johnson that he wondered if any bullets were aimed at him in Dealey Plaza as proof that he wasn't the mastermind of the JFK plot. DiEugenio also fails to mention LBJ's "personal and often emotional connection to Israel."

It turns out that LBJ had been a Zionist sympathizer since he was a little boy. Any serious discussion of Johnson needs to include this vital information about his background.

Lyndon Johnson: Our First Jewish President?

Morris Smith of *5 Towns Jewish Times* posted an article called *Our First Jewish President Lyndon Johnson?* Per Smith:

> *Most students of the Arab-Israeli conflict can identify Johnson as the president during the 1967 war. But few know about LBJ's actions to rescue hundreds of endangered Jews during the Holocaust—actions that could have thrown him out of Congress and into jail. Indeed, the title of "Righteous Gentile" is certainly appropriate in the case of the Texan, whose centennial year is being commemorated this year. Appropriately enough, the annual Jerusalem Conference announced this week that it will honor Johnson.*
>
> *Historians have revealed that Johnson, while serving as a young congressman in 1938 and 1939, arranged for visas to be supplied to Jews in Warsaw, and oversaw the apparently illegal immigration of hundreds of Jews through the port of Galveston, Texas . . . .*

Research into Johnson's personal history indicates that he inherited his concern for the Jewish people from his family. His aunt Jessie Johnson Hatcher, a major influence on LBJ, was a member of the Zionist Organization of America. According to Gomolak, Aunt Jessie had nurtured LBJ's commitment to befriending Jews for 50 years.

As young boy, Lyndon watched his politically active grandfather "Big Sam" and father "Little Sam" seek clemency for Leo Frank, the Jewish victim of a blood libel in Atlanta. Frank was lynched by a mob in 1915, and the Ku Klux Klan in Texas threatened to kill the Johnsons.

The Johnsons later told friends that Lyndon's family hid in their cellar while his father and uncles stood guard with shotguns on their porch in case of KKK attacks. Johnson's speechwriter later stated, "Johnson often cited Leo Frank's lynching as the source of his opposition to both anti-Semitism and isolationism."

According to historian James M. Smallwood, Congressman Johnson used legal and sometimes illegal methods to smuggle "hundreds of Jews into Texas, using Galveston as the entry port. Enough money could buy false passports and fake visas in Cuba, Mexico and other Latin American countries. Johnson smuggled boatloads and planeloads of Jews into Texas. He hid them in the Texas National Youth Administration. Johnson saved at least four or five hundred Jews, possibly more."

. . . . Soon after taking office in the aftermath of John F. Kennedy's assassination in 1963, Johnson told an Israeli diplomat, "You have lost a very great friend, but you have found a better one." Just one month after succeeding Kennedy, LBJ attended the December 1963 dedication of the Agudas Achim Synagogue in Austin. Novy opened the ceremony by saying to Johnson, "We can't thank him enough for all those Jews he got out of Germany during the days of Hitler."

Lady Bird would later describe the day, according to Gomolak: "Person after person plucked at my sleeve and said, 'I wouldn't be here today if it wasn't for him. He helped me get out.'" Lady Bird elaborated, "Jews had been woven into the warp and woof of all [Lyndon's] years."

. . . . According to Jewish law, if a person's mother is Jewish, then that person is automatically Jewish, regardless of the father's ethnicity or religion. The facts indicate that both of Lyndon

Johnson's great-grandparents, on the maternal side, were Jewish. There is little doubt that he was Jewish.

During WWII Johnson shipped arms to "freedom fighters in Palestine" and later in the Senate he blocked the Eisenhower administrations attempts to impose sanctions on Israel after the 1956 Sinai campaign.

Lyndon certainly had a track record of doing anything he possibly could to help Jews before he became Vice President and later President. As we shall see this pattern continued once he was in the Oval Office.

The USS *Liberty* Attack

Damaged USS *Liberty* one day (9 June 1967) after attack.

On June 8, 1967, under Johnson's orders, Israeli planes bombed the American spy ship USS *Liberty* off of the coast of Egypt. 34 of the 294 crewman aboard were killed in the attack. If not for some ingenuity and dumb luck the ship would have been sunk and the attack would have been blamed on Russia or Egypt.

It appears that the attack on the *Liberty* was going to be used to justify the nuclear bombing of Cairo which may have led to World War III.

From Judy Morris' article *The USS* Liberty, *Israel & President Johnson's Order to Destroy the USS* Liberty:

The real story is that President Johnson, who was being battered in the polls over the Vietnam War and facing a general election loss and even losing the DNC primary, ordered the Israelis to bomb the USS Liberty *to create a casus belli to secure a Gulf of Tonkin style resolution to explode the world into war because in America everybody loves an outraged and indignant president who will use the full force of the military at the slightest provocation, even a government planned false flag attack.*

The USS Liberty, *however, encompasses far more than a murderous psychopathic American president resorting to hideously evil deeds to get re-elected. In addition to ordering the total destruction of the USS* Liberty *and sending 294 Americans*

> *to a watery grave in the Mediterranean Sea, LBJ also ordered the nuclear bombing of Cairo, an event specifically designed to create a nuclear war by blaming the entire USS* Liberty *affair on Russia or Egypt.*
>
> *More horrifying, it's documented that U.S. planes were on emergency standby orders as pilots waited on the runways in their planes armed with nuclear weapons.* ***The nuclear bombing of Cairo was called off only three minutes before the nuclear bomb drops.***
>
> *As fate would have it, LBJ's plan blew up in his face and the world got a reprieve from a nuclear U.S. induced holocaust.*

Clearly Lyndon would stop at nothing (not even nuclear war) to ensure Israeli domination of the Middle East. If he had no qualms about nuking an innocent city, certainly organizing a plot to assassinate JFK and ascend to the Presidency would not be a stretch for LBJ.

Encounter with the Israel Lobby

JFK got on the bad side of the Zionists long before he was elected to the presidency. In 1957 during his first Senate term he spoke of the need for Algeria to gain its independence. That speech did not sit well in certain quarters. From Michael Collins Piper's book *Final Judgment*:

> *Israel, of course, saw the emergence of another independent Arab republic as a threat to its security and anyone favoring Algerian independence was, thus, advocating a policy deemed threatening to Israel's survival.*
>
> *Some of Kennedy's critics said that the speech was a political move and that he chose the topic of Algerian independence as the subject of his first major foreign policy address because there was neither a "French" vote nor an "Algerian" vote to contend with in his home state of Massachusetts or in the nation as a whole.*
>
> *While the latter observation is correct, of course, the fact is that there was one particularly powerful American voting bloc (and source of financial contributions) that did take note of Kennedy's support for Algerian Arab independence: the powerful American lobby for Israel.*
>
> *As we shall see, in the end, it may have been JFK's initiative on the Algerian question that, in fact, played a major part in shaping the entirety of the conspiracy that ended his life in Dallas, Texas on November 22, 1963.*

This gesture by the young senator also angered many French nationalists who wanted to retain French colonial control of Algeria. Many of these nationalists later banded together in the so-called Secret Army Organization—the Israel-backed OAS—and fought against French President Charles DeGaulle who ultimately granted Algerian independence.

We can see a distinct pattern here: Johnson doing everything in his power to help the Zionist cause and Kennedy standing up to the Zionists and acting in the best interests of the U.S. as well as African and Middle Eastern countries. Certainly the Algerian situation irked the Zionists but that paled in comparison to Kennedy thwarting the Zionist's desire to produce nuclear weapons.

Confronting Ben-Gurion Over Dimona

Kennedy's letter to Israeli Prime Minister David Ben-Gurion regarding U.S. visits to Dimona:

Dear Mr. Prime Minister:

I welcome your letter of May 12 and am giving it careful study.

Meanwhile, I have received from Ambassador Barbour a report of his conversation with you on May 14 regarding the arrangements for visiting the Dimona reactor. I should like to add some personal comments on that subject.

I am sure you will agree that there is no more urgent business for the whole world than the control of nuclear weapons. We both recognized this when we talked together two years ago, and I emphasized it again when I met with Mrs. Meir just after Christmas. ***The dangers in the proliferation of national nuclear weapons systems are so obvious that I am sure I need not repeat them here.***

It is because of our preoccupation with this problem that my Government has sought to arrange with you for periodic visits to Dimona. When we spoke together in May 1961 you said that we might make whatever use we wished of the information resulting from the first visit of American scientists to Dimona and that you would agree to further visits by neutrals as well. I had assumed from Mrs. Meir's comment that there would be no problem between us on this.

We are concerned with the disturbing effects on world stability which would accompany the development of a nuclear weapons capability by Israel. I cannot imagine that the Arabs would refrain from turning to the Soviet Union for assistance if Israel were to develop a nuclear weapons capability—with all the consequences this would hold.

But the problem is much larger than its impact on the Middle East. Development of a nuclear weapons capability by Israel would almost certainly lead other larger countries that have so far refrained from such development, to feel that they must follow suit.

As I made clear in my press conference of May 8, we have a deep commitment to the security of Israel. In addition this country supports Israel in a wide variety of other ways which are well known to both of us. [4 1/2 lines of source text not declassified]

I can well appreciate your concern for developments in the UAR. But I see no present or imminent nuclear threat to Israel from there.

I am assured that our intelligence on this question is good and that the Egyptians do not presently have any installation comparable to Dimona, nor any facilities potentially capable of nuclear weapons production. But, of course, if you have information that would support a contrary conclusion, I should like to receive it from you through Ambassador Barbour. We have the capacity to check it.

I trust this message will convey the sense of urgency and the perspective in which I view your Government's early assent to the proposal first put to you by Ambassador Barbour on April 2.

Sincerely,

John F. Kennedy

Ben-Gurion eventually resigned from office over tensions with Kennedy regarding the Dimona reactor. Kennedy was determined to keep Israel from becoming a Nuclear Weapon State and, had he lived, it's likely that Israel would have had to abandon its nuclear ambitions.

Vanunu: Israel Behind JFK Assassination

However, Kennedy did not make it out of Dallas alive. Israeli dissident Mordechai Vanunu stated in a 2004 interview that Israel was indeed behind the JFK assassination:

> ***Comments by freed nuclear spy Mordechai Vanunu that Israel was behind the assassination of U.S. President John F. Kennedy failed to bring smiles to government officials Sunday.***
>
> *One would expect that such claims would portray Vanunu as a man with a credibility problem, but as far as the defense establishment is concerned, the former nuclear technician still has secrets to reveal and a declared goal of ending Israel's nuclear program. He shouldn't be talking to the media and is actually barred from meeting with foreigners.*
>
> Nevertheless, the London-based *Al-Hayat* published Sunday an interview it claims it had with Vanunu. According to the interview which appeared in its Arabic supplement *Al-Wasat*, Vanunu said that according to "near-certain indications", Kennedy was assassinated due to pressure he exerted on then head of government, David Ben-Gurion, to shed light on Dimona's nuclear reactor."

Israeli involvement in JFK's assassination appears to be the dark secret that forces behind the assassination 50 years down the line are still desperately attempting to cover it up.

Closing Thoughts

Many people in the JFK research community have remarked that JFK was the last real American President. After Kennedy, a steady stream of mediocre men whose loyalties certainly appeared to lie elsewhere

(Israel) have occupied the Oval Office. Certainly Lyndon Johnson's loyalty was greater to Israel than the U.S. Johnson's lust for power and ruthlessness are well known.

However, there appears to be a method to the madness. Johnson's actions primarily benefited the Zionists. He showed great compassion and selflessness in getting Jews out of Europe before WWII. The men aboard the USS *Liberty* saw the other side of Johnson—one willing to kill his own countrymen in order to justify military action on behalf of Israel. There can be no disputing Johnson's central role in the JFK assassination as Phil Nelson and others have pointed out. Closer examination into Johnson's motives show that he was most likely acting in the interests of Israeli Prime Minister Ben-Gurion and his quest to build nuclear weapons. Certainly the Israeli nuclear program flourished under Johnson.

Why does an otherwise meticulous researcher like DiEugenio avoid the topic of Israel's involvement in the JFK assassination? Perhaps Michael Collins Piper is on to something.

Why is there not more discussion of the Mossad's role in the JFK assassination in the research community? Perhaps this is a case where most Americans are blinded by our national ego; the thought being that some tiny country in the Middle East has no ability to set our national agenda or assassinate our Presidents. The reality is that Israel does indeed appear to have the power to influence U.S. elections and if necessary assassinate our duly elected President at high noon in the streets of Dallas.

If anyone doubts the ability of Israel to play kingmaker, look at the steady stream of 2016 Presidential hopefuls who visited Israel. Ted Cruz made at least two trips to Israel. Rand Paul was there in January 2013, and Rand started backpedaling on his rhetoric about ending foreign aid to Israel in short order. Rick Perry was in Israel in October 2013, traveling with Houston businessman and former U.S. Holocaust Memorial Council Chairman Fred S. Zeidman (who is also a large Republican fundraiser). And so it goes.

Source note: This chapter previously appeared as "The JFK War: The Disturbing Case of Jim DiEugenio, LBJ and Israel," *http://jamesfetzer.blogspot.com/2015/09/the-jfk-war-disturbing-case-of-jim.html.*

21

What's going on with Len Osanic and Black Op Radio?

by Jim Fetzer

For five years or more, I was the informal co-host with Len Osanic on Black Op Radio, which in my view has overall had a positive impact on JFK research. Since Len has begun co-hosting with Jim DiEugenio, however, I have been concerned that Black Op Radio has gradually—like a boiling frog—slipped from a forum for objective and dispassionate exchange to one in which it has become a platform to advocate indefensible positions about controversial issues, such as that of the authenticity of the Zapruder film.

When I traveled to Vancouver for The Vancouver Hearings in June of 2012, I was delighted to visit with Len at his studio and to create three segments for his *50 Reasons for 50 Years* to believe that JFK was taken out by a conspiracy and that the Warren Commission (1964) is indefensible. One was on 15 indications that the Secret Service set him up for the hit; another was on evidence of the fabrication of the Zapruder film; the third was on proof that Lee Oswald was standing in the doorway at the time of the shooting.

Imagine my surprise when Len released his *50 Reasons* and I discovered, not only had my second and third segments been excluded from his sequence, but even my first on the Secret Service had been edited to cut off some of the most important points I was making, where he left in that the driver had pulled the limousine to the left and to a halt, but had cut it there to exclude my elaborating on that point and several others, which were further additions to the proof that the Secret Service set up JFK for the hit.

The Groden Deception

My presentation was cut at the very point I mentioned that the driver, William Greer, had pulled the limo to the left and to a halt—not even adding, "to make sure that he would be killed". I am quite certain that I added, "During the limo stop, he was hit twice in the head—once in the back of the head (and fell forward), where Jackie eased him back up and was looking him right in the face when he was hit in the right temple by a frangible—exploding—bullet that blew his brains out the back of his head to the left/rear with such force that, when they impacted Officer Bobby Hargis riding there, he initially thought that he himself had been shot".

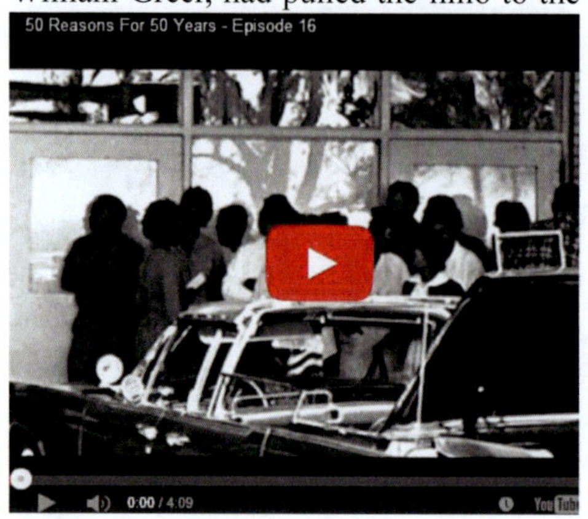

Here's what survived of that interview: *https://youtu.be/AdFgPDTr458*

When I discovered that the second and third of my segments were not included at all, I asked Len what had become of them. He told me that "important people" had refused to participate at all if I were included, but that he had managed to keep the one segment in the sequence (but had dropped the others). I found that to be extremely offensive, because the points I was making are extremely well-founded and those who oppose them have not been able to fault any of the arguments that I have made on their behalf. But he featured Robert Groden making the unsubstantiated charge that all of the claims that have been made of film fakery are "easily refuted", which is completely false. (see: *https://youtu.be/LSAbhc-9K39A*)

It also struck me as odd that Len would position Groden's segment about the films that were taken during the assassination earlier in the sequence (as "Episode 11") than my explanation about the Secret Service setting him up for the hit ("Episode 16"), since it was important to understand how he was set up. Indeed, one of the most important points I had made about all of this was that the vehicles were in the wrong order, since the presidential limousine should have been in the middle, where the lower-ranking dignitaries, such as the Mayor and the Vice President, preceded him. And that the cars were of different makes and models, which enabled the conspirators to keep track of where everyone was in the motorcade. That point seems to have been lost as well.

Concealing the blowout

Len told me that something must have gone wrong with the camera, but he had double-checked it at the time. Since the key points I was making concerned the motorcade and the limo stop, they appear to have been deliberately removed from my segment. Interestingly, the medical evidence supports and substantiates the alteration of the film, where the defect at the back of the head has been blacked out in most of the frames of the Zapruder film. The Parkland physicians had observed a fist-sized blowout at the back of the head and slightly to the right. These diagrams were drawn by Robert McClellan, M.D. (on the left) and by Charles Crenshaw, M.D. (on the right), who were present in Trauma Room #1 during JFK's treatment.

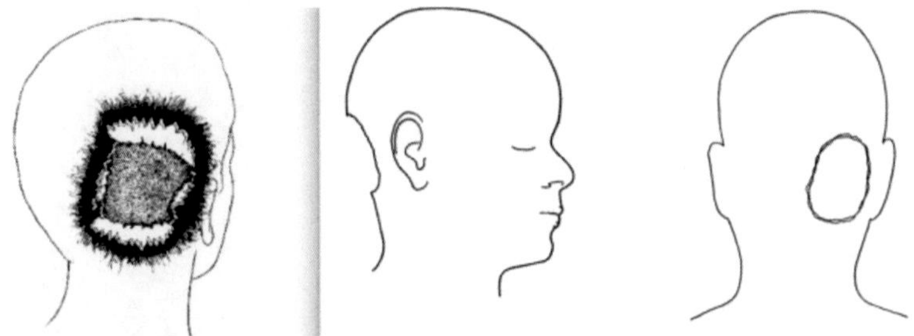

Just two days later, Dr. Crenshaw would be responsible for the treatment of JFK's alleged assassin, Lee Oswald, in Trauma Room #2. They were discounted by the Warren Commission and the HSCA on the ground that the autopsy X-rays did not confirm them. However, as the extraordinary research by David W. Mantik, M.D., Ph.D., *Assassination Science* (1998), on the basis of meticulous optical densitometry studies have established, those X-rays were "patched" to conceal the blowout, which has now been confirmed by my discovery of the visible blowout in late frame 374, which I emphasized in *The Great Zapruder Film Hoax* (2003).

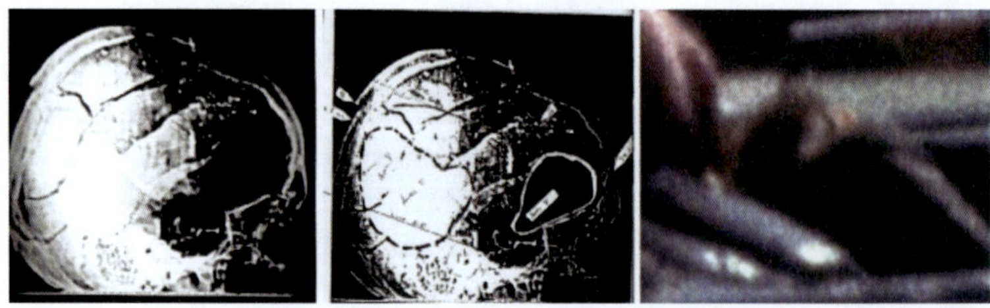

Notice how closely "Area P" (for "patch") defined by the series of broken lines corresponds to the blow out as seen in that frame. For those who prefer evidence-based history, there is no longer any room for doubt who got it right—the Parkland physicians, the Bethesda pathologists, or the HSCA!

Zapruder vs. the medical evidence

What means—repeating the points for emphasis—is that critical medical evidence in the assassination of John Fitzgerald Kennedy has undergone an astounding evolution from the appearance of the wounds to thoroughly competent and highly experienced physicians at Parkland Hospital—who were used to dealing with gunshot victims—to the Bethesda autopsy report–by physicians who had never dealt with one!–and then was unjustifiably contracted by the HSCA. Consider the absurdity:

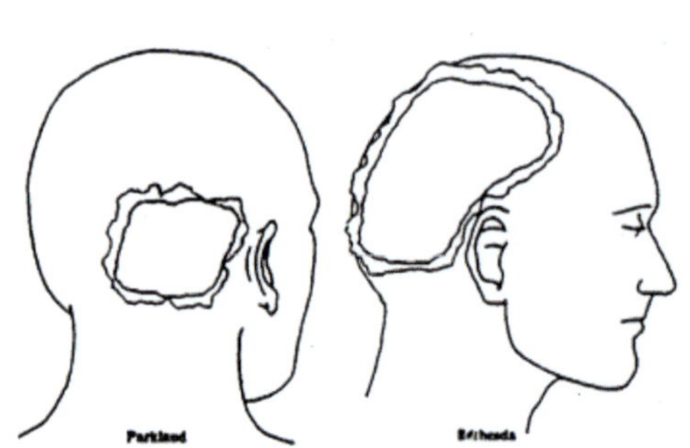

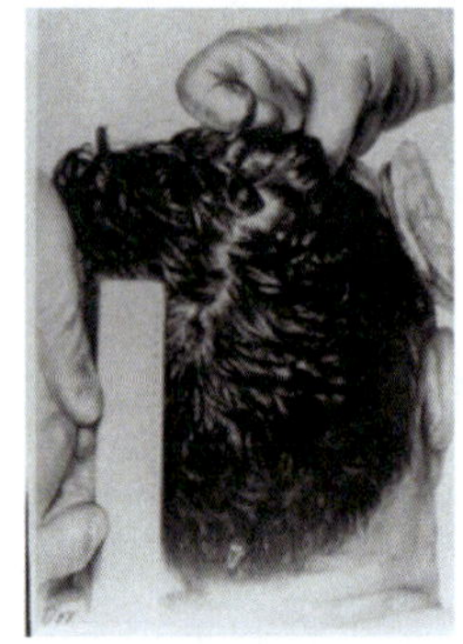

Indeed, we now know from depositions conducted by the ARRB, that Humes took a cranial saw to the skull of JFK and enlarged the wound to make it more consistent with the appearance of (what could have been) a shot fired from behind, since the Parkland observations were obviously of an exit wound from a shot fired from in front. Humes performed that grisly task in front of two witnesses, one of whom was Thomas Evan Robinson, the mortician.

This comparison of earlier frames with frame 374 demonstrates that the blowout observed at Parkland was taken out by the simple expedient of painting over the wound in black—as the Hollywood restoration experts have confirmed.

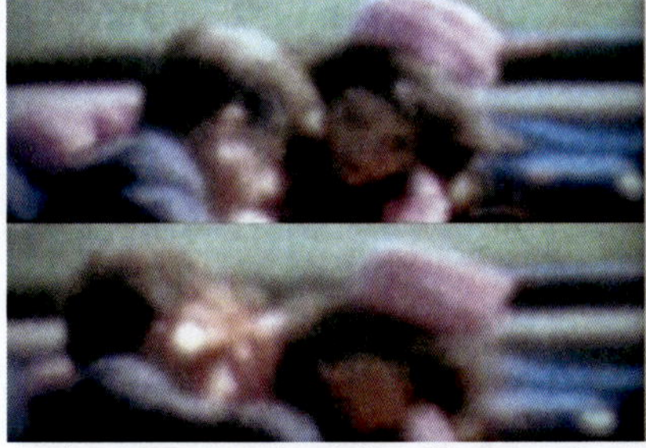

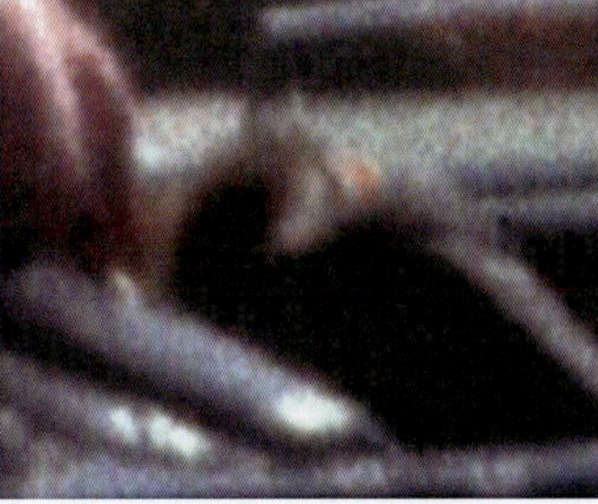

This means that the film is not even internally consistent, which makes it all the more incredible that experts on film and photos, such as Robert Groden, would persist in contending the film is authentic, when it is provably false.

Further proof of film fabrication

So much proof that the film is a fabrication has been published—where at least some of those proofs are as simple and straightforward as the one I have just presented—that I shall simply summarize some of the most important proofs that have appeared since the publication of *The Great Zapruder Film Hoax* (2003), where it is beyond belief that any serious student of the assassination of JFK, much less experts on film and photos, would continue to deny them. Consider:

(1) We have more than 60 witnesses who reported seeing the limo slow dramatically or come to a complete stop, where it slowed dramatically AS it came to a complete stop, where those witnesses include all four of the motorcycle escort officers: See: *What happened on Elm Street? The Eyewitnesses Speak*, compiled by John P. Costella, Ph.D.

(2) We also know that Officer James Chaney motored forward to inform Chief Curry the President had been shot, which was confirmed by Chief of Police Jesse Curry, Secret Service Agents Winston Lawson and Forrest Sorrels, as well as Motorcycle Officers Bobby Hargis, James Chaney, and Marrion Baker: See *New Proof of JFK Film Fakery*.*

(3) We know that, for nearly 50 years, Clint Hill has

described climbing on the trunk, pushing Jackie down, lying across their bodies, peering into the wound, observing a fist-sized blowout and giving a "thumbs down", all before the limo had reached the Triple Underpass: See *JFK: Who's Telling the Truth: Clint Hill or the Zapruder Film?* (https://youtu.be/lYpY8zI_wwA)

(4) We know that the original 8mm, already split film developed in Dallas, was taken to the NPIC on Saturday, the 23rd, and that a substitute 16mm, unsplit film, developed in Rochester, N.Y., was taken there on Sunday, the 24th, where two different teams worked on the different versions: See *U.S. Government Official: JFK Cover-Up, Film Fabrication.*

How much proof do we need?

(5) We also know that a half-dozen or more have viewed another film, apparently the original, including William Reymond, Rich DellaRosa, Gregory Burnham and several others, where Rich DellaRosa's description of its content appears as an Appendix to *The Great Zapruder Film Hoax* (2003): See *Did Zapruder Film "the Zapruder Film"?*

(6) We have John Costella's precise visual tutorial about evidence internal to the film that explains how we can know that the film is a fabrication, where all of its frames had to be reshot to create the right sequence of "ghost panels": See *The JFK Assassination Film Hoax: An Introduction.* Here's an informal discussion of his research on the film: https://youtu.be/UnnxwijxG7Q

(7) We know that they not only removed the limo stop but painted over the blowout in early frames and that the "blob" and the blood spray were painted in, but that they overlooked that in later frames, especially in frame 374, the blowout can be seen, as I explain in many places, including *What Happened To JFK And Why It Matters Today.*

(8) More recently, in *The Two NPIC Zapruder Film Events: Signposts Pointing to the Film's Alteration* (2012) and *The Two NPIC Zapruder Film Events: Analysis and Implications* (2012), Doug Horne has substantiated that the original was taken to the NPIC on Saturday, the 23rd, and the substitute was brought there on Sunday, the 24th.

The timeline argument—that there was no opportunity for

the film to have been faked, which Josiah Thompson has endlessly promoted—has no basis in fact and was merely a gambit. We know that the film was altered, which can be proven by multiple lines of argument. We also know when and where it was altered and when and where the fake film was substituted for the original. Since rationality requires that we revise our beliefs with the acquisition of new evidence and alternative hypotheses, the time has come to abandon the fantasy that the Zapruder film is authentic.

And it might be appropriate for Len Osanic to publish the proof in the segment that I provided for *50 Reasons for 50 Years*.

* Recent research by Larry Rivera, including on the Jack Daniel's film (which was only released in 1979), shows Cheney well behind the limousine, where this appears to have been a cover story that cannot be sustained.

Source note: This chapter previously appeared as *The JFK War: What's Going on with Len Osanic and Black Op Radio?, http://jamesfetzer.blogspot.com/2015/09/the-jfk-war-whats-going-on-with-len_30.html.*

Epilogue

Operation 40: Origins of CIA's Ultra-Secret Hit Teams

by Ole Dammegård

Before we end this fascinating book, I would like to show some more or less unknown, direct connections with many other major assassinations. The implications of these connections are enormous.

Just before the Bay of Pigs Invasion, a super-secret special team of skilled killers was put together under the name Operation 40. One of the leaders of the group was CIA's David Atlee Philips, a key player in the plot against JFK.

It is now clear that he was also the so-called controller/handler of none less than the patsy, Lee Harvey Oswald, as well as being the controller of one of the shooters, the man behind the fence on the Grassy Knoll—James Files!

James Files

He was also the handler of the young Michael Vernon Townley, who has been very active in many other extremely violent assignments, one of which appears to be the Palme assassination as well as the poisoning of Chilean Nobel Prize-winning poet Pablo Neruda.

The poet died aged 69 on 23 September 1973, just 12 days after General Pinochet's military coup. His death certificate says he died of prostate cancer, a view widely accepted for nearly four decades. But his former personal assistant Manuel Araya says the poet was given a lethal injection in hospital by a "Dr Price". Michael Vernon Townley is now suspected of have been this mysterious and deadly doctor and Neruda's remains are being examined for evidence.

Pablo Neruda

This assassin was active very early in life. In the late 1960s, David Atlee Philips (backed by Henry

Kissinger) sent Michael Townley to Chile with many covert tasks, one of them organizing covert groups to take part of the overthrow of president Salvador Allende. Two of the group members were Roberto Thieme and Julio Izquierdo Menéndez, both on location at the time of the Palme assassination.

Michael Vernon Townley

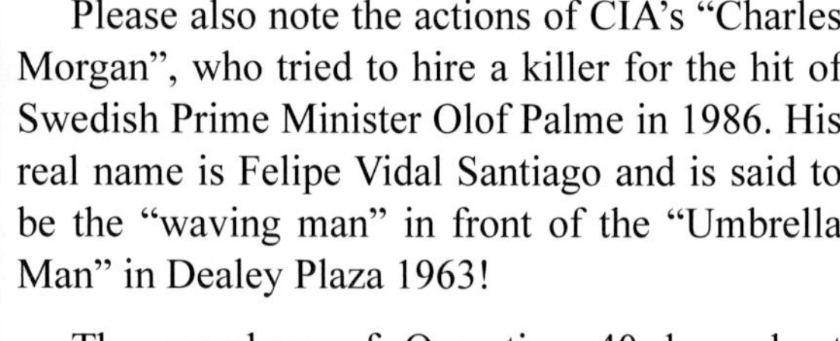

Please also note the actions of CIA's "Charles Morgan", who tried to hire a killer for the hit of Swedish Prime Minister Olof Palme in 1986. His real name is Felipe Vidal Santiago and is said to be the "waving man" in front of the "Umbrella Man" in Dealey Plaza 1963!

The members of Operation 40 have kept themselves very busy and were involved in the murders of John Lennon, Che Guevara, Salvador Allende, Orlando Letelier, General Prats, South African Robert Smit, the 1976 bombing of a Cuban airliner, the Watergate burglary, the Iran-Contra scandal, 9/11 and onward. Even attempts to kill De Gaulle and the murder of Italian Enrico Mattei have been mentioned.

Che Guevara

Not to forget several hundred people who have died in mysterious ways in connection with the JFK assassination. Who killed them? Let's take a closer look at this sinister group, which has left a long trail of blood stains through modern history. We will find that some of them are still around.

Robert Smit

Operation 40 and its Evil Spider Web

Operation 40 was a CIA-sponsored undercover operation started in the early 1960s, which was to become active in the United States, Central America, and Mexico as well as Europe and South Africa.

Roberto Thieme

Allen W. Dulles, the director of the CIA, established Operation 40 after a confidential memorandum from Colonel J. C. King, chief of CIA's Western Hemisphere Division. It obtained its name because originally there were 40 agents involved, mainly Cuban exiles.

It was approved by President Dwight D. Eisenhower and was presided over by Vice

President Richard Nixon. George Herbert Walker Bush was asked to cooperate in funding the group. The man assigned to him for his new mission was Féliz Rodríguez. This included finding private funding as a result of pressure from American corporations which had suffered at the hands of Fidel Castro.

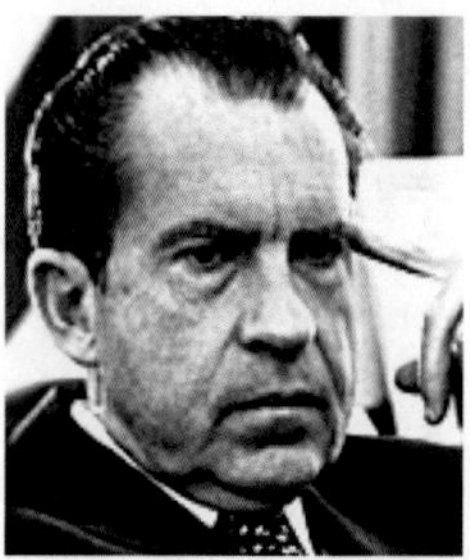

Richard Nixon

One member, Frank Sturgis, allegedly told author Mike Canfield: "This assassination group would upon orders, naturally, assassinate either members of the military or the political parties of the foreign country that you were going to infiltrate, and if necessary, some of your own members who were suspected of being foreign agents. . ."

George H. W. Bush

Some Members of Operation 40

David Atlee Philips, a.k.a. "Howard Benson": The head of Operation 40. Central in countless covert operations, including the hit on JFK. Rose to become the CIA's chief of all operations in the Western hemisphere.

Here is the only known group photograph of some of the members of Operation 40, the CIA's super-secret assassination squad, taken in the Mexico City nightclub, La Reforma, January 1963. To the left (with glasses) is Porter Goss, Barry Seal is seated behind him. Leaning over the table laughing is Felix Rodriguez. The fourth from the right is said to be Jorge Robreno, the third Alberto 'Loco' Blanco. Covering his face with his sport coat is Tosh Plumlee and to the far right is William Seymour.

David Atlee Philips

Theodore "Blond Ghost" Shackley: Station chief of CIA's Miami Station, a three-time recipient of the Distinguished Intelligence Medal, the CIA's highest honor. In nearly three decades of service, he was on "the front lines".

E. Howard Hunt: A front-line CIA supervisor of the Kennedy assassination and many, many other covert operations, including the Watergate burglary.

Ted Shackley

David "El Indio" Sanchez Morales: Deeply involved in the CIA covert operation that overthrew President Jacobo Arbenz Guzmán of Guatemala. Acquired a reputation as CIA's top assassin in Latin America. Through the 1960s and mid-1970s, Morales was involved at top levels in plots to assassinate Fidel Castro, the Bay of Pigs Invasion operation, the JFK assassination, the CIA's secret war in Laos, the capture of Che Guevara as his real killer, and the overthrow of Salvador Allende.

E. Howard Hunt

"Stories about him permeated the Agency", remembered CIA agent Tom Clines. "If the U.S. government as a matter of policy needed someone or something neutralized, Dave would do it, including things that were repugnant to a lot of people."

David Sanchez Morales

In November 2006, BBC's Newsnight presented a report by filmmaker Shane O'Sullivan, alleging that three senior CIA operatives were present at the Ambassador Hotel on the night Robert F. Kennedy was assassinated: JMWAVE Chief of Operations David Morales, Chief of Maritime Operations Gordon Campbell, and Chief of Psychological Warfare Operations, George Joannides. The program featured an interview with Morales's former attorney, Robert Walton, who quoted Morales as having said, "I was in Dallas when we got the son of a bitch and I was in Los Angeles when we got the little bastard".

Féliz "Max" Rodríguez Mendigutia: A former Cuban cop under the Batista regime, a notorious "freedom fighter" who later became a key Iran-Contra operative and a special confidant of President George

H.W. Bush. Was a helicopter pilot in Vietnam and later involved in much of the illegal drug handling around the Mena airstrip in Arkansas together with Bill Clinton and Barry Seal among others, as well as being in charge of the capture and execution of Che Guevara. Since 2004 president of the Bay of Pigs Veterans Association.

George Joannides

Frank Fiorini, a.k.a. "Frank Sturgis": CIA operative, mercenary. Heavily involved in planned attacks on Fidel Castro, the Bay of Pigs Invasion, the JFK assassination and later, a member of the team that broke into the Watergate complex in 1972.

Felix Rodriguez

Orlando Bosch, aka "Dr. Death": Founder of the counterrevolutionary Coordination of United Revolutionary Organizations that organized the 1976 murder of Chilean former minister, Orlando Letelier.

Bosch was also present in Dallas at the JFK assassination as well as guilty of hundreds of bombs and terror acts against Spain, England, Japan, Mexico, Poland, and other countries that traded with Cuba.

Felix Rodriguez

Barry Seal: Was recruited at the age of 17 along with Lee Oswald by CIA agent David Ferrie. According to his wife, Deborah, "Barry Seal flew a getaway plane out of Dallas after JFK was killed". Barry Seal was a very successful cocaine smuggler and helped facilitate the exchange of drugs for arms in support of the Contras in Nicaragua. He also helped launder that drug money in some of the Arkansas banks tied to the Bill Clinton family. Seal was later willing to testify against George H.W. Bush in the matter, and was shot dead in his car on 19 February 1986, just a few days before Swedish Prime Minister Olof Palme was taken out.

Orlando Bosch

Luis "El Bambi" Posada Carriles: Cuban-born anti-communist extremist. CIA agent involved in the Bay of Pigs Invasion and many other covert operations. Present in Dallas 22 November 1963. Convicted in absentia in Panama of various terrorist attacks and plots in the Americas, including the 1976 bombing of a Cuban airliner that

Barry Seal

killed 73 people. Admitted involvement in a string of bombings in 1997 that targeted fashionable Cuban hotels and nightspots. A key figure in the Iran-Contra scandal alongside Felix Rodriguez. In addition, he was jailed under accusations related to an assassination attempt on Fidel Castro in Panama in 2000. Has been referred to as "one of the most dangerous terrorists in recent history" and the "godfather of Cuban exile violence."

Luis Posada Carriles

Porter Goss: Later appointed to CIA Director by President Bush, only to mysteriously resign. He served for a time as the chairman of the House Intelligence Committee. Goss was a co-sponsor of the USA PATRIOT Act and a co-chair of the Joint 9/11 Intelligence Inquiry. Goss was also present at the infamous breakfast meeting at the Capitol, on the morning of September 11, 2001, with General Mahmoud Ahmad, head of the Pakistani ISI (Inter-Services Intelligence).

Portor Goss

Marita Lorenz: Operation 40's only female member. Had an affair with Fidel Castro and was part of an attempt on his life. She later had a child with the Venezuelan former dictator, Marcos Pérez Jiménez. In the 1970s she testified about the John F. Kennedy assassination, stating that she was involved with a group of anti-Cuban militants, including Lee Harvey Oswald, shortly before the assassination.

Marita Lorenz and Fidel

Tosh Plumlee: Piloted and co-piloted clandestine CIA flights for over 31 years. Picked up Johnny Roselli from Tampa, Florida, early on 22 November 1963. After picking up three more men in New Orleans, Plumlee took them to Redbird Airport in Dallas. In an interview in April 1992, Plumlee claimed that he was told that the objective was "to abort the assassination" of John F. Kennedy.

Herminio Díaz García: Worked as a bodyguard for mafia boss Santos Trafficante. Killed "Pipi" Hernandez in 1948 at the Cuban Consulate in Mexico. In 1957 he was involved with an assassination attempt against President José Figueres Ferrer of Costa

Rica. Garcia was also part in an unsuccessful attempt to assassinate Fidel Castro. Garcia moved to the United States in July 1963, where he worked for Tony Varona, another infamous member of Operation 40. Believed to be one of the shooters/spotters on the sixth floor in the TSBD in Dallas.

Tosh Plumlee

"Handsome Johnny" Roselli: Middleman between the Mob and the CIA, worked with Mob figures like Al Capone, Meyer Lansky, and was later a close associate of Santos Trafficante. Is said to have been in the Dal-Tex Building when JFK was shot, next to shooter Chuckie Nicoletti and possibly George H.W. Bush! Ended up cut into pieces and stuffed in an oil barrel. In an interview in April 1992, Tosh Plumlee claimed that Roselli had been killed because he knew too much.

Herminio Díaz García

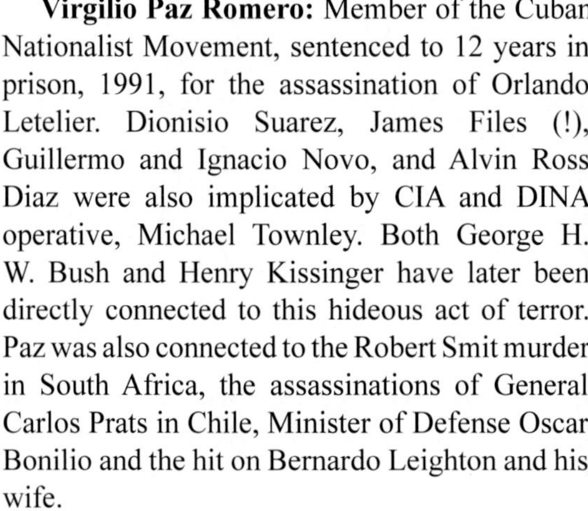

Virgilio Paz Romero: Member of the Cuban Nationalist Movement, sentenced to 12 years in prison, 1991, for the assassination of Orlando Letelier. Dionisio Suarez, James Files (!), Guillermo and Ignacio Novo, and Alvin Ross Diaz were also implicated by CIA and DINA operative, Michael Townley. Both George H. W. Bush and Henry Kissinger have later been directly connected to this hideous act of terror. Paz was also connected to the Robert Smit murder in South Africa, the assassinations of General Carlos Prats in Chile, Minister of Defense Oscar Bonilio and the hit on Bernardo Leighton and his wife.

Johnny Roselli

Virgilio Paz Romero

Jose Perdomo: Chief of Police during Cuban President Carlos Prio's regime. Member of Brigade 2506 during the Bay of Pigs Invasion. Worked closely with Frank Sturgis for many years on CIA's payroll. Is cited by multiple sources as the doorman on duty at John Lennon's Dakota residence on the night in 1980 when the rock star was murdered. Doorman Jose Perdomo was standing to the left of Lennon and patsy Mark Chapman to the right. All shots that hit Lennon were fired from the left. The hit is claimed to have

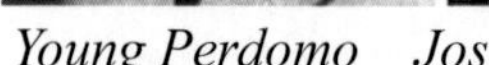
Young Perdomo *Jose Perdomo (1980)*

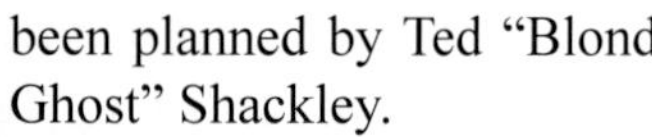
been planned by Ted "Blond Ghost" Shackley.

Eladio "Lado" Ceferino del Valle: Allegedly involved in the JFK assassination as a shooter on the sixth floor of the TSBD, together with Herminio Díaz García and Richard Cain from the Chicago mafia. He was violently murdered on the same day as David Ferrie.

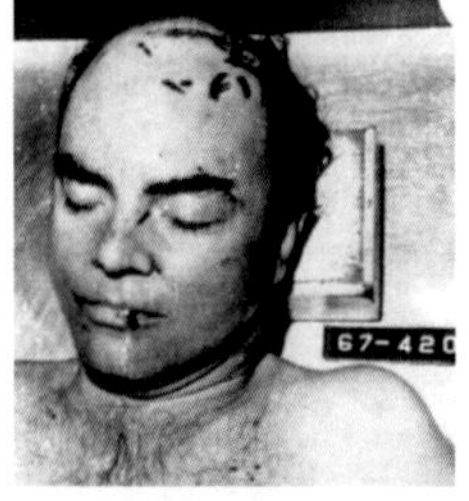
Eladio del Valle

Guillermo "Mister Bill" Novo Sampol: Has taken part in countless violent acts of terror, together with his brother Ignacio. Sentenced to life imprisonment for his involvement in the murder of Orlando Letelier. However, his conviction was later overturned.

Ignacio Novo Sampol

Ignacio Novo Sampol: In 1964, he fired a bazooka at the United Nations building as Ernesto "Che" Guevara prepared to address the General Assembly.

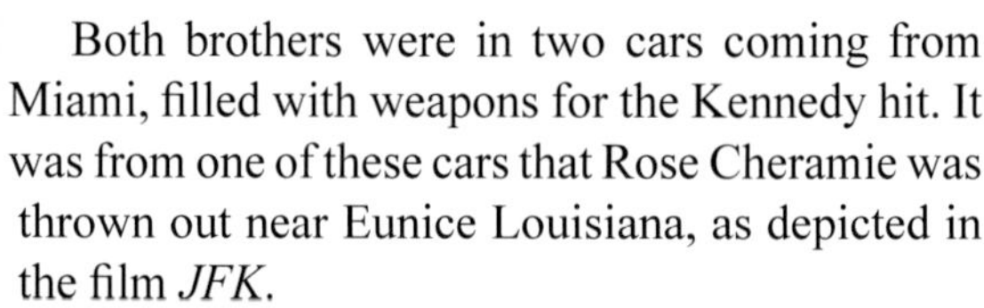
Both brothers were in two cars coming from Miami, filled with weapons for the Kennedy hit. It was from one of these cars that Rose Cheramie was thrown out near Eunice Louisiana, as depicted in the film *JFK*.

Guillermo Novo Sampol

William Seymour: Experienced soldier, took part in training exiled Cubans for attacks on Cuba. Member of Interpen.

Accused by some researchers of having been part of the JFK assassination and is regarded as one of the men who on several occasions impersonated Lee Harvey Oswald.

Bernard L. Barker: Heavily involved in the Bay of Pigs Invasion. Dallas Police Deputy Constable Seymour Weitzman identified Bernard Barker as the fake Secret Service agent behind the fence just seconds after JFK was shot. Later worked for the FBI. Was one of the Watergate burglars.

Antonio Veciana: Cuban exile, founder of CIA-backed Alpha 66. Had close connections with David Atlee Philips. Named in E. Howard Hunt's deathbed confession as one of the key participants in the planning of the JFK assassination.

William Seymour

Tom Clines: Joined Ted Shackley, David Atlee Phillips, and David Sanchez Morales at JM WAVE. During the Vietnam War, Clines worked as Ted Shackley's deputy in charge of the CIA's secret war in Laos.

In 1972, Clines was in charge of CIA operations in Chile, and helped overthrow President Salvador Allende. Later, a key person in the Iran-Contra scandal. In 1977 he stood accused of shipping 42,000 pounds of the plastic explosive C-4 directly to Libyan dictator, Moammar Gaddafi.

Bernard Baker

Eugenio "Muscolito" Martinez: One of the convicted Watergate burglars.

Jorge Mas Canosa: Dedicated to overthrow Castro, first in armed plots and then in the halls of Congress. Became a familiar presence on Capitol Hill and for years Presidents Reagan, Bush, and Clinton sought his advice on Cuban affairs to such an extent that many critics considered him the principal architect of a very rigid American policy.

Antonio Veciana

Edwin P. Wilson: CIA officer who was later convicted of illegally selling weapons to Libya.

Virgilio "Villo" Gonzalez: One of the Watergate burglars.

Rafael "Chi Chi" Quintero: In an article published in *Granma* in 2006, Rafael Quintero stated: "If I was to tell what I know about Dallas and the Bay of Pigs, it would be the greatest scandal that has ever rocked the nation."

Eugenio Martinez

José Dionisio "Bloodbath" Suárez Esquivel: Convicted for the murder of Chilean Marxist leader Orlando Letelier. Michael Townley placed the bomb underneath the car. Suarez Esquivel and his accomplice, Virgilio Paz, detonated it.

Jorge Mas Canosa

Edward P. Wilson

Dionisio Suarez Esquivel

Jose Miguel Battle

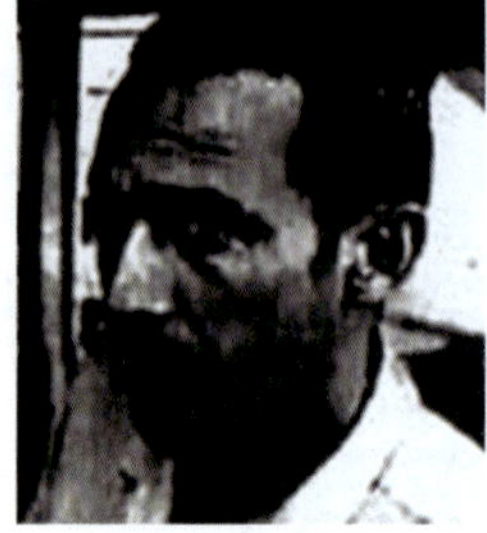

Felipe Vidal Santiago

Roy Hargraves

Pedro Diez Lanz

Virgilio Gonzalez

Nestor Izquierdo

Manuel Artime and President John F. Kennedy

Manuel Artime Buesa: A political leader of Brigade 2506 land forces in the Bay of Pigs Invasion in April 1961. Later organized the Miami Defense Relief Fund for the Watergate burglars.

Close associates

Felipe Vidal Santiago: aka "Charles Morgan": Directly involved in the JFK assassination as the man standing shaking his fist in front of Umbrella Man, mercenary Roy Hargraves, who marked the exact point for the crossfire. Years later he appeared in Stockholm, searching for the killers of Olof Palme.

Nestor "Tony" Izquierdo: Member of Brigade 2506. Worked with David Morales in many advanced raids. Mercenary Gerry Hemming claimed that "Tony" was the spotter in the Dal-Tex Building in Dallas in 1963.

"Still going strong . . . ?" Alvin Ross, Guillermo Novo Sampol and Virgilio Paz Romero. Photo taken in 2012.

SOME OF THE MEN WHO KILLED JOHN F. KENNEDY

After many, many years of research, I hereby present some of the participants in the John F. Kennedy assassination.

This case is like an extreme, multi-layered labyrinth inside an enigma, so some researchers may not agree, but in my humble opinion, here are some of the most important people involved (there were many more, especially from the military-industrial complex, on the Mob side, and from the so called 'Elite').

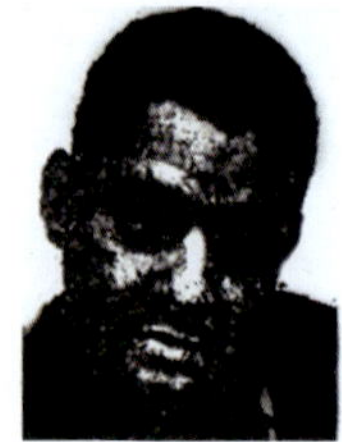

Richard Cain (1) Shooter, the sixth floor Herminio Diez Garcia (2) Spotter, sixth floor (3) Eladio del Valle Shooter, the TSBD Chuckie Nicoletti (4) Shooter, the Dal-Tex Building Nestor Izquierdo

(5) Spotter, the Dal-Tex Building (6) Frank Sturgis Shooter (?), the Grassy Knoll (7) Lucien Sarti Shooter, the "Badgeman" (8) Roscoe White Shooter (?),

In the manhole (9) James Files, Shooter, behind the fence (10) Bernard Baker Fake Secret Service Man (11) Roy Hargraves Umbrella Man (12) F. Vidal Santiago "The Fist Shaking Man"

Dealey Plaza, Dallas, Texas. Numbered position of shooters, etc. The Xs marks possible additional shooters.

Lyndon B. Johnson; Cord Meyer CIA agent; David Atlee Philips, CIA; William Harvey CIA coordinator

Allen Dulles CIA Director; George H.W. Bush Later CIA Director; E. Howard Hunt CIA Coordinator; David Morales CIA, Operation 40

Edward Lansdale General; J. Edgar Hoover FBI Director; Richard Nixon Future President; Charles Cabell General

H.L. Hunt Oil tycoon; Guy Banister FBI, ONI; Jack Ruby Mafia, CIA; Clint Murchinson Texas millionaire

Santos Trafficante Organized crime; Carlos Marcello Organized crime; Sam Giancana Organized crime; Meyer Lansky Organized crime

Clay Shaw CIA, etc.; Jimmy Hoffa Organized crime; Richard Helms CIA; Tony Varona CIA, Mob, etc.

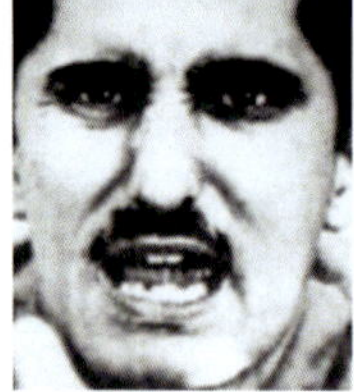

Antonio Veciana Coordinator; Chauncey Holt "The old tramp"; Charles Harrelson "The tall tramp"; Charles Rogers "The first tramp" ONI

David Ferrie CIA, pilot etc.; Robert Mahau Coordinator; William Greer Limo driver; Jim Hicks Radio operator

Guillermo Novo Present in Dallas; Ignacio Novo Present in Dallas; Gerry Hemming Present in Dallas; Orlando Bosch Present in Dallas

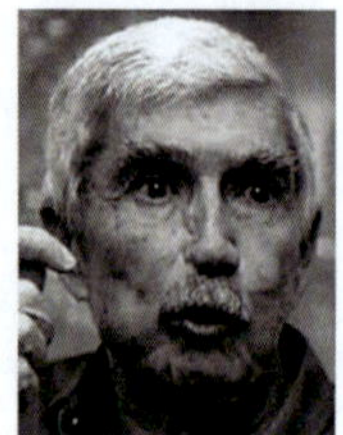

Marc Wallace Present in Dallas; Luis P. Carilles Present in Dallas; Pedro Diez Lanz Present in Dallas; Earle Cabell Dallas Mayor

Source note: This part first appeared in Ole Dammegard's epic book *Coup d'etat in Slow Motion, Part I and II,* connecting the dots between the assassination of the Swedish Prime Minister Olof Palme and many, many more murders of top political individuals and other people standing up against the New World Order.

Additional Findings and Conclusions

I would like to continue with some observations and conclusions I have made over the years, things I have not encountered elsewhere, so hopefully they might be useful pieces of this giant jigsaw.

In November 2016, I had the immense pleasure and honor to be invited as one of the speakers to the JFK Assassination Conference in Dallas. Here I met incredible people like Judyth Vary Baker, Beverly "The Babushka Lady" Oliver, St. John Hunt (son of E. Howard Hunt), and many others.

Amazing encounters with world history: Judyth Vary Baker and Beverly Oliver

French hit man Lucien Sarti was dressed in a black Dallas Police uniform

It also gave me the opportunity to visit Dealey Plaza to check out different angles and locations.

The author located in the exact position as the infamous Badge Man / Black Dog

Please compare some of the photos where I placed myself in the exact positions of the shooters. A very eerie feeling . . . As far as I can see, the photos and the proportions of the so-called Badgeman fits perfectly.

Who the railroad worker next to him was is still a mystery. Regarding the sniper behind the picket fence, I truly believe this to be James Files, whom I have recently been in direct contact with. To not listen to his story is, in my humble opinion, a major mistake.

Files and Badgeman—two of the shooters.

Enlargement and coloring of the photo

Positioned exactly as James Files, the shooter behind the picket fence

An additional shooter was placed not far from Badgeman, behind the same wall

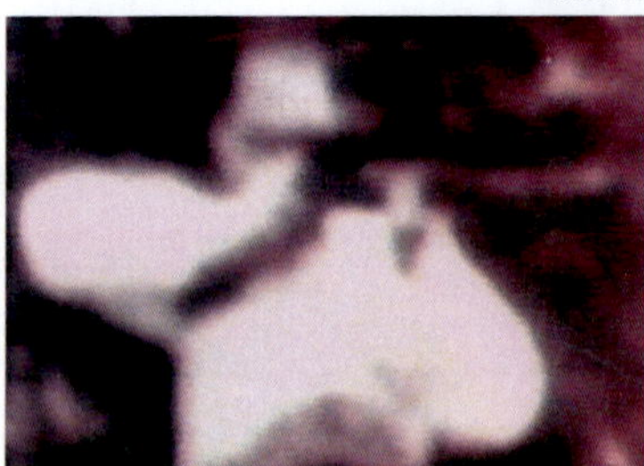

According to a reliable witness, this shooter is Canadian assassin Clyde Forshaw

Two more shooters, unknown to many most, were close by. One was standing not far from Badgeman and Railroad Worker, leaning up against a white car: Clyde Forshaw. And on the other side of the lawn was his cousin, Walter Tabinski who has been identified as the same mysterious individual who acted as Lee Oswald at the embassy in Mexico City.

The man equipped with a big bulletproof vest fires at the car, then calmly walks away

He has been identified as the same man who acted as Oswald in Mexico City

Lee's rooming house at 1026 North Beckley Avenue and the additional house behind it

I also went to the rooming house where Lee was staying, at 1026 North Beckley Avenue a few miles from Dealey Plaza. The current owner and grandchild of Earlene Roberts told me that there are actually no less than 18 (!) rooms in this plain house, including the additional house

Lee's room is very small and narrow

The cupboard where he 'had his gun'

In the living room of the boarding house

The elevator at the TSBD

behind it. She denied it having been used as a CIA safehouse in the 1960s, contrary to what both Operation 40 member and pilot Tosh Plumlee and author Jim Marrs claim. But then again, she was only 11 years old in 1963, so I believe it must have been quite easy to keep such a secret from her.

By the way, I believe the reason why Lee was found in the lunchroom, was that his task was to make sure no one would use the elevator, since the shooter team was rappelling down inside it after the attack (the reason for why the power was cut as well). They then left from the back of the building, being observed by several witnesses.

In Dallas, just like in many other places, like Memphis, Tennessee, Freemasonic symbols like obelisks, the eternal flame and pyramids are discreetly erected after the brutal killings of 'enemies'. Hidden in plain sight, only to be understood by the secret members of the dark forces... . . .

Hidden in plain sight—powerful Masonic pyramids and sculptures in Dallas

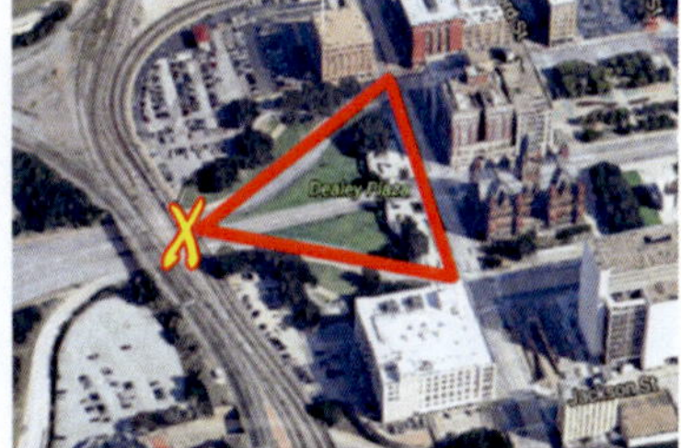

The glass pyramid can only be seen at the exact top of the pyramid-layout

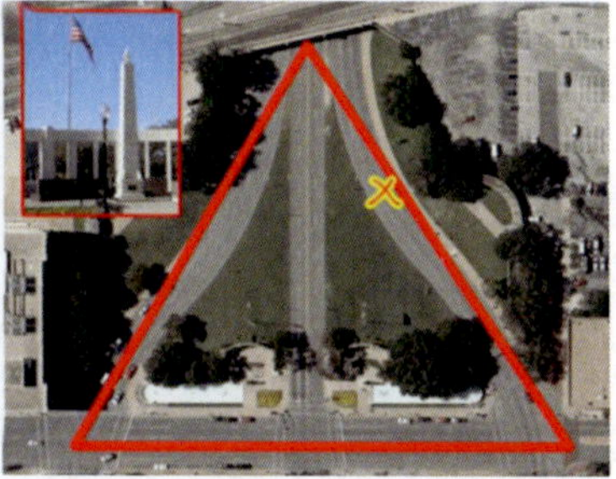

Change the angle and it will point you straight to an 'obelisk with the eternal flame'

The Cyprus Lodge, a massive pyramid erected near the Martin L. King, 'death place'

Mary's Mosaic: A Litmus Test for JFK Research Integrity

by Peter Janney

"There are very few human beings who receive the truth, complete and staggering, by instant illumination. Most of them acquire it fragment by fragment, on a small scale, by successive developments, cellularly, like a laborious mosaic."—Anaïs Nin

Some issues within JFK research represent litmus tests that separate the competent from the frivolous, the courageous from the cowardly, and the honest from the dishonest, where some estimates have gone so far as to suggest that as much as 95% of members of the JFK research community are promoting an agenda to sow confusion and uncertainty, even in those cases where the evidence for a conclusion has made the question beyond reasonable doubt, precisely because, once the evidence has been properly understood, no alternative explanation is reasonable.

That, I (Jim Fetzer) submit, is the case in relation to the fabrication of the Zapruder film and the other home movies, as I have documented over and over again.

Courtesy Peter Janney

The 60 witnesses to the limo stop, a series of actions taken by Clint Hill, Officer James Chaney's motoring forward (none of which are present in the extant film) and the blacking out of the fist-sized wound at the back of JFK's head in frames after 313 (but where the wound itself can actually be seen in later frames such as 374–serves as a litmus test that differentiates between researchers who are competent, courageous and honest from those who are not.

Another now appears to be the murder of Mary Pinchot Meyer, where the evidence of CIA complicity in her death, as in the assassination of JFK, persuasively presented by Peter Janney in *Mary's Mosaic: The CIA Conspiracy to Murder John F. Kennedy, Mary Pinchot Meyer, and Their Vision for World Peace* (2012), is simply overwhelming.

I submit that anyone who reads this book is going to be astonished at the depth, the passion and the intelligence with which it has been written—and the rigor and detail with which it explains her assassination by the CIA.

Mary was the former wife of Cord Meyer, who began his career dedicated to the promotion of world peace but ended it working for the military-industrial-intelligence complex as the Director of Plans for the CIA.

In his *"Last Confessions"* in *Rolling Stone* magazine, E. Howard Hunt confided in his son, St. John, that those who had been responsible for the death of JFK had included Lyndon B. Johnson, Cord Meyer, David Atlee Phillips, William Harvey, David Sanchez Morales and Frank Sturgis, among others. Cord Meyer and JFK had both enjoyed enormous success early in their careers, where JFK would enter the political arena as a candidate for office, first as Senator from Massachusetts, later as President of the United States, while Cord would be induced by Allan Dulles to join the CIA.

Mary Pinchot was a remarkable woman who fascinated them both, where she would marry Cord Meyer but later divorce him and subsequently become involved with JFK in what was far more than an affair, where she appears to have become enormously important to him as he became a statesman for peace.

In the aftermath of his assassination, she became determined to expose those who had been responsible for his death, which led to her death, in turn, which, as Peter Janney explains, involved high-level officials of the CIA, including his own father, Wistar Janney, and James Jesus Angleton (who apparently authorized her murder), but where even Ben Bradlee, who was married to Mary's sister, helped to cover it up.

Mary was found on a towpath adjacent to a pond on 12 October 1964, which she used to walk from her Georgetown home to her artist's studio, where she had been apprehended and, after a brief struggle, during which she cried out for help, was shot in the left temple. Remarkably, the bullet did not kill her outright. She crawled to a nearby tree and tried to regain her footing, but was dragged back to the path and shot again, this time through her back and into her heart, killing her instantly.

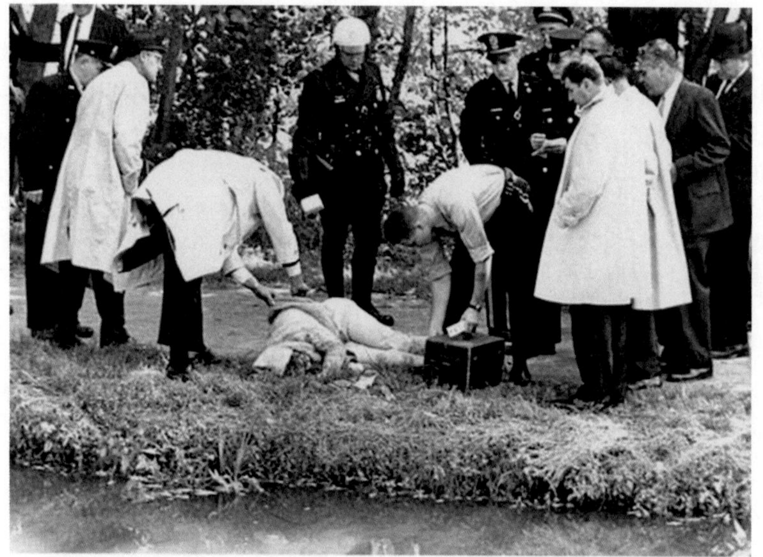

The crime scene on the C & O towpath within 30 minutes after the murder of Mary Pinchot Meyer on October 12, 1964.

Her cry for help had brought Henry Wiggins, Jr., who had come to fix a falsely stalled Nash Rambler on the roadway above the crime scene, to look over the wall and observe a man standing over her, whom he described (and as was broadcast by the police) as a Negro male wearing a dark baseball cap, light-colored jacket and dark shoes, who appeared to be 5'8" or 5'10" tall and weighing about 185 pounds (*Mary's Mosaic*, p. 42).

When he was taken into custody in the vicinity by the Washington, D.C. police, however, Raymond Crump, Jr. was only partially attired as the person Wiggins had described. He was weighed in at 5'5.5" tall and weighed 145 pounds, which may have been exaggerations, because his driver's license showed him to be only 5'3.5" tall and weighing only 130 pounds (*Mary's Mosaic*, p. 51).

Subsequently, a man who identified himself as "Lt. William L. Mitchell", who claimed to have been jogging on the towpath and to have passed by a person fitting the description that Wiggins had provided (but whose name and identity would turn out to be fabrications), likewise described him as a Negro male, wearing a baseball cap, a light-colored jacked and dark shoes (*Mary's Mosaic*, pp. 61-62).

When Ray Crump was apprehended, soaking wet, with his fly still open from the sexual escapade he had been engaged in with "Vivian", a married woman, who confirmed their tryst on the rocks not long before the murder—in a sworn affidavit—but was unwilling to testify because she feared her husband would kill her if he found out (*Mary's Mosaic*, pp. 95–96), he was wearing neither the baseball cap nor the light-colored jacket, which had been temporarily lost when he had fallen into the water upon awakening on the rocks.

You don't have to be a rocket scientist to realize that both Wiggins and "Mitchell" are describing someone other than Ray Crump, who was not only substantially shorter and far lighter in weight than the man Wiggins, in particular, had described, but could not have been wearing the dark baseball cap or the light-colored jacket at the time.

As "Vivian" had confirmed, they had been having a sexual dalliance on the rocks. He had fallen asleep and she departed, where he lost both cap and jacket in the water when he awakened disoriented and fell into the pond.

The police and the DA's Office realized that they had a weak case, where there was no forensic evidence that tied Ray Crump to the crime: there was no weapon; he did not own a gun; his height and weight did not match; even the jacket, when recovered from the water, had no signs of blood, even though they believed the killer would have been coated with it.

While there was a trace of lipstick on his jacket (which was no doubt Vivian's or even Ray's wife's), they did not pursue it—and even acknowledged in a memorandum that their case against Ray Crump "was very weak" (*Mary's Mosaic*, p. 398).

Nevertheless, they assigned their strongest, most aggressive prosecutor, Al Huntman, Assistant Chief of the Criminal Division, U.S. Attorney's Office, Washington, D.C., to the case.

While Ray Crump was defended by a brilliant attorney, Dovey Roundtree, who emphasized the kinds of discrepancies that I have noted here, it is difficult to believe that anyone today, unless they have either an inadequate understanding of the evidence or a powerful bias against truth and justice, would continue to maintain Ray Crump had actually committed the crime. (see, for example Lisa Pease's deplorable review on *amazon.com*)

Even then, in the highly impoverished state of the evidence—Dovey was able to create sufficient reasonable doubt—that Ray Crump was unanimously acquitted at trial.

And, as readers will discover for themselves, the additional evidence that Peter Janney was able to uncover makes the case for Ray Crump's innocence simply overwhelming and beyond reasonable doubt. I am aghast at the dimensions of the distortions in this review.

Lisa Pease, the closest collaborator of Jim DiEugenio, begins her review as follows: "Peter Janney wrote a book entitled *Mary's Mosaic: The CIA Conspiracy to Murder John F. Kennedy, Mary Pinchot Meyer, and their Vision for World Peace*.

"From the subtitle, researchers can be forgiven for thinking that Janney's book is a serious contribution to our side, as many of us believe that the CIA killed John Kennedy in part because he was trying to end the Cold War and rein in covert operations.

"But Janney's book is such a frustrating mix of fact, fiction, speculation and unverifiable data that I [Lisa Pease] cannot recommend this book. Indeed, I'd rather it came with a warning label attached" (amazon.com). Having investigated more than one strange death myself, I (Jim Fetzer) must say that I find these introductory passages both grotesque and irresponsible.

Given the consideration that, by the end of *Mary's Mosaic*, the actual assassin had apparently confessed and explained in detail how it had been done and that Peter Janney has convincingly established the complicity of the CIA—which had to silence Mary Meyer, because she was uncovering its role in the assassination of JFK and was in a position to do something about it—I find her complaints to be virtually incomprehensible.

While Lisa Pease does her very best to create the impression that Ray Crump (who had no motive) could actually have committed the crime, the kinds of things she says about Peter Janney's brilliant book (where Peter had known Mary in his childhood and whose research would lead led him to the agonizing realization that his own father had been complicit), which is a completely unwarranted characterization of *Mary's Mosaic*, appear to me to be completely justified in relation to her own review, where I (Jim Fetzer) would fashion a parallel complaint about her review as follows:

> *"Researchers can be forgiven for thinking that Lisa Pease's CTKA review is a serious contribution to JFK research.* Mary's Mosaic *provides ample substantiation that the CIA killed John Kennedy in part because he was trying to end the Cold War and rein in covert operations. But her review of Peter Janney's book is such a frustrating mix of fact, fiction, speculation and*

> *unverifiable data I cannot recommend it. I'd rather that it came with a warning label attached".*
>
> *Indeed, it is inconceivable to me that anyone who has actually read the book completely to its end, where crucial aspects of what Peter Janney reports there about uncovering the actual plot to murder Mary Pinchot Meyer are presented, could continue to regard Ray Crump as anyone other than the "patsy".*
>
> *Since those include the detailed confession of the actual assassin, who was the very "Lt. William L. Mitchell", who explains how it had been done, including the use of spotters and luring the auto repair man to the scene to witness Mary's screams, I am baffled how anyone could entertain reasonable doubts about it.*

There is no reasonable alternative explanation for what happened to Mary and, instead of attempting to debunk his landmark research, she and her associate ought to be touting it as a major contribution to JFK research, which I would liken to *an insider's view* that confirms the findings of Noel Twyman, *Bloody Treason* (1997).

What also stuns me is that I find a pattern emerging from the work of Lisa Pease and Jim DiEugenio. I have had several encounters with Jim over the years, one of which occurred sometime back on an extended thread devoted to Judyth Vary Baker, who has authored *Me & Lee: How I Came to Know, Love and Lose Lee Harvey Oswald* (2010).

Jim DiEugenio sought to debunk a fascinating report of a woman who remained sitting in a car during the visit of Lee Oswald to State Representative Reeves Morgan—whom Judyth claims to have been herself—whose presence was witnessed by his daughter, Mary, where Mary's report surfaced during the trial of Clay Shaw.

Jim DiEugenio attempted to debunk Mary's corroborating testimony on the ground that she had later repudiated it, which, as I observed to him at the time, was a violation of the principle that earlier testimony is preferable to later, especially when witnesses have been subjected to pressure to change it.

And, in another case, I faulted the biased research of Jefferson Morley and David Talbot related to the presence of CIA officials at the Ambassador Hotel at the time of Bobby's shooting—he would die the following day—where I had to reprimand him for his irresponsible acceptance of their shameless efforts to whitewash the identifications, which was supported by overwhelmingly more evidence than they produced against it.

Why Lisa Pease would attempt to cast doubt on Peter Janney's thoroughly researched and meticulously documented study, which carefully ties together the murder of Mary Pinchot Meyer, the CIA and the assassination of JFK, is difficult to fathom.

But there is a troubling pattern here, which suggests to me that, whatever their motives may be, Lisa Pease and Jim DiEugenio, who has been praising Lisa's review, appear to be undermining research (and not in this case only) concerning major advances in our understanding of the *modus operandi* of the CIA in events of this kind.

The Autodafé of Lisa Pease and James DiEugenio

Tomas de Torquemada and the Spanish Inquisition return in a new era of suppression of freedom of thought and adherence to a rigid dogma—namely their own prejudices!

by Peter Janney

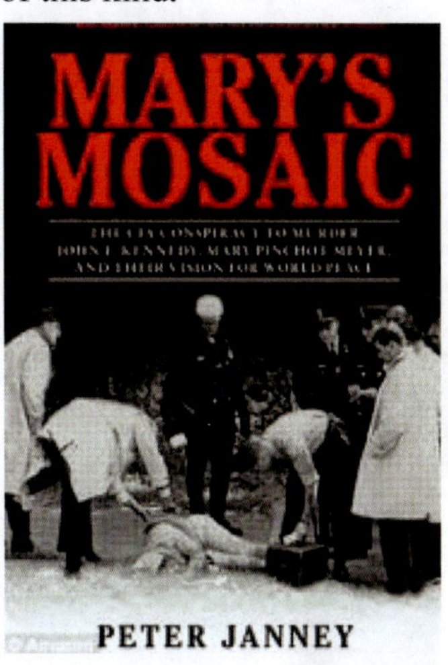

Lisa Pease's six-page diatribe against me and my recent book, *Mary's Mosaic: The CIA Conspiracy to Murder John F. Kennedy, Mary Pinchot Meyer, and Their Vision of World Peace* (2012) is, at the very least, a marvel of subjective distortion and shoddy criticism, fueled by her own personal vendetta that someone dared not follow her as she, and her partner James DiEugenio, have attempted over the years to appoint themselves as the ultimate "guardians of truth" in all things Kennedy (see the review).

And as usual, Lisa Pease's only fallback source in her vain attempts to substantiate anything she writes is James DiEugenio, whom she seems to always regard as unassailable.

Together, nothing that these two write can ever be challenged or debated—without one of them launching some kind of personal diatribe against anyone who challenges it, establishing a different opinion.

Indeed, during his last appearance on Len Osanic's "Black Op Radio" program (28 June 2012), DiEugenio gushes over "Lisa Pease's wonderful—and I really think it's a really wonderful piece of work . . . because it's done in her usual very intelligent, very elegant, very incisive kind of a style. And I'm going to be doing Part II to which I am actually working on right now . . ." We wait with bated breath.

What's particularly revealing in Pease's latest piece of writing is that she first announces to her readers that she "check[s] every fact, . . . dare[ing] the author to prove his case to me," and then goes on to continue (along with her partner DiEugenio) to make the absurd claim that JFK was not a womanizer, or sexually promiscuous, but always "adorable and sweet," (quoting Angela Greene).

We are now, after years of revelation by such authors as Ralph Martin, Seymour Hersh, Nigel Hamilton, and Presidential historians Michael Beschloss and Robert Dallek—to say nothing of the women who have come forward (the most recent is Mimi Beardsley Alford in 2012)—supposed to go on believing "The Doctrine of Pease and DiEugenio" that this was all just a "Republican Party" or "CIA" plot to discredit President Kennedy.

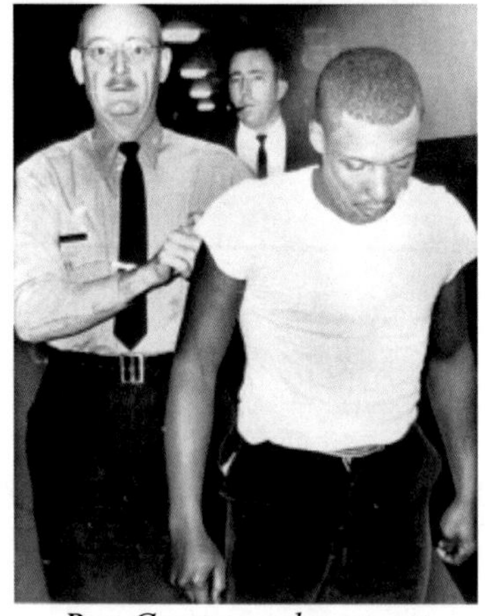

Ray Crump under arrest

Following "the two McCarthyites of the JFK assassination research community," as one researcher recently put it, is like walking into a never-ending fantasy world of ignorance, hopefully having been convinced that the real truth has just been dispensed, when all that has taken place in this case is Pease's fabricating evidence in order to gin up "facts" to support her delusions.

I am not going to try your patience as a reader by writing six pages of rebuttal, though I easily could take issue with every aspect of Pease's tangled web of claims where she can't even correctly restate what I wrote.

Indeed, it becomes clear that Pease's greatest talent is attempting to bestow upon her readers her own vitriolic projections that have no basis or understanding of fact. In doing so, she identifies herself as an intolerant critic who must torture (and therefore misconstrue) the facts in an effort to win an argument, so typical of a fanatical mindset that can't consider any real alternative other than its own projections.

And so, despite the fact that there was absolutely no forensic evidence whatsoever (as documented in the FBI Crime Report, which was withheld from the defense until the beginning of the trial nine months after the murder) linking Ray Crump, Jr. to the bloody crime scene or to the body of Mary Pinchot Meyer, Lisa Pease wants her readers to believe, as she does, that Ray Crump was actually guilty, because some of the clothes he was wearing that day matched what eyewitness Henry Wiggins, Jr. saw when he viewed the man standing over Meyer's body within 30 seconds after the two gunshots had ended her life.

Wiggins was 126.5' away from the murder scene. This was all documented in 1,200 pages of trial transcript, something that Pease fails to mention to her readers, because she never read or studied it.

Still, Pease omnisciently claims that in viewing just one picture of Ray Crump in my book, she (and she alone) has decided to proclaim that Crump does, in fact, have a "medium build," and that Wiggins' description is completely accurate.

Wiggins obviously saw somebody who wore similar clothes to Crump that day, but I maintain it wasn't Ray Crump. Then, ignoring everyone else's disposition toward Crump, including his attorney Dovey Roundtree, public defenders George Peter Lamb and Ted O'Neill, and anyone else who actually had contact with Crump at the time of the murder, Pease becomes convinced he was only acquitted because he had "a very astute lawyer."

Never mind the lack of any real evidence, or the fact she was shot execution-style with a gun that was never recovered, or that no one in Ray Crump's family or community had ever seen Crump with any firearm.

A younger Mary

To further make her case, Pease invokes the authority of author Nina Burleigh, who like Pease is sure of Ray Crump's guilt, but who can't even correctly document the jury's composition, in addition to a number of other important neglected facts.

Then, hanging her hat on the fact that because Crump lied (he was concealing a tryst with a married woman) about why he was in the vicinity of the towpath that morning, this is further proof to Pease of Crump's guilt.

Our Dick Cheneyesque "cherry-picker" of facts then takes her distorted proclamations even further. Creating her own testimony, Pease suppresses that Crump had an organic brain impairment before the murder took place and that he was actively alcoholic, which in the perception of his attorney Dovey Roundtree made him "incapable of clear communication, incapable of complex thought, incapable of grasping the full weight of his predicament, incapable most of all, of a murder executed with the stealth and precision and forethought of Mary Meyer's [murder]." (*Mary's Mosaic*, p. 318).

Further accusing me of concealing the fact that Crump had a criminal record before the Meyer murder (which consisted of the unspeakable, heinous crime of having been twice arrested for disorderly conduct, along with having served a 60-day jail sentence for shoplifting—all of which I mention on page 53), Ms. Pease wants her followers to believe that because of Crump's subsequent career in crime, this is the ultimate *sine qua non* proof of Ray Crump's having murdered Mary Meyer.

The only thing that becomes clear here is that any psychological understanding and sophistication of the human condition completely eludes Lisa Pease; she's unable to comprehend how an already psychologically impaired individual subjected to continued abuse over a nine-month period in jail (which according to his attorney Dovey Roundtree likely included sexual assaults) could damage someone to the point of becoming a hardened criminal.

Mary Pinchot Meyer and Cord Meyer

And so in Pease's fantasy world, nothing matters (or is able to be grasped) except her distorted perception of her own opinions that have no real basis in factual evidence.

But not yet content, Pease wants her supporters to believe that all of this "illustrates Janney's shortcomings as a researcher."

She goes on to attempt to prove that I next have "distorted the math" and time intervals in showing that there was a second "Negro male" eluding capture by police immediately following Meyer's murder. Either Pease didn't read carefully what I wrote, or she is intellectually challenged by the English language. In either case, she proves only one thing: she hasn't read the trial transcript.

Indeed, her own shortcomings as a researcher won't even allow her to be factually accurate when quoting what I wrote. "Detective Warner arrested Crump at 1:15 p.m.," writes Pease, which is not only incorrect (and not what I wrote), but reveals how little Pease actually understood what she read.

Very simply (*Mary's Mosaic*, pp. 122-128), I demonstrate through an extensive study of the trial transcript, and in an interview with police officer Roderick Sylvis for this book, how he and his partner Frank Bignotti arrived at Fletcher's Boat House at approximately 12:30 p.m. in order to block the exits of anyone trying to leave the towpath area.

That's what they were supposed to do: wait in their patrol car and guard the exits, a concept that Lisa Pease again is unable to grasp.

They waited for about "four or five minutes" and then began hatching a plan whereby Sylvis would begin walking eastward toward the murder scene via the towpath and Bignotti would do the same along the adjacent railroad bed and woods that separated the two.

This planning and positioning of themselves, according to Sylvis, took another five minutes or so. We are now at approximately 12:40 p.m. As soon as they started out, the two officers spotted a young white couple walking westward on the railroad tracks, who they then approached and began talking to.

In an interview with Sylvis in 2008, I asked him specifically how long this interrogation had taken. "At least five minutes, probably more," said Sylvis. It is now conservatively past 12:45 p.m., and very possibly later, approaching 1:00 p.m., before the two officers start their journey eastward toward the murder scene.

Sylvis told the court that he walked "approximately a mile east on the towpath, at which point he saw "a head jut out of the woods momentarily, just for a second . . ." (*Mary's Mosaic*, p.123).

When I queried Sylvis about how long it took to walk the mile, he was very clear that he had walked "very slowly" and vigilantly, intermittently stopping to peer into the woods, and periodically calling out to his partner Frank Bignotti.

During the interview, Sylvis told me he had to have been walking for "about 20 minutes." In my book, I gave him the benefit of the doubt and stated that "it has to have been at least 15 minutes or more" (p. 123), before he spotted the head of a second "Negro male."

That meant that the time was likely to be at the very least 1:15 p.m. (the time Ray Crump was arrested, 7/10 of mile away) and likely significantly later.

Yet in Lisa Pease's reverie, this too becomes incomprehensible for her to grasp. Furthermore, Ray Crump—according to the trial transcript—was already in the company of Detective John Warner sometime before 1:15 p.m. at a location of 1/10 of a mile east of the murder scene.

I maintain that it could have been as much as 10 to 15 minutes before 1:15 p.m. that Warner first spotted Crump (who Warner said "wasn't running" when he first spotted the about-to-be defendant), before he started interrogating him—first asking him to produce his driver's license, which Warner studied, then asking him a series of seven questions, before deciding that he would walk with Crump to his alleged fishing spot in order to help him retrieve his fishing gear that Crump said had fallen into the Potomac River.

The trial transcript repeatedly documents that Crump was officially arrested at approximately 1:15 p.m. by Detective Bernie Crooke, but he was in the company of Detective Warner before that time.

Therefore, the "Negro male" spotted by officer Sylvis, who successfully eluded capture by police, couldn't have been the defendant Ray Crump.

This isn't rocket science, but for the challenged Lisa Pease, it's too much to tolerate, given her desperation to find some way to discredit me, whereby she finally resorts to attacking my educational credentials.

In addition, Ms. Pease can't even seem to fathom or consider how "Lt. William L. Mitchell," a man who told police he was jogging on the towpath when he passed Mary Meyer—allegedly just before the murder took place—told police that a "Negro male" matching Wiggins' description was following her in an effort to frame Ray Crump.

"Mitchell" would then testify against Crump at the murder trial nine months later in July 1965 as part of the CIA's assassination operation. It doesn't seem to matter to Pease that "Mitchell" has never been able to be located since the trial, or that his known address during that time was documented as a "CIA safe house" by three separate former CIA employees.

At the time of trial in July 1965, Mitchell told a reporter that he had since retired from the military and was now a mathematics instructor at Georgetown University—yet no record of his employment there could ever be located, nor was there ever any *bona fide* military service record located for "Mitchell," either in the Pentagon where he was listed in the directory at the time of the murder, or in the main military data base in St. Louis.

This was thoroughly researched by the Peabody Award-winning journalist Roger Charles, as discussed in my book, a fact that Pease fails to mention in one of her many deliberate omissions, which also included Damore's consultation with L. Fletcher Prouty (as documented by Damore's attorney James H. Smith) to finally understand who

"Mitchell" was, before Damore confronted him. Of course, Lisa Pease is entitled to whatever flawed point of view she wants to embrace, but she's not entitled to her own set of facts.

The author's father, Wistar Janney

The rest of Pease's long-winded misstatements criticizing author Leo Damore, Timothy Leary, Robert Morrow, Gregory Douglas and other sources who I attempted to unravel—explicitly noting their deficiencies and limitations—completely obfuscates the clarity of the emerging picture:

Placed in a larger context, and juxtaposed with firm documentation, the aggregate unfolding scenario clearly indicates that Mary Meyer's life was ended by a CIA assassination.

But in the Pease-DiEugenio fantasy world, people are either all white or all black, complete truth-tellers or liars, completely reliable or unreliable. There are no shades of gray; there is no ambiguity; and there is no room for the analysis of intricacy and complexity.

And this is why the Pease-DiEugenio brand of journalistic sophistication (or lack thereof) can't seem to fathom how JFK advisor Kenneth P. O'Donnell could somehow go on the official record after the 1976 *National Enquirer* exposé about the Meyer-Kennedy affair and defend the shining Camelot myth in his attempt to negate that there had been a romantic affair between Mary Pinchot Meyer and President Kennedy; yet only a year later, shortly before his death, confide to author Leo Damore some of the intimate details of their relationship.

In the same way that O'Donnell never talked publicly about how the FBI had discounted his testimony that the Presidential motorcade in Dallas was driving into an ambush where at least two shots had come "from behind the fence [on the grassy knoll]," in front of the motorcade, O'Donnell only mentioned this reality to insiders, which was confirmed 25 years later by Speaker of the House Tip O'Neill in his 1987 memoir *Man of the House: The Life and Political Memoirs of Speaker Tip O'Neill*.

Both Leo Damore and his attorney James H. Smith worked on one of O'Donnell's Massachusetts gubernatorial campaigns where the three had become good friends. Yet Lisa Pease can't fathom that there were many things O'Donnell didn't want to share publicly, and would only confide privately to the people he trusted. Fabricating evidence is a fatal error for any kind of investigative reporter or critic. What kind of a mindset (or person) would do this?

Only a callow, dogmatic "true believer" in the childish Camelot myth, who cannot tolerate being challenged, resorts to a riddled analysis that is filled with factual errors and deliberate omissions and misstatements. This episode in their increasingly virulent and intolerant criticism is both tragic and unfortunate, because some (but not all) of the work of Pease and DiEugenio has made a significant contribution to JFK assassination historical research.

James Jesus Angleton, Chief of Counterintelligence at CIA, answering questions on September 25, 1975 before the Senate Intelligence Committee in Washington. Angleton was answering questions concerning the CIA's cover-up of reading the mail of many prominent Americans, including the mail of Richard M. Nixon. (Photo Credit: George Tames (*The New York Times*))

For example, James DiEugenio's deconstruction of Chris Matthew's recent book on JFK was an insightful analysis of a flawed work.

In addition, DiEugenio and Pease together edited a useful anthology of articles on the assassinations of the 1960s.

However, what they have done to *Mary's Mosaic* is all too similar to what they do to other first-time authors writing about the JFK assassination: they delight in subjecting those who dare to write about the Kennedy assassination (in a way that conflicts with their own historical interpretations) to the "CTKA buzz-saw."

So, readers and followers beware (those of you who have the patience to read many of their long and pompous reviews): these two Los Angelinos have an extremely inflated opinion of their own importance in the JFK assassination debate.

Fortunately, books last; and reviews are forgotten weeks after they are written (if not sooner). Moreover, we are living in the 21st century. In spite of the fact that Pease and DiEugenio would surely resurrect book burnings for those works of which they disapprove—establishing a modern-day JFK assassination *Index Librorum Prohibitorum* if they could do so—modern-day JFK researchers and the American public do not hunger for another Torquemada or Cardinal Bellarmine.

I dare say that if Pease and DiEugenio had been in charge of Galileo's heresy trial in Rome, he would have been sentenced to burn at the stake, instead of to the life imprisonment (house arrest) levied on him by the Holy Office.

Source note: This chapter previously appeared as "Mary's Mosaic—A Litmus Test for JFK Research Integrity," *http://jamesfetzer.blogspot.com/2015/09/marys-mosaic-litmus-test-for-jfk.html.*

Appendix A

A Review of David Talbot's *The Devil's Chessboard*

by Phillip F. Nelson

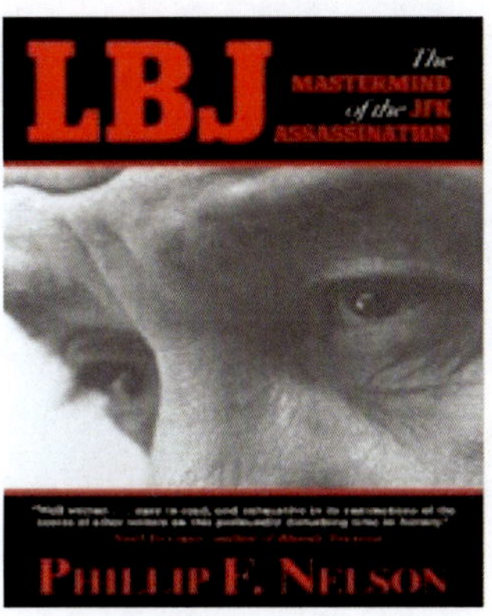

There are so many great attributes of this richly detailed book that any criticism of it seems like something only a graduate-level "nitpicker" could even attempt to do. One of the best is the very title of the book: clearly Allen Dulles was a personification of the "Devil" himself; that his game was played on a global chessboard with thousands of pawns at his disposal certainly cannot be denied, thus the book's title is very fitting. And certainly one of those pawns was Lee Harvey Oswald, whose moves were closely monitored by none other than one of Dulles' top king's men, James Jesus Angleton. Which brings us to an axiom that is understood by anyone who has ever played a game of chess: It is virtually impossible for any pawn to ever successfully kill the king.

I've never been a graduate level anything—at least in the world of academia—but a, but I have earned something of a reputation as a "nitpicker" nonetheless. And as much as I believe that Talbot is a great author, and that both his latest book as well as his previous book *Brothers: The Hidden History of the Kennedy Years* are proof of that, I do have a few comments to make regarding a single sentence that appears on p. 504: "But Johnson was certainly not the mastermind" [of the JFK assassination].

That "not a mastermind" sentence comes toward the end of Chapter 18, "The Big Event"—25 pages devoted entirely to Dulles' putative role in the JFK assassination. The single-most referenced source that Talbot used in that chapter was from one of the bishops—to continue the chess metaphor—E. Howard Hunt, who worked for Dulles (and Angleton, Helms, Wisner, et al.), who finally "confessed" to his son, Saint John Hunt, that he was . . . ahem, a "benchwarmer" in that particular caper. But, thanks to an article in *Rolling Stone* (2 April 2007), the whole world should know by now that Mr. Hunt actually drew a chart that had "LBJ" in the top-most position of the cabal which developed the plan for the "Big Event" and subsequently executed it—and John F. Kennedy, in the process.

In fact, nearly every point that Mr. Talbot made within that chapter reinforced Johnson's purported role, particularly this passage on p. 503:

While the Miami ["JM/WAVE," the CIA station there] conspirators made it clear that Bill Harvey was playing a central role in "the big event," they assured Hunt that the chain of command went much higher than Harvey. Vice President Johnson himself had signed off on the plot, [David Sanchez] Morales insisted."

It was on this point (and practically only this point) that Talbot demurred from Hunt's statements, saying "This is where Hunt began to obfuscate. There is no evidence that Lyndon Johnson and Bill Harvey [the man designated to plan "The Big Event] were ever in close contact. . . .It is simply not credible that a man in Johnson's position would have discussed something so extraordinarily sensitive as the removal of a president with a man who occupied Harvey's place in the national security system."

Then he allowed that, well, yes, Lyndon B. Johnson was a very close confidant of Allen W. Dulles, a man who had the "stature and clout to assure a man like LBJ that the plot had the high level support it needed to be successful." In my opinion, Talbot has reversed those roles: It was Dulles who needed the reassurance that LBJ was on board for the project to go forward.

There were several reasons that "no evidence" existed that Lyndon Johnson had ever had close contact with Bill Harvey. First, Johnson had, since his college days back in San Marcos, practiced every tenet of secrecy protocol ever invented, chief among them was rule No. 1: "Never commit anything to writing" when it came to the most unethical, immoral or criminal actions that one might employ to accomplish his objectives. In fact, on the most brutally deadly acts, he did not even like to use the telephone, unless he could be certain that it wasn't tapped. Which is why he often required "face to face" meetings to reach certain "understandings."

And that would undoubtedly explain an item that Talbot noted on p. 493 of his latest book: ". . . in the summer of 1963, Johnson hosted Dulles at his ranch in the Texas Hill Country . . ." which, he also noted, ". . . did not appear in his [Dulles'] calendar." Talbot never reflected on just "why" such a notation was not made in Dulles' calendar. Nor did he further note that Dulles returned to LBJ's ranch just three weeks before the assassination, as contemporaneously reported in the *Fort Worth Press*.

But the larger point, as Talbot went on to acknowledge, was that the question was moot, regardless. Because Johnson was indeed so close to Dulles that the need for him to ever meet personally with Bill Harvey was never at issue, thus this point was, actually, a non sequitur. Not to be pedantic, but the point was pointless—other than being put into the narrative as a means to undermine the issue of Johnson's possible role as the "mastermind" of JFK's assassination.

While author Talbot never attempted to advance the notion that Dulles—or anyone else—was the "mastermind," he did assert (unconvincingly) that Dulles was higher up the totem pole amongst Washington officialdom:

"Howard Hunt was fully aware of the seating arrangements at the Washington power table. He knew, in fact, that Dulles outranked Johnson in this rarefied circle."

Talbot did acknowledge that LBJ might have been either a "passive accessory" or "even an active accomplice" in the "crime of the century." So if it was the latter, then he and I might not be that far apart in our respective arguments. That's because, as I've stated at least a thousand times before, in order to qualify for the term "mastermind" (i.e., the dictionary definition) one need not have personally designed and overseen every aspect of the planning and execution of this kind of operation, any more than a CEO of a major enterprise would have to personally know every detail of every management position throughout the organization: It's called "delegation," as one learns in Business Management 101.

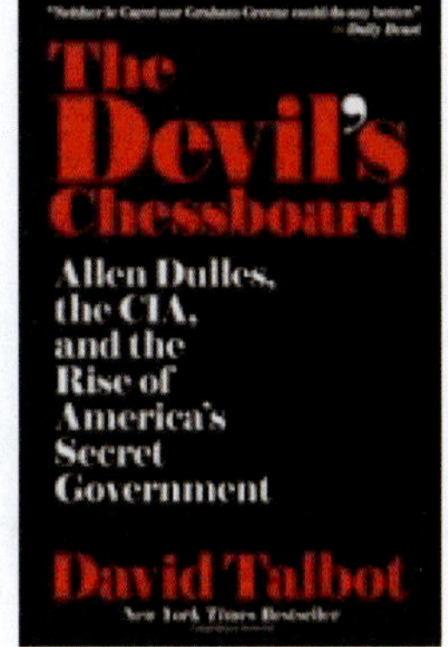

There has been more misrepresentation, disinformation, obfuscation and general confusion about that term than any other that I have ever witnessed, even after having spent three decades in a corporate environment where resolving the confusion between different departments, and the people who populated them, seemed like a daily ritual. When I first used that term, in a discussion with Noel Twyman, the author of one of the best books of the genre, *Bloody Treason*, I was warned of the possible repercussions of doing so because of that very phenomenon. But I thought it fit the subject well and elected to use it despite the pitfalls. Mea culpa.

To support my own view of Johnson's supremacy regarding "the seating arrangements at the Washington power table" I offer the following comments, excerpted from my own book, *LBJ: From Mastermind to The "Colossus"*:

"It took someone with extreme powers of persuasion, who had built a lifetime record of experience pulling people together to accomplish his schemes—the criminal ones like stolen elections, flagrant abuse of campaign fund handling, murders of people who got in his way, as well as the more conventional politicking skills—to have pulled together and led the powerful men already alluded to throughout this book to agree to the plan to kill Kennedy.

Such a person had to be driven by passion, and there was no one in Washington who even came close to him in that qualification—certainly not the rather introverted, cerebral, pipe-smoking, tweed-jacketed Princeton alumnus who had previously presided over the CIA, nor the equally deluded and aged head of SOG (his term for "Seat of Government," being his own government-issued heavy-duty desk chair) J. Edgar Hoover—who also had tentacles throughout the federal bureaucracy but not nearly equal to the powers that Johnson had amassed.

"The catalyst behind the assassination had to have been a singular "driving force" who had to have connections to all the key people in multiple agencies of the federal government as well as to local officials in Dallas, Texas (the previous schemes in Chicago and Miami were most likely merely test runs to assure that all contingencies had been anticipated and that the men involved had been properly prepared for the real event). The "key man" had to have the ability to push all the right buttons and get those people—some unwittingly, with only a limited scope of knowledge of the overall plan—to take actions on his command.

He was acting as a forceful CEO of an enterprise that would primarily benefit himself, but sold to the others as being necessary for accomplishing their own interests, whether that be a more aggressive foreign policy, especially toward Vietnam, an end to the "peace process" with the USSR that Kennedy had implemented, a stop to the threat he had introduced to the power of the Federal Reserve, or simply a change to the apparent slippage toward socialism that many feared. Only a very powerful force, a "colossus" as described by none other than Bill Moyers, could have possibly been the driving force that was the essential ingredient, the "critical mass."

"The enterprise, like all major undertakings of humanity, required a powerful catalyst to give it momentum, direction, and the subsequent promise of protection that all the players would expect, a promise that only LBJ could make effectively. That catalyst would have to reach into not only all the federal agencies, especially the military and intelligence organizations, but just as certainly into the state and local authorities in order to simultaneously ignite the fuses within each; it would take a unified "driving force" to do that, and Lyndon Johnson was uniquely capable of providing that kind of reach into every such entity.

That element could have only come from a very powerful and dedicated single person, a very forceful person, one who could bring all the elements together. Some may prefer other terms, such as a "CEO," a "Key Man," a "Linchpin," or even the term I've used, a "Mastermind," but that person, regardless of the label one prefers, could only have been a man consumed by power and obsessed for decades about becoming president.

"The accumulated evidence [as presented in earlier chapters of this book and its predecessor, *LBJ: The Mastermind of the JFK Assassination*], demonstrates beyond doubt that Lyndon Johnson really was smart enough to have "masterminded" the plot to kill JFK (a point that many incorrectly believe excludes him from being a worthy candidate for this title). No other candidate for that role comes close to the manic Johnson, pushing and pulling the other key people to stay on task, including the trial runs ("beta tests" as they might be called today) planned for Chicago and Miami in the weeks before the Texas trip.

"For those who insist it was the introverted Allen Dulles—someone without personal connections to such other key people as James Rowley in the Secret Service, or even J. Edgar Hoover, with whom he had battled for turf that he considered his own—a man who in 1963 only had sway with others through an established linear hierarchy, within which he could receive input and issue orders, an obvious question arises: How could he do that when he had been fired two years earlier from his position of power and authority over many others?

The premise would necessarily require the existence of an entirely separate organization, an enterprise dedicated to a presidential assassination. If that were the case, does it not follow that the authority residing within such a structure designed to carry out the mission of this "invisible government" had to be conferred upon him when he was chosen for the position by some very powerful men?

"Are we to infer, in that scenario, that Allen Dulles issued his deadly orders as the enigmatic, albeit secret, CEO, through an amorphous group of anonymous men at the helm of this invisible government? It may be instructive, as to who reported to whom, to note that Allen Dulles visited Dallas and Fort Worth and the LBJ Ranch just three weeks before the assassination. This was reported in the *Fort Worth Press* a few days before JFK's trip to Texas. Johnson had spent the better part of four weeks at the ranch before JFK's Texas trip as he made plans, focused primarily on the Dallas motorcade. For Dulles to go there to consult with him speaks volumes about who was the CEO and who was merely a high-level facilitator.

"In 1963, Lyndon B. Johnson was the most powerful man in the United States, in some ways even more so than John F. Kennedy, owing to the "back channel" alliances he had developed within the Pentagon and CIA. If indeed the "invisible government" were behind the assassination of the president, Lyndon B. Johnson would be at the head of the line for being the CEO of that invisible government.

His direct connections to the military and intelligence organizations and law enforcement agencies of the federal government and the state of Texas were unimpeded by the many clashes that John F. Kennedy had experienced with those same chieftains. This kind of power was best illustrated by Johnson's close connections through J. Edgar Hoover, Clint Murchison, H. L. Hunt, Irving Davidson, Fred Black, and Bobby Baker to Mafiosi throughout the country such as Carlos Marcello and Sam Giancana, et al., and through Angleton, Bill Harvey, Johnny Rosselli, and David Morales on down to the numerous Cuban exiles.

"These were all men whom Lyndon Johnson had developed for many years, decades even, insinuating himself as closely and personally as he could, using methods (or Johnson "Treatments") customized for his selected prey. That kind of power was unique to Lyndon Johnson, no one else in Washington had worked so hard to accrue it and practice it and hone its edges with every iteration: He alone possessed that kind of power in 1963. The record of his astounding success stands, even now, half a century later, and thus becomes the biggest proof of his pivotal role:

The claim of the title "Mastermind" is proven, ironically, by the even grander title "Colossus," which best represents his real legacy of having achieved the highest office in the land, his resolve established when he was merely a child and later a high school bully. His lifetime of corruption and criminal behavior attest to the fact that his character traits were consistent over his entire lifetime."

Addendum: There was one other issue that I did not catch on my first, "fast" read of the book that needs to be added: The death of James Forrestal, which Mr. Talbot quickly writes off as a "suicide" as though that is an undisputed fact. Such is simply not the case, and the most compelling, thoroughly researched and documented treatise on the subject was written by G. David Martin, Ph.D., a six-part series which can be found at this link: *www.dcdave.com/article4/021110.html.* (I have summarized the facts he presented in my own book *LBJ: From Mastermind to The "Colossus"* as noted above).

I want to reiterate that I thought Mr. Talbot did an outstanding job of describing just how devilish Allen Dulles was. My original quibble was with that one sentence. Although I initially gave Mr. Talbot's book a "4.5" rating—which rounded back up to a "5"—I have since adjusted it downwards and must revise the rating to a "4" due to the combined deduction for both of these areas of substantive disagreement. The matter of James Forrestal's death, as noted above in the "update" has been very controversial for too long to be ignored as something trivial, as to not affect the rating, and it is with some regret that I decided to make this change, for a work that is otherwise quite well done.

Source note: This chapter previously appeared as "A Nitpickers Review of David Talbot's The Devil's Chessboard"

Appendix B

The Zapruder Film: "No" to Copyright

by Mike Pincher

[Editor's note: *Mike Pincher is a graduate of SUNY Albany who earned his J.D. at the San Fernando Valley College of Law. He contributed a co-authored study (with Roy Schaeffer) concerning the Zapruder film to* Assassination Science *(1998). He practices as a trial attorney in the Los Angeles area and prepared this study in late 2003 specifically for publication in* Assassination Research, *where it appears in print for the first time. It is an important contribution.*]

Introduction

This chapter aims to show that copyright protection should not generally apply to the Zapruder film ("Z-film") record of the 22 November 1963 assassination of President John F. Kennedy. The predominant reason is legislation popularly known as "the JFK Records Act" that was a direct countermand to the veil of secrecy pervading the subject-matter (arguably placing the film in the public domain), but also because of language contained in judicial case law.

As shown below, while one 1968 federal district court case called it copyrightable, it is doubtful, based on subsequent case law, that even its own United States Court of Appeals for the Second Circuit would agree. More significantly, it is doubtful that the U.S. Supreme Court would agree. Arguably, it was never properly copyrightable to begin with, both because of its great public interest as a news event, and, even more importantly, in that the assassination cannot be properly understood without public access to this source *in toto*. The idea of the event and its precise Z-film depiction cannot be properly treated separately.

More targetedly, copyright is especially inappropriate where the Z-film's very authenticity as an accurate record of the JFK assassination is impeached as it is in the Fetzer treatment by resort to the very Z-film itself. Hence, even if for some applications it could be considered copyrightable, the scope of its protection should not extend to the Fetzer treatment. This principle also illustrates that copyrightability of subject-matter and scope of copyright protection can be two distinctly different factors. In this case, however, it seems that the Fetzer treatment wins in both arenas.

While arguments can be made for Z-film and frame copyright "waiver" or "abandonment" based on either selective enforcement or perhaps even abuse of copyright, given the strength of the supporting arguments otherwise militating toward free First Amendment use of it, that thread has not been pursued here.

Finally, "fair use" is not addressed because of this writer's conviction toward non-copyrightability. Historically, that element expands the actionability issue even where technical infringement might exist. But the virtual wholesale use of the Z-film frames in the Fetzer treatment almost hinges on non-copyrightability rather than "fair use" (since extent of use is one of the statutory factors and case law considerations for "fair use"), though not necessarily because of the uniqueness of his application. While a source for interesting debate, it is not considered necessary for purposes of this essay.

The Economic Market Effect: Copyrightability vs. Actionability

Regardless of infringement or not, once the inevitable "fair use" defense enters the fray, there must be an adverse impact on the marketability of the infringed product, be it directly through the film itself or indirectly through impairment of derivative rights [1]. On its surface, an attack such as Fetzer's on the very integrity of the film as an historical document would probably promote interest in the film for the alteration ramifications of such a finding.

While for reasons discussed below, copyrightability should be adversely impacted should his thesis find acceptance, lack of detrimental market effect is an element that must be considered if it does not.

Z-Film Lineage and Exposure

While by no means exhaustive, a tracing of official Z-film disposition and other relevant facts of historical interest appears in order. Circa 24 November 1963, Zapruder agreed to a $150,000 purchase price for television and movie rights plus royalties. The first $25,000 was donated to Dallas police officer J. D. Tippit's widow. Tippit had been murdered on the same day as JFK, and allegedly by Oswald [2].

Interestingly, actual copyright of the original Z-film itself was not registered until 15 May 1967, by Time, Inc., the parent company of *Life* magazine [3]. On 6 March 1975, Geraldo Rivera showed Groden's Z-film version for the first time on national television on his *Good Night America* talk show [4]. In April of 1975, Time transferred the copyright back to the Zapruder family [5], purportedly through assignment that reserved to Time unlimited non-exclusive print rights to Zapruder frames [6]. On 13 July 1998, a digitized Z-film produced by MPI Home Video debuted as a documentary [7].

On 1 August 1998, Z-film ownership was officially transferred to the National Archives and Records Administration (NARA) [8]. On 3 August 1999, a Department of Justice (DOJ) special arbitration panel headed by Philadelphia lawyer and former federal judge Arlin Adams and also composed of former Department of Justice official Walter Dellinger and Kenneth Feinberg, a Washington D.C. lawyer and law professor, announced that it had determined eminent domain compensation to the Zapruder family (without copyright purchase) to be $16 million plus interest, describing the film as "a unique historical item of unprecedented worth" [9].

While the Arbitration Agreement states that "[n]othing in this Arbitration Agreement alters LMH's right to fully enforce its Copyright" [10], that does not in itself imbue by law a valid copyright if none existed by law at the time of said Agreement, which it is argued herein that it did not. The provision might just as well have more artfully read, "nothing in this Arbitration Agreement alters LMH's right, be there any, to fully enforce whatever copyright enforcement rights it may have". Eminent domain rights were at issue and nothing more. As will be described later, the Archivist no longer treats the Z-film as though there were copyright rights that remain to be respected.

Dellinger disagreed with the settlement figure, saying it was "simply too large an amount". He purportedly would have assigned its value between $3 million and $5 million [11]. While the panel said it reached its decision on 6 July 1999, that was coincidentally the same tragic day that the airplane carrying JFK, Jr. and his wife crashed off Martha's Vineyard in Massachusetts, killing them both, so the announcement had been postponed in deference to the Kennedy family [12].

Jeff West, director of the Sixth Floor Museum (converted from the infamous Texas School Book Depository in Dealey Plaza in Dallas, the assassination situs), was quoted as saying the $16 million purchase price, plus interest, was a "good, fair price for the family and the government" [13].

On 30 December 1999, the copyright to the Z-film was donated by the Zapruder family, along with various artifacts, to the Sixth Floor Museum [14].

Constitutional Significance of Copyright

Copyright is not a matter of right but of statutory privilege as Congress has been enabled to enunciate it through Art. I, Section 8 of the U.S. Constitution. Therefore, the extent to which it has addressed both the assassination itself and the general goals of copyright law is paramount to ascertaining the scope of copyright protection toward that subject.

Congress Speaks

That statement was dramatically made with the passage of the President John F. Kennedy Assassination Records Collection Act of 1992 ("JFK Records Act" or "Act"). Its need was perceived by Congress as urgent. Otherwise, Congressional records would not be disclosable until at least 2029 [15]. The government's secrecy in treating assassination records had undermined public confidence in its very integrity.

As the Assassination Records Review Board ("ARRB", but hereafter "Review Board" or "Board") that was created by Congress to help implement the Act wrote in its Final Report, the removal of secrecy was the *sine qua non* of its existence. It explained: "Numerous records of previous investigatory bodies such as the Warren Commission, the Church Committee, and the HSCA were *secret*. Yet members of these commissions reached conclusions based on the investigatory records. *The American public lost faith* when it could not see the very documents whose contents led to these conclusions." [16] (Emphasis added.)

The Act is designed to specifically address the shortcomings of both the Freedom of Information Act ("FOIA") and Executive Order #12356 as applied by the Executive Branch so as to favor disclosure of JFK assassination records ("records") [17]. It recognizes that "legislation is *necessary* to create an *enforceable*, *independent*, and *accountable* process for the public disclosure of such records." [18] (Emphasis added.)

It seeks to place *all* records into the National Archives [more formally, the National Archives and Records Administration ("NARA")] and requires their "*expeditious* public transmission to the Archivist." [19] (Emphasis added.) To satisfy a "compelling" public interest [20], each record bears a "presumption of immediate disclosure" [21] only rebuttable by "clear and convincing evidence" [22], a standard above the normal civil one of "preponderance of the evidence" (more likely than not).

To exclude for security, privacy or other overriding purposes, each applicant has to present written reasons to obtain a "Postponement of Disclosure" subject to periodic review to sustain its status and only specifically enforceable as to those portions of a record reflecting the exclusionary purpose. Even then, paraphrasing has to be made of the deleted areas. The Board was specifically empowered to "direct Government offices to transmit to the Archivist assassination records as required under this Act, *including segregable portions of assassination records*, and *substitutes and summaries of assassination records* that can be publicly disclosed to the fullest extent" [23]. (Emphasis added.) Even sealed court records are petitionable by the U.S. Attorney General [24].

So as to preserve the truthfulness and reliability of the collection, it is the duty of the Archivist to "ensure the physical integrity and original provenance of all records" [25]. In general, "no assassination record shall be destroyed, *altered*, or mutilated in any way" [26] and "no assassination record created *by a person* or entity outside government . . . shall be *withheld, redacted, postponed for public disclosure*, or reclassified" [27]. (Emphasis added.) The Act is not sunseted until the Archivist certifies to the President and Congress that all records have been made available to the public. The Review Board considered this pivotal. ("This provision is significant because it underscores the continuing obligation of federal agencies on the assassination after the Review Board's term expires." [28])

So as to remove all doubt as to its predominance over the JFK assassination subject, the JFK Records Act contains a Supremacy Clause at Section 11(a) [29]. When time threatened the Review Board's task, the President John F. Kennedy Assassination Collection Extension Act of 1994 was passed, with yet a final extension granted the Board until 30 September 1998 through the passage of Public Law 10525.29 [30]. Congress never expressed doubts as to the primacy of its initial task.

The scope of "assassination record" is treated at section 1400.1(a) of 36 CFR (Code of Federal Regulations) 1400 (which the Review Board itself formulated)— Guidance for Interpretation and Implementation of the President John F. Kennedy Assassination Records Collection Act of 1992 [31] and entails "… all records, public and *private*, regardless of how labeled or identified …". (Emphasis added.) Section 1400.4(b) and (c) specifically identifies "photographs" and "motion pictures" [32].

Subject to availability, Section 1400.6(4) calls for storage of the original camera and 1400.6(5) of the original video recordings [33].

Of significance is the release of records in their entirety. In pertinent part, Section 1400.5 states "... no portion of any assassination record shall be withheld from public disclosure solely on grounds of non-relevance ..." [34]. Also of seminal importance is Section 1400.8(c), which states: "In determining such designation of records as assassination records, the Review Board must determine that the record or group of records will more likely than not *enhance*, *enrich*, and *broaden* the historical record of the assassination." [35] (Emphasis added.)

With the Z-film being the most complete photographic record, its prominence escaped neither the Review Board nor Congress. In Chapter 6, Part 11 of its Final Report, the Board said: "The Zapruder film, which records the moments when President Kennedy was assassinated, is perhaps the single most important assassination record." [36] In a policy statement, the Board strove to transfer the original to the archives on 1 August 1998 and to work with Congress to achieve this [37].

In a letter to Frank W. Hungar, Assistant Attorney General for the Civil Division of the DOJ dated 5 June 1998, Congressman Dan Burton, Chairman of the House Committee on Government Reform and Oversight, a Review Board watchdog, wrote that Congress supported the "Board's commitment to ensuring that the original Zapruder film *remains* in the custody of the American people *as the most important assassination record*" [38]. (Emphasis added.)

As a corollary, the Board vowed to establish tests for film authenticity. In short, assurances of the integrity of the film were important before it was to be transferred to the Archives. Again, in Chapter 6, Part II of its Final Report, the Board highlighted the significance it placed on JFK students' concerns over three major evidentiary areas:

(1) the medical evidence; (2) the ballistics evidence; and (3) assassination film recordings taken at Dealey Plaza.

It wrote: "The Review Board believed that, *in order to truly address the public's concern relating to possible conspiracy and cover-ups relating to the assassination*, it would need to gather some additional information on all three of these topics. The pages that follow detail the Review Board's efforts to develop additional information on *these highly relevant and interesting topics*." [39] (Emphasis added.)

In a letter to James Moore dated 10 July 1978, Zapruder's son Henry G., while retaining legal ownership, deposited the original Z-film with the National Archives for safekeeping. After passage of the Act, separate attempts for its return were unsuccessfully made, in March of 1993 by Henry personally and in October of 1994 through his counsel. The Board noted, "NARA declined to return the original film, knowing that the JFK Records Act may have affected the legal ownership status of the film." [40]

Joint efforts between NARA, the Board, and the DOJ were undertaken to clarify the status of the original film under the JFK Records Act, including whether the U.S. government could legally acquire the original film and what the value of compensation to the Zapruder family would be under the takings clause of the Fifth Amendment [eminent domain].

In addition, the U.S. government had numerous discussions with legal counsel for the Zapruder family regarding a legal 'taking' of the film, the compensation to be accorded the family, and the copyright issues regarding the film." [41]

By 1997, the Board concluded that the Zapruder film had to become an official Government document. It wrote: "In 1997, the Review Board deliberated, and ultimately asserted, its authority under the JFK Records Act to acquire legal ownership of the original Zapruder film. . . . The Review Board also had to consider how to acquire the film *for the American people,* whether through the exercise of a takings power or through negotiations with the Zapruder family." [42] (Emphasis added.)

Returning to their "Statement of Policy and Intent with Regard to the Zapruder Film", its third resolution was "that the Board would work cooperatively with the Zapruder family to *produce the best possible copy for scholarly and research purposes,* establishing a base reference for the film through digitization …" [43].

It was hence expected that scholarship would be stimulated by the Board's work and the Archival Collection. In fact, that would be the barometer of whether or not the Act was an overall success. As the Board stated: "Ultimately, it will be years before the JFK Collection at NARA can be judged properly. *The test will be in the scholarship that is generated by historians and other researchers* who study the extensive documentation of the event and its aftermath. . . . Will the mass of documentary evidence answer the questions posed by historians and others? . . . *What do the records tell us about the 1960s and the Cold War context of the assassination?"* (Emphasis added.) The Board added: "The creation of the JFK Collection at NARA establishes a large records collection *undergoing intense use by researchers."* [44] (Emphasis added.)

Regarding agency reviewers, it was noted that not only did the Republic withstand the scrutiny, but "… perhaps, they will also note that openness is itself a good thing and that *careful scrutiny of government actions* can strengthen agencies and the provisions of government, not weaken it." [45] (Emphasis added.)

Perhaps most ringingly, the Board commented: "Formation of a historical record that can augment understanding of important events is central not only to openness and accountability, *but to democracy itself.*" (Emphasis added.)

That it was legislation that empowered it to act played a critical role, as "standards set through agency recommendation and presidential inclusion in an executive order would have limited the Board's ability to compel disclosure." [46]

The Final Report at Review Board Recommendations, No. 8, emphasizes that government accountability should be a continuing concern.

"The public stake is clear in creating a mechanism such as the Review Board to inform American citizens of the details of some of the most controversial events in American history. *Moreover, the release of documents enables citizens to form their own views of events, to evaluate the actions of elected and appointed officials, and to hold them to account.* There will not be a large number of such events, but there must be procedures grounded in experience that might be used to uncover the truth when these events, tragic as they are, occur. The provisions of the JFK Records Act have fostered the release of such documents, and the Board's experience demonstrates that similar legislation would be successful in the future." [47] (Emphasis added.)

The Board definitively concluded at Review Board Recommendations, No. 10, that government suppression of records had been overreaching in the JFK controversy. "The Review Board's experience leaves little doubt that the federal government needlessly and wastefully classified and then withheld from public access countless important records that did not require such treatment.

Consequently, there is little doubt that an *aggressive policy* is necessary to address the significant problem of lack of accountability and an uninformed citizenry that are created by the current practice of excessive classification and obstacles to releasing such information." It added: "Change is long overdue and the Review Board's experience amply demonstrates the value of sharing important information with the American public. *It is a matter of trust.*" [48] (Emphasis added.)

Court Rulings

A. Deference to Congress

As to the overall copyright scheme and other copyright legislation enacted by Congress, the U.S. Supreme Court has overall deferred to that body's judgment. In *Sony Corp. of America v. Universal City Studios, Inc.* [49], the Court said: "It is Congress that has been assigned the task of defining the scope of the limited monopoly that should be assigned authors . . . in order to give the public appropriate access to their work product."

In analyzing the constitutionality of the Sonny Bono 1998 Copyright Term Extension Act ("CTEA"), the Court noted in *Eldred v. Ashcroft* [50]: "we turn now to whether it [the CTEA] is a *rational* exercise of the legislative authority conferred by the Copyright Clause. *On that point, we defer substantially to Congress.*" [51] (Emphasis added.) The Court elaborated: "We have also stressed, however, that it is generally for Congress, not the courts, to decide how best to pursue the Copyright Clause's objectives. See *Stewart v. Abend,* 495 U.S. [207] at 230 [(1990)] ('Th[e] evolution of the duration of copyright protection tellingly illustrates the difficulties Congress faces .... [I]t is not our role to alter the delicate balance Congress has labored to achieve.'); *Sony,* 464 U.S., at 429 ('[I]t is Congress that has been assigned the task of defining the scope of [rights] that should be granted to authors or to inventors in order *to give the public appropriate access to their work product.*') [emphasis added]; *Graham [v. John Deere Co. of Kansas City]*, 383 U.S. [1] at 6 ('Within the limits of the constitutional grant, the Congress may, of course, implement the stated purpose of the Framers by selecting the policy which in its judgment best effectuates the constitutional aim.')." [52]

Precisely what scope the Constitutional Copyright Clause should have in its overall application, both generally and specifically, is subject only to rational scrutiny by the courts due to its Art. I, Section 8 deferential derivation. "The Copyright Clause," said *Eldred*, empowers Congress to *define* [emphasis original] the scope of the substantive right. See *Sony,* 464 U.S., at 429. Judicial deference to such congressional definition is '*but a corollary* to the *grant to Congress of any Article I power*.' *Graham*, 383 U.S., at 6." (Emphasis added.)

The Court wrapped this theme up by saying, "As we read the Framers' instruction, the Copyright Clause empowers Congress to determine the intellectual property regimes that, overall, in that body's judgment, will serve the ends of the Clause. See *Graham,* 383 U.S., at 6 (Congress may 'implement the stated purpose of the Framers by selecting the policy which *in its judgment* best effectuates the constitutional aim.' " [53] (Emphasis added by *Eldred* to *Graham*.)

Almost all 1976 Copyright Act terms for both existing and future copyrights were extended 20 years by the CTEA, which the petitioners to the Court derided as "very bad policy". Weighing such factors as the historical analysis by Congress indicating that extended terms favored greater public dissemination by private copyright holders than shorter ones, that the CTEA established parity with international copyrights assigned by the European Union, and that the greater durations were still within "limited Times" allowances prescribed by Art. I, section 8, the Court upheld the CTEA time extensions. As to the "very bad policy" charges of the petitioners, the Court returned, "*The wisdom of Congress' action, however, is not within our province to second guess.* Satisfied that the legislation before us remains inside the domain the Constitution assigns to the First Branch [Congress], we affirm the judgment of the Court of Appeals [which also upheld the CTEA]." [54] (Emphasis added.)

Therefore, how Congress treats the Z-film copyright issue bears great weight with the courts, who are loathe to interfere with its implementation of its Constitutionally-based mandate.

B. Judicial Postures Toward the Z-Film

The only court to make an official ruling as to the Z-film's copyright status found in the affirmative; but for reasons to be submitted below, the vitality of that designation is open to serious question, not only in terms of the age of the opinion but also as to other expressions that have come from the appellate courts in the same Second Circuit as that District Court sits, as well as from other federal circuits and the United States Supreme Court itself.

In 1968 (and, among other things, *long* before the JFK Records Act), the Southern District Court of New York found in *Time. Inc. v. Bernard Geis Assocs* [55] that the Z-film was indeed entitled to copyright protection. No liability was imposed, however, because to the degree that unauthorized frames and sketches of frames were used by Josiah Thompson and his publisher Geiss in *Six Seconds in Dallas*, District Judge Wyatt upheld the defense of "fair use" and awarded summary judgment to the defendants.

The creative requirement for copyright protection was found in the decisions Zapruder made as to the type of camera he used (movie rather than still), the type of film (color rather than black and white), his use of a telephoto lens, his determination of the time they would be taken, and his selection of the general area and specific location for the filming (choosing among several experimental positions) [56]. The court also correctly found that photographs generally are subject to copyright.

The distinction made by the Court in differentiating this from non-copyrightable news events is itself pivotal. "All that *Life* claims is a copyright is the particular *form of expression* of the Zapruder film." Notably, *Nimmer on Copyright* is referenced to establish that sketches may be a form of infringement. Yet, he (this is before son David assisted father Melville) is curiously and *importantly not* referenced regarding his specific comments as to the Zapruder film as they are discussed below.

Even *Geis* acknowledged public interest in the assassination: "There is a public interest in having the fullest information available on the murder of President Kennedy. Thompson did serious work on the subject and has a theory entitled to public consideration. While doubtless the theory could be explained with sketches of the type used at p. 87 of the Book [*Six Seconds in Dallas*] and in *The Saturday Evening Post*, the explanations actually made in the Book with copies is easier to understand. The Book is not bought because it contained the Zapruder pictures; the Book is bought because of the theory of Thompson and its explanation, supported by Zapruder pictures." [58] Fair use here also was based on non-comparable markets. Time does not sell Zapruder pictures [59]. This is not a categorization that would necessarily receive universal acclamation, even within its own federal Circuit.

Before turning to the Second Circuit, however, also of interest is the statement made by *Geis* itself in articulating why defense claims of oligopoly cannot be considered by it: "All that *Life* claims is a copyright on the particular form of expression of the Zapruder film. If this be 'oligopoly', it is specifically conferred by the Copyright Act and for any relief address must be to the Congress and not to this Court." [60] How well it could be argued that since the government's secrecy and concealment of documents prompted passage of the JFK Records Act and the fact that now the Z-film is government property for disclosure to the public also because of said Act, that Congress has indeed addressed and retaliated against the very oligopolic practices the defense presented in *Geis*. Logically, it seems that even that court would have considered copyrightability in a different light with that input.

While the Court of Appeals for the Second Circuit [covering New York, Vermont and Connecticut] would have probably upheld the end result of non-liability in *Geis*, it is unlikely they would have arrived at it under the same premise. The Court noted in *Iowa State University Research Foundation. Inc. v. American Broadcasting Cos., Inc.* [61] that in the "almost unique instance" of the Zapruder film "it is at least arguable that the informational value of that film cannot be separated from the photographer's expression."

Therefore, while *in dicta*, an argument for the Z-film falling outside of the scope of copyright protection altogether was alluded to.

More recently, the Z-film appeared in further *dicta* while the Second Circuit factually distinguished the case before it in *Twin Peaks Productions. Inc. v. Publications Internat., Ltd.* [62] by saying that its instant case was not the "extraordinary" situation overcoming the principle that fair use encompasses all First Amendment arguments. "Whatever non-protectable information PIL [defendant] seeks to disseminate is hardly inseparable from TPP's [Plaintiff's] copyrighted expression, *as perhaps is the case with the Zapruder film of the Kennedy assassination*." [63] (Emphasis added.) The supporting cite of *Roy Export Co. v. Central Broadcasting System. Inc.* [64] was also made by the court [65].

There is language in *Geis* that is useful in evaluating the effect of the JFK Records Act on the copyright issue. During the 1968 period in which its decision was rendered, the court said that the Archivist's practice was to instruct anyone requesting a copy of the complete Z-film as deposited by the Warren Commission that it could not comply. It would instead respond with the statement: "*Life* Magazine has advised us that while it will permit the film to be shown to qualified researchers, it cannot permit the reproduction of the film." [66]

The Archives' posture has now changed considerably. A person is allowed to copy the Z-film for free if he has his own equipment. Otherwise, he must rent out Archives equipment for $9.95 for two hours usage.

If one cannot directly access the Archives, an outside vendor is required. The copying of the film, however, is not restricted in any manner. This is highly probative evidence that the government no longer regards copyright as a viable issue.

Interesting *dicta* emanates from the federal Ninth Circuit (covering Washington, Oregon, Idaho, Montana, California, Nevada, Arizona, Alaska, Hawaii, Northern Mariana Islands, and Guam) case of *Los Anqeles News Service v. Tullo* [67] as well. Therein, the court noted that the Fair Use doctrine itself, which normally encompasses all First Amendment considerations, can be inadequate to protect First

Amendment issues and Nimmer treatise's examples of the My Lai massacre and Kennedy assassination were referenced regarding times when the demands for a *democratic dialogue* dictate less stringency in copyright application.

The court said in pertinent part: "... where the 'idea' of a work contributes almost nothing to the democratic dialogue, *and it is only its expression which is meaningful*, copyright protection should be limited in the interest of public access to information *necessary to effective public dialogue*. (1 Nimmer §1.10[C][2] at 1-82–1-84.)" [68] (Emphasis added.)

The court quoted Nimmer as to the treatise's Z-film posture at 1-83–1-84: "Similarly, in the welter of conflicting versions of what happened that tragic day in Dallas, the Zapruder film gave the public authoritative answers that it desperately sought; answers that no other source could supply with equal credibility.

Again, *it was only the expression, not the idea alone,* that could adequately serve the needs of an *enlightened democratic dialogue*." [55] (Emphasis added.) In such instances, the expression and idea are not dichotomous at all but essentially a "unity", inseparable from one another.

While *Tullo* acknowledged that no court referencing Nimmer in this capacity had ever applied the treatise's premise to the particular matter before them, it is important to realize that the facts before them were never on point. Nimmer's prominence and influence in the copyright area, however, is undeniable, as attested by the numerous references to the Nimmer treatises.

U.S. Supreme Court Posture

Even the U.S. Supreme Court, again *in dicta*, has given some indication it would entertain the Z-film as outside copyright protection even on the basis of the copyright statute itself and the idea–expression unity principle. In *Harper & Row, Publishers, Inc. v. Nation Enterprises* [69], the court said, in recognizing a possible qualification for some of the minor extractions *The Nation* made from Gerald Ford's yet-unpublished memoirs (although imposing liability overall):

"Some of the briefer quotes from the memoirs are arguably necessarily adequate to convey the facts; e.g., Mr. Ford's characterization of the White House tapes as the 'smoking gun' is *perhaps so integral to the idea expressed as to be inseparable from it.* Cf. 1 Nimmer Section 1.10[C]." (Emphasis added.)

If the U.S. Supreme Court were indeed convinced that the expression and idea as conveyed by the Z-film were so inseparable, it would probably rule for no copyright infringement. This would apply regardless of the extent of usage as long as some form of analysis could be reasonably associated with the respective footage.

While the Supreme Court reversed the Second Circuit in *Harper & Row* and found infringement without an adequate "fair use" defense regarding the Ford memoirs, it agreed with some of the copyright principles espoused therein. It, too, recognized "that copyright is intended to increase and not to impede the *harvest of knowledge . . .* The rights conferred by copyright *are designed to assure contributors to the store of knowledge a fair return for their labors. Twentieth Century Music Corp. v. Aiken*, 422 U.S. 151, 156 (1975)." [70] (Emphasis added.)

In quoting from the dissenting opinion in its earlier case of *Sony Corp. of America v. Universal City Studios, Inc.* [71], the court said: "*The monopoly created by copyright thus rewards the individual author in order to benefit the public*." [72] (Emphasis added.). It also quoted from p. 429 of *Sony*: "[This] limited grant is a means by which *an important public purpose may be achieved*. It is *intended to motivate the creative activity of authors* and inventors by the provision of a special reward, and to allow the public access to the product of their gains after the limited period of exclusive control has expired." [73] (Emphasis added.).

It also wrote: "By establishing a marketable right to the use of one's expression, copyright supplied the economic incentive to create and disseminate ideas."

While the freedom of thought and expression includes the right *not* to speak, it also stated: "We do not suggest the right not to speak *would sanction abuse of the copyright owner's monopoly as an instrument to suppress facts*." [74] (Emphasis added.)

The implications of this last statement are monumental. Suppression of facts is something Z-film copyright holders might well be challenged on. There have been licensing fees for Z-film use of $15,000 on up for a 26-second film that have been staggering in comparison to what would be ordinarily considered reasonable by industry standards.

As of the time that the Declaratory Relief petition was filed by the Assassination Archives & Research Center and Passage Productions, L.L.P. against The LMH Company and the DOJ on 23 November 1998 with the Washington, D.C. District Court, the NBC News standard rate card, if the petition was accurate, called for a licensing fee of $73 per second, for a respective fee of 26 x $73 or $1898. [75] Even adjusting for not readily apparent other extraneous factors reveals an outrageous and arguably abusive and suppressive sum for Z-film usage.

Supreme Court rulings in other areas of copyright also strongly suggest other bases for holding that various Z-film analyses, including Fetzer's, would be considered outside the ambit of copyright protection. E.g., most recently, the majority in the *Eldred v. Ashcroft* opinion decided 15 January 2003 stated that, in distinguishing some of the features of patent and copyright, "… copyright gives the holder no monopoly on any knowledge. A reader of an author's writing *may make full use of any fact or idea she acquires from her reading.* See [17 U.S.C.] §102(b); [1976 Copyright Act]." [76] (Emphasis added.) That opinion also states:

"Due to this distinction [the idea–expression dichotomy], every *idea*, *theory*, and *fact* in a copyrighted work becomes instantly available for public exploitation at the moment of publication. See *Feist* [*Publications. Inc. v. Rural Telephone Service Co.*, 499 U.S. 340], at 349–350 [(1991)]." [77]

The reader may recall the court's language in *Geis:* "The Book is not bought because it contained the Zapruder pictures; the Book is bought because of the *theory* of Thompson and its explanation, *supported by Zapruder pictures*." [78] (Emphasis added.) Thompson's theory was derived from the evidence *ascertained specifically from the Z-film itself.* It would seem for that reason alone that the U.S. Supreme Court would conclude Thompson's usage outside of the scope of copyright protection for the Z-film.

In the Fetzer treatment, it can be amply argued that the knowledge, idea, theory or fact of alteration is observable and hence emanates from the many oddities appearing internally within the Z-film itself. Just a few of the examples convincingly cited and readily observable on their face are Presidential limo driver William Greer's impossibly fast backward head-turn in Z-frames 302–303; his equally impossible forward head-turn in Z-frames 315–317; the too rapidly dissipating blood spray in Z-frame 313 and thereafter; the absence of blood and other debris on the limo's trunk, even though the President's brains were blown out to the back and left; and spectators such as the Franzens who are not responding at all to the horrific event that is unfolding before them. (See Z-frame 369—JFK's head has already exploded but that reality is totally undetectable judging from the lack of reaction by the Franzens and the other spectator in view in the frame.)

For that matter, there is a row of spectators who are unresponsive to JFK's presence around the proximity of the Stemmons Freeway sign, which is best explicable by his not being present when this portion was filmed and for which he was introduced only later using a "floating matte" technique.

These observations are elicited from a close visual inspection of the film itself and comprise a far different and more expansive argument than "scholarship" or "criticism" encompassed within the "Fair Use" doctrine.

Fetzer goes even further than the patently observable by applying advanced photographic technology to show Stemmons sign anomalies that are also symptomatic of alteration in terms of correction for pincushion distortion that results in the "twitching" of the sign because the sign was introduced prior to said correction. Z-frame lamppost verticality anomalies are also revealed by comparing their verticality to Dallas Police Department photographs of Dealey Plaza. All of these and *many more* research findings were initially prompted by the plethora of patently pronounced peculiarities replete in the Z-film, again transcending "Fair Use" boundaries.

Feist also stars in another capacity, of in part defining that which is copyrightable. 499 U.S. at 345 states that the "*sine qua non* of copyright is originality".

At p. 359, it goes on to say that copyright protection is lacking for "a narrow category of works in which the *creative spark* is utterly lacking or so trivial as to be virtually nonexistent". (Emphasis added.)

From this, it may be legitimately queried, "How can a fraud of an historical document (which would be the case if it is altered) present any 'creative spark' at all that would be recognized by any court of law?" By implication from *Feist*, such a debauchery is devoid of copyright protection.

Put another way by Copinger [79] as presented in *Eldred*, "… the reader of a book is not by the copyright laws prevented *from making any full use of any information* he may acquire from his reading." [80] Arguably, the "information" leading one to conclude the Z-film has been altered is self-contained in the Z-film.

From there, further research procedures were prompted and utilized to both reinforce and expand upon this basic premise. This appears entirely consistent with a reader or viewer's right to make "full use" of the "information" elicited from the work under review.

Conclusion

A. Generally

There are powerful reasons for concluding that the Z-film is not now subject to copyright protection, if, indeed, it ever was. The one court case that found that it was, *Geis*, is questionable in its rationale. Even in its own Second Appellate circuit, there are reasonable expectations that the circuit would follow the Nimmer premise that idea and expression are inseparable (or a "unity" as this writer prefers to say it) and that crucial public debate is impermissibly quenched contrary to the design of the copyright statute if such protection is extended.

Further, its own explanation of how Thompson's theory is promoted by using the Z-frames themselves suggests that under today's standards, such a use is not copyright protectable at all even if the Z-film itself would be otherwise protectable.

While, to date, no case at any level has directly applied the Nimmer unity principle to the Z-film, it has received strong mention *in dicta* that certainly suggests that only the proper fact scenario awaits its implementation.

The U.S. Supreme Court has shown a recognition that there are circumstances wherein idea and expression are inseparable. It has also indicated that the right not to publish would not be allowed to suppress the truth and has recognized the general need to disseminate news information. It seems inevitable that it would find the JFK assassination idea and its expression on the Z-film to be First Amendment protectable to the outweighing of copyright monopoly restraints.

Arguably, the truth has been suppressed in this instance in a number of ways, but for the narrow purposes of this particular thread, it has been in the sense that the copyright holder, save for when the Zapruder family licensed the film to MPI Home Video in 1998, *35 years after* that fateful event, has never aggressively tried to market the Z-film, but simply has acted, when it has at all, to contain its usage.

Even if the judicial presumption espoused above is successfully rebutted, there remains the virtual Congressional declaration that copyright is no longer a viable position regarding the Z-film based on the JFK Records Act. One of the Board's pronounced purposes is to make government actors accountable for any questionable conduct concerning the assassination. Even the Archivist's handling of the Z-film has changed. Anyone for reasonable copying costs can now obtain a copy of the original. It no longer can be withheld.

The value of this expansion of public access cannot be underestimated.

Even the Zapruder family could not claim repossession of it. It is now an official Archival and hence government document. Government documents do not enjoy copyright protection and would not in this case anyway and remain consonant with the goal of stimulating public debate and scholarship in this field. On 3 August 1999, a DOJ special arbitration panel pursuant to eminent domain provisions awarded the Zapruder family $16 million plus interest for the taking. While the purchase price did not include the copyright transfer, the point appears moot.

Still further, the original copyright holder no longer owns the copyright. The Zapruder family donated it along with certain artifacts to the Sixth Floor Museum on 30 December 1999. While it would seem ludicrous that an institution so self-professedly dedicated to preserving the JFK legacy would wish to also suppress the Z-film, they would have little to no practical right to assert such anyway.

The newsworthiness of the event (as recognized by *all* courts that have addressed the issue), public interest in the item (now recognized as "compelling" by Congress), the unity of idea and expression, and the fact that any creativity was exercised by their predecessor Zapruder (for whom he and his family have been, under seemingly *any* measure, enriched enough), rather than themselves, would appear to be a fatal combination working against them. While it is possible to transfer legal ownership in a work without also conveying copyright ownership, the dynamics of such a transaction to this specific set of facts would not favor the Museum.

As aforementioned, one of the pronounced purposes of the JFK Records Act, as emanating from the very mouths of its appointed Board, is to enhance scholarship regarding the JFK scenario and to put it in its proper context as to the 1960s and the Cold War. The Board itself recognized the Z-film as probably the single-most prominent piece of evidence in the case.

The inability to utilize Z-film frames (as well as the film itself) to discuss whatever elements of the assassination are consistent with these targets, regardless of extent, would defeat these purposes. Public dissemination of scholarly findings is the only practical way these goals are accomplishable. There cannot be public debate without public exposure, a hallowed purpose for NARA's creation. As the Review Board stated at Chapter 1 of its Final Report, page 9 of 15, "The JFK Collection's purpose would be to make records available to the public."

Otherwise, in essence, the Zapruder family would have received a $16 million windfall with nothing accomplished. Researchers have always had their own access to the film through the Archives.

A number of books have, without garnering a license, already shown many frames of the film as it is, far beyond anything exercised by *Six Seconds in Dallas*. Numbered among them are *Assassination Science*, *Murder in Dealey Plaza* and *The Great Zapruder Film Hoax*, as well as Stewart Galanor's *Cover-Up* (which includes 40 Z-frames) and Fetzer's video, *JFK: The Assassination, The Cover-Up, and Beyond* (which includes the entire film three times). Official confiscation by the government only makes sense if it is done for all aspects and purposes, where it makes a difference not only as to formal status but in practical usage as well. In this manner, eminent domain should equate with public domain, taking the film (and constituent frames) outside of the ambit of copyright protection.

That copyright not extend in this instance is also consonant with the principle that Congress controls copyright and may exercise all rights "corollary" to it. It is incongruous and oxymoronic to enable it to force relinquishment of possession of the original for total public access and then allow the copyright holder to have a stranglehold on usage. That would render nugatory the Statute's very declaration that it was necessary to create "enforceable" legislation for public disclosure and then make the public (researchers and scholars among them, but the public at large as well) impotent thereafter to share its findings.

Even more tellingly, it would divest Congress of the powers ordained it by the U.S. Constitution. The Supremacy Clause of the Act, well within Congress's powers to enact, resolves all potential conflicts with the Copyright Act. The JFK Records Act prevails. The Archives have treated the copying of the film as having disposed of copyright as an issue. During the time of *Geis* and for years afterward, the copyright holder had controlled that aspect. This changed government posture therefore has powerful probative value.

B. As To the Fetzer Treatment Specifically

Applied to the Fetzer treatment, exposure of the Z-film as altered and a fraud even accomplishes specific JFK Records Act goals. The Archivist cannot certify its pedigree as one of his duties under the Act. But this is not to say that this frustrates the Act. On the contrary, it accomplishes accountability. *The provenance (chain of custody) aspect inevitably leads to government actors, be they individuals, agencies, or a combination thereof. This is important on more than one level.*

Foremost, it becomes a government document for copyright purposes *ab initio*. There is nothing to protect for Zapruder (or any other copyright holder) because the film purported to be his is not his—it is not a true depiction of what he filmed. It is not his creation. As *Feist* would describe it, it does not demonstrate his originality and thus lacks his "creative spark".

As the federal Seventh Circuit court (covering Wisconsin, Illinois and Indiana) in *Baltimore Orioles v. MLB* [81] put it at p. 668, footnote 6, "A work is original if it is the *independent* creation of its author." (Emphasis added.) Government tampering has caused the Z-film to lose its "independent" creation. Hence, being a government document to begin with, it is not entitled to copyright protection.

Second, it conclusively shows, in and of itself, that the JFK assassination was the result of a conspiracy that the government actively participated in, especially in terms of, though not necessarily confined to, the cover-up.

Minimally, it also lends credibility to the other elements of the conspiracy claimed by some researchers—that some of the X-rays and autopsy pictures were faked. If the Z-film was altered, why not the rest of the evidence as well?

Again, government actors become primary suspects. This is the exact kind of accountability striven for by the JFK Records Act and as enunciated by the Board. The Board raised serious questions with how the medical evidence was treated by the Warren Commission.

Put another way, this is an "enhance[ment], enrich[ment], broaden[ing] of the historical record of the assassination". The realization of the doctoring of the Z-film tells *volumes* more than mere words could describe about the dynamics of politics in the 1960s, and comparing the conditions for this event from then to today. In essence, the Z-film becomes more important in its *il* legitimacy than it even was in its legitimacy.

Due to the foregoing, it seems conclusive that, concerning the Fetzer treatment, at worst, First Amendment concerns would prevail over copyright protection even outside of "fair use" doctrine. At best, *a fraudulent historical document is not entitled to copyright protection*. The public does not benefit directly from authors perpetrating a fraud. Copyright allows for creativity to flourish and rewards honest effort. It is not intended to reward dishonest effort. The "information well" espoused by the U.S. Supreme Court in *Harper & Row* has been irrevocably polluted.

If the Z-film is a fraud as Fetzer proposes, it is not a contribution to the "store of knowledge" as contemplated by copyright law and recognized by the U.S. Supreme Court. Nor does one "motivate the creative activity of authors" within the meaning of the copyright statute and as interpreted by the courts by perpetrating a fraud. While it would frankly seem impossible to envision any court in the land at this point in time, especially in light of the JFK Records Act and its goals and ramifications, ruling for a copyright infringement with any use of the Z-film, this is particularly so in the case of the Fetzer treatment. To impose copyright obstacles in such an instance with such a revolutionary finding "would [particularly] sanction abuse of the copyright owner's monopoly as an instrument to suppress facts", especially as to a work described as "a unique historical item of unprecedented worth".

C. The Tragic and Resounding Theme

As to the overall message to be pondered in the JFK Aftermath, never have the words of James Madison written in a letter to W. T. Barry dated 4 August 1822 played more powerfully: "A popular Government without popular information or the means of acquiring it, is but a Prologue to a Farce or a Tragedy or perhaps both. Knowledge will forever govern ignorance, and a people who mean to be their own Governors, must arm themselves with the power that knowledge gives." [82]

How true. How *sadly* true! The JFK Records Act reflects not only the imperatives of Congress but also of our Constitutional forebears. For it to supersede copyright for all of its collection—not the least of which is the Z-film—is more than just a matter of trust; it hits, as the Review Board itself asserted, at the very core of a democratic republic.

Source note: This appendix originally appeared under the title, "*The Zapruder Film: 'No' to Copyright Protection*", *https://www.assassinationresearch.com/v3n2/v3n2pincher.pdf.*

References

[1] *Harper & Row v. Nation Enterprises*, 471 U.S. 539, 566, 567 (1985).
[2] The Sixth Floor Museum at Dealey Plaza, *Abraham Zapruder Film Chronology*, *http://www.jfk.org/Research/Zapruder/Zapruder_Film_ Chrono.-*
htm, at p. 4 of 12.
[3] *Id.*, at p. 6 of 12.
[4] *Id.*, at p. 7 of 12.
[5] *Id.*, pp. 7–8 of 12.
[6] Mark Zaid, James Lesar, and Charles Sanders, "Zapruder Film Civil Suit
Filed," *Assassination Research* Vol. 2, No. 2 (2003).
[7] *Ibid.*, Sixth Floor Museum, at p. 11 of 12.
[8] *Id.*, at p. 11 of 12
[9] *Updates*, "Big Bucks for Z-Film," *http://www.acorn.net/ jfkplace/09/fp.-*
back_issues/29th_Issue/updates.html, at pp. l–2 of 2.
[10] *Ibid.*, Zaid *et al.* Civil Suit, at p. 9 of 15.
[11] *Ibid.*, "Big Bucks for Z-film," at p. 2 of 2.
[12] *Id.*, at p. 1 of 2.
[13] *Id.*, at p. 2 of 2.
[14] *Ibid.*, Sixth Floor Museum, at p. 11 of 12.
[15] *Final Report of the Assassination Records Review Board*, Chapter 1: "The
Problem of Secrecy and the Solution of the JFK Act," *http://www.fas.-org/sgp/advisory/arrb98/part03.htm*. at p. 12 of 15.
[16] *Id.*, at p. 2 of 15.
[17] *Ibid.*, Final Report, Appendix C: "The President John F. Kennedy Assassination Records Collection Act of 1992 (JFK Act)," Section 2: "Findings, Declarations, and Purposes," (a)(5)(6), *http://www.fas.org/ sgp/advisory-/arrb98/part15.htm*, at p. 1 of 23.
[18] *Id.*, (a)(3), at p. 1 of 23.
[19] *Id.*, Section 2(b)(2), at p. 2 of 23.
[20] *Id.*, Section 3: "Definitions," (10), p. 4 of 23.
[21] *Ibid.*, ARRB, Chapter 1, p. 9 of 15.
[22] *Ibid.*, Appendix C, JFK Act, Section 9, (c)(l), at p. 16 of 23.
[23] *Id.*, Section 7: "Establishment and Powers of the Assassination Records
Review Board," (j)(B), at p. 12 of 23.
[24] *Id.*, Section 10: "Disclosure of Other Materials and Additional Study,"
(a)(1), at pp. 18–19 of 23.

[25] *Id.*, Section 4: "President John F. Kennedy Records Collection at the National Archives and Records Administration," (a)(1), at p. 4 of 23.
[26] *Id.*, Section 5: "Review, Identification, Transmission to the National Archives, and Public Disclosure of Assassination Records by Government
Offices," (2), at p. 5 of 23.
[27] *Id.*, Section 5(4), at pp. 5–6 of 23.
[28] *Ibid.*, ARRB, Chapter 1, at p. 12 of 15.
[29] See also *Id.*, at p. 12 of 15.
[30] *Id.*, at p. 9 of 15.
[31] ARRB, Final Report, Appendix D, *http://www.fas.org/sgp/advisory/-arrb98/part16.htm*.at p. 1 of 6.
[32] *Id.*, at p. 3 of 6.
[33] *Id.*, at p. 4 of 6.
[34] *Id.*, at p. 4 of 6.
[35] *Id.*, at p. 6 of 6.
[36] *http://www.fas.org/sgp/advisory/arrb98/part09.htm*, at p. 5 of 9.
[37] *Id.*, at p. 6 of 9.
[38] *Id.*, p. 6 of 9 (see also endnote 6).
[39] *Id.*, at p. 1 of 9.
[40] *Id.*, at p. 5 of 9.
[41] *Id.*, at p. 5 of 9.
[42] *Id.*, at p. 5 of 9.
[43] *Id.*, at pp. 5–6 of 9.
[44] Final Report of the Assassination Records Review Board, Recommendations, *http://www.fas.org/sgp/advisory/arrb98/part12.htm*, at p. 3 of 10.
[45] *Id.*, at p. 3 of 10.
[46] *Id.*, at pp. 3–4 of 10.
[47] *Id.*, at p. 9 of 10.
[48] *Id.*, at p. 10 of 10.
[49] *Sony Corp. of America v. Universal City Studios, Inc.* [49], 464 U.S. 417,
429 (1984).
[50] *Eldred v. Ashcroft,* 537 U.S. 186 (2003)
[51] *Id.*, pp. 13–14.
[52] *Id.*, p. 22.
[53] *Id.*, pp. 31–32.
[54] *Id.*, p. 32.
[55] *Time. Inc. v. Bernard Geis Assocs*, 293 F.Supp. 130 (SDNY 1968); *www.law.cornell.edu/copyright/cases/293_FSupp_130.htm.*
[56] *Id.*, at p. 14 of 18.

[57] *Id.*, at p. 15 of 18.
[58] *Id.*, at p. 17 of 18.
[59] *Id.*, at p. 18 of 18.
[60] *Id.*, at p. 15 of 18.
[61] *Iowa State University Research Foundation. Inc. v. American Broadcastinq Cos., Inc.* 621 F.2d 57, 61 n.6 (2d Circuit 1980).
[62] *Twin Peaks Productions. Inc. v. Publications Internat., Ltd.,* 996 F.2d 1366
(1993); *http://www.tourolaw.edu/2ndCircuit/Pre95/92-7933.html.*
[63] *Id.*, at p. 10 of 18.
[64] *Roy Export Co. v. Central Broadcasting System. Inc.,* 672 F.2d 1095,
1099–1100 & n.8 (2d Cir.), cert.dnd., 459 U.S. 826 (1982).
[65] *Id.*, at p. 10 of 18.
[66] *Id.*, at p. 4 of 18.
[67] *Los Angeles News Service v. Tullo,* 973 F.2d 791 (1992).
[68] *Id.*, at p. 4 of 11.
[69] *Harper & Row, Publishers, Inc. v. Nation Enterprises*, 471 U.S. 539, 565
(1985).
[70] *Id.*, at pp. 545–6.
[71] *Sony Corp. of America v. Universal City Studios, Inc.*, 464 U.S. 417, 477
(1984).
[72] *Id.*, at p. 546.
[73] *Id.*, at p. 546.
[74] *Id.*, at p. 559.
[75] *Ibid.*, Zaid Civil Suit, at p. 8 of 15.
[76] *Ibid.*, Eldred, at p. 26.
[77] *Id.*, at p. 29.
[78] *Ibid.*, Geis, at p. 17 of 18.
[79] W. Copinger, Law of Copyright 2 (7th ed. 1936).
[80] *Ibid.*, Eldred, at p. 26.
[81] *Baltimore Orioles v. MLB*, 805 F.2d 663 (1986).
[82] G.P. Hunt, ed. IX, *The writings of James Madison*, no. 103 (1910).

Appendix C

Forrest Gump on the Grassy Knoll

by Jim Fetzer

As a huge fan of actor Tom Hanks, I have admired him in many roles, including in *Charlie Wilson's War* and *Saving Private Ryan*. I am also a fan of Leonardo DiCaprio, who became a worldwide phenomenon in *Titanic*.

But I was distressed and dismayed to learn that they had committed to films about the death of JFK—in Tom's case, one based on Vincent Bugliosi's *Reclaiming History* (2008), and in Leonardo's, based on Lamar Waldron and Thom Hartmann's *Legacy of Secrecy* (2008)—which are indefensible books.

According to Bugliosi, the Warren Commission got it right: Lee Harvey Oswald was indeed "the lone assassin," where he claims to have refuted alternative "conspiracy theories."

According to Waldron and Hartmann, JFK was planning to assassinate Fidel, when the Mob learned of the plan and took JFK out first, using its insider's knowledge of the plot against Fidel to silence Bobby and preclude his pursuit of the guilty. The problem is that both theories are false.

Not only am I a fan of these actors but I have met Vincent Bugliosi. In my library downstairs, for example, I have a framed photo of Jesse Ventura, Vince and me at dinner in a restaurant in Min-

neapolis, when he came to present a lecture at the Hamlin University School of Law on 7 April 2003.

We had a great time, and I admire many of his books, from *Helter Skelter* (about the Charles Manson case) and Outrage (why O.J. Simpson was guilty of killing both Ron and Nicole) to *The Prosecution of George W. Bush for Murder* (for war crimes and other atrocities).

The Great Zapruder Film Hoax

DECEIT AND DECEPTION IN THE DEATH OF JFK

I like most of his books and have greatly admired him in the past. Similarly, I enjoy listening to Thom Hartmann over our local progressive radio station, "The Mic" at 92.1 FM in Madison, including his "Brunch with Bernie" Friday segments.

I share many beliefs and values with Vince and with Thom about truth, justice and the American way. But on JFK, they are trading in fiction, not fact.

I know because I organized a research group consisting of the best-qualified students to ever study the case, including Robert B. Livingston, M.D., a world-authority on the human brain and an expert on wound ballistics; David W. Mantik, M.D., Ph.D., who is board certified in radiation oncology and an expert on the interpretation of X-rays; Charles Crenshaw, M.D., who had attended the moribund president when he was brought to Parkland Hospital after the shooting and then, two days later, his alleged assassin after he, too, had been shot; a legendary photo-analyst, Jack White, who testified before the House Select Committee on Assassinations (HSCA) when it reinvestigated the case in 1977–78, explaining a dozen or more indications that the infamous "backyard photographs" were fake; and another Ph.D. in physics, John P. Costella, whose specialization in electromagnetism, the properties of light, and the physics of moving objects enabled him to help prove the Zapruder film is a fraud.

On 3 March 2010, *The Huffington Post* published a piece about Tom Hanks, which included his comments about producing a television mini-series based on Bugliosi's *Reclaiming History*: "We're going to do the American public a service," Hanks says. "A lot of conspiracy types are going to be upset. If we do it right it'll perhaps be one of the most controversial things that has ever been on TV."

Whether or not he knew it, I knew that I was one of those he had in mind, having published three books on the assassination, chaired or co-chaired four national conferences about it, and given hundreds of lectures and interviews about it.

On more than one occasion, I appealed to Vince not to publish his book on JFK, but to no avail. Even though he did acknowledge that mine are the only three "exclusively scientific" books about the death of our 35th President—in which I publish studies on different aspects of the case by qualified experts—he sailed ahead in reckless disregard for our findings.

The Falsifying Findings

According to the Warren Commission (1964), a lone, demented former Marine named Lee Oswald fired three shots from the sixth floor of the Texas School Book Depository, with a World War II vintage Italian-made, 6.5mm Mannlicher-Carcano, scoring two hits and killing JFK.

Originally, the FBI and the Secret Service concluded that all three shots had hit, one striking JFK in the back about 5.5" below the collar, the second hitting Texas Governor John Connally in the back, and the third hitting JFK in the head.

When it was discovered that one shot had missed and pieces of curbing had slightly injured bystander James Tague, the commission had to revise those findings and claim that the bullet that hit JFK in the back actually struck the base of the back of his neck and had exited his throat and injured Connally—a bullet that emerged virtually pristine and has come to be known as the "magic bullet."

Our research has demonstrated, however, that this account cannot possibly be true:

- According to the Warren Commission, the *Final Report of the Select Committee on Assassinations U.S. House of Representatives*, and articles in the *Journal of the American Medical Association*, our 35th President was killed by high-velocity bullets, which have muzzle velocities of 2,600 fps or higher. The Mannlicher-Carcano only has a muzzle velocity of 2,000 fps, however, which means that it is only a medium velocity and not a high-velocity weapon, as other authors—Harold Weisberg, *Whitewash* (1965), Peter Model and Robert

Groden, *JFK: The Case for Conspiracy* (1976), and Robert Groden and Harrison Livingstone, *High Treason* (1989)—have also observed. Insofar as this is the only weapon that Oswald has ever been alleged to have used to shoot JFK, if those official sources are correct, then he cannot possibly have fired the bullets that killed him; and if they are wrong, then how could they be regarded as reliable on any other aspect of the case?

• According to the Warren Commission, the *Final Report of the Select Committee on Assassinations U.S. House of Representatives*, and other sources, the assassin was situated in the southwest corner of the TSBD during the assassination, which took place at 12:30 PM on 22 November 1963. William Shelly, however, saw Oswald on the second floor near the lunchroom when he (Shelly) came down to eat lunch; at noon, Eddie Piper saw him on the first floor, when he (Oswald) told him (Piper) he was going up to eat; at 12:15 PM, Carolyn Arnold, the executive secretary to the vice president, saw him sitting in the lunchroom; and again at 12:25 she observed him, but on the first floor near the front door. Within 90 seconds after the assassination, Motorcycle Officer Marrion Baker confronted him in the lunchroom and held him in his sights until Roy Truly, his supervisor, assured the officer that he belonged there. They both reported that Oswald was not breathing heavily or perspiring but acting normally—not what would be expected if he had run down from the sixth floor.

• Later, when she was interrogated, his wife, Marina, stated that Lee admired JFK and bore him no malice. During his excellent *"Conspiracy Theory"* program on the assassination, broadcast on TruTV on Friday, 19 November 2010, Jesse Ventura had the opportunity to talk with Marina, who did not want her face shown on television because she lived in fear for the life of her children—nearly 50 years later. Jesse had 2.5 hours to talk with her, however, and she said that, although at one time she had thought Lee had done it, she was now convinced he was innocent and had been working undercover for the government. This conjecture had even been confirmed by the Attorney General of Texas, Waggoner Carr, who had

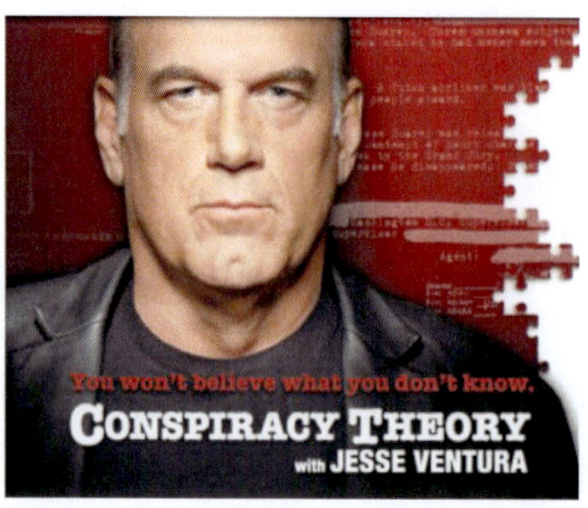

launched his own investigation and found that Lee was working as an informant for the FBI, had been assigned informant No. 179, and was being paid $200 per month right up to the time of the assassination. That may be why his W-2 forms have never been released, as if the IRS couldn't get hold of them, which is a unique event in American history!

More Problems for Bugliosi

What this means is that the man the Warren Commission fingered for the crime had neither the means, the motive nor the opportunity to have committed the crime. Most of what I have just said, however, has long been known to serious students of the assassination—on some issues—as long ago as the book by Mark Lane, *Rush To Judgment* (1967).

The reason why it has been so difficult to crack is that the government produced X-rays and photographs that suggested the two bullets that hit JFK had been fired from above and behind—the official location of the shooter. It would not be until 1992 when David W. Mantik began to study the X-rays in the National Archives and discovered that they had been altered and Robert B. Livingston announced that the brain shown in diagrams and photographs could not be the brain of JFK—based upon his study of the doctors' reports from Parkland Hospital—that the case the Commission had endorsed began to suffer its most significant damage.

Mantik obtained permission to study the autopsy X-rays, borrowing a technique from physics known as optical densitometry that enabled him to identify regions of the X-rays that were abnormal, including a region on the right lateral-cranial X-ray (of his skull taken from the side), which had been "patched" to conceal a massive blowout at the back of the head, which corroborated the reports from the Parkland physicians that he had a major defect at that very location.

When he studied the anterior-posterior X-ray (of the skull taken from the front), he found a 6.5mm slice of metal, which had apparently been added to the X-ray (in the darkroom) after they were taken from the morgue by Secret Service Agent Roy Kellerman.

So the reason the HSCA had discounted more than 40 eyewitness reports of a massive blowout at the back of his head was wrong and could no longer be defeated by the X-rays.

Livingston studied the reports from the physicians at Parkland, who, unlike the pathologists at Bethesda, were well-experienced with gunshot wounds.

One after another—including Charles Crenshaw, M.D., Marion Jenkins, M.D., Charles Carrico, M.D., Malcolm Perry, M.D., Robert McClelland, M.D., Charles Baxter, M.D., and Kemp Clark, M.D., the Director of Neurosurgery—they reported that both cerebral and cerebellar tissue had been extruding from the wound.

When Livingston compared their consistent and detailed reports with the diagrams and photographs of a brain at the National Archives, which shows only slight damage and a completely intact cerebellum, he was obligated to conclude that the brain shown in the diagrams and photographs could not be the brain of John Fitzgerald Kennedy. Once they had "patched" the massive defect to the back of the head, there was no place for that tissue to go, so they simply substituted another man's brain.

These discoveries were astonishing enough, but an even more important discovery would follow from them: that the home movie of the assassination (associated with Abraham Zapruder) had been edited to conceal the true causes of JFK's death.

There were reasons to suspect the film had been re-created—by removing some events and adding others—since there were more than 60 witnesses who reported that the vehicle either had slowed dramatically or had come to a complete stop. It had to slow dramatically *as it came to a complete halt,* where some saw more, some less.

The back-and-to-the-left motion of the body, moreover, was not reported by any of the witnesses in Dealey Plaza, even though it is the most striking feature of the extant film. And his brains had been blown out to the left-rear and had struck a motorcycle patrolman with such force he thought he himself had been shot. Yet the film shows brains bulging out to the right-front, giving the impression of a shot from above and behind.

He Should Have Known Better

What bothers me is that these crucial findings—for which we have adduced abundant proof—had been published in *Assassination Science* (1998), *Murder In Dealey Plaza* (2000), and *The Great Zapruder Film*

Hoax (2003) at least five years before Bugliosi published his massive tome.

As David W. Mantik observed in his review of *Reclaiming History*, although I had laid out "16 smoking guns" in the Prologue to *Murder In Dealey Plaza*, "authentic discussion of our paradoxes was, by and large, quite off limits. There was a lot of palaver about many other things but little at all about the central 16—or [his] '20 Conclusions [after nine visits to the National Archives].' Nor did he take up the challenge of defeating our argument about the fabrication of the film, which includes a visual tutorial by John P. Costella explaining how we know that the film has been faked. This means our major findings remain unchallenged."

Instead, Vince placed his faith in an argument about several bullet fragments that had been found on the front floor of the limousine. The claim that neutron activation analysis (NAA) had shown the fragments to have come from allotments of WWII Mannlicher-Carcano ammunition (on the basis of the analysis of its trace mineral composition with respect to their percentage of zinc, arsenic, lead and other elements) had convinced Robert Blakey, Executive Director of the HSCA, that Oswald had been the lone assassin.

Alas, as Mantik explains, the assumption of homogeneous composition of the Italian ammunition—which used recycled lead—was seriously flawed and therefore NAA could not be used to justify claims about their common origin. (Indeed, a recent article by Gary Aguilar, M.D., *"Is Vincent Bugliosi Right that Neutron Activation Analysis Proves Oswalds Guilt?"* has put the final nail in its coffin.)

And, as I observed in my review of Bugliosi's book, had they come from a Mannlicher-Carcano or even from the same weapon, that would not have proven the location from which they were fired or by whom. But this means that Bugliosi's principal scientific argument was misconceived from the beginning.

Indeed, Bugliosi contends that Oswald was too unstable and insufficiently reliable for the CIA or the Mafia to have depended upon him to carry off the biggest murder in American history. After all, given the official story, he had defected to the Soviet Union, slashed his wrist trying to commit suicide, behaved erratically in New Orleans, and lived the life of a loner. Why would the CIA or the Mafia have trusted him?

If Lee had been part of a conspiracy, as soon as he departed from the building, a car would have been waiting to take him to his death. Instead, he becomes the first successful assassin in history to make his escape by public transportation!

Bugliosi, alas!, appears unable to appreciate that the same reasons he offers for why Oswald might not have been an appropriate choice to serve as an assassin are excellent reasons why he would have made a great selection in a conspiracy to serve as the patsy! Jesse Ventura made this point with devastating effect during his stunning exposure of Vince during their confrontation in the JFK segment of *"Conspiracy Theory"*.

Impending Disaster

If the planned mini-series based upon *Reclaiming History* starring Tom Hanks should make it to the small screen, his own remarks ("A lot of conspiracy types are going to be upset. If we do it right it'll perhaps be one of the most controversial things that has ever been on TV.") are going to play out in ways he no doubt did not intend, an opinion shared by many other experts.

On 19 November 2010, alas, an announcement appeared that Leonardo DiCaprio is set to star in and produce *Legacy of Secrecy*, a movie based on the book by Lamar Waldron and Thom Hartmann about the assassination of President John F. Kennedy.

The authors claim that JFK and RFK were planning a covert coup in Cuba that the Mob got wind of it and whacked JFK, then covered its back by threatening to expose the coup plans if RFK went after them. And they insist that LBJ and the FBI were not complicit in the crime. It has received rave praise, such as the following:

> *"I believe Waldron's heavy-to-lift book is actually all but the last word on these troubling assassinations which have been so wildly speculated about since 1963 . . . Lamar Waldron, indefatigable public servant and author deserves his own Pulitzer Prize for his great work."—Liz Smith,* New York Post
>
> *"They've done a service by digging up the deepest, darkest, most disturbing archival evidence to support their Mob hit theory."—Ron Rosenbaum*
>
> *"Staggering!"—Mark Crispin Mill*
>
> *"Exhaustively researched"*—New York Observer

"[Legacy of Secrecy contains] over 800 pages of intricately documented data. Their findings add pieces to one of our most perplexing puzzles, and suggest where the key missing pieces may be found."—Ronald Goldfarb, Daily Beast

Unfortunately, their scenario is completely ludicrous.

(1) After the abortive "Bay of Pigs" fiasco, JFK had entered into agreements with the Soviet Union that the U.S. would not invade Cuba, which he could not have broken, even covertly, without profoundly tarnishing his reputation and that of the U.S.

(2) There are more than 15 indications of Secret Service complicity in setting him up for the hit.

(3) The autopsy X-rays were altered to conceal a massive blowout to the back of the head and by adding a 6.5 mm metallic slice.

(4) The home movie of the assassination was re-created to remove incriminating evidence, including that the driver, William Greer, brought the limousine to a halt after bullets began to be fired.

Once JFK was dead, RFK was rendered powerless, sandwiched between his powerful superior, LBJ, and his nominal subordinate, J. Edgar Hoover, both of whom appear to have been deeply involved in planning for JFK's death and then covering it up. None of this could have been arranged by the Mob.

No doubt, the Mob wanted to regain control of its resorts and casinos in Havana, where it had been running the largest money-laundering operation in the Western Hemisphere. If JFK and RFK were going to take out Castro, the Mob would have waited until after that had been accomplished.

The book appears to have been inspired, in part, by a misunderstood contingency plan for an operation of this kind, one that was filed and forgotten. Even Robert McNamara had never even heard of it; yet its execution was allegedly only weeks away when the Mob took Jack out.

The idea that JFK could be planning something like this without the knowledge of his close and trusted Secretary of Defense verges on the absurd. And, as other, more qualified sources, including Robert Dalleck, *An Unfinished Life* (2003), have also explained, JFK was planning to promote a new era of less stressful and far more peaceful relations with the USSR, including the normalization of relations with Cuba.

Tom Hanks and Leonardo DiCaprio have now embarked upon a voyage into the unknown, which is rife with hazards of which they

Jesse Ventura, Vince Bugliosi, and Jim Fetzer

appear to be blithely unaware. Bugliosi is an impressive prosecutor, but he knows very little about the alteration of X-rays or the fabrication of films.

He produced a brilliant brief in his zeal to convince his readers that Oswald committed the crime. If Oswald didn't do it, then the Mafia would be a serious alternative, which Robert Blakey pushed when the *Final Report of the Select Committee on Assassinations U.S. House of Representatives* (1979) appeared.

But the mob could not have altered X-rays under control of medical officers of the U.S. Navy, agents of the Secret Service, or the President's own personal physician. Neither pro- nor anti-Castro Cubans could have substituted another brain for that of JFK.

And even if the Soviets had the capacity to fabricate movies comparable to that of the CIA and Hollywood, it would have been unable to get its hands on the Zapruder film. These things could only have been done with complicity from the highest levels of the American government.

There are books worth producing as mini-series and as films, especially ones by James Douglass, *JFK and the Unspeakable* (2008), and by Phillip Nelson, *LBJ: Mastermind of JFK's Assassination* (2010). The situation is not unlike that of those who controlled a magnificent ship, thought to be unsinkable, steaming blissfully ahead and unaware of its destiny. They bought the wrong books.

Special thanks to David W. Mantik for his comments and suggestions on this chapter.

Source note: This appendix previously appeared as "Forrest Gump on the Grassy Knoll", *http://jamesfetzer.blogspot.com/2015/09/forrest-gump-on-grassy-knoll.html.*

Index

Symbols

A

B

C

L

M

N

T

U

V

W